*Fascism in Spain*

Publication of this volume has been made possible in part by grants from the Program for Cultural Cooperation between Spain's Ministry of Education and Culture and United States' Universities and from the Humanistic Foundation Fund.

# Fascism in Spain

## 1923–1977

*Stanley G. Payne*

THE UNIVERSITY OF WISCONSIN PRESS

The University of Wisconsin Press
2537 Daniels Street
Madison, Wisconsin 53718

3 Henrietta Street
London WC2E 8LU, England

Printed in the United States of America

Illustrations for this book are reproduced courtesy of the following sources:
Editorial Planeta, Barcelona: pp. 64, 72, 84, 99, 241, 243, 296,
302, 313, 315, 322, 324, 360, 369, 386, 416, 439, 450
Historia 16, Madrid: pp. 26, 57, 76, 112, 217, 251,
335, 338, 341, 383, 466

Library of Congress Cataloging-in-Publication Data
Payne, Stanley G.
    Fascism in Spain, 1923–1977 / Stanley G. Payne.
        pp.        cm.
    Includes bibliographical references and index.
    ISBN 0-299-16560-4 (cloth)
    ISBN 0-299-16564-7 (pbk.)
    1. Spain—Politics and government—20th century.  2. Fascism—
Spain—History—20th century. 3. Francoism. 4. Falange Española
Tradicionalista y de las Juntas Ofensivas Nacional-Sindicalistas—
History.   5. Falange Española—History.   I. Title.
DP243.P39   1999
946.08—dc21        99-23078

To
Juan J. Linz
*Magister studiorum Hispaniae*

# Contents

*Illustrations*                                                      ix
*Preface*                                                            xi

### I. NATIONALISM IN SPAIN:
### LIBERAL, AUTHORITARIAN, FASCIST

1. The Problem of Spanish Nationalism                                 3
2. Origins of Authoritarian Nationalism in Spain                    16
3. The Fascism of the Intellectuals                                 51

### II. JOSÉ ANTONIO PRIMO DE RIVERA AND
### FALANGE ESPAÑOLA, 1933–1936

4. José Antonio Primo de Rivera and the Founding
   of the Falange, 1933–1934                                        69
5. Jefe Nacional, 1934–1936                                        115
6. From Clandestinity to Civil War                                 185
7. The Death of José Antonio                                       209

### III. THE FALANGE ESPAÑOLA TRADICIONALISTA
### IN THE FASCIST ERA, 1936–1945

8. Francisco Franco and the Formation
   of the Falange Española Tradicionalista                         239
9. The FET during the Civil War, 1937–1939                         273
10. The FET during the Climax of European Fascism,
    1939–1941                                                      310
11. The First Phase of a Long Defascistization, 1941–1945          363

IV. THE MOVIMIENTO NACIONAL DURING
THE POSTFASCIST ERA, 1945–1977

12. Partial Eclipse and Frustrated Resurgence, 1945–1958          401
13. The Last Phase of the Movimiento, 1959–1977                   431

    *Conclusion*                                                  469
    *Notes*                                                       483
    *Index*                                                       565

# Illustrations

Lieutenant General Miguel Primo de Rivera y Orbaneja,
Dictator of Spain, 1923–1930                                    26
Ramiro Ledesma Ramos, founder of the Juntas de Ofensiva
Nacional-Sindicalista (JONS)                                    57
Onésimo Redondo Ortega                                         64
The Primo de Rivera family                                     72
José Antonio Primo de Rivera in his law office                 76
Julio Ruiz de Alda                                            84
The Falangist triumvirate in 1934                              99
Funeral of Matías Montero Rodríguez, the "fallen student,"
in Madrid, February 1934                                      108
Republican Assault Guards searching citizens in Madrid        112
The Falangist triumvirs lead a mass demonstration
in the center of Madrid to support Spanish unity,
7 October 1934                                                121
Agustín Aznar, the Falangist national militia chief in 1936   217
General Francisco Franco and Colonel Juan Yagüe (the
chief Falangist in the military), in the streets of Seville,
August 1936                                                  241
Falangist militia in Salamanca                                243
Manuel Hedilla Larrey, head of the Falangist Junta de
Mando, 1936–1937                                             251
Women supporters of the Nationalists                          296
Pilar Primo de Rivera, head of the Sección Femenina          302
Falangist leaders in 1939                                     313
Falangist membership card, February 1939                      315
Assembly of leaders of the Frente de Juventudes              322
A parade of the Falanges Juveniles in 1940                   324
Hitler and Franco at Hendaye, 23 October 1940               335
Serrano Súñer, Franco, and Mussolini at Bordighera,
12 February 1941                                              338

Falangist demonstration in Madrid to support the German
    invasion of the Soviet Union, 24 June 1941                         341
The propaganda elite: Dionisio Ridruejo, Antonio Tovar,
    and Serrano Súñer                                                  360
Falangist mass assembly                                               369
General Agustín Muñoz Grandes as commander of the Blue
    Division                                                          383
Arrese meets Hitler, January 1943                                     386
SEU student demonstration in Madrid to protest continued
    British rule over Gibraltar, 27 January 1954                      416
José Solís Ruiz and Torcuato Fernández de Miranda                     439
The party's national headquarters on Madrid's calle de
    Alcalá, during the final years                                    450
The last public demonstration on behalf of Franco,
    October 1975                                                      466

# Preface

In 1961 I published a study of the early history of the Falange that was based on a doctoral dissertation for Columbia University and grounded particularly in extensive research in oral history in Spain during 1958-59. Though it could not, for political reasons, be published in Spain at that time, a translated edition was brought out in Spanish by Ruedo Ibérico in Paris in 1962. The study soon became relatively widely read by both left and right[1] and in fact remains in print and on sale in Spanish after nearly four decades.

The passage of time, the availability of an infinitely broader range of sources and materials, and the appearance of a series of new studies on aspects of the history of the Falange and the Franco regime have inevitably revealed the limitations and deficiencies of the work of 1961, but the present study is not a mere revision of the earlier book. The present volume is a substantially new study, much broader in range both chronologically and thematically, based on a much broader range of sources, and also different and broader in analytic focus and in interpretation.

The present work also owes a very great deal to the imagination, encouragement, and friendship of Rafael Borràs, who first conceived of the project at Planeta. Indeed, without his encouragement and support the book would not have been written. It also draws heavily on the work of other scholars who have published key studies that touch on the history of the Falange, beginning with Javier Tusell—the real leader of the field of twentieth-century political history in Spain—and including many others. My debts to them are acknowledged in the notes, but my gratitude for their work extends well beyond that.

Most of all this book is indebted to Juan J. Linz, to whom the English-language edition is dedicated. Since I first set foot in Madrid at the beginning of October 1958, he has been an unfailing source of advice, information, analytical insight, and personal friendship. He is the outstanding Spanish social scientist of the late twentieth cuntury, and I am particularly grateful for the very careful attention that he has devoted to this study, even though in a few instances I was unable to implement his suggestions.

This English-language edition is abridged and somewhat revised from the earlier and even lengthier version that appeared in Spanish entitled *Franco y José Antonio. El extraño caso del fascimo español: Historia de la Falange y del Movimiento Nacional, 1923–1977* (Madrid: Planeta, 1997). General and comparative introductory material has been eliminated, some additional data included, and a few errors corrected.

# Part I

## Nationalism in Spain:
## Liberal, Authoritarian, Fascist

# One

# The Problem of Spanish Nationalism

The political culture of Spain has seemed unique among European countries because of the absence or weakness of Spanish nationalism for much of the modern period. The Spanish crown and state are more than half a millennium old, and for non-Spaniards the identity of Spain has seemed clear enough from the sixteenth century on. Yet at both the beginning and the end of the twentieth century, nationalism in Spain has commonly referred to "peripheral" or "centripetal" nationalism, that of Catalans, Basques, or others, rather than to an inclusive all-Spanish nationalism.

The origins of Spanish institutions lie in the Middle Ages and in the formation of the Christian principalities of the "Reconquest"—a term that chronologically may be considered synonymous with Middle Ages in Spain. Territorial and dynastic kingdoms were the basic political unit of western civilization for approximately its first thousand years, so that the formation of the Hispanic kingdoms may be considered a natural western political development. Particularism and localism were at the same time characteristic of medieval society, and this was certainly the case in the Hispanic peninsula, though not necessarily to any greater extent than in any other equivalent part of continental Europe. Under those circumstances the development of five distinct Christian kingdoms (Asturias-Leon, Castile, Navarre, Aragon-Catalonia, and Portugal) was a natural feature of the peninsula's difficult history on the border of western civilization, particularly in view of its divisive geography.

"Spain" or "Hispania" (as derived from the Latin term for the entire peninsula) certainly existed as a concept during the medieval period, first of all as a general geographic term but also, more vaguely, as a reference to a certain common identity among the population of the Christian states. This had to do with a historical background in the Roman empire and the Visigothic kingdom, common religion, certain common cultural-institutional forms (law and writing script, for example), and to some

3

extent a common orientation toward Reconquest (though the character and scope of this remain highly controversial among historians).[1] Though Castile emerged as far and away the largest kingdom—more than two-thirds of the entire peninsula—and thus provided the most commonly spoken language, it had to borrow a basic term for Spaniard or Spanish (*español*) from Catalan.

The union of the crowns under Fernando and Isabel in 1478–1479 was the seed of a general Spanish state, which, after incorporating cis-Pyrenean Navarre in 1512, included all the peninsula save Portugal. The united crown, however, may be considered a kind of dynastic federation, for the only common institutions were the Church and to some extent the military. The separate laws, institutions, and governments of the non-Castilian principalities (Aragon, Catalonia, Valencia, and Navarre) continued unaltered. Moreover, the three Basque provinces, crown lands of Castile from the later Middle Ages on, thereafter enjoyed a more formalized and codified provincial autonomy as royal corregidores assisted in the codification of the *fueros* or autonomous rights.

The united crown nonetheless created a state system, though not a centralized state administration, and began to foster some further sense of unity. It remains very difficult to evaluate the degree and character of any broader sense of a "Spanish" identity, which would have been based on the general sovereignty of the united dynasty, common religion, and the zeal for empire. This was apparently expanded somewhat by the Habsburg crown in the sixteenth century, with the broad extension of empire and mission, the growth of Castilian ("Spanish") as a common peninsular language (at least at the level of high culture), and the rise of a general xenophobia in the second half of the sixteenth century, buttressed by the Inquisition determined to eliminate heretical (and to some extent foreign) influences. There also appeared the first common or prenational histories, such as Padre Juan de Mariana's *Historia de España* (1598), while Cervante's play *La Numancia* (1584) presented pre-Roman Iberians as recognizably heroic Spaniards, exhibiting what were by that time considered to be the fundamental Spanish values of religiosity, honor, and valor.[2] All this perhaps amounted to what two historians have recently called "Habsburg paleonationalism."[3]

Running as a major subcurrent through Leonese-Castilian and Spanish history from at least the end of the ninth century was the sense of historic mission and reconquest, the fundamental responsibility to expand Christendom and roll back Islam. This would later take the form of the crusading ideal, reaching its height in the imperial Spain of the late fifteenth to the seventeenth centuries. This broadly expansive ideal eventually amounted to what I have elsewhere called the "Spanish ideology,"[4] though it was not fully formulated until the era of high imperial Spain. Since that time it has variously waxed and waned, with a general tendency to wane until it was vigorously revived in the early years of the Franco regime.

By the end of the sixteenth century, if not well before, a tenuous identity apparently existed for a large part—not all—of the population of the homelands of the crown of Spain, though this was not at all the same sort of thing as a modern unified national identity. Moreover, the Habsburg dynasty was never able to construct a fully unified state. A major effort in that direction precipitated the political and military crisis of 1640. Portugal, briefly incorporated under the crown in 1580, broke away for good, and twelve years of fighting were necessary to drive out the French and regain Catalonia. But Catalonia was not merely "conquered," and the constitutional status quo returned as Spanish power declined rapidly.

A united and largely centralized Spanish state was the achievement of the new Bourbon dynasty after 1700. In the long War of the Spanish Succession, the Aragonese principalities—unlike Castile, Navarre, and the Basque provinces—opted for the losing Habsburg dynasty, leading to the Nueva Planta decree of 1716, which abolished separate laws and institutions in the Aragonese states[5] and created the first common legal and political structure for nearly all the Spanish crown territories in the peninsula and the adjacent islands—the sole remaining exceptions being Navarre and the Basque provinces.

Bourbon "prenationalism" instituted common Spanish programs of development through the reforms of "enlightened despotism." It also created common new institutions such as the Royal Academies, the National Library, the Museum of Science, the Botanical Garden, and the Astronomical Observatory. Though in 1729 Padre Feijóo declared that national passion was a "delinquent affection,"[6] the eighteenth century was the time of the first common modern historiography of Spain in the work of Mayans, Burriel, Masdeu, P. Flórez, and, at the close, Llorente. Other figures revalorized seventeenth-century Spanish art, while José Cadalso repeated Cervantes' themes concerning the identity and unity of Spanish history and culture; his *Cartas marruecas* (1768–1774) used the term "nación" for this common identity. Thus when the French *Encyclopédie méthodique* (1782) rhetorically asked what civilization owed to Spain, Cadalso and Juan Pablo Forner led the response.[7]

This was also part of a broader cultural expansion within the peninsula. Just as the eighteenth century produced the first modern work on common Spanish history and the history of Spanish law,[8] it was also the time of the first modern writing on the history, culture, and institutions of Catalonia and the Basque Country.[9]

The enlightenment intelligentsia and elite reflected one side of what soon became a kind of bipolarity, as they participated in a cosmopolitan culture and mentality that was more broadly international in scope than anything seen in Spain since the early sixteenth century. This tendency of the elite to ape sophisticated French culture and manners in turn elicited a nativist reaction during the second half of the century. In larger cities such as Madrid and Seville, this reaction was expressed on the popular level by the rise of lower-class "Majeza." The aggressively nativist "majo" and his "manuela" developed their own styles of clothing, behavior, and mores that were related to, though also a distinct new development of, more traditional Spanish culture in disdainful rejection of the Frenchified elite and the "petimetre" (the French cultural arbiter or *petit maitre*). By the latter part of the century, native Spanish styles and songs had become "camp," and were even a new vogue among the aristocracy. Similarly, these decades saw the crystallization of the modern form of the *corrida de toros* (bullfight), the most exclusively Spanish of modern popular sports. The dress and style of the new plebeian torero, fighting on foot, were a direct expression of the dress and mannerisms of the majo, while the construction of the new urban plazas de toros produced what might be called the first modern sports stadiums or arenas, all of this a unique blend of the traditional and the modern.[10] On the elite level, a sharp religious and philosophical rejection of the liberal and radical features of the Enlightenment had begun by the 1790s;[11] on the level of popular culture, the "tipista" and "castizo" (nativist) were stressed; together, something like a new nativist cultural synthesis was under way. In the initial war against the forces of the French Revolution, there developed a strong patriotic reaction—just as strong in Catalonia,[12] Navarre, and most of the Basque Country as elsewhere. This neotraditional "casticismo" was highly patriotic, but also provincial and not truly nationalist for lack of modern political content.

The political turning point came with the War of Independence, which temporarily eliminated the traditional state and produced a three-way split in political identities. Most of the militarily active or politically conscious population held to a xenophobic and royalist patriotic traditionalism. In the cities under French domination, conversely, a small minority of the elite and the educated supported a new French-dominated centralizing and modernizing seminationalism in strong opposition to traditionalism, while in free Spain the main forces of the educated elite achieved the breakthrough to an independent new liberalism.

The Cortes de Cádiz may be said to have provided the first expression of a kind of modern Spanish liberal nationalism. The authors of the constitution of 1812 projected a vision of Spain as a continuous historical and political development, guided in the past by its historic fueros and liberties and a concept of the sovereignty of the people (if admittedly more in latent theory than in practice), now organized into a single modern and progressive centralized unit.

The modern centralized Spanish state was thus in large measure the creation of nineteenth-century liberalism. It developed centralized institutions and modern national law codes on the basis of the "Spanish nation," which became a constant reference. Borja de Riquer and Enric Ucelay da Cal call this a sort of "institutional nationalism."[13] The language of liberal politicians was "españolista," and the concept of the nation was especially expressed in historiography, with the teaching of history organized around the idea of the common historicocultural evolution and identity of all the regions of Spain,[14] often accompanied by an "essentialist" understanding of the role, character, and identity of Castile.[15] This historiography reached a kind of apotheosis in the thirty-six-volume *Historia de España* of Modesto Lafuente, which was still being printed and sold into the 1920s. In imaginative literature, the "Episodios nacionales" of Galdós were the highest expression of the concept.

The obvious weakness of liberal nationalism lay in the elitist character of nineteenth-century Spanish liberalism. It was incapable of educating and mobilizing the masses of the population, as occurred in France during the second half of that century. The Spanish liberal system was either too weak and disunited or perhaps too liberal, depending on one's point of view, to impose a standard history or civics manual, a "libro único," as might have been found in other "state-building" polities. Even had one existed, there were no schools for the majority of Spanish children during most of the century, and thus only the most limited opportunity for the bulk of the society to be instructed in a common modern civic identity or a historically conscious nationalism. Under elitist liberalism there was no flag until 1843, no real national anthem, few new national monuments, a very weak national school system, and no genuine universal military service.[16] With the Catholic revival of the second half of the century, much of the educational system remained in the hands of the Church, but the latter remained antagonistic to the development of a strong modern liberal (and always potentially anticlerical) state, and this further weakened the unifying and modernizing potential of the liberal system.

In contrast to liberals, Carlists used the terms "patria" and "patriótico,"[17] for "nación" was part of the discourse of the French Revolution—liberal, modernist, even radical. As the years passed, however, Carlists accepted the latter term more and more. With the development of the liberal regime and the growth of new movements even farther to the left, Carlists after mid-century presented themselves as the only "true Span-

iards." A form of neotraditionalist Carlist nationalism, invoking traditional Spanish institutions and corporatism in place of liberalism, had
become their centerpiece by the time of the last Carlist war,[18] with
Carlism the "glorious national movement."[19] The Carlist emphasis on
regionalism and decentralization was presented as the genuine expression of Spanish historical institutions, and the only way to reconcile all
Spaniards.

By the end of the reign of Isabel II, reaction against the strongly centralized character of liberalism was widespread, culminating in the federal
republican movement. Federal republicanism, however, did not challenge
the broader identity and general national unity of Spain, but sought only
to decentralize the internal structure. Thus the original federalist Pacto de
Tortosa (1869) recognized one Spanish nation and one national state,
though the latter was envisioned as a republican confederation of regional
states or "provincias" (the latter corresponding to the historic regions,
not the fifty provinces of the modern state). Francisco Pi y Margall did
declare that the former provinces were "nations, for centuries,"[20] but this
was a historical reference, not a plea for a modern multinational state.
Federal republicanism in power (1873–1874) nonetheless quickly began
to break down into a *reductio ad absurdum,* the new cantonalist movement fractionalizing the federalists' "historic provinces" on the atomistic
basis of the smaller provincial units of the nineteenth century.[21] The Federal Republic became a byword for failure, while the movement for a
broader Iberian federalism that would include both Spain and Portugal—
at its height between 1854 and 1874—later declined drastically.[22]

The Restoration era that followed succeeded in stabilizing elitist liberalism and continued to foster the liberal concept of the nation. National
education expanded, but still slowly. Increased attention was devoted to
the major national commemorations, such as the anniversaries of the
death of Calderón (1881), of Recaredo's establishment of the Catholic
unity of Spain (1889), and of the discovery of America (1892). None of
the limitations on development and education were, however, overcome
during the late nineteenth century, and there was still no incorporation of
any sizable proportion of the population into any new nationalist project.

The leading statesman of the Restoration, Antonio Cánovas del Castillo, held so firmly to the concept of a united Spanish nation that his
attitude has sometimes been defined as one of Spanish/Castilian "essentialism."[23] Cánovas was a historian of some accomplishment, and his historical works reveal an interpretation of Spanish unity and identity derived not so much from any specific essence as from the institutions,
culture, and course of Spain's history. Unlike Lafuente and many earlier
historians, Cánovas did not dwell on great men, leaders, and wars, finding

many of the latter catastrophic, but focused instead on the processes of development that had eventually created the Spanish nation.[24]

A philosophical counterpoint to Cánovas's approach, even though it agreed with him on certain fundamental points, may be found in the beginnings of a form of Catholic cultural nationalism as developed by the Catholic revival of the second half of the century and the leading Catholic thinkers of the period. Chief among the latter was the most wide-ranging humanist of the late nineteenth century, Marcelino Menéndez Pelayo. He recognized the historical and cultural diversity of Spain and supported the regionalist cultural revivals, but sought to "integrate" Portugal with Spain and devoutly believed that it was above all religion that provided the basis for Spanish identity and unity. His studies of Spanish decline, whether in the seventeenth or nineteenth century, convinced him that the country had failed to develop fully the possibilities of its own culture, allowing itself to become exhausted by trying to do too much (as in the seventeenth century) or confused and nonfunctional by uncritically importing foreign ideas and institutions (as in his own times). As against the pure traditionalists of Carlism and orthodox neo-Thomism, however, Menéndez Pelayo sought to harmonize tradition and modernity without losing the former. He tried to come to terms with conservative liberalism, before the profound depression of his last years.[25]

The only truly overt and active nationalism in the last years of the nineteenth century was the imperialist nationalism focused on Cuba. This issue brought together journalists, leading politicians, and major economic interests, but was represented most stridently by sectors of the military. Carried to the greatest extreme in the military journals and publications of the 1890s, this attitude marked a shift toward a more right-wing, militarist, and imperialist nationalism, parallel with similar changes in the character of nationalism in many other European countries in these years. More unique to the Spanish case was the shallowness of the response generated among the middle classes and the ordinary population.

Throughout the century, meanwhile, romanticism had projected its own images and symbols of Spanish identity, often at considerable variance from those employed by elite politicians and intellectuals. "Romantic Spain" had both a domestic and an international dimension, for its most widely read and influential expressions often came from foreigners—Englishmen, an occasional German or North American, but especially Frenchmen. The travel literature on Spain had roots in the late Middle Ages but began to take its modern form during the eighteenth century. Most eighteenth-century travel accounts, however, strove for objectivity and a degree of detachment, almost like scientific expeditions into uncharted territory; early nineteenth-century treatments throve on emotion and intensity. After 1823, trips into "romantic Spain" became almost de rigueur for the French intelligentsia. The newly mythified "Spaniard," particularly as described by the French, was deemed a being unique in western Europe. Stendhal declared, "I love the Spaniard because he is an archetype; he is not a copy of anyone."[26]

It is highly debatable whether the images and concepts of romantic Spain really had much to do with Spaniards or Spain as a whole. The romantic stereotype was in fact appealing as a form of European "orientalism," directed especially toward Andalusia and more particularly toward gypsies, as well as relying heavily on Arab remnants, which were often considered to be a dominant influence. It was above all the scent and combination of perceived cruelty, sensuality, and violence that created the special *frisson* of romantic Spain. The most famous, and virtually archetypical, expression was Prosper Mérimée's *Carmen* (1845), which became to romantics what the concept of the noble savage had been to Rousseauians. Established by the 1840s, this set of images would continue into the middle of the twentieth century and even after.[27]

Very similar motifs were adopted by Spanish romantic writers from the 1830s, as they proved eager to portray gypsies, Moors, historical legends, the loves and deaths of young rebels, and equivalent forms of melodrama, along with the usual scenes of bulls, toreros, and dancing. On a slightly higher literary level, mid-nineteenth-century "costumbrismo" recorded these images of Andalusia but also tried to reflect the styles of other regions as well, contributing to the regional cultural revivals that preceded the development of the peripheral nationalisms. The Andalusian style nonetheless became popular within Spain as a whole, reflected in the growth of the late nineteenth-century zarzuela and even more in the flamenco style. As far as can be determined, modern flamenco emerged in the larger Andalusian cities during the 1860s and 1870s but soon moved on, particularly to Madrid, where it had gained great popularity by the 1890s.

As Alvarez Junco and others have noted, the romantic perceptions were gratifying enough to patriotic Spaniards because—despite their exoticizing and orientalizing qualities—they neatly reversed standard European stereotypes of the Black Legend. What was once denounced as Spanish cruelty was now celebrated as bravery; the avarice of the conquistadors was celebrated as Spanish adventurousness; Castilian arrogance was now honored as a kind of dignity unknown in bourgeois Europe; and the fanaticism of earlier times was transmuted to a spiritualized religiosity of which materialistic Europeans were incapable. All this may have contributed to the relative complacency of the Restoration era, a complacency that was patriotic and rhetorical but not really nationalistic, more interested in consolidating the status quo than in transformation. Thus, as has been mentioned, such developments as the formation of the Unión Ibero-Americana or the celebration of the Quadricentennary in 1892 were sources of national pride but generated little in the way of modern nationalism.

By the 1890s, however, a new critical generation was emerging, increasingly prone to the conclusion that the nominally liberal Spain of the nineteenth century had failed to achieve progress and modernization. What became known as the "disaster literature" was not simply touched off by the debacle of 1898 but had begun several years before. The disaster nonetheless gave it impetus. During the 1820s, a period of transition away from traditional society, there had been scant reaction to the loss of most of America, a limited response similar to that of France in 1763 or England in 1783. By contrast, the disaster of 1898 may be considered the first modern postcolonial trauma in western Europe, even though to critics in Spain it seemed as though the country had basically failed in the modernization process itself. Spanish critics at the close of the century were thus more alarmed and pessimistic than the original liberals of 1810. The most censorious wondered if the basic history and culture of Spain for a century—or even three centuries—had been founded on false premises, if the very categories of "casticismo" and "españolismo" were mistaken and inferior. The sense of national historical and cultural failure approached that of Islamic countries in modern times.

This sense gave rise to the Regenerationist movement that officially began with the efforts of Joaquín Costa and others in 1899. Regenerationism to a large extent dominated Spanish affairs during the early twentieth century, with the goal of achieving honest and authentic government, practical reform, and modernization. More than a little was accomplished, but the basic problems were far from eliminated during the first two decades of the new century. Though some basic Regenerationist goals were widely accepted, organized political consensus proved impossible. With each step toward reform and predemocracy, fragmentation increased. The old elites still refused to yield control, and the major breakthrough never occurred. Regenerationism never became a unified movement, and generally failed to take the form of a new, modern nationalism.

The "problem of Spain" became a fundamental preoccupation of the distinguished new group of litterateurs who emerged from the fin-de-siècle—the celebrated "noventayochistas," or "Generation of Ninety-Eight." Unamuno's dictum "Me duele España" (Spain pains me) was a leitmotiv. The Generation of Ninety-Eight generated some of the qualities needed for a cultural nationalism, with their invocation of Castile and the "tierra de España." They sought to identify what was most authentic and creative in Spanish social and cultural tradition, finding it more in the Middle Ages and early Renaissance than in the Golden Age. They sought the salvation of Spain and wished to combine the traditional with the modern, but they were essentially critics and esthetes, writers and not men of action. They rejected history in favor of Unamuno's concept of unchanging "intrahistoria" and lapsed ultimately into estheticism, internal spirituality, and interiorismo. They rejected the traditional Spanish baroque, which "Azorín" denounced as full of "pompous declamation" and "bombastic boasting," and Valle-Inclan as "vain and boastful literature," with its dramas based on an arid "cruelty." Unamuno feared that Spaniards had more "individuality than personality," lacking depth and development. Some of them celebrated an "African" element in Spain that they could little define or develop, and this made the cultural nation ever harder to bring into focus. As critics, they feared nationalism itself as a form of excess, aggression, and the manipulation of special interests, as Unamuno once indicated, the product of corrupt large cities, "the bourgeois," and of "great landlords."[28] So they relapsed not into complacency, but into "reverie."

The leading historians of the early part of the century, led by the liberal Rafael Altamira, generated more of a unified national vision, and more yet emerged from the intellectual critics of the second and third decades of the new century, the "Generation of 1914," led by José Ortega y Gasset. Ortega was much more focused and empirically minded than the estheticizing, subjectivist noventayochistas. His concern, expressed first in the Liga de Actuación Politica of 1914, then in his initial praise of Primo de Rivera, and finally under the Republic, was the modernization and development of Spain under more capable government. Though he joined in the initial rush of enthusiasm for Primo de Rivera in 1923, Ortega was basically a centrist liberal with elitist tendencies. The latter feature, in fact, was the counterpoint of his analysis of the "ills of the fatherland," which he thought stemmed above all from lack of leadership and of creative elites, a problem that he erected into a general interpretation of the history of Spain. More than the noventayochistas, he had a certain sense of nationalism, intuiting that major changes would not occur until Spaniards became united in some great common enterprise. As he would declare in *España invertebrada* (1922):

> In every authentic incorporation, force has a merely adjectival character. The truly substantive strength that drives and sustains

the process is always a national dogma, a suggestive project of a common life. Let us repudiate every static interpretation of national co-existence and learn to understand it dynamically. People do not live together for no reason or out of inertia; a priori cohesion only exists in the family. Groups that form a state live together for some purpose: they constitute a community of goals, of aspirations, of great purposes. They do not coexist merely to be together, but to accomplish something together.[29]

This concept would later become a powerful force in Spanish extremist nationalism, constituting the root of José Antonio Primo de Rivera's doctrine of "unity of destiny in the universal." For Ortega, Spain was not a nation created by some unchanging essence, but the product of a common history, a joint national enterprise.

Yet Ortega refused to become a Spanish nationalist. Though less paranoid in his opposition to nationalism than Unamuno, he nonetheless perceived it as a force for aggression, oppression, and excess, declaring that "nationalism presupposes the desire for one nation to rule over others."[30] All that can be said is that his writings and speeches reveal nationalist elements but never an endorsement of nationalism per se.[31]

If nearly all the leading intellectuals, writers, or politicians tried at one time or another to deal with "el problema nacional," their efforts produced no consensus, no hegemonic reform group, and no focused nationalist organization. Though Francisco Silvela's famous newspaper article "Sin pulso" ("Without Pulse"), written to decry the apathy of the Spanish on the morrow of defeat, was clearly exaggerated, it nonetheless reflected a very problematic situation. In the first years of the twentieth century, it was above all army officers who were given to nationalist sentiments, but they felt completely unsupported by political and cultural circles. Symptomatic of the dismay of the nationalist military was an editorial in *El Heraldo Militar* on 23 November 1908 entitled "Worse Than Anywhere." It declared: "Wherever we look, we find greater virility than in our own people. . . . In Turkey, Persia, China, the Balkan states—everywhere we find life and energy. . . . Even in Russia! In Spain there is only apathy and submission . . . ! How sad it is to think about the situation in Spain!"

It is easy enough to summarize the factors in Spanish history and culture that discouraged a modern kind of nationalism during the late nineteenth and early twentieth centuries:

1. Spain's situation of absolute independence since the eleventh century, permitting it later to become the first true world empire in history and to rank among the major established powers for an extended period

2. The nature of the traditional Spanish state as a sort of dynastic confederation of strongly pluralist character despite so-called Habsburg absolutism and even, to some extent, Bourbon centralization

3. The exclusive mutual identity of traditional Spanish culture and religion, which created a climate of national (or prenational) Catholicism that endured for centuries and ended only with the full secularization that occurred late in the twentieth century

4. The absence of foreign threat after the Napoleonic wars

5. The nearly century-long domination of classical liberalism, conditioning formal culture and discouraging new military ambition or the development of a modern radical right

6. The unique role of peripheral nationalism, which absorbed much new energy

7. Neutrality in World War I

8. All this influenced and conditioned by, and to some extent even predicated upon, a slow pace of modernization, accompanied by the absence of new political, economic, or cultural ambitions that might have stimulated nationalism

During the course of the nineteenth century, the character of both internal political conflict and the broad development of romantic culture and costumbrista literature and art had the effect of emphasizing the plurality and internal differentiation of Spain. Though the state apparatus had become centralized, writers, artists, and sometimes politicians as well referred to the diversity and distinct characters of the historic regions. Though formal historiography and patriotic rhetoric tended to be Castilianist in character, in everyday practice and in both low and high culture the "patria chica" or "local fatherland" received great emphasis.[32] For regenerationists and noventayochistas alike, it became an accepted truism that the real life of Spain, both historically and at present, lay in the provinces, and that the provinces and regions were diverse and fragmented. Ortega's new book of 1931 was entitled *La redención de las provincias* (The Redemption of the Provinces), emphasizing that national reform must begin by facing the problems and the diversity of the provinces.

In some of the most distinctive regions, particularly in those with a different language and with distinctive social and economic structures, the last years of the nineteenth century saw the rise of peripheral nationalism. Even within its own strongholds, Carlism, for example, was unable to hold its own as a program of decentralized and traditionalist all-Spanish nationalism. Its emphasis during the last Carlist war on the perfection and distinctiveness of the traditional provincial structures of the Basque Country became a major factor in the eventual emergence of a Basque nationalist movement in Vizcaya.[33]

Those who were pessimistic about the cohesiveness of a Spanish nation seemed to be correct as the slow but steady rise of peripheral nationalism provoked no reaction in favor of Spanish nationalism but merely a negative and divisive anti-Catalanism and anti-Basquism. The moderate Catalanists, however, sought to respond with a broader common Spanish project of which the regular Spanish politicians themselves seemed incapable. The first important Catalanist party was the Lliga Regionalista,[34] which adopted the adjective "regionalist" rather than "Catalan" or "Catalanist" to avoid unnecessarily offending sensibilities in other parts of Spain. Certainly the Lliga's leaders were in their own way good citizens of Spain. Their goal was autonomy, never separatism (for which Arana Goiri, founder of Basque nationalism, bitterly denounced them). The Lliga's goal was a free and modern Catalonia in collaboration with a free and modern Spain, and in a sense it had conceptualized Ortega's notion of a grand, progressive all-Spanish enterprise before he did. Enric Prat de la Riba, chief ideologue of the Lliga, propounded a kind of "federal imperialism" to foster broader goals for all Spain.[35] Francesc Cambó, political head of the movement, waged the Lliga's electoral campaign of 1916 under the slogan "Per l'Espanya Gran." Cambó was, in fact, probably the greatest Spanish statesman of the early twentieth century, with a broader and more inclusive, more constructive vision of Spain than that advanced by any of the politicians centered in Madrid.[36] As will be discussed in the next chapter, Barcelona before 1923 was the leading center of nationalism in Spain, whether Catalan or Spanish.

# Two

# Origins of Authoritarian Nationalism in Spain

At the beginning of this century, liberal political culture in Spain was challenged only by the revolutionary extreme left and by the Carlist extreme right, both equally impotent. The generally liberal orientation of the Spanish intelligentsia was accentuated by the philosophical vogue of Krausist pantheism and progressivism, increasingly influential since the last decades of the nineteenth century. By contrast, the radical new fin-de-siècle culture, associated with what some scholars have called the "cultural crisis" of the 1890s, invoking secular neo-idealism, vitalism, and nonrationalism, was comparatively weak.

Nonetheless, a minor current of authoritarianism underlay Regenerationist thought. Joaquín Costa had once called for a dictatorship that would be "ideologically neutral" in order to carry out a "revolution from the government." Of the major works of the era, *El problema nacional* (1899) of Ricardo Macías Picavea was perhaps the most antiparliamentary, proposing an "organic" system of both political and economic corporatism. He stressed the need for "a man" to provide leadership; should the latter not appear, Macías Picavea urged the Spanish bourgeoisie to carry out its own "national revolution." Similarly, *Problemas del día* (1900), by César Silió y Cortés, was overtly nationalist and urged leadership by "caudillaje" (a strong man). These ideas, repeated by others from time to time, were satirized in the 1912 Madrid comedy by the Cuevas brothers entitled *¡Aquí jase farta un hombre!* (*A Man Is Needed Here*), in Andalusian dialect.[1]

In the two countries that most resembled Spain—Italy and Portugal—nationalism and nonleftist authoritarianism were finding clear expression. Before the end of the nineteenth century, several Italian conservatives had made proposals for a more authoritarian kind of liberalism. The new culture of the fin-de-siècle was strong in Italy, producing a wave of intense nationalism among some sectors of the intelligentsia. Italian political theorists and sociologists were among the leaders in Europe in developing new theories of elitism. Formation of the Associazione Nazionalista Italiana in 1910 led within four years to espousal of a clear doctrine of the authoritarian nationalist corporate state. Nationalism even invaded minor sectors of the left, as some revolutionary syndicalists moved toward national syndicalism. The outbreak of World War I then sparked the phenomenon of nationalistic "left interventionism."

In Portugal there was proportionately more support for political authoritarianism, as well as distinctly more nationalism, than in Spain. The Portuguese "Generation of 1870"—in some respects a limited precursor of the Spanish noventayochistas—made a number of calls for a dictator or dictatorship that could regenerate the country in a more modern or progressive form. Calls for an "iron surgeon" were much more frequent there than in Spain.[2] By 1890, forms of reactionary or authoritarian liberalism were more in vogue in Portugal than in Italy, let alone Spain, and temporary parliamentary "dictatorships"—the closing of parliament for brief periods to permit government by decree—were not uncommon. This was climaxed by the "dictatorship" of João Franco during 1907–1908, in which the regular parliamentary prime minister was authorized by the crown to govern by decree[3] until the spectacular double assassination of King Carlos and the heir to the throne at the Lisbon dock in 1908 removed all support.

In Portugal a more organized nationalism was championed by the Republican movement, which had developed in response to the British "Ultimatum" of 1890 that crushed hopes for an even greater Portuguese empire in southern Africa—a setback sometimes called "Portugal's 1898." Thus in Portugal, where problems of nationalism, independence, and international competition were more keenly felt than in its larger, more self-enclosed Iberian neighbor, regenerationism took the form of a categorical political alternative. However, Portuguese nationalist republicanism paralleled "left interventionism" in Italy in its incorporation of part of the revolutionary collectivist left. Members of the small Portuguese anarchist movement were attracted to republicanism because of its militancy and capacity for subversion of the political establishment. As the movement grew, Portuguese republicanism stressed paramilitary activity, somewhat in the tradition of the nineteenth-century progressivist citizen militias in both Spain and Portugal. The republican "Carbonária," not sympathetic rebel sectors of the Portuguese military, did most of the fighting in the overthrow of the monarchy in October 1910.

Despite its temporary association with the extreme left, the "First Republic" in Portugal (1910–1926) was never democratic. It maintained a restricted suffrage to exclude illiterate but conservative and Catholic peasants from the vote, while the largest sector of republicans continued to rely in part on volunteer militias (and the clandestine "formigas"—literally "ants") to maintain power or overthrow rightist forces.

Military pretorianism, always weaker than in Spain, also returned under the Republic, beginning with the bloodless "Movement of the Swords," which temporarily placed the aged Gen. Pimenta de Castro in power in January 1915. The call to military revolt was also important in the two attempted monarchist rebellions led by Gen. Paiva do Couceiro from Spanish sanctuary and in the brief civil war waged by the so-called Monarchy of the North in 1920. During the final years of the parliamentary republic, military conspiracy on the right became endemic.

The new authoritarian radical right also emerged earlier than in Spain, starting with the organization of Integralismo Lusitano in 1917. This elitist formation was inspired by the Action Française and sought the installation of a monarchy that would be authoritarian, nationalist, and corporatist.[4] Doctrinally, it constituted a Portuguese antecedent of the journal *Acción Española* and the Renovación Española party under the Spanish Republic. By contrast, the main Catholic corporative organization was more moderate and pragmatic, led by the Centro Académico da Democracia Cristã at Coimbra University and later expanded into the Portuguese Centro Católico in 1917.[5]

A unique but abortive breakthrough was accomplished when Sidonio Pais introduced the República Nova in 1917–1918. This took the form of a brief presidentialist republic with a stronger government based on populist charisma and democratic plebiscitarianism—a moderate right-authoritarian form of republicanism whose transient existence left an example not readily forgotten by the Portuguese right.

Other minor forms of nonleftist authoritarianism emerged briefly after World War I. The right-radical Cruzada Nun' Alvares Pereira, was formed in 1919 with the goal of a nationalist authoritarian regime under a powerful leader. Two years later a small group of army officers created a Nationalist Republican Presidentialist Party to restore the República Nova, but failed in an abortive coup attempted in conjunction with the monarchist Integralists. Neither of these two postwar groups was a regular organized political party, and their followings were very limited. This was even more the case with Nacionalismo Lusitano, a tiny proto-fascist movement formed in Lisbon in 1923 in imitation of Italian Fascism.[6]

Prior to 1923, such initiatives found little counterpart in Spain, where the last Carlist bands had been formed unsuccessfully in 1906.[7] Nineteenth-century theorists of authoritarian liberalism—in such figures as Jaime Balmes, Juan Donoso Cortés, and Francisco Bravo Murillo—had no significant counterparts during the fin-de-siècle. Apart from the

vague appeals mentioned at the beginning of this chapter, the nearest examples were the various attempts to form citizen defense leagues to protect property and public order in several provinces, and particularly in
Barcelona, where the most important initiative was the creation by royal
decree in 1905 of the Somatén de Cataluña as a regional militia and auxiliary police force of volunteers.[8]

The end of World War I, followed by the offensive of the revolutionary
left, led to the organization of numerous volunteer paramilitary and parapolice forces in diverse parts of central, eastern, and southern Europe.
The most famous were the various German Freikorps. In neutral Spain,
the situation was much less likely to get out of control, and the Spanish
counterparts of such organizations were correspondingly feeble. Conservative middle-class forces organized a new Acción Ciudadana in Barcelona and a Unión Ciudadana in Madrid during 1919, but these had little
significance. Their only political goals were to maintain order. The main
focus of sociopolitical conflict was the class struggle in Barcelona, featuring numerous street killings by the gunmen of the anarchosyndicalist
CNT (National Confederation of Labor) and of the Barcelona Patronal.[9]
A unique development was the growth of the Sindicatos Libres, a rightist
Catholic worker movement of Carlist origins that was not simply another
paternalist Catholic group but a militant and aggressive syndical movement determined to wage battle with the anarchist left.[10]

The nearest thing to a nationalist grouping among the main parliamentary parties was Maurism, which took form after the split in the Conservative Party in 1913. Antonio Maura was the only politician of his
time whose name became an "ism," though he himself never shared all
the tenets of what subsequently became "maurismo." Formally, the self-
righteous Mallorcan politician stood for a reformist conservatism that
emphasized strict law-and-order constitutionalism, more honest politics
and elections, a degree of responsible politico-administrative decentralization, strong support for Catholic values, and overriding concern for the
higher interests of the Spanish nation and its economic development. A
singular feature of maurismo was the Jovenes Mauristas, the only significant youth group among the establishment parties. The Jovenes Mauristas were more militant and nationalist than adults in the movement, with
a demand for leadership and strong government, and a sharp note of pugnacity. Maura's only opportunity for a genuinely maurista government—
in 1919—ended in complete failure, for it was a narrowly based minority
administration that developed no social program to cope with the country's increasingly severe societal problems. Thereafter the mauristas
tended more and more to divide, a minority veering toward Christian
democracy and participating in the founding of the Partido Social Popu-

lar in 1922. Others took a more authoritarian direction, championing a pronounced nationalism, strong leadership, and the need for a government of authority. Maura himself never supported extreme maurismo, and always maintained scrupulous respect for established constitutional procedure, but some of his followers eventually supported an authoritarian alternative.[11]

The breakpoint in Spanish affairs came during the extended postwar political crisis, the six years of proto-democratization, social conflict, and political fragmentation between 1917 and 1923. Like other political systems of nineteenth-century elitist liberalism in southern and east-central Europe, the Spanish system was incapable of accepting or undergoing sufficient reform to permit a genuine transition to democracy, while, partly because of the country's neutrality in the war, the established elites nonetheless managed to cling to political power. Yet as processes of social, economic, and cultural change accelerated, it was impossible to maintain stability. An archaic system could neither fully maintain itself nor reform itself, but limped along from year to year with increasing difficulty.

## A BARCELONA AMBIENCE

After 1913 the Liberal and Conservative parties became hopelessly fragmented, despite the slowly but steadily growing challenges of democratic reformers, the revolutionary left, and peripheral nationalism in Catalonia and the Basque Country. It was in Barcelona following World War I that new and radical forces clashed most directly. Barcelona was the center not only of Catalan nationalism, but also of the first significant organized expressions of a more radical Spanish nationalism in opposition to it. Street fighting between rival nationalists first occurred there in January 1919. Radical Catalanists held largely peaceful nightly demonstrations on the central avenue of Las Ramblas, prompting the formation of a group of right-wing *españolistas* made up of local army officers and others calling itself the Liga Patriótica Española. It soon turned to violence, provoking counterviolence from the radical Catalanists (in this case assisted by Barcelona Carlists, who aided them on behalf of regional liberties).[12] This brief phenomenon was, however, quickly superseded by the violent outbreak of organized class struggle, whose most extreme form was organized murder by CNT hitmen, the "policía patronal," or the regular police (and, later, the Sindicatos Libres). From that point on, normal political demonstrations were usually made impossible by patrols of police or the middle-class Catalan militia, the Somatén.

By the end of World War I, the old establishment parties in Barcelona and Bilbao had begun to join together in new "españolista" coalitions, the Liga de Acción Monárquica in Vizcaya (1918–1919)[13] and the Unión Monárquica Nacional (1919) in Catalonia. What was distinctive about these two entities was that, being formed in regions where battlelines were being drawn with both peripheral nationalism and the revolutionary left, they tended to adopt a position more oriented toward Spanish unity and a form of right-wing nationalism than other sectors of the establishment parties did.[14]

During these years the new initiatives in Catalanism were drawing steadily away from the moderate Lliga Regionalista toward more radical positions. In 1922 the more youthful and dynamic or democratizing sectors of the Lliga itself split off to form a more militant party, Acció Catalana, which would launch an activist and democratic appeal to the Catalan lower middle classes. By the following year it had defeated the Lliga in Catalan elections. One sector of intellectuals in Acció Catalana, led by the poet J. V. Foix and the essayist Josep Carbonell, was more elitist and tried to follow the radical politics of esthetics preached by the French radical right of Charles Maurras and Action Française. Foix had been a key leader in the convening in the spring of 1922 of the Conferencia Nacional de Catalunya, which had created Acció Catalana, and he served as director of the party's official journal, *Acció Catalana*, in 1922–1923.

Though not merely anti-Spanish, Foix found the old Lliga too españolista, and looked toward a fully autonomous Catalan nation that would participate in an Iberian Federation and also cooperate with "Occitania" (southwestern France) in a "Confederació Llatino-Occidental." He and Carbonell adopted the federal imperialist line of Prat de la Riba, advocating the modern transformation of the entire peninsula, to a considerable extent under Catalan leadership, with a special emphasis on education and accompanied by a new nationalist military mobilization, following a drastic reform of the Spanish army. This would require a sort of multinational revolution in which "the radical de-hispanization of Catalonia would have to be followed by the de-hispanization of geographical Spain."[15] It could not be accomplished merely by Catalan dominance but would require the complete reorganization of the entire peninsula under a "strong state" of federal characteristics that would permit a national policy for Catalans, as well as for Basques, Portuguese, and Andalusians. Each member unit would have to accept its relative "subordination" under the strong new state and plurinational community, which would be destined to expand in North Africa and increase its influence in the Mediterranean, while also cooperating internationally with a revival of other Latin nations.

At this time the rise of Fascism in Italy fascinated Foix:

> In its origins Fascism enjoyed the complete sympathy and
> theoretical admiration of Foix, who saw it as a social movement born
> to rebuild a country faced with disorder and the "dissolution of the
> patria." . . . As a social movement it gave voice to a vein of mysticism
> and idealism that exalted the concept of the patria and its full
> realization. According to Foix, between 1920 and 1922 Fascism
> "offered the spectacle of national restoration" where syndicalism and
> nationalism converged.[16]

Nonetheless, the elitist Foix was not pleased with the plebeian and demagogic character of Italian Fascism, and after it moved in 1924 toward
dictatorship and institutionalized violence, he dissociated himself from
it.[17]

If Acció Catalana stood generally to the left of the Lliga, still farther
left was an extreme Catalanism that spoke of absolute self-determination
and even of independence. This was composed of a number of small
groups whose common denominator, in addition to extreme nationalism,
was an orientation toward social issues and some concept of social democracy, with a laborist appeal to the working classes. These currents
came together in 1922 in the organization of the Estat Català (Catalan
State) movement under the leadership of the retired army officer Francesc
Macià; in the following year, nationalist socialists formed their own Unió
Socialista de Catalunya (USC). Estat Català sought broad populist mobilization and also employed direct action. At that time the Catalanist left
felt considerable interest in the style and organization of Italian Fascism,
and in its use of *squadristi* for direct action. Though Estat Català did
not invoke any Fascist doctrine of therapeutic violence, and though the
"national socialism" of some of its members was oriented more toward
social democracy than toward corporatism, it represented the only coherent form of direct-action nationalism in Spain. By 1923 Estat Català leaders spoke of the need for a separate Catalan military and for military
action. Theirs was the only form of directly mobilized nationalism in the
peninsula that sought to appeal to all social classes and later, under the
Dictatorship, even to employ violence and terrorism to a limited extent.[18]

Españolista activists in Barcelona sought a more effective radical alternative of their own. In December 1922, two months after Mussolini's
March on Rome, a publication called *La Camisa Negra* (*The Black Shirt*)
appeared in Barcelona in imitation of Fascism; it was unable to print a
second number. In a manner rather similar to the launching of the Cruzada Nun' Alvares Pereira in Lisbon four years earlier, a small number
of military officers formed El Cruzado Español (The Spanish Crusader)

in Barcelona in 1923–1924, but in fact their symbolism was more specifically traditionalist and quasi-Carlist than Fascist. Meanwhile, in the spring of 1923 a few officers in the local garrison (possibly encouraged by Alfonso Sala Argemí, the leader of rightist Catalan españolista monarchism)[19] formed a circle called La Traza (The Project). The tracistas adopted a blue shirt as their uniform and hoped to extend their tiny group throughout Spain, in October 1923 changing their name to the more benign Federación Cívico-Somatenista.[20] It would be an exaggeration to call La Traza a fascist organization, but it was clearly inspired by Italian Fascism, the first radical nationalist group to be formed in Spain through such inspiration.

## THE PRIMO DE RIVERA DICTATORSHIP, 1923–1930

The only major institution that could be said to support Spanish nationalism directly during the first part of the twentieth century was the officer corps of the army. Military commanders had often served as the backbone of liberal government prior to 1875, in the so-called epoch of pronunciamientos. The Spanish army had been the most "pretorian" in Europe during that period, and a major achievement of the restored monarchy had been to end overt military intervention in politics. Pretorianism had been more the result of the weakness of the liberal parties than of the ambition or egotism of the military; most officers had always been patriotic and relatively conservative. As Spanish society and politics changed, the military found themselves increasingly placed toward the rightist side of the political spectrum.[21]

One factor moving many officers toward a more authoritarian political position was the rise of the revolutionary left from the 1890s on. Though the military press, for example, accepted some leftist social and economic claims (the military were also somewhat anticapitalist), army officers demanded suppression of the left's disorder, violence, and subversion of national unity.[22]

The parliamentary conflict and stalemate in public affairs also affected the military. From 1917 officers were themselves divided politically and internally, not so much between liberals and conservatives (only a minority of officers were by this point genuinely liberal) as between combat officers with experience in Morocco (africanistas) and bureaucratic peninsular officers whose advancement was based only on seniority. The latter had turned to military syndicalism in 1917, forming "Juntas militares" of officers.[23]

The military generally supported a nationalist position, urging stronger government, an end to internal subversion, and a more powerful and effective national policy, particularly in the Protectorate. Since the establishment of the small Spanish zone in northern Morocco in 1913, it had never been possible to occupy and pacify the territory fully. By 1921 the Riffi insurrection of Abdul Karim had become the strongest rebellion anywhere in the Afro-Asian world, inflicting a severe defeat on Spanish forces at Annual in which approximately nine thousand soldiers perished.[24]

During 1922–1923 Spanish affairs seemed stalemated. The effort to reunify the Liberal Party did not succeed,[25] and yet the established elites still dominated the electoral system, preventing true reform or democratization. Frustrated, King Alfonso XIII began to embrace the concept of military government. Major sectors of the military also demanded changes, or at least a stronger government. Yet the internal division and lack of leadership were so great that no commander stepped forward to lead the pronunciamiento that many had begun to talk about. One group of four senior generals, known as the "Quadrilateral," conspired during the summer of 1923 to promote a temporary military government that would press the struggle in Morocco to a victorious conclusion and silence critics at home, but it lacked sufficient support or leadership for a coup.

The pronunciamiento of 13 September 1923 that overthrew constitutional government thus depended on the personal initiative of Miguel Primo de Rivera, captain general of Barcelona. Descended from an illustrious military family with roots in the region of Jerez de la Frontera, Primo de Rivera was the product of a military career that had spanned more than three decades. He had inherited the title of marqués de Estella from his uncle, a hero of the final Carlist war and a major figure in the military hierarchy. Tall and heavyset but rather distinguished looking, he was a bluff, hearty, and frank military man of good nature and authoritarian ideas who also harbored a streak of slyness. Primo de Rivera had served with distinction and unusual courage in Cuba, Morocco, and the Philippines. Partly as a result, he harbored few illusions about Spanish imperialism,[26] but slowly developed political ambitions, which only fully crystallized in the spring of 1923. Strongly influenced by the regenerationist spirit and also by the tradition of nineteenth-century liberal pretorianism, he became convinced that only a temporary military government could achieve unity, solve problems, and institute necessary reforms.[27]

The timing of the pronunciamiento was triggered by several key events: the resignation of three ministers of the Liberal government on 3 September to protest against renewal of the military initiative in Morocco, the parade of left Catalanists in Barcelona on 11 September, at which the Spanish flag was dragged on the ground without remonstrance from the authorities, and the impending release (scheduled for 26 September) of a parliamentary commission's report concerning culpability for the military disaster of 1921. Mussolini's threat of force in taking over the Italian government in the preceding year, following the seizure of power by military elements in Greece, and France's invasion of the Ruhr only a few months before all may have encouraged the use of force in Spain, though there is little direct evidence of this. The decision to act was apparently made on 8–9 September when Primo visited the Quadrilateral in Madrid.[28]

The revolt began in Barcelona as a classic pronunciamiento, with a local takeover in the Catalan capital by its captain general, who called upon the rest of the army and other patriotic Spaniards to rally round. In fact—also in the traditional style—all but one of the other captains general at first sat on the fence. The pronunciamiento succeeded above all because the Liberal government did almost nothing to defend itself. The issue was finally decided two days later by the crown, as Alfonso XIII, without invoking constitutional limits or procedures, transferred power to what would become the first direct military dictatorship in Spanish history.[29]

Primo de Rivera gave no evidence of any explicit theory or plan. His assumption of power was at first predicated on a ninety-day emergency military directory to deal with such problems as attempted subversion, the stalemate in Morocco, administrative corruption, and political reform. In fact his only professed ideology was constitutional liberalism. He insisted that the constitution of 1876 remained the law of the land and initially denied that he was a dictator in any genuine sense, insisting in his first public statement, "No one can, with justice, apply that term to me."[30]

It is generally agreed that the introduction of "la Dictadura" (the Dictatorship)—as it would for years be known in Spain—was greeted with relief and broad, if shallow, support from the public. This was true even among the moderates and many liberals. Ortega y Gasset hailed the new government in *El Sol* as a splendid opportunity to cut the Gordian knot restraining modernization and regeneration. The "iron surgeon" had arrived. More than a little nominally enlightened opinion at first seemed to agree.

The regular government was replaced by a Military Directory composed of eight brigadier generals and one admiral. Public order was quickly controlled by martial law, which as it developed was maintained for two years, until 1925. The Catalan Somatén eventually was expanded into a national Spanish institution.[31] Beginning in October 1923, the first of what would be approximately fourteen hundred military "delegados gubernativos"—officers of junior or middle rank—were appointed to su-

Lieutenant General Miguel Primo de Rivera y Orbaneja, Dictator of Spain, 1923–1930

pervise local administration and the judiciary. Soon all municipal councils would be abolished, and later the same would be done with nearly all provincial assemblies. New personnel were appointed by decree, subject to the supervision of the military delegados. Government thus became much less representative than before, and was not necessarily more efficient, for most of the new delegados lacked administrative skills. Their number would later be reduced, but in some areas delegados continued to function until the end of the Dictadura.[32]

For several years the Dictator himself would be a generally popular figure with many admirers. His bluff, informal manner and sly sense of humor were appreciated as he appeared frequently in public and made an effort to communicate directly with the citizenry. Even some of the comparatively mild punishments he imposed on conspirators against his regime resembled practical jokes, and at first this reinforced his public image.

During the first two years of the Dictadura, however, Primo found that he had to devote a large part of his attention to Morocco. During 1924 the Spanish forces conducted a strategic retreat and then underwent reorganization to improve their performance. That year Abdul Karim made the ultimately fatal mistake of invading the French zone in a bold bid to liberate more of Morocco. The commitment of massive French forces made possible for the first time a Spanish–French collaboration that broke the back of the insurgency in 1925–1926, though all resistance was not put down until 1927–1928. The Moroccan problem had finally been solved, thanks to hard fighting, military reorganization, and French assistance.[33] Yet the Dictator's second Moroccan objective—to enhance the status of the Spanish Protectorate and incorporate the international enclave of Tangier—encountered almost complete frustration.[34]

Though its main success lay in military affairs, the fate of the Dictatorship would ultimately depend on its domestic achievements. There the key was the search for a political alternative, and at first Primo de Rivera denied that Italian Fascism was a prime influence. When an excited journalist asked on the first day of the pronunciamiento if it had been inspired by the March on Rome, Primo replied: "It has not been necessary to imitate the Fascists or the great figure of Mussolini, though his actions have been a useful example to all. But here in Spain we have the Somatén and we have had Prim, an admirable military and political figure,"[35] thus invoking the name of the greatest liberal reformer among the Spanish generals of the past century.

Despite such occasional references to liberalism, Primo de Rivera made clear his admiration of Mussolini. Alfonso XIII and the Dictator visited Rome within two months of Primo's takeover, marking the first official visit abroad by any Spanish chief of state in the twentieth century (and, aside from Franco's meetings with Salazar and Mussolini, the last until the reign of Juan Carlos). Don Alfonso is supposed to have remarked to King Vittorio Emanuele of Primo: "This is my Mussolini." The Italian Duce hailed him as the "chief of Spanish fascism," while Primo called Mussolini his inspirer and teacher.[36] Both the Spanish Dictator and the king viewed Mussolini's regime as the most friendly foreign power, if for no other reason than that it was the only other authoritarian west European state. Primo de Rivera was even more fulsome in an interview with the Fascist journal *Impero,* expressing his desire that "Spain should follow in the footsteps of Italian Fascism," and that "Spanish fascism" (which he otherwise failed to identify or define) would help to "liberate the country from harmful elements." "Fascism is a universal phenomenon that ought to conquer all nations. . . . Fascism is a living gospel."[37] In Rome he further extolled Mussolini as a "world figure" and "apostle of the campaign against revolution and anarchy" who had achieved "order, work, and justice."[38]

Though part of this was rhetorical exaggeration to please his Italian hosts, there is clear evidence that from the time of the Italian visit the Dictator developed expansive if vague ambitions to create some permanent alternative in Spain. Because he was a military man, his first interest lay in the middle-class Catalan militia of the Somatén, and on 1 December 1923 he was quoted as saying that "fascism is precisely our Somatén."[39] He subsequently spoke vaguely of converting the latter into some sort of national political organization, perhaps to be called a "partido cívico-somatenista" (civic Somatén party).

The initiative in forming some sort of political or civic organization to support the Dictatorship was, however, already being taken in the final months of 1923 by members of the Asociación Católica Nacional de Propagandistas (ACNP) under the leadership of Angel Herrera. Though most of the established political elites had rejected the new government, much ordinary middle-class opinion, particularly among Catholics (though not restricted to them), greeted it warmly. The effort begun by Herrera and other activists of the ACNP in the conservative and small-town society of Castile and León under the banner "Unión Patriótica Castellana" was soon expanded into a national organization, the Unión Patriótica (UP), in a meeting at Valladolid in April 1924.[40] It was joined by the tiny Spanish nationalist La Traza of Barcelona and several other small groups, and was quickly adopted as the new political front of the regime.

The UP was not so much a political party as the civic organization of a dictatorship opposed to political parties. It was based on patriotism, religion, and the established institutions (except parliament), and its program was never fully and explicitly developed. "Law" still ultimately meant the liberal constitution: thus Primo's declaration to the press on 15 April 1924: "There is a place in the party for all who respect the constitution of 1876," a qualification repeated five months later.[41]

The Unión adopted as its slogan "Monarquía, Patria y Religión" (Monarchy, Fatherland, and Religion), which sounded like nothing so much as a rewording of the traditional Carlist "Dios, Patria y Rey" (God, Fatherland, and King). In a set of programmatic norms issued on 1 May 1925, Herrera declared that the purpose of the Unión must eventually be to serve as the transitional "civil dictatorship" after the military dictatorship came to an end.[42] During the next five years, the UP functioned, officially at least, in every province of Spain, and at its height claimed to have 1,700,000 members, even though the real figure was probably scarcely a third of that.[43]

The members of the Unión Patriótica were primarily middle-class, Catholic, and conservative. In some provinces, sectors of the old political elite did join and dominate, but the organization also incorporated ordinary middle-class people who had not previously been politically active. The most distinctive new note was perhaps the role of middle-class Catholic leaders who had played little or no role in the old elitist parties. Overall, it would be accurate to say that the affiliates stood clearly to the right of the former parliamentary parties.[44]

The UP's doctrines reflected an attempt to revive historic Spanish Catholic ideology and to create a sense of positive nationalism. They emphasized hierarchical and authoritarian leadership, with Primo de Rivera as Jefe Nacional (National Chief), and the ultimate goal of some kind of corporative system. Though the *upetista* doctrines remained vague in detail, they pointed toward a permanent right-authoritarian alternative for Spanish government, far from the moderate liberal constitution of 1876.[45] In the process, the UP became the first significant force for twentieth-century Spanish nationalism, and it inaugurated a new style of mass rallies that would reappear among both left and right during the Second Republic.

Nonetheless, the UP bore little resemblance to Italian Fascism, and by 1928 several leading spokesmen would stress the differences between the two. Primo de Rivera himself emphasized that the UP was not "an armed force like Fascism."[46] His semiofficial newspaper, *La Nación*, came to insist that the two regimes differed "in very important aspects."[47] The UP ideologue José Pemartín, who admired Fascism, nonetheless criticized the latter's "disciplined, active exaltation," as well as the absence of any check

on the power of Mussolini's government, since such restraints were "necessary in every state"; moreover, Fascism's conflicts with the Church were
"absolutely reprehensible."[48]

The cordial relations between the two dictators did not yield very positive results. Though trade between their countries more than doubled between 1923 and 1926, the increase stemmed in good measure from the
general economic expansion of the period. A Treaty of Friendship and
Conciliation between Rome and Madrid was signed in 1926, but Spain
refused to yield to Italy a most-favored-nation status exempting it from a
very high tariff and had to turn toward collaboration with France to put
down the revolt in Morocco.[49] In 1928 Mussolini would announce officially that Fascism "is not goods for export."

During the later phase of the regime its spokesmen and apologists
would nonetheless draw encouragement from the large number of countries in southern and eastern Europe—Italy, Greece, Bulgaria, Poland,
Lithuania, Portugal, and Yugoslavia—in which more authoritarian new
systems had been established, sometimes transitorily, since 1922. This
provided confidence that national authoritarianism was the new trend,
even the wave of the future, in the less developed countries with major
social, political, and economic problems.

The chief alternative to direct parliamentary liberalism that had been
discussed in Spain increasingly since the 1890s was not something as violent and authoritarian as Fascism but rather the introduction of varying
degrees or aspects of corporative representation. Modern corporatist representation in economics was advocated in Spain as early as 1872 by Eduardo Pérez Pujol, professor of law at the University of Valencia. The Va-
lencian chapter of the Sociedad Económica de los Amigos del País, which
in the late eighteenth century had along with its counterparts pressed for
elimination of the traditional guild system, in 1879 recommended a reorganized guild system to rectify the excesses of rampant individualism.
From the time of Leo XIII, recommendations for some form of corporatism were frequent in Catholic ranks, and the most prominent traditionalist politician and ideologue of the early twentieth century, Juan Vázquez
de Mella y Fanjul, corresponded with the internationally known theorist
Albert de Mun and formulated corporatist doctrine for Carlism. Corporatism had figured ever more prominently in proposals for electoral and
parliamentary reform, particularly on the municipal and provincial levels,
where it was introduced by various elements in the main parties. For example, Primo de Rivera's eventual labor minister, Eduardo Aunós, had
earlier been a maurista and then a member of the Catalanist Lliga. Both
of these groups had favored the introduction of partial corporatist representation within the liberal system. Spain's most esteemed intellectual,

Ortega y Gasset, had at least temporarily come out for corporative reform in 1918,[50] and at approximately the same time the Socialist Party had urged the government to form state labor regulation boards and mixed juries of labor and employer representatives. In earlier years, the Dictator himself had been a devotee of corporatist ideas.[51]

After gaining control of the situation in Morocco, Primo de Rivera was farther than ever from relinquishing his "temporary" rule. In December 1925 he replaced the Military Directory with a "civilian" government—civilian at least to the extent that it was composed of regular government ministers. Five of the nine portfolios were held by conservative and rightist civilian appointees; the rest, by military men. The Dictator himself was still of little help in political definition. He was given to dicta such as "First live, then philosophize,"[52] bearing heavily on the regime's "simplicity." His supporters used the terms "intuicism" and "intuitionism" to describe this approach.[53] Though one of his ablest associates, the thirty-three-year-old finance minister José Calvo Sotelo, warned that a merely government-created party was "condemned to futility,"[54] Primo de Rivera was determined to expand the UP into a stronger base for his regime, stressing that the Unión was to be neither of the left nor the right and would even welcome nonmonarchists. In August 1927 he defined the UP as "an organized behavior."[55] It was not "doctrinaire" or "personalist," but somehow "apolitical" and purely patriotic. Compared with the "armed force" of Italian Fascism, the UP was a Christian movement, "virtually a cleansing civil crusade."[56] It encouraged, theoretically, the participation of women—a notable innovation—and stood for "la España una" (a united Spain), as well as the expansion of Spanish influence abroad and closer ties with Latin America.

The Dictatorship featured close association with Catholicism, not merely breaking with liberal precedent but virtually reassuming the norms of the ancien régime. Religion, in fact, became the main single ideological force invoked to legitimize the new regime, with official support for Church activities and the formation of numerous local "juntas ciudadanas" (citizen committees) to ensure the orthodoxy of social and cultural activities. The Catalan and Catholic statesman Cambó, who had no illusions about the long-term viability of the Dictatorship, observed with dismay how "the Church, ignoring all its traditions, placed itself at the service of force, against law and justice."[57] This, he feared, might result in an anticlerical eruption when the Dictatorship was over,[58] and such indeed proved to be the case in 1931.

For five years the regime rode the crest of the great prosperity of the 1920s, which achieved the most rapid economic expansion in all Spanish history to that point. A parliamentary regime might have presided over equal prosperity; the unique approach of the Dictatorship was to develop the first statist, nationalist economic policy since the enlightened despotism of the eighteenth century.[59] "Spain's economy was to be brought under an unprecedentedly high level of *dirigisme* and tutelage. State-assisted monopolies and a wide range of excessively bureaucratized regulating committees supervised economic activities down to their most minute details."[60] A strongly protectionist National Economics Council was instituted in 1924, and a state petroleum monopoly, CAMPSA, was created in imitation of a similar initiative in Italy. An effort was made to institute a concerted national hydraulic policy for dams and reservoirs, though the Second Republic would be more successful in actual development.

Virtually all sectors of national production registered significant increases, but the most notable was that of industry, which expanded from an index of 102.5 in 1923 to 142.0 in 1929, a rate of expansion not to be seen again until the 1960s. One of the most progressive aspects of the regime's economic policy was the introduction of a tax reform that for the first time tried to shift part of the burden from excises and property taxes to slightly graduated income taxes. Though the change was comparatively modest, it marked the only reform of any particular significance in this area until the 1980s. Altogether, the taxes collected increased approximately 50 percent under the Dictadura, making possible a wide variety of new initiatives, including the beginning of a modern highway system. Yet some of the new initiatives were poorly conceived and costs were heavy, producing a significant rise in the national debt. Once general conditions began to change in 1929, Spanish entrepreneurs were quick to turn against intrusive and controlling state policies, even though the Dictadura's activism had not resulted in any significant inflation.

Social programs and expenditures were impressive. Between 1920 and 1930 state expenditure on education more than doubled, school attendance increased 23 percent, and outlays on public health tripled. There were major increases in social services, with resultant significant declines in both infant mortality and the general death rate.[61] The Dictatorship initiated the first significant program of housing subsidies in Spanish history and also enhanced workers' rights and the scope of workers' insurance.[62]

A notable innovation was the beginning of a limited system of state-supervised labor arbitration, arguably the most directly corporatist measure the Dictatorship undertook. Labor Minister Aunós became especially interested in the Italian system of national syndicalism then being developed, and in April 1926 visited Italy, where he was received by Mussolini and the Italian minister of corporations, Giuseppe Bottai, who made available extensive information and advice.[63]

Partly as a result, a decree-law on economic corporations, promulgated in November 1926, theoretically divided the Spanish economy into twenty-seven corporations. Within each were to be formed freely elected "comités paritarios" (equal committees) for both workers and employers on the local level, "comisiones mixtas" (mixed commissions) on the provincial level, and corporation councils on the national level.[64] Aunós liked to point out that this was a theoretically more complete and hierarchical structure than that of Italy, and also more democratic.[65]

In fact, the Spanish corporative system remained largely undeveloped. The largest syndical organization in Spain, the CNT, had been formally dissolved and driven underground by the Dictadura. Its rival, the much smaller, more moderate and disciplined Socialist General Union of Labor (UGT), was willing to participate in the new system. In the process, it was able to elect numerous local delegates to the comités paritarios and expand its own membership by more than a third.[66] The other well-represented sector comprised the Catholic labor groups. Altogether, by May 1929 a total of 450 comités paritarios had been formed, representing more than 320,000 workers and nearly 100,000 employers.[67] This amounted to only about 15 percent of the national labor force and not even half the industrial workers, the ones primarily represented.

The condition of Spanish labor under the Dictadura varied widely. General wage levels did not rise, despite relatively high production and employment in industry. Overall real wages declined 3 percent between 1925 and 1930. Skilled workers in Vizcayan industry, strongly represented by Socialist and Basque unions, gained a nominal increase of 8 percent in wages over five years. The addition of not inconsiderable fringe benefits meant an even greater increase in real income. Yet the destitute farm laborers of the south may have seen their meager incomes rise very little or not at all. Most noteworthy perhaps was the more careful regulation of female labor, and the wages of women in some fields increased 12 percent over five years.[68]

After three years in power, Primo de Rivera showed not the slightest inclination to return to military life, and so finally had to consider the issue of presenting a permanent political alternative through constitutional reform. King Alfonso was reluctant, for he had begun to realize that the Dictatorship was lasting too long and might eventually lose whatever legitimacy it once had, not in law, but in large sectors of public opinion. According to Calvo Sotelo, Rome strongly encouraged the Dictator to hold some sort of legitimizing elections:

> When Aunós returned from Italy [in May 1926] . . . , the Duce, who not for nothing is an eminent politician, firmly advised Primo de

> Rivera through our minister of labor to convene a parliament, no
> matter what the system or procedure was. The essential thing, in his
> judgment, was not the style but the actuality. It is the suit which
> one must wear in international company, said Mussolini. This
> recommendation made a great impression on the mind of Primo de
> Rivera, not because he had such extraordinary regard for the Italian
> statesman but because their two regimes had a similar origin, and it
> seemed logical that they would evolve by analogous standards. At one
> point, then, Primo de Rivera decided to call for elections. . . . But his
> UP advisers and possibly some other friend—there are friendships
> that are fatal—turned him away from the proper course.[69]

Rather than regular elections, Primo eventually opted to convene a new National Assembly to deliberate on constitutional reform. None of this had been hinted at in the first phases of the Dictatorship, and Primo de Rivera sought to legitimate the maneuver through a national plebiscite held in September 1927. Women over eighteen years of age would be allowed to vote for the first time, and the regime utilized all its resources to gain a positive outcome. Of more than 13 million people legally recognized to vote, well over half—nearly 7.5 million—were proclaimed to have participated and given their approval. The government relied more on a certain amount of old-fashioned vote fraud than the heavy-handed police tactics of some other new dictatorships.

A tug-of-war then took place over the composition of the Assembly. The king wanted the leaders of the old parliamentary parties to participate, but they would insist on regular elections. Instead, the Dictator decided on a corporative assembly, made up of appointed or indirectly chosen delegates. More than half were representatives of the national or provincial governments or were appointed ex officio; about a third were corporatively selected representatives of what were euphemistically called national "Actividades, clases y valores" (social, economic, and cultural organizations), and forty-nine were representatives of the upetistas. Consequently the Assembly that convened in Madrid in October 1927 was a very conservative gathering of middle- and upper-class elites.

By the time of its final session in June 1928, the Dictator had announced a new twenty-point political program that called for completely corporative organization of the Spanish political and economic systems. He then appointed a constituent committee to prepare the draft of a new constitution. This body was dominated by ultra-rightist monarchists under the secretaryship of the right-wing Andalusian writer and politician José María Pemán. The new constitution eventually made public in July 1929 declared that sovereignty resided in the state, with a drastic increase in royal executive power. The crown was to have full responsibility for

appointing the government, its approval would be necessary for all legislation, and it would even hold a certain amount of authority over the
judiciary. There would be no parliamentary votes of confidence. Parliament would consist of a single chamber, half its members chosen by corporate representation and half by direct elections, the latter based on full
universal (including female) suffrage. The Senate would be replaced by a
small consultative Council of the Realm, which would also have extensive
authority in ratifying new government and judicial appointments, and in
judging the constitutionality of new legislation. Half its members would
be appointed by the government and half chosen by corporative elections.

During the summer of 1929, the proposal was subjected to extensive
criticism in the only lightly censored Spanish press.[70] It found little favor.
Primo de Rivera himself seemed to prefer corporative selection of all the
members of parliament, yet at the same time hesitated to give all-out support to such a basically illiberal document. He also did not favor giving
so much authority to the crown, while Don Alfonso was also skeptical,
doubting that he could accept greater authority in such a manner.[71]

Primo de Rivera formally denied any intention of copying Italian Fascism, declaring to an Italian journalist: "I am not creating a state like
your Mussolini. The conditions of Spain and Italy are different; here it
was only necessary to reestablish public morality and cure the country
of the infirmity of politics."[72] As Tusell has observed, "In Italy the most
important press organs were scornful of the Spanish regime as much for
its incapacity for institutional change as for individual aspects of policy,
such as its cowardice in facing disorder in the universities."[73]

The Dictator was particularly interested in gaining advice from his Italian counterpart on the constitutional reform.

> Thus even before the National Assembly published the results of its
> first deliberations, the Spanish Dictator transmitted the constitutional
> project to the Italian ambassador so that the Duce might see it and
> give his opinion, even to the point of suggestions for modifying the
> text. . . . Mussolini did not read the text of the Spanish constitutional
> project, but ordered that a report on it be prepared. Its conclusions
> pointed out the great differences between the two countries. In Spain
> there had been no revolution, nor a war ending in frustration, nor a
> great collective national myth, nor was there a political leader of
> charismatic appeal. Thus the Spanish project stood "half-way"
> between fascist principles and democratic electoral principles, and
> therefore whoever prepared the report for Mussolini recommended
> that he write to Primo de Rivera in vague and noncommittal terms.[74]

Meanwhile the Dictatorship began to drift into crisis, due in part to
a deteriorating financial situation, even though 1929 marked the apex

of the industrial boom and Spanish exports reached an all-time high, not to be seen again for more than thirty years. Easy credit and the entry of more and more foreign capital had encouraged the government to maintain a high rate of exchange for the peseta (a modest reflection, one might say, of Mussolini's artificially high "Quota Novanta" for the lira in 1926). Rumors that the peseta would be placed on the gold standard only encouraged more money to enter Spain, at least for the time being. Yet prosperity was also raising imports to unprecedented levels, while the government's heavy expenditures were now placing its budget severely in the red. By the end of 1928, it was clear that there could be no conversion to gold, and the government had to resort to increasingly interventionist measures to try to maintain the peseta's value, as more and more money flowed out. During the course of 1929 the peseta lost more than a third of its value on the international market, despite massive efforts at artificial support. Though most of the economy remained prosperous well into 1930—suffering little from the first phase of the international depression—prices dropped steadily in the stock exchange during the course of 1929.

By 1929 the regime had lost the confidence of businessmen and financiers. There was growing rebellion over the Dictatorship's interventionism and statist policies, which were now declared to be holding the economy back, and some Spanish producers even challenged the high tariff policy, demanding lower prices and more support for exports. Paradoxically, some praised Mussolini's economic policy for its relative liberalism, compared with the growing statism and restrictiveness of the Spanish regime.

Though by this point the business interests were clearly disaffected, the most overt opposition during 1929 came from the intelligentsia and university students. Part of the intelligentsia had not opposed the Dictatorship in the beginning, but the latter showed no interest in trying to win over intellectuals, and by 1929 opposition in their ranks was almost universal. University students became a political factor for the first time, partly because their number had more than doubled under the Dictatorship, from fewer than 19,000 in 1922 to more than 42,000 in 1929. Their ire was initially directed against an educational reform that for the first time in modern Spain would allow Catholic colleges to confer full academic degrees. Beyond that, the Federación Universitaria Española (FUE) soon came simply to oppose the Dictatorship itself, as evidenced by a series of student riots. Though the government announced cancellation of the proposed change at the beginning of the 1929–30 academic year, riots later broke out again. "Primo de Rivera's eventual downfall, as the Italian organ *Critica Fascista* rightly pointed out, owed much to the fact that his was essentially a movement of quinquagenarians devoid of any meaningful support either on the campuses or among youth in general."[75]

The Dictator did not intend to give up without a struggle, and the only further alternative he could conceive in the waning weeks of the year was to try to radicalize the regime on the Italian model. Italian diplomatic correspondence from Madrid in the final days of 1929 reported that Primo de Rivera was indicating that he would soon begin a fundamental reorganization of the UP along the lines of the Fascist Party. This reorganization never got started. As Javier Tusell and Ismael Saz have written:

> What the Spanish Dictator felt for Mussolini was considerably more than Platonic admiration. He was pathetically incapable of transferring Italian institutions to Spain and was often infantile in his effusive expressions to Mussolini. Nonetheless, the degree of his enthusiasm for the neighboring peninsula in the area of politics and ideology motivated actions that frequently have not been fully taken into account, such as, for example, the creation of the National Assembly, partly a consequence of Mussolini's advice, the request for the latter's advice on the constitutional project of 1929, the close collaboration in repressing their respective oppositions, and, finally, his farewell telegram to Mussolini. In the final phase of the regime there existed a real possibility of the "fascistization" of Primo de Rivera's government, though this always stemmed much more from the personal desires of the Dictator than from the Spanish historical context.[76]

Though Primo de Rivera indicated his willingness to scrap the new constitution altogether and changed some of his cabinet ministers, opposition grew on almost every front. The king had been increasingly restless for some time, as had sectors of the military. By the beginning of 1930 a military conspiracy was under way, possibly encouraged by the crown itself. The Dictator had lost the personal popularity of earlier years and was now sixty years of age, suffering severely from diabetes, with greatly diminished energy. All backing from the army gone, Don Alfonso was able to obtain his resignation on 30 January 1930.

### THE LEGACY OF THE DICTATORSHIP

It had been the first direct dictatorship of any length in Spanish history, and had won a difficult colonial war, instituted a number of reforms, and presided over a period of remarkable prosperity for millions. Yet the Dictatorship ended in complete failure due to its inability to legitimize itself or create any political alternative.

It had been one of the most moderate of all twentieth-century dictator-ships, one that infringed civil liberties as little as possible, produced few political prisoners, and refrained from political executions. To that extent even his enemies spoke well of Primo de Rivera after he was gone. The Socialist leader Indalecio Prieto termed Primo "a dictator without execu-tions," which was true enough, and added, "if only all dictatorships—though I desire no more of them—were like his."[77] His labor minister Aunós even suggested that the Dictatorship failed because Primo had never fully escaped the mental boundaries of liberalism. Nearly two de-cades later, in a lecture in Madrid entitled "The Ideology of Primo de Rivera as the Principal Obstacle to His Work," he emphasized that "it is not a secret to anyone that the marqués de Estella was fundamentally a liberal. He passed his life amid principles, theories, and facts of liberal import."[78] This interpretation was exaggerated, but there is no doubt that the Dictator was a victim of his own contradictions.

Though the Dictatorship was a failure, it marked a turning point in Spanish history. First, it ended the legal continuity of liberalism and the parliamentary monarchy, reasserting arbitrary rule in Spain for the first time in fifty years. Once that legality and continuity had been broken, stable parliamentary government would not reappear for more than half a century. By eliminating constitutional rule, it radicalized sectors of middle-class liberalism, reviving republicanism as a serious alternative for the first time in fifty years. Even more, much of the new middle-class re-publicanism drew its political lessons not from the old liberalism but from the recent dictatorship. Much republican opinion would soon hold that it was moderate liberalism that had failed, because it did not prevent the Dictatorship, and that therefore only a radical liberalism could succeed. The result was simply a new round of arbitrary government from the re-publican left starting in 1931, continuing the cycle of arbitrary rule begun by the Dictatorship, a process that continued for two more rounds until it erupted in complete conflagration. From this perspective—which is a compelling one—the Dictatorship was the first step in the coming of the Civil War of 1936.

Despite the Dictator's difficulty in achieving clear political definition, his regime nonetheless began to develop an alternative version of authori-tarian nationalism with which to replace the liberal state, seeking how-ever uncertainly to create a Spanish equivalent of some of the other new dictatorships in southern and eastern Europe.

It advanced a social approach that viewed the care of the popular classes as a mission that should be accomplished through a

corporatist reorganization of labor relations; it advocated an
economic policy based on control, planning, and *dirigisme* on a scale
never attempted before; and it defended a political system based on
direct democracy (through the plebiscite), organic as opposed to
individual suffrage, a strong executive, and a single official state party
that should hold the monopoly of key administrative posts as well as
of the political and ideological truth.[79]

It served not merely as a sort of ideological laboratory for the new authoritarian right, but also began to create a new style of symbolism, propaganda, and rhetoric, and it also brought to the fore a cadre of activists
who would subsequently play dominant roles in the radical right during
the following decade and in certain aspects of the Franco regime as well.

Though Primo de Rivera's own relations with the military were uncertain and ultimately adversarial,[80] he restored military dominance in politics for the first time since 1874. The formerly "abandonista" Dictator
led the army to victory in Morocco, helping to consolidate a new officer
corps that was more nationalistic and authoritarian. He also created a
new General Military Academy in Zaragoza to mold the psychology and
training of new officers, led by Francisco Franco, who became the youngest brigadier in Europe under the Dictatorship. "This army—let it not
be forgotten—was the one that seized the initiative in the revolt of 1936
and bore the main burden of the Civil War. In that sense, the Dictatorship
not merely bore the germ of Francoism but even gave it the means to
triumph."[81]

Francisco Franco was an attentive student of the Dictatorship, in which
he saw Primo de Rivera frequently hailed as the "Jefe Nacional" and
"Caudillo glorioso" of what was sometimes called a "glorioso movimiento nacional." Its successes, however temporary, provided him with
living proof that an authoritarian nationalist regime could achieve unity,
law and order, military victory, and national prosperity, together with
technical modernization. Its failures provided him with a cautionary example of how not to run a dictatorship. A new regime should develop a
clear-cut ideology and a more fully articulated political system, thus
avoiding what he would later term "el error Primo de Rivera."

Nor was the example of the Spanish Dictatorship lost on Mussolini.
Despite all the differences between their two regimes, it had been the
south European system most similar to Fascism and most congenial to
the Duce. After the king and most of the possessing classes turned against
it, the Spanish experience strengthened Mussolini's growing conviction
that his regime could not forever rest on a semipluralist compromise but
must become more authoritarian and revolutionary. To that extent the

Spanish experience was at least a minor factor in the Duce's turn toward a more radical policy in 1932.[82]

As a political type, Primo de Rivera's dictatorship lay somewhere between that of Mussolini, on the one hand, and the other regimes in southern and eastern Europe induced by the military, such as the República Nova of Sidonio Pais (1917–1918) and the military dictatorship of 1926 in Portugal, the short-lived Pangalos regime in Greece (1926), the authoritarian governments introduced by military revolt in Poland and Lithuania that same year, and the Uriburu regime in Argentina (1930–1932), on the other. These and other military coups in primarily agrarian countries in no case rested on a fascist movement, nor did they directly create an institutionalized new authoritarian regime, though the takeovers of 1926 in Poland, Portugal, and Lithuania did eventually lead to more institutionalized authoritarian regimes some years later. It was clear to reflective contemporaries that the Spanish dictatorship could not be fully compared with Fascism for lack of institutionalized mobilization and categorical doctrine.[83] Rather it should be compared with the initial breakdown of the liberal system in Italy and elsewhere, which in the cases of Italy and Portugal partially occurred during World War I. That in turn led to institutional destabilization followed by further democratization, political mass mobilization, and prerevolutionary conditions, at least in the Italian case, just as were produced by the aftermath of the Primo de Rivera regime and the depression and the Second Republic in Spain.

Most of the early efforts at overriding parliament and establishing authoritarian regimes in southern and eastern Europe failed to produce absolutely clear-cut alternatives that could endure for more than a few years, and in this once more the first Spanish dictatorship was typical. They succeeded to a greater extent, in most cases, only during the second, more radicalized phase of the 1930s, the primary early exception being Italy. Virtually an entire generation ahead of the rest of southern and eastern Europe in modernization, Italy led the way in introducing a stable noncommunist authoritarian regime, thereby also giving rise to the confusing terminology that labeled all such regimes fascist.

Another even more decisive consequence of Spanish affairs during the 1920s was the enormous social, cultural, and political impact of accelerated modernization. Spain changed more rapidly and decisively during that decade than in any equivalent period of its long history; only forty years later, during the 1960s, would such a rate briefly be recovered. This produced the most rapid proportionate expansion of the urban population and the industrial labor force in all Spanish history. Between 1910 and 1930 industrial employment almost doubled, from 15.8 percent of the labor force to 26.5 percent. By 1930 the portion of the active population engaged in agriculture and fishing had dropped to less than half for the first time, having shrunk from 66.0 percent in 1910 to 45.5 percent in 1930—a proportional decline never equaled before or after. Spain was no longer the overwhelmingly rural, agrarian society that it had been before 1910. Thanks to urban expansion and the boom in transportation and communication, growth was even more rapid in service employment than in industry, increasing from 20.8 percent in 1920 to 28.0 percent in 1930. As indicated, there were rapid improvements in education. Illiteracy dropped by almost 9 percent during the 1920s, again apparently the most rapid improvement within ten years in all Spanish history. The proportion of women in the labor force grew by almost 9 percent during the 1920s, and the percentage of women university students doubled between 1923 and 1927.

Though Spain remained seriously underdeveloped compared with northwestern Europe, these rapid changes were producing a new and more modern society that was better educated and increasingly urban, and also more socially and politically conscious. The limited experience of a broader prosperity during the 1920s produced a society now much more ambitious for change and further improvement than ever before, a society undergoing the most profound of psychological revolutions—the revolution of rising expectations. This resulted in a growing demand for political democratization and further improvement, leading to the democratic Republic in 1931, and mounting political and social demands in the years that followed.

## THE AUTHORITARIAN NATIONALIST RIGHT, 1930–1933

The collapse of the Dictatorship brought the downfall of the Spanish monarchy within fifteen months, for the crown's recognition of the Dictatorship in 1923 had seriously compromised the legitimacy of the reign of Alfonso XIII. Had the state moved vigorously to restore the political system through full and free elections soon after the Dictator's departure, it is at least theoretically possible that constitutional monarchy might have survived. Yet seven years of dictatorship had undone the old parliamentary parties, and they were being replaced by more radical new semiclandestine republican organizations. Alfonso feared to proceed directly to new elections and passed more than a year under an epigonic "dictablanda" (a mildly authoritarian government) that eroded the monarchy's remaining credibility. When municipal elections were eventually held in April 1931, the victory of republican candidates in the larger cities was accepted by much of Spanish opinion as a valid plebiscite. Without formally abdicating, Alfonso XIII quickly departed and the Second Republic was inaugurated. Though elsewhere in southern, eastern, and central Europe, forces of authoritarian nationalism were either in power or rapidly growing in strength during the depression year of 1931, Spain seemed to be registering the triumph of liberal democracy.

In 1930 only one small group of diehard supporters of Primo de Rivera stood against the left-liberal tide. In April 1930 they organized a new Unión Monárquica Nacional (UMN), reviving the name of the Maurist-rightist organization that existed in Catalonia from 1919 to 1923, although the UMN's monarchism was sui generis, for it vehemently opposed the liberalizing line of the gravely weakened monarchy. Led by the conde de Guadalhorce, public works minister of the Dictatorship, the UMN stood forthrightly for a new regime of strong monarchism based on outright authoritarian rule and the willingness to use violence. It glorified the historic Spanish ideology of Catholic identity and Catholic mission, seeking the full restoration of traditional Spanish values, initiating what would soon be termed the "neotraditionalist" school of monarchism. Though Fascism was hailed, a particular interpretation of religion formed much of its ideological basis. The economic program of Primo de Rivera was invoked to demonstrate the path to further development, a path that would harmonize the interests of all classes. Government should rest on popular support but not on political parties and direct elections. The UMN proposed to repress all regionalism in the name of "España, Una, Grande e Indivisible," reviving a slogan of the Dictatorship. Its position was categorical: if an atomistic, democratic Republic was inaugurated even by means of free elections, the new regime should be crushed through armed force.[84] The leading theorists and propagandists of the UMN were drawn from the front echelon of ideologues of the Primo de Rivera regime: José María Pemán, Victor Pradera, and Ramiro de Maeztu.

The UMN was flanked by various other tiny rightist-monarchist groups such as Reacción Ciudadana and Acción Nobiliaria, some of which briefly carried over into the early Republican years. Its most notable counterpart, however, was the tiny new Partido Nacionalista Español (PNE), founded in the same month by José María Albiñana, a physician and sometime medical school professor. The PNE shared the general right-radical ideology of the "umenistas," its two main features being an extreme emphasis on Spanish imperialism and the formation of a small political militia called Los Legionarios de España, the first of the radical new "shirt" formations, left and right, of Spain in the 1930s.[85]

What distinguished the UMN and the PNE from fascists in Italy and elsewhere was, first, their rigorously right-wing defense of vested interests and opposition not only to socialism but also to any form of significant economic reorganization, and second, their extreme ideological reliance on traditional culture, especially Catholicism. They were obviously opposed to any fascist "recirculation of elites." Thus they formed the first new Spanish variants of the radical-right movements then flourishing in continental Europe, sometimes in conjunction with, sometimes in competition with, fascism.

The former dictator died of natural causes in Paris in March 1930, only a few months after leaving Spain, exhausted by disease and disappointment. His eldest son, José Antonio, served as vice secretary general of the UMN. Young José Antonio's primary political passion was and would long remain the vindication of his father's work, which he was now trying to conceptualize in a radical, authoritarian, nationalist form. The fact that the UMN emphasized the role of monarchist youth made the new organization still more appealing.

The UMN admired the example of Italian Fascism and, like Albiñana's group, tried to copy aspects of fascist style. Mass meetings, heroic and violent rhetoric, and efforts at paramilitary organization (this last largely wanting in the UMN) were of course characteristic of many different forms of radical movements in Europe between the wars. The UMN's attempts to win popular support, beginning in the summer of 1930, were quite unsuccessful and failed to incorporate the main sectors of monarchists and conservatives. When the Republic began, there was once more little alternative to neoliberalism (now of a more radical kind) and the left in Spain.

Perhaps the only effort to articulate a more active Spanish nationalism from a more liberal perspective during the developing political crisis of 1929–1930 came once more from the moderate Catalanists. Joan Estelrich, at this point the leading theorist and intellectual of the Lliga, came out in 1929 for the "authentic revolution" of a partly corporative, partly liberal "federal, imperial" Spain, based on a completely new two-chamber legislature, a corporative chamber for economic interests and a directly elected chamber for political issues and national/regional interests. Like the Acció Catalana writer J. V. Foix, Estelrich spoke favorably of aspects of Italian Fascist organization and achievements, but considered the Italian regime too authoritarian to merit imitation.[86]

In general, by the end of the 1920s the concept of nationalism had been so thoroughly embraced by rightist and authoritarian forces that Spanish liberals generally refused to accept the concept, as was often the case with genuine liberals elsewhere. In the new 1927 edition of his classic *History of European Liberalism,* the distinguished anti-Fascist Italian historian Guido de Ruggiero declared that he would no longer use the term "nationalism" to describe the "national sentiments" of nineteenth-century liberals, saying that it now "has acquired a meaning very different from and even opposed to" that found in nineteenth-century liberal nationalists.

Under the Second Republic, for the first time in Spain's history, the main political movement of Spanish conservatism took the form of mass mobilized political Catholicism. The main Catholic group formed for the first Republican elections in mid-1931 was Acción Nacional, based especially in the conservative north-central provinces. The right in general remained in severe disarray, which permitted the new Republican–Socialist coalition to sweep these elections, but Acción Nacional was able to elect a handful of delegates to the parliament, and its principal leader, the eloquent, mentally nimble young university professor José María Gil Robles, soon began to make a reputation as the chief parliamentary spokesman for the right. After the government forced it by decree to change its name in April 1932, the party held its first national assembly as Acción Popular in October of that year. It pledged to work legally within the system and rejected violence but adopted an officially "accidentalist" position on the form of government. The position of the leadership was that monarchism was by that point inadequate as a political banner, but as Gil Robles admitted years later in his memoirs, "In theory I was and am a monarchist," while "the immense majority of those joining Acción Popular were decidedly monarchist."[87]

Since there was a strong tendency for political Catholics to organize around regional groups, Acción Popular soon joined with a variety of other Catholic political organizations to form a large new umbrella party, the Confederación Española de Derechas Autonómas (CEDA—Spanish Confederation of Autonomous Rightist Groups), which convened its first national congress in Madrid on 28 February 1933. Delegates claimed to represent a total of 735,058 members, which, even if somewhat exaggerated, still made the new party the largest new independent political group in Spanish history. Though the left Republican leader Manuel Azaña had declared in parliament that Spain as a whole had ceased to be Catholic— which in one sense was correct—more Spaniards still believed in Catholicism than in any other single creed or ideology. Militant Catholics made up no more than a large minority of Spanish society, but with most of them organized by the CEDA, they would constitute the largest single voting bloc in the country, as demonstrated in the two remaining Republican elections. Catholicism was particularly effective in the political mobilization of women, who were said to make up 45 percent of the CEDA's membership in Madrid; if correct, this was by far the highest proportion of female membership in any group.

The controversy that soon developed over the CEDA had to do with its true identity and real intentions. Moderate Republicans hoped to win it for a moderate liberal Republic of equal rights for all. Left Republicans and the worker left categorized the CEDA as the Trojan horse of rightist authoritarianism, "objectively fascist," and the controversy continued in historiography long after.[88]

In fact, it seems fairly clear that the CEDA's basic intentions were to win decisive political power through legal means—the exception being an ill-defined "emergency situation"—and then to enact fundamental revisions to the new Republican constitution (which restricted Catholic rights) in order to protect religion and property and alter the basic political system. The CEDA was not a truly democratic party, as some of its friends and allies hoped; nor was it in any genuine sense "fascist," as its enemies charged. The CEDA's platform was that of Catholic corporatism (as had been that of the Dictatorship, to a considerable degree), not merely in economic structure but also in political organization. Though the CEDA spokesmen were usually coy in defining their long-term goals, their aim was neither a fascist state nor restoration of the monarchy, but a corporative and conservative Catholic Republic, reordered by corporative representation that would mean some limitation of democratic rights. This would be far from the initial Republic of 1931–1933, but it was not the Mussolinian or Hitlerian state that its enemies alleged. If there was a model for the CEDA (and if a major Spanish party had been capable of taking the Portuguese seriously), it might have been the conservative and authoritarian "Estado Novo" in neighboring Portugal (which will be treated below in this chapter). By 1934 the one new authoritarian regime that *cedistas* unreservedly endorsed was the new Catholic corporative state of Dollfuss and Schuschnigg in Austria, which wrote God into the first article of its constitution.

Though publications associated with the CEDA sometimes carried favorable articles on Fascist Italy, Gil Robles went to some lengths to distinguish the movement from fascism. Charges of fascism, in the sense of arbitrary power, were in fact sometimes leveled in the parliament against Azaña's Republican administration. The Catalan Christian democrat Carrasco Formiguera referred to what he called Azaña's "fascist concept of the state," the old Liberal politician Royo Villanova termed the new regime a "fascist republic," and Basque nationalist spokesmen would call the 1933 education bill (which banned Catholic religious orders from teaching) an expression of "Gentilean etatism" (referring to Mussolini's first education minister) and "pure fascism."[89]

The CEDA's position on fascism and authoritarianism seemed equivocal. Gil Robles visited Rome at the beginning of 1933 and in September attended the annual Nazi Party rally at Nuremberg. He nonetheless insisted that the CEDA rejected statism, whether communist or fascist, and early in March 1933 declared, "Marxism is not combated with Hitlerian militia or fascist legions, but with an advanced social program,"[90] reiterating this stance at a meeting in Barcelona on the twenty-first. The CEDA press never directly endorsed Mussolini or Hitler as models, as later became the tendency with part of the extreme right-wing press, but its treatment of them was normally more favorable than unfavorable, and by the autumn of 1933 Gil Robles was saying that much could be learned from them, though he always avoided any clear-cut endorsement. His most sinister remarks came in a major campaign speech in Madrid on 15 October 1933: "We want a totalitarian patria, but it is strange that we are invited to look for novelties abroad when we find a unitary and totalitarian policy in our own tradition," referring to the new concept, adopted by ideologues of the radical right in recent years, that Spain's first unified monarchy under Fernando and Isabel in the late fifteenth century was itself somehow a "totalitarian regime" (in fact, a gross misreading of Spanish history). He went on: "For us power must be integral. For the realization of our ideal we shall not be held back by archaic forms. When the time comes, parliament will either submit or disappear. Democracy must be a means, not an end. We are going to liquidate the revolution."[91] The CEDA's ambiguity concerning fascism was symbolized by the official salute of their youth movement, Juventudes de Acción Popular (JAP—Youth of Popular Action): the right arm was raised only half-way, then drawn back across the chest.

## THE MONARCHIST REALIGNMENT

It was only natural that a semimoderate rightist movement like the CEDA would attract the bulk of middle-class Catholic and conservative opinion. By definition, the conservative middle classes wanted to avoid trouble, and a technically legalistic alternative reflected their habits and values. Small groups of the more extreme monarchist right could not accept the CEDA's relative moderation. While most ordinary monarchists followed the CEDA, a smaller, more doctrinaire sector organized a more clear-cut solution for the radical right.

This formed around a journal called *Acción Española* that began publication in December 1931. The activists of *Acción Española* were drawn from three areas: former followers of the monarchist Conservative leader Antonio Maura, the more ultra-conservative wing of social Catholicism, and Carlism. Each of these earlier Spanish sources had been superseded in the thinking of the new group; classical maurismo had been too legalistic and parliamentarian, the nascent Spanish social Catholicism of the early 1920s too heterogeneous, squeamish, and even democratic,[92] and Carlism too reactionary and backward-looking.[93] Financial backing came from wealthy rightists, and above all from the well-organized Bilbao industrial-financial elite.[94]

The very title of *Acción Española* made obvious the inspiration of the French Maurrasian radical right. Italian Fascism was a more distant secondary influence. Chief foreign collaborators were members of Action Française, followed by Portuguese Integralists and National Syndicalists and a few Italian Fascists. *Acción Española* generally approved of Hitlerism but criticized the German movement for its secularism and demagogy, holding that the Führerprinzip was no substitute for a monarchy.

*Acción Española* adopted what it conceived as a modernized neotraditionalism, pledging to revive the traditional Spanish ideology, grounded in religion and in strong monarchist institutions. It derived much inspiration from the Primo de Rivera regime, with which nearly all its members had been associated; in turn, the critique of the regime's failure was a prime goal.[95] Blame was placed on the lack of elite support and the absence of a clear vision of a modern new authoritarian structure.

The editor of *Acción Española* was Ramiro de Maeztu, formerly a leading noventayochista writer who had converted to the principles of authority and religion at the time of World War I. Maeztu was to give the final major historical definition to the traditional Hispanic ideology in his *Defensa de la Hispanidad* (1934), a polemic in defense of traditional Hispanic culture and religion, both European and American, as opposed to Soviet communism and Anglo-American materialistic liberalism.[96]

All this first took an organized political form with the initially semiclandestine founding of the Renovación Española party in February 1933. The chief political leader in this first phase was Antonio Goicoechea, former head of the authoritarian right wing of the Juventudes Mauristas. A variety of small extreme-rightist sectors came together to found the new monarchist party.[97]

Authoritarian *alfonsino* monarchism hoped to broaden its base by incorporating the other sector of Spanish monarchism—traditionalist Carlism. The onset of a radically anticlerical Republic had the effect of reviving Carlism, which most observers had considered already passé, doomed by processes of social change. Though Carlism had split in three directions during the late nineteenth and early twentieth century, all three sectors had come together by 1932 in an expanded new Comunión Tradicionalista, and Carlism showed greater vigor and activism than at any time since the late nineteenth century. Since the last pretender in the direct male line was elderly and without a direct heir, the direct Carlist male line would soon become extinct. Neotraditionalist alfonsismo carried on negotiations during 1931–1932 to try to obtain unified Carlist recognition of and support for an alfonsino monarchism that now rejected liberalism and incorporated key Carlist principles.

Most Carlists remained suspicious of the formerly liberal dynasty, however, and alfonsino neotraditionalism proposed a formula of centralized authoritarianism that was far from identical with the noncentralist traditionalism of Carlism. By 1934 the pretender, Don Alfonso Carlos, recognized the comparatively young Seville lawyer Manuel Fal Conde as jefe-delegado, or national leader, of the Carlist movement within Spain. Fal Conde was a Carlist purist and intransigent who sought to avoid any compromise and to expand a revitalized Carlism through an energetic national organization. Though Carlists might on occasion establish temporary alliances with other rightist groups, they refused to yield to alfonsino neotraditionalism, which from their point of view remained illegitimate, opportunistic, and excessively influenced by modern centralized dictatorship.

The principal new statement of traditionalist doctrine would be the dissident Carlist Victor Pradera's *El Estado nuevo* (1935), a work that made some impression on Francisco Franco, even though he rejected its theoretical limits on authoritarianism. Pradera defined Spain's Catholic identity and presented a system of societal corporatism, under monarchy, that would be autonomous from the state though partially regulated by it and also compatible with partial regional decentralization. Though the Carlist youth organization, like the CEDA's Juventudes de Acción Popular, suffered from aspects of the vertigo of fascism and sometimes used fascist-like slogans, the Carlists differentiated their traditionalist, ultra-Catholic, monarchist, and partially decentralized corporatism from the radical, centralized, modern authoritarianism of Italy and Germany.[98]

## THE PORTUGUESE ALTERNATIVE:
## AN AUTHORITARIAN NATIONALIST REPUBLIC

In underdeveloped Portugal the transition to a republic had occurred more than two decades earlier than in Spain. Portugal's reduced scale often had the effect of focusing issues, while its weakness meant that foreign and imperial affairs usually had greater impact than in Spain. The elitist censitary constitutional monarchy in Portugal had been very similar to its Spanish counterpart, had stabilized itself earlier, and maintained relatively uninterrupted stability longer, until its final crisis. A high rate of illiteracy reduced pressures for democratization, but by the same token the narrowness of elitist liberalism remained unrelieved, and Portuguese liberals were incapable of the regenerationist tendencies found in Spain.

After the 1890s republicanism developed as the main new force within Portuguese nationalism, yet it never became democratic. Throughout the history of the parliamentary republic of 1910–1926, suffrage remained restricted, primarily through the exclusion of the large number of illiterates. Portuguese republicanism soon fragmented badly. Facing an increasingly authoritarian opposition, it became increasingly authoritarian itself, and in the early 1920s extremist republicans revealed radical tendencies in their relations with more moderate republicans. Despite the prosperity of the decade elsewhere, Portuguese republicans could not achieve unity or deal with basic financial and economic problems. They eventually became discredited even among moderates.

A united and well-organized military coup seized power on 28 May 1926 almost without violence, undoubtedly encouraged by the movement toward political authoritarianism in Spain and other parts of southern and eastern Europe.[99] The parliamentary regime was so discredited that at first the new military government was praised by diverse opinion from right to left. It rested, nonetheless, on the particular support of rightist authoritarian elements among the officer corps and civilian politics, though these were considerably divided among themselves. Several small authoritarian nationalist groups from earlier years, such as the Integralists and the Cruzada Nun' Alvares Pereira, still survived. A new right radical movement, the Liga Nacional 28 de Maio, was formed in 1928 to try to guarantee the permanent rule of authoritarian nationalism.[100] The military, however, proved no more successful than parliamentary liberals in solving financial and political problems.[101]

In 1928 the military dictatorship installed as new finance minister Dr. Antonio de Oliveira Salazar from Coimbra University, a leading figure among Catholic corporatists. He immediately made himself the system's indispensable administrator, balancing the budget and stabilizing government finance. In 1932 Salazar became prime minister, and from that point he sought to create a permanent new system of institutionalized moderate authoritarianism—something that neither Primo de Rivera nor the Portuguese military had been able to achieve. Given the very limited support for monarchism in Portugal, that was not a viable option. Instead, Salazar introduced in 1933 a new corporative constitution for the Portuguese Republic—the first new corporative constitution in Europe, anticipating that of Austria by one year. Salazar, who was devoutly Catholic and opposed to any form of radicalism, sought to reconcile economic corporatism and a controlled authoritarian political liberalism by introducing both a corporative chamber for the representation of social and economic interests and a directly elected national assembly. A National Union—very similar to Primo de Rivera's Unión Patriótica—was organized to support the government, help win elections, and provide administrative personnel,[102] but elections were held regularly, even though they were carefully controlled. Church and state remained separate. Salazar's system might best be described as one of "authoritarian corporatism" or even of "authoritarian corporative liberalism."[103] It would withstand all challenges for many years. With a total lifespan longer than that of the Franco regime, it would last longer than any other European right-authoritarian system.

*Three*

# The Fascism of the Intellectuals

The appeal of fascism in Spain was limited by the weakness of Spanish nationalism, by the country's lack of involvement in World War I, and by the lesser impact there of the cultural crisis of the fin-de-siècle. Radical Catalanism had by the 1920s created the first direct-action nationalism in Spain, but this had not assumed a fascist form. Thus reaction to the frustrations of liberalism, to the anarchist left, and to the struggle in Morocco had been led by one sector of the military and had taken the form of rightist authoritarianism, eschewing fascist revolutionism. In Spain, as in some other countries, a genuine fascist doctrine would first be disseminated by small circles of intellectuals and a few activist allies.

## ERNESTO GIMÉNEZ CABALLERO

The first intellectual to espouse directly fascist ideas in Spain was Ernesto Giménez Caballero. Born to a prosperous family in Madrid in 1899, Giménez Caballero had the generally liberal education of the Spanish intelligentsia of his time. He first came to attention with the publication of his *Notas marruecas de un soldado* (1923), a personal memoir written after he had served a year as a recruit in the fighting in the Protectorate. This original and well-written memoir raised pertinent questions about the confused and poorly organized struggle in Morocco—making its author an overnight success among the stylish liberal intelligentsia—but it also raised questions about Spain's role and place in the world, and concluded with a whiff of *trincerocrazia* (Mussolini's term for the elitism of the trenches) that was originally passed over by most readers. Arrested by a military court, the young author was released by the new Dictator himself and quickly went off for a year as Reader in English at the University of Strasbourg. There he soon reacted against a foreign ambience, embracing an inchoate *españolismo*. He also met his future wife, sister of the Italian consul, whom he married in 1924 and who introduced him to Italian culture and Fascism. Back in Madrid, Giménez Caballero moved promi-

51

nently among the literary avant-garde. In 1929 he published a book entitled *Los toros, las castañuelas y la Virgen* (The Bulls, the Castanets, and the Virgin), his first direct inquiry into the character of *españolismo* and—more significantly in the eyes of most—became the director of a new journal, *La Gaceta Literaria,* which quickly established itself as the foremost literary avant-garde journal in Spain, perhaps the premier voice of what would later be called the literary "Generation of 1927."

José-Carlos Mainer has judged that Giménez Caballero was "surely the most lucid of all the young writers of 1929 with regard to the political meaning of the vanguard position: in the first place, for what his work did to try to politicize the ultra-contemporaneity of the movement . . . ; in the second place, for his concern to find a historic role in promoting something which defined itself as marginal to such an enterprise, but which he effectively associated directly with the intellectual rupture of the fin-de-siècle."[1]

For Giménez Caballero this involved a combination of the most extreme manifestations of avant-gardism with increasing attention to issues of cultural nationalism, for he was becoming increasingly obsessed with the backwardness of Spain and the problem of finding the keys to its resurgence and modernization.[2] At first his nationalism was culturally and even politically pluralistic, for Giménez Caballero recognized the vitality of Catalan and Portuguese culture, as well as that of other parts of the peninsula. He was fascinated by Catalan modernism and the Catalan avant-garde, and wanted to incorporate Catalan modernization into the framework of a sort of federal nationalism perhaps at first not altogether dissimilar to that of the Lliga. Giménez Caballero led in organizing expositions of Catalan, Portuguese, German, and Argentine books in Madrid during 1927–1928. He thought that Barcelona might become the Spanish Milan and, as he had written in 1923, that the regions and peoples of the peninsula might unite in a single "haz" (bundle)—the literal Spanish equivalent of the Italian "fascio" (though Unamuno preferred "fajo").

Yet another aspect of his early pluralist nationalism was his discovery of Sephardic culture in Morocco, an interest dating from his year of military service. The *Gaceta* drew attention to this aspect of emigre minority national culture, and Giménez Caballero sought to collect Sephardic materials from other parts of the Mediterranean.

*La Gaceta Literaria* quickly acquired an international audience, and in 1928 its director—now becoming colloquially known from his initials as "Gece"—undertook a tour of several countries in which he had been invited to speak, ending in Italy. For "Gece," this was the road to Damascus. He was completely dazzled.[3]

"After a few days, Rome became everything for me. It was the imperial and Caesarean Madrid that Madrid would never be."[4] Rome was the seat of both western civilization and Latin Christendom, the light obscured by four centuries of Protestantism and the Germanic north. There Italian Fascism was providing the new political and cultural forms to achieve modernization and coherent internal development, uniting the cultural elite and the masses. Fascism was the true revolution of modernity, but also the genuine expression of a Latin and Catholic people that transcended materialism and artificiality, elevating popular culture and national ambience into a violent and transcendent mission. It could also show the way to Spain, whose weakness came from copying outworn models from northern Europe. Giménez Caballero had earlier written on the eve of the pronunciamiento of Primo de Rivera: "Currently Spain can be considered one of the most liberal nations in Europe; consequently, Spain is at this moment one of the most backward countries on the European continent."[5] Things had changed little for him in that regard by 1929; the regime of Primo de Rivera was merely "archiburgués" (ultrabourgeois).

Part of the concept behind *La Gaceta* was that contemporary art would lead to a "new man" and help to revitalize Spain. After his trip to Italy, Giménez Caballero came to doubt that this could be achieved primarily by cosmopolitan avant-garde esthetics. He officially announced his conversion to fascism on 15 February 1929 in *La Gaceta,* publishing the prologue to his new translation of the Fascist writer Curzio Malaparte's *Italia contro Europa.* To achieve a "haz," a real "fascismo hispánico," would require going far beyond anything suggested by Primo de Rivera. "Gece" now espoused the violent, populistic national syndicalism of Malaparte, calling this a "hacismo" for Spain, though he acknowledged that his country was not yet prepared for it.

This declaration created a political and editorial crisis for *La Gaceta,* inspiring the resignation of part of the staff and causing some scandal. Trying to control the damage (all the more because he recognized the inviability of a genuine fascism in Spain at that point), "Gece" editorially reiterated that the *Gaceta* was a literary journal and would not become a vehicle for fascist or any other political ideas. This was only partly correct; certainly the attention earlier given to Catalan, Galician, and Portuguese literature had virtually disappeared. Amid the liberalization that followed the end of the Dictadura, Giménez Caballero tried to recover lost ground by declaring himself a "demo-liberal," but this convinced few. By 1929 the only Catalan to be regularly published by the *Gaceta* was the elitist Eugenio d'Ors, while the genuinely proto-fascist young intellectual Ramiro Ledesma Ramos began to appear on the front pages. During 1929–1930 Giménez Caballero generally tried to avoid use of the term "fascist" but more and more frequently turned to the theme of violence in cultural and national change. He seems to have maintained an underlying concern for a kind of "pan-Latin fascism," but his observations on German Nazism were often quite critical, rejecting Nazi racism and anti-Semitism. As a sort of historical and cultural Catholic, he was also opposed to Protestant countries generally. Whereas communism tended to be merely destructive, Italian Fascism was held to have created a new synthesis of western and Latin civilization.[6]

Amid the left-liberal effervescence of 1931, Giménez Caballero became increasingly isolated. For six months, beginning in August, he alternated biweekly publication of the *Gaceta* with a sixteen-page publication written entirely by himself, entitled *Robinson Literario* (alluding to his condition, marooned like Robinson Crusoe). This mainly gained him a further reputation for opportunism and irresponsibility, since one of its main objects was to court the politically dominant left. Manuel Azaña, strong man of the Republican left, was hailed as the closest thing to a fascist leader in Spain (a judgment in which Mussolini concurred, however ridiculous this may seem in retrospect), and the Socialist labor minister Largo Caballero was acclaimed for his effort to "nationalize socialism," as "Gece" liked to put it.

His two major works on Spanish nationalism appeared in the years immediately following: *Genio de España* (1932) and *La nueva catolicidad* (1933). While he did not officially propose a program for a "Spanish fascism," he passed in review the high points of national history and the various regenerationist proposals, finding nearly all wanting. The basis for national renewal lay in developing "true Catholicity," the institutions and culture of Spanish, Italian, and Latin Catholicism within a framework of strong nationalism, unity, an authoritarian state, and an armed militia and a strong army. The CEDA was too moderate and semiliberal to serve this purpose, while its Catholicism was too theological and narrow. Giménez Caballero was trying to sketch a broad historical, cultural, and political outline for a sort of Spanish fascism that might be naturally allied with Italy and with certain others, but his nostrums were so general—and sometimes vague—with so little practical political content that their impact was very limited.

## RAMIRO LEDESMA RAMOS AND THE BIRTH
## OF NATIONAL SYNDICALISM

The fascist project for Spain that Giménez Caballero was unable to define coherently was given a different but much clearer form by the intense and rigorous young philosophical essayist and writer Ramiro Ledesma

Ramos. If "Gece" was the first clear-cut Spanish fascist intellectual, Ledesma was the first intellectual to define a relatively clear-cut Spanish fascism.

Ledesma was born in a small town in Zamora province in 1905, son of a schoolteacher who was also the son of a schoolteacher. At first he followed the typical career of the precocious student in provincial surroundings. Unable to afford an elite higher education, he completed secondary school by examination in Salamanca at the age of sixteen, then moved to Madrid to prepare for and take the examination for a junior position in the Cuerpo de Correos y Telégrafos (the Postal and Telegraph Corps). Despite his youth, he took first place in the national competition and was given a position as soon as he reached the minimum age of qualification in 1922. For several years he was moved about to various cities and served a brief period of mandatory military service in the army's Centro de Automóviles in Barcelona at the time of Primo's coup before later being assigned permanently to Madrid. His family moved to the capital in 1924, and for the remainder of his brief life he lived at home in the family apartment in north-central Madrid.

At the age of eighteen Ledesma had written a dramatic philosophical novel presented as the memoir of a pessimistic intellectual who eventually commits suicide. An indulgent uncle subsidized the publication of this early effort, *El sello de la muerte* (*The Seal of Death*), in 1924. Ledesma later wrote another philosophical novel, doomed to remain unpublished. From a conventional youthful and Nietzschean *Weltschmerz,* he soon moved to more serious studies. He completed a formal bachillerato at a prestigious Madrid institute and then enrolled in the university, gaining a licenciatura in philosophy in 1930. Philosophy became his passion, as he moved from Cartesian rationalism to the neo-Kantian idealism of Hermann Cohen to more recent German mathematical philosophy. He developed fluent reading skill in German, and his ability in mathematics enabled him to deal with complex logic with relative ease. During the later 1920s Ledesma may have been the best-read young intellectual in Madrid, devouring works by Spanish, German, French, and Italian authors. (In contrast, the culture of Anglo-Saxon empiricism did not interest him.) Spare, tense, and abstract, this green-eyed young intellectual of medium height and reasonably attractive—though not conventionally handsome—appearance seems to have had little or no private life and no known sex life. Mornings were devoted to his work as a civil employee, while afternoons, evenings, and weekends were given over to university classes and to incessant reading and writing.[7]

Still in his early twenties, Ledesma began to make a name for himself as a translator of German philosophical works and as an essayist and critic of new philosophical trends. His writings found ready acceptance in the capital's leading cultural-philosophical journal (Ortega y Gasset's *Revista de Occidente*), the leading avant-garde literary journal (*La Gaceta Literaria*), and the leading newspaper (*El Sol*).[8] He found a welcome in the salons of both Ortega and "Gece."

By the time the Dictatorship ended, Ledesma was well placed either to follow a career like the earlier one of Manuel Azaña—divided between an undemanding bureaucratic position and intellectual and literary affairs—or to extend his university studies in preparation for an academic career. In fact, he did neither, for 1930 was the year of a different decision.

Whereas the dilemmas of subjectivism and objectivity had once been important issues in his philosophical studies, his later readings in Husserl and Heidegger encouraged him to move directly into the realms of existence and experience, leaving aside epistemological problems. By 1930 he was focusing on Heideggerian *Angst*. Anguish and the threat of nothingness could be overcome only by will and achievement, by an action that would increasingly become direct action.

For some time Ledesma had been preoccupied with "el problema de España" that had haunted other Spanish intellectuals before him, without resolution. At first this concern had focused on Hispanic culture, as he lamented: "We are the only great people who have still not borne the philosophical scepter. And who, therefore, have still not projected an intellectual dictatorship over the world."[9] He is said to have completed the manuscript of a book called "Filosofía del Imperio," dealing with the diversity of worldwide Hispanic culture and its extensive bibliography, which was subsequently lost by a press considering it for publication.[10] Ledesma adopted the standard "españolista" critique, holding that decline had been due not to internal decadence but to external military defeat, and that national frustration stemmed from disunity and the aping of northwestern European models. Eventually, however, he became convinced that Spain could find no solution in trying to return to its cultural past, that it needed a popular modern revolution of unity, authority, and central leadership, with a revolutionary economic program to reintegrate the masses, and the readiness to affirm willpower, violence, and the conquest of a new place in the world. What Spain needed was something like fascism.

The first public expression of Ledesma's extreme nationalist and philofascist sentiments came in January 1930 at a large literary banquet in honor of Giménez Caballero, attended also by significant members of the liberal intelligentsia. His declaration created something of a scandal, though accounts differ. Ledesma was well aware of the danger of being

Ramiro Ledesma Ramos, founder of the Juntas de Ofensiva Nacional-Sindicalista (JONS)

merely dismissed with the pejorative label of "fascist," and wrote to the *Heraldo de Madrid* that "we," meaning principally himself, "are not fascists." The entire year was one of self-debate, the word "rigor" appearing frequently in his writings, and Ledesma's last philosophical article was published in the *Revista de Occidente* in December 1930. Soon afterward he made the decision to abandon scholarship and philosophy for political activism, and to "save Spain."

The sudden catharsis shocked some of Ledesma's acquaintances, who could not conceive of this obsessive young intellectual as anything other than scholar, philosopher, or writer, but the die was cast. Early in 1931 he drew together nine young collaborators, all about his own age. The fledgling journalist Juan Aparicio, who served as secretary of the little group, would later observe that what they had in common "was their youth and their university background." [11] They signed their first manifesto by candlelight in an office consisting of four largely unfurnished rooms. Their new organ was called *La Conquista del Estado* (*The Conquest of the State*) in imitation of the Italian Fascist Curzio Malaparte's weekly *La Conquista dello Stato;* only a few pages in length, it appeared on 14 March 1931. Money was a desperate problem, the first small subsidy being provided by the Comisaría Regia del Turismo (Royal Council of Tourism). [12]

The "Political Manifesto" in this first number bombarded the reader with slogans and apodictic declarations, proclaiming "SUPREMACY OF THE STATE. . . . Ultimate sovereignty will reside in it, and only in it. . . . It is up to the state to accomplish all the political, cultural, and economic goals that the people have. We therefore defend panstatism, a state that achieves all our ends." "We will affirm Spanish culture with imperial goals." "EXALTATION OF THE UNIVERSITY. The university is for us the supreme creative organ of cultural and scientific values. Peoples without a university remain at the margin of superior achievement. Without culture there is no tension of spirit, as without science there is no technique." "DEVELOPMENT OF THE PROVINCES OF SPAIN. The prime reality of Spain is not Madrid, but the provinces. Our most radical goal, therefore, is to articulate and foster the vital interests of the provinces. . . . The new state will consequently make the complete and integral autonomy of the municipalities the indispensable basis of its structure," to revive the old Hispanic tradition of local autonomies. "SYNDICAL STRUCTURE OF THE ECONOMY. . . . The new state will impose a syndical economic structure. . . . The new state will break the back of the fearsome and tremendous agrarian problem that presently exists. Through the expropriation of large landlords." Expropriated land was to be given directly to the rural population under supervision of local municipalities "and with a preference for communal and cooperative cultivation." "We do not seek votes, but brave and audacious minorities. We seek militant young squads without any hypocrisy about guns and military discipline. Civil militias that can break the anachronistic bourgeois pattern of pacifist antimilitarism. We want to embrace politics with a military sense of responsibility and struggle. Our organization will be built on syndical cells and political cells." Members would have to be between eighteen and forty-five years of age.

Ledesma has been described even by friends as a man of "cold personality," and though he normally dressed correctly in suit and tie, was sometimes slightly unkempt or careless about his appearance.[13] Later he would be remembered as "a man of harsh temperament and steel-like intolerance."[14] There is no question that he was the most aggressive and tough-minded of all the nationalist intellectuals in Spain. In one of the first numbers of *La Conquista,* he paid homage to the intellectual life that he had abandoned, observing that the intellectual "constitutes a magnificent human type, and is of all social strata [sic] the most indispensable," but that a national crisis demanded more than mere theorizing.[15] Thus there would be considerable irony in the fact that nearly all Ledesma's brief political career would be devoted to propagandistic theorizing and the repetition of simple and general radical ideas.

The first number of his new publication had little impact, except to arouse mirth among some of Ledesma's intellectual acquaintances, who referred to the new organ as "La Conquista del Establo" (The Conquest of the Stable). Giménez Caballero sent his support from Barcelona and contributed to several numbers, but in Madrid almost the only voice to speak favorably on its behalf in the press was that of the right-authoritarian Ramiro de Maeztu.

Ledesma and his associates refused to apply the term "fascist" to themselves, even though their terminology made the Italian inspiration perfectly obvious. One of the group, Antonio Bermúdez Cañete, was the first Spanish translator of Hitler's *Mein Kampf,* of which Ledesma hoped to become the first publisher in Spain.[16] Nonetheless, he was aware of the need to do more than imitate a foreign movement and sought to develop his own form of revolutionary Spanish nationalism.

Though *La Conquista del Estado* demanded the extirpation of Marxism as materialist, anti-Spanish, internationalist, and subversive, it hailed all revolutionary regimes abroad, including the Soviet Union, and even declared that it would prefer a Soviet-type economic system in Spain, if purely Spanish, than the continued dominance of the "foreign bourgeoisie." The fourth number (4 April) demanded immediate revocation of all concessions to foreign capital and was banned by the police—hardly surprising, since the preceding number had emphasized the group's intention "to impose its policies violently."

By 4 June the little journal was shrilling:

> Long live the new world of the twentieth century!
> Long live Fascist Italy!
> Long live Soviet Russia!
> Long live Hitler's Germany!
> Long live the Spain that we will make!
> Down with the bourgeois parliamentary democracies!

*La Conquista del Estado* stressed that "the individual has died" and that its goal was "the collectivist state," hoping to win sectors of the left to revolutionary nationalism. It looked especially to the CNT, free of Marxist internationalism. Ledesma may even have been aware that some anarchists had, like himself, been attracted to Malaparte's fascist book, *The Technique of the Coup d'Etat.*[17] Winning over anarchosyndicalists was to become a long-cherished goal of Spanish fascism, lasting well into the 1940s but never achieving much success. Despite the "Sorelianism" of some anarchists, only one local leader, Nicasio Alvarez de Sotomayor, was seduced by Ledesma into joining his group. Meanwhile, *La Conquista* urged farm laborers to demand expropriation of large estates, announcing formation of a "Bloque Social Campesino" (Social Peasant Bloc), which, like most of its projects, never materialized.

By the end of May, as the movement toward Catalan autonomy gathered force, *La Conquista* had launched what would be an ongoing, shrill campaign against "separatism." At the same time, declaring that "we affirm our will to empire," it assured Catalans that their region would have "a privileged place" in an imperial Spain that would stretch "from the Pyrenees to the Sahara." By mid-July his anti-Catalanist activities, including a minor abortive effort at terrorism, would lead to Ledesma's first detention by police.

Though he had to spend only three days in jail, the publication was now the target of three separate indictments and had run out of funds. In September, however, Ledesma received a small subsidy from young Spanish nationalists in Bilbao, such as José Félix de Lequerica and José María de Areilza, who had access to wealthy circles in Vizcaya.[18] This sufficed for four more numbers during October, at which point *La Conquista del Estado* ceased publication permanently.

Years later, Areilza presented a vivid pen portrait of Ledesma the revolutionary nationalist:

> Ramiro was nearly thirty, not very tall, firm and vigorous in
> appearance, with a pale face, prominent nose, strong chin, high

forehead, abundant dark chestnut hair and a steely gray look, profound and inquisitive, like a man deep in reflection, attuned to inner meditation. This sensation was heightened by extremely poor hearing, which placed a perpetual question mark on his face when he listened to a conversationalist, reading the movements of the latter's lips. He spoke with a slight accent somewhere between Galician and Extremaduran, typical of the Zamora district from which he came. He swallowed his "r's" a bit and his diction had a slightly nasal tone. His mind was clear, orderly, and methodical. . . . He seemed a man accustomed to manipulating mental schemes and maneuvering between mathematical correlates.[19]

Ledesma had launched the idea of revolutionary national syndicalism tied to state dictatorship and extreme nationalism, the glory of empire, anticapitalism and land expropriation, the creative role of youth and the importance of violence—even though his group was so tiny that scarcely any violence could be practiced. It had broadcast many new slogans, coining phrases that would be repeated for many years. It was less successful in the search for visual symbols, coming up only with the "garra hispánica" (a sort of lion's claw) and the "imperio solar" ("empire of the sun"— a metaphoric reference that seemed almost Japanese).

The only authoritarian nationalist worker group in contemporary Spain had been the Sindicatos Libres of Barcelona, which had engaged in violent battle with the CNT before 1923 and then expanded briefly into a national movement under the Dictatorship. Of Carlist origins, the Libres were not, as their detractors maintained, a "yellow syndicate," but in their own way a genuine worker organization. During the late 1920s their doctrines had shifted to an españolista and authoritarian corporatism, though one that was to be weighted against capital. Though originally friendly to Italian Fascism and generally opposed to existing Spanish Catholic syndicates as too rightist and capitalist-dominated, most Libre leaders retained a certain Catholic orientation and generally avoided embracing fascism. The coming of the Republic had in fact ended all hope for their movement, choked off by the mass organizations of the CNT and UGT, and also by anarchist violence, which murdered twenty-two Libre members in Catalonia during the first weeks of the Republic.[20] The Libres would provide individual recruits for Spanish fascism, but nothing in the way of organized support.

One other tiny extreme nationalist group had been founded in Valladolid during the summer of 1931 by Onésimo Redondo Ortega. Redondo came from a rural and Catholic background. Only three months older than Ledesma, he too obtained a civil service position at an early age, in the Ministry of Finance, while taking law courses at the University of Salamanca. In 1927–1928 he worked for a year as an assistant in Spanish language courses at a school of commerce in Mannheim, where he became acquainted to some extent with Nazi ideology. Before completing his military service in 1929–1930, Redondo worked as the secretary of the Syndicate of Sugar-Beet Growers of Old Castile, giving him some experience in economic organization and establishing a professional connection that he would maintain for the rest of his life. Redondo was a voracious reader but not a professional intellectual like Ledesma. He was also a very devout and extremist Catholic, and led a normal married life as husband and father.[21]

Redondo's passions were nationalist unity, the primacy of traditional Spanish values, and social justice. Defense of the rural society of León and Old Castile formed the social base of his political activism, while a kind of "Castilian essentialism" lay at the root of his Spanish nationalism. Catholic Action, with which he had earlier been associated, came to seem pale and compromising. Redondo sought a radical nationalist youth movement, religiously conservative but violent in style and tactics. With extremely limited resources and a few supporters, he founded a weekly called *Libertad* whose first number appeared on 13 June 1931, just three months after the inception of *La Conquista del Estado*.[22]

"Castile! Save Spain!" shouted the headlines of *Libertad*. The remedy for Spain's ills lay "in the people," meaning the Catholic rural society of Old Castile, whom Redondo called on to save the rest of Spain from the materialistic, "pornographic," and "Jewish" influences corrupting the land. He hailed *La Conquista del Estado* but condemned its lack of anti-Semitism, which he termed indispensable for a genuine nationalism. Similarly, Republican coeducation was "a governmental crime against decent women. It is another chapter of Jewish action against free nations. A crime against the health of the people, for which the traitors responsible should pay with their heads."[23] If anything, *Libertad* was more bellicose than Ledesma's organ, its second number declaring, "We are enamored of a certain healthful violence."

Redondo declared that Spain already lived in a state of civil war and exhorted true Spanish youth to gird for battle. With the support of a few radical students and a handful of other supporters in Valladolid, in August he organized a tiny group called the Juntas Castellanas de Actuación Hispánica (Castilian Committees of Hispanic Action). It was not at all a mirror image of Ledesma's small nucleus, for though both claimed to be radical nationalists opposed to materialism, decadence, and the bourgeoisie, there were differences of emphasis. Ledesma's sloganeering was in some ways more purely abstract, but also more clearly statist and economically revolutionary, completely secular and not anti-Semitic. Redondo's group was less interested in the state (perhaps reflecting its Catholic origins), intolerantly Catholic, vehemently anti-Semitic, and even more categorical about the call to violence.[24]

Despite these differences, the two groups obviously needed each other. They were clearly differentiated from the middle- and upper-class monarchist radical right, and in its penultimate issue of 10 October, *La Conquista* announced the impending fusion of the two bands in the Juntas de Ofensiva Nacional-Sindicalista (JONS)—again a sort of verbal analogue, in this case, of the Italian "Fasci di Combattimento," with a different (if quite fascist) adjective added. The new organization was to be governed by a national council, but in practice by a triumvirate, with Ledesma and Redondo remaining in more or less mutually autonomous command of their respective groups.

The "jonsistas," as the few members were called, belonged to the first political organization in Spain officially bearing the national syndicalist label. For their symbol they selected the "Yugo y flechas" (yoke and arrows) of the Reyes Católicos, a fitting symbol for those who dreamed of reviving Spain's imperial grandeur.[25] During this period Ledesma also coined several slogans—such as "¡Arriba!" (Upward) and "España, Una, Grande y Libre" (Spain, One, Great, and Free)—which would become standard in the movement for many years.[26] To symbolize further their revolutionary aims, the jonsistas adopted as their colors the red-black-red device of the anarchists. Their opening manifesto declared that their intention was to build "squads of national offensive, which, by invoking violence, can destroy subversive germs through the direct action of the people."

With Ledesma's rasping voice momentarily silenced because of lack of funds, the chief spokesman of the JONS at first was Redondo. Ledesma was not sanguine about this, later observing that the Valladolid group, because of its rightist and ultra-Catholic background, "did not offer many guarantees of faithfulness to the spirit and principles of the JONS."[27] But to any who drew attention to that background, Redondo would emphasize that the JONS was in no way tied politically to either the Church or the monarchy. Nationalism was declared to be pragmatic, scorning old doctrines and rigid schematism. Spain's two greatest ills were "foreignization and the cult of formulas."[28] Redondo demanded a "popular dictatorship" that would develop its own leader and its own program out of the process of its own dialectic, a typically fascist plea for a pragmatic vitalism.[29]

As Ledesma later admitted, "During all of 1932, the activity of the JONS was virtually nil."[30] He continued to frequent Madrid's Atheneum, which had served for some time as his main library, though his presence had become unpopular. On 2 April, wearing a black shirt, he gave an

Onésimo Redondo Ortega

Atheneum lecture on "Fascism Facing Marxism," which eventually degenerated into disorder, the twenty-five jonsistas present engaging in combat with a somewhat greater number of leftists. So few activists, however, could scarcely practice any noteworthy violence; their activity was limited to burning an occasional kiosk that sold leftist literature or trying to disrupt a cinema showing a Soviet film. Ledesma had had to abandon his first office for lack of funds in May 1931; although he rented a second, the same thing happened twelve months later.

Redondo's students in Valladolid were rather more active and engaged in several brawls with their opponents. The first fatality of Spanish fascism was suffered there on 11 May 1932, when jonsistas defied a ban against demonstrating in opposition to Catalan autonomy. A detachment of Assault Guards was ordered from Madrid to contain them and opened fire on their demonstration in front of the city hall, killing a sixteen-year-old jonsista.[31]

Nor was this time of frustration used to elaborate their ideas more precisely. No theory of syndical organization was worked out, and their propaganda remained at the level of vague generalizations.[32]

A new temptation developed in the summer of 1932, when a confused conspiracy against the new Republic began to take shape among monarchists and a small sector of the military. The revolt of Gen. José Sanjurjo on 10 August in Seville and Madrid, often called the "sanjurjada," was easily aborted. Redondo, who was marginally implicated, fled to Portugal. Ledesma, who probably thought it an absurdly reactionary gesture, had nothing to do with it, but was subsequently arrested along with hundreds of others. By the end of 1932, the jonsista movement was barely alive.

*Part II*

José Antonio Primo de Rivera
and Falange Española
1933–1936

# José Antonio Primo de Rivera and the Founding of the Falange 1933–1934

Ramiro Ledesma's achievement was to define the program of a Spanish fascism, something that no other sympathizer or would-be Spanish fascist had been able to accomplish. Yet Ledesma was clearly no Duce; though he possessed clarity, intensity, and decisiveness, he lacked charisma. He could define a sort of Spanish fascism in doctrinaire terms, but it was quite doubtful that he could give it successful political leadership. That would require more sensitive and charismatic direction, and also more favorable opportunities. Such a combination of factors first began to coalesce under the leadership of José Antonio Primo de Rivera.

José Antonio, as he would eventually become known to friend and foe—the only figure in contemporary Spanish history customarily referred to by his first name—was born in 1903 into an upper-class family with a strong military tradition dating back at least three hundred years. The Primo de Riveras were socially prominent in Andalucia, having intermarried with large landowners and merchants in the district of Jerez de la Frontera. Most recently the family had been brought to prominence by José Antonio's grand-uncle, Lt. Gen. Fernando Primo de Rivera, a major figure of the military hierarchy during the Restoration who had been granted the title of marqués de Estella for bringing the last Carlist war to a close with a victory in 1876. This title, upon his death in 1921 elevated to the rank of grandeza de España, passed to the future Dictator and then, following his demise nine years later, to José Antonio, who became third marqués in that line.

José Antonio was the oldest of five surviving children (three sons, two daughters) of a mother who died very young, after giving birth to six children (including a set of twins, one of whom failed to survive childhood) in little more than five years. All five siblings were then raised by their beloved aunt, Tía "Ma" (María Jesús Primo de Rivera y Orbaneja, sister of the future Dictator), who served as surrogate mother until all reached maturity and beyond. Despite his family's Andalusian roots, José Antonio was essentially a madrileño, having been born in a commodious apartment in a building on the calle de Génova, near the glorieta de Colón. His early life was divided between residence in the capital and in Andalusia, where his father drew several military assignments. A significant part of his future political orientation was determined by his family upbringing, in which an affectionate but stern and authoritarian father (who required that his children address him as "usted") inculcated an unswerving sense of extreme patriotism, deep respect and affection for the military, and belief in the importance of militant service for the patria. Nearly all his early education was obtained at home through private tutors, and he obtained his secondary school diploma in September 1917 after a series of examinations in private schools.[1]

Since his father had discouraged the military vocation that was his first love, José Antonio entered the Faculty of Law at the University of Madrid. In his first major experience with organized classes, he struggled academically during the first two years. These problems may have been exacerbated by the time he devoted for some three years to paid employment—employment required by a family income that was not altogether commensurate with the public prestige of his father. An uncle imported automobiles from the United States, and José Antonio, an able linguist who had learned English from an English governess during his childhood, was responsible for the firm's English-language correspondence. His grades subsequently improved markedly, allegedly at first with the assistance of a new friend, the brilliant student Ramón Serrano Súñer. Serrano was two years older than José Antonio and according to some was the best student in Spain, having gained "Matrículas de honor" in every single course. Later, in his final courses for the licenciatura (1922) and the beginning of the doctorate (1923), José Antonio also did very well, gaining "Matrículas de honor" in all but one course.

His military and patriotic upbringing notwithstanding, José Antonio shared the elitist liberal orientation common to Spanish university students in the early twentieth century, and this was reflected in his first political activities in the university. After the autonomy decree of 1919 permitted student organization, he later served as general secretary and member of the governing committee of the Asociación Oficial de Estudiantes in the Faculty of Law, his friend Serrano becoming the committee's president. Though a devout Catholic, José Antonio believed in the distinction between religious and secular activities, and vigorously opposed the rival Asociación de Estudiantes Católicos. This was the first occasion on which he competed with the young Catholic leader José María Gil Robles, though it would be far from the last. Serious and sometimes seemingly almost timid, José Antonio would nonetheless readily express much more passion and vehemence than the more intellectual and purely calculating Serrano, and his official biographer would later remark upon "the abrupt fisticuffs with which José Antonio ended many discussions."[2]

After his father had become captain general of Barcelona, José Antonio spent the summer of 1922 there, being exposed to a very different cultural and political ambience. Ending his legal studies the following year (he never completed a thesis for the doctorate), José Antonio performed his military service as a volunteer in a cavalry regiment in Barcelona during 1923–1924 and then in the elite "Húsares de la Princesa" in Madrid during 1924, the latter assignment evidently stemming from family connections. With the aid of his university degree and a brief officer-candidate course, he achieved the rank of reserve second lieutenant. Military service completed, José Antonio returned to civilian life, devoting one more semester to formal study in the Faculty of Law and then opening his own law office in Madrid on 3 April 1925, just before his twenty-second birthday, in the new family home on the very central calle de los Madrazo. He soon participated in arguing a case before the Tribunal Supremo, highly unusual for a novice lawyer. His status as son of the Dictator was a source of both complications and benefits, though the latter did not take the form of any official positions or emoluments. José Antonio seems to have had a genuine sense of vocation as a lawyer and grew increasingly interested in legal theory. His legal practice prospered and expanded, eventually employing three or more assistants.

Tall, handsome, athletic, and physically vigorous, by all accounts José Antonio also possessed a winsome and charming personality that only in extreme situations gave way to fits of anger and physical outbursts. Unlike Ledesma, he had an extensive personal and social life, moving in the highest circles, where he possessed the talents to cut a wide swath. Withal, he was a serious and often studious young man, much better read than most others of his generation and social class, influenced by Regenerationist literature and by Ortega, and with a taste (though only a limited talent) for poetry. By 1928 he was evidently reading diverse theorists, from the Spanish traditionalists—who always influenced his thinking—to Spengler, Keyserling, Marx, and Lenin.[3]

## DEFENDING THE DICTATORSHIP

There is no record of José Antonio's initial political reaction to his father's Dictatorship, which may at first have mildly offended his elitist liberal

The Primo de Rivera family. *Standing:* Miguel, José Antonio, General Primo de Rivera, and Fernando; *seated:* Carmen, "Tía Ma," and Pilar.

sensibilities.[4] He was nonetheless a loyal supporter of Don Miguel, whom he idolized, and by 1929, at the very latest, was thoroughly identified with the main thrust of the Dictatorship's policies. Yet his incipient political career was initiated not so much by the Dictatorship itself as by its failure. The collapse of the regime in January 1930 was quickly accompanied by the absolute prostration of his ailing father. The man who had governed Spain for more than six years became the object of scorn and derision, and died in Paris on 16 March 1930, only five weeks after leaving Madrid. As the eldest son of a dying and humiliated father, José Antonio felt an understandable need to defend the family name, stand up for his father, and in some fashion vindicate and continue his father's labors. Vindication of family honor involved more than one bout of fisticuffs with his father's detractors, the most notable being his altercation with Gen. Gonzalo Queipo de Llano. After the general had challenged an elderly uncle, José Antonio, accompanied by two friends, approached Queipo's tertulia in a central Madrid cafe and knocked the general down, leading to a brief brawl. Other incidents followed. Thus "during the spring and summer of 1930," José Antonio "would get a reputation as a bully and a man of violence that would accompany him to his grave."[5] This also brought him a military court martial, which stripped him of his reserve officer's commission in the army. He began to write newspaper articles in defense of his father, but his first public appearance after the collapse of the Dictadura was to present an abstract, purely juridical and philosophical lecture before the Atheneum of Albacete on the theme "What is just?" To this most basic and fundamental of questions, José Antonio presented no unique or one-sided answer, but a complex and balanced philosophical discourse, concluding that "that which is just . . . can be found in the combination of norms."[6]

Even before his father's death, he had announced that his only public ambition would be to defend his father's record and to continue his work.[7] His course was thus to some degree decided from the moment the Dictatorship fell, and the first organization at hand was the Unión Monárquica Nacional, created in April 1930. Within less than a month, on 2 May, José Antonio accepted the position of vice secretary general of the UNM, declaring it a personal and family obligation, since all but two of the ministers who had served his father were members of the Unión.[8] During the next few months his duties involved wide travel and a series of public meetings from Madrid to Barcelona, Andalusia, and Galicia. There were a number of incidents, and several people were injured in these meetings. In his first political speeches, José Antonio called for a program of strong national unity, the recovery of economic "independence," and the strengthening of the army and the navy (despite economic challenges and the lack of any military threat to Spain). From the beginning, then, his posture was one of an authoritarian and militarist nationalism, coupled with strong economic demands.

A tendency toward extremism began to surface, perhaps most notably in an article in *La Nación* on 29 July in which he savagely chastised intellectuals as a group for their opposition to the Dictatorship. He characterized them as unidimensional and even inhuman, so totally isolated from reality and human sentiments that if a child should break into an intellectual's study, "the irritated intellectual would desire the child's death." This absurd claim was even more ironic in view of José Antonio's undeniable intellectual interests, even though he was not a professional intellectual.

In defense of the Dictatorship, José Antonio insisted shrilly that all that really mattered was Spanish unity and a strong nationalist government. In Barcelona on 3 August he declared: "Don't hold back before any superstition or even the shrieking of the vestal virgins of legality! . . . We must say: 'Save Spain, even if all constitutional principles perish!' "[9] Later, on 5 October, he proclaimed in Bilbao that Spain was faced with its greatest challenge in centuries: "There are only two paths in these transcendent moments: either revolution or counterrevolution. Either our traditional order or the triumph of Moscow."[10] As the republican movement gained force during the final weeks of 1930, he declared in the journal *Unión Monárquica* (15 December) that the crucial factor was not the nominal form of government but an integrated and unified national program. Lacking that, "the monarchy is the same as the republic, or as the revolution."

At the same time, José Antonio recognized that the unified national system that he invoked so vaguely, yet so categorically, could not be reactionary or merely authoritarian in a negative sense, but must have progressive, modern social content and could not simply ignore the rights of the individual. In a speech in Madrid on 16 January 1931, he invoked traditional thought, on which he frequently drew, to define a true democracy as a "life in common not subject to tyranny, peaceful, happy, and virtuous," but then emphasized the superiority of what he called a "politics of content" as opposed to one "which hopes to achieve it all by a magic formula."

> If democracy as a form has failed, it is because, more than anything else, it has not been able to provide a truly democratic life in its content. Let us avoid extreme exaggerations that extend their hatred of electoral superstition to everything democratic. The aspiration to a free, peaceful, and democratic life will always be the goal of political science, beyond any temporary fashion.
>
> Attempts to deny individual rights, gained through centuries of sacrifice, will not prevail. What is important is that we seek, through new structures of content, the democratic results that one form has not been able to provide. Let us therefore seek a different path, not through improvisation, but through persevering study, with diligence and humility, because truth, like bread, must be earned every day through the sweat of our brow.[11]

Until this new formula was found, it would be impossible to continue and to transcend the frustrated efforts of the Dictatorship.

Thus, like much of the right, José Antonio stood aside not merely from the coming of the Republic but also from its first elections. Even though Don Alfonso had dismissed his father from office, José Antonio and his siblings remained loyal to the royal family to the end, accompanying the queen as she boarded a train a short distance outside the capital. José Antonio then played only a passive role in the organization in Madrid of Acción Nacional, the new Catholic party that was the precursor of the CEDA.

The new regime pursued a policy of vengeance against the monarchy, the Dictatorship, and the principal figures of the latter. In this gale José Antonio firmly dismissed Republican denunciation of the authoritarian character of the Dictatorship as ingenuous or hypocritical, on the sophistical grounds that Spain had always been ruled by arbitrary government, under every regime[12]—a gross exaggeration, by any standard. The decision of the Cortes Constituyentes, the first Republican parliament, to prosecute the leading figures of the Dictatorship soon led him to seek a public role in opposition. When special by-elections to fill vacancies in parliament were announced in September 1931, José Antonio announced his candidacy in Madrid:

> to defend the sacred memory of my father. I know that I lack the merits to aspire to represent Madrid in the Cortes simply by myself. I am not presenting my candidacy due to vanity or the love of politics, which every moment attracts me less. God well knows that my vocation lies among my books, and that to tear myself from them to launch myself temporarily into the steep vertigo of politics causes me genuine pain. But it would be cowardly or insensitive to sleep quietly while in parliament, before the public, false accusations continue to be hurled against the sacred memory of my father.[13]

José Antonio insisted publicly that his intention was not to oppose the Republic itself and admitted candidly, "My own convictions are not formed. I do not consider myself adequately informed in many areas to define myself politically."[14] He had been reading Ledesma's *La Conquista del Estado* and at one point had sent a law clerk from his office to establish personal contact, but he in no way associated himself with the shrill little fascist group. Though José Antonio stood as the only rightist candidate in the by-election, the right was not yet fully mobilized, and the liberal Republican candidate, the venerable academician Bartolomé Manuel de Cossío, bested him easily, drawing twice as many votes. Approximately a month later, on 11 November, José Antonio was suddenly arrested and held incommunicado for twenty hours, nominally on suspicion of participating in a monarchist plot, before being released with no charges filed. This may simply have been a gesture of intimidation, which the Republican leadership had publicly announced that it would employ against supposed enemies of the new regime.

For the remainder of 1931 and 1932, José Antonio withdrew into his legal practice, which, by dint of skill and hard work, became even more

José Antonio Primo de Rivera in his law office

successful under the Republic than under the monarchy. His office enjoyed a strong reputation and became somewhat fashionable among sectors of the elite. By the end of 1932, his extensive clientele was earning him an annual income of nearly 250,000 pesetas—an impressive sum for the period—with a widely varying case load ranging from criminal cases to ordinary civil suits (including what was apparently the first divorce case under the new Republican legislation, in which he took the role of the defense).[15]

His most notorious public case was the defense of Galo Ponte, one of his father's ministers, before the newly created ad hoc Tribunal de Responsabilidades Políticas de la Dictadura. José Antonio argued, among other things, that Ponte could not be accused of violating the constitution of 1876, whose functioning had been suspended by the monarchy's installation of the Dictatorship, so that when Ponte became minister in 1925 he was doing no more than obeying what was then the recognized and established law. José Antonio also underscored the less than complete recognition of civil rights under the new Republic, accompanied by arbitrary arrests, abuses, and censorship, and in certain respects worse than under the Dictatorship.[16] All this was for naught; the ministers all received sentences ranging from six to eight years, which in the case of the elderly and ailing Ponte was reduced to six years of internal exile at least 250 kilometers from Madrid.

At the time of the abortive monarchist-military revolt against the new system in August 1932 (the "sanjurjada"), a politically uninvolved José Antonio was taking his usual upper-class summer vacation in San Sebastián. José María de Areilza, who first became acquainted with him on this occasion, has described the José Antonio of that summer as "physically arrogant, with a graceful manner and a distinguished bearing, a firm step and a blue gaze that gave him a certain sportive and Nordic air. . . . He gave the appearance of living a carefree existence, with many plans involving women and incessant summertime participation in parties and dinners."[17] At this point he and his brother Miguel were suddenly arrested and jailed for two months in the massive roundup that followed the failed coup (they were eventually released without any charges being filed). José Antonio pointed out with his customary sense of irony that their younger brother Fernando, who had followed his father in becoming a career army officer, had been publicly praised for correctly following orders while serving at the Getafe airdrome during the revolt. Since the three bachelor brothers lived together, it seemed unlikely that one would respect the laws of the Republic while the other two were supposedly conspiring to restore the monarchy.[18]

## DEFINING A FASCIST MOVEMENT

The first wave of interest in fascistic politics in Europe had been set off by the March on Rome in 1922, yet all efforts to form a new movement in imitation of Italian Fascism elsewhere had failed, partly because the prosperity of the 1920s did not encourage them. Whenever parliamentary liberalism had been overthrown in other countries, it had occurred at the hands of military coups in the less developed lands of southern and eastern Europe, the government of Primo de Rivera in Spain having been one of the first examples.

Hitler's accession to power in Germany on 30 January 1933 touched off a second and much more powerful wave of interest in fascistic politics. By this time radical authoritarian ideas had been more widely disseminated in Europe, and the depression crisis made nationalists and antileftists much more receptive to a categorically authoritarian alternative.

This ambience encouraged a relative expansion of the JONS in Spain for the first time, as well as a formal proclamation of fascist identity by Dr. Albiñana's tiny right-radical Partido Nacionalista Español. The PNE's youth group, Juventud Nacionalista, actively espoused a fascist identity, and Albiñana himself, for a considerable period exiled to Las Hurdes by the new regime, issued a manifesto in March 1933 entitled *Hacia la nueva España: El fascismo triunfante*. This was less than convincing, for there was no indication of fundamental change in the monarchist and rightist position of his tiny organization.

The most visible response in Madrid to the triumph of Hitler was undertaken by the newspaper editor Manuel Delgado Barreto. He had been a close friend of the former Dictator and the founding editor of *La Nación*, mouthpiece of the Unión Patriótica, in 1925. After his father's death, José Antonio had inherited the largest portion of shares in the newspaper, which had published his first political articles during 1930–1931. Delgado Barreto decided to capitalize on the excitement generated by Nazism to start publication of a new weekly entitled *El Fascio: Haz Hispano*, devoted to the discussion of fascism.

The first number appeared on 16 March, third anniversary of the death of Primo de Rivera, whom the editor of the new organ hailed as "the first Spanish fascist." Articles were solicited from Ledesma and other jonsistas, from Giménez Caballero, from Rafael Sánchez Mazas (a novelist and writer on nationalist themes who resided in Bilbao and Madrid), and from José Antonio. Ledesma decried the mimicry of the title but contributed an article, while one anonymous entry (probably by Giménez Caballero) lauded "Haz" as the Spanish equivalent of "Fascio." All articles tended to agree that a fascist solution—more or less similar to Italy's—was the appropriate goal for Spain, though some of the pieces were rather vague. José Antonio's article was signed "E." (for "Estella") and entitled "Orientations: Toward a New State," proclaiming the need for a strong state of national unity to overcome the fragmentation and lack of conviction in liberalism and democracy.[19]

*El Fascio* apparently attracted numerous subscriptions, and its first number enjoyed a huge press run, but it never survived the day of its birth. All issues were confiscated and the publication prohibited. According to the monarchist daily, *ABC*, opposition was led by the Socialists in the government, who were determined to eliminate any expression of fascism in Spain. The draconian Law for the Defense of the Republic made it easy for the government to impose broad censorship. Ledesma would later insist that the suspension had been fortunate, for the genuinely fascistic JONS was finally beginning to expand, whereas the backers of *El Fascio* were merely rightist and reactionary.

On the following day *ABC* carried extensive commentary on fascism, its editor Juan Ignacio Luca de Tena rejecting fascist authoritarianism and violence, and further declaring that conditions in democratic Spain would discourage a Spanish fascism. José Antonio replied immediately with an article defending fascism, whether in its Italian form or more generally, holding that:

> Fascism is not a tactic—violence. It is an idea—unity.
>
> In a fascist state victory does not go to the strongest class or to the most numerous party—which just because it is more numerous is not necessarily justified, though a stupid electoral system may say otherwise. What triumphs is the orderly principle common to all, consistent national thought, of which the state is the expression.
>
> The liberal state believes in nothing, not even in itself. It watches with folded arms all sorts of experiments, even those aimed at the destruction of the state itself.
>
> Fascism was born to light a faith, neither of the right (which at bottom aspires to preserve everything, even the unjust) nor of the left (which at bottom aspires to destroy everything, even the just), but a collective, integral, national faith. Its fruitfulness lies in this faith, against which all persecution is unavailing. . . . If there is anything that deserves to be called a workers' state, it is the fascist state. Therefore, in the fascist state—and this is something that workers will come to learn, no matter what—worker syndicates are raised to the dignity of organs of the state.[20]

The much wiser, more experienced, and more prudent Luca de Tena was friendly but categorical in his response:

> We repudiate all violence, whatever its source. "Fascism," you say, "is not a tactic—violence; it is an idea—unity." I understand, on the contrary, that what characterizes fascism and all other antiliberal regimes is, precisely, their tactics. The difference lies in the tactics. By what means, through what procedures, does the nascent Spanish *fascio* expect to conquer power? By means of persuasion? And if, eventually, it did conquer, how would it retain power to impose its ends? How would it annihilate Marxism and liberalism, which is its goal? In Italy and Germany, we already know. Using the same means of repression that in Spain the Socialists try to use against the legal propaganda of the *fascio*.

Luca de Tena observed that the socioeconomic radicalism expressed by José Antonio differed little from that of the revolutionary left: "Just putting the word 'socialist' where you say 'fascist,' many supporters of Marxism could espouse the same concept." He concluded with some generous words for the attractive young aristocrat with whom he was debating: "What comes from the heart is not subject to reason. And I suspect that your fascism has sprung from your great heart rather than from your brilliant intelligence."[21]

This was a shrewd observation. On the one hand, José Antonio had continued to read widely, with ever-increasing attention to Italy,[22] but also extremist literature from Germany (Hitler and Rosenberg) and from the Soviet world (Lenin and Trotsky). The only balance to this was the continuing influence of Ortega and some of the Spanish traditionalists. Though he was increasingly convinced of the cogency of the new revolutionary ideas, there is little doubt that much of his political orientation was existential and familial, a personal commitment to devote himself to the completion of the heroic task that his father had been unable to carry out. And, like all adherents of fascist and other antimaterialist doctrines, he would emphasize the primacy of faith and spirit over intellectual analysis and material interest. More than three years of uncertainty were coming to a close. Though his professional career was extremely successful and lucrative, it did not satisfy his deepest aspirations, which he would no longer deny.

It is a moot point whether this change was influenced significantly by his frustrated romance with Pilar Azlor de Aragón, the duquesa de Luna. This Aragonese aristocrat, member of a family of grandees descended from a natural son of Fernando el Católico, seems to have been the principal love interest of his life. José Antonio had made her acquaintance late in 1927, but at the point at which he might seriously have proposed marriage, he found the road blocked by her father, the duque de Villahermosa. The duke was an extreme right-wing monarchist who detested the Primo de Riveras as mere upstarts, and particularly detested the former Dictator as a parvenu adventurer who had brought discredit on the monarchy and initiated social reform policies harmful to certain vested interests. During the first two years of the Republic, José Antonio had nonetheless persisted in his surreptitious courtship. His affections seem to some extent to have been reciprocated by this young woman of high family, whom he privately praised not merely for beauty and charm but also for literary sensibility. Since the duke had moved his family back to Aragon with the coming of the Republic, José Antonio was aided in his contacts by his close friend Ramón Serrano Súñer, then state attorney in Zaragoza. José Antonio in turn served as a witness when Serrano married Zita Polo, younger sister of the wife of Gen. Francisco Franco, in Zaragoza in February 1932.

Despite the obstacles in his path, it appears that José Antonio had still not given up hope for the marriage, sooner or later, and the attractive Pilar seems not to have seriously cultivated rival suitors for a number of years. Only in 1934, it has been said, after José Antonio had become fully committed to political leadership in a country ever more torn by violence, did he renounce the prospect of matrimony, and even at that time he initially thought that this renunciation would be temporary.[23]

On 24 March 1933, a week after the appearance of *El Fascio,* he authorized a good friend and distant relative, Sancho Dávila, to act as his representative in drawing together relatives and family friends in Seville and Cádiz who might be sympathetic to a radical nationalism. Dávila did not find the assignment particularly easy, and on 2 April José Antonio wrote to his cousin Julián Pemartín, who was helping Dávila:

> The truth is that the working out of this idea is something probably reserved for a man of popular background. The role of caudillo has something of the prophet in it, and requires a commitment of faith, enthusiasm, and anger that is incompatible with refinement. I, for my part, would be better fit for anything than for being a fascist caudillo. The attitude of doubt and the sense of irony, which never leave those of us who have had intellectual curiosity, incapacitate us for launching the robust and unflinching affirmations that are required for leaders of masses. So, if in Jerez, as in Madrid, there are friends whose liver suffers from the prospect that I might want to make myself Caudillo del Fascio, you can reassure them on my behalf.[24]

José Antonio is also supposed to have observed elsewhere that "he had too many intellectual concerns to be a leader of masses," and that: "My scholarly vocation is of the worst kind to combine with that of a caudillo."[25]

There were already monied interests in Spain who had indicated willingness to help finance a new nationalist movement, but some showed little enthusiasm about backing another Primo de Rivera. It was argued that a fascist leader must indeed be a man of the people, as José Antonio admitted—someone like Mussolini, or a front-line soldier, like Hitler.

Bilbao businessmen at one point wanted to consider the pragmatic Socialist Indalecio Prieto as leader of a nationalist socialism that might oppose the extreme left. Having made his way up from poverty, Prieto fit the working-class description. Moreover, as a practical politician he had never lost contact with Vizcayan finance and industry and had combated the agitation of incendiary revolutionaries within the Socialist Party. In return, members of the Bilbao elite had sheltered him from police in the last days of the monarchy. In 1932 they had hoped he might become sufficiently disillusioned with the left wing of the Socialist Party to consider developing an alternative "national" socialism. Prieto, however, was dedicated to his party and, though more broadly national in his outlook than most Socialists, refused even to consider participating in any variant of "social fascism," [26] though he later showed a certain personal interest in the leader of the national syndicalist movement, with whom he came to enjoy a special relationship.

Another possibility was Demetrio Carceller, director of a petroleum company in the Canary Islands, who had risen from modest origins. Carceller was talented, with considerable drive and energy, and not averse to entering politics. However, the absence of any concrete political preparation behind certain vague proposals made to him caused him to lose interest in politics, particularly in comparison with his successful business career.[27]

Ramiro Ledesma, who had looked more deeply into fascist politics and radical politics in general than any of the others, publicly warned those interested in a new "Spanish fascism" of all the difficulties involved in trying to develop a radical new nationalism based on a foreign model. He also correctly prophesied that a serious effort to create a "Spanish fascism" would encounter more violent resistance from the left than the irrelevant posturing of a rightist physician with no significant following had:

> Let those comrades currently interested in launching fascism in
> Spain think about the grave risks involved: more than by Marxist
> bullets, more than by the poison of opportunists and traitors, the
> potential movement will be weakened by relying on foreign
> slogans, ceremonies, and forms. Be very careful, comrades, of such
> associations! . . . There are things that may be permitted to an
> Albiñana, because of his comical style, but would never be permitted
> to those in Spain who try to carry out a serious effort with genuine
> youth, and generous ideals and talent.[28]

During the spring of 1933, José Antonio's political contacts and discussions normally took place either at his law office or in the offices of *La Nación*. There he met with old friends and relatives such as Raimundo Fernández Cuesta and Julián Pemartín, and with new acquaintances such as the able young Bilbao writer Rafael Sánchez Mazas, who like Giménez Caballero was married to an Italian woman and became something of a mentor on Italian Fascism, as well as the wealthy marqués de la Eliseda, son of one of his father's ministers. Army officers loyal to his father who had retired early under the new Republican legislation, such as Emilio Alvargonzález and Emilio Rodríguez Tarduchy, also played a role, as did a number of young nationalist writers who frequented his regular literary tertulia at "La Ballena Alegre" (The Jolly Whale) in the basement of the Café Lyon on the calle de Alcalá across from Madrid's central post office.

The most important new collaborator, however, was the former artillery officer and aviation hero Julio Ruiz de Alda, co-pilot on the famous trans-Atlantic flight led by Ramón Franco from Spain to Argentina in 1926.[29] For the Spanish-speaking world, this exploit was the South Atlantic equivalent of Charles Lindbergh's epic journey. Subsequently Ruiz de Alda was president of the Federación Nacional Aeronáutica and filled minor technical posts under the Dictatorship. A bluff and hearty military man, he was a strong nationalist who was repelled by the subsequent leftist radicalism of General Franco's younger brother; by the time the Republic was founded, he had declared that Spain needed "a totalitarian system."[30]

The link between fascism and aviation has been commented on by various historians. Ruiz de Alda made contact with Ledesma's initial group in 1931 and was briefly enrolled in it, but had nothing to do with the subsequent JONS. He helped to organize a new company to undertake an aerial survey of the country to supply hydraulic data, which fell through when government aid was suspended in 1931, partly because of the political sympathies of Ruiz de Alda and his principal associates, the monarchist Ansaldo brothers. Embittered, they established an aviation armaments group to lobby for nationalization and expansion of the tiny Spanish aircraft industry.[31] By the first months of 1933, Ruiz de Alda was being sounded out by several figures on the extreme right. In an interview conducted by Giménez Caballero for *El Fascio*, Ruiz de Alda declared that he favored "a violent and high-spirited movement, directed at the younger generation and with a strong social background that integrates workers and intellectuals. A movement led by ardent spirits ready to sacrifice to keep it from becoming a simple action of class defense or of cowardly capitalism."[32]

He and José Antonio complemented each other and got along well together. Ruiz de Alda was no intellectual and had limited ability for public speaking, but was down-to-earth and had a certain amount of organizational ability. He could also sometimes reduce José Antonio's grandiloquent rhetoric to more practical terms. Whereas José Antonio would speak of the nation in grand Orteguian terms as "a unity of destiny in the universal," the aviator would opt for the simpler "unity of mission." The two agreed that Spanish fascism must be clearly distinct from the right and make a strong appeal to workers.

A more prestigious collaborator, in political and intellectual terms, appeared in the person of the sometime liberal intellectual Alfonso García Valdecasas, a former member of the Agrupación "Al Servicio de la República," the parliamentary group organized by Ortega y Gasset. Ortega had

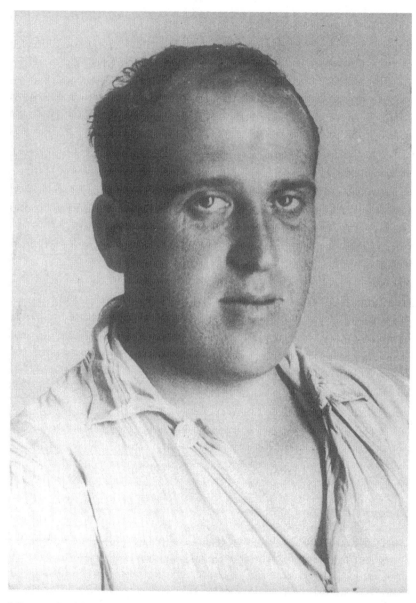

Julio Ruiz de Alda

preached a kind of "national Republicanism," propounding a national politics above factionalism. During 1932 he became profoundly disillusioned with the sectarianism of Republican politics and called for its "rectification." He dissolved his parliamentary body in October 1932 and called vainly for the formation of a grand national Republican movement above the parties. In disillusionment Ortega soon withdrew from politics altogether and even refused a medal awarded to him by the Republican government. His younger follower García Valdecasas, a law professor, struck out on his own. After the dissolution of the Agrupación, he and a few associates late in 1932 formed the tiny Frente Español (Spanish Front), seeking a "national Republicanism." This resembled nothing so much as the "New Party" formed that year in England by Sir Oswald Mosley, a disillusioned young leader of the Labour Party, who subsequently organized the British Union of Fascists. One or two of Ledesma's followers abandoned the JONS to join the Frente Español, but the latter foundered somewhere between liberalism and a more integral nationalism, and failed to gain any following. By the spring of 1933, it was already being split between those who still wanted to work with the Republic and others, led by García Valdecasas, who sought a more authoritarian kind of nationalism.

During the summer of 1933, José Antonio and Ruiz de Alda, together with a handful of collaborators, founded an entity that they called the "Movimiento Sindicalista Español" (MES):

> Before everything, and above all ideology . . . , fascism is the
> resolute will to create a virile, harmonious, and totalitarian state. . . .
> We come with a necessary but humanitarian violence, raw but
> chivalrous, as is the nature of all surgical violence. . . . Our party is
> the authentically Spanish form of what has become a normal crusade
> in great countries to redeem Europe, to redeem the fatherlands of
> Europe, from the spiritual degradation and material ruin in which
> they have been sunk by the poisonous, antinational left and the
> cowardly, obtuse, and egotistical right.

It sounded like a direct effort to transcribe Italian Fascism into Spanish.

This initiative coincided with the first significant wave of activism for the JONS. Though Ledesma had to spend another month in jail for his anti-Catalanist agitation (January–February 1933), he would later declare that "the year 1933 was the true year of the JONS."[33] Hundreds of Spanish youths—particularly students—began to join after Hitler's rise to power. For the first time, on 10 March, a large, disorderly jonsista demonstration could be organized in Madrid's Faculty of Law. According to Ledesma, it encouraged 400 students to register as jonsistas in the following week. The new members raised 2,000 pesetas from their meager incomes, enabling the little movement for the third time to rent an office in Madrid and also to begin publication of a monthly devoted to doctrine, entitled *JONS*.[34] It tried to popularize Ledesma's slogan of "La Patria, el Pan y la Justicia" (The Fatherland, Bread and Justice). Sales of the monthly at the university produced more clashes, during one of which a jonsista armed with a pistol wounded three students. The Madrid JONS were able to organize their first twenty direct-action squads, composed of five members each. One militant raised 1,500 pesetas through subscriptions sold in Argentina, and by autumn local JONS publications were appearing in Valladolid (the other center), Granada, Valencia, and Santiago de Compostela, with small groups also organized in Bilbao, Barcelona, and several smaller towns. In Galicia the JONS were led by the young professor and former Communist leader Santiago Montero Díaz.[35] Further funding was obtained from the monarchist radical right and big business in Bilbao and San Sebastián.[36]

Outside the university, the most direct provocation carried out was the ransacking of the Madrid offices of the Friends of the USSR by pistol-wielding jonsistas on 14 July. In response to this and to inflammatory actions by anarchists, between 19 and 22 July the government carried out approximately 3,000 detentions nationwide. The targets included Ledesma and several of his chief collaborators, a number of anarchists, a few "social Catholics," a wide variety of rightists, and several individuals connected with the nascent MES. Most were soon set free, though some ninety were held for a week or two. José Antonio and Ruiz de Alda were not detained but found it prudent to remove themselves from circulation for a brief period. As a result, the MES—which had involved numerous contacts with ex-upetistas, jonsistas, and even a few Carlists—never took any clear form.

José Antonio took his accustomed vacation in San Sebastián during August, but this time used the occasion for political contacts. He and Ruiz de Alda reached agreement with García Valdecasas, and also discussed plans and financing with acquaintances among the españolista radical right of Bilbao, such as the young José María de Areilza. After the recent arrests, the JONS was beginning to run out of money once more, and at the end of the month Ledesma—who rarely vacationed for more than a few days anywhere—made another trip on his motorcycle to Bilbao to seek further funding. There the question of uniting the JONS with the initiative of the would-be fascist triumvirate was discussed in direct conversations, but Ledesma was convinced that the latter were little more than reactionary upetistas manipulating a naive and imported fascist rhetoric. He especially resented the tall, suave, affluent, and aristocratic

José Antonio, whom Ledesma—prototype of the revolutionary proletarian intellectual—considered a "millionaire aristocrat,"[37] to the combined frustration and amusement of José Antonio himself.

Full-time commitment to politics would probably bring a drastic decline in José Antonio's personal income, so that a reliable source of financing became indispensable. The monarchist radical right of Renovación Española would be more useful than the uncertain and limited support of a handful of financiers and businessmen in Bilbao, and it may have been just before or after the vacation trip that José Antonio signed a ten-point agreement at El Escorial with Pedro Sainz Rodríguez, the witty, enormously obese literary scholar who served as *éminence grise* of the alfonsino monarchists. Sainz Rodríguez sought to bind the nascent fascist movement to a set of principles that would not conflict with a monarchist restoration. These included the goal of "a system of authority, hierarchy, and order," and elimination of direct elections and political parties, to be replaced by a new corporative system that was otherwise not defined, official support for Catholicism, and the conclusion that "violence is justified in the service of truth and justice."[38]

The result was a situation in which Renovación Española was financing both the JONS and the new MES, part of its strategy to encourage the development of fascist-type groups as shock troops for a monarchist restoration. Antonio Goicoechea, the party's leader, would soon accept an invitation to a juridical conference in Leipzig and a personal interview with Hitler, while the party's monies were doled out in calculating fashion by "El Técnico," the hard-core monarchist Lt. Col. Valentín Galarza, formerly of the General Staff.

To strengthen their hand during their vacation trip to the north, José Antonio and Ruiz de Alda had also visited in Biarritz two key monarchist activists who were especially interested in a radical fascist alternative, the aviator Juan Antonio Ansaldo and José Antonio's wealthy aristocratic acquaintance Francisco Moreno Herrera, marqués de la Eliseda. They both favored the clear-cut "fascism" of the MES over the revolutionary nationalism of the JONS, which tended to reject the Italian label, and criticized the tendency of the Renovación Española leaders to favor the senior movement. In a subsequent letter to the emigré alfonsino leadership in France, Ansaldo reported that in his circle

> we have been subsidizing the JONS and the fascists, supporting more the former than the latter. Some leaders seem to be jealous of the latter. We had agreed to give two thousand pesetas [per month] to each group, but then I was told two for the JONS and four for the *fascio*, but the latter have not received that much, sometimes not even two. This month Paco [Eliseda] and I between ourselves have attended

to their needs, and in previous months I have even had on several occasions to give them three thousand pesetas, since they lacked resources for urgent matters. Of course they are not treated with the same interest as the others. As I said before, I see an intention or a scheme to create rivalry between them, which seems to be occurring. In my judgment, this is prejudicial. I think that both should not be stirred up so as not to create competition between them; in so far as possible we should maintain a hold on both as allies with each preserving its own ideology. . . .

Fascism has much more of a future than the JONS, but for that reason we think that we should inject ourselves into it, since as a political party it might develop a life of its own without us, whereas no one knows where it might end up if some success should encourage its leaders. Today it can serve us and it may serve us in the future as an action group, but we must be involved in its growth and evolution so that it will not escape our tútelage and support.[39]

José Antonio was fully aware that his plunge into politics would divert most of his working time from his legal practice exactly at the point at which his prestige as a lawyer had reached its height. To several positions that he already held in professional associations had been added in June 1933 his election by acclamation to the Committee for Culture of the Bar Association in Madrid. But there, too, his activity had become increasingly political, as he had led a campaign to force the liberal moderate Angel Ossorio y Gallardo from its presidency.[40] This was another destructive gesture on his part; Ossorio, who later resigned, was exactly the kind of moderate liberal desperately needed in positions of leadership in Spain at that moment.

Though the MES had been stillborn, in September support developed for a new organization to be led by the triumvirate of José Antonio Primo de Rivera, Julio Ruiz de Alda, and Alfonso García Valdecasas. José Antonio had earlier declared in an interview that it was a matter of adapting "the magnificent Italian enterprise" to the needs of Spain,[41] and on the tenth anniversary of his father's pronunciamiento insisted that the Spanish Dictatorship had been the precursor of what were now "leagues of entire peoples."[42] One further step that José Antonio felt was necessary before the public launching of a new movement was a personal meeting with his new role-model, Mussolini. Seeking the assistance of the Italian embassy, he declared that he wished to "obtain informative material on Italian Fascism and the accomplishments of the regime," as well as "advice about the organization of an analogous movement in Spain."[43] He had accompanied his father on a brief state visit to Rome ten years earlier and allegedly said to an Italian journalist on this second occasion, "I'm like the disciple who is going to visit the master. How much help, if he wants, and I am sure he would want, he can give to me, to my movement, to my country. He was the friend of my father, he will certainly help me."[44] The interview with Mussolini took place on 19 October and lasted about thirty minutes, during which it may be doubted that Mussolini was able to impart much practical wisdom concerning how to develop a fascist movement in such complex circumstances as those of Spain. José Antonio met briefly with the vice secretary of the Fascist Party, Arturo Marpicati, and was given a brief tour of several Fascist institutions.[45] It all served as an inspiration, for immediately on his return he declared in *La Nación* (23 October):

> Fascism is not just an Italian movement: it is a total, universal
> sense of life. Italy was the first to apply it. But is not the concept of
> the state as an instrument in the service of a permanent historical
> mission valid outside of Italy? . . . Who can say that such goals are
> only important for Italians?

Here one of his principal concerns was to defend Italian Fascism from recent charges by Gil Robles and other CEDA leaders that it was non- or anti-Catholic. José Antonio pointed to the Lateran Pacts of 1929, which nominally healed the breach between church and state for the first time since Italian unification, ignoring altogether the conflicts of the past two years in which the Fascist state had severely curtailed the activities of several Catholic lay associations. More convincingly, he stressed the differences between Italian Fascism and German Nazi racism, repeating the common Fascist slogan that Fascism was based on universal *romanità*, like Catholicism itself—though this claim might technically have been considered sacrilegious. He declared that Fascism was "eminently traditionalist . . . because what is universal in fascism is this revitalization of all peoples, this attitude of rediscovering what is in one's own culture." Finally, José Antonio concluded that the CEDA's attitude toward Fascism was hypocritical, since the CEDA also sought an authoritarian corporatism:

> When Sr. Gil Robles, in contradiction with himself, says that
> democracy must submit or die, that a strong social discipline will rule
> over all, and other fine truths, he is proclaiming "fascist" principles.
> He may reject the name, but the name does not make the thing. Sr.
> Gil Robles, when he speaks thus, is not speaking like the leader of a
> Christian democratic party.

All this was probably not deliberate mystification on José Antonio's part, for, though he wanted to introduce a genuine Spanish fascism, his own conception of fascism remained somewhat vague. It seemed to amount to a radical and authoritarian nationalism with a modern social and economic program of radical reformism, audacious and modern in culture but still somehow in harmony with Catholicism and traditionalism, and ready to employ whatever violence was necessary. At this point his admiration for Mussolini was at its height. For some time the autographed photograph the Duce gave him would remain on his office wall just below that of his father,[46] and he wrote the prologue to a volume of Mussolini's writings soon to appear in Spain under the title *El fascismo*.

It had been agreed that the party must soon be launched as a regular movement under a more appropriate new name. An initial plan was to hold the first meeting in Burgos, "capital of Castile," on 7 October, but the civil governor refused to authorize it. Soon afterward, new parliamentary elections were announced for November, and it was decided to use the full freedom of the electoral campaign for the first public meeting.

This took place in the Teatro de la Comedia in the center of Madrid on Sunday, 29 October 1933. Free use of the theater had been provided by its owner, a friend and supporter of the late Dictator, and national radio coverage was arranged. A full house of two thousand people were present, most of them sympathetic rightists with a tendency toward the radical right. In addition, Ledesma and a group of jonsistas were present. All three of the new, unofficial triumvirs addressed the meeting. Though they were greeted by the audience with the fascist salute, Valdecasas insisted in his remarks that "we do not want to live off foreign formulas," and while José Antonio personally returned the salute, he avoided use of the terms "fascism" and "fascist."

His oratory formed the centerpiece, its rhetorical and romantic style setting the tone for much of early Falangist discourse:

> The liberal state came to offer us economic slavery. . . . Therefore socialism had to be born, and its birth was just (for we deny no truth). Workers had to defend themselves from that system, which only promised them rights but made no effort to give them a just life.
>
> But socialism, at first a legitimate reaction against liberal slavery, lost its way, first, in the materialist interpretation of life and history; second, in its sense of reprisal; third, in proclaiming the dogma of class struggle.
>
> . . . The Patria is a total unity . . . ; it cannot be in the hands of the strongest class or the best organized party. The Patria is a transcendent synthesis. . . . This is what our total sense of the Patria and of the state which must serve it requires:
>
> That all the peoples of Spain, however diverse, be harmonized in an irrevocable unity of destiny.

That political parties disappear. No one was ever born a member of a political party, but we were all born as members of a family, we are all residents of a municipality, we all toil at our professions. . . .

We want less liberal verbiage and more respect for the profound liberty of man. Because the freedom of man is only respected when he is esteemed, as we esteem him, as the bearer of eternal values, when he is esteemed as the corporeal vessel of a soul that may be condemned or saved. Only when man is considered thus can it be said that his freedom is truly respected, and all the more if that freedom is associated, as we intend, with a system of authority, hierarchy, and order.

. . . And finally we intend, if it is sometimes necessary to achieve this through violence, that we not shrink from violence. For who has said—speaking of "anything but violence"—that the supreme hierarchy of moral values lies in amiability? Who has said that when our values are insulted, rather than reacting like men, we are obliged to be amiable? Dialectics are perfectly good as the first instrument of communication. But no dialectic is admissible other than the dialectic of fists and pistols when justice or the Patria is outraged.

. . . Yet our movement would not be understood at all if it were thought to be just a way of thinking; it is not a way of thinking but a manner of being. . . . We must adopt, before all of life, in every act, a profound, humane, and concrete attitude. That attitude is the spirit of service and of sacrifice, the ascetic and military sense of life. Let no one imagine that here we recruit in order to offer perquisites; let no one imagine we are meeting here to defend privileges. I would hope that this microphone before me could carry my voice to the farthest corners of working-class homes, to say to them: Yes, we wear neckties; yes, you may say that we are señoritos. But we bear the spirit of struggle precisely for that which does not concern us as señoritos. We come to struggle to impose harsh and just sacrifices on many in our own classes, and we come to build a totalitarian state whose resources can deal equally with both the humble and the wealthy. This is our task, for thus the señoritos of Spain have been throughout their history. . . .

I think that the banner has been raised. Now we shall defend it joyfully, poetically. Because there are some who think that in the face of the advance of the revolution . . . one should avoid in propaganda whatever might excite emotion or arouse an extreme and energetic attitude. What a mistake! Only poets have ever been able to move the peoples, and woe to those who, in the face of the poetry that destroys, do not know how to present the poetry that creates!

In a poetic movement, we shall raise this fervent zeal for Spain, we shall sacrifice, we shall renounce, and ours will be the triumph, a triumph that—need I say it?—will not be won in these next elections. In these elections vote for whoever seems to you less bad. But our

Spain will not arise from that, nor is it our model. The elections produce a fetid, morbid atmosphere, like a tavern at the end of a dissolute night. That is not our place. Yes, indeed, I am a candidate, but I am one without faith in or respect for the system. I tell you this now, when it might cost me votes. That does not matter. We do not intend to go to quarrel with the habitués over the rotting remains of a sordid banquet. Our place is outside, although sometimes we may have to go within. Our place is in the fresh air, under the clear night, weapon on our shoulder, with the stars above. Let the others go on with their amusements. We, outside, in tense, fervent, and secure vigilance, already feel dawn breaking in the joy of our hearts.[47]

The liberal caretaker government provided police protection for the meeting, which passed without incident. The rightist pundit José María Carretero observed: "It seems a bit strange that the first public fascist meeting should end in an atmosphere of peaceful normality. On leaving the Comedia and finding a calm and tranquil street outside, I had the feeling of having attended a lovely literary soirée at the Atheneum."[48]

The rightist press generally described the event as the founding of a Spanish fascist movement, and the correspondent of Mussolini's *Il Popolo d'Italia* termed it "the first propaganda meeting of the Spanish fascist movement."[49] *El Sol,* Spain's leading liberal newspaper, dismissed it as "A Poetic Movement," largely concerned with style and outward form, adding, "We reject it in the first place for wanting to be fascist . . . and in the second place for not really being so, for not being a deep and authentic fascism."[50]

The movement did not receive an official name until four days later (2 November), when the official organizational meeting took place. After some debate, it was decided to retain the mimetic initials "F. E." but to change their meaning from "Fascismo Español" to "Falange Española" (Spanish Phalanx). Though the Falangist version would later claim that the leaders thought this up themselves, "falange" was a term used not infrequently by precursors, "falange" or "falanges" having been employed any number of times by Giménez Caballero in earlier writings as well as in the pages of *La Conquista del Estado* (while in 1929 the right-authoritarian Jeunesses Patriotes in France had organized their student activitists as Phalanges Universitaires).[51]

The "Puntos Iniciales" of the new party emphasized organic unity and the replacement of parliament by an authoritarian system, while invoking the Catholic religion:

> We are all born in a *family.*
> We all live in a *municipality.*
> We all work in a *trade* or *profession.*

> But no one is born or lives, naturally, in a *political party*.
>
> . . . Thus the new state must recognize the integrity of the family as a social unit, the autonomy of the municipality as a territorial unit, and the syndicate, the guild, the corporation as authentic bases of the organization of the state.
>
> . . . For everyone, true freedom, which is only achieved by forming part of a strong and free nation.
>
> For no one the freedom to perturb, poison, or incite destructive passions, or to undermine the cohesion of an enduring political organization. These bases are *authority, hierarchy, and order.*

The Puntos added, "All reconstruction of Spain must have a Catholic character."

Though commonly considered a movement of "Spanish fascism," an aura of vagueness surrounded the new party. Its announced doctrines, vague and general, were less distinctively fascistic than those of the JONS, and might have been more representative of a corporative and authoritarian right-wing Catholic party than of a specifically fascist movement.[52]

García Valdecasas, one of the three co-founders, disappeared almost immediately. He would later claim that he had not realized that a full-scale party was to be organized at that time, and had only been asked to participate in a meeting of "national affirmation." Within a fortnight he married a marquesa and went off on a long honeymoon. He never returned to the party until after the Civil War began, fearing, he later said, that the somewhat amorphous new movement would either fall apart or degenerate into violence, or both.[53] Moreover, on his return to Madrid he found José Antonio in control as leader and chief ideologue of the Falange, effectively displacing any role for Valdecasas as an intellectual leader.

For the elections of November 1933, José Antonio was personally offered a place on the rightist lists in both Madrid and Cádiz, and accepted the latter because the list included family friends and allies in the Primo de Rivera home district, providing somewhat greater freedom and independence. Even so, José Antonio did not campaign as a fascist or Falangist, but simply as a nationalist and a Primo de Rivera on one of the most ultra-right, not to say reactionary, electoral lists in all Spain.

The campaign was marred by several incidents. The worst occurred prior to his speech in San Fernando on 13 November, when a leftist gunman attempted to fire at the speakers but succeeded only in killing one spectator and wounding four others, one of whom, a female relative of José Antonio, was left permanently blind. This may be considered the first of several attempts on José Antonio's life, for an accomplice of the killer, later arrested, declared that the action was a protest against the appearance of a fascist candidate. There was no response or reprisal by those attacked, so that the cleverly sardonic columnist of *ABC*, Wenceslao Fernández Flórez, sarcastically commented: "So that everything will be incongruous, here it is the fascists who were made to swallow castor oil," referring to the early Italian Fascists' practice of forcing their enemies to swallow large draughts of castor oil in public. "If fascism responds to two corpses only with verbal protests, then it is not fascism but franciscanism."[54] José Antonio shot back, "The Spanish fascists will make it perfectly clear, without boasting, that even symbolically they do not swallow the slightest dose of castor oil."[55]

The victory of the right and center in the Cortes elections of November 1933 facilitated José Antonio's fairly easy victory in his own district, where he placed second on the rightist list.[56] Though it was probably not necessary, his success was eased by a certain amount of old-style corruption: Ramón Carranza, the former Conservative Party cacique of Cádiz, made a comeback in these elections and followed former practices by distributing a certain amount of money among local anarchosyndicalists to accentuate their tendency toward abstentionism.[57] Amused by this essay in mutual corruption, José Antonio would later begin a brief comic novel in English entitled "The Anarcho-Carranzists."[58] The nascent Falange nominally gained another deputy when the marqués de la Eliseda, elected on the same Cádiz list as José Antonio, affiliated himself with the party, though in fact he remained closely associated with the monarchists as well. Eliseda then spent the balance of that month of November in Italy, where, like José Antonio previously, he gained an audience with the Duce.

The biggest winner, however, was the new Catholic CEDA, which emerged as the largest single political party in the country. The triumph of the moderate right would prove highly detrimental to the Falange, for it seemed to prove that moderate, legalist tactics would suffice to defeat the left in democratic Spain. For that matter, the elections also strengthened the radical right of monarchism, on whom the Falange was dependent for financing but who might now feel less need of a militant fascist force. José Calvo Sotelo, finance minister for Primo de Rivera, gained a seat in parliament and was immediately hailed by part of the radical right as the real leader of an authoritarian nationalism in Spain.

The gadfly Giménez Caballero could not resist satirizing the appearance in the autumn of 1933 of the two latest messiahs of what was termed "Spanish fascism":

> As soon as Dr. Albiñana, under the Berenguer government, entered a movie theater throwing punches, the newspapers said: "Fascism is imminent!"

Then when Sanjurjo took over Seville on the tenth of August and coughed vigorously for twenty-four hours, all Spain said: "Fascism!"

When Lerroux won the elections, the socialist-communists shouted everywhere: "This is fascism!"

When Maura buttoned his jacket more angrily than on other occasions and walked out of parliament, people exclaimed: "Behold it comes!" (Even Ortega y Gasset, in the opera house, had sung a magnificent aria on "national laborism" that awakened much suspicion.)

When Gil Robles triumphed with his party, the entire population of Spain was not slow to muse: "This must be fascism!"

When the JONS attacked the office of the Friends of the USSR, it was immediately said: "Fascism is starting there!"

When José Antonio Primo de Rivera presided over a lovely meeting in the Comedia and some of his friends then gave him a banquet, sensible Spanish opinion did not vacillate: "Fascism is on the march!"

And then, when Señor Calvo Sotelo, living in Paris, won a parliament seat in the last elections, the well-informed could not restrain themselves from proclaiming: "Fascism will soon be here!" [59]

Within the first month or two, the Falange gained about two thousand members, but many of these were younger ex-upetistas or other rightists and monarchists who lacked any clear-cut fascist identity. The main counterbalance to this rightist nucleus came from the only other significant source of new members: the students, mainly from the universities, who were more energetic and revolutionary in their aspirations. A student affiliate, the Sindicato Universitario Español (SEU), organized in November, became the first Falangist syndicate and the first auxiliary organ of any type. It would play a key role in the early years of the party.

The official publication of the new party was the weekly *F. E.*, which, following an initial embargo by the ever-present Republican censors, was allowed to appear on 7 December 1933. A total of fifteen numbers, each about twelve pages in length, came out between December 1933 and 19 July 1934, subject to constant censorship, relatively frequent wholesale suspensions or prohibitions by the government, and increasing street affrays over its sale, which became more lethal than the skirmishes over *JONS* the preceding year. All this rather contrasted with the predominantly literary and esthetic tone of much of the writing that appeared in *F. E.*, a reflection of the stylistic scruples of José Antonio, and different from the shrill and aggressive polemics that many members and observers expected. It is a commonplace of historians that fascism was the most "estheticizing" of modern radical movements, but in this case what was intended to be the major propaganda organ of an aggressive new nationalist movement had more the tone of a literary review.

*F. E.* did make clear the political and ideological character of the movement, acknowledging its debt to Italian Fascism, running a regular column on "Fascist Life" that dealt with Italy and other countries, and also reporting on "the movement," as fascist and proto-fascist groups were referred to, in various countries. Of all references to foreign lands, 40 percent of the space went to Italy, with entire speeches of Mussolini reprinted. France came second with approximately 15 percent, and Nazi Germany a poor third with 10 percent.[60] In addition, a series of articles by Giménez Caballero concerned his doctrine of fascism as the new Rome, for both Italy and Spain. Numerous articles—though none by José Antonio—used the term "fascist" or some qualified form thereof to refer to the movement and to what was said to be needed for Spain. At the same time, there was considerable sensitivity to the charge of being merely fascist or imitating Italy, and in the very first number an unsigned editorial declared, "*F. E.* does not intend to imitate any foreign movement." Nonetheless, all doctrine presented in *F. E.* was completely parallel to or similar to that of Italian Fascism, and there was no criticism whatsoever of any aspect of the latter's policies or ideology.

Unlike Onésimo Redondo's *Libertad, F. E.* was not particularly anti-Semitic, though it was not opposed to anti-Semitism, either. While it recognized that anti-Semitism was what was most "distinctive" about German National Socialism, differentiating it from Italian Fascism and some other fascist-type movements, there was no criticism of Nazi policy, except to point out that in Spain the historic "Jewish problem" did not have to do with race but with religion. There does not seem to have been a full appreciation of the character and extent of Nazi racism, either vis-à-vis the Jews or in general. An occasional reference in *F. E.* articles might denounce Jews for "usury" or "parasitism," but there was never any proposal to imitate Nazi anti-Semitism. *F. E.* was always more comfortable with Fascist Italy, and its constant goal was to propagate doctrines and attitudes drawn from the Italian experience.

The appearance of the Falange did not seem particularly impressive to German and Italian diplomatic observers resident in Madrid. The counselor of the German embassy, Hans Hermann Völckers, reported on 15 December 1933 that there were currently three organizations of the fascist type in Spain, the least significant of which was Albiñana's PNE.

> A second group is constituted by the so-called JONS. . . . This group, which, like its equivalent in Portugal, calls itself "national-syndicalist," is perhaps the nearest to German National Socialism, since it also tries to attract workers. . . . It has a left-nationalist program and has developed corporatist principles. . . .
>
> The third group is led by the oldest son of Primo de Rivera and has

only existed for a few weeks. Young Primo de Rivera is about thirty years old, a lawyer, intelligent and a good speaker. He is called "el señorito," because he is young and elegant. It is possible that he may develop well; everyone appreciates his good qualities of character but says that, as a politician, he is too young and has little experience. His father's name helps him in some things, but constitutes an obstacle for him with regard to those who rejected the Dictatorship and see in his initiative a return to his father's regime. Primo de Rivera openly proclaimed himself fascist during the last elections and declared that the latter do not interest him at all since parliamentarianism is of little use to Spain. His supporters are mostly young aristocrats, but he is trying to develop roots for his movement among the armed forces, though he says he is only interested in the officers. Behind him he has the well-known rightist newspaper *La Nación,* with its director Delgado Barreto, who certainly does not have an impeccable reputation.[61]

Italian embassy officials naturally felt somewhat closer to the nascent Falange than did the Germans, and the Italian chargé, Geissler Celesia, reported to Rome on 1 February 1934:

There is evidence of some intensification of fascist propaganda, with a certain effectiveness despite the dubious means they have adopted. I have spoken with the two young fascist deputies. Primo de Rivera and Eliseda, both young, good orators, full of good intentions, but inexpert and too open to the accusation of being "señoritos," rather than representatives of something new. They complain that Gil Robles gives them no money, that the Grandes de España have provided no funding for their propaganda since the elections. . . . They assure me that they are holding frequent meetings and have enthusiastic followers, that their propaganda is gaining ground in Catalonia, and that they are making progress among the armed forces. But, in my opinion, they are not sufficiently aware of the need for propaganda and recruitment among the workers and rural sectors and of the need to have young people who are well organized and strongly combative, and, above all, of the need for a well-defined program that can win the support of the masses. Certainly, opposed to that is the problem of not antagonizing the large landowners, whom they ask for economic assistance and who still dream of retaining their lands, privileges, and subjugated peasants. Moreover, many of their new supporters are motivated not by positive convictions but by fear of the worst, and in such conditions their combat value is not equivalent to their numbers, which, for that matter, even their own leaders cannot calculate.[62]

By this point, despite the positive construction that he placed on the party's activities when talking with Italian diplomats, José Antonio was already becoming somewhat discouraged. Privately he complained to Ruiz de Alda and other associates that the founding of the movement may have been premature, that there should have been deeper preparation in the areas of culture and propaganda to overcome the basic left–right polarization and the strength of conservatism generally—though what effective form such preparation might have taken remained obscure. The less sensitive Ruiz de Alda was not as discouraged, pointing to the beginning, at least, of what could become national organization and recommending greater militancy and direct action.[63]

The one thing that the Falange had accomplished during its first three months was to seize the initiative in fascistic proselytization from the JONS, which it quickly surpassed in numbers. Its supporters among the radical right had won the battle for financial assistance, at least as compared with the JONS.[64] The Falange could exhibit more famous names and invest in more propaganda, so that, as Ledesma later admitted, "the entry of new members and the rise of the JONS both declined visibly after the appearance of F. E."[65] Though both groups suffered from the great success of the CEDA, the JONS was affected more drastically.

Thus, during the winter of 1933–34, pressure increased on the leaders of the JONS to agree to a fusion, which both José Antonio and Ruiz de Alda favored. Privately, Ledesma had earlier cast all blame for the rivalry between the two groups on the "ideological confusion" of José Antonio (too rightist and Italianist, too imitatively fascistic, and inadequately revolutionary) and his compromises with "reactionaries."[66] But jonsismo's main prop, its student following, was being seduced by the rhetoric and charisma and more active propaganda of the Falange. As incidents attending the sale of F. E. in Madrid mounted, attention focused more and more on the Falange, and the prospects of the JONS were becoming "paralyzed."[67] Thus Ledesma reached the conclusion that

> the enormous defects noted in F. E. were, perhaps, transitory, and could be overcome. With regard to its influx of new supporters, they were lacking in vigor and historical consciousness, and thus it should not have been difficult to displace them from positions of leadership. Furthermore, the JONS, managing the more resonant propaganda platform of F. E., could manage to popularize its slogans much more easily.[68]

Finally, he judged that the military mentality and enthusiasm for direct action of Ruiz de Alda were favorable to jonsismo, and might help tilt the balance of power.

On 11 February 1934, the Consejo Nacional (National Council) of the JONS, representing the nine local jonsista groups then in existence,

The Falangist triumvirate in 1934: José Antonio, Ledesma, and Ruiz de Alda

met in Madrid to consider a merger.[69] A majority of its fifteen members voted to pursue possible terms of unification, while condemning "grave errors" in the Falange that they proposed to rectify. There was little difficulty in arriving at terms. The unified movement would be called Falange Española de las Juntas de Ofensiva Nacional-Sindicalista, or, in moments of fatigue, F. E. de las J. O. N. S. Thus was born the most peculiar and long-winded name of any fascistic movement in Europe.

The party would henceforth be directed by a unified Junta de Mando (Command Council) composed of four former Falangists (José Antonio, Ruiz de Alda, Sánchez Mazas, and Fernández Cuesta) and two former jonsistas (Ledesma and Redondo), with day-to-day leadership in the hands of a Triunvirato Ejecutivo Central composed of José Antonio, Ledesma, and Ruiz de Alda. José Antonio insisted that Ledesma take membership card number 1 in the united party because of his political seniority (though he was two years younger than José Antonio). José Antonio then became number 2, Redondo number 3, Ruiz de Alda number 4, and so on. Each local unit of the Falange was to be called a "Jons," and in March Fernández Cuesta was named the first party secretary.[70]

The unification agreement specified that the party must adopt "a revolutionary economic line" (something the original Falange had not done), and all the jonsista slogans and emblems—superior to anything thought up by the Falangists—were incorporated by the united movement. These included the Yugo y flechas, the red-black-red banner, and the slogans that Ledesma had coined: "España, Una, Grande y Libre," "Por la Patria, el Pan y la Justicia," and "¡Arriba!" (The later slogan "¡Arriba España!" is said to have been coined by Sánchez Mazas.)[71]

The two entities were sufficiently similar that the fusion was effective, though the monarchists and other rightists who had joined the original Falange to work for "Spanish fascism" (who were often considerably older than the party leaders) were not enthusiastic about the revolutionary dialectic of the JONS. The only notable defection from Ledesma's small following was Santiago Montero Díaz, professor of classical history and ex-leader of a Communist youth group, who headed the small JONS group at the University of Santiago de Compostela. Announcing his resignation in a letter to Ledesma, he declared that national syndicalism could only thrive on the basis of "revolutionary rivalry" with Marxism. The "rightist limitations" of the Falange would be fatal, he said. "In spite of all verbal declarations to the contrary, the members, content, and political style of the Falange are in open opposition to the national revolution."[72]

The unification would in fact be decisive in the political future of José Antonio and the Falange, for it meant a decisive turn from the semirightist direction of the original Falange and the beginning of a fuller adoption of a revolutionary fascism. Despite what he called the "coarseness" of the JONS,[73] José Antonio welcomed the fusion. He recognized the need for a more radical approach that would work free of the rightist framework, and abandoned his musings of the previous month about the possibility of some sort of understanding with the CEDA youth movement (in which his old friend Serrano Súñer played a leading role).[74] Falangist propaganda began to move in a more jonsista direction, taking its esthetic tone from José Antonio but much of its practical content from Ledesma. Moreover, the terms of unification stipulated that all leaders and active members had to be between eighteen and forty-five years of age. Though this rule was not enforced immediately, it was aimed at the retired rightist army officers and older ex-upetistas who had formed part of the initial Falangist leadership.

The first major meeting of the united movement was an expression of solidarity held at the JONS stronghold of Valladolid, which had the second-largest party leadership after Madrid. On 4 March busloads of Falangists from all over central and northern Spain converged on the Teatro Calderón in Valladolid. The setting had been well prepared by Redondo's followers: the meeting opened in the electric atmosphere of a hall full of new Falangist banners and emblems, and when the four top leaders entered, they received the fascist salute from an audience of between two and three thousand enthusiasts who packed the building. The Falangist journalist Bravo Martínez would later call this "the first purely fascist meeting."[75]

José Antonio delivered the major address. After some rhetorical flourishes on the landscape of Castile in the style of the Generation of Ninety-Eight, he began by denouncing the right:

> They deem us reactionaries because they hope that, while they vegetate in their casinos and fret over privileges that have partially disappeared, we would become the Assault Guards of reaction and snatch their chestnuts from the fire, replacing on their estates those same people now scrutinizing us. . . .

Then he turned to Redondo's concern that the Falange might copy foreign ideologies:

> What characterizes our enterprise is its temperature, its spirit. What does the Corporate State matter to us, what difference does it make if parliament disappears, if that is only to go on producing the same cautious, pale, shifty and smirking young people, incapable of being inflamed for the Patria, or even, no matter what they say, for religion?
>
> Be very careful with all that about the Corporate State, be very careful about all those canned phrases repeated by those who are trying to convert us into just another party. Onésimo Redondo has already warned of that danger. We cannot achieve our goals simply by restructuring the state. What we seek is to restore to Spain an optimism, a faith in itself, a clear and energetic project of a common life.[76]

As the Falangists left the theater, shots broke out and there was some fighting in the streets.[77] Though one Falangist was killed, the leaders considered the meeting a successful baptism of fire for the newly unified movement. On the way back to Madrid, José Antonio proposed that from that day forward all Falangists employ the familiar (second-person) form or *tuteo* in speaking to each other.[78] A relative anomaly in the formal Spanish society of that day, the proposal also paralleled to some extent Mussolini's campaign to generalize the familiar *voi* in place of *Lei* all over Italy. José Antonio himself was already becoming widely known simply as José Antonio, and he would be increasingly referred to in this familiar way, not merely within the movement, but also to a certain degree outside it.[79]

The truly militant sector of the Falange, as of the JONS before it, was the students. Spanish university students had first achieved a political impact in the last phase of the Dictadura. The left-liberal Federación Universitaria Española (FUE), founded in 1931, was one of the most ultra-

Republican groups in Spain and had become a dominant force among non-Catholic students. It first introduced direct action into the universities, though without fatal violence. By the end of the first Republican biennium, however, attitudes were beginning to shift. One indication had been the successful formation of the JONS student syndicate in May 1933.

Ruiz de Alda supervised the formation of the Sindicato Español Universitario (SEU) during the first days of the new party. The initial student organizers were Manuel Valdés Larrañaga, an athlete and champion swimmer, and the former jonsista Matías Montero Rodríguez, both at the University of Madrid. The formal statutes, which required official independence from any political party, were presented to the authorities on 19 November 1933, though the latter did not legally authorize the SEU until 5 March 1934. It quickly established a following in Madrid and also in Seville, and then incorporated the jonsistas at the University of Valladolid.[80]

Its main enemy was the FUE, which the SEU set out to undermine by taunts, propaganda, and physical provocation. In this it was willing to accept the assistance of the Catholic students, who had been slightly more numerous in the elitist university system of those years than the FUE, but much less active politically. In a talk to the Madrid SEU a few months after its organization, Ruiz de Alda declared: "Our objective is the destruction of the FUE, which must disappear either by absorbing it, dividing it, or suppressing it. . . . And we must drag the Asociación de Estudiantes Católicos into the combat."[81] In the university there were to be no neutrals.

### THE ERUPTION OF VIOLENCE

The level of political violence under the Second Republic was very high; the journal *Historia Contemporánea* has referred to "the militarization of politics during the Second Republic."[82] This was begun by anarchists and Communists in 1931 and reached its two points of climax in 1934 and 1936.[83] From their first days Falangists—as befitted generic fascists— talked of violence. In the Comedia meeting, José Antonio had spoken of engaging the left in "the dialectic of fists and of pistols," and Ruiz de Alda had declared that leftists would be treated as "enemies in a state of war." Point IX of the party's "Puntos Iniciales" stated:

> Violence can be justified when it is employed on behalf of a legitimate ideal.

> Truth, justice, and the Patria will be defended with violence when
> they are attacked by violence—or by ambush [*insidia*].
>    But Falange Española will never employ violence as an instrument
> of oppression.

The Falange thus spoke of violence as justified by the ends it served
rather than simply as a means of defense. In the first number of *F. E.*
José Antonio had declared that violence was of minor importance in the
Falangist program but definitely justified in the right time and place. Earlier, he had written in a personal letter that "violence is not to be censured
categorically. Only when it is employed against justice"[84]—a highly ambiguous standard at best.

The jonsista leaders had been rather more direct. Ledesma's philosophy
of violence has been explained by his friend Emiliano Aguado as requiring
that the nationalist who employs violence must freely accept equal risk
for himself. Violence "is only to be employed to achieve ends superior to
those defended by the enemy and to the life of man itself" and must be
"carried out in an orderly manner." "Violence" should be used "as a historical force," based on "sentiments that transcend the combatants themselves, superior to the personal trajectory of each of them." What Ledesma ultimately sought was "a religious justification; thus he appealed
to higher values beyond any individual . . . beyond which there was no
higher belief."[85]

Like some Spanish anarchists, Ledesma had been influenced by the
Italian Fascist Curzio Malaparte's *Technique of the Coup d'Etat,* and his
goal was a nationalist revolutionary insurrection. He had outlined the
prerequisites for this "conquest of the state" in the journal *JONS* only
two months before the founding of the Falange:

> 1. The insurrection must be led by a party with armed squads
> capable of controlling the situation, even if part of the army supports it.
>    2. Training in insurrection is indispensable, along with political
> development to guarantee the party's discipline.
>    3. Insurrectional squads must undergo frequent mobilization to
> ensure their effectiveness at the decisive moment.
>    4. Surprise and direct takeover must be the prime elements of
> insurrection, and one of the primary goals will be to achieve at least
> the neutrality of the coercive arms of the state.
>    5. The objectives of the insurrection must be popular, known to
> the national masses, and the product of the people's dissatisfaction
> with the regime. To achieve this, the party must undertake an intense
> informational campaign.
>    6. The insurrectional party must be totalitarian, that is, organized
> hierarchically and dictatorially, prepared to do away with other

parties and fuse itself with the state so that its use of violence appears justified and moral.[86]

Onésimo Redondo was in some respects the most explicit of all the Falangist leaders, announcing that "we are enamored of a certain salutary violence"[87] and that "a situation of absolute violence is approaching."[88] In December 1933 he shrilled:

> Young workers! Young Spaniards! Prepare your weapons, get used to the crack of the pistol, caress your dagger, be inseparable from your vindicative club!
> Young people must be trained in physical combat, must love violence as a system, must arm themselves with whatever they can, and must be prepared to finish off by whatever means a few dozen Marxist impostors.[89]

One month later he insisted that "it is impossible to live without war"[90] and that "youth, furthermore, needs the tonic of real combat, of physical struggle, without which all creative energy perishes. A national and youthful violence is necessary, is just, is convenient."[91]

The first fascist direct action in Spain was that of the students of the JONS and later of the Falange, chronicled by David Jato: "Along with books, a lead-tipped club or a pistol were inseparable companions. Some hollowed out an old book, carving room for a pistol inside, and in this way could carry weapons more safely and discreetly, hiding them at home, where their families by natural instinct would otherwise complement the police."[92]

Perhaps the Falangist leaders had not thought that their talk would be taken so seriously by the left, but, if so, they were mistaken. The UGT trade union and the left wing of the Socialist Party had already begun to speak vaguely of violent revolution as early as the summer of 1933, and this had been the position of the tiny Communist Party since its founding. Since the takeover of the CNT by the revolutionary Iberian Anarchist Federation (FAI) in 1931, the anarchosyndicalists had attempted two abortive revolutionary insurrections, with a third following in December 1933, only a month after the founding of the Falange. The sharp leftist defeat in the elections of 1933 only increased radicalization among the Socialists, who had seen the much larger Italian movement suppressed by Mussolini and the German party, largest in the world, succumb to Nazism only a few years later. Similarly, Austrian socialism—the intellectual distinction of its leaders notwithstanding—had also fallen to the right, and in February 1934 would lose completely a desperate effort at insurrection. Spanish Socialist leaders had clearly stated in 1931 that one of the basic goals of the new Republic was to reverse the trend toward nationalist authoritarianism and fascism in Europe. They were in no mood to accept passively the emergence of a Spanish fascism. The Socialists could afford largely to ignore jonsismo, but the Falange seemed more serious; it was capable of making a lot of noise, and it apparently had financial backing. Given the trend of recent political developments in central Europe and in Spain, the Socialists were increasingly prepared to take the offensive.[93] In these months the Madrid press carried many notices advertising firearms.

The left had already drawn first blood when a jonsista government employee was stabbed to death by a Socialist at a Socialist meeting in Daimiel in Ciudad Real province on 2 November 1933.[94] This had not been a planned killing so much as a crime of political passion. One month later Ruiz de Alda barely escaped being attacked while passing through the town of Tudela; his car was seized and burned by the assailants.[95] On 4 December a jonsista baker was killed in Zalamea de la Serena (Badajoz province), and a third jonsista was killed in Villanueva de la Reina (Jaén province) on 26 December.[96] The first fatalities were jonsistas—apparently because they were better known and in some cases more aggressive than the new Falangists; the fact that these first acts of deadly violence by the left took place in smaller towns and cities was an indication of the level of social and political tension building in Spain. The first fatality in Madrid occurred with the sale of the first number of *F. E.* on 7 December 1933, when a student—apparently not a Falangist but simply an interested reader—was killed soon after buying a copy.

From this point the ambiguity and contradictions in José Antonio's attitude toward violence would become increasingly apparent. He was obviously a strong believer in direct action on the level of personal violence as expressed in fist-fights, showing pronounced aggressiveness ever since his student days toward those who strongly disagreed with him or disparaged him or members of his family. José Antonio was also well acquainted with the use of firearms, for, like many in his social class, he enjoyed hunting game in the countryside. The contradictions began with the dilemma over use of deadly force, rather than personal fisticuffs, in political disputes, for that was a level of violence with which the young fascist leader was frankly uncomfortable, as compared with Ruiz de Alda, Ledesma, or Redondo.

Strange though it may seem, José Antonio appears to have thought or hoped that the Falange—perhaps with the assistance of allies—might somehow capture the state without employing the systematic and deadly violence employed by Italian Fascism between 1920 and 1922. He is said to have explained privately that the "dialectic of fists and pistols" of which he had spoken was intended primarily as a rhetorical metaphor,[97] as though he were innocently unaware of what all this meant in the climate of Spanish radical politics in 1933–1934. He wanted to differentiate the Falange from the small bands of the sometimes armed "Legionarios de España" of the right-radical Dr. Albiñana or the earlier pistoleros of the Sindicatos Libres, and found the prospect of a future of indiscriminate political violence dismaying. Thus when police raided the Falangist Center in Madrid on 3 January 1934, they found twenty clubs but no pistols.[98]

Political opponents put so much pressure on kiosk dealers that *F. E.* was virtually barred from retail trade, and SEU students had to hawk each number on the streets. Several squads of activists were formed to protect the vendors, and when the fifth number of *F. E.* appeared on 11 January, José Antonio and Ruiz de Alda personally joined the escorts to encourage their youngsters. Several major brawls erupted, and later in the day a twenty-two-year-old student, not a member of the party or the SEU but apparently a sympathizer, was shot and killed on the central calle de Alcalá after buying a copy.[99] As a sympathizer of the Falange, he was treated as the first official "caído" (fallen member) of the new party. Falangists attended his funeral and for the first time chanted the ritual "¡Presente!" borrowed from Italian Fascism, which would be a permanent feature of ceremonies for the Falangist dead.

Violent incidents also occurred around the universities of Seville and Zaragoza, where the SEU was active. Falangist militants began to demand a policy of direct reprisals—an eye for an eye—but José Antonio was reluctant to follow the tactics of Italian Fascists, German Nazis, or the Spanish revolutionary left. An article in the next number of *F. E.* (18 January) was entitled "Enough martyrs":

> Readers of *F. E.* have criticized its mildness of tone. Our reply is that we are not given to bravado. What we are about to say is therefore no bravado: it is nothing more or less than the calm expression of a firm decision, adopted in all tranquility: we are not willing to have more of our members' blood spilled in the streets without response. We already have enough martyrs. We cannot prevent another from falling, but it shall not take place with impunity.

The same day a SEU student was seriously wounded outside the University of Zaragoza, where the rector temporarily closed the FUE center. Before the month was out, four more Falangists had been slain in different parts of the country.[100] On 1 February José Antonio responded soberly in *F. E.*:

> Death is an act of service. . . . A reprisal can be something that in a given moment might set off an endless series of other reprisals and counterstrokes for an entire people. Before unleashing on our people a state of civil war, those with responsibility for leadership must

calculate how much can be suffered and when anger provides sufficient excuse.

That day, in one of his rare speeches before the Cortes, José Antonio admitted that the appearance of the Falange was associated with "that phenomenon of fascism which is being produced in Spain as all over Europe," but insisted that in a recent assault by the SEU at the University of Zaragoza, out of "between 200 and 300 assailants," only two "had a pistol."[101] This seemed ingenuous at best, for, as Ledesma would observe a year and a half later, the Falange had appeared "with excessive optimism and gesticulation" and a "vocabulary of violence"[102] that José Antonio was not at first prepared to back up in practice.

Not long before, the Madrid daily *Luz* had published an internal document from the party militia, probably prepared by the retired Lt. Col. Luis Arrendondo, the ex-upetista in charge of paramilitary training, which contained detailed instructions for what would later be called urban guerrilla warfare.[103] In fact, the Falange was not at all prepared for any such activity at that time, but this well-publicized document helped convince the left of the seriousness of the fascist threat in Spain. The climate in at least four universities had become very tense, and on 25 January an assault was carried out in Madrid against the office of the FUE affiliate in the School of Medicine. It was led by one of the chief SEU and Falangist militia leaders, Agustín Aznar, Castile's Greco-Roman wrestling champion, and left one opponent seriously wounded. Later, on 7 February, a banner appeared that had been hung on the principal Socialist Casa del Pueblo (House of the People) in Madrid. It read, "F. E. Viva el Fascio."

Two days later Matías Montero Rodríguez, the medical student who was one of the principal founders of the SEU, was shot five times and killed while returning home from selling copies of *F. E.* Only twenty years of age, Montero had been a charter member of the JONS[104] before switching to the Falange. His funeral was well attended and very moving. Though the invocation of "¡Presente!" was copied from Italian Fascism, José Antonio's terse elegy achieved a somber, laconic eloquence:

> Brother and comrade Matías Montero y Rodríguez de Trujillo! Thank you for your example.
>
> May God grant you his eternal rest and deny rest to us until we learn to harvest for Spain the seed sown by your death.
>
> For the last time: Matías Montero y Rodríguez de Trujillo.
> (All respond: "¡Presente!")
> ¡Viva España!
> (All respond: "¡Viva!")[105]

So far as is known, the tall, handsome Montero was the first Falangist to die in a planned assassination. Because he was also the most prominent

Funeral of Matías Montero Rodríguez, the "fallen student," in Madrid, February 1934

of the first Falangists killed, he would become the official martyr of the movement (some would later say the "Spanish Horst Wessel," after his Nazi counterpart). Later, under the Franco regime, the anniversary of his murder would become the annual SEU day of commemoration ("Día del Estudiante Caído," or Day of the Fallen Student). Somewhat unusually, in this case the killer was arrested, convicted, and given a long prison sentence until amnestied by the Popular Front in 1936.[106]

This succession of unavenged attacks caused certain commentators to suggest that F. E. should stand for "Funeraria Española" (Spanish Funeral) and its principal leader be known as "Juan Simón the gravedigger." The pundit Fernández Flórez had already suggested that the new party smacked more of "franciscanism" than of "fascism." The day after Montero's killing, Alvaro Alcalá Galiano inquired in *ABC*, "Where are the mysterious fascist legions? Where can their organization be seen?" On 13 February the same organ concluded that "such a fascism is no more than literature, presenting no risk for its adversaries." Alcalá Galiano added that "a purely theoretical fascism, without violence as a tactic, may be whatever it pleases, but is not fascism," [107] and in this he was undeniably correct.

José Antonio's response remained unvaried. He simply dispatched to

*ABC* a copy of a paragraph that he had earlier published in the third number of *F. E.*: "Falange Española will accept and wage combat on terrain of its own choosing, not on that selected by its adversaries . . . Furthermore, Falange Española has nothing to do with a criminal organization and does not intend to copy the methods of such organizations, however extreme the provocations."

Such high-minded equanimity was not characteristic either of other leaders or of rank-and-file militants. As one veteran later observed, "The lads who first signed up were much more sportive than scholarly."[108] When *ABC* declared "its astonishment, shared by many, at the state of defenselessness in which F. E. leaves its spirited youth,"[109] many of the "spirited youth" must have agreed.

By the end of February, the Falangist leadership in Madrid began to organize more seriously for violence that would go beyond student riots or brief street skirmishes over selling papers. According to Ledesma, the first measures had been inept. The initial militia chief was the middle-aged Lt. Col. Luis Arredondo, who, seconded by other older retired officers, had some tendency to conduct formal infantry drills.[110] A new tone was added, however, by Juan Antonio Ansaldo, a daredevil monarchist aviator who had earlier won the Gran Cruz Laureada de San Fernando for aerial combat in Morocco and was a business associate and friend of Ruiz de Alda. He had encouraged substantial financial support for the Falange and formally joined the party at the beginning of February. Ansaldo soon became the movement's "jefe de comandos," or the leader of small direct-action and reprisal squads. During the spring of 1934, these units became known, in typically blood-curdling fascist style, as the "Falange de la Sangre" (Phalanx of Blood). Though under the general supervision of Ruiz de Alda, the actual planning was done by Ansaldo and by Arredondo and the retired officers who functioned as militia leaders.

Within a few days of the Valladolid meeting in early March, at which, as was indicated, one Falangist had been killed, a second was slain in Gijón and then a third in Madrid.[111] Later that month, Falangists carried out raids in the capital against the FUE center in the Faculty of Law and against one of the Casas del Pueblo in the hope of being able to seize firearms allegedly hidden there. In the latter affray, a Falangist secondary school student named Jesús Hernández was shot; he later died. Only fifteen years old, but large for his age, Hernández had been carrying a loaded pistol, and his death at such a tender age in a Falangist "comando" created something of a sensation. By the close of April, civil governors had prohibited Falangist activities in a number of provinces, and the party's center in Seville was closed altogether.

The continuing casualties produced a letter to the party's leadership by one SEU student who complained that "if *F. E.* continued to have that literary and intellectual tone, it was not worth risking one's life to sell it."[112] José Antonio replied in the 19 April issue with an article entitled "Letter to a Student Who Complains That F. E. is Not Harsh," repeating his earlier position and stressing the importance of maintaining the quality of the party weekly.

To this point the escalation of political violence under the Republic had not included direct assassination attempts against party leaders, with the exception of the violence at José Antonio's election meeting in November. Now, however, a fascist leader was considered a fair target by the extreme left. On 10 April two small bombs that failed to explode were thrown at José Antonio's car as he was driving near the center of Madrid, and a series of shots smashed the windshield. The Falangist leader leaped out of his car, accompanied by his two law clerks, and gave chase to the assailants, even exchanging gunshots with them.[113] Two months later, in June, a second bomb was hurled against his car outside the Model Prison, where he had attended a judicial hearing involving a detained Falangist. Yet a third attempt took place subsequently, a late-night attack in the fashionable Chamartín district after a party. On that occasion confused assailants fired by mistake at the car of the noted physician Dr. Luque, who had left the gathering just ahead of José Antonio.[114] These brushes with death had little effect on the Falangist leader. He had inherited the extreme boldness and sang froid of his father, who had won "Méritos de guerra" (combat merits) for unusual bravery on the battlefield. José Antonio never exhibited the slightest degree of physical fear—a quality that enhanced his reputation among his juvenile followers—and was in fact emotionally exhilarated by the scent of danger. He often went about Madrid without an escort, and in his new ground-floor law office, he often kept the window open to the street, almost inviting an attack—though he did keep a large loaded revolver on his desk.[115]

José Antonio had continued his active social life after entering politics. Thus at the time one Falangist was killed he was at a high-society dance, and on the day of Montero's death he was participating in an aristocratic hunting party. Eugenio Vegas Latapié, the monarchist intellectual who directed the journal *Acción Española* sought, like most of the radical right, a more aggressive and violent role for the Falange. He made a sarcastic comment to José Antonio about the latter's "social frivolity" while his followers were being killed. This led to the severing of personal relations between the two,[116] though José Antonio did take Vegas's point. He subsequently swore to personal friends that he would put frivolous activities behind him because of the seriousness of the political struggle and the loss of life; in fact, however, he did not fully live up to his oath.

José Antonio would remain socially and sexually active down to the time of his final detention in March 1936, though he increasingly restricted such activities. In addition, during 1934 he apparently came to the decision that the marriage that he had long sought was impossible.

Organization of the Falangist militia of the "Primera Línea" (Front Line) slowly went forward in Madrid, replacing the small "patrullas de asalto" of the JONS. Several hundred members were now organized in "centurias," and the first formal review was held on Sunday, 3 June, at Carabanchel airfield outside Madrid. It was eventually terminated by the police, and subsequently the party leaders were fined 10,000 pesetas for illegal assembly, but the review drew considerable attention in the press and provided extensive publicity about the "mobilization of fascism" in Spain, even though only a few hundred people were involved. More serious was Ansaldo's Falange de la Sangre, but it still encountered problems, as much internal as external. Ansaldo later claimed that so many of the early actions were either leaked or betrayed that he had to adopt the practice of locking his men in a room during the hours between instruction and execution of any action. Eventually, also according to Ansaldo, a traitor was identified and promptly executed.[117]

The point of inflection in the political violence took place on Sunday, 10 June. The "Chíbiris"[118] of the Young Socialists had been prohibited by authorities from marching in the streets of Madrid but during the warm weather organized regular weekend outings to the Casa de Campo recreation area on the west side of Madrid. On the tenth a group of Falangists intercepted them, and the usual fight took place. An eighteen-year-old Falangist, Juan Cuéllar, son of a police inspector, was killed, and his corpse was subsequently mutilated, his head apparently crushed with rocks. One of Ansaldo's squads was quick to respond, allegedly without obtaining approval from the triumvirs who directed the party. Later that evening, as a bus transporting the Young Socialist excursionists unloaded some of them in Madrid, a car full of Falangist pistoleros, personally led by Ansaldo,[119] was waiting. It slowly passed the young people on the sidewalk, spraying them with bullets. A twenty-year-old shop clerk, Juanita Rico, was killed; the Falangists claimed she had been involved in desecrating the corpse. Her twenty-one-year-old brother was left permanently disabled, and several others were wounded.[120] Four days earlier, a Falangist smallholder in Torreperogil (Jaén province) had been killed during a farmworkers' strike, so that Cuéllar was the fifteenth or sixteenth jonsista or Falangist killed since a jonsista teenager had been slain by Assault Guards in Valladolid in May 1932. All the others had been killed by the left. Though numerous leftists had been injured by Falangists in street affrays and university assaults, Rico was the first leftist fatality at their hands.

Republican Assault Guards searching citizens in Madrid

For years she would be commemorated as "the first victim of fascism in Spain,"[121] but she would be far from the last. Late that same night, the third attempt against José Antonio took place as mentioned above, the gunmen mistakenly targeting Dr. Luque.[122] Later, on the day of Rico's funeral, five gunmen passed the Falangist Center in a taxi, firing on members in the garden area and wounding two.[123] Before the close of the month, José Antonio had to veto plans to assassinate Indalecio Prieto, the Socialist leader, and to explode a fifty-kilo bomb in the basement of the Socialist Casa del Pueblo.[124] On the first of July, Manuel Groizard, a retired army doctor who was Ansaldo's chief lieutenant in the Falange de la Sangre, was gravely wounded on the sidewalk in front of his home.[125] Action and counteraction continued on into July.

The liberal Madrid daily *Ahora* commented:

> The cult of violence has its practitioners in both bands. The Falangist militia practiced it with arrogant brazenness. The Young Socialists do the same, despite the pacific character of their slogans of international fraternity. . . . We can no longer tolerate the legal existence of political organizations who boast of their warlike training and military tactics, with the goal of subverting the structure of the state through a terrorist coup d'état. Whether they call themselves Socialists or fascists, such elements have no right to organize military parades and disrupt public order.[126]

In the summer of 1934 the centrist government of the Radicals, supported by the votes of the CEDA, struggled with some desperation to maintain Republican legality in the face of a constitutional challenge in Barcelona and the threatened Socialist insurrection, which would finally occur in October. It was not disposed to accept a further challenge from nascent fascists. On 10 July Assault Guards raided the Falangist Center in Madrid, arresting sixty-seven members of the party, including José Antonio and the marqués de la Eliseda, its two Cortes deputies, and seizing a variety of weapons and explosives. The two deputies soon had to be released because of their parliamentary immunity, and eventually all the detainees were freed, but by mid-July the government had ordered the closing of all Falangist centers throughout the country and prohibited all Falangist publications and public meetings, although the party itself was not declared illegal. The government also subsequently banned membership in political organizations for those under sixteen years of age and decreed that permission from parents would be required for all under twenty-three (at that time the legal age of majority in Spain).

It was clear that after less than a year the Falange was locked in a desperate struggle in which it was failing to make any real headway, and that José Antonio's approach to this struggle and to the issue of violence had been based on a naiveté that bordered on irresponsibility. He repeated at various times the standard Falangist slogan that "life is militia," but premeditated murder repelled him and made him question the nature of his enterprise, though never quite to the point of abandoning it. The writer Heleno Saña, a strong opponent of Falangism, has offered a balanced commentary:

> José Antonio wanted to convince, not to impose, as did many of his supporters and followers. At bottom he was a seducer, not a dictator. He believed in the dialectic of fists and pistols as a last resort, but

such bravado must be understood as a concession to the times, not as an essential expression of his way of being. Violence and *pistolerismo* were a common instrument in his time, employed by all the radical parties, not just the Falange. In fact, José Antonio always opposed the violence introduced in Spain by the bands of the Sindicato Libre, the anarchosyndicalist gunmen, the albiñanistas, and the extremist students of the FUE. Before organizing its own repressive squads, the Falange was the victim of physical reprisals by the extreme left. Anyone who does not keep this decisive fact in mind disqualifies himself from judging honestly the evolution of aggression and political crime. . . . José Antonio delayed such vengeful methods as long as he could, but the terror practiced by the extreme left did not favor his initial moderation. The violent squads of the Falange de la Sangre were finally accepted by José Antonio as a purely practical necessity, but not out of inner conviction.[127]

Clearly the other Falangist leaders—Ledesma, Redondo, Ruiz de Alda, Ansaldo—sought a harsher line.[128] It has even been alleged that after the killings of 10 June, José Antonio sought to make contact with the Socialist leader Largo Caballero to reduce the violence. That José Antonio believed that a fascist-style movement could be developed without deadly violence on a large scale may have reflected a certain idealism, but also confusion, naiveté, inexperience, and bad judgment. Ramiro Ledesma suffered from no such illusions. José Antonio and many thousands of others would pay the price for the miscalculations of both sides about the cost of revolutionary confrontation.

# Five

# Jefe Nacional, 1934–1936

By mid-1934 it seemed that José Antonio's earlier pessimism had been justified. Whatever initial momentum may have existed had been lost, and the letters to the Madrid office pledging affiliation had declined to the merest trickle. The left expressed its hostility in the most violent manner, the right was critical and disdainful, while the centrist government of the Radicals showed a heavy hand, momentarily paralyzing the party's activities with its prohibitions. The Falange would soon be able to resume its activities, but the immediate future was not encouraging.

Thanks to José Antonio's place on the rightist list, the party had a voice in the Cortes, but a vote or two in parliament (counting the temporary affiliation of Eliseda) was of scant use to a strongly antiparliamentary movement. José Antonio cut a curiously contradictory figure in the Cortes, where he refused to join any rightist minority—he emphasized that in many matters the Falange was as much opposed to the right as to the left—and hence played a completely solitary role. He also had some initial difficulty adjusting to the practical dialectic of parliamentary debate, since the two most salient characteristics of his public discourse were a tendency toward philosophical abstractions on the one hand and the use of lyrical and poetic forms of expression on the other, neither of which was very useful in the prosaic repartee of the Cortes. Though most of his infrequent speeches were carefully prepared and not extemporized, they achieved little. This is particularly true of his first interventions. As his rival Gil Robles put it:

> José Antonio Primo de Rivera was a much more academic than
> parliamentary orator. His careful intellectual formation, the doubts
> that many times assailed his sincere spirit, and his repugnance
> at living in an ambience that violated his sensibility all reduced
> considerably the effectiveness that his parliamentary interventions,
> correct and incisive, merited. He faced the tumult that his speeches
> sometimes provoked with more personal courage than skill in
> dialectical fencing.[1]

115

Even his close friend, the cedista Serrano Súñer, would write later that his presentations were "stylized, too academic, and lacking in vigor" and sometimes created a "painful" impression.[2]

One of his initial concerns remained the defense of his father and of the Dictatorship. When, in one of the early sessions of the new Cortes, Indalecio Prieto condemned as "systematic robbery" the Dictatorship's concession of the Spanish telephone contract to ITT, José Antonio was infuriated and literally leaped across three rows of seats in an attempt to physically assault the obese Socialist. Others stopped him short, but a general brawl broke out between left and right. This resulted in perhaps the worst scene that ever took place on the floor of the second Cortes and, to the left, no doubt seemed a perfect expression of "fascism." Once order was restored and José Antonio had gained control of himself, he presented a perfectly judicious speech criticizing the constant denunciations of the actions of the Dictadura. In an interview with journalists immediately afterwards, he insisted that he harbored no "instincts of a bully," but would always respond to what he considered an insult.[3]

José Antonio could never overcome the contradictions of his nature, an unstable combination of careful, elegant lawyer and direct-action tough. It was the former image that he normally tried to present in the Cortes, where his personal charm soon won him friends, not merely on the right, but also among the center and occasionally on the left as well. Except when trying to assault a fat, middle-aged Socialist, he normally did not present the appearance of a fascist in parliament. He worked to improve the effectiveness of his infrequent Cortes remarks, and later the ultra-rightist Ramiro de Maeztu would remark that in eloquence of figure and gesture, the Falangist leader reminded him more of the British Labourite Ramsay MacDonald, when the latter was young, than of Mussolini or Hitler. José Antonio's antagonistic monarchist comrade Ansaldo told him, with some sarcasm, that he perfectly embodied the image of a proper president for the International Anti-Fascist League.[4]

By June 1934, however, José Antonio felt the full weight of the government's pressure, when the investigating committee of the Cortes submitted a report authorizing his impeachment for illegal possession of firearms. He had declared ownership of six guns found on Falangists serving as guards and escorts. The government was seeking strenuously to deradicalize and depolarize the current political situation by reducing the means of violent conflict. All spring the police had been conducting a campaign to reduce the large number of firearms held without license, and during a three-hour search in downtown Madrid, 103 firearms were removed from passing pedestrians.[5] Many political leaders now maintained bodyguards, and though José Antonio still often went about Madrid without an escort, this was not always the case, while Falangists maintained a twenty-four-hour guard around his residence.[6] In the ensuing Cortes ballot on 3 July, Radicals and cedistas voted in favor of the report, which would strip him of his parliamentary immunity and very likely send him to jail. This danger, which might have totally derailed his chance of becoming the "jefe único" of Spanish fascism, was averted when Indalecio Prieto intervened to couple his case with that of a young Socialist deputy under indictment on a similar charge, carrying a motion to delay any further consideration until the end of the parliamentary session. A month earlier, José Antonio had delivered a very striking speech insisting that the day on which the Socialist Party "would assume a national destiny" and become a national socialism would be the day on which the mission of the Falange was completed. This infuriated the right and some Falangists as well, but marked the beginning of an unusual mutual regard between Prieto and the Falangist leader, who on 3 July rushed over to thank the Socialist and shake his hand.[7]

During the spring and summer, tension grew between José Antonio and the monarchist right, both inside and outside the Falange. The newest leader of the extreme right to emerge in 1934 was José Calvo Sotelo, finance minister of the Dictadura. Election to the Cortes had brought him home from Parisian exile, where he had been strongly influenced by Action Française and by Italian Fascism. He was young (only ten years older than José Antonio), energetic, hard-working, and intelligent, a capable writer and orator, well-positioned to become the new leader of the alfonsino radical right. On the occasion of his return and maiden speech in the Cortes on 18 May, monarchists arranged a sumptuous banquet at the Hotel Ritz, José Antonio sitting near the guest of honor at the central banquet table. Calvo Sotelo sought to lead the monarchists toward a more extreme position that would use such terms as "totalitarian" and even be willing to embrace some form of fascism, so long as the latter would be more elitist than revolutionary. He consequently asked to be admitted to the Falange.

Ruiz de Alda and even Ledesma were in favor of allowing Calvo Sotelo to join, but José Antonio strongly opposed it. He resented the monarchist, first for having failed to support his father fully during the final year of the Dictatorship, and second for having fled into exile. More directly, he alleged that Calvo was too sedentary to be a leader, did not know how to ride a horse, "only understood numbers and didn't know a single poem." More to the point, he sought to avoid the latter's competition for leadership, claimed that he was a reactionary representative "of the grand bourgeoisie and of the aristocracy," and effectively barred his admission.[8]

By July the tension between José Antonio on the one hand and the rightist and most extremist sectors of the party on the other neared the boiling point. The latter were led by Juan Antonio Ansaldo, the jefe de comandos of the Falange de la Sangre, who was supported by various of the monarchists, many of the activists in his comandos, some of the retired military men, and also a sector of the most radical students, especially some ex-jonsistas.[9] Their complaint was that José Antonio was too moderate and failed to encourage enough direct action, meaning violence. Ansaldo's plan was to collect a dozen or so of his commando leaders and burst into José Antonio's office, deposing him by force, dissolving the Executive Triumvirate and replacing it with a new configuration in which the more militant Ruiz de Alda would be head of the party, and Ledesma general secretary. One rumor even had it that José Antonio was to be assassinated by the radical Falangists.

As soon as José Antonio got the first word of this, he ordered Ansaldo to appear before a meeting of the triumvirs. José Antonio had the strong support of various key leaders in Madrid, such as Sánchez Mazas, the party secretary Fernández Cuesta, and others. Ansaldo did not deny either his position or his plan, and José Antonio had him expelled from the party forthwith. Ruiz de Alda was against this, and so, to a lesser degree, was Ledesma, but José Antonio threatened either to split the party completely or to abandon it, and quickly got his way. With Ansaldo departed a few other monarchist military men, such as Lt. Col. Luis Arredondo, the first leader of the Falangist militia.[10]

The way in which the crisis had been resolved nonetheless raised the question of whether the party would continue to enjoy financial support from the monarchists, its main source of funds. The proceeds from José Antonio's legal practice declined as he devoted most of his time to politics, and his personal resources were completely insufficient for the party. Members were few, and the most ardent were underage students, who had little or no money to contribute. It was already becoming necessary to reduce expenditures, and the elimination of monarchist funding would threaten disaster.

As it turned out, Ansaldo's expulsion had not burned the bridges between José Antonio and the monarchists of Renovación Española, who were still interested in promoting the Falange as a shock force and possible progenitor of a nationalist worker organization. For a decade José Antonio had enjoyed good relations with Antonio Goicoechea, the chief monarchist leader, and Sainz Rodríguez, the intellectual *éminence grise*. He therefore took advantage of these relationships to resolidify the Falange's financial support by signing a detailed political and financial pact with Goicoechea on 20 August.

Among other points, the agreement specified that:

Falange Española de las J. O. N. S. will not attack either the Renovación Española party or monarchist doctrine in its oral or written propaganda, pledging itself not to do anything that would create an obstacle to carrying out the program of said party.

The Right Honorable Antonio Goicoechea, in so far as is possible within the means that he administers for such purposes, will economically assist Falange Española de las J. O. N. S. . . . As long as this sum does not exceed TEN THOUSAND PESETAS MONTHLY, it is at liberty to distribute it in the manner judged convenient, but if that sum is exceeded, Falange Española de las J. O. N. S. agrees that of the surplus 45 percent be applied to the expenses of militia organization, another 45 percent to anti-Marxist syndical labor organization, with 10 percent remaining at the free disposition of the organization's leadership.

The agreement stated that Renovación Española thought it particularly important to combat "Marxist violence and power" and "to supplement . . . the functions of the state, now shamefully abandoned by the Republican administration."

It therefore desires the maximal expansion of the combat militia, which, by their public character and collective cooperation, can lift the spiritual tone of the country. As a logical consequence it shares no moral responsibility whatever for violent actions of a different type which might be carried out by members of Falange Española de las J. O. N. S.

It was also stipulated that "to achieve the most effective cooperation . . . , a technical liaison will be appointed to act in permanent contact with the command of Falange Española de las J. O. N. S., principally with regard to military and shock activity."[11]

The "technical liaison" would in fact be Sainz Rodríguez, and in theory all this seriously compromised the independence of the fledgling movement, but José Antonio is said to have remarked to party comrades, "It is necessary to be bribed . . . the better to deceive the bribers."[12] In addition to providing financial assistance, the agreement had the advantage for him that he was the sole signatory on behalf of the Falange, thus reinforcing his internal preeminence.

Sainz Rodríguez later wrote:

For some time José Antonio and I met at least once a month to examine the accounts of the aid given and also to exchange impressions about political issues. In those conversations I learned to appreciate the clarity, moderation, good judgment, and tact of José Antonio. Generally, on public occasions in parliament and elsewhere, he tried to display a forceful, even violent, attitude, but in reality, if

he sometimes adopted such gestures, it was because he thought
it necessary for the prestige of his party, not because he was an
impulsive person incapable of reason or compromise. . . . He was a
cool and moderate person of good judgment, with very solid juridical
training and of a general cultural level very superior to what was
normally found among politicians.[13]

Encouraged by the terms of the pact, Falangist leaders set out to
expand their new workers syndicate, the Confederación de Obreros
Nacional-Sindicalistas (CONS—Confederation of National-Syndicalist
Workers), first tentatively set up two months earlier. Perhaps because of
his partially Andalusian background, José Antonio tended to think of
"the people" as being composed primarily of peasants and farm laborers,
and he particularly enjoyed conducting meetings in small rural towns.[14]
Ledesma, however, with his radical modernism, was more eager to organize a nationalist proletarian revolution in the cities, and for months had
been pressing his fellow triumvirs toward formation of a worker organization. The CONS began virtually without members, but this mattered
little to Ledesma, who, like most radical intellectuals, thrived on abstractions. An office was thus opened for the CONS, and propaganda was
printed. A previous JONS syndicate of Madrid taxi-drivers served as the
first section, with a similar syndicate planned for waiters. Tiny though
these were, they represented a beginning, and other syndicates were soon
created in Valladolid and Zaragoza.

Falangist leaders sought to avoid any comparison between the CONS
and earlier Catholic syndicates, many of which had been "company
unions." CONS propaganda declared full agreement with the economic
claims of the leftist organizations; the only difference was that the CONS
was determined to bring nationalist priorities into the proletarian revolution. The earlier Carlist Sindicatos Libres, which had engaged in lethal
street warfare with the CNT, were specifically denounced, even though
the Libres had been a genuine worker organization, something that in
general could not be said of the Falangist movement. The small Catholic
syndicates replied in leaflets of their own, calling the Falangists traitors
to religion and to the nation.[15]

The CONS enjoyed one brief flurry of activity in Madrid. Though the
Spanish economy would soon emerge from its delayed and somewhat limited depression, unemployment continued to grow, most notably within
the large construction industry that had developed in the bigger cities
during the 1920s. Worker resentment was rapidly rising, and by the beginning of September 1934 groups of the unemployed started to gather
around the Falangist Center in Madrid, perhaps thinking that the Falangist association had a special relationship with employers. The CONS
leaders at first had little idea what to do with them, but eventually decided

The Falangist triumvirs lead a mass demonstration in the center of Madrid to support Spanish unity, 7 October 1934

to give them certificates supposedly entitling them to employment on public works projects in the capital. Thus equipped, possibly as many as a thousand unemployed workers were sent out on the morning of 3 September. This was a hopelessly provocative gesture by the Falangists, for public works and other projects were strongly organized and dominated by the UGT and CNT. The certificates were, of course, patently illegal and no more than a propaganda ploy; fights immediately broke out at work sites, and a number of the unemployed bearing the phony Falangist certificates were injured. The CONS leaders were forced to suspend their futile strategy with a public announcement.[16]

After this incident the UGT exerted heavy pressure on both workmen and employers to boycott the CONS. Since both classes already generally distrusted the Falange, it was not difficult to isolate the national syndicalist confederation, which made no impression on the organized leftist worker syndicates.

The situation was almost worse in the provinces. Whenever Falangists succeeded in forming a small syndicate of construction workers in a city, it would usually collapse under a combination of pressure from organized leftist workers and refusals by employers to risk further labor strife with a small, unpopular union. Though the CONS did manage to form several very small syndicates, they completely failed to achieve any general break-through,[17] and served only to demonstrate that the national sydicalist movement existed more in theory than in practice. A plan announced on 1 November to organize a Confederation of National-Syndical Employ-ers[18] failed even more completely.

Street violence had abated temporarily following the severe restrictions placed on Falangist activity in July, but began to expand once more the next month. On 29 August the sculptor Joaquín del Grado, a member of the Communist Party central committee and head of the party's important Radio Norte (northern sector) in Madrid, was killed in a street clash with Falangists. Two weeks later the local leader of the Falange in San Sebas-tián was slain, and in revenge Falangist gunmen struck down the vaca-tioning Manuel Andrés Casaus, a former director general de seguridad (national police chief) under the Azaña government who was much hated by nationalists and the right. Del Grado's elaborate public funeral became the occasion for one of the first public scenes of fraternization between Communists and Socialists, one of the initial harbingers of the Popular Front.

As the Falange neared its first anniversary, prospects were no more encouraging than ever. Both Ledesma and Ruiz de Alda continued to press for a policy that was more aggressive and, they hoped, more dema-gogic and revolutionary. Although Ledesma had agreed that there was some wisdom in José Antonio's plan to stage a series of seven or eight provincial meetings during the preceding spring, he had refused to partici-pate in them.[19] Ledesma was well aware of Ruiz de Alda's annoyance at the expulsion of his old friend Ansaldo and therefore suggested that the time had come to get rid of José Antonio, or at least force him to take a back seat, thus freeing the Falange from the restraint of his rather liberal temperament. Ruiz de Alda was tempted but hesitated to break from José Antonio simply in order to build a partnership with the tough-minded Ledesma.[20]

Despite varied opposition, José Antonio's status in the movement re-mained preeminent. His combination of physical courage, personal charm, vigor, and eloquence might yet make him the "jefe único," and, despite earlier disclaimers, there was little doubt that this was what he sought. The rough, rather unprepossessing Ruiz de Alda and the harsh, cold, abstractly intellectual Ledesma stood little chance in a popularity contest. Ledesma's intellectual force was not reflected in any aptitude for public speaking, partly because of a speech defect (shared with his brothers) that prevented him from pronouncing properly the Spanish "r," which he rendered with a guttural, somewhat aspirate sound. José Antonio had bested his critics, and his law office often doubled as the Falangist center, for the official center was kept closed by the authorities much of the time. Ledesma and Ruiz de Alda were occasionally forced to go into hiding, while José Antonio's parliamentary immunity (ironically preserved by the Socialists for their own separate purposes) allowed him to remain fully active and in the public eye.

José Antonio therefore seized the initiative once more during the vacation period. Returning to Madrid after a brief holiday in San Sebastián, he called a meeting of the Falange's Junta de Mando (Executive Committee) on 28 August. The committee, in turn, approved the convening of the party's first Consejo Nacional (National Council) in Madrid from 4 to 7 October. Its task was to perfect the editing of the party statutes, adopt an official Falangist program, and decide whether the leadership of the party should remain collective or take the form of a jefe único, as increasingly demanded by José Antonio's partisans. In the interim, the functions of both the Executive Triumvirate and the Junta de Mando would be suspended, with José Antonio, acting in his capacity as president of the Consejo Nacional, as the single leader of the party.

In Spain talk of fascism was increasingly in the air, but this rarely referred to the Falange. The left pointed to the danger of "fascism on the march," but the only sizable potentially authoritarian force increasing significantly in power and influence was the Catholic CEDA, which had the largest parliamentary delegation of any party—democratically elected—and thus would soon have to be permitted representation in the government. For the left, the CEDA represented "objective fascism"—admittedly not something equivalent to Italian Fascists or Nazis per se but a right-wing authoritarian force capable of converting the Spanish Republic into a more authoritarian system (as the Socialists sought on the left), much more like the regime of the Christian Social Party in Austria or that of the Catholic corporatist Salazar in Portugal.

Luis Araquistain, soon to become the chief theorist for the "bolshevizing wing" of the Socialist Party, had published an article in the North American journal *Foreign Affairs* in April 1934 that correctly judged that a true fascism, Italian or German style, was probably impossible in Spain:

> In Spain a fascism of the Italian or German type cannot be
> produced. There exists no demobilized army, as in Italy, there are no
> thousands of university students without a future, nor millions of
> unemployed, as in Germany. There is no Mussolini nor even a Hitler;

there exist no imperial ambitions, nor sentiments of revenge, nor problems of expansion, nor even a Jewish question. Of what ingredients could a Spanish fascism be made? I cannot imagine the recipe.[21]

But to the left, massed rallies of the CEDA—such as those at El Escorial (22 April) and Covadonga, birthplace of the Reconquest (9 September)—replete with such slogans as "antiparliamentarianism" and "the chief [Gil Robles] is never wrong," seemed menacing enough.

The spring and summer of 1934 had seen numerous strikes, disorders, and acts of violence, mainly initiated by the left in the name of better working conditions or "antifascism." The liberal *El Sol* editorialized on the morrow of a political general strike in Madrid:

A weapon employed too often for improper ends up becoming too worn to be used at the proper time, for not only does it become blunted and its edge dulled, but it also provokes a reaction that learns how to deal with it and perfect an opposing weapon.

. . . When all the revolutionary techniques are used with mindless frequency to combat a fascism that does not even exist, except as a pale imitation, the eventual result may be to produce all the necessary conditions—the ground, the climate—for the genuine emergence of fascism. Not this feeble, upper-class fascism that we now have for reasons of fashion, but a real and fearful fascism, against which the weapons of the liberal state are useless. In a similar way fascism has been engendered in other countries.

Thinking to follow the lessons of history, the Socialists, who were organizing an anti-CEDA insurrection, grew more confused by the month and ended up completely ignoring the real lessons of history—even though innumerable moderates attempted to warn them. After three CEDA ministers entered a coalition government of the Radicals on 4 October, the Worker Alliance of revolutionary worker groups now led by the Socialists launched an armed insurrection to overthrow the new parliamentary government and seize control of the Republic. Though it only held power for a brief time in Asturias, this revolt proved much more powerful than the "sanjurjada" or any of the previous anarchist mini-insurrections. It initiated an almost irreversible process of revolutionary–counterrevolutionary polarization in Spain.

Fearful that the present government would lack the strength to resist a serious armed assault, on 24 September José Antonio wrote a private letter to General Francisco Franco, at that moment military commander of the Balearics. Franco was one of the most respected figures in the military hierarchy, and reliably antileftist. The letter, which José Antonio dispatched by way of his good friend and Franco's brother-in-law Serrano Súñer, did not seek to convert the general to Falangism but urged him to be prepared to take action to safeguard the unity and integrity of Spain.[22] Franco sent a verbal reply in much the same vein, urging Falangists to maintain faith in the military, and to support it whenever the crisis broke. By that point Franco was in Madrid, coordinating the repression of the insurrection as special adviser to the Ministry of War.

Just at this moment, the first Consejo Nacional of the leaders of the Falange was convened in Madrid. Delegates had been asked to submit memoranda on a variety of doctrinal and structural problems, and the first day was devoted to discussing the question of party leadership.[23] José Antonio and his partisans defended the jefatura única (single or sole leadership) at all levels, but this was vigorously resisted by Ledesma, Giménez Caballero, the former jonsistas, and others, who even referred to the pluralism of Spanish history in support of maintaining the triumvirate. On the second day, the first item of business was approval of the new permanent Statutes, which were accepted over the opposition of the ledesmistas.

A formal motion then proposed establishment of the jefatura única for national leadership of the party, described as the most appropriate expression of "the totalitarian, hierarchical, and military ideals of an organization of combat, hostile to all democracy."[24] The discussion was heated and the vote very close, with José Antonio abstaining. With the ballots evenly divided at sixteen each, the deciding vote in favor of the jefatura única was cast by the youngest council member, Jesús Suevos, who was also the secretary of the Consejo and voted last.[25] Once the office of Jefe Nacional had been created, however, there was no conflict over whom to select to fill it, for the primacy of José Antonio was by that point readily admitted. As Areilza would put it, "He had an aura, expressive magic, leadership, 'sex appeal,' strength, ascendancy, imperiousness and finally *le physique du role*, the visible and external signs of a great political leader."[26] Ledesma himself seized the initiative and proposed that the Consejo unanimously acclaim José Antonio as Jefe Nacional for a period of three years. This was done without hesitation. José Antonio immediately assumed the office that he had in fact sought for some time, declaring to the consejeros that "what you have done saves the Falange from decomposition, possibly from extinction." His first act of command was to name the president and half of the members of the Falange's new Junta Política (Political Council), as stipulated in the new Statutes; the other half of the twelve-member Junta was to be named by the Consejo. Ledesma was appropriately made president of the Junta. On the final day of the meeting, 6 October, the symbols and slogans of the party were reaffirmed, and a shirt color was selected. José Antonio declared that the color should be "clear, whole, and proletarian," and at the suggestion of Ruiz de Alda adopted the navy blue worn typically by mechanics.[27]

The atmosphere of the Consejo was made especially tense by the imminent outbreak of the leftist insurrection, which began on 6 October and cut the sessions short. This occasioned the first successful mass demonstration in Falangist history, when on the afternoon of the seventh José Antonio, Ruiz de Alda, and Ledesma led hundreds of Falangists on a march from the Center down the boulevard of the Castellana in support of the unity and integrity of Spain. Since this was not a specifically fascist demonstration but a gesture of patriotic unity, the few hundred had swelled into several thousand by the time they reached the Ministry of the Interior in the Puerta del Sol. Though the government refused each of two requests by José Antonio that Falangist auxiliaries be armed, the party's provincial leaders had standing orders to cooperate fully with government and military officials to defeat the insurrection. Falangist volunteers helped maintain vital services in various parts of the country and took an active part in the fighting in Asturias, where five Falangists were killed[28] out of a total of more than 1,200 fatalities. Six of the most valiant Asturian Falangists were awarded the Palma de Plata (Silver Palm), the party's highest decoration.

Meanwhile, the almost instantaneous collapse of the Catalanist insurrection in Barcelona had exposed the futility of hopes expressed by Raffaele Guariglia, the Italian ambassador, that the most promising center for a Spanish fascism, or at least a Spanish pro-fascist center, was Barcelona. Guariglia had pointed out to superiors in Rome that dynamic and modern Catalonia was much more like the northern Italy in which Fascism had first arisen than was the rest of Spain, and that a Catalanist society of "Amics d'Italia" existed. The officially supported Casa de Italia and other Italian schools and institutions in Catalonia were larger and better funded than those in Madrid. Certainly the first interest in Italian Fascism had been expressed there by small circles of españolistas and also by some of the more radical elements in Catalan nationalism.[29] There had always been an elitist, potentially violent, and to some extent authoritarian sector in Estat Català, the main radical Catalanist group. During 1933–1934 that sector had been led by Dr. Josep Dencàs, councillor of health and sanitation in the Catalan government. The Estat Català youth group, Joventut d'Esquerra Republicana–Estat Català (JEREC—Youth of Republican Left–Catalan State), took the name "Escamots" for its activists. They wore olive green shirts and sometimes engaged in strong-arm tactics against anarchosyndicalists, leading some to term them "Catalan fascists." Dencàs was quoted as saying:

> Am I a communist? Am I a fascist? I myself don't know. What I do
> realize, however, is that any political line, to triumph, needs to move
> young forces, to give them a mystique, a discipline, and bring them
> into action. That's what I want to do in Catalonia. I want to escape
> the old molds of republicanism. I don't want to enter the molds—
> untried at home—but old in other countries of dogmatic Marxism.
> To form a strong and ardent political movement based on two
> fundamental principles: nationalism, socialism, is what I want.[30]

Dencàs had been in charge of organizing the insurrection in Barcelona.
Its complete and indeed pathetic failure totally discredited him, as well
as his groping notion of Catalan "national socialism." Italian policy in
Catalonia had not sought to stimulate a true Catalan fascism so much as
simply to turn Catalanism in a more pro-Fascist and pro-Italian direction,
but Catalanism for the moment lay shattered.

Despite its sometimes harsh repression of the revolt, José Antonio vigorously criticized the new center–right government, declaring that its victory would be rendered sterile by "Cedo-radical mediocrity."[31] In the
Cortes, he pointed to what he considered the crux of the problem:

> The strength of the revolution . . . was that the revolutionaries had a
> mystical sense—if you prefer, a satanic sense—but a mystical sense
> of the revolution. In the face of that mystical sense of the revolution,
> society had been unable, and the government has been unable, to
> counter with a mystical sense of duty that would be permanent and
> valid for all circumstances.
>
> . . . Do people become revolutionaries to earn two pesetas more or
> work one hour less? . . . No one risks his life merely for material
> goods. . . . People place their lives on the line when they are moved by
> mystical fervor for a religion, for a Patria, for their honor, or for a
> new sense of a society in which to live. For this reason the miners of
> Asturias have been strong and dangerous.[32]

An uncompleted task left over from the Consejo Nacional was redaction of the "definitive program" of the Falange, a task that José Antonio
assigned to the new Junta Política. Its president, Ledesma, edited the initial drafts into a unified program, but the final text was considerably
amended by José Antonio,[33] who gave the resulting Twenty-Seven Points
their final form. They emphasized the following principles.

Point 2 reaffirmed José Antonio's concept that "Spain is a unity of
destiny in the universal" and that all separatism and weakening of that
unity must be overcome.

Point 3 proclaimed "We have a will to empire. . . . We claim for Spain a
preeminent place in Europe. . . . With regard to the countries of Hispano

America, we propose a unification of culture, of economic interests, and of power. Spain affirms her condition as the spiritual axis of the Hispanic world with a right to preeminence in universal enterprises."

Point 4 was succinctly militarist, declaring that "our armed forces . . . must be as large and strong as is necessary to assure for Spain at all times her complete independence and the world leadership which she merits." Point 5 added that "Spain must aspire to be a great maritime power in the interests of her security and her commerce."

Point 6 asserted, "Our state will be a totalitarian instrument in the service of the integrity of the Patria. All Spaniards will participate in it through military service, their municipalities, and their syndicates." Political parties and "inorganic suffrage" (direct elections) would be abolished.

Point 7 affirmed that "human dignity and the integrity of human liberty are eternal and untouchable values. But one is only truly free when he forms part of a strong and free nation," and liberty could never be used "against the unity, strength, and freedom of the Patria."

Point 9 declared that "we conceive Spain in economic terms as a gigantic syndicate of producers." All society would be organized "through a system of vertical syndicates by branches of production, in the service of national economic integrity."

Point 10 announced that "we repudiate the capitalist system" and "Marxism as well." Points 11 and 12 promised to eliminate class struggle and achieve the economic well-being of all.

Point 13 promised that "the state will recognize private property" for individual, family, and social ends, and "will protect it from the abuses of grand financial capital."

Point 14 announced the goal of "the nationalization of banking and, through the state corporations, of the great public services."

Point 15 proclaimed that "all Spaniards have the right to work" and promised to maintain all benefits provided by existing Republican legislation.

Points 17 to 19 dealt with the need to improve agricultural conditions drastically, promising "to carry out without delay the social and economic reform of agriculture," protecting farm prices, establishing "a true national agrarian credit bank," stimulating technical education, maintaining a protective tariff, "rationalizing units of cultivation," "accelerating hydraulic projects," "redistributing cultivable land to solidify family property, and energetically stimulating the syndication of cultivators," "redeeming the rural masses from the misery in which they live today as they exhaust themselves working sterile soil, transferring them to new units of cultivation."

Point 20 proposed strong campaigns to stimulate cattle production and reforestation.

Point 21 guaranteed that "the state will expropriate without indemnity lands that have been acquired or exploited illegitimately."

Point 22 promised that the state would give preference to restoring the communal properties of rural municipalities and districts.

Point 23 insisted that "an essential mission of the state is to achieve a strong and united national spirit and inculcate in future generations pride and joy in the Patria. All men will receive premilitary education that prepares them for the honor of serving in the national people's Army of Spain."

Point 24 promised that "culture will be organized so that no talent is wasted for lack of economic resources. All meritorious students will have easy access to higher studies."

Point 25 declared that "our movement incorporates the Catholic sense—of glorious and predominant tradition in Spain—of national reconstruction. Church and State will concord their respective responsibilities without admitting any interference or activity that might lessen the dignity of the state or national integrity."

Point 26 announced that the Falange "aspires to a national revolution. Its style will privilege the direct, ardent, and combative. Life is militia and must be lived with an unblemished sense of service and of sacrifice."

The final point (27) dealt with the question of political alliance in gaining power (both Mussolini and Hitler had to form initial alliances): "We shall strive to triumph with the forces subject to our discipline alone. We shall make very few pacts. Only in the final drive for the conquest of the state will the command negotiate necessary collaboration, so long as our predominance is assured."

This program, which generally fits within the fascist "ideal type," was merely a systematization of existing doctrine and produced no surprises. Though José Antonio now announced publicly that the Falange was not "a fascist movement" in order to avoid being stereotyped with foreign fascist movements, by November 1934 it was in fact all the more important to define the Falange programmatically as a fascist-type movement—which, in reality, was what the Twenty-Seven Points did—in order to distinguish it from new efforts to expand the nonfascist radical right. From José Antonio's point of view, the "revolutionary" character of the Falange distinguished it from the latter, as well as from "fascism," though on more private occasions he would make no effort to maintain the latter distinction.

The new initiative of the radical right in the closing months of 1934 was led by José Calvo Sotelo, who had earlier been denied admission to the Falange and was competing, not entirely successfully, with Goi-coechea for the leadership of the monarchist Renovación Española. Calvo Sotelo sought to overcome his personal impasse, as well as that of the extreme right in general, by leading the formation of a new "Bloque Naci-onal," which hoped to incorporate all the organizations of the radical right in a broader "social, national, nationalist, and nationalizing force" in order to "conquer fully and possess completely the state,"[34] building a state that would be "integrative" and "totalitarian." In practice, however, the Bloque Nacional was only to gain the support of the most extremist alfonsino monarchists, a sector of the Carlists willing to participate in a broader alliance, and the tiny Partido Nacionalista Español of Albiñana. It proposed to organize its own militia units, the "Guerrillas de España," led by the redoubtable Ansaldo, but in practice Ansaldo had even less success with his new group than with the preceding Falange de la Sangre.

José Antonio completely rejected the Bloque Nacional as rightist and reactionary, announcing in *ABC* on 28 November that the Falange would not join it, "being so very far from being a rightist party." During the weeks and months that followed, the Falangists would ridicule the Bloque's mimicking of fascist terminology, or what José Antonio would call their "talk of unity of command, of the Corporate State, and other fascist expressions."[35]

This stance, together with the official adoption of the Twenty-Seven Points, initiated a new state of tension with the monarchist right, and placed in jeopardy the financial agreement reached only three months ear-lier. The Falangist program was at best neutral on the issue of monarchy versus Republic, did not reject a republican form of government per se, and took a semirevolutionary position on social and economic issues. This would result in an increasing distance between the Falange and the radical right.

The new tension was first signaled by the abrupt withdrawal of José Antonio's wealthy and aristocratic childhood friend and longtime asso-ciate, the marqués de la Eliseda, who announced in a note to the press on 29 November that the position of the new program on religion was "frankly heretical," reflecting "a secular attitude toward religion and sub-ordination of the interests of the Church to those of the State."[36] This echoed the remarks of Gil Robles in the Cortes earlier that year that "the Falange is not Catholic."

There was in fact no novelty whatsoever in Point 25 of the new pro-gram, for José Antonio had always emphasized his own Catholic religious convictions and his determination that a Falangist state would negotiate an appropriate concordat with the Church.[37] The very first number of *F. E.* a year earlier had addressed the issue directly:

The Catholic interpretation of life is, in the first place, the true one, but it is, also, historically, the Spanish one.

. . . Thus any reconstruction of Spain must be Catholic in nature.

This does not mean that there will be any revival of religious persecution against those who are not. The era of religious persecution has passed.

Neither does it mean that the State will take charge of religious functions that belong to the Church.

And even less that it will tolerate interference or machinations by the Church with possible damage to the dignity of the state or to national integrity.

It does mean that the new State will be inspired by the Catholic religious spirit traditional in Spain and will accord to the Church the respect and support that are due to it.

That statement had never previously been an obstacle for Eliseda, or for the radical-right supporters of Falangism in general, and in fact local priests had played some role in helping to organize the initial Falangist groups in Pamplona, Oviedo, and one or two other places.[38] Thus the religious argument had merely become an excuse in November 1934 to act on the increasing criticism and rejection of radical Falangism in general by the monarchist right. José Antonio sprang to the defense of the Catholic orthodoxy of the movement, replying acidly in *ABC* one day after Eliseda's declaration that the Falangist position coincided with that of Spain's most Catholic kings (which was entirely correct) and with that of the doctors of the Church, "among whom, to this point, the Marques de la Eliseda is not to be found." Most Falangists were believers and some belonged to Catholic organizations; very few followed Eliseda's example.[39]

The Bloque Nacional, in fact, proved to be a failure, unable to achieve unity among the various groups of the radical right. Calvo Sotelo none-theless forged ahead, becoming during the next year and a half the principal spokesman for a modern Spanish radical right, with a clear project, as outlined in the alfonsino neotraditionalist organ *Acción Española,* for the *instauración* (installation) of a corporative authoritarian monarchy, as distinct from the mere "restoration" of a constitutional parliamentary monarchy. The installed monarchist system would build an "integral state," replacing parliament with an "organically" organized corporate chamber, social and economic problems being resolved through state regulation, corporative institutions, and state intervention and reflationary policies. Calvo Sotelo clearly understood that this was not likely to come about merely through political mobilization but would probably require forcible intervention by the military. The new monarchist state would adopt a militantly nationalist program and foster the development of the armed forces in particular. It would reject secularism and restore the Catholic identity of Spanish government.[40]

The radical right of *Acción Española* and Renovación Española differed from generic fascism not in any squeamishness about violence and authoritarianism, but in their concepts of leadership and legitimacy, their distinct socioeconomic strategies, and their cultural formulae. *Acción Española* invoked a traditional monarchist legitimacy rather than the charisma of mass revolutionary nationalism, together with the leadership of traditional rightist elites. Both the neomonarchists and Falangists strove for a corporate state, but for the latter this meant the mobilization of labor and a drastic new mobilization of national interests behind national syndicalism. In religious and cultural matters, the neomonarchists were clerical and neotraditionalist, and the Falangists formally Catholic but nonclerical and zealous to combine traditionalism with cultural modernization.

Unlike many other rightists, however, Calvo Sotelo was sometimes willing to be labeled a fascist. His own definition of fascism seems to have been loose, referring rather vaguely to authoritarian nationalism and corporatism. Calvo Sotelo drew the line, however, against fascism in the sense of a political movement based directly on the masses, declaring in June 1935 that "the masses should not command. For that reason I am not a fascist."[41] In fact, any analysis of the subsequent Franco regime— especially the "high phase" of the Franquist system from 1937 to 1959— will reveal that it was built in a fashion more nearly corresponding to the ideas and doctrines of Calvo Sotelo and the *Acción Española* group than to those of Falange Española, even though Franco would adopt the latter as the basis of his own state party. The reliance on the military, aversion to revolutionary mass mobilization, creation of a corporate Cortes, and instauración of an authoritarian monarchy all corresponded to this doctrine. Even the national syndical system functioned primarily as an agency of state control more or less along lines conceived by Calvo Sotelo. Similarly, the intensely Catholic character of the Franquist system in its heyday corresponded much more to the concepts of *Acción Española* than to those of the Falangists.

More clearly than either the moderate Gil Robles or the increasingly utopian and revolutionary Ramiro Ledesma and José Antonio, Calvo Sotelo grasped that the most feasible alternative to the Republican system was neither conservative parliamentarianism nor a popular revolutionary national syndicalism but an integrated mobilization of all the resources of the counterrevolutionary groups for a military-led neorightist solution. The difference, of course, was not a matter of tactics alone but also of values. To the CEDA leader such an extreme form of dictatorship was repugnant, while for the Falangists it was inadequate and reactionary. Calvo Sotelo's politics became those of catastrophism. The rightist reaction of the military on which he came to rely could be achieved only in a situation of intense polarization and impending cataclysm. Hence the irony that Calvo Sotelo's own eventual assassination formed an integral part of the very process on which he depended to realize his ideas and achieve his goals.

Authoritarian alfonsino monarchism in support of the exiled king and his heir was not the only significant sector of rightist monarchism, however, because traditionalist Carlism revived and took on new life under the Republic. As Spain's classic radical right, indeed the original nineteenth-century prototype of such a force, Carlism had been the only mass movement in the peninsula for much of the preceding century. Defeats in two major civil wars, combined with extensive social and cultural change, had eroded Carlism's following considerably, but just as the emergence of the anticlerical First Republic had reawakened Carlism in 1873, so the anticlericalism and mass leftist mobilization of the Second Republic revived Carlism in the early 1930s. A more contemporary and integrated doctrinal base had been provided during the early years of the century by the theorist and political leader Juan Vázquez de Mella y Fanjul, who cast Carlist principles fully in the mold of right-wing Catholic corporatism under the leadership of traditionalist but theoretically decentralized monarchy.

During the first phase of the Republic, the main branches of Carlism were reunited and given vigorous leadership by a new leader in Seville, Manuel Fal Conde. Popular support was disproportionately concentrated in the historically autonomous northeastern province (formerly kingdom) of Navarre. Since *Acción Española* to a large extent adopted a neotraditionalist philosophical and political position, its directors hoped to encourage the Carlists (whose only remaining Pretender was elderly and childless) to join them in supporting a reorganized alfonsino monarchism. Carlists, however, continued to reject the formerly liberal main branch of the dynasty and were not overly impressed by its discovery of a highly centralist authoritarianism. Carlists provided little support for Calvo Sotelo's broader Bloque Nacional, which soon broke down.

The principal new statement of Carlist doctrine was Victor Pradera's *El Estado nuevo* (*The New State*) of 1935. In it he defined Catholic identity and a form of societal corporatism, under monarchism, that would be relatively autonomous from the state though partially regulated by it and also compatible with partial regional decentralization. Though he disagreed with the latter point, General Franco would later comment very favorably on Pradera's book. The Carlist youth organization, like the CEDA's Juventudes de Acción Popular, suffered from aspects of the vertigo of fascism in these years and sometimes used fascist-like slogans, but the Carlists differentiated their traditionalist, ultra-Catholic, monarchist, and partially decentralized corporatism from the radical, secular, centralized, ultra-statist, and modernistic authoritarianism of Italy and Germany.[42]

The immediate reaction to the October insurrection had strengthened the antileftist parties, and for about sixty days the Falange enjoyed its first significant influx of new members in nearly a year. The political climate seemed momentarily favorable, but internal disagreement over strategy persisted. At one point Ruiz de Alda wanted to take advantage of the disturbed situation in Asturias, currently under military occupation, to use that area as the base for an uprising against the divided and procrastinating government.[43] Ledesma was even more exasperated at the limited scope of Falangist activities. He urged José Antonio to do more to fill the gap in revolutionary action resulting from the defeat of the left.[44] Though secret contacts were maintained with the CNT dissident Angel Pestaña and a few other current or ex-cenetistas, nothing came of such conversations.

Ledesma held that the Falange should engage in mass agitation, more incendiary propaganda, and more direct action. Above all, it should begin to prepare for the grand nationalist revolutionary insurrection, even though that might take the form more of a coup d'état than an insurrection. This required development of a true "totalitarian party," aiming for a new state that would be anticapitalist, though protective of private property.[45] Ledesma wanted to target potentially more radical junior army officers, and apparently expected José Antonio to use family connections to try to win over part of the military.

The new Jefe Nacional dismissed most of these radical suggestions as grandiose and irrational. Persistent efforts had been made to proselytize the military, and José Antonio did prepare a "Carta a un militar español" (Letter to a Spanish Officer) in mid-November to distribute among targeted officers,[46] but he also knew that the military had abandoned his father, had initially accepted the Republic, and had failed to rally to Sanjurjo in 1932.

At the close of 1934, the Falange had scarcely five thousand members, recruitment had clearly begun once more to decline, and its propaganda had failed to make the slightest dent either on the right or on the organized worker groups of the left. Though José Antonio was not a pessimist by nature, he had once more fallen into a pessimistic mood about the possibilities for the movement. Near Christmastime he expressed his gloom in the bar of the Cortes to his friend Serrano Súñer, who would later remember his saying something to the effect that "if blood had not been shed, today I would dissolve the Falange. What would be the fate of these lads if they triumphed? What could they do in normal times? Many would have to be packed off to the Congo."[47]

The rupture with the radical right was complete, so that the financial subsidy from Renovación Española lasted a mere four months.[48] By the close of the year, the party was in arrears in rent for its Madrid Center and lacked the funds to pay for electricity; heating was also shut off for several weeks. José Antonio is said to have told Ruiz de Alda that it might be necessary to make concessions to the Bloque Nacional after all, though this tactic was rejected.[49] The year 1935 would open grimly, with no new sources of funding or support in sight. The CONS had dwindled to scarcely two thousand members.[50]

At this point Ledesma finally decided that his differences with José Antonio could never be reconciled. They were not merely a matter of short-term tactics, but had as much or more to do with José Antonio's personal dominance; his personality and style, his aristocratic and rightist background and contacts (though Ledesma had relied on funding from the same sources), and his general attitude of moderation and restraint. Ledesma met privately with his old partner Redondo and with the CONS leaders Nicasio Alvarez de Sotomayor and Manuel Mateo. Rather than trying to split the Falange directly, they agreed that they would encourage as many ex-jonsistas and others as possible to leave the party in order to recreate a new and independent JONS. Alvarez Sotomayor and Mateo would then separate the CONS from the Falange and associate it with the new party, though Redondo warned that he might not be able to persuade his followers in Valladolid to join them. A note appeared first in the *Heraldo de Madrid* on 14 January, signed by Ledesma, Redondo, and Alvarez Sotomayor, announcing "the need to reorganize the JONS outside of the orbit of Falange Española and of the authority of its Jefe, José Antonio Primo de Rivera."

Once more the latter reacted swiftly, convening on the sixteenth a meeting of the Junta de Mando, that officially expelled Alvarez Sotomayor and Ramiro Ledesma from the national syndicalist movement which the latter had originally founded.[51] Redondo was not included because he had indicated uncertainty. At this crucial juncture, the loyalty of the large Valladolid "Jons" (local section) was critical to the future of the party. José Antonio's closest supporters worked feverishly, and successfully, to maintain the support of the Valladolid section and of the Madrid SEU. Altogether, no more than two dozen students and ex-jonsistas joined Ledesma in abandoning the party.

On the seventeenth José Antonio appeared with a few of his most loyal friends at the CONS center, dressed as usual in a parliamentarian's gray suit, with white shirt and tie. Some of the workers lounging outside tried to prevent him from entering, but he pushed his way through. He then made a short, intense speech explaining the present situation in the party, the goals he had set for the national syndicalist movement, and the type of discipline and ethical conduct he expected. José Antonio's personality and oratory could be quite convincing at close quarters, and Ledesma lacked his personal charisma and oratorical eloquence. Redondo, Ruiz de Alda, and the other leaders hastened to reaffirm their loyalty. For the next year and more, José Antonio would dominate the Falange.

He announced to the press that the expulsion of Ledesma and a few of the latter's followers had removed those—rather like Ansaldo the summer before—who were sullying the party's name with direct action and criminal activities:

> Falange Española is doing well. I can guarantee that all punishable actions which lay in the sphere of the most common crime and in which some members of our organization appeared as protagonists will not be repeated, because in this last purge we have cleaned out all those elements that sought to give our movement, which ought to have an ascetic, poetic, and military character, a disturbing tint of delinquency and the underworld.[52]

It then became Ledesma's turn to have to duck into the Telefónica on one occasion to avoid a possible physical assault by Falangists loyal to José Antonio. He had little alternative but to turn once more to the usual rightist sources for financial backing for his own national-syndicalist alternative. By 16 February Ledesma was publishing a small organ of a few pages called *La Patria Libre,* subtitled "Organ of the JONS," with the announced goal of mass mobilization of the workers and of "all the people." He had apparently sold his motorcycle to finance the first issues. Subsequently a small meeting was held under the banner of the JONS at Valladolid on 2 March, with the assistance of Javier Martínez de Bedoya, an early activist. It claimed to represent a complete break with the Falange, proposing a "National Wheat Syndicate" and the "democratization" of a truly national SEU. After only six issues, however, Ledesma announced that he was leaving Madrid—which he denounced as being full of all kinds of bureaucracies (of the state and of political parties) and unrepresentative of Spain—for Barcelona, the most revolutionary city in the peninsula. In this revolutionary center, however, he would find the competition for support even more difficult.

He began his memoir *¿Fascismo en España?* in March, and it appeared in print in November. In this work Ledesma declared that he had sought to found "a political movement with deep national roots and great social—better said, socialist—perspectives. What people here call fascism."[53] He went on to explain that "whenever we use here the word 'Fascism' we do so as a concession to the worldwide polemical vocabulary, without any great faith in its necessity, since, for our part, we are inclined to deny to Fascism, strictly speaking, any universal characteristics"[54]—in certain respects a perfectly accurate distinction. Since fascism was based on extreme nationalism, "there is not and can never be a Fascist International." *"Hence fascism can have no other universality than what is provided by the 'national' support with which it is born"* (Ledesma's italics).[55]

At the same time, he recognized that on a certain level of comparative analysis it was possible to identify a generic fascism, observing that "we can . . . list a series of characteristics, of ideals, of goals, and of dreams that give us with perfect clarity the exact profile of fascism as a world phenomenon. In the sense of that concept, and only that, is it appropriate to speak of fascism outside Italy, that is, giving the word a universal meaning."[56]

In his formulation, fascism was an "organized and hierarchical democracy" that employed syndicalism and corporatism for a "totalitarian concept of the state." Above all, *"fascism seeks a new meaning of authority, of discipline, and of violence"* (his italics) to achieve a "totalitarian state, socializing credit, transportation, great landed property, and as far as possible the means of exchange." He stressed the importance of winning the workers, since "in Italy and in Germany the expansion of fascism" had converted many "revolutionaries" from Marxism.[57]

Ledesma accurately noted the tendency of other groups, usually on the right but sometimes on the left, to try to appropriate the trappings of fascism and hence appear "fascistized." In fact, to that point in Spain there had been virtually an inversion of fascist-type activity between left and right. *"In Spain, the rightist groups are apparently fascist, but in many respects essentially antifascist"* (his italics), for, though they borrowed certain trappings of fascism, they were moderate, rightist, and essentially reactionary. Conversely, *"the leftist groups are apparently antifascist, but, in many aspects and pretensions, essentially fascist,"*[58] because of their violence, authoritarianism, and revolutionism. Ledesma particularly praised the new book *Hacia la segunda revolución* (*Toward the Second Revolution,* 1935) by the non-Soviet independent Leninist Joaquín Maurín, co-founder of the new Workers' Party of Marxist Unification (Partido Obrero de Unificación Marxista—POUM). He quoted Maurín as stressing the underpopulation of Spain and Spanish workers' need for a "patria." Maurín had written that "what is reactionary in our days would be the dissolution of Spain, the anti-Spain. Our proletariat must complete a broadly national task."[59] Ledesma cited with approval Maurín's insistence that the "liberal plutocracies" were not the allies of Spain, which Maurín declared should stand with such lands as Portugal, Italy, Germany, and Russia.

During May Ledesma wrote a book-length essay entitled *Discurso a las juventudes de España* (*Address to the Youth of Spain*), published later that year in Barcelona. It stressed an intense social nationalism that would nationalize "large industry," transport, banking, and foreign commerce,[60] with the goal not of mere expropriation but of using revolutionary change to begin to create new wealth, a goal that Ledesma claimed distinguished his strategy from that of the left. Spain needed a larger population to achieve military strength; its youth should become accustomed to direct action and violence, which were justified:

> A) As a moral value of rupture, of breaking free and rebelling against decrepit, treacherous, and unjust values.
> B) As a necessity, that is, as an obligatory principle of defense, as an unavoidable tactic in the face of armed enemy camps (Spain today is full of veritable armed camps, ready for war).
> C) As a test, as a demonstration of historical wholeness, ability and preparation to move the soldiers of the national revolution.[61]

Ledesma acknowledged "religious faith and Empire" as "the two most powerful motivations of history," but insisted that Spanish nationalism could not be merely Catholic, for the Church failed to support it. Hence "the yoke and the arrows, as an emblem of struggle, can be advantageously substituted for the cross to preside over the days of the national revolution," which would appeal to "the messianic consciousness of youth."[62]

Ledesma hailed Communism as the national revolution of Russia but found it woefully inadequate. He defined Italian Fascism as revolutionary but limited by the fact that it had to fight the organized Socialist workers to gain power, after which the movement had been joined by many conservatives, leaving Fascism with the future task of winning the workers back and carrying out the revolution from the state itself. Perhaps most puzzling was "the socialist racism of Germany," for Ledesma could not discern its ultimate form. He was correctly convinced of the numerous similarities between Spain and Italy, but emphasized that all these movements in other lands were primarily national revolutions, "without breadth or worldwide meaning."[63] He was thoroughly convinced that Spain could yet create its own revolution to achieve a new modern form and status for the country, and concluded ¿*Fascismo en España?* with the declaration: "We would say, to conclude, that for Ramiro Ledesma and his comrades, the red shirt of Garibaldi fits better than the black shirt of Mussolini."[64]

Apparently subsidized by the German consulate in Barcelona, Ledesma eventually returned to Madrid in the spring of 1936, where through intermediaries he achieved a reconciliation of sorts with José Antonio, though he did not rejoin the Falange. His new publication *Nuestra revolución* (*Our Revolution*), six pages in length, appeared on good-quality paper on 11 July, though he had trouble finding someone to print it. The outbreak of the Civil War made a second number impossible. Ledesma was arrested at the beginning of August and killed on 29 October in one of the great Soviet-style "sacas" (clean-outs) of political prisoners, his corpse being dumped into the common pit at Aravaca.[65]

Ramiro Ledesma was a man of genuine intellectual ability and force who presented an extreme example of the radical intellectual of early twentieth-century Europe. The North American polemicist H. R. Southworth described him as:

> the real genius of the movement. In a short space of time, he founded the movement, established its principal doctrines and invented its most effective slogans. It has been said that he lacked the political personality of José Antonio Primo de Rivera, but the image of the latter in Spain was created artificially after his death. José Antonio applied the term intellectual to himself, and subsequently all his biographers accepted that definition, but Ledesma Ramos was a much more serious intellectual and a more disciplined thinker. José Antonio Primo de Rivera possessed the gift of making more poetic phrases than Ledesma, but that is not always a guarantee in politics.[66]

Perhaps the best epitaph was later penned by his friend Emiliano Aguado:

> Ramiro . . . could never find the frontiers that separate the fluidity of real life from imagined existence, which only possesses us in fleeting moments of enchantment. . . . One cannot well ascertain if Ramiro dreamed in order to act or longed for action in order to dream. Nor could he himself.
>
> It is difficult to find in the work of Ramiro, so tied to the concrete, a concrete norm about anything in ordinary life. When he talks of social affairs he loses himself in vague rhetoric that would never satisfy anyone who is in open struggle with life, and when he speaks to us on his own account of the economic order of the state, the same thing happens. The worst occurs when, perhaps taking note of this vagueness, he endeavors to tell us something concrete about things he has not studied, for then one sees only too clearly that he has wanted to convince us with an artificial argument.[67]

It is difficult to resist the conclusion that his radical nationalism was forged as a means of overcoming personal isolation. "Ramiro's work . . . did not propound anything concrete; it was rather the expression of a human lack we shall continue to feel so long as the present spiritual state of Europe endures."[68]

Ledesma would never receive full canonical recognition as the real founder of fascist politics and doctrine in Spain. The Franco regime never gave him official honor and status commensurate with his original contribution to the movement, in large part out of concern that this would encourage the more radically fascistic elements in the Falange. Only a few of his journalistic pieces and one book would be republished in Spain during the first thirty years of the ensuing dictatorship, though some of the more ardent zealots in the party would recurrently look to and invoke his example of a more categorical and intransigent fascism.

## JOSÉ ANTONIO, JEFE ÚNICO

With his election as Jefe Nacional, the departure or expulsion of the right-wing monarchists, and the expulsion of Ledesma, José Antonio had become—after fifteen months—the uncontested leader of the Falange. Though he complained both publicly and privately of the trials and indignities of public life,[69] he also enjoyed the exhilaration of leadership. Though he could never adopt the arrogant style of a Duce or a Führer, he was an attractive and dashing figure even to some who opposed his political philosophy,[70] and a number of his opponents in other parties acknowledged his personal charm and sincerity.[71] What he could never fully overcome, however, was the label of "señorito" attached to his background, his aristocratic title, and his family name.[72]

Though José Antonio was neither a professional intellectual nor a writer, he was more intellectual than most politicians and was seriously concerned about literature, esthetics, and style (which many would, of course, consider typically fascist concerns). The poetry that he occasionally wrote was little more than amateurish, and the two novels he began remained uncompleted.[73] His chief works were his speeches and political essays, which often reveal a genuine gift for phrasing and imagery.

His most intimate associates were a small set of personal and family friends and Falangist writers. Though Ansaldo would ridicule his "court of poets and litterateurs,"[74] José Antonio's tertulia at La Ballena Alegre, continued to expand during 1935. His chief literary crony was the talented writer and journalist from Bilbao, Rafael Sánchez Mazas, whom Ledesma sneered at as the "provider of rhetoric for the Falange,"[75] but whom José Antonio referred to in his own final trial in Alicante as "the leading intellectual of the group"[76]—a possibly damaging admission. Other leading writers in his circle were José María Alfaro, Agustín de Foxá, Eugenio Montes, Samuel Ros, and, in later months, Dionisio Ridruejo.

When he had spoken in the Comedia of a "poetic movement," José Antonio was not merely coining a phrase. After the founding of F. E. in December 1933, he fretted considerably about finding the right tone and format, a preoccupation that never entirely left him in the turbulent years that followed.[77]

Falangist writing repeated the Castilianist themes and imagery of modern Spanish historiography and nationalism, providing the movement with a vocabulary of mystical exaltation, sacrifice and violence, national mission and revolution—a mixture that sometimes proved intoxicating to the young. From the beginning, it was students who responded most fervently to Falangist propaganda, as in fascist movements in a number of other countries. It was they who made a political idol of José Antonio, and they who provided the idealism, the radicalism, and the first martyrs, establishing the mystique of the party. Though no more than a minority of university students, and only a very small minority of secondary students, were ever enrolled in the Falange, their enthusiasm did much to set the tone.

Despite or because of the scorn they had heaped upon his father, José Antonio hoped to attract leading intellectuals, and avoided repeating the hysterical denunciations he made in his first political statements of 1930 and 1931. Unamuno received him personally on the occasion of a rally in Salamanca in March 1935, though he would later accuse the Falange of contributing to the "dementalization" of Spain's youth.[78] For José Antonio, Ortega y Gasset was even more important, since he had been heavily influenced by the latter's *España invertebrada* and his concept of the nation as a "unity of destiny." His essay "Homenaje y reproche a D. José Ortega y Gasset" ("Homage and Reproach to D. José Ortega y Gasset"), which appeared in *Haz*, the SEU journal, in December 1935, recognized his debt to Ortega but reproached him for abandoning public life and withdrawing once more into intellectual affairs.

In some ways nascent Falangism managed to connect better with the artistic elite in San Sebastián and Bilbao than in Madrid, perhaps due to the españolista orientation of the Basque upper class. José Antonio's main contact there was Sánchez Mazas, but there were other Falangist writers from the region, such as Pedro Mourlane Michelena, while the leading avant-garde painters in Guipuzcoa, Cabanas Erauskin and Julián Tellaeche, worked with the Falange. The inauguration of San Sebastián's foremost avant-garde group of painters, "Gu," which was pro-Falangist, brought together in the summer of 1934 such disparate figures as José

Antonio and Pablo Picasso.[79] More decidedly Falangist was the noted "rationalist" architect from Guipuzcoa, Manuel Aizpurúa.

The question has subsequently been asked many times—was José Antonio a "real" or "genuine" fascist? The basic answer is yes, in so far as he believed in the goals of the revolutionary nationalist movements that the Falange paralleled and that in a broader sense composed generic fascism. That generic movement was a category which he, like Ledesma, recognized, though in some ways he became increasingly uncomfortable with it. Certainly his aim in 1933 had been to introduce the forms, values, and goals of Italian Fascism into Spain, but at the same time he did not possess what would conventionally be considered a "fascist temperament." He was too generous, too broad-minded, too liberal with friends, and nominal enemies (in the classic sense of the term "liberal"). He continued to dine, albeit secretly, with politically more liberal friends; he was too willing to admit that the opposition was human, was too friendly in personal relations, to fit the stereotype.

Counselors like Francisco Bravo Martínez kept telling him to be "fascist," to be more stern and distant,[80] for *El Sol* opined that "José Antonio, as his intimates call him, is a fascist *malgré lui*. . . . He is a parliamentarian unknown to himself."[81] In the words of the liberal Reuters correspondent Henry Buckley: "Tall, thirty, soft-voiced, courteous, José Antonio was one of the nicest people in Madrid. He looked very unreal in his role of fascist leader."[82] Unamuno agreed, observing that "he is a lad who has adopted a role that doesn't suit him. He is too refined, too much of a señorito, and basically too timid to be a leader, much less a dictator." The sage of Salamanca concluded that to be head of a "partido fajista," it was necessary to be "epileptic."[83]

His more intemperate followers would say that "neither Unamuno nor Ortega—nor, in fact, all our intellectuals—are worth as much as one zealous twenty-year-old, fanaticized with Spanish passion"; José Antonio, however, would joke, "We want a happy and short-skirted Spain."[84] Party activists thought up plots for assassinating Prieto or Largo Caballero, but José Antonio would not countenance them. At one demonstration he threw his arms around a young leftist who got in the way, to protect the youth from his own Falangist following. After the first months he would not permit extravagant talkers like Giménez Caballero to address Falangist meetings, and he discouraged language like "Down with . . ." or "Death to . . ." at rallies that he attended:

> The anti-something, whatever it may be, seems to me imbued with
> reminiscences of Spanish *señoritismo*, unthinkingly but actively

opposed to anything different. I am neither anti-Marxist, nor anticommunist, nor anti . . . anything. The "antis" are banished from my vocabulary, as if they were plugs to ideas.[85]

Ramiro Ledesma's trenchant prose provided one of the most acute analyses of the seemingly impossible contradictions of José Antonio as a fascist leader:

Primo de Rivera is characterized by the fact that he operates on a series of insoluble contradictions due to his intellectual background and the politico-social circumstances in which he grew up. He shows firmness in his goals and is motivated by a sincere desire to achieve them. The drama or the difficulties arise when it becomes clear that these goals are not the ones best suited to him, that he is the victim of his own contradictions and that, because of these, he is capable of destroying his own work and—even worse—that of his collaborators. Behold him organizing fascism, that is, a task born of faith in the virtues of forcefulness, of a sometimes blind enthusiasm, of the most fanatical and aggressive national and patriotic spirit, of deep anguish over the social problems of the entire people. Behold him, I repeat, with his cult of the rational and the abstract, with his tendency toward moderate and skeptical approaches, with his preference for adopting the most timid forms of patriotism, with his bent for renouncing anything purely emotional or based on the impulse of willpower alone, and so forth. All that, with his courteous temperament and legal training, should have led him to political forms of a liberal and parliamentary type. Various circumstances nonetheless have impeded such a path. Being the son of a dictator and living in the social milieu of the highest bourgeoisie are sufficiently weighty matters to influence one's destiny. The effect that they had on José Antonio was to oblige him to distort his own sentiments and to seek a politico-social policy that might reconcile his contradictions. He searched for such an approach through intellectual means and found it in fascism. From the day of this discovery he has been in intense conflict with himself, forcing himself to think that this belief is true and profound. At bottom, however, he intuits that it has to come to him through artifice and patchwork, without roots. This explains his vacillations and what happens to him. These vacillations at one time made him prefer the leadership of a triumvirate, repressing his own aspiration to the *jefatura única*. Only when, as a result of the internal crisis, he saw his own position and preeminence in danger did he determine to establish his personal leadership. It is curious and even dramatic to see how a man not lacking in talent struggles against his own limits. Only, in reality, after winning that struggle might he one day really achieve political victory.[86]

## THE IDEOLOGY OF JOSÉ ANTONIO

During the last regular phase of the independent Falange (1935–1936), the party's doctrine was dominated by the ideas and speeches of José Antonio. The concepts he expressed were often categorical but also sketchy, abstract, and doctrinaire, and were never developed systematically or in detail. Only in this period did his political ideas take their fullest form, but they were still evolving. Had José Antonio lived, some of these might have been considerably modified. Ironically, then, the sketchy outlines of his ideas that the Franco regime later presented as a sort of *summum* of Spanish political wisdom were hastily developed and never systematically expressed. The resulting corpus of ideas was therefore very general and often surprisingly vague in application.

Ramiro Ledesma may have had more political and intellectual impact on José Antonio than he had thought, for by mid-1935 José Antonio had come more and more to espouse four specific attitudes and proposals earlier formulated by the stern leader of the JONS. José Antonio was becoming increasingly aware of the problems of mimesis involved in the use of the term "fascist," increasingly critical of the conservative compromises of the Mussolini system in Italy, steadily more oriented toward a strongly revolutionary social and economic position, and increasingly interested in planning for an insurrection or a coup état.

Like many Europeans during the 1920s and 1930s, José Antonio was heavily influenced by Oswald Spengler's concept of the history of civilizations and of their historical rise and fall. Like Spengler himself, however, José Antonio rejected mere resignation to historical and cultural processes, which he believed could be fundamentally altered by political and cultural will. He seems to have divided the history of civilizations into three cycles of classical plenitude, decline, and the gestation of "middle ages" until a new classical plenitude was achieved. As a Spaniard, however, his approach varied from those who found the full plenitude of western civilization in modern times, for to José Antonio complete harmony and plenitude had been achieved by imperial Spain. In this key regard he fully followed traditionalist Spanish thought as it had been developed since the late eighteenth century. More recent European history was thus a record of fragmentation, confusion, and decline, beginning with the destructive ideas of the late eighteenth century, climaxed by rampant capitalism and industrialization, the fratricidal slaughter of World War I, the challenge of the Russian Revolution, and the relativism and nihilism of early twentieth-century European culture.[87]

It was nonetheless possible for Spain and other western countries to save themselves once more by restoring classical cultural harmony and strength, averting the impending breakdown, and defeating the new barbarian invasion of cultural nihilism and the revolutionary left. The strength and health of Spain could be restored only by a program of nationalism and unity. José Antonio had declared on 19 July 1934 that

> Spain is "irrevocable." Spaniards can decide about secondary matters, but about the very essence of Spain they have nothing to say. . . . Nations are not "contracts," rescindable by the will of those who grant them: they are "foundations," with their own substance, not dependent on the will of the few or the many.[88]

This basic concept was repeated, with variations, many times.

Though Ortega had rejected overt nationalism because he believed that it inevitably implied that a given nation "rule over the others," José Antonio drew an important part of his thesis from Ortega. His concept of the nation was not primarily racial or ethnic (as to some extent had been the case in the Spanish prenationalism of the sixteenth and seventeenth centuries), but was derived from history, culture, and institutions (as in fact had been understood by the liberal Spanish nationalism or protonationalism of the nineteenth century). Its origins, character, and goals were, however, transhistorical and transcendental, for a true nation represented a mission or goal and was project-oriented; it was in fact "unity of destiny in the universal."[89]

Though José Antonio was a strong nationalist in the general sense of that term, he derided what might be called "mere nationalism." In a major speech of 17 November 1935 in Madrid, he insisted: "We are not nationalists, because nationalism is the individualism of the peoples."[90] He derided what he termed "romantic nationalism" based on ethnic racialism, language, local culture, or folklore, which were merely local physical features that limited and divided and lacked all sense of transcendence. Thus Basque nationalism, based on what he viewed as local, possibly transitory, characteristics—"ultra-Catholic in the religious, ultra-conservative in the political, ultra-capitalist in the social"—was "for the misfortune of its own people and of Spain, the least intelligent of all."[91]

He preferred the neologism "españolidad" to the old "españolismo," with its right-wing associations, for a true "españolidad" must be based on broader, more universal, and eternal principles. "Spain needs to unite in a common ambition the multiple variety of the peoples who form it." "When those peoples [of imperial Spain] united, they found in the universal the historical justification of their own existence. Therefore Spain as a whole was the nation."[92] "A nation is not a language, or a race, or a territory. It is a unity of destiny in the universal."[93] "Spain, since it first existed, is and will always be a task; . . . Spain is justified by a mission to fulfill."[94] "Without an enterprise there is no Patria."[95]

The "enterprise" ultimately reached a metaphysical level because of its universally broad historical dimension, and duration, and because it was centered on enduring truths and values. In that sense José Antonio would speak of what he called "the eternal metaphysics of Spain." Though the Falangist system was to be revolutionary within the new requirements of the twentieth century, it could not be totally original, for it would have to draw on the perennial principles of Spanish tradition. A palingenetic project for Spain must be founded on traditional truths and values, combined with new institutions and policies for the contemporary world. It would be Catholic in an orthodox sense,[96] but at the same time a modern doctrine that would not attempt to revive inquisitorial Spain. Just how the revolutionary and the traditional were to be combined and expressed José Antonio did not attempt to explain in any but the most vague and summary way.

It was axiomatic to him that Spain could regain unity and a sense of mission only through the direction of an elite. Ortega's concept of "invertebrate Spain" lay at the core of José Antonio's thought, whose aim consequently was to "vertebrate Spain." A revolutionary kind of new authoritarian elite was needed because the country had failed to generate an effective historical elite on the more liberal English or French pattern. To speak of liberalism in either the political or the economic sense was a waste of time in Spain, where liberalism "was almost able to forgo the trouble of disintegrating, since it scarcely ever existed."[97] Hence a militant minority must guide: "It is not necessary for Spain to congregate masses, but select minorities. Not many, but few, but ardent and convinced, for so everything has been done in the world."[98]

The creative minority itself would require strong leadership and ultimately one dominant leader. An appropriate "unity of command" had once been achieved by the monarchy of imperial Spain, though at the present time a more modern and charismatic figure would be needed. Even though all leaders err from time to time, the necessary great leader should enjoy predominant and relatively unquestioned authority, for only thus could he realize the mission of the historic nation:

> No revolution produces stable results if it does not find its Caesar. Only he is able to determine the historic course beyond the ephemeral clamor of the masses.[99]

> The chief should not obey the people: he ought to serve it, which is something quite different. Serving it means to orient the exercise of command for the good of the people, achieving the best for the

people ruled, though the people themselves may not know what is good for them.[100]

Leaders may make mistakes, because they are human; for the same reason, those called to obey may be mistaken when they judge the leaders to be wrong. The difference is that whereas the personal error is always possible in a leader, the added disorder created by refusing or resisting obedience is much more probable.[101]

Despite his emphasis on elitism and authoritarian leadership, José Antonio often referred to the importance and uniqueness of the human individual. This was one of his most attractive features and made it clear that he did not endorse the Ledesmian notion of the mass-man or a mere "statist pantheism." Point 7 of the first Falangist program of December 1933 declared "Falange Española considers man as a unity of body and soul; that is, as capable of an eternal destiny, as the bearer of eternal values. Hence we accord maximal respect to human dignity, to the integrity of man and his freedom."[102] José Antonio would subsequently repeat that "human dignity, the integrity of man and his freedom are eternal and untouchable values,"[103] that "the new order starts from the existence of man as bearer of eternal values. We do not, therefore, agree with statist pantheism."[104] Later, in April 1935, he declared that "in the face of Lenin's disdainful 'Liberty, for what?' we begin by affirming the freedom of the individual. We, who are accused of defending statist pantheism, begin by accepting the value of the free individual, bearer of eternal values."[105]

This rhetoric, like so much of José Antonio's speech-making, could be quite deceptive, for what he meant by "freedom" and "the free individual" had nothing to do with the liberty of liberalism or political democracy. To José Antonio the individual merited a certain respect yet achieved true significance only when occupied in some noble collective task: "Life is not worth living if it is not to be consumed in the service of a great enterprise."[106] Great enterprises were formed by the enthusiastic union of individuals, who, when bound together by historical tradition, institutional cooperation, and mutual destiny formed a nation. Only a true nation could guarantee the genuine freedom, well-being, and security of individuals and their families, because law and justice could arise only from its historical development and could be enforced only by its superior moral authority,[107] a doctrine rather similar to that of German historical jurisprudence but in this case not limited to the concept of the partially restricted *Rechtsstaat*. Thus "man must be free, but freedom exists only within order."[108] Only a strong national system would be able to "defend in the long run the rights and liberties of the individual personality against the abuses of authority by social and economic collectivities."[109]

Each human being was a "bearer of eternal values," but not merely as an individual; his rights and values could only be affirmed, expressed, and defended in a strong and unified national society.

The eulogists of José Antonio would later claim that such principles distinguished his position from that of fascism, but in fact the position of Italian Fascism on this issue differed comparatively little. In the grand polemic between Italian Fascism and German Nazism during 1934–1935, for example, Fascist writers strongly attacked Nazism for being too "socialist," for denying the rights of the individual and of spiritual freedom that were supposedly protected by Italian Fascism.

José Antonio constantly reiterated his basic theme of life as community, as service, and as sacrifice, for no individual lived alone, nor was one single existence the ideal and ultimate goal of any individual life: "Those who understand existence as service, as a path toward a higher goal, have made an offering of their lives, so that the sacrifice of their lives may serve the fulfillment of a higher end." [110] In his thinking this paralleled both the teaching of Ortega and that of the Church that all life is struggle to be placed in the service of a higher project and a broader, more inclusive destiny.

To serve great ideals required maintaining constant tension and a perpetual commitment to struggle—qualities characteristic of nearly all revolutionaries. It demanded "a military and ascetic sense of life, and a disposition for service and sacrifice, which, if necessary, will lead us as knights errant to renounce all reward until we have rescued the beautiful captive who is no other than Spain." [111] Struggle must be so constant that even paradise would bring no respite, for struggle must be part of paradise itself:

> Paradise is not rest, Paradise is against rest. In Paradise one cannot lie down; one must remain vertical, like the angels. Well, then, we, who have already borne the lives of our best comrades on the road to paradise, desire a difficult, erect, implacable paradise; a paradise where one never rests and which has, by the jambs of its gates, angels with swords. [112]

Any valid struggle would have to be founded on voluntarism, faith, spirit, and a religious conception of life. The "Puntos Iniciales" had declared that the Falange "does not accept the materialist interpretation of history. The spiritual has been and remains the decisive motivation in the life of men and of peoples. The preeminent aspect of the spiritual is the religious." In his final public statement as a free man on 14 March 1936, José Antonio proclaimed:

> Today two total concepts of the world face each other. . . . Either
> the western, Christian, and Spanish spiritual concept of existence
> triumphs, with all that it means of service and sacrifice, but with all
> that it gives of individual dignity and patriotic decorum, or there
> triumphs the Russian materialist concept of existence.[113]

This higher goal and this form of community could not be achieved through political liberalism and democracy, for the latter were forms of pure relativism without normative content. Doctrines based on mere economics, such as capitalism and Marxism, were worse, for they were based on outright lies. José Antonio had declared in March 1933: "The liberal state believes in nothing, not even in itself. It watches with folded arms all sorts of experiments, even those aimed at the destruction of the state itself."[114] All public doctrine must be based on "a permanent truth," but in liberalism "political truth ceased to be a permanent entity."[115] The present political chaos was what resulted "when one denies the existence of certain permanent truths,"[116] and hence the importance of recognizing that "what is necessary is to have a great truth that can be served, and a truth that can be the axis, the pole of attraction of an entire people."[117]

Under present conditions this "great truth" could be established only through a strong and totalitarian state. In an interview on 25 August 1933, shortly before the founding of the party, he had declared: "I see the remedy in an authoritarian state, not at the service of a single class. . . . In a strong state, at the service of the historic idea of the Patria."[118] On other occasions he spoke of an "integral state," while the Puntos Iniciales referred to "the new state, which, being of all, is totalitarian," though this concept of the "totalitarian" was defined as a state that "will consider as its own goals the goals of every one of the groups that are part of it and will strive for the interests of each one as for itself." This became his standard definition of the state. Thus in his interview of 11 November 1934, he endorsed "a totalitarian state that achieves internal peace and national optimism, making the interests of everyone its own."[119] No explanation or blueprint was ever presented to explain how the state could become so omniscient. He would later use the term "totalitarian" to try to spur the military to action, arguing that "just as the Army . . . is national, integrating, totalitarian, and opposed to classes (since within it all classes organically coexist in the warmth of a religion of patriotic service), the Spain which comes from the hands of the Army must seek, from the start, an integral, totalitarian, and national destiny."[120] So vague a doctrine of the totalitarian was mythic rather than precise and instrumental. In an interview of 16 February 1934, he recognized that more moderate political solutions "do not represent the danger that the fascist experience brings with it, but neither do they have our spiritual force nor that of the Social-ists." [121] At least in his franker moments, he might admit that this was potentially a two-edged sword.

José Antonio was undoubtedly influenced by the fact that, in the calmer 1920s, his father had controlled Spain dictatorially with compara-tively limited violence. His whole political career was predicated on the fact that an effective authoritarian nationalism would have to be much more programmatic and ideological, and much more organized, than the simple system of his father. At first he seems to have believed that a broad popular movement might be created, but in 1935 he moved more and more to Ledesma's position on insurrection, coup d'état, or both, though the two positions were not mutually exclusive. José Antonio seems to have failed altogether to appreciate how much more violence and repres-sion would be required to dominate the more advanced, better educated, much more politically conscious and mobilized Spanish society of the mid- or late 1930s. Decisive changes had occurred in Spain during the intervening decade, some of them due to the achievements of, and others to the reaction against, the first dictatorship. When José Antonio finally had an opportunity to see the level of violence required, he would be appalled.

A valid authoritarianism for José Antonio could not rest on strength or force alone. "Nowadays people talk about strong states, but I say to you that a state that relies only on its armed forces and does not generate spiritual support is condemned to be conquered by its enemies." [122] A valid state must incorporate an organic form of representation of family, syndi-cate, and municipality: "The individual, then, participates in the state by fulfilling a function, and not by means of political parties; not as the representative of a false sovereignty, but by having a profession, and a family, by belonging to a municipality." [123] "Thus the new state must rec-ognize the integrity of the family as a social unit; the autonomy of the municipality as a territorial unit, and the syndicate, the guild, the corpo-ration as authentic bases of the organization of the state." [124]

Moreover, José Antonio had the notion that a system of national syndi-calism would relieve the state itself of responsibilities: "The Spanish state can restrict itself to fulfilling the essential functions of power, handing over not merely the arbitration but the complete regulation of many eco-nomic matters to entities of great traditional lineage, to the syndicates." [125] "Thus the state is relieved of a thousand tasks that it now pursues un-necessarily. It only retains those of its mission before the world, before history." [126] "All those who form part of the normal economy will be organized in vertical syndicates, which will need neither arbitration com-mittees nor liaison groups, because they will function organically, like the

Army, for example."[127] Thus the state was to be "totalitarian" but also decentralized vis-à-vis municipalities and the syndicates. The latter would function on their own, but be as tightly organized as the army.

Like all fascist movements, the Falange proclaimed itself to be neither of the right nor the left, though, like the left, it was opposed to "capitalism" and "the bourgeoisie." The "capitalism" to which it was opposed was not simply private property, which was to be respected, but impersonal and transnational "big business" and monopolies, which should in various ways be controlled. The "bourgeoisie" to which the movement was opposed were not ordinary owners of private property but those who represented materialism, skepticism and self-indulgence, and a style of life based on compromise and opposition to self-sacrifice. Being "antibourgeois" was almost more a psychological and a moral position than an economic one.

During 1935 Falangists increasingly emphasized their program of sweeping quasi-utopian economic changes, which they called a revolution. The phrase "Spain has a revolution pending" became a leitmotiv of José Antonio's public remarks. The most important single speech that he delivered on the economic aspects of the "national revolution" was presented before a large rally at the Cine Madrid on 19 May. In it he explained:

> When we speak of capitalism, as you know, we are not talking
> about property. Private property is the opposite of capitalism:
> property is the direct projection of man over things: it is an elemental
> human attribute. Capitalism has been devoted to replacing this
> human property with capital property, for the technical instruments
> of economic domination.[128]

Earlier, in a big meeting at Salamanca on 10 February and again before the Círculo Mercantil of Madrid on 9 April, he stressed that national syndicalism did not propose a socialized economy but only a certain amount of state socialism for vitally needed reforms. He repeated previous statements that the corporatism of Fascist Italy would represent no more than a point of departure.[129] Falangist national syndicalism would differ from and be superior to Italian Fascist syndicalism because it would incorporate both capital and labor within the same syndicates.

José Antonio thought Falangist economics compatible with the thinking of the moderate wing of the Socialist Party, while frequent efforts were made to maintain contact with some of the more moderate leaders of the CNT or its adjacent groups. According to José Antonio, differences with the Socialists were not over economics, but over recognition of the primacy of the nation. In June 1934 he had declared: "The day on which the Socialist Party assumes a national destiny, like the day on which the Republic, which professes to be national, assumes a socialist content— on that day we would not need to leave our homes to raise our arms or expose ourselves to stone throwing or, even worse, to be badly understood."[130]

José Antonio became comparatively well-informed on certain agrarian problems, and his recommendations were commended by at least one agrarian expert.[131] He tried to collect information on agricultural affairs in various regions, and understood that poor land probably required larger units of cultivation, while fertile soil might be more widely distributed. He believed that large holdings forming natural units of cultivation should be protected, while excessively small strips should be consolidated; some sections, he thought, would have to be taken out of production altogether. Though the state should recognize the priority of agrarian reform, the latter would also release redundant workers, and rapid industrial expansion would be needed to absorb them.

José Antonio held that a strong and authoritarian nationalist state founded on unity need not centralize all aspects of Spanish life:

> Spain is varied and plural, but its various peoples, with their languages, with their customs, with their characteristics, are irrevocably united in a unity of destiny in the universal. The loosening of administrative bonds is not a problem, with one condition: that the region which is given the greatest leeway have so well formed in its consciousness the unity of destiny that it will never use that freedom to conspire against it.[132]

> There can be no conflict between love for one's native region, with all its particularities, and love for the common Patria, with all that it means for the unity of destiny. Nor should this unity stoop to abolish local characteristics, such as customs, traditions, languages, customary law, nor in order to love these local characteristics should one turn one's back—as do [Catalan and Basque] nationalists—on the glories of common destiny.[133]

Yet he never made the slightest effort to describe precisely and in detail what elements of autonomy might be retained by different regions under a powerful nationalist authoritarian state.

All Spanish nationalists were aware that Spain had achieved world greatness as empire. The palingenesis of Spain required the revival of empire, and so the Twenty-Seven Points proclaimed: "We have the will to empire." But what would "empire" mean for Spain in the twentieth century? In *JONS* Ledesma had demanded Tangier, Morocco, and a big chunk of Algeria, as well as Gibraltar, but his ultra-Catholic co-leader

Redondo had more modestly explained that this would be primarily a spiritual and cultural empire, in line with the thinking of some pan-Hispanists since the turn of the century:

> We believe in the imperial power of our great culture. And so that those who draw back or laugh at this great concept of "the imperial" may dismiss the idea that to say "empire" is to mean the conquest of lands and nations by armed conflict, we take this occasion to define more clearly the firm, enduring value of that word.
>
> Empire is, of course, domination, or, at least, a superiority exercised among a group of peoples.
>
> But the importance—indeed the utility—of "empire" is *positive and multiple*. It means, needless to say, a willing hegemony, and a glorious sensation of power that benefits and elevates the race that exercises it before others. It is also—and here, without doubt, is its greatest and truest political utility—a source of generous national ambitions and the supreme motor of the great energies latent in every race: it is the maximum ideal for a people and, therefore, the greatest stimulant for outstanding individualities, both a spur and, at the same time, a platform for great men to arise and exert their beneficent influence. . . .
>
> And "the empire," so understood, does not mean, *is not*, an external enterprise that would divert energies amply needed to live in peace and prosperity at home. This is the crude deception of timid temperaments.[134]

José Antonio could subscribe to such a concept but in fact, like Ledesma, hoped for a good deal more. The Twenty-Seven Points announced Spain's claim to be the "spiritual axis of the Hispanic world," and José Antonio invoked for Spain "the participation, with a preeminent voice, in the spiritual enterprises of the world,"[135] even "leadership in the universal enterprises of the spirit,"[136] but his thinking went beyond that. One of his frankest statements occurred in an interview of February 1934, when he admitted that "there are no more continents to conquer," yet added:

> But in international affairs the democratic idea promoted by the League of Nations is in decline. The world is once more tending to be led by three or four racial entities. Spain can be one of those three or four. It is situated in an extremely important geographic keypoint, and has the spiritual strength to enable it to aspire to one of those places of command. That is what may be proposed. Not to be a mediocre country, because either it becomes an immense country that fulfills a universal mission or it is a degraded country without significance. The ambition to be a leading country in the world must be restored to Spain.[137]

On at least one occasion—probably more—he privately told intimates that Spain would rule over the entire Iberian peninsula, with the capital to be Lisbon, the flag that of Catalonia ("the oldest, with the most glorious military and poetic tradition, of the peninsula"), and the dominant language Castilian.[138] On 2 October 1935 he strongly defended Italy's invasion of Ethiopia in the Cortes, insisting that "colonizing is a mission, not merely a right, of civilized peoples."[139]

Since José Antonio was at first more moderate on the issue of violence than some other European fascist leaders, it has sometimes been alleged that he did not hold to a fascist, or Sorelian, view of the need and benefits of violence—that is, of violence as an intrinsic good as well as a necessary means. This, however, was not the case, as José Antonio tended to become increasingly categorical about war and violence. "Life is militia" was one of the most basic Falangist slogans, and José Antonio made various references to the need for a "military sense of life." In one of his final newspaper interviews, on 14 February 1936, which presumably reflected the more developed phase of his thinking, he came out strongly in favor of war in a discussion of women's suffrage:

> War is inalienable from man. It cannot and will not be evaded. It
> has existed since the world was the world, and will continue to exist.
> It is an element of progress. It is absolutely necessary!
>     . . . Men need war. If you think it an evil, because they need the
> evil. From the eternal battle against evil rises the triumph of good,
> says St. Francis. War is absolutely necessary and inevitable.[140]

José Antonio held to a basically fascist concept of war and violence; what he believed by August 1936, however, may have been another story.

It has been seen that in 1933 José Antonio routinely referred to the new political movement as "fascismo" or "Spanish fascism," since it was clearly inspired by the Italian model. In such generic terms, he was quoted in January 1934:

> Fascism has been nourished up to now by the modest middle
> class, and the workers will be convinced later. The wealthy classes will
> have to support el fascio with their history and their prestige. They
> will have to regain their lost hierarchy through sacrifice and effort.
>     If we triumph, rest assured that the señoritos will not triumph with
> us. They must find worthy employment for their gifts, restoring
> hierarchies that they wasted in idleness.[141]

Only a few months had been required—particularly after the antifascist violence of 1934—to convince him that Ledesma was correct to emphasize the purely Spanish identity of the movement. Thus he would later say that "F. E. does not intend to imitate any foreign movement," and try to explain to the Cortes on 3 July 1934 that

> it so happens that we have entered the world at the time when fascism is prevailing—and I assure Señor Prieto that this handicaps us more than it favors us, because fascism has a series of external interchangeable inflections that we do not at all wish to adopt. People who are little inclined to make careful distinctions cast upon us all the attributes of fascism, without seeing how we have only taken from fascism those qualities of permanent value that have also been assumed by yourselves, who call yourselves the men of the [Republican] biennium.[142]

He would later try to distance the party from the Italian model, while at the same time recognizing the greater utility of and affinity with Italian Fascism compared with German National Socialism. Following his visit to Germany in April 1934, he demonstrated concern about and aversion to Nazism (as at that time did many Italian Fascists), criticizing it as a purely "romantic" political doctrine based on "racial instinct," which he associated generally with German romanticism and the Protestant Reformation.[143] German racism might even lead to a peculiar sort of racial "superdemocracy," which by implication might be worse than liberal democracy. In a speech at Santander on 14 August, he declared that only Italy could safeguard the principles of western civilization, for German Nazism was racial and romantic, and might even fall prey to its main adversary, the Soviet Union.[144]

Though, like Ledesma, José Antonio continued to recognize the common identity of a purely generic fascism, by 1935 he became increasingly critical in private conversation of the rightist compromises and tendencies of the Italian regime, while in public he backed away from facile references to the totalitarian state. In a speech at Zaragoza on 17 February 1935, José Antonio observed:

> There are also efforts toward a totalitarian state, but I am not referring to Italian Fascism, which is an experience that has still not taken firm shape.
>
> It is necessary to examine very carefully all the attempts carried out so far: Italian Fascism and German National Socialism, and to point out the differences that exist between both ideological movements. The Italian movement is, above all, classical, tending toward the classical. . . .
>
> The German is just the opposite. It comes from a romantic faith, from the capacity for divinizing a race. Therefore it is just to assert that Hitlerism is a mystical movement, very consubstantial with German psychology. Germany, moreover, is not like what people who

prefer simplistic interpretations believe, the country of discipline, though it may appear to be judging from external signs. Germany is a very special people. They sing in choruses very well, march at the same military step, yet all the movements of insubordination, of rebellion in the world, in the Spartacus manner, have come from Germany.

Neither can the totalitarian state save us from the invasion of the barbarians, all the more because the truly totalitarian cannot exist.[145]

Beyond his point that a completely totalitarian state was probably a physical impossibility, he added that "the life of Spain must be based on the municipalities and the syndicates, since corporatism is a timid solution, not at all revolutionary. It is necessary to cement our life once more on religion and the family."[146]

On another occasion José Antonio would emphasize the need to "be very careful with all those canned phrases like the Corporate State":

Another pretended solution consists of the totalitarian states. But the totalitarian states do not exist. There are nations who have found brilliant dictators who have served to substitute for the state, but this cannot be copied, and so far in Spain we still have to wait for such a genius to appear. Examples of what are called totalitarian states are Germany and Italy, and note that they are not only not similar, but are even radically opposite each other, for they start from opposing points. That of Germany starts from the capacity for a people's faith in their racial instinct. The German people live in a paroxysm of themselves; Germany lives as a superdemocracy. Rome, on the other hand, has passed through the experience of having a genius with classical mentality, who seeks to configure a people from the top downward.

Neither social democracy on the one hand, or the effort to create—lacking a genius—a totalitarian state on the other, would suffice to prevent catastrophe. . . .

Other political blocs call themselves corporatists. That is no more than a phrase: let us ask the first person who brings this up—What do you understand by corporatism? How does it work? What solution, for example, does it offer for international problems? Up to now the best attempt has been made in Italy, and that is no more than an adjunct part of a perfect political machinery.[147]

These and other statements would later be used to demonstrate that José Antonio was opposed to totalitarianism, but they also express the most extreme admiration for Italian Fascism, classifying the Duce as a "genius" and his regime, somewhat grotesquely, as "a perfect political machinery."[148]

If José Antonio was proud to say that "to be Spanish is one of the few serious things one can be in the world"[149] (words remarkably similar to those Franco used in his last public appearance in October 1975), he was sometimes at pains to indicate that he was not the mindless chauvinist that he often seemed. Publicly his remarks were frequently extreme and intemperate, sounding like a right-wing ultra whose attitude might be termed "the Black Legend in reverse": that is, rather than seeing Spain as the source of manifold ills, instead blaming many of Spain's problems on other countries, who might be seen paranoically as engaging in constant conspiracy and exploitation. Yet José Antonio had been educated in the relative Anglophilia of one sector of the Spanish aristocracy, knew English well, and admired important aspects of the Anglo-Saxon world, perhaps most of all the British empire (a trait he shared with many others, including Adolf Hitler). He was fond of Rudyard Kipling, premier poet of the empire, and liked to recite, in English, Kipling's "If," a poem of manly challenge. For some years a copy hung on his office wall.

At bottom he largely accepted the fact that Spain's problems were above all its own fault. He once remarked to the Reuters correspondent, "You see, Mr. Buckley, there are a group of typical Spaniards talking, talking eternally. It is very difficult to organize our race for constructive work."[150] Though he often criticized those whom he perceived as Spain's antagonists abroad, he had little praise for contemporary Spain and contemporary Spaniards:

> I say to you that there is no fruitful patriotism if it does not follow
> the path of criticism. And I will say to you that our own patriotism
> has also followed the path of criticism. We are not at all motivated
> by that operetta patriotism which delights in mediocrities, with the
> present pettiness of Spain and simplistic interpretations of the past.
> We love Spain precisely because it does not now please us. Those who
> love their patria because it merely pleases them love it with a desire
> for carnal contact, love it physically, sensually. We love it with a will
> to perfection. We do not love this misery, this decadence of our
> physical Spain of today. We love the eternal and immovable
> metaphysic of Spain.[151]

In conclusion, the ideology of José Antonio, as it reached its fullest form in 1935 and the first weeks of 1936, revealed two contradictory orientations. The greater part of it lay within the spectrum of the general ideal-type of fascism, but also defined itself as one of the more moderate expressions of generic fascism—as was typical generally throughout western Europe, as distinct from the more extreme forms typical of central and eastern Europe. In religious and cultural matters, however, José

Antonio's thought was informed to a large extent by neotraditionalism,[152] which resulted in a tension and a contradiction that could not be resolved. Of all the existing political doctrines in Spain (aside from the purely socioeconomic doctrine of the more moderate Socialists and syndicalists), he found those of Carlist traditionalism the most valid and truly Spanish, but rejected Carlism for its dynasticism and lack of new social and economic content.[153] (In both respects his attitude toward Carlism was remarkably similar to that of Franco.) He thus recognized the need to incorporate traditional religious, cultural, and institutional principles into his form of "españolidad," which would never become a mere copy of foreign fascism, though its general coincidences with Italian Fascism were extensive.[154]

## FOREIGN RELATIONS

José Antonio had initially so modeled his political enterprise on Italian Fascism that, as we have seen, he had hurried to Rome on the very eve of the founding of the movement for a personal interview with the Duce and a quick inspection of several Fascist institutions. Four months of direct experience led him to be more cautious. At the big rally in Valladolid on 4 March 1934 to inaugurate the fusion with the JONS, he had gone out of his way to emphasize that each nation had its own manner of realizing its political aspirations. Using the kind of literary analogy that came most easily to him, he had referred to certain verse forms in the poetry of the sixteenth century that had originated in Italy but were later developed even more fully in a somewhat different and authentically Spanish style. Scarcely two weeks earlier, he had declared to the Madrid press: "Fascism is a universal attitude of return to oneself. They tell us that we imitate Italy. Yet we do so in our search for our own intimate reason for being within ourselves. But that attitude, copied, if you like, though eternal, offers the most authentic results. Italy has found Italy. We, turning toward ourselves, will find Spain."[155]

The other possible prototype was Germany. Gil Robles and Goicoechea had already visited the Third Reich during its first year of existence, and at the beginning of 1934 José Antonio approached the German embassy to arrange a trip to Berlin. The ambassador, Welczeck, reported that "today Primo sees in our Führer his teacher" and sought to "transfer the ideological bases of the National Socialist Party to the situation and conditions of Spain."[156] It was arranged that the visit would receive no publicity. Accompanied by the Falangist writer Eugenio Montes, José Antonio traveled to Germany by rail at the close of April, having a very brief and purely protocol meeting with Hitler on the thirtieth. His host seems to have been a low-ranking Nazi Party member who worked as a German commercial representative in Barcelona. The contacts with National Socialism were few, so that most of the visit seems to have been devoted to tourist-type activities. Though a German woman living in Spain and associated with the political right had earlier made several contacts with German authorities to request financial support for the Falange, there is no indication that José Antonio made any such request himself, despite the deteriorating financial condition of his party.[157]

José Antonio's reaction to the visit seems to have been mixed. He apparently indicated to some of his companions that his previously high opinion of Nazism had been damaged,[158] though the very opposite was reflected in the first edition of his official biography by Felipé Ximénez de Sandoval, published at the height of Nazi power in Europe. He was definitely impressed by a brief visit to the University of Heidelberg, and after his return made sharply critical remarks about the languid state of Spanish higher education. The example of Nazi vigor may have served as a stimulus, but he had few illusions concerning the appropriateness of the German model. Even while he was in Berlin, the major Italian Fascist journal *Ottobre* had published an interview on 1 May in which José Antonio declared himself much closer to the Italian Fascist concepts of *romanità* and *cattolicità* (ideas propagated in Spain particularly by Giménez Caballero).

José Antonio's last public acceptance of the term "fascist" for the Falange may have taken place in an *ABC* interview of 11 April 1934. By June Falangist propaganda had generally ceased to refer to the party as fascist, and, as indicated earlier, José Antonio had rejected the label in his Cortes speech of 3 July. From that point, he began the series of often unfavorable comments on Nazism and on German culture generally (some of which have been quoted in the preceding section). In August he was recorded in a Barcelona newspaper as declaring: "Hitlerism is not Fascism. It is anti-Fascism, the counterfigure of Fascism. Hitlerism is the ultimate consequence of democracy, and a turbulent expression of German romanticism. Conversely Mussolini is classicism, with his hierarchies, his following, and, above all, reason."[159] José Antonio's aversion to Nazism and to German culture generally, as well as the degree of ignorance he sometimes exhibited about the history of ideas, was further revealed in a subsequent declaration:

> The German movement is of the romantic type, its course the same
> as ever. From there came the Reformation and even the French

Revolution, since the Declaration of the Rights of Man was copied
from the North American constitutions, daughters of German
Protestant thought.[160]

The most important contact between a Spanish group and a foreign
government that year (aside from the activities of the Comintern) was not
made by the Falange, but was rather the secret agreement signed in Rome
on 31 March 1934 between Antonio Goicoechea of Renovación Española, two Carlist leaders, and the retired monarchist Gen. Emilio Barrera on the one hand and, on the other, Italo Balbo, top Fascist *gerarca*
and Italian air minister, on behalf of the Italian government. This pledged
Italian assistance in money and arms for an eventual Spanish monarchist
revolt to overthrow the Republic. One and a half million pesetas were
promised (of which 500,000 were immediately disbursed). Some fifty
Carlist Requetés were given military training in Libya, and arms were also
sent there prior to transshipment to Spain (though in fact the final ship-
ment never arrived).[161] The only significance for the Falange of this ultimately abortive arrangement was that it presumably helped to facilitate
the financial subsidy provided by Renovación Española for approximately four months beginning in August.

For the Falange, the principal issue in its international relations during
1934 was its relationship to the Comitati d'Azione per la Universalità di
Roma (CAUR—Action Committees for the Universality of Rome), the
new Italian organization for "universal fascism." Leaders of the CAUR
had some difficulty in defining fascism for themselves. With regard to
Spain, they reviewed the various new nationalist groups that had appeared, the Italian ambassador reporting that the Falange had formed
"the first effective nucleus of action squads of the fascist type,"[162] adding
the fantastic estimate that it had 100,000 members. When Guido Cabalzar, a representative of the CAUR, came to Spain in May 1934, José
Antonio informed him more prudently that at the moment it had some
50,000 members in thirty-two provinces[163]—still a considerable exaggeration. The Falangist chief signed a membership form and received a membership card from the CAUR, though, as Gil Pecharromán observes, this
might be considered little more than a gesture of good will or courtesy.
The Italians decided to create a Comitato of the CAUR in Spain, headed
by Giménez Caballero, the Spanish fascist intellectual best known in Italy,
described as "one hundred percent fascist and very loyal to the Duce,"[164]
with leaders of the various Spanish nationalist groups as individual members, but in fact this plan never came to full fruition. When the Spanish
Comitato was reconstituted in March 1935 as a nonparty group, its new
director was the playwright Jacinto Benavente, who had also recently

been a member of the Association of Friends of the USSR. The only Spanish representative at the first international meeting of the CAUR at Montreux on 16–17 December was Giménez Caballero, listed by the Italians as "delegate of Falange Española." The Fascist press announced that José Antonio had sent "his support for the work of the congress."[165]

José Antonio released a statement that was published in the Spanish press on 19 December:

> The head of the Falange was asked to attend, but he firmly refused the invitation, since he believes that the genuinely national character of the movement that he leads must reject even the appearance of international direction.
>
> Furthermore, Falange Española de las J. O. N. S. is not a fascist movement. It coincides with fascism in essential points of universal value, but every day continues to define its own specific character and is confident that by such a course it will develop its most fruitful possibilities.[166]

Though they had become increasingly aware of the problems attending use of the term "fascist," Mussolini's Italy was still the only point of reference the Falangist leaders had. Moreover, as the party's financial situation grew increasingly desperate in the first months of 1935, it might be the sole possible source of funds. A general party circular of 8 February emphasized the Falange's penury, claiming that the stronger and more fully defined the party became (one is tempted to add: and the more radically fascist), the more reluctant other elements were to fund it. The circular asked all affiliates to make regular contributions.[167]

In search of financial support, José Antonio made his second trip to Rome at the end of April and spent several days there, accompanied by Sánchez Mazas and Montes. He met with Eugenio Coselschi, president of the CAUR, but otherwise did not obtain the same elite interviews he had enjoyed in October 1933; his request for another meeting with the Duce was not granted. Mussolini did, however, personally approve his financial request. Beginning in June, the Falange was promised a payment of 50,000 lire (then about 30,000 pesetas) a month, to be paid through the press attaché of the Italian embassy in Paris.[168] The Italian regime subsidized a number of foreign movements, such as the Francistes of Marcel Bucard, the only categorically fascist movement in France, and proportionately even smaller than the Falange. Because of their small size and dim prospects, the Francistes received only 10,000 lire per month.[169]

Only two months earlier, Mussolini had decided to cancel the pledge of assistance to the Spanish monarchist conspirators that had been made during the preceding year. The subsidy to the Falange was a safer and cheaper way to try to influence Spanish affairs; because of continuing pressure on Italy's foreign exchange, it was cut in half in January 1936,[170] but it rescued the Falange from extreme poverty in the winter of 1935.

In an interview published in *Il Lavoro Fascista* on 25 May, José Antonio declared:

> We regard Italian Fascism as the most outstanding political development of our time, from which we seek to draw principles and policies adapted to our own country, otherwise very similar to Italy. Fascism has established the universal basis for all the political movements of our time. The central idea of Fascism, that of the unity of the people in a totalitarian state, is the same as that of Falange Española. Our adherence to the Comitati per la Universalità di Roma is proof of our sentiments.[171]

Though there does not appear to have been a regular Falangist delegate to the second and last "universal fascism" meeting of the CAUR held at Montreux in September 1935, José Antonio himself made a brief appearance on 11 September. His remarks have been reported as follows:

> I feel very moved by your reception and transmit to you the very sincere greetings of Falange Española and of myself. For the moment, I am obliged not to participate in the work of your commission. The president has explained the reasons. Spain is not yet prepared to unite itself, through my mediation, with a movement of not merely international but supernational, universal character. And this is not just because the Spanish character is too individualistic, but also because Spain has suffered a great deal from the Internationals. We are in the hands of at least three Internationals that intervene in Spanish affairs—one Masonic, another capitalist, and perhaps of other powers, of an extranational character. If we appeared before Spanish opinion as united with another movement, without slow, careful, and complete preparation, the Spanish public conscience, and even the democratic conscience, would protest. It is necessary, therefore, to prepare people's thinking in view of these supranational labors.[172]

This was a very frank recognition both of the generic fascism of the Falange and at the same time of the need to pretend inside Spain that the movement was not fascist. José Antonio was more specific yet in a special report that he had prepared in the preceding month (August) for the Italian embassy. In it he affirmed decisively that "Falange Española de las JONS has succeeded in making itself into the only fascist movement in Spain, which has been difficult in view of the individualistic character of the Spanish people."[173]

That the Falangist leaders were always fully cognizant of the fact that theirs was a specifically fascist-type movement does not mean that they were always completely comfortable with all aspects of fascism or of the Mussolini regime itself. This had always been the case particularly with Redondo, who was aware of some of the major contradictions and compromises of Italian Fascism.[174] Even as he acknowledged outside Spain the fascist identity of the Falange, José Antonio was becoming somewhat better informed about Italian Fascism. By the end of 1935, he told some of his intimates that he realized that Mussolini had neither created a new juridical system nor effected a genuine revolution yet; rather, he had constructed a useful myth that the Spanish movement might exploit to its own benefit.[175] If that indeed represented his considered opinion, it was rather more realistic than some of his earlier assessments.

## THE FALANGE IN 1935

During its first full year, the Falangist organization had taken clear form. Members were divided between "militants" and "adherents," the former being full active members and the latter less involved but willing to participate in "accessory activities," such as distributing information. All healthy young "militants" were automatically to be enrolled in the Primera Línea, the basic militia organization. The "Segunda Línea" (Second Line) was composed of those not fit for such physical activism (because of age or infirmity); these were expected to contribute in other important ways, through financial assistance or political activities. The most important auxiliary organization was not the CONS but the SEU, which also enrolled all the underage students legally banned from party membership. Sections of the SEU might also form their own direct-action squads apart from the Primera Línea. A tiny "Women's Section" had been started by José Antonio's younger sister Pilar and several of her friends in June 1934.

The Primera Línea was modeled on the tercios or battalions of the Legión Española in Morocco and on the *squadre* of the early Italian Fascist Party. Two militants or escuadristas with a jefe formed an "elemento"; 3 elementos plus a jefe and subjefe composed an "escuadra" of 11; three escuadras then made up a "falange" of 33; and 3 falanges plus a jefe de centuria amounted to a "centuria" of 100. Three centurias were to be combined for a tercio of 300 (in towns and regions where there were enough members to form one), while three tercios in theory would compose a bandera and three banderas in turn a legión. The latter two units existed only on paper, however, and no banderas would be formed until after the Civil War began. Even the two largest centers, Madrid and Valladolid, did not organize genuine tercios.

The Primera Línea was originally directed by Col. Luis Arredondo and several other retired military officers, but the crisis of November 1934 had produced the departure of most of the latter, who joined either the alfonsino monarchists or the Carlists. The first young Falangist jefe nacional of militia was appointed in February 1935 in the person of the burly Agustín Aznar of the SEU. Aznar, son of the last authoritarian president of government before the advent of the Republic and himself a Greco-Roman wrestling champion, had excelled in violent brawls in the university.

General membership statistics have not survived, but at the beginning of 1935 it is doubtful that the Primera Línea numbered many more than 5,000. Officially, there were 743 registered members in Madrid, possibly four or five hundred in the city of Valladolid, and a few hundred in Seville. There were Falangist groups in almost every provincial capital, and a few rural provinces, such as Badajoz and Cáceres, claimed to have over 500 members per province, but such density, if it really existed, was rare. Significant nuclei existed in Santander and Burgos, but the party had done poorly in Catalonia, the Basque Country, and, to a lesser degree, Galicia.[176]

Membership increased modestly during 1935, but remained insignificant compared with the major parties. By February 1936 the Primera Línea probably numbered well under ten thousand, supplemented by the small Segunda Línea and a sizable membership in the SEU. All this probably did not amount to as many as ten thousand adults, though the total following, including several thousand students and the adherents, may have amounted to nearer twenty thousand.[177] By February 1936 the membership in Madrid had grown to 1,040 (plus 63 women in the Sección Femenina), from the following professions:

| | |
|---|---|
| Workers | 431 |
| Office employees | 315 |
| Skilled workers | 114 |
| Professionals | 106 |
| Students of legal age | 38 |
| Small businessmen | 19 |
| Officers and aviators | 17 |

In fact, at least half the total following in Madrid, where the university was comparatively large, came from students at either the university or the secondary level.[178]

Below the Jefe Nacional, the party was directed by a National Council and an executive advisory group, the Junta Política. All leadership positions were appointed from above, the jefes locales (local chiefs) being directed by jefes provinciales (provincial chiefs), with jefes territoriales (territorial chiefs) for each region of Spain. Each jefe had a secretary of corresponding rank. The secretary general, José Antonio's chief administrative assistant, was his lifetime friend and fellow lawyer, Raimundo Fernández Cuesta.

The party was strikingly immature; much of the total following was less than twenty-one years of age. These youngsters were poorly indoctrinated, as José Antonio realized. When Unamuno warned him that the Falangists with whom he had talked had no clear conception of what they really wanted, José Antonio replied that they had "much more heart than head."[179] All that most of them knew of their program was that it was radical, ultra-nationalistic, and stood for social reform. They knew that the party planned some sort of economic new order because José Antonio and their other leaders told them so, but they often had the vaguest of ideas about the nature of that order. Their enemies were the left, the center, and the right, but they hated the left and "separatists" most of all, because the latter most disparaged their exalted concept of the patria.

José Antonio privately recognized that the movement had failed in considerable measure to attract high-quality adherents, observing late in 1935:

> We have to try harder all the time to find better people. Many magnificent comrades of today, even National Council members, would have to be "retired with full honors" on the day of our triumph. They risk their life and liberty with such generosity that it causes pain even to think of it. But there would be no alternative. They will receive the Gold Palm, they will receive a special certificate, they will have a reputation within the Falange as being semidivine . . . but their time will have ended. Some could not even be city councilmen in their home towns, while there will be surprises, many surprises, about other people who no one thought were that close to us.[180]

The party was led in Madrid by personal friends and "incondicionales" of José Antonio, who was not at all immune to the vice of cronyism. After the rivalry over command during the first year and a half of the Falange, he surrounded himself with old friends and relatives, such as Fernández Cuesta in Madrid and Sancho Dávila in Seville, together with devoted young admirers, such as the SEU chiefs Manuel Valdés Larrañaga and Alejandro Salazar. A sycophantic clique had developed around José Antonio, composed of old personal friends, litterateurs, his law clerks, and other flatterers. This was a comfortable arrangement for the Jefe Nacional, though probably not the most productive for the party.

There was an equally pronounced tendency for the Madrid directors of the second rank, as well as the territorial and provincial chiefs, to guard their own preeminence jealously. The Madrid leaders in turn tended to distrust Onésimo Redondo, the most important chieftain in the provinces. Some of them tried to convince José Antonio that Redondo's reluctance to break with Ledesma and discontinue his autonomous local weekly showed a lack of loyalty. Furthermore, they complained, Redondo had never really left the path of clerical reaction, and his continued authority augured ill. Though *Libertad*, the Valladolid weekly, ended publication in March 1935—ostensibly for lack of funding—some of the Madrid leaders encouraged two student activists (aspiring young leaders themselves) who were plotting rebellion against Redondo among the young Valladolid militants.

In the summer of 1935 Redondo informed José Antonio that he would tolerate no more of this; he intended either to expel or to severely punish the two dissidents and whoever sided with them. José Antonio did not want to lose Redondo, arguably the most able leader in the party after himself, and authorized him, in accord with the Falangist *Führerprinzip*, to proceed as he saw fit. Relations between Madrid and Valladolid nonetheless remained strained throughout the year.[181]

That summer José Antonio intervened in party affairs at Málaga and Santander, where the provincial organizations had fallen under the control of rightist cliques. In each case, the Jefe dismissed the rightist leaders, replacing them with Falangists of more modest social background.[182]

The unsuccessful efforts at negotiation with the CNT persisted (and would continue until well after the Civil War). CNT affiliates in fact complained of reports linking their activities with those of the Falange,[183] and occasionally there was more than a little similarity between some of the slogans and the language of the two groups.[184]

José Antonio was not so much interested in the anti-Marxist but anarchist-controlled CNT itself as in the moderate, responsible "Treintistas"—dissident syndicalists who had split off after the anarchist FAI largely took over the Confederation in 1931–1932. Angel Pestaña, one of the top Treintista leaders, had even formed a separate Partido Sindicalista and was said to think well of José Antonio, who returned the compliment. The Falangist chief had made his first effort to deal with Pestaña during a visit to Barcelona only a few weeks after founding the party. Pestaña had been wary, and the two never actually met; further contacts were made by Ruiz de Alda and Luys Santa Marina, a writer and a Falangist leader in Barcelona (whose cultural review *Azor*, published from 1932 to 1934, had served as a propaganda vehicle for Falangism). Pestaña refused any cooperation. A major attempt was made to influence him once more at the end of 1935, but he and his small party insisted on an entirely independent voting list in the upcoming elections. Some agreement may momentarily have been reached on a brief statement of joint principles—which affirmed a national Spanish worker movement and condemned anticlerical violence—but this did not go very far. Thinking that the Falange had more money than it really did, Pestaña wanted it to defray expenses for his party's electoral candidacy in Barcelona, which was quite impossible.[185]

The right–center coalition that governed Spain during 1935 sought to discourage extremism and kept the Falange on a short leash. Its publications, like those of left extremist groups, were constantly censored and frequently fined; entire editions were sometimes confiscated. Provincial centers might be closed after any outburst of violence—sometimes even in the case of very moderate incidents—and authorization for meetings was sometimes withheld until the last minute, and occasionally denied altogether.

The movement nonetheless maintained as much activity as finances and general conditions permitted, and managed to organize more public meetings than in the preceding year. José Antonio's personal appearances were more than ever the centerpiece of major occasions. Though more meetings and speeches took place in Madrid and in provincial capitals than before, José Antonio devoted considerable energy to rallies in smaller provincial towns, convinced that there he encountered the true and uncorrupted "people," more receptive to the message of "españolidad" than the decadent materialists of the cities.

The rupture with the radical right deprived the Falange of the publicity it had previously enjoyed in the right extremist press, and by early 1935 its only publications were a few modest provincial weeklies or biweeklies, none of which survived very long. Hence the importance of *Arriba*, the official new party weekly that appeared in Madrid on 21 March. Though shorter than *F. E.*—normally only four pages in length—it once more provided a central organ, publishing about 5,000 copies of each issue, with occasional runs of twice that length. *Arriba* lasted almost exactly one year, though it was closed by the government for nearly all of July to October.

Compared with the newspapers of the major parties, however, *Arriba* had little impact, and at the close of May the party announced a campaign to fund a Falangist daily, which would be financed through the sale of 3,000 shares at 50 pesetas each. José Antonio saw this as vital, complaining privately on 20 August of "a closed agreement against us which extends from the government to the extreme right."[186] At that point there appeared in Madrid the first book on party doctrine written by a

Falangist, José Pérez de Cabo's brief *¡Arriba España!* In his Prologue to this work, José Antonio admitted that it was a far from complete or perfect treatment of Falangist ideology, but expressed his sense of desperation to find any means of generating greater attention to the movement: "In vain have we traversed Spain wearing out our voices in speeches; in vain have we published papers: the Spaniard, firmly set in his first infallible impressions, denies us, even as alms, what we would have most desired: a little attention." A leaflet distributed on the first of October insisted that "our most hidden enemy crouches behind the curtains of the capitalist press." Yet the results of the campaign for a daily newspaper were disappointing; by February 1936 only 9,000 pesetas had been raised.[187]

Falangist spokesmen raged against the moderate parliamentary right of the CEDA, which enjoyed most of the votes and financial contributions of the Catholic middle classes. José Antonio was particularly annoyed by the way his old rival Gil Robles dismissed the Falange as a fascist movement that was non- or anti-Catholic and worshiped a pantheist state. He announced that he had given up all hope that Gil Robles would ever rise to the stature of a national leader (probably referring above all to his refusal to join forces in violently overthrowing the Republican state). The CEDA youth, the khaki-shirted JAP, unaggressive and employing a half-fascist salute, was dismissed by Falangists as a bad joke. José Antonio sneered that "this is the only case in which the most decrepit sector of a party is made up of its youth."[188] *Arriba* published side by side, and over interchangeable titles, a picture of a JAP picnic and a photo of hogs scrambling for the slop trough. As early as 28 March, José Antonio had predicted that the right–center government would fail and the left would return to power within a year; this proved entirely correct.

The Falangist leadership took its first major stand on foreign policy in October at the time of the Italian invasion of Ethiopia, springing to the defense of Fascist imperialism. José Antonio and other spokesmen had always ridiculed the pacifist and internationalist foreign policy of the Republic, whose constitution renounced war "as an instrument of national policy"—the exact reverse of the Falangist "will to empire." He met privately with the Italian ambassador to offer his support and, in a major speech to the Cortes on 2 October, insisted that "colonizing is a mission, not merely a right, of civilized peoples" and that Italy had the duty to raise Ethiopia from "barbarism." He insisted on strict neutrality for Spain, for joining in sanctions by the League of Nations would only benefit Great Britain, occupant of Gibraltar and foe of Spain. Indeed, should the League approve sanctions, José Antonio warned melodramatically and somewhat grotesquely that such an action "will assuredly unleash a European war."[189] This gesture, like all Falangist activities in 1935, proved futile. Spain supported the sanctions voted by the League of Nations, and Italy then completed the conquest of Ethiopia, but there was no "European war."

Though the Falange could not deliver a "European war," it had within its power the ability to increase the amount of conflict in Spain. Violent incidents continued through 1935, though at a lesser rate than during the preceding year. The most difficult situation developed in Seville. After a street skirmish outside the city's Falangist center on the Día de la República in the preceding year (14 April 1934), 110 members had been temporarily arrested and the Center closed for thirteen months. In a recurrent cycle of violence, Falangists killed the president of the Casa del Pueblo and two other Socialists in the nearby town of Arija on 8 April 1935. Three weeks later, on 29 April, a group of Falangists from the city of Seville entered the town of Aznalcóllar, from which their propagandists had been expelled shortly before. In the ensuing conflict, one Falangist and one of their adversaries were killed, and a number of people on both sides were wounded. Thirteen Falangists were arrested. José Antonio served as their defense lawyer and awarded a large number of party decorations to those involved in the fight. Falangists apparently also killed two Socialists in the province of Badajoz during the next two months, one of them a Socialist deputy in the Cortes.[190]

Later, on 6 November, two Falangists—a student and a mechanic— were killed in Seville, allegedly by Communists, while posting propaganda. In the Cortes, José Antonio drew attention to this particular incident, claiming that it was only one of a series of attacks on Falangists in that region and that, in his words, "the Falange is proud that not even once has it initiated an aggression. The Falange can say that not even once has an aggression been proven."[191] Here José Antonio was apparently placing all killings by Falangists in the category of acts of reprisal, which in a certain narrow, technical sense may have been correct, but conveniently overlooked the fact that Falangists were constantly taking the initiative in acts of provocation, even if not normally those of lethal violence. He complained that there was no punishment for leftist assailants, while a Falangist response had drawn the arrest of fifteen leaders, a 5,000 peseta fine, and the closing of all Falangist centers in the province. The government did, however, replace the civil governor.

In March the party had to relinquish its national center in Madrid, a two-story building with a garden at 16 Marqués de Riscal, on the corner of the Castellana. (Its rent had been paid by the now-departed marqués de la Eliseda.) They moved into a much more modest apartment on the Cuesta de Santo Domingo. In the interim before the Italian subsidy became available, José Antonio had to pay a considerable part of the cost of operations from his own pocket, and even afterward funding remained very tight, at a level distinctly lower than during the first period of the party.[192] It was certain that the party could never emulate Mussolini's rapid rise to power; at the very least, its struggle would have to parallel Hitler's much longer road. Once more José Antonio privately admitted discouragement. In the normal course of events, five or ten years of intensive work would be needed to gain any influence in national affairs.[193]

### PLANS FOR ARMED REVOLT

The only possibility for rapid change would come from armed revolt. Thus far the military had shown little interest in rebelling, but toward the end of 1933 a clandestine professional officers' organization, the Unión Militar Española (UME), was created and slowly but steadily expanded. The UME was nominally apolitical but in fact clearly antileftist. Its first director had been the retired Falangist Captain Emilio Tarduchy, a strong partisan of the former Dictator, assisted by, among others, fellow retired Falangist officers such as Arredondo and Ricardo Rada. Regarded as too sectarian and rightist, Tarduchy was soon replaced by a captain in the General Staff, Bartolomé Barba Hernández (also very antileftist). Though the UME continued to grow, it remained a rather small minority within the officer corps, and included few if any generals.[194]

Though the Falangists had always cultivated contacts among the military, in the spring of 1934 José Antonio had shown limited interest, saying that generals could rarely be trusted.[195] The prospect of the Socialist insurrection had led him to write to General Franco, however, and in the aftermath of the revolt he had given in to Ledesma and Ruiz de Alda, who, as indicated above, had pressed for armed revolt. The Falangists made contact with several senior commanders who were trying to plot a coup, and in November 1934 José Antonio had written his "Carta a un militar español," decrying the situation in Spain, where the bourgeoisie was allegedly dominated by foreign ideas and the "proletarian masses completely won over by Marxism." In this rather lengthy missive he assured the military that they were "the only historic instrument to achieve the destiny of a people," and that theirs was the duty to *"replace a nonexistent state"* (his italics). They must fulfill "an integral, totalitarian, and national destiny." "This will be the decisive moment: either the sound or the silence of your machine guns will determine whether Spain is to continue languishing or will be able to open its soul to the hope of dominion. Think about these things before giving the order to 'Fire!' "[196] Yet very few of the military were interested in acting.

Just as he had adopted various of Ledesma's principles and slogans, so by mid-1935 José Antonio had begun to consider more seriously the possibility of a Falangist initiative in armed insurrection. In mid-June he called a special meeting of the party's Junta Política at the Parador de Gredos, a mountain resort west of Madrid. (The great irony of this occasion, as he soon found to his immense discomfort, was that his former unofficial sweetheart, Pilar Azlor de Aragón, the duquesa de Luna, had finally looked elsewhere. She had just married an aristocratic naval officer in Madrid, and that night she and her new husband were staying at the Parador on the first leg of a long honeymoon. José Antonio later described it as the worst night of his life, but pressed ahead with the meeting.)[197]

Gathering in a pine grove near the Parador, members of the Junta were told that the present political situation was hopeless and would only deteriorate. In remarks prepared earlier, José Antonio declared:

> Spain is irremediably headed toward the dictatorship of Largo Caballero, which will be worse than that of Stalin, since the latter wants to build a state and the former has no idea what he wants. We shall be fodder for the Russian hordes, who will sweep us away, and thus we have no alternative but to move to civil war.
>
> . . . In the next elections the left will win and . . . Azaña will return to power. . . . I think that instead of waiting for the persecution, we should prepare to revolt, counting, if possible, on the military, and, if not, on ourselves alone. Our duty is, consequently, and with all its consequences, to move toward civil war.[198]

Only a few of the Junta members, such as Ruiz de Alda and the SEU chief Salazar, were strongly in favor. According to the diary of the latter, most revealed their characteristic uncertainty when faced with bold decisions,[199] but they agreed to support José Antonio's proposal. He then issued instructions to the territorial and provincial leaders to prepare a second parallel clandestine formation of militants for paramilitary activity (though this in fact did not begin to take any real shape until the spring of 1936).

The precise details of the Falangist plan have never been clarified. The basic concept seems to have been to concentrate Falangist militia at Fuentes de Oñoro in the province of Salamanca. This would make it easier for the exiled Gen. Sanjurjo (resident in Portugal) to join and possibly lead them, while it also facilitated a defensive alternative. Should the revolt fail, the rebels would fight a defensive action, which, if necessary, might retreat into Portugal. There were contacts with Generals Goded and Mola (though neither had direct command of troops in the peninsula) and discussion of the provision of ten thousand rifles.[200] It was also known that in Navarre Col. José Enrique Varela and the ex-Falangist Lt. Col. Rada were engaged in helping to train Carlist volunteers.

The goal of this (at best quixotic) venture was a Falangist-led government, which in José Antonio's planning would be more a fascist party government than the first governments of Mussolini or Hitler had been, because—unlike the March on Rome or Hitler's rise to power—it would be the product of direct insurrection aiming to establish a dictatorship. At one point, either late in 1934 or in 1935, he drew up a tentative government list with the following names:[201]

| | |
|---|---|
| National Defense | General Franco |
| Foreign Affairs | Bárcena (professional diplomat) |
| Justice | Ramón Serrano Súñer (CEDA, but friendly to the Falange) |
| Education | Eduardo Aunós (monarchist and Primo de Rivera minister) |
| Undersecretary | Manuel Valdés Larrañaga (SEU and Falange) |
| Economics | Demetrio Carceller (Falange) |
| Interior | General Emilio Mola |
| Security | Vázquez |
| Public Works | Lorenzo Pardo |
| Corporations | Manuel Mateo (CONS and Falange) |
| Undersecretary | Rafael Garcerán (Falange) |
| Communications | Julio Ruiz de Alda (Falange) |
| Undersecretary | José Moreno (Falange) |
| Morocco and colonies | General Manuel Goded |

If José Antonio headed the government, this would have given the Falange and its close sympathizers six out of nine civilian portfolios, with four others (presumably including navy) held by the military, though the cabinet was not complete. In negotiations with Capt. Barba Hernández of the UME, José Antonio tried to gain the UME's support for a revolt to establish a new Falangist–military government, with the Falangists predominating. Not surprisingly, Barba Hernández categorically refused to underwrite Falangist predominance. José Antonio is then said to have agreed to an arrangement that would merely give the Falange priority of propaganda under a new government, with the possibility of effecting further changes at some point in the future,[202] but the entire scheme for revolt had to be dropped because of the lack of support among senior army commanders.

Shelving the "Gredos plan" did not, however, put an end to preparations for armed revolt, for by the summer of 1935 this had in fact become a major part, if not indeed the key, to Falangist strategy, the only real means of victory in the political struggle. In August, at the request of the Italian press attaché in Paris (from whose hands José Antonio personally received the Italian subsidy), the Falangist leader prepared a personal analysis of the situation in Spain. As was apparently customary in his reports to the Italians, he somewhat exaggerated the recent achievements of his party, declaring that the SEU "now holds the majority in most of the universities"—which was perhaps only a slight exaggeration—and maintaining that there was a significant growth in sympathy for Falangism among the military and the Civil Guard. José Antonio insisted that another leftist revolutionary insurrection, led by the Socialists, was inevitable, probably early in 1936, regardless of the date or the winner of the next elections. The next major violent leftist outburst nonetheless would be "the precise moment for the triumph of a fascist movement." At that time "the Falange, at the side of the Civil Guard, will be able to take over a number of towns, perhaps even a province, and proclaim the national revolution against an impotent state." A nonleftist government engaged in repressing a leftist insurrection "will find it very hard to send troops against fascism," whose own insurrection would then generate so much support that it could seize power. If a leftist government was already in power, "the entire Army, as long as it is headed by the present leaders, will readily follow the first group that launches the slogan of national rebellion. All the rightist political parties would hesitate, and the Army would not take the initiative by itself. The Falange would be the one to do so." José Antonio calculated that "an integral plan" would be ready "beginning in October."[203] His timing was obviously badly off, but this proposal was the first presentation, more or less *ab ovo*, of the kind of plan eventually developed by the Falangists and by military conspirators during the following spring. The flaws in José Antonio's original concept were at least threefold. First, further difficulties would not arise until after the moderate left had returned to power. Second, the consequence would be numerous changes in personnel in top military commands, which, together with many other uncertainties, would mean that only about half the army, not "all," would join the revolt. A third and even more fundamental miscalculation stemmed from José Antonio's superiority complex vis-à-vis the professional military, for, contrary to his analysis, the military would indeed, under Mola and Franco, "take the initiative," almost inevitably relegating the Falange to a secondary position. The rudiments of the rebellion of 1936 were present in José Antonio's report to Rome the preceding August, but the eventual result would be the division of the military and of all Spain in a total civil war, led on the side of the right by the military and not by the Falange.

It is more than doubtful that an "integral plan" was ready by October, but the Falangist leaders continued to consider alternative scenarios for revolt. At a meeting of the Junta Política in Madrid on 27 December, José Antonio presented yet another proposal to begin the revolt in nearby Toledo, where the Falange enjoyed numerous sympathizers among officers and cadets at the Military Academy. The following morning Fernández Cuesta and the Falangist writer José María Alfaro talked in Toledo with Col. José Moscardó, the director of the Army Gymnastics School and acting military governor, to urge him to seize control of the Academy, bring the cadets out in armed revolt in conjunction with the Falangist Primera Línea of Toledo, and then join forces with a column of Falangist militia from Madrid. A national appeal would then be made by radio for all the military and other patriotic forces, together with all the rest of the Falangist militia, to join together in support of a strong new nationalist government in Madrid. Moscardó, a strong nationalist and antileftist, labeled the plan "magnificent" and requested that the Falangists wait in Toledo while he consulted with military superiors in Madrid. Moscardó was then driven to a meeting in the capital with the chief of the General Staff, Franco, who was reported to have approved the concept of the plan in theory but labeled it altogether "premature" and forbade any action at the present time.[204] A Falangist initiative was once more canceled because of lack of support from the military.

A few weeks later, José Antonio made a personal attempt to remedy the problem by going directly to the top, arranging a personal interview with the chief of the General Staff in the home of the father of his good friend Serrano Súñer (Franco's brother-in-law). There José Antonio is reported to have made a strong case that the Falange was the only completely reliable, new, modern antileftist force in the country but that it would inevitably need the armed support of the military in order to "save Spain." Franco responded with great caution, deflecting the entire conversation. He had no desire to be involved in a technically criminal revolt so long as a nonleftist government remained in power, and so devoted the conversation to his customary patter of small talk, recounting military anecdotes, criticizing various other military leaders, and going on at great length about a particular type of new artillery piece developed by the French that he thought the Spanish army should acquire.[205] José Antonio was both disgusted and disillusioned, and his already low opinion of the political acumen of the military sank. The truth of the matter, of course, was that whereas José Antonio was a rash and radical politician, Franco was a very cautious one (whose caution and dissimulation would eventually prevail over all, including the Falange). At this point, very early in 1936, plans for a Falangist insurrection had to be temporarily—but only temporarily—discontinued.

## THE DESTRUCTION OF PORTUGUESE
## NATIONAL SYNDICALISM

The Falangist leaders could not have been encouraged by the final destruction of their Portuguese counterparts in 1935. The national syndicalist movement in Portugal was largely initiated by students, as in Spain, and in the very same years (1931–1932). Its founders were dissatisfied with the moderate character of the Salazar regime, which was just beginning to institutionalize itself, inaugurating the Estado Novo in 1933, with the first new corporative constitution in Europe. They were also dissatisfied with the more extreme right-radical Liga Nacional 28 de Maio, formed in 1928 to commemorate the Portuguese military coup of two years earlier and to lead it to a permanent hard-line rightist authoritarian system. Salazar basically seized control of the latter during 1931–1933, forcing its dissolution and incorporating its members into his own National Union, a sort of more organized Portuguese version of the former Spanish Unión Patriotica.[206]

To challenge Salazar's moderation and rightism, Portuguese National Syndicalism had been officially constituted in September 1932 under Rolão Preto, a former leader of monarchist integralism who had moved "left." Preto had declared that "nationalism can no longer signify 'Tradition'—but a breaking of the mold—and a break with the old ideological restraints so that the spirit may fly and rise ever higher."[207] Like the Falangists, the National Syndicalists adopted blue shirts (though of a lighter color) and generally identified themselves with fascism, even though Preto sometimes claimed that he was "beyond Fascism and Hitlerism," since they divinized a totalitarian state whereas National Syndicalists sought to synthesize their movement with Portuguese Catholic values and "our dignity as free men"[208] (in a manner not unlike José Antonio's distinction). The Blue Shirts proclaimed their own revolution, emphasizing social and economic transformation, though in terms vaguer than those of the Falange. They welcomed contacts with other fascist movements and, despite an occasional remark by Preto, seem to have identified almost completely with Italian Fascism, while maintaining their distance from Nazism and condemning the excesses of the Legion of the Archangel Michael in Romania. Relations with the Falange were conflictive. Ledesma had feared that the Blue Shirts were potentially reactionary, while Preto himself had criticized José Antonio for being perhaps too "capitalist."

Moreover, the Portuguese had certain designs on Spanish Galicia, whereas some, at least, of the Falangists believed that Spain should rule the entire peninsula.[209] This uneasy relationship was somewhat similar to that between the Arrow Cross in Hungary and the Legion of the Archangel Michael in Romania.

The National Syndicalists grew fairly rapidly in 1933 and at their high point may have had twenty-five thousand members—proportionately a much larger membership than that of the Falange—whereas the government's National Union then had only about twenty thousand. Militancy was centered in Lisbon and in the conservative northern cities of Braga and Bragança. Of those members for whom data are available, the largest minority came from the working class, followed by white-collar employees and students, and next by shopkeepers, petty entrepreneurs, and farmers. There was also a not inconsiderable membership among junior army officers. By contrast, the National Union was made up more of professional men, landowners, and other conservative middle- and upper-middle-class elements.[210] In political background, the largest single sector of leaders and militants stemmed from the old monarchist Integralist movement, and more than a few local National Syndicalist centers seemed interested in a monarchist restoration, which tended to dilute genuine fascist identity. The National Syndicalists organized small "shock brigades," but rarely engaged in direct action.

Salazar, the prime minister and virtual dictator, made clear his rejection of fascist "pagan caesarism" and its "new state that knows no juridical or moral limits."[211] Catholic leaders also strongly denounced National Syndicalism. While inaugurating his Estado Novo in 1933, Salazar put strong pressure on the Blue Shirts, closing their newspaper, firing some of their leaders who held government positions, and tightly censoring their activity. He also created his own more moderate student organization, Accão Escolar Vanguarda (AEV), to outflank them.[212] Salazar then permitted the National Syndicalists to hold a national congress in November 1933, indicating a willingness to co-opt them if they would moderate their position and renounce a categorical fascism. By the first months of 1934, he had succeeded to some extent in splitting the movement; those who broke off were then incorporated in many cases into positions within the regime (where for the remainder of the decade some of them constituted a sort of de facto fascistic pressure group within the state syndical system). On 29 July 1934, Salazar announced dissolution of the National Syndicalist organization. The government's decree rejected their fascistic "exaltation of youth, the cult of force through so-called direct action, the principle of the superiority of state political power in social life, the propensity for organizing masses behind a single leader."[213]

At the same time Salazar felt a need to give his own system a somewhat more dynamic, mobilized appearance. This was provided initially by the AEV, which also, somewhat contradictorily, maintained contact with the CAUR organization in Rome promoting "universal fascism." Thus, while the Falange, a genuine fascist-type party, sent no official representative to the CAUR conference at Montreux in December 1934, the AEV, not a generically fascist organization, sent one of their own leaders, Antonio Eça de Queiroz (son of Portugal's leading novelist). His presence created an anomaly, the only case of a delegate who was not representing an ostensible fascist movement in opposition to the government in power in his home country. Eça de Queiroz was even announced as the delegate of the "National Syndicalists, led by Salazar." It is not clear whether Salazar himself had personally approved the initiative, and during 1935 relations with the CAUR lapsed, while the AEV itself was downgraded.[214] The Portuguese government condemned Mussolini's invasion of Ethiopia, and a Portuguese diplomat chaired the League of Nations committee charged with coordinating economic sanctions against Italy.

The regular National Syndicalists meanwhile maintained a clandestine existence, though a number of their militants were placed under arrest. Preto helped to organize an extremely heterogeneous conspiracy against the Portuguese regime. This was led by the National Syndicalists and a small circle of monarchists but was also supported by some right-wing republicans and even a few Socialists and anarchists interested simply in toppling the existing regime. Preto may have hoped for decisive support from the military, but the revolt of 10 September 1935 was backed by only a very small sector of the armed forces and collapsed, leading to the effective repression of the National Syndicalists.[215] Fascism had failed completely in Portugal. Repressed by the more moderate authoritarian right in control of the state, it had suffered the same fate as its counterparts in Austria, Hungary, and Romania.

In Portugal fascism had played no role in either the overthrow of the parliamentary regime in 1926 or the construction of the new authoritarian system, functioning instead as a movement of opposition against the moderation of the latter. After 1935 National Syndicalism could survive only as a tiny semiclandestine sect; former Blue Shirts within the regime were not very influential, apart from their role in the state syndical system. Salazar personally rejected the support of a fascist movement, was hostile to genuine fascist culture, and rejected any concept of a charismatic Führerprinzip, as well as cultural modernization in general and any priority for accelerated economic development. He similarly rejected militarism and aggressive new imperialism as simply opposed to Portuguese interests, which should center on law and order and the status quo to maintain

the large empire that Portugal already held. Though he would briefly employ certain organizational and choreographic trappings of fascism during the Spanish Civil War, he was categorical in his rejection of its most
distinctive and determining features. Salazar's ideology was that of Catholic corporatism (much like Gil Robles and the CEDA). Though his caution and moderation prevented him from formally reunifying church and
state, his Estado Novo should be seen as a new Catholic corporative regime analogous to that of Dollfuss in Austria.

After the opposition of the regime itself—which was decisive—the
possibilities of a fascism in Portugal were limited by other basic factors:
the relatively low level of mobilization in a country where genuine mass
politics had never fully emerged; the comparative weakness of the threat
from the worker left (compared with Italy, Germany, Austria, or Spain);
the fact that Portugal had been on the winning side in World War I, so
that any lingering traumas from that conflict had dissipated by the late
1920s; an imperial position that was satisfied and defensive, concerned
only to retain the empire already occupied; and finally the overwhelmingly agrarian structure of Portuguese society, less amenable to mass mobilization (even though fascist movements generated agrarian support in
Italy, Hungary, and Romania).

It is doubtful that José Antonio and the other Falangist leaders were
especially impressed by the fate of Portuguese National Syndicalism, but
the complete failure of the September revolt, together with its inability to
gain much assistance from the military, could not but further have discouraged any prospect of success for the "Gredos plan" of an insurrection
in Spain.


THE ELECTIONS OF 1936

By the closing months of 1935, the Falange had taken clearer form as a
utopian, revolutionary fascist party. Though for domestic political reasons its leaders rejected the formal label of fascism, they continued privately to recognize their fascist identity, a fascism modified primarily by
religious, and to some extent cultural, neotraditionalism. The Falange's
politics were those of catastrophism, and its leader deliberately assumed
the goal of "civil war" in internal party communications.

In national politics, José Antonio sought to break the CEDA–Radical
coalition, isolating and reducing the democratic center while encouraging
the parliamentary right toward a position of absolute polarization and
an authoritarian break with the Republic. The first goal was also encouraged by the president of the Republic, Niceto Alcalá Zamora, who
sought to destroy the Radical Party in order to be able to take over indi-

rectly the leadership of the center himself. The two financial scandals that broke during the autumn of 1935, the "Estraperlo" concession and the Nombela-Tayà affair, were comparatively minor issues in themselves but were deliberately fueled by the president and others to discredit the Radicals, who despite their name were the only large moderate democratic party in Spain, the true fulcrum of a democratic Republic. The financial scandals had all the more impact—unlike similar issues in France a year earlier—because in Spain a state of ideological polarization was developing in which public issues were being argued in apocalyptic terms of absolute and ultimate morality. Those on both left and right who decried the "immorality" of the Radicals found it perfectly moral to propose to deprive their fellow citizens of freedom, to steal their property, or even to murder them. The Radicals were, in fact, the least morally corrupt large political group in Spain, because they were the only one that respected the rights and liberties of their fellow citizens. José Antonio eagerly joined in the assault on the Radicals, declaring that they must "disappear from public life,"[216] expediting the polarization and extremism of the political atmosphere. As it soon turned out, the Radicals were irremediably discredited, while the president refused to allow the CEDA, despite its parliamentary plurality, to form a government. The only alternative was the installation of a nonparliamentary caretaker coalition in mid-December, which must soon lead to new elections.

On 15 November the Falange's Second National Council was convened in Madrid. The main item of business was to discuss the desirability of forming a "Spanish National Front" with rightist forces, above all the CEDA, against the left. The crises of the preceding fifteen months had produced many changes among the party's elite; only eleven of the fifty councillors who met in November had participated in the first Council a year earlier. As recently as September, José Antonio had privately expressed fear of "a new schism,"[217] but this did not occur, for by the autumn he had renovated the leadership structure and achieved a party elite that was personally loyal to him, however much else it may have left to be desired. The proposal of an electoral National Front, "as Hitler had done in Germany in a similar situation" (as Bravo Martínez put it),[218] was approved.

The sessions were climaxed by a large meeting in the Cine Madrid on 17 November, at which José Antonio delivered the keynote address. It presented the National Front proposal and went on to elaborate the Falangist concept of "the national revolution," the revolutionary "left fascism" that had become a leitmotiv. José Antonio promised rapid prosecution of agrarian reform and nationalization of banking and credit, accompanied by "urgent disarticulation of capitalism itself." He explained that "the easiest of all is to dismantle rural capitalism; next easiest, to dismantle or replace finance capitalism; the hardest, to dismantle industrial capitalism. But since God is on our side, it turns out that in Spain there is scarcely any industrial capitalism to dismantle, since very little exists."[219] Though such simplistic formulae were the stock-in-trade of Falangist propaganda, this was in fact one of the most substantive speeches José Antonio ever presented. It was of course inherently contradictory, proposing a temporary electoral alliance with the most rightist parties in order to develop strength for drastic economic changes, and, like nearly all of José Antonio's speeches, was generally ignored in the media and in the political world.

Approximately two weeks later the party anthem, "Cara al Sol" ("Face to the Sun"), was composed, much of it prepared at a session on 3 December in the Cueva del Orkompón, a Basque bar in Madrid. The music was written by Juan Tellería, with lyrics provided by the collective effort of José Antonio, Agustín de Foxá, Dionisio Ridruejo, and Pedro Mourlane Michelena.

The Falangist proposal for a National Front was ignored, but Gil Robles announced his own version of a similar proposal in mid-December. *Arriba* declared on the nineteenth the willingness of the Falange to participate so long as its independence was respected and it was not assigned "the role of a guerrilla force or light infantry for other, wiser parties." After dispatching a questionnaire to members of the Junta Política on 24 December, José Antonio convened a meeting of the Junta and once more gained approval for negotiating an electoral pact with the right, with the stipulations that the party be able to wage an independent campaign, negotiate alliances on the local and provincial level rather than on a national basis, and obtain a minimum of twenty-five to thirty candidacies nationwide.[220] This would have been roughly equivalent to the representation of Italian Fascist candidates in the Italian election of 1921.

Early in January the government announced that elections would be held on 16 February. The Falangist electoral manifesto appeared on 12 January, announcing its continued willingness to negotiate National Front pacts but also insisting on the party's semirevolutionary platform, which made cooperation with the right difficult. Since its offers were being universally ignored, the Falangist leadership announced two days later that though it was still willing to negotiate, it was planning to present independent candidacies in a total of nineteen electoral districts.

The party leaders had few illusions about the weakness of an independent small-party candidacy in an electoral system structured to reward large parties and coalitions disproportionately. This situation was most dangerous of all to José Antonio, for, should he lose his seat in the Cortes, he would also be stripped of parliamentary immunity, leaving him liable for the charge of illicit possession of firearms pending since July 1934, and potentially subject to arrest on other grounds as well. Therefore on the day the independent campaign was announced, José Antonio paid a personal visit to Gil Robles on his own initiative, seeking to negotiate an arrangement that would permit the Falange approximately eighteen candidacies nationwide. Gil Robles was receptive in principle, but rejected so many candidacies as out of the question for a tiny party, offering instead a total of six candidacies, of which three or four would be in districts with a reasonable possibility of success. Moreover, he offered to include José Antonio in the "safe" list that would be led by Gil Robles himself in his home district of conservative Salamanca. According to Falangists, José Antonio rejected this, since he was denied a place on the "prestige list" in Madrid, where Gil Robles proposed that the only Falangist on the rightist coalition list would be Ruiz de Alda, in last place.[221] According to Gil Robles, however, José Antonio initially accepted what was a perfectly reasonable proposal, only to return a few days later to declare that the Falange must refuse so limited an offer, since other Falangist leaders rejected an arrangement that might safeguard José Antonio personally but would benefit few other Falangist candidates.[222] Even so, José Antonio returned on 7 February to discuss with the CEDA leader a limited set of arrangements that might also give him a place on the rightist list in Madrid. This proved impossible.[223] Nor could he recover his old position on the rightist list in Cádiz, his nominal home district. There the rightist forces were more tightly organized than in 1933, and there seems to have been considerable animus against him for devoting his attention in parliament to national issues, ignoring the local interests that had been attended instead by the other rightist deputies from Cádiz.[224]

The Falange thus stood alone in the final elections of the Republic. Its official list of candidates was in fact not entirely finalized until 13 February, though José Antonio and others had begun to campaign well before that. Candidacies were listed in Madrid and in eighteen other provinces where there seemed a slight possibility of electing a Falangist. José Antonio stood in Madrid and in seven other areas, and among the Falangist candidates were such party luminaries as Redondo, Ruiz de Alda, Sánchez Mazas, Sancho Dávila, and Manuel Hedilla (in Santander).[225] As it turned out, the only electoral agreement made with any other group was arranged in Santander, where Hedilla withdrew on behalf of a Carlist, leaving Ruiz de Alda the only Falangist candidate in the province.[226]

The party attempted an active campaign, though its financial and other resources were slight, with José Antonio contributing some thousands of pesetas out of his own pocket. Public meetings were emphasized, accompanied by the party press, leaflets, and posters. Manpower was sometimes also in short supply, so that it proved impossible in certain provinces even to spend the limited funding available. Often, however, it was difficult to make a convincing case for voting for the parliamentary candidates of an antiparliamentary movement.

By far the most active candidate was the Jefe Nacional, who threw himself into a frenzy of campaigning, appearing in large and small cities in eight provinces, including two fairly large rallies in Madrid. José Antonio emphasized the party's semirevolutionary economic program, declaring that "if we base ourselves on this just doctrine of universal destiny we will see how communism—considered only as an economic system, to the exclusion of its philosophy—is less distant from Christian morality than is capitalism." To this sophistry he added that "communism is only more opposed by the fact of proclaiming and professing atheism," going on to emphasize that "liberal capitalism necessarily ends up in communism." Now was the time to introduce a new order for Spaniards, based on "their moral units, their family, their guild, their municipality." "The nation that is the first to speak the words of these new times will be the one to place itself at the head of the world." Spain could do what even Italy and Germany, much less the Soviet Union, had not accomplished: "Here is where, if we wish, we can place Spain once more at the head of the world." [227]

Falangist propaganda ridiculed the rightist coalition, which "supposed that the union of various midgets was sufficient to form a giant." [228] Falangist tracts alleged that "the rightist parties only joined together for fear of the common enemy; they did not understand that in the face of an aggressive faith it is necessary to oppose another active and combative faith, not the inert slogan of mere resistance." "It's not enough to come chanting hymns." [229] At Cáceres José Antonio cried: "Less 'Down with this,' and 'Against that' and more 'Upward Spain!' " He emphasized that the old battle cry had not been "Down with the Moors!" but "St. James and Spain charges!" [230]

On the eve of election day, many conservatives urged the Falangists to withdraw their candidates altogether, insisting that the only consequence of Falangist obstinacy would be to split the antileftist vote. *ABC* flattered the Falangists by saying that their activists were worth several times as many of the more timid conservative youth, but it urged them to take the long view, since their ideology was fundamentally antiparliamentary:

> Falange Española is not in a condition to expect that its four candidates in Madrid will be elected. To persist in the contest nonetheless will result in inevitable damage, not merely to the vote for

the candidacy of the united right, but also to the spiritual strength
with which Falange Española can present itself to public opinion after
the elections.[231]

A significant number of conservatives presented themselves at José Antonio's office and at various Falangist centers to reiterate this proposal.

The only agreements made, apart from the Carlist accord in Santander,
were certain vague understandings on the provincial level, which provided
that the Falangist militia would support the military should the left win
the election and the military declare martial law. In his last major speech
of the campaign, José Antonio warned: "If the result of the balloting is
contrary, dangerously contrary, to the eternal destiny of Spain, the Falange with its forces will relegate the results of the balloting to the lowest
depths of contempt."[232] Revolutionary Socialists and anarchosyndicalists
made equally clear their own contempt for parliamentary procedures.

In the balloting of 16 February, the left won a rather close but clear
plurality, which, as a result of the plurality/majority list system for appor-
tioning representation, gave the leftist parties a clear majority of seats.
The CEDA remained the largest single party, but its lack of influential
allies left it in the minority. The left's strong majority of seats (about 60
percent) was turned into a sweeping majority of some two-thirds following the deliberations of the new parliament's Electoral Commission,
which began on 16 March. Under the constitution, representatives of the
parties that were returned in each election met in a special commission
to review the results. In this case, the leftist majority simply acted to transfer a sizable number of seats from right to left, ordering new elections for
the disputed provinces of Cuenca and Granada.[233]

The electoral outcome was a disaster for the Falange, which garnered
only 44,000 votes in all Spain, or about 0.7 percent of the popular vote.
The Falangist vote was proportionately strongest in Cádiz (4.6 percent,
7,499 votes), where José Antonio was standing alone for reelection, Valladolid (4.19 percent, 5,435 votes), Santander (1.9 percent, 2,930 votes),
and Madrid (1.2 percent, 4,995 votes). Not a single Falangist was elected.
José Antonio was grievously disappointed, for he had hoped for 35,000
votes in Madrid alone.[234]

Given all the talk about fascism in Spain during the past three years, it
may be asked why so few Spaniards were willing to vote for the only
clearly fascist-type party. One reason was that the antileftist vote was
dominated by the hegemonic CEDA, and further absorbed on the nationalist right by the Carlists and alfonsino monarchists. Compared with the
situation in Italy and Germany, or for that matter Hungary, rightist and
nationalist opinion was considerably less secularized, and political Ca-

tholicism was thus the favored vehicle. Clear-cut nationalism had always been weak in Spain, and the lack of involvement in World War I further diminished the appeal of a radical, not so very Catholic, nationalism. Another factor was the role of the "voto útil," which led many voters to choose the main list of either the left or right as the force most likely to win; more than a few voters simply chose the side they were less opposed to. This, together with the peculiar character of the electoral system, also worked against the liberal center, now reduced to little more than a handful of parliamentary seats.

The Falange made a poor showing: fascist parties did proportionately better even in such democratic northern countries as Britain, Holland, Norway, and Sweden during those years. According to the electoral results of February 1936, categorical fascism was weaker in Spain than almost anywhere else in western and northern Europe.

# Six

# From Clandestinity to Civil War

The victory of the Popular Front was at first not viewed as a total disaster by Falangists, for they could now argue that their tactics had been proven correct and the moderate electoral policy of the CEDA a failure. Some party militants were convinced that their hour was approaching. As the local chief of Seville later wrote:

> After the February elections I had absolute faith in the triumph of the Falange, because we could now consider the right, our most difficult enemy, defeated and eliminated. Their failure provided us with a great advantage, as well as the inheritance of the greater part of their best youth. Moreover, we were absolutely certain that the Popular Front would also fail, given its internal divisions and antinational position, openly opposed to the sentiments of a large number of Spaniards. Our task simply consisted in broadening our base among the workers.[1]

It is clear that José Antonio himself did not see the situation as one of final polarization leading to civil war. Like many others, he was still at least partially captive to the myth of Manuel Azaña as the great statesman of the left who might provide creative leadership. His article "Here Is Azaña," which appeared in *Arriba* on 23 February, was surprisingly positive, declaring that experience would enable Azaña to do better than in his first government, and that if he established a broad national base— not just a sectarian leftist one—he would have a chance to enact important reforms. José Antonio recognized Azaña's talents as "exceptional," as he had in the past, and declared that "in spite of all its great defects, universal suffrage this time has shown signs of good sense and justice," almost balancing the popular vote (if not the parliamentary representation) between left and right, giving the middle-class left better representation than the revolutionaries, and repudiating the Radicals. This was another of the disastrously inaccurate political analyses to which José Antonio was so prone. Privately, Alejandro Salazar (Jefe Nacional of the

SEU) wrote in his diary, "he has expressed to us his blind faith in Azaña. He thinks he will manage to carry out a work of national revolution."[2] The other Falangist leaders were more skeptical, so that their first meeting after the elections was fairly gloomy, and in fact in less than two weeks José Antonio would radically change his evaluation. As it turned out, the only initial advantage for the Falange was that the amnesty for political prisoners declared by the new government resulted in cancellation of the charges pending against José Antonio since July 1934 for illegal possession of firearms.

The most immediate concerns for the Falangist leadership were, first, that the new leftist government might proceed to outlaw the fascist party, and, second, that the defeat of the right and the resultant rightist movement toward extremism might swamp the Falange with new rightist members. José Antonio told the editorialists of *Arriba* to concentrate their fire on the right and go easy on the leaders of the Popular Front. In a circular of 21 February to local leaders throughout Spain, he directed:

> The leaders will take care that no one adopt any attitude of hostility toward the new government, nor of solidarity with the defeated rightist forces. . . .
> Our militants will completely ignore any request to take part in conspiracies, projects of coup d'état, alliances with forces "of order," or any similar things.[3]

All new members—and soon there would be many new members from the right—were to be required to pass through a probationary period of four months before enjoying any role of responsibility within the party.

The attempt to nationalize the left remained a basic priority, and at some point after the elections José Antonio made contact with the moderate prietista sector of the Socialists through the physiology professor Juan Negrín. The aim was somehow to split the Socialist Party, uniting the Falange with true "national Socialists"—as José Antonio conceived the prietistas to be—even to the point, it was alleged, of offering Prieto the leadership of any such fusion. The moderate Socialists, however, refused to negotiate; "social fascism" was not an object of attraction.[4]

José Antonio was perfectly aware that the new government might adopt strong measures against the Falange, and hence his concern to avoid the slightest provocation, to the extent of warning against the wearing of external emblems on the lapels of jackets. This concern was reasonable, for on 26 February the newly rented Falangist Center was raided by police during a meeting of the Junta Política. On the following day the Center was officially closed by the authorities on the charge of illicit possession of firearms, though there is no indication of any similar effort to monitor the centers and activities of the revolutionary left. The last number of *Arriba* appeared on 5 March. In it José Antonio acknowledged his error of a fortnight earlier, declaring that the new Azaña government was becoming even more arbitrary and sectarian than that of the first biennium. Demonstrating the accuracy of that analysis, the government decreed the permanent suspension of the Falangist organ.

Neither the revolutionary left nor many of the rank-and-file Falangists shared José Antonio's commitment to moderation. The government would soon announce that "some fascists" had been killed in Almoradiel, though it is not clear whether they were Falangists. The latter have claimed that four of their members in Seville were soon killed by the left, but that reprisals were authorized by José Antonio only after a fifth was slain.[5]

Events now escalated rapidly. On 6 March members of the Falangist syndicate CONS, who had failed to support a leftist strike and were employed in the demolition of the old Plaza de Toros in Madrid, were attacked. Three workers plus a fourth Falangist guard were shot, the latter and one of the workers fatally.[6] On the following day a member of the SEU shot in an earlier attack on a SEU meeting in Palencia also died of his wounds. Four days later, on 11 March, two young law students, one a Falangist and the other a Carlist, were shot to death in Madrid, allegedly by members of the Socialist Youth. Even though this was the third Falangist fatality in Madrid in five days, the party leadership did not order reprisals, but one was quickly carried out by militants of the SEU. On the morning of 13 March, several gunmen fired on the prominent Socialist leader and law professor Luis Jiménez de Asúa, one of the principal authors of the Republican constitution. He managed to flee unharmed, but his police escort soon died of his wounds. The police moved rapidly to arrest a total of fourteen Falangists, though the genuine authors of the deed escaped by plane to France.[7] Burial of the slain policeman then became the occasion for a leftist demonstration and riot in which two major churches were torched. Yet the subsequent official statement by the national police bureau, the Dirección General de Seguridad (DGS), placed the matter in clearer perspective than have some subsequent writers, relating the attempt on Asúa to the preceding deaths of "some fascists" in Almoradiel, the killing of two Falangists on the sixth, and of the two students on the eleventh.[8] Two Communists were said later to have been slain in a bar in a second Falangist attack.

The attempt on Asúa's life attracted enormous attention because it represented an escalation in violence. Aside from the earlier attacks on José Antonio in 1934, major party leaders had not been the targets of assassination attempts, and now the authorities reacted swiftly. Though the great bulk of the political violence under the Republic had always come from the left, the Azaña government reasoned that the abolition of the Falange—the one categorical fascist-type movement in the country— would only improve public order and reduce the provocation and excuses of the leftist revolutionaries. On the night of the thirteenth, therefore, orders were given for the arrest of the national leaders of the Falange and the SEU. On the following day most of those in Madrid were taken into custody, only a very few for the moment managing to elude the authorities. The arrest report on José Antonio simply read, "Detenido por fascista" (arrested as a fascist),[9] though no law at that time declared such identity or affiliation to be illegal.

The official justification for the arrests was that the party leaders had violated the order of 27 February that had closed the Falangist Center, because the official seal of closure placed on the front door had been broken. For two days the Falangist leaders were held in cells in the basement of the DGS but were allowed to receive the many visitors who came to offer assistance and condolences. To one of these, Antonio Goicoechea, José Antonio joked that the seals had been broken by José Alonso Mallol, the director general of DGS, "with his horns." This remark was overheard by a corporal of the Assault Guards, who exclaimed, "The little jokes of this *señorito flamenco* are over, and he will find out what it's going to cost him!"[10] This remark would in fact be used against José Antonio in one of the six judicial indictments filed against him that spring.

On 17 March the Falangist leaders appeared in court to face the charge of leading an illicit political organization whose official program, the Twenty-Seven Points, threatened to subvert Republican legality. The presiding judge, Ursicino Gómez Carbajo (who four months later would initiate the investigation into the killing of Calvo Sotelo), agreed with the indictment, ruling that the defendants should be held under preventive arrest pending trial on these charges. He also ordered the closing of all Falangist centers and offices and the "suspension of regular functions" of the party, which, though not technically dissolved, had now been shut down as a political organization. That same morning Falangist gunmen sought to carry out an attack on Largo Caballero in reprisal, but finding his residence too closely guarded, settled for firing into the windows of his apartment instead. Once more the authorities reacted swiftly, arresting thirty more Falangists in Madrid. Within the next few weeks, hundreds more would be arrested all over the country.

The intention was to keep Spain from following the path of Italy and Germany. "Fascism" would simply be abolished, though in fact the matter was not so simple. The Falange could no longer operate as a legal organization, but the Second Republic—despite the draconian police and censorship powers that could be invoked under the Law for the Defense of the Republic—was not a police state. Though the party was driven underground, new recruits far exceeded the number of those arrested. Hundreds and thousands of former affiliates of JAP, the CEDA, and Renovación Española began to join, while many more made common cause, showing their sympathy and support. Outlawing the party helped to effect a momentary decline in violence during the latter part of March, but the rate picked up again by mid-April and then continued at a high level as Spain began its descent into civil war.

The government, dependent on the revolutionaries' votes in parliament, could not take the same approach to them as to the Falangists. Though leftists might grumble (sometimes with reason) about conservative judges who were too lenient with imprisoned Falangists, the police were in fact much more rigorous with the latter, while more often than not overlooking leftist attacks on Falangists.[11] The bourgeois left Republicans were in turn increasingly bewildered by the unwillingness or inability of the leaders of the revolutionary organizations to control their own activists. *Política,* the organ of Azaña's party, declared on 27 March:

> It is almost a commonplace to say that fascism is not fearful for what it represents numerically, but for what, as a phenomenon of social breakdown, it generates in demagogy and sterile agitation. Consequently the tactic based on the theory of "permanent revolution" has been discredited for its disastrous results in Germany and in other countries affected by fascism. . . . Thus it becomes impossible to understand how forces that in the past never represented worker extremism now turn to failed methods and succumb to the illusion of a revolution that does not even correspond to the process predicted by Marx.

Violence began to escalate once more in mid-April. After a seuísta law student was sentenced to twenty-six years imprisonment for the attack on Asúa (the actual gunmen having been flown to France), the presiding judge in the case, Manuel Pedregal, was shot to death on a street in the center of Madrid on 13 April. Three days later a first cousin of José Antonio was one of six people killed and thirty-two wounded in a running battle in the streets of the capital after leftists opened fire on Falangists and others escorting the bier of a Civil Guard killed by leftists.[12] After a Falangist was killed by Socialists in Carrión de los Condes (Palencia) at the beginning of May, a special Falangist commando squad dragged the president and several other members from the local Casa del Pueblo and lynched them on a public street. On 8 May the leftist army captain Carlos

Faraudo, a weekend instructor of the Socialist militia, was shot down in Madrid. As nearly as Falangists were able to calculate later, approximately forty of their members were slain by the left in a ninety-day period;[13] the number killed by Falangists was probably greater. By 1 June the party's death toll since its founding had reached at least seventy,[14] and altogether there were nearly three hundred political killings in Spain as a whole between February and mid-July.[15] The left blamed all this on the Falange, when in fact there were numerous participants, with the Socialists playing a leading role. There is no question, however, that the now-clandestine Falange had become a lethal and murderous organization, more purely oriented toward violence at this point than any other in Spain. The most vehement denunciation of the fascist movement stemmed not from the Socialists but from the Communists, whose organ *Mundo Obrero* had begun on 13 March to call for the "complete elimination" of the Falange and of the "señorito sangriento" (bloody señorito), José Antonio Primo de Rivera.

On 16 March the "señorito sangriento" and most of the other Falangist prisoners in Madrid had been moved to the Cárcel Modelo, the country's most modern penal institution. There the members of the Junta Política were assigned to the comfortable quarters reserved for political prisoners, José Antonio occupying the same cell inhabited only a short time before by Largo Caballero. The "Modelo" was indeed an exemplary institution in which the prisoners enjoyed every reasonable consideration, including an hour almost every day for receiving visitors, the ability to have special food brought in, and extensive recreation facilities. José Antonio was active in soccer. The measures taken against the Falange awakened strong sympathy for the Falangists throughout the right and even in some sectors of the center. Visitors appeared literally by the hundreds, and money was no longer a problem, as sizable amounts became available to encourage violent reaction against the left.[16]

This made it possible for José Antonio to maintain to some degree the direction of the clandestine movement, using numerous messengers, many of whom were female visitors. For party administration he relied at first on Mariano García, the administrative secretary in the office of the secretary general (who had not been arrested, in one of the typical contradictions of government policy). Soon, however, he turned to his very able and energetic brother Fernando. The youngest Primo de Rivera had resigned his army officer's commission sometime earlier and had entered medical school, where he had compiled an outstanding record and had become an assistant to Spain's most famous physician, Gregorio Marañón. Now, for the first time, he associated himself with the Falange as his brother's chief lieutenant. (The acting secretary general was now the SEU leader Alejandro Salazar, who temporarily avoided arrest.) Fernando soon found that so many japistas were entering the Falange that the JAP's chieftain, Pérez Laborda, came to discuss a formal collaboration between the two groups. He was sent to the Modelo to discuss the matter with José Antonio and Fernández Cuesta, who rejected any compromise, insisting that the japistas must simply continue their transfer en masse into the ranks of the Falange.[17]

On 20 March a secret circular was dispatched to all territorial and provincial leaders, calling for the reorganization of the party as a clandestine organization on the basis of a communist-type cell structure of three members per cell. The Primera Línea was to be reorganized for active combat, with its ranks broadened by incorporation of all SEU members, and measures were to be taken to obtain "arms and means of transport."[18] Though the Italian subsidy could not be received after January, the new contributions guaranteed that there would be no serious shortage of funds. By the time the Civil War began, however, approximately two thousand party members were in prison, so that the maintenance of the party's administrative system became increasingly difficult.

When Azaña was replaced as prime minister in mid-May by his personal crony, the consumptive and highly emotional Casares Quiroga, the latter officially declared that the government was "belligerent against fascism." Had he specified the Falange alone, that might have been justifiable, but Casares well knew that the rhetoric of his Popular Front allies extended the term to anything right of center. He thus announced a policy of hopeless sectarianism, in which civil rights would increasingly become a dead letter.

At this point the Falange regained its voice, as José Antonio was able to edit from prison a four-page clandestine paper entitled *¡No Importa!* (*It Doesn't Matter*). The first of three short numbers was published on 20 May. Ruiz de Alda contributed an article on his favorite theme, "The Justification of Violence," which declared that Spain was already living in a state of civil war. He received hundreds of telegrams of congratulation addressed to the Modelo, mainly from enthusiastic rightists.[19] In even more sinister fashion, *¡No Importa!* published "blacklists" of enemies of the Falange, in such circumstances an incitement to their murder. Even so, José Antonio still occasionally acted to moderate his subordinates, vetoing from his prison cell a new plan to assassinate Largo Caballero.

The government meanwhile drew its coils tighter around the Falangist leader, together with many of his associates. The first of a series of formal prosecutions had taken place before a special court in the Modelo on 21 March. This accused him of a "crime against the press law," because of a clandestine "Manifesto" dated 14 March (written the evening of the day of his arrest) "from the dungeons of the Dirección General de Seguridad" and distributed in published form on 16 March. The Tribunal sentenced him to the penalty of two months and a day requested by the prosecution, but this was immediately appealed, and on 19 May the Second Chamber of the Tribunal Supremo reversed the verdict, absolving José Antonio of the charge.[20]

The second prosecution, held in the same venue, took place on 28 March. This stemmed from José Antonio's private joke in the DGS about its director, Mallol, now used to fuel a charge of "insults and lack of respect for authority." As in the preceding case, José Antonio acted as his own defense attorney and, without accepting the validity of the accusation, labored with considerable erudition and wit to cite a variety of honorable uses of the term "horns" in history. Once more he received a sentence of two months and a day, and once more the case was appealed, eventually drawing a second acquittal from the Tribunal Supremo.[21]

On 30 April José Antonio and other members of the Junta Política were tried before the Tribunal de Urgencia on the more serious charge of directing an "illegal association." The prosecutor did not challenge the legality of the party's original statutes, but indicted Points 2, 3, 4, and 26 of the Twenty-Seven Points as aimed at subversion of the constitutional order. José Antonio maintained that the Points were merely a "political sheet," not the official program of the party, which was untrue, but of course similar charges might have been brought against many other extremist organizations in Spain. This time the court was not convinced by the indictment and acquitted the accused, an absolution that, after appeal by the prosecution, was upheld by the Tribunal Supremo on 8 June.[22]

This verdict was a severe blow to the government's policy of suppression of the Falange, though José Antonio had to remain imprisoned because of the two earlier verdicts, pending their final dismissal by the Tribunal Supremo. To prevent his imminent release, the authorities quickly introduced that same day (30 April) a new indictment, this time for "illegal possession of firearms." Three days earlier the police had conducted a thorough search of José Antonio's home, allegedly finding three loaded pistols in a bookcase. As the object of three earlier assassination attempts, the Falangist chief had long possessed a license to own weapons, but on 10 March the new government had abruptly canceled all existing permits, allowing a grace period of fifteen days for their renewal. José Antonio had been arrested four days later, and had little time to renew his permits.

The distortion of procedures that was becoming increasingly common in Republican judicial and police administration then followed. Strong pressure was exerted on the president of the Territorial Court of Madrid, who on 22 May transferred this indictment to a different section of the

Provincial Court that was presumed to be more hostile to the defendant. The court heard the case on 28 May and sentenced José Antonio to another five months imprisonment. Appearing in formal judicial toga as his own defense counsel, José Antonio flew into a towering rage and shouted abuse at the judges while he dramatically tore part of his toga and threw his lawyer's cap on the floor, stamping on it and refusing to sign the judicial record. When the court secretary observed, "A ruffian like his father," or words to that effect, José Antonio struck him on the head and threw him to the ground. When the secretary recovered, he threw an inkpot at his adversary, opening a cut on his forehead. During the course of this scene, part of the audience joined the uproar, and nine of the spectators (eight of them women) were briefly arrested. The outburst then led to two further indictments, one for "contempt of court" and another for an "offense against authority." The verdict of the court was meanwhile appealed, and the Tribunal Supremo eventually scheduled a hearing on the case for 23 July. José Antonio soon came to regret the spectacle he had created and obtained the agreement of the president of the Bar Association, the veteran liberal Melquiades Alvarez, to represent him as defense attorney on the resulting charges.[23]

The government clearly had no intention of releasing José Antonio, for whom the lack of parliamentary immunity now constituted the gravest of handicaps. The Electoral Commission of the new Cortes, while arbitrarily reassigning a number of rightist seats to the left in March, had been unable to reach a decision on the results in Cuenca and Granada, where grave irregularities had allegedly occurred, and it was eventually decided that new elections would be held in both provinces in May. Cuenca was a relatively conservative area that had voted decisively for the right in 1933, so that Ramon Serrano Súñer, Antonio Goicoechea, and other friends now arranged with the CEDA to include José Antonio's name on the rightist list for the new elections. If they were fairly conducted, he would have every hope of triumphing. Serrano Súñer also arranged to include his brother-in-law, General Franco, as an "independent rightist" on the list. The goal was to present a powerful rightist slate of candidates; Franco was one of the most respected figures in the military and was also interested in the advantages of parliamentary membership, as he remained hesitantly and skeptically just inside the boundary of the military conspiracy that was now developing. José Antonio, however, strongly objected to Franco's inclusion, arguing that such an electoral list would constitute too grave a provocation to the left and that, even if Franco won, he might be seriously embarrassed in the parliament, where experience, quick wit, and verbal eloquence were at a premium. By the same token, such a candidacy might reduce José Antonio's own chances for the electoral victory that he so desperately needed: he was not entirely unaware that this might be a question of life or death. Serrano Súñer, sent to reason with his brother-in-law at the latter's new military command in Tenerife, obtained his somewhat reluctant agreement to withdraw.[24]

In the meantime, though it became a foregone conclusion that Azaña would be chosen as the new president of the Republic following the left's deposition of the centrist liberal Alcalá Zamora, the rightist daily *Ya* conducted its own poll among its readers. José Antonio was the hands-down favorite, with 38,496 votes, followed by Calvo Sotelo and Gil Robles with more than 29,000 votes each. There was little doubt that the Falangist leader personally, and the Falange generally, were becoming "fashionable" in rightist circles. In various parts of the country young ladies from respectable conservative families were now wearing Falangist emblems on their dresses.[25]

The government decreed that no changes could be made in the list of candidates for the new elections, making José Antonio, who had of course not appeared on the original rightist list in February, ipso facto ineligible for the special election, even though that would be irrelevant in view of the way the elections were conducted. The rightist leadership announced Franco's withdrawal but insisted on maintaining José Antonio's candidacy, an indication both of his growing prestige in rightist circles and of the increasing obstinacy of both right and left in their political behavior.

The campaign in Cuenca was notable for a speech by Indalecio Prieto warning the left that it needed to moderate its tactics to avoid a catastrophe, but the left, including Prieto's own Socialist followers, were determined to dominate the elections totally. A considerable number of the Socialist militia group known as "La Motorizada" were officially given deputy police status as "governmental delegates." The local CEDA center and several other rightist offices, together with at least one church, were burned on 1 and 2 May. The deputized delegates arrived on the evening of the first and for the next four days ruled with an iron hand, making campaigning difficult for the right. As Prieto himself later wrote: "When I reached the theater, nearby there were smoking ashes from the bonfire made from the furnishings of a rightist club assaulted by the masses. In a hotel near the center of town important monarchists had been under siege since the night before. The atmosphere was frenzied."[26] Several companies of Assault Guards had been assigned to patrol the province, and the Republican government ordered the preventive arrest of scores of rightists, so many that special jails had to be created to contain them until the balloting was over. A sweeping victory for the Popular Front was recorded amid armed coercion and blatant electoral fraud. Supporters claimed that

José Antonio's name led the rightist list, if not both lists, in the vote totals, though the evidence remaining does not support the latter conclusion,[27] and the issue became moot because the government simply ordered that all his votes be thrown out. In a subsequent parliamentary debate of 1 June, rightist deputies denounced the fraud and coercion that had characterized the Cuenca elections. Serrano Súñer presented a complicated set of figures to try to demonstrate that José Antonio deserved a seat, and even introduced a motion to exchange the seat of one CEDA deputy for the Falangist chieftain, but all this was rejected.[28]

Luis Romero has provided the best commentary:

> The May elections in Cuenca were an episode that can be properly described as shameful, in which Prieto played a leading role, taking much of the responsibility. Every kind of outrage and abuse was committed, with extreme coercion and bold-faced illegalities. The civil governor, the electoral board, and, as a fitting climax, the young men of the "Motorizada," pistols in hand, won those elections ignominiously. Primo de Rivera was deprived of a seat that he had won in popular votes, after the governor announced that his votes simply would not be counted, as occurred in various districts, and that announcement by the leading authority in the province intimidated others.[29]

Though José Antonio failed to win the election, in one sense he had philosophically and politically won the broader contest. Free elections are the lifeblood of a democracy, but the Cuenca elections were no freer than the Nazi elections of March 1933 in Germany, and they provided further indication that democratic practice and civil rights would not obtain under the Popular Front in Spain. They further illustrated the point made by Ledesma in the preceding year that in Spain "fascist practice" was in fact followed by the theoretically antifascist left. For some time José Antonio had preached that democracy was ultimately fraudulent; in Cuenca, at least, the Popular Front had proven him correct.

Despite the role of Prieto's followers in the electoral coercion, José Antonio was impressed, as usual, by the moderation of the Socialist leader's public remarks and his appeals to Spanish patriotism and national well-being. In a clandestine publication of 23 May, José Antonio entitled an article "Prieto Draws Near the Falange," claiming that despite the official suppression of the movement, Falangist nationalism now in one way or another was influencing a large audience:

> First, defeated; then, persecuted; finally, according to what they say, dissolved. We are nothing and have no importance. . . . But since they said we ceased to exist there is not a single aspect of Spanish life

that is not tinged with our presence. I am not talking any more about fascism and antifascism. I am talking, specifically, about the ideas and vocabulary of the Falange. . . .

. . . In this moment, there is not a single Spanish politician who has not adopted, more or less explicitly, certain points from our vocabulary.[30]

José Antonio was presumably referring to the increasing calls for greater concern about the unity and economic health of the nation, but he would also have been correct in referring to rhetorical appeals to fascist arguments by the extreme and even the moderate right. "Gaziel," the respected conservative editor of *La Vanguardia*, would write on 12 June:

How many votes did the fascists have in Spain in the last election? Nothing: a ridiculously small amount. . . . Today, on the other hand, travelers returning from different parts of Spain are saying: "There everybody is becoming a fascist." What kind of change is this? What has happened? What has happened is simply that it is no longer possible to live, that there is no government. . . . In such a situation, people instinctively look for a way out. . . . What is the new political form that radically represses all these insufferable excesses? A dictatorship, fascism. And thus almost without wanting to, almost without realizing it, people begin *to feel themselves* fascist. They know nothing about all the inconveniences of a dictatorship, which is natural. They will learn about those later on, when they have to suffer them.

. . . Fascism is, in the cases of France and Spain, the sinister shadow projected across the land by democracy itself, when its internal decomposition turns into anarchy. The more the rot spreads, the more fascism expands. And therefore the deluded concern that the triumphant Popular Front shows about a defeated fascism is nothing more than the fear of its own shadow.

Ever since the arrest of the leadership and the suppression of the party in mid-March, the goal of the Falange was an armed revolt to overthrow the Republic, but it had no greater means at its disposal than in the preceding year, when several successive plans had to be rejected. The ideal project was not merely to overthrow the Republic but to replace it with a Falangist regime, yet the potential for accomplishing this through the efforts of the party alone ranged from extremely limited to nonexistent. Thus on 19 March a message had been transmitted to the air attaché of the Italian embassy, with whom José Antonio maintained friendly relations, asking help in arranging an interview for his brother Miguel with Mussolini himself in Rome, "to explain a plan with regard to the internal Spanish situation"[31]—presumably to request Italian support for a Falangist insurrection. This request was rejected, however; the Italian ambassador had a low opinion of the Falange's prospects and was reluctant to encourage any Italian interference in Spanish internal affairs.

After another month, it became even clearer than in 1935 that Falangist hopes for revolt would have to rely to a large extent on the military, and by the end of April José Antonio had come to accept this conclusion.[32] A clandestine circular by José Antonio entitled "Letter to the Military of Spain," dated 4 May, was widely distributed among the military. It made no effort to convert them to the specific doctrines and goals of Falangism, but sought simply to galvanize their interest in an armed revolt to "save Spain." The "Letter" insisted that the present revolutionary plans that threatened the country "come from outside, from Moscow," and promoted "an unlimited right of self-determination" of the regions of Spain "that even permits them to declare independence." The revolutionaries sought to "foment the collective prostitution of young women workers," which "undermines the family," in the interests of "free love." Only the military had the means to rescue the patria: "At the last moment, Spengler has said, it has always been a platoon of soldiers that has saved civilization."[33] Whereas in the preceding year José Antonio had sought a certain amount of military assistance for a Falangist insurrection, by May 1935 he had come to accept the fact that the Falange must encourage and assist a military revolt per se, though still attempting to exercise some degree of political influence over it, even if very limited.

José Antonio began to realize that, given the endless series of indictments and prosecutions to which he was being subjected, he very likely would not be able to leave his jail cell until freed by an armed revolt, and that would require extensive contacts with a variety of rightist organizations, as well. Thus on 20 May he wrote to his longtime friend Goicoechea—who had no seat in parliament and had lost active leadership of the monarchists to Calvo Sotelo—to ask him to "assume my representation" in dealing with other rightist sectors.[34]

For some time the Falange had maintained a small "Servicio EE" (Army Service) for political contacts with the military. This kept up liaison with sectors of the UME and with Lt. Col. Juan Yagüe of the Legión in Morocco, one of the very few relatively senior officers who were members of the party and the person recommended by Franco for political contact. There were several different strands to the conspiracy developed by sectors of the military during March and April, but what nearly all of them had in common was the resolve that an armed revolt would be led initially by the army alone, without compromise with political groups. They first began to come together at the close of April when Gen. Emilio Mola, commander of the Pamplona garrison, was recognized as overall coordinator. A month or so passed before José Antonio learned of this, and on 19 May he sent one of his clerks, Rafael Garcerán, to establish contact with Mola in Pamplona and offer 4,000 Falangist militiamen to assist the rebellion.[35] Though there is no indication of any clear political agreement with Mola at that time, preliminary instructions concerning the manner in which the party's Primera Línea would take part in the rebellion were issued the following day.

José Antonio's most direct invocation of civil war would appear in the next number of ¡No importa! dated 6 June:

> THERE ARE NO LONGER ANY PEACEFUL SOLUTIONS. War has been declared and the government has been the first to proclaim itself belligerent. . . . The government does not waste its time swatting flies; it rushes to destroy anything that might constitute a defense of Spanish civilization and the historic permanence of the Patria: the Army, the Navy, the Civil Guard . . . and the Falange.
> Then let there be this war, this violence, in which we not only defend the existence of the Falange, . . . but the existence of Spain itself . . . ! Continue fighting, comrades, alone or together. . . . Tomorrow, when brighter days dawn, the Falange will wear the fresh laurels of primacy in this holy crusade of violence.

This dithyramb to violence was one of the last of José Antonio's political writings to be published during his lifetime.

On the night of 5–6 June, José Antonio and his brother Miguel, who had also been incarcerated in the Modelo, were abruptly transferred to the provincial prison of Alicante, only hours after José Antonio's most recent appearance before the Tribunal Supremo. (The latter's final decree three days later that the Falange was a legal organization had no effect on government or police policy.) It was a somewhat irregular procedure, since only a few days earlier José Antonio had been indicted by the Provincial Court of Madrid on two new charges stemming from the courtroom incident on 28 May, and he would later be scheduled to return to the capital at the end of July for the hearing on these charges. José Antonio screamed that he was being taken away to be murdered, and the other Falangist prisoners made a great row, while he shouted at the Modelo's director that his "squads" of Falangists would eventually come to hang the latter in the courtyard of his own prison.[36] The transfer was then accomplished without further incident.

The Alicante prison contained no special section for political prisoners, but for two months the Primo de Rivera brothers received special treatment. The director showed genuine personal regard for them and allowed one of the other young Falangists being held in his institution to serve the brothers as a personal orderly.[37] During his first six weeks in Alicante, prior to the outbreak of the Civil War, more than 1,500 individual requests were made to visit José Antonio,[38] who also received hundreds of letters, as well as packages, that were apparently not opened by the authorities. After it became evident that he was passing political messages and even sending out articles for the clandestine Falangist press, tighter security was instituted on 2 July, and henceforth visitors who did not enjoy parliamentary immunity were carefully frisked. The Alicante prison director would later be arrested and prosecuted for his leniency toward the brothers, though he was eventually absolved.

On 16 June José Antonio responded to a questionnaire from a journalist that the Falange now had 150,000 members, of whom at least 48 had been killed and 500 wounded in the political violence since the elections.[39] In fact, no one really knew what the current membership was, but the party continued to grow rapidly and even underground had several times as many members as in February. José Antonio probably had sufficient sense of irony to appreciate the paradox of a movement's reaching prominence only at a time and in a situation in which it had lost normal freedom of action. The initiative lay more than ever with the right and with the military. Even though José Antonio knew that the latter were indispensable to any attempt to overthrow the Republic, he had few illusions about the character of a new military regime and was presumably aware of the fate of fascist movements under nonfascist right-authoritarian regimes in other Catholic countries such as Austria and Portugal.

Thus, even though his rage at his confinement was expressed through increasing efforts to encourage armed revolt, his fundamental ambivalence did not disappear in these final months. He apparently did not hide from himself the fact that an insurrection might fail, might produce instead a national disaster such as a long civil war or a triumphant leftist revolution. The only viable alternative would be for Azaña to come to his senses and replace the politically monocolor government of the disastrous Casares Quiroga with a "government of national concentration with full powers," which would stretch from the prietista Socialist left to the monarchist right. According to Serrano Súñer, he discussed this alternative during the latter's final visit,[40] and there seems to have been some discussion of the possibility that José Antonio's three closest friends and associates in the CEDA—Serrano Súñer, the conde de Mayalde, and Fermín Daza (all of them visitors to his cell in Alicante)—might withdraw from the CEDA and form a new Falangist minority in the Cortes.[41]

Whether the armed revolt took place or not, however, José Antonio was determined that the Falange retain its newly established primacy as the only major force of a modern revolutionary and authoritarian nationalism—that is, of a Spanish fascism. Thus in some ways he resented the emergence of the hard-line Calvo Sotelo as the principal spokesman for the right in the new Cortes and was particularly offended by Calvo's declaration in parliament on 16 June, which outlined the latter's version of an alternative political system and concluded: "Many call this kind of state a fascist state; well, if that is a fascist state, then I who share this idea of the state, I who believe in it, declare myself fascist."[42] Though for tactical reasons the Falangists had for some time denied that they themselves were fascist, they were gravely offended by the arrogation of this adjective by other groups, and were said to have published leaflets accusing the monarchists of "wanting to usurp the glory and triumph of those who have worked and suffered for it."[43]

José Antonio immediately lashed out in the final number of ¡No Importa! on 20 June with the announcement: "Look to the right. A warning to opportunists. The Falange is not a mercenary force." His article went on: "The opportunist will try to say: But I believe what the Falange believes! I too want a corporate and totalitarian state! I am not even reluctant to proclaim myself a 'fascist.' " He concluded that the "fascistized right" (as Ledesma would have put it) merely sought to exploit and dominate the Falange.

In an article possibly written by the monarchist army officer Jorge Vigón (later a minister of the Franco regime), the rightist newspaper La Epoca shot back with a description of the Falangist leader as "the essayist." It declared that

> the essayist . . . is not an achiever. . . . The task to which he devotes himself most assiduously is that of convincing those around him that this, or that neat expression reveals his fertile genius. At times—though not frequently—he even claims maternity of an idea.
>
> Maternity—we must underline—is not written here by mistake. The temperament of this kind of essayist is essentially feminine. He likes what is shiny, flashy, and new; his spiritual life is a tourney of coquetries, a career of intrigues, and an inferno of jealousies.[44]

Since he had little opportunity to respond publicly, José Antonio vented his spleen in a personal letter to the director of La Epoca, José Ignacio Escobar, marqués de las Marismas, a sometime personal friend, to whom he spat: "What pains you is your consciousness of your resentful inferiority: to you, personally, being ugly, foolish, useless, defeated a thousand times in amorous adventures, and, finally, son of a mother and father of whom you cannot be proud," but he apparently had enough discretion not to mail the letter.[45]

Equal cause for concern was the near inevitability, in the confused and desperate circumstances of that "tragic spring," that local Falangist leaders in various provinces would become involved in collaboration and co-conspiracy with local sectors of the military, the monarchists, or the Carlists.[46] José Antonio himself was rather more willing at this point to deal with the last of these, whose ideology he respected, than with the main sector of alfonsino monarchists, though there is no clear evidence of any general agreement with the Carlists.[47]

Worst of all was the growing fear that the military, who were the key to everything, would lack the courage or determination to rebel. José Antonio correctly prophesied that most of the senior generals holding active commands would not revolt, and he expected little from Franco, observing that "it is useless to count on the generals on active duty. They are chickens, and Franco is the biggest chicken of all."[48] This pessimism was shared by Fernando Primo de Rivera, responsible for much of what little coordination the Falange maintained. The Falangist chief in Burgos wrote of him:

> He did not think that the military would rebel; he had no faith in
> them. When I assured him about Burgos, he said to me: "All right,
> that may be for Burgos, Alava, and Logroño and some other place,
> but in general there is nothing that can be done with the military. In
> Madrid the situation is hopeless."[49]

With each passing day anxiety increased that local and provincial sectors of the party might be compromised in abortive plots by sectors of the right and the military that would not produce the decisive insurrection and the revolutionary new nationalist regime that José Antonio sought. On 24 June he dispatched a circular to party leaders throughout Spain:

> The plurality of machinations in favor of more or less confused
> subversive movements being developed in diverse provinces of Spain
> has come to the attention of the Jefe Nacional.
>     . . . Some, carried away by an excess of zeal or a dangerous
> ingenuity, have gone ahead to draw up plans for local action,
> compromising the participation of comrades in certain political
> schemes.
>     . . . The respect and consideration of the Falange for the Army
> have been proclaimed so repeatedly that they need no further
> elaboration. . . . But admiration and esteem for the Army as an
> essential organ of the Patria does not mean agreement with all the
> thoughts, words, and projects that every officer or group of officers
> may profess or present. The withdrawal from politics that the Army
> has imposed on itself has had the effect of placing the military,

generally, in a state of dialectical defenselessness in the face of charlatans and opportunists from the political parties. . . .

Hence the political projects of the military (except, naturally, those developed by a well-prepared minority that does exist in the Army) are usually not accompanied by accuracy. These projects almost always start from an initial error: the idea that the ills of Spain are due to simple problems of domestic order that can be solved by handing over power to those previously alluded to, charlatans lacking all historical consciousness, all authentic formation, and the necessary zeal for the Patria to return to the great paths of its destiny.

The participation of the Falange in one of those premature and simplistic projects would involve a grave responsibility and would bring *its total disappearance, even in the event of victory.* For this reason: nearly all those who count on the Falange for such enterprises merely consider it an auxiliary shock force, a sort of assault troop of youthful militiamen, destined on the morrow merely to parade before the arrogantly presumptuous who have installed themselves in power.

All comrades must realize how destructive it is for the Falange to be asked to participate as a mere auxiliary in a movement that will not lead to establishment of the national syndicalist state.[50]

He concluded by warning that any party leader, even of the highest rank, would be immediately expelled if he participated in any conspiracy without approval from the "central command." José Antonio required that all provincial and territorial chiefs notify him within five days of receipt of this circular that it had been received and its instructions fulfilled.

Four days later he wrote to his liberal friend Miguel Maura of his forebodings (Maura had recently proposed in the pages of *El Sol* a centrist "national republican dictatorship" to save the country from breakdown):

But you will see how the terrible lack of culture, or, worse yet, the mental laziness of our people (in all its strata) ends up either giving us an experience of cruel and filthy Bolshevism or a flatulent representation of shortsighted pseudo-patriotism by some puffed-up figure of the right. May God free us from the one and the other![51]

General Mola, who was a relatively moderate conservative, was not impressed by José Antonio's hard line, for he did not consider the Falange important or its fascist program that desirable for the future of Spain,[52] and he was not particularly impressed by its paramilitary potential.[53] Mola was rather more interested in the assistance of the Carlist Requetés, and the top Carlist leader in Navarre, the conde de Rodezno, was eager to support an army-led revolt. At this point Rodezno visited José Antonio in the Alicante prison to urge the Falangists to collaborate without making exclusive demands.[54] Almost simultaneously, a clandestine meeting of the remaining members of the new Junta Política met at José Antonio's request in Madrid and agreed by a clear majority that it would be preferable for the Falange to participate in Mola's military-led revolt.[55]

Whatever the immediate motivation was, José Antonio finally decided that there was no alternative to such a course. He dispatched a new circular on 29 June:[56]

> As a continuation to the circular of the twenty-fourth, instructions will now be given to the provincial and territorial chiefs concerning the conditions in which they can concert pacts for a possible rising against the present government.
>
> 1. Each provincial or territorial chief will deal *exclusively* with the superior commander of the military movement in his province or territory, and with no one else. . . .
>
> 2. The Falange will participate in the movement, forming its own units, with its own natural commanders and emblems.
>
> 3. If the provincial or territorial chief and that of the movement agree that it is indispensable, part of the forces of the Falange, which will never exceed one-third of the members of the Primera Línea, may be placed at the disposal of the military leaders to enter the units under their orders. The other two-thirds must scrupulously follow what was stipulated in the previous point.
>
> . . .
>
> 5. The military commander must promise his Falangist counterpart in the province or territory that civil government of the province or territory will not be handed to anyone for at least three days after the triumph of the movement, and that during that period the military authorities will retain the civil government.
>
> . . .
>
> 7. Unless renewed by a specific new order, the present instructions will become completely without effect on the tenth of July at twelve noon.

In his next "confidential report" to the military leaders of the conspiracy, Mola would then declare that with "the director of a certain combat force . . . intelligence is absolute,"[57] apparently referring to José Antonio and the Falange.

The deadline set in this last circular could not be observed, because on the sixth of July two Falangist provincial chiefs were arrested carrying copies of the document as well as other militia instructions, and Mola therefore postponed the date until the fourteenth. This also proved impossible, for Mola was still unable to reach agreement with the Carlists—whose national leader Fal Conde proved even harder to deal with than José Antonio—and Mola considered their paramilitary support almost indispensable for the revolt in the northern part of Spain.

The final catalytic acts of violence took place in Madrid, where on the evening of 2 July gunmen of the Juventud Socialista Unificada (United Communist–Socialist Youth) fired on a café frequented by Falangists, killing two Falangist students as well as two non-Falangists.[58] On the following day two corpses were discovered outside the city. One was that of the son of the owner of a popular amusement center, Circo Price, an eighteen-year-old student who was not a Falangist but a friend of Falangists. The other cadaver was that of a thirty-year-old retired army officer, either a member or a sympathizer of the Falange, who had been abducted and then stabbed 33 times.[59] On 4 July Falangists retaliated by killing two Socialists outside a Casa del Pueblo. During the next three days police arrested some 300 more Falangists and rightists in the province of Madrid alone, though as usual there is no indication of any Socialists arrested. By this time more than two thousand Falangists were in prison in Spain as a whole.[60]

The climax of violence occurred on the night of 12–13 July. A Socialist officer in the Assault Guards, José del Castillo, who had been active in recent police measures, was shot to death about 10 P.M. by gunmen who were either Falangists or Carlists. Members of the Assault Guards and other leftist militants demanded vengeance, inducing the minister of the interior to approve the arrest of a number of leading rightists, even though some of the latter enjoyed parliamentary immunity. One police squad was led by a Socialist Civil Guard captain, Fernando Condés, only recently reinstated after having been convicted of subversive activities during the revolutionary insurrection of 1934. Still in civilian clothes, he led a detachment of Assault Guards and Socialist activists, who increasingly were being included in regular police activities in further violation of the constitution. They arrested Calvo Sotelo; and as the rightist deputy was being driven away in an Assault Guard truck, he was shot in the back of the head Soviet-style and killed by one of the Socialist militiamen.[61]

This was a crime without precedent in the history of European parliamentary government, but by this time the Spanish Republic had to a considerable extent ceased to be a constitutional state. The killing of Calvo Sotelo was for Spain the equivalent of the Matteotti Affair in Italy twelve years earlier. The latter precipitated the onset of the full Fascist dictatorship; the former precipitated the beginning of the Civil War. That Matteotti was slain by Fascists and Calvo Sotelo by a Socialist underscored the difference in a principal source of violence in the two systems. This grave act decided many of the undecided, not least "Miss Canary Islands," as General Franco was sarcastically known among some of the military conspirators because of his reluctant coquetry about committing himself to the revolt. Franco now apparently concluded that it was more dangerous not to be involved than to be fully involved. During the next three days final obstacles to the participation of the Carlists and other rightist groups were also overcome.

José Antonio had already had to extend the deadline of 10 July that he had earlier set for participation in the revolt, and on that date he received a visit from his brother Fernando. On the following day in Madrid, the latter told Manuel Hedilla, a new national inspector of the party who was helping Fernando to coordinate Falangist participation, that the rebellion would take place very soon, probably between the fifteenth and the twentieth.[62]

On 12 July José Antonio wrote to Giménez Caballero that he had been able to use his four months in prison to develop strong connections with the most patriotic forces in Spain, "to the point that without the Falange nothing can be done at the present time." He denounced as inadequate any "national republican dictatorship," as advocated by moderate liberals such as Miguel Maura and Felipe Sánchez Román, but added that "another danger that I fear is the implantation through violence of a false conservative fascism, without revolutionary valor or young blood."[63] In fact, the "false conservative fascism" would largely be what Spain would get, and there is no indication that Mola ever promised anything more than complete freedom for Falangist organization and propaganda. He was in fact so skeptical about the extent or value of Falangist paramilitary assistance[64] that he did not decide to give the final orders until arduous, last-minute negotiations finally achieved an agreement of sorts with the Carlists.[65]

News of Calvo Sotelo's murder had the same effect on José Antonio that it did on many others. That same day (13 July) Fernando Primo de Rivera was arrested in Madrid. Early on the fourteenth José Antonio was visited in Alicante by his old friend (and CEDA deputy) José Finat, conde de Mayalde, who, thanks to his parliamentary immunity, was able to smuggle in two pistols and was then dispatched posthaste to Pamplona to tell Mola that the revolt could not be delayed. The Falangist chief declared that, if Mola refused, he himself would initiate the insurrection with the Falangists in Alicante.[66]

By the time Finat arrived in Pamplona on the fifteenth, Mola had reached the same conclusion, and his own emissary may have reached José Antonio later that same day with word that the revolt would begin in Morocco and the southern garrisons on the eighteenth. By 15 July José Antonio had already prepared his Manifesto for the insurrection. It did not once use the word "Falange" but emphasized broad national goals, assuring readers that these were not a matter of "replacing one party with another" and that "our triumph will not be that of a reactionary group nor mean for the people the loss of any advantage"; rather, it would elevate the life of the entire nation.[67]

This was a desperate undertaking, without the slightest guarantee as to either the military or the political outcome. With the army divided, only about half the military units effectively joined the revolt, which in fact began in Morocco on the afternoon of 17 July and slowly spread to peninsular garrisons during the next three days. Most of the navy and air force could not be brought into the rebellion, which was, however, supported by about half the Civil Guards and Assault Guards. It was initially successful only in the Moroccan protectorate, the Canaries, and about one-third of peninsular Spain (mainly in the north, though with several Andalusian bridgeheads around Cádiz, Córdoba, Granada, and Seville). To make matters worse for the rebels, most military equipment and munitions remained in the larger depots in or near the big cities, mostly in the power of the left.

Like the leftist insurrection of 1934, the rightist revolt of 1936 was a preventive blow, aimed at seizing power before the main enemy could take over the government. In this case, the main enemy was the revolutionary left, and the preemptive revolt had the paradoxical consequence of precipitating the very revolutionary takeover it was designed to avoid. In one respect, however, the triggering of revolution in what would henceforth be called the Republican zone was—in the second paradox—of great immediate advantage to the rebels, for two reasons. First, the outbreak of the revolution in the Republican zone temporarily eliminated most of the remaining authority of both the Republican government and any form of central military organization; second, the revolution, with its disorder, seizures of property, and mass killings, had the political and psychological effect of driving some millions of moderates into the political camp of the rebels.

Even so, the military resources of the rebels were at first so limited that within a week both Mola, commanding the insurgent forces in the north, and Franco, head of the Army of Africa in the Protectorate, dispatched representatives to Rome and Berlin asking for limited assistance, particularly munitions and planes. By 26 July Hitler and Mussolini, independently of each other, had agreed to send arms to the rebels. This support slowly increased, responding by November to a Soviet escalation of support for the Republicans with a counterescalation, until it reached major proportions, thus identifying the rebel movement increasingly in the minds of many abroad with Fascism and Nazism. It is important to note, however, that neither Italy nor Germany had anything significant to do with the background and initial development of the revolt, and that direct support came in response to urgent requests only after the fighting had begun.[68]

To lead the insurgent movement, Mola set up a Junta de Defensa Nacional in Burgos on 23 July. Pursuant to his original plan, this was composed only of senior army commanders. No political party was represented, though all the rightist groups, as well as small sectors of the Radical and Basque Nationalist parties, supported the rebels.

As soon as the fighting began, the Falange was decapitated politically. José Antonio, Ruiz de Alda, and many other leaders were in Republican prisons and would soon be executed, while Onésimo Redondo was killed in a skirmish with Republican militiamen on 24 July. While leadership failed, the rapid rise in membership that had been going on for four or five months only accelerated in the new Nationalist zone. The militant program of the Falange, based on extreme nationalism, violent antileftism, and direct action, seemed the natural political counterpart of civil war—a political ideology, like that of the revolutionary left, founded on civil war and mobilized for military struggle. Falangist cadres imprisoned in jails within insurgent territory were immediately freed, but even so the old cadres were in danger of being swamped by the influx of new members. It was reported that two thousand volunteers presented themselves for service in the party and its militia within the first twenty-four hours of recruiting in Zaragoza.[69]

It was not only the radicalism but also the novelty of the Falange that seemed attractive. There was little or no time for indoctrination; most new members knew only that the Falange was patriotic and stood for something "new" or "social."[70] By 11 September a German diplomat reported that "one has the impression that the members of the Falangist militia have no real aims and ideas; rather they seem to be young people for whom mainly it is good sport to round up Communists and Socialists."[71]

Mercedes Fórmica, one of the early leaders of the Falange's Sección Femenina, has written:

> In the weeks between the eighteenth of July and the end of August,
> Falange opened wide its arms and gates, in a gesture poorly
> understood and worse utilized. The absence of the best leaders and
> the lack of political sense of others permitted the party of José
> Antonio to be infiltrated by all sorts of people looking for shelter:
> "those who had never joined anything," those who had never risked
> their skin, throwing the rock but hiding their hand, those who had
> much to hide, the saboteurs, even those of opposing ideas. This mass
> corrupted the essence of the Falange, and the few remaining idealists
> were overwhelmed.[72]

Some of the top surviving Falangist leaders in the northern provinces met on 1 August in Valladolid and ratified the authority of Agustín Aznar as the jefe nacional of militia. At the end of the month (29–30 August), Aznar and Andrés Redondo, brother of the slain Onésimo and now de facto territorial chief for much of León and Old Castile, traveled to Seville to meet the surviving southern leaders.[73] This in turn led to a major meeting of all remaining leaders of the rank of provincial chief or higher that convened in Valladolid on 2 September. Remnants of the original Madrid leadership, headed by Aznar, still wanted to maintain the pro forma leadership of José Antonio, even though he remained imprisoned far behind Republican lines. Other jefes feared that powerful regional leaders, such as Andrés Redondo in Valladolid or Joaquín Miranda in Seville, might usurp power. It was therefore agreed to create an interim Junta de Mando (Command Council) under Manuel Hedilla, the former provincial chief of Santander who had served as national inspector for the northern provinces, rallying the clandestine party during the spring and early summer. Hedilla would not be acting Jefe Nacional but simply jefe de la Junta de Mando, which was to include Aznar, Redondo, José Moreno (provincial chief of Navarre), Jesús Muro (national councillor and provincial chief of Zaragoza), and José Sainz (national councillor and provincial chief of Toledo—the latter province still held by the Republicans).[74] This would provide interim leadership to try to reconstruct the party amid the chaos of civil war until—they hoped—José Antonio could be liberated.

# Seven

# The Death of José Antonio

During the final weeks before the outbreak of Civil War, several plans were conceived to enable José Antonio to escape from prison. What the variants had in common was reliance for the initial passage to freedom on the complicity of some of the prison personnel—a possibility that apparently continued to exist. Thus at the beginning of July, Falangist leaders in Mallorca tried to develop a scheme that would permit José Antonio to flee from Alicante harbor in a boat, though this proved too complicated,[1] while the party chieftains in Barcelona looked into the possibility of arranging for his old nemesis, the monarchist aviator Ansaldo, to fly him to safety. In Alicante, local Falangists and their allies proposed to make use of an official troop truck of the Assault Guards, though that plan is said to have been vetoed by José Antonio himself, who may have wanted to avoid having to flee and hide himself before the revolt began, which would temporarily sever his main political contacts and communications.[2]

What seems to have been the most serious plan was developed in the final days before the cataclysm by José Antonio's good friend, the conde de Mayalde, and his brother Fernando. As usual, it counted on the complicity of prison officials, who are said to have even provided duplicate keys for the main door. Arrangements would be made for an airplane— according to some versions a seaplane from a nearby naval base (since the prison was very near the coast)—to fly the Falangist chief to safety.[3] Miguel Primo de Rivera has characterized this scheme as "perhaps the only sensible one of all that we planned."[4] It may have been designed to coincide approximately with the outbreak of the revolt and was more acceptable to José Antonio because it would enable him to fly immediately to the headquarters of the insurgent movement. Fernando, however, was arrested on 13 July, and the pace of events quickened. According to Miguel Primo de Rivera, José Antonio subsequently dispatched a message through his sister Carmen and Margarita Larios (the wife of Miguel), who together with Tía "Ma" had earlier taken up residence in Alicante,

209

to Lt. Santiago Pascual, a Falangist officer who was the main contact in the local garrison. This requested Pascual to arrange for the regular military prison guard to be composed as much as possible of Falangist or pro-Falangist troops.[5] A final variant of the plan would supposedly have had José Antonio taken to a boat in the harbor by sympathetic police and military personnel.[6] According to Miguel, however, a message was received on 17 July from Major Barba Hernández, the UME chief in Valencia, asking José Antonio to make no premature attempt to escape, for the garrisons in Valencia and Alicante would join the revolt and then free him immediately.[7] Thus the Falangist chief received his final visits from couriers on 16–17 July, and a prison official later testified that José Antonio was observed on those days organizing his papers and suitcases, as though he expected soon to be leaving.[8]

As it turned out, the military conspirators in Valencia were overconfident and proved comparatively weak both there and in Alicante, being unable to bring either garrison out in revolt. Early on the morning of 19 July, two crowded truckloads of members of the Falangist Primera Línea in the province approached the city of Alicante, hoping to join forces with the rebel military. One of the trucks broke down from mechanical difficulties; the second, hiding outside the town, was discovered and virtually surrounded by a large detachment of Assault Guards loyal to the government. In the firefight that followed, three Falangists were killed and fifty-two captured.[9] Though José Antonio had been told the night before that orders had reached the prison to hold him incommunicado, one last messenger was permitted to speak with him later on the nineteenth. Told that the local garrison was not rebelling because its commander, Gen. José García Aldave, insisted on awaiting instructions from divisional authorities in Valencia, an enraged José Antonio replied: "Well, if he continues to resist and you don't shoot him, we are lost."[10] He was later heard to shout within the prison "Aldave has reneged!" The rebellion had failed in most of the eastern half of Spain, and there would be no liberation of José Antonio. To make matters worse, on the seventeenth he had sent the close relatives who were staying near the brothers in Alicante to carry a message to the Falangists in Alcoy. Returning later that weekend, they were stopped by one of the new roadblocks of leftist militiamen and placed under arrest. All three—Carmen Primo de Rivera, Margarita Larios, and Tía "Ma"—were later moved to the Adult Reformatory on 1 August.

Though the Primo de Rivera brothers were now placed together in the same cell, they continued to enjoy relatively privileged treatment for two more weeks and were even allowed to receive further correspondence, though no visitors. On 2 August some of the common prisoners rioted against the "fascist" brothers and the special conditions they had enjoyed, and their contact with the outside world was further reduced. On 16 August, a search of the cell revealed the two pistols that Mayalde had smuggled in, as well as the map of Spain on which the brothers charted the advance of the insurgent forces. From that point they were separated once more and were now held completely incommunicado.

A worse fate was befalling thousands of Falangists throughout the Republican zone. Some two thousand or more veterans of the party, as well as many of the new affiliates of the spring of 1936, were executed in the mass slaughters that took place during the first six months of the Civil War. According to one account, fifty of the fifty-two Falangists captured outside Alicante on 19 July were executed as a group on 12 September.[11] Altogether, more than three hundred Falangists were executed in the province during the Civil War,[12] so that it was not surprising when a rumor developed that, under the pretext of moving José Antonio to a different prison, the authorities would apply to him the "ley de fugas" (supposedly, "shot while resisting arrest"). In fact, Alicante prison was not subject to invasions by revolutionary mobs and mass "sacas" (cleanouts) as some other Republican jails were, and for the moment José Antonio was in little danger. Some of the more moderate Republican leaders, such as Azaña, Prieto, and the new prime minister, José Giral, apparently made inquiries concerning his personal safety.

The conspirators had planned to seize full power within a week or two, and we have no documentation whatever on José Antonio's first reactions to what became a full-scale civil war. Failure of the initial rebellion in so much of Spain must have shocked and depressed him, while the growth of such an extensive conflict must also have been a surprise and possibly an increasingly tormenting problem. Julio Gil Pecharromán has provided the fairest commentary:

> The consequences of his acts—and of those of many other thousands—had not brought a swift and bloodless pronunciamiento, like the one led by his father, or a distant and triumphal war, like the invasion of Ethiopia that he had on occasion praised. This conflict was devastating the soil of his own country, and, whoever might be the victor, he began to see more and more clearly that it would not result in the national syndicalist state preached by the Falange, but would leave the nation divided and reduced to ruins.
>
> It was not a matter of *repentance*, and even less of abandoning his firmest convictions. But there are numerous indications that, once he had confirmed the disastrous effects of the war, he tried to contribute to a swift resolution.[13]

José Antonio was allowed to receive letters from such major figures as Santiago Alba and Miguel Maura, both by this time in Paris, asking him to consider some effort to mediate in the conflict. Therefore on 9 August he wrote to Diego Martínez Barrio, president of the Cortes and since 22 July the president delegate of the new Delegated Council for the Government of the Levant (a new ad hoc administration for the entire central part of the eastern coast, including Alicante). Martínez Barrio was generally recognized as the most moderate of the major middle-class Republican leaders within the Popular Front (and had also become Azaña's prime minister–designate on the night of 18–19 July in a belated and failed attempt to form a compromise moderate government that could avoid civil war). José Antonio's missive read:

> After careful deliberation with my conscience and with concern for the Spain of all of us, so gravely threatened in the present days, I have decided to seek an audience with you. This would not be difficult to arrange: I could be moved some night to the civil government, as though I were to be interrogated by the governor and there be received by yourself without anyone else learning of it. The audience might be helpful and in no case prejudicial. At any rate, it will be up to you to decide; I have done my duty by writing these lines.[14]

Martínez Barrio has declared that he immediately took the matter to Prime Minister Giral and that the government decided that the interview should be conducted instead by the secretary of the Delegated Council, Leandro Martín Echevarría. The latter met with José Antonio a few days later, at which time the Falangist leader asked to be temporarily freed under his "word of honor" to proceed immediately by airplane to the rebel zone to negotiate an end to hostilities, leaving as hostages his brother Miguel and the latter's wife, as well as his aunt and foster-mother, all of whom were now imprisoned in Alicante.[15]

In connection with this initiative and a subsequent letter to Echevarría, José Antonio drafted a general political analysis, discovered among his papers after his execution. This read:

> Situation: I have not sufficient facts as to who is doing better. Therefore, a purely moral synthesis:
>
> A: If the Govt. Wins. 1) Shootings; 2) predominance of the workers' parties (of class, of discord, of war); 3) consolidation of certain Spanish castes (unemployed functionaries, Republicanization, etc.).
>
> It will be said: The Govt. is not to blame. The ones who rebelled are *the others*.
>
> No, a rebellion (especially one so extensive) is not produced without a powerful motive.
>
> Social reaction?
>
> Monarchist nostalgia?
>
> No, this rebellion is, above all, of the middle classes. (Even

geographically, the regions in which it has most firmly taken root (Castile, León, Aragon), are regions petit-bourgeois in character.)

The determining cause has been the insufferable policy of Casares Quiroga.

. . . One cannot increase indefinitely the pressure in a boiling pot. The thing had to explode.

And it exploded. But now:

B. What will happen if the rebels win?

A group of generals of honorable intentions but of abysmal political mediocrity.

Pure elementary clichés (order, pacification of spirits . . .).

Behind them: 1) Old Carlism, intransigent, boorish, antipathetic. 2) The conservative classes, fixed on their own interests, short-sighted, lazy. 3) Agrarian and finance capitalism, that is to say: the end for many years of any possibility of building a modern Spain; the lack of any national sense of long-range perspective.

And then, after a few years, as a reaction, once more the negative revolution.

The only way out:

An end to hostilities and the start of an era of national political and economic reconstruction without persecutions, without a spirit of reprisal, which can make of Spain *a peaceful, free, and industrious* country.

My offer:

1. General amnesty.

2. Reinstatement of the functionaries fired since 18 July.

3. Dissolution and disarmament of all the militias. . . .

4. Lifting of the state of alarm and of prevention. (If, for reasons of public order, this is not considered possible, modification of the law of Public Order to provide: 1) that government imprisonment may not last more than fifteen days, nor be imposed more than twice each six months; 2) that the closing of political centers be subject to the same norms; 3) that government fines are to be imposed only after proper resolution and, not being imposed in application of prosecuting orders, are not to be effective until all legal recourse is exhausted; 4) revision of the attachments of properties during the abnormal period, in order to accommodate them to the precepts effective prior to 18 July.

5. Declaration of the permanence in office of all government employees, save for the provisions of the organic regulations of the various bodies effective on 18 July.

6. Suppression of all political intervention in the administration of justice. This will be dependent on the Tribunal Supremo, constituted just as it is, and will be regulated by the laws effective prior to 16 February last.

7. Immediate implementation of the law of Agrarian Reform.

8. Authorization of religious teaching, subject to the technical inspection of the state.

9. Formation of a government presided over by D. Diego Martínez Barrio, of which the Señores Alvarez (D. Melquiades), Portela, Sánchez Román, Ventosa, Maura (D. Miguel), Ortega y Gasset, and Marañón form a part.

10. Preparation of a program of national political pacification and reconstruction.

11. Closure of the Cortes for six months and authorization for the government to legislate within the lines of the program approved.

José Antonio also drew up a list of cabinet members for a government of "national pacification":

Presidency: Martínez Barrio
Foreign Affairs: Sánchez Román [one of Spain's most eminent jurists]
Justice: Melquiades Alvarez [conservative liberal]
War: the President
Navy: Maura (M.)
Interior: Portela [centrist Republican]
Agriculture: Ruiz Funes [technical expert]
Finance: Ventosa [noted moderate Catalinist financier]
Public Instruction: Ortega y Gasset
Public Works: Prieto
Industry and Commerce: Viñuales [economist]
Communications, Labor and Health: Marañón [celebrated liberal intellectual][16]

This was a government that would have been led by moderate Republicans and would have included two of the country's most respected intellectuals as well as a few technical experts. It came very close to the proposals made by such Republican leaders as Sánchez Román and Maura before the Civil War began, and indeed was rather more liberal than the broad national coalition government that José Antonio had earlier considered a remote possibility. Yet he never had an opportunity to present this compromise formally, because the left Republican ministers flatly ignored his proposal, either because they did not trust him or because they believed his plan had no chance of succeeding, or both.

Was all this an elaborate ruse to engineer his escape? With four family members to be left in Alicante, this seems doubtful. Though José Antonio often sounded harsh and fanatical in public, his private doubts and ambivalence are well documented. Though he had endeavored to develop a systematic doctrine of authoritarian and radical nationalism, it is not surprising that the effects of mass violence left him with second thoughts. He had never been hostile to a serious reform government of notables of the Republican parties and the moderate left. His admiration for Azaña and Prieto is well documented. Both before and immediately after the elections, he had declared both publicly and privately his support for an effective Republican national reform government led by Azaña (whom he greatly overestimated, as have many others then and now), if it could maintain national unity and devote itself to the country's major problems. José Antonio's turn toward a program of moderate Republican unity under the pressure of long imprisonment and a horrible civil war was not entirely surprising, for it reflected a frequently suppressed but longstanding alternate polarity or contradiction within his own thinking. Thus the tragedy of Spain had also become his own personal tragedy.

During his final trial, José Antonio summarized the position he took in the negotiations with Martínez Barrio and Echevarría:

> I am watching Spain break into pieces, and I can see that this may be the return to the old civil wars between Spaniards, and that by this path we can fall back in the social, political, and economic order into a state of confusion and darkness. I can only do one thing: ask you to provide me with an airplane, so that I can go to the other zone pledged to return, backed up by my deep concern for my family, since my brother, sister-in-law, and the aunt who has acted as my mother are all here. I leave these hostages; I go to the other zone and try to intervene to put an end to all this.
>
> I was told: the government will not accept this proposition.
>
> I replied: If I can provide this service, not to the Republic but to the peace of Spain, I will not feign sudden piety, but here I am.
>
> My service was not accepted. What I offered may not have been possible, but I offered it and they never came to give me a reply.[17]

Republican authorities were not blind to the potential importance of José Antonio. No effort was made during the first weeks of the Civil War to bring him to trial, but internal disagreements among the Republican leaders prevented their making use of him, and the formation of the first true government of the Popular Front under Largo Caballero on 5 September marked a shift to the left and a harder line.

The first phase of the Civil War was too desperate and confused for the surviving Falangist leaders to give great priority to plans for the rescue of their Jefe Nacional, but by September affairs in their zone were becoming better organized. In the meantime, the first initiatives had been taken in Paris by Miguel Maura and the Falangist writer Eugenio Montes, who encouraged Sánchez Román to get in touch with Prieto about the possibility of an exchange. Prieto is said to have stipulated the freeing of thirty prisoners in the hands of the Nationalists and the payment of six million pesetas. Montes returned to the Nationalist zone and obtained the approval of Hedilla, Franco, and Mola, but when Sánchez Román then reestablished contact with Prieto, the latter declared that anarchists were now in charge of the Alicante prison and would never release José Antonio.[18]

Montes remained active in Paris. After Largo Caballero became Republican prime minister on 5 September, it was brought to light that a son of his, who had been performing his military service in an army unit that had joined the revolt, was being held prisoner in Seville. The Junta de Defensa in Burgos approved an exchange of José Antonio and the son, who is said to have written to his father to encourage the transaction. The matter was eventually discussed in a Republican council of ministers in which the new president refused to intervene, allegedly declaring, "Don't force me to play the role of Guzmán el Bueno." The ministers could not agree and therefore decided to reject the proposal.[19]

After 1 September Falangist leaders, now reorganized under their new Junta de Mando in the Nacionalist Zone, arranged for representatives of the Nationalists to take other initiatives. On 5 September the German legation in Lisbon received a request for use of a German boat to transfer a Falangist delegation to Alicante to arrange for José Antonio's exchange or escape. Alicante had in fact become one of the major escape routes from the Republican zone. Three members of the Primo de Rivera family (including José Antonio's sister Pilar, founder of the Sección Femenina) had gained safe passage through the port,[20] as had an even larger number of members of the Pascual de Pobil family (the relatives of the wife of Nicolás Franco, the general's older brother).

Thanks to the German naval command, by 16 September a second Falangist rescue team was aboard the small German torpedo boat *Iltis*, bound from Algeciras to Alicante. It was led by the militia chief Agustín Aznar, whose fiancée, Lolita Primo de Rivera, a cousin of José Antonio, had recently escaped through Alicante, and it included José Antonio's law clerk Rafael Garcerán, who had himself escaped through Alicante the preceding month. Aznar, who was blond, and another light-haired Falangist had been provided with German passports, and Aznar also held one million pesetas from the Banco de España in Seville (provided by Gen. Queipo de Llano) with which to bribe Republican authorities. By this time, however, the official German embassy had also been evacuated to Alicante and was under the direction of Chargé d'Affaires Völckers, who was convinced that the Falangist enterprise was doomed to failure and, fearing diplomatic complications, confiscated the two German passports.

The initiative was then seized by the honorary German consul in Ali-

Agustín Aznar, the Falangist national militia chief in 1936

cante, Joachim von Knobloch, who was strongly pro-Falangist and enabled Aznar, minus the passport, to be transferred from the boat into
the city of Alicante. The Falangist leader met with several Republicans,
including the leader of the Socialists there, Cañizares (whom Prieto credited with having prevented an earlier anarchist attempt to murder José
Antonio). Aznar offered Cañizares an eventual payment of six million
pesetas and guaranteed passage for himself and his family to the Nationalist zone in return for José Antonio's escape. The Socialist leader replied
that the prison was totally controlled by the FAI, though he was said to
have made further futile inquiries. On 22 September Aznar was recognized by a captain of the Assault Guards and, escaping the first attempt
at his arrest, was finally transferred back to the *Iltis* in the uniform of a
German sailor.[21] Some days later von Knobloch himself was expelled from
Alicante by Republican authorities.[22]

During the next two months Falangists and others undertook a variety
of efforts to achieve the liberation of José Antonio. The new Generalissimo and chief of state in the Nationalist zone left the initiative in their
hands. One Falangist veteran later wrote: "For Franco the matter was
very delicate, given the limited political confidence the Falange had in
him. If he took charge of the operation and it failed, the responsibility
would fall on his shoulders. If he did nothing, he would be blamed for
omission. . . . He left the initiative to the Falange and helped to the extent
that he could."[23] Paul Preston agrees, observing that "early attempts to
liberate José Antonio were approved by Franco. His grudging consent was
given for the obvious reason that to withhold it would be to risk losing
the good will of the Falange."[24]

One approach that was considered and abandoned was that of gaining
Italian citizenship for the Falangist leader on the dubious basis of his two
very brief visits to Italy. Early in October Hedilla asked Franco for funding to support another trip to Paris by Eugenio Montes to seek foreign
assistance. The request was granted, and, after some confusion, Montes
carried on a series of negotiations with various French and Spanish Republican personalities. Over a period of some six weeks, these involved
such dissimilar go-betweens as Ortega y Gasset, the French cabinet minister Yvon Delbos, and the wife of the Romanian ambassador to Spain
(herself a British aristocrat who was a personal friend of José Antonio).
Prieto remained the chief, but not the only, contact on the Republican
side, and inquiries extended to the Spanish royal family and even to the
Papacy.[25]

The most ambitious plan was hatched by a meeting of Falangist territorial chiefs at Seville near the beginning of October. It authorized Aznar
to prepare a Falangist commando squad that would proceed to Alicante

aboard a Spanish merchant vessel and try to rescue José Antonio by force. This dubious operation was also approved by Franco, enabling Aznar to begin training some fifty commandos, including the renowned heavy-weight boxer Paulino Uzcudun. Security was lax, however, and after some indication that the newly reorganized Republican intelligence had learned of the operation, as well as a manifest lack of interest among either the German or Italian naval authorities in providing support for it, the enterprise was soon canceled.[26]

It was replaced by a new scheme of von Knobloch's, first broached to Aznar on 6 October, which would seek to make use of the personal friendship known to exist between Gabriel Ravelló, director of the Seville office of the Ybarra steamship line, and the Republican governor of Alicante. Von Knobloch and Sancho Dávila once more obtained Franco's approval, as well as German naval assistance, so that by mid-October another German vessel was anchored in Alicante harbor, bearing the somewhat unlikely quartet of von Knobloch, Aznar, Pedro Gamero del Castillo (a rising young neo-Falangist leader from Seville who had joined the party only weeks before), and Ravelló. There matters were temporarily halted by Karl Schwendemann, the counselor of the German embassy, who declared that a more promising new scheme was under way to bribe the anarchist authorities in Alicante. Chargé Völckers reported to the Wilhelmstrasse on 17 October:

> Knobloch alleges that the liberation of Primo is a vital question
> for Spain Fascism, which must bring about a National Socialist
> revolution of the people now, during the Civil War, since otherwise,
> after victory, reactionary elements . . . would hinder Franco in the
> execution of his program. This is allegedly also the opinion of
> authoritative Party circles in Germany.[27]

Aznar retained 800,000 of the one million pesetas given him in the preceding month (the other 200,000 pesetas was allegedly spent on preparations in Seville), but it was decided to ask Franco for two million more to guarantee success.

At this point, for the first time, Franco began to interpose restrictions.

> On the nineteenth and twenty-first of October, Lt. Col. Walter
> Warlimont, in charge of coordinating German military activity in
> Spain, sent a telegram to the commander-in-chief of the German naval
> units in Spanish waters, Rear Admiral Rolf Carls, indicating to him
> that Franco wanted the rescue operation to be carried out with as
> little money as possible, without the participation of von Knobloch,
> with maximal precautions concerning the identity of the prisoner
> to be rescued, and, should the liberation of Primo de Rivera be

completed, with his immediate isolation from all human contact
except for "a Spaniard sent from here," since there were doubts about
the mental health of Primo de Rivera.[28]

Franco was convinced that von Knobloch was meddling excessively in
Spanish affairs and probably had become increasingly concerned that the
whole operation was getting out of control. He may also have learned of
José Antonio's offer to mediate and feared that either his mental state or
his political views had altered. On 22 October the Republican governor
finally boarded the German vessel in Alicante harbor, but was not allowed
to speak with the Spanish delegation, who were confined to their cabins.
He was allowed to speak only with the German captain, while Völckers
awaited further instructions from Berlin. Ernst von Weizsäcker, chief political secretary of the German Foreign Office, informed the latter on the
twenty-sixth that "there is no question of any authorization of Knobloch
by the [Nazi] party to work there toward a National Socialist revolution
in Spain."[29] By that time this mission had been terminated.

Even so, neither Franco nor the German authorities turned their backs
entirely on these efforts. On 4 November Warlimont informed Carls that
Franco was now proposing that the ransom money—which indeed might
be increased to three million pesetas—be used in connection with a new
scheme to exchange José Antonio for Graciano Antunia, a Socialist Cortes deputy from Asturias being held by the Nationalists.[30]

Ramón Cazañas, Falangist chief in the Moroccan Protectorate, learned
of efforts by relatives of Gen. José Miaja (soon to become Republican
commander of Madrid) to obtain the exchange of his wife and daughters,
who were being held in Melilla. Falangist leaders proposed to Franco that
they be exchanged for José Antonio and the other members of his family
in Alicante, together with a large bribe and the possibility of a lifetime
pension from the Nationalist army for Miaja. Franco, however, rejected
this as impracticable and dishonorable, as he rejected the proposal from
the Falangist press official Maximiano García Venero for mounting a major international press campaign on José Antonio's behalf.[31] This was held
to be too disproportionate, and likely to draw too much attention toward
the Falange and its leader, which was clearly undesirable politically for
Franco at that time.

Further suggestions and initiatives were forthcoming. The conde de
Mayalde proposed to visit the French premier, Léon Blum, but Franco
continued to delay approval until it was too late.[32] It has also been alleged
that the heir to the throne, Don Juan de Borbón, sought to arrange
through the good offices of his mother, the British princess and former
Spanish Queen Victoria Eugenia, the sending of a British warship to Ali-

cante to attempt an exchange, and that he later reported categorically that this initiative had been vetoed directly by Franco.[33]

The attitude of leaders in the Republican zone remained unclear.[34] Whereas the FAI–CNT chiefs in Alicante were intransigent, from as far away as Buenos Aires came requests from Argentine anarchists that the national CNT leaders in Spain consider intervening on behalf of the Falangist chief.[35]

Largely cut off from the outside world, José Antonio devoted much of his time during the last four months in Alicante to reading and writing. As contrasted with the numerous letters and topical political articles of his first months in prison, those of José Antonio's last writings which have survived are much more philosophical, speculative, and interpretive in character. Bearing the date of 13 August[36] is an essay entitled "España: Germanos contra Bereberes." It outlined a general ethnosocial and cultural interpretation of Spanish history that advanced an extreme (some would say "fascistoid") version of the emphasis on the Germanic Gothic element so frequently found in medieval chronicles, Spanish nationalist writings, and the historical speculations of José Antonio's sometime mentor Ortega y Gasset.

The essay championed a racial concept of Spanish history—strongly joined with historical, religious, and cultural features—that José Antonio had never discussed publicly. In it he contended that the Reconquest had been a struggle of the Germanic (Visigothic), Roman Catholic, and European north against a south dominated by an Arab elite, but essentially composed of "an indolent, imaginative, and melancholy people" of Hispano-Berber Andalusians, a different ethnic stock that was either Islamic or increasingly indifferent in religion. "In that struggle Berbers and aborigines took part sometimes as footsoldiers and other times merely as resigned subjects of one set of conquerors or the other, though with a marked preference, at least in much of the territory, for the Saracens." "On the Christian side, the preeminent leaders were all of Gothic blood. . . . The Reconquest was a European enterprise—that is, at that time, Germanic. Many times, in fact, free knights from France and Germany came to help fight against the Moors. The kingdoms that they formed had undeniable Germanic foundations. . . . Considerable parts of Spain, especially Asturias, León, and northern Castile had been Germanized . . . for a thousand years . . . , quite aside from the fact that ethnic affinity with north Africa was much less than that of the population in the south and east."

The united Spanish monarchy of the fifteenth century had continued the historic mission of Catholic Christian and European culture, first in uniting Spain and then in creating the universal empire and championing the cause of Catholicism both in Europe and throughout the world. "The conquest of America" was also a Catholic and Germanic enterprise, possessing "a sense of universality without the slightest Celtiberian or Berber roots. Only Rome and Germanic Christianity could transmit to Spain the expansive, Catholic vocation of the conquest of America."

Yet Spain had never become homogeneous ethnically and culturally, the social and political conflicts of modern times representing in large measure the revolt of the plebeian Berber substratum of southern Spain, which had been conquered but never entirely convinced. "The Berber line, more apparent the more the opposing force declines, appears in all the leftist intellectuals from [the poet Mariano José de] Larra to the present. Not even fidelity to foreign fashions manages to hide the resentment of the conquered in all the Spanish literary production of the last hundred years. In any leftist writer one finds the morbid intent to demolish, so persistent and tasteless that it can be fueled only by the animosity of a humiliated caste. . . . What they hate, without realizing it, is not the failure of the institutions they denigrate, but their previous triumph; a triumph over them. . . . They are conquered Berbers who will not pardon the fact that the conquerors—Catholic, Germanic—bore the message of Europe."

A later essay, "Aristocracia y aristofobia," expanded on aspects of the earlier piece. In Spain the rebellion of the masses was in full force, and "the aristocracy no longer counts." Conversely, one found among the "aristophobes": "Envy. Rancor. Lack of moral vigor." The result was that "the masses will destroy themselves." What was needed was an "open aristocracy. The desire to be imitated. Free access. Patronage without irony," which would give an "example of good manners—of refinement—of beneficence (e.g., nurses . . .)." "Aristocracy is in *service,* one must accept it as a *mission* and not only as a *privilege.*" The goal should be to "aristocratize the middle class" with "a very severe regimen." [37]

These final essays would tend to confirm Ledesma's contention that José Antonio's rightist, aristocratic, elitist, and neotraditionalist proclivities were too deep-seated to be completely overcome by his (ultimately superficial) fascist political choices. At the same time, not too much should be made of the final writings, produced under completely abnormal conditions during a period of general isolation and growing anguish. If he had had a chance to lead the insurgents to victory, José Antonio might have said and written something considerably different.

The most interesting political speculations are contained in a series of notes under the general heading "Notebook of a European Student." [38] The adjective was carefully chosen because the notes dealt with historical, religious, and cultural problems of Europe in general. Here he returned to the Spenglerian cyclical concept of history that he had mentioned in public speeches during the preceding year:

> Classical ages and middle ages. The middle ages end in classical ages.—The classical do not become middle: they end in catastrophe, in invasions or barbarians. Afterward, within a new, barbarous culture, the best constants of the submerged classical age operate and then begin a new material, ascendant middle age.—The signs are all of the sinking of a world (foretold by Marx).—But not everything in it is lost: much ought to live and even to survive the catastrophe. Very well, must we resign ourselves to trusting in a remote resurrection? Must we allow the torrent to arrive and, for the moment, annihilate *everything*? That is, must we *resign ourselves* to be witnesses of the catastrophe predicted by Marx?

A significant part of José Antonio's thinking may be explained by the impact of Marx and Spengler on a fundamentally elitist, religious, and traditionalist temperament. In these notes he sought to reach "the religious essence of the crisis." The ultimate philosophical and spiritual solution lay in "Catholic unity," which had achieved a "total sense of religious life in the Middle Ages, that is, neither the sacrifice of the individual to the collectivity nor the dissolution of the collectivity into individuals, but a synthesis of individual and collective destiny in a higher harmony, which the one and the other serve." "And perhaps one day Catholic joy will reignite itself over a unified Europe."

> Then, say the traditionalists, the only thing is to return to tradition. Of course! As the language teachers say, "Faites comme moi" to slow students of phonetics. This is to suppose, *irreligiously,* that religion can be put on one day like a colored necktie following a period of mourning. No. Religion is, fundamentally, a *gift of God;* one must hope for it and ask for it, but it cannot be acquired overnight. Moreover, inculcating religious fervor among the peoples is not a political task. What can be attempted politically is *to create conditions* for the hope of grace (Pascal advises that those who do not feel charitable should behave as though they did.) Ascesis: innocence and penitence.

Then, in the typical neotraditionalist Catholic manner, José Antonio went on to find the roots of many of the major ills of the modern world in Protestantism.

He had never wished to present Falangist "españolidad" as merely "nationalism," conceiving the true Spanish principle to be supranational and universalist, Catholic religiously and empirically:

What is Spain? A nation? But first: what is a nation? Nationalism = the individualism of the peoples. The individual, the native; the nation, the native: before the individual, the person; before the nation (this nation), unity of destiny = a number of unities of destiny in the universal. Among them, Spain = the destiny of Spain = the incorporation of a world to culture, to Catholic culture. Spain was exactly ready (in *form*) when the world presented that conjuncture. Spain then resolutely assumed the cause of Catholic unity.

"Fascism" had become distant, an object of observation and analysis:

Attitudes.—Anarchism: it pretends to resolve the lack of harmony between man and his environment by dissolving the collectivity into individuals.—Fascism: it pretends to resolve that by absorbing the individual in the collectivity (communism is not yet a third attitude: it is *the very invasion of the barbarians* as the dictatorship of the proletariat); anarchism—utopian—as a remote aspiration.— Anarchism is unrealizable.—Fascism is fundamentally false: it succeeds in glimpsing that this is a religious phenomenon, but it wants to substitute idolatry for religion. Nationalism. Nationalism is romantic, anti-Catholic: therefore, at bottom, antifascist. Hence its multitudinous character, fatiguing in the permanence of its tension. False furthermore in economics, because it does not get at the real base: capitalism. All this about the *corporative system* is just a phrase: it preserves the duality management–labor, although magnified into syndicates. That is, the bilateral scheme of labor relations persists and, attenuated or not, the capitalist mechanism of *surplus value.*— But fascism glimpses (most of all, perhaps, in Germany) that there is something of an ascetic nature to acquire. An effort will be made to clarify this in the following chapter.

In his final return to the theme, he observed:

Fascism: absorption of the individual into the collectivity. The great achievements of the fascist systems and their internal failure: religious appearance *without religion.* Germany: it will become a profound and stable system if it achieves its ultimate goals: the return to the religious unity of Europe; that is to say, if it departs from the nationalist and romantic tradition of *the Germanies* and resumes the imperial destiny of the house of Austria. In the contrary case, the fascisms will have a short life.

Beginning in 1934, José Antonio had slowly but increasingly become aware of some—not all—of the deficiencies of political fascism. He correctly perceived from the beginning that the fascist enterprise involved, among other things, an attempt to recapture the spiritual in a materialist world, but eventually came to grasp the hollow and artificial character of fascist spirituality. Yet he could still speculate about Nazism's attempting to achieve a universal European spirituality, even though his largely negative public remarks about Nazism during 1934 and 1935 came much nearer the mark.

Like many during the 1930s, José Antonio was convinced that liberal capitalism was doomed and must be replaced by some new and superior form of organic and collective, or semicollective, social and economic organization. This would, however, require not merely a new political form but also a new cultural form that could recapture the full dimension of Catholic spirituality, without which a new harmony could never be achieved and could never endure. In the search for this utopia, he sought more and more to transcend the political form of fascism, which he found increasingly inadequate to the task, but, like many other new theorists and visionaries of the period, was unable to find the formula.

The last person to visit José Antonio from the outside world was the American journalist Jay Allen, reporter for the *Chicago Daily Tribune* and the London *News Chronicle,* who interviewed him on 3 October. It was clear that the Falangist leader was poorly informed on current events; he asked Allen for news, saying that he could not be sure what was happening in the rest of Spain. The reporter, whose political sympathies lay with the left, parried by inquiring what José Antonio would say were he told that Franco's forces merely represented old conservative Spain fighting selfishly to retain traditional privileges. José Antonio replied that he doubted whether that was true, but that if it was, the Falange had always worked for something very different. Allen then recounted a mixture of true and false reports concerning the gory exploits of the Falange's execution squads in recent months. José Antonio said that he believed, and wanted to believe, that none of this was true, but he pointed out that his young men now had no real leader and had suffered great provocation. Reminded that he himself had introduced the term "the dialectic of fists and pistols" in his founding speech, José Antonio retorted (quite accurately) that the left had struck first. He declared that if the Franco-led movement were in truth reactionary, he would withdraw the Falange from it and would shortly end up in a different prison.

José Antonio still seemed confident of receiving his freedom within a short time. Allen thought his performance "a magnificent bluff." After finishing the interview, Allen asked the jailers: "What are you going to do with him?"—to which they replied "There will be a trial." Allen accurately concluded: "It will be a trial, not only of the man, but of Spanish Fascism. I cannot for the life of me imagine any circumstances which would save this young man. His situation is very bad. The least I can do is not aggravate it."[39]

Early in November several newspapers in the Republican zone printed second-hand accounts of the Allen interview, highlighting criticisms of Gil Robles and potential criticism of Franco. Even earlier, on 24 and 25 October, several newspapers had printed charges that Sanjurjo and José Antonio had earlier negotiated support in Berlin for the rebellion, and that José Antonio had also taken part in a public meeting with the British Fascist leader Oswald Mosley.[40] In his final trial, José Antonio could with complete accuracy deny the main charge, pointing out that his only trip to Germany had taken place much earlier, in May 1934. The prosecutor would later allege that José Antonio had made statements in the Allen interview to counter the effects of the "revelations" of 24–25 October, since the fuller reports of the Allen interview appeared in Spain only in November; the prosecutor did not understand that the interview had taken place on 3 October.[41]

The Republican authorities were in fact slow in bringing José Antonio to trial, and this delay in Alicante may have been due to the attitude described by the Socialist Julián Zugazagoitia:

> In Alicante the first furious fits of collective anger that demanded the immediate execution of the Falangist leader had passed, giving way to the conviction that, as long as he lived, the city would not be bombed from the air. Such suppositions were frequent then. The municipal authorities of Cartagena showed signs of rebellion on learning that the family of General Pinto was about to be exchanged, thinking that the absence of air attacks on the city was due to the presence of the general's family. When the exchange was carried out, a storm of angry resignations took place. With Primo de Rivera something similar happened. Moreover, in one of those reactions so frequent in the sensibility of the Spanish people, hatred had turned into sympathy. Sympathy for a man who, without weakness or vacillation, was facing a harsh fate. His conduct in prison had been liberal and generous. During hours of imprisonment he conjured up dreams of peace: he sketched out a government of national concord and drew up a new political outline. He feared the victory of the rightist military.[42]

The Republic's new revolutionary system of Popular Tribunals was introduced in Alicante at the beginning of September. These retained most features of normal court process, though proceedings were accelerated. The most notable innovation was that juries would be drawn exclusively from members of Popular Front parties and syndicates, also including the FAI–CNT, and were given special powers. This was a new politicized system of justice, though one that did not abandon all judicial guarantees. By the fifth of October, the Popular Tribunal had voted the death sentence for at least sixty-one Falangists in the province, and the penalties were swiftly carried out.[43]

The prosecution of José Antonio and Miguel Primo de Rivera for the crime of "military rebellion" was initiated with a preliminary investigation that began on 3 October. The Tribunal Supremo assigned a special magistrate from Madrid, Federico Enjuto Ferrán, to hear the case, and he arrived in Alicante on the eleventh, where he continued the investigation.

November was a month of decisive change in the Spanish conflict. The battle for Madrid provoked the flight of the Republican government to Valencia—nearer Alicante—and a further radicalization of the struggle. In the Madrid region this led to the most extensive series of executions in any phase of the Civil War—the "Spanish Katyn" of some thousands of mass executions at Paracuellos del Jarama and other sites during the first days of November[44]—though there is no evidence of any linkage between events in Madrid and the death of José Antonio.

Some evidence has been presented that the immediate catalyst for the official trial was Alicante's sudden loss of immunity from air attack. The very first minor bombing of the city by a Nationalist airplane took place on 5 November. Though most bombing attacks during the Spanish conflict caused little damage compared with those of World War II, they often infuriated the local populations in the target areas, particularly those in the Republican zone, which was the more frequently attacked. The only large-scale killings in Republican Bilbao, for example, took place after bomb attacks, and on the very day of the first raid on Alicante the Commission of Justice of Alicante sent a telegram to the undersecretary of the Ministry of Justice of the Republic, stating: "Given situation of feelings after bombardment, important name special prosecutor, don Vidal Gil Tirado, in case begun magistrate Enjuto,"[45] to proceed with local prosecutions. Moreover, the new Republican minister of justice was the faísta Juan García Oliver, who was pleased to expedite the prosecution of fascists. According to a subsequent declaration by Tomás López Zafra, court secretary of Alicante, he and other local court officials were severely criticized by García Oliver for having proceeded slowly with the case of José Antonio.[46]

However that may have been, José Antonio's formal trial began on 16 November under the terms of the Code of Military Justice before a jury of the Popular Tribunal of Alicante. Miguel Primo de Rivera and his wife, Margarita Larios, were included in the same indictment, while lesser charges were brought against a number of prison officials accused of laxness during the first two months of his detention in Alicante. The definitive conclusion of the prosecutor was that José Antonio had plotted to overthrow the Republic during his visits to Rome and Berlin in 1933 and

1934 (a charge that technically was not true but that was typical of the wartime hysteria in both zones of Spain) and of having participated through messengers in the preparation of the revolt during the spring and early summer of 1936. The penalty for "military rebellion," particularly in wartime, was death.

As a professional lawyer, José Antonio took charge of his own defense, employing all his forensic skill to try to establish his innocence of a charge that, while somewhat exaggerated, was nonetheless in basic substance correct. He read his strongest articles from *Arriba* condemning the rightist groups and differentiating the Falange from them. He pointed out that the military forces in the Alicante region had made no attempt to free him and noted that newspapers in rebel territory had published lists of possible cabinet members for the future insurgent government without ever, to his knowledge, including him. José Antonio ingenuously proclaimed himself innocent "by the very simple fact of being in jail, something that had been directly sought by the rightist forces in revolt. They wanted to take advantage of the spirit and combative energy of the lads of Falange Española, blocking my control over them."[47] (This latter assertion would become even more correct than José Antonio ever knew.) He then went on to mention the letters and offer of mediation to Martínez Barrio and Echevarría.

After the second long day of hearings, the jury retired after 10 P.M. on the evening of the seventeenth to deliberate on its verdict. More than four hours passed before it returned with a decision, indicating disagreement among the members; nonetheless, they had found all three of the defendants guilty as charged. The court then sentenced José Antonio to death, and decreed life imprisonment for his brother and a term of six years and a day for Margarita Larios. In his final effort, at nearly 3 A.M. on the morning of the eighteenth, José Antonio invoked article 238 of the Code of Military Justice, which permitted the commutation of his sentence to life imprisonment. Under the present regulations, such a request would be decided by the jury, whose members were to cast black balls for denial and white balls for acceptance of commutation. Though several of the latter were cast, the black balls were in the majority, and the request was denied.

Only at this point, at the very end, did José Antonio briefly lose control of his nerves. The only direct account of this final session was written by a local journalist:

> Oblivious to the beehive of such a large, heterogeneous crowd
> packed together in the chamber, José Antonio Primo de Rivera reads
> a copy of the prosecutor's closing statement during a brief pause

ordered by the court. He does not bat an eyelash. He reads as though those pages dealt with some banal problem that did not concern him. Not the least trace of a squint or a raised eyebrow, not the slightest gesture, alters his serene face. He reads, reads intently with concentrated attention, the incessant buzzing of the chamber not distracting him for an instant.

. . . Primo de Rivera hears the courtroom ritual like someone listening to the rain. It does not appear that this affair, all this frightful affair, moves him. While the prosecutor reads, he reads, writes, and arranges his papers, all without the slightest expression, without nervousness.

Margarita Larios hangs on the reading and on the eyes of her husband Miguel, who listens, perplexed, to the reading, which must seem to him eternal.

The prosecutor reads on, before the emotion of the public and the attention of the jury.

José Antonio only raises his head from his papers when the accusation against the prison officials is dismissed and he sees them depart freely amid the approving clamor of the public.

Yet that expression, not of surprise, but only, perhaps, of a brief hope, lasts no more than a moment.

Immediately he begins to read aloud, with tranquility and composure, his own closing statement, to which the public listens with close attention.

. . . Margot raises a small handkerchief to her eyes, which are filling with tears.

Miguel listens, but does not look at the prosecutor; his eyes are turned toward the face of his brother, which he searches avidly for an optimistic gesture or a sign of discouragement. But José Antonio continues to be a sphinx, who only becomes animated when it is his turn to speak in defense of himself and the other two persons on trial.

His report is clear and direct. Gesture, voice, and word fuse in a masterpiece of forensic oratory to which the public listens carefully, with evident signs of interest.

. . . At last the sentence.

A split sentence in which the jury has fixed the penalties according to the differing responsibilities of the accused.

And here the serenity of José Antonio Primo de Rivera was shattered before the eyes of his brother Miguel and his sister-in-law.

His nerves broke.

The scene that followed may be imagined.

His emotion, and the pathos of it, touched everyone.

José Antonio nonetheless quickly regained control of himself and, turning with some satisfaction toward his brother and sister-in-law, declared, "You are saved!"[48]

The case against José Antonio had been reasonably clear, even though partially based on circumstantial evidence: during much of 1935 and from March to July in the current year, José Antonio preached a policy of civil war and had worked actively to prepare an armed insurrection. Death is not an uncommon penalty in wartime for helping to foment a major insurrection to overthrow the state. Telegrams of appeal were nonetheless dispatched to the highest Republican authorities, the one sent by José Antonio alleging a grave error in judicial procedure in the court's formulation of one of its final questions to the jury. Almost to the final moment, José Antonio hoped to win a reprieve—which indeed might have been in the political interest of the Republican government.[49]

On the eighteenth, José Antonio prepared his personal testament, naming Fernández Cuesta and Serrano Súñer as executors. In this final statement he gave no indication that he had changed his basic political values, and repudiated some of the remarks attributed to him by Jay Allen and the versions of Allen's article published in Republican Spain:

> Until I studied five or six days ago the full indictment that had been prepared, I was unaware of the statements imputed to me, for neither the newspapers that printed them nor any others were available to me. On reading them now, I declare that, among different paragraphs presented as mine, uneven in their interpretation of my thought, there is one that I reject completely: the one that condemns my comrades of the Falange for cooperating in the movement of insurrection with "foreign mercenaries." I never said such a thing, and yesterday I so declared categorically before the court (though such a declaration did not favor me). I cannot speak ill of military forces who have lent heroic service to Spain in Africa. Nor can I here cast reproach on comrades who—I know not now whether wisely or erroneously led—but who undoubtedly try to interpret with the best faith, despite the lack of communication between us, my permanent instructions and doctrine. May God will that their ingenuousness never be used in any service other than that of the great Spain to which the Falange aspires.
>
> I pray that mine may be the last Spanish blood shed in civil discord. I pray that the Spanish people, so rich in good and endearing qualities, may find *la patria, el pan y la justicia* [the fatherland, bread, and justice].
>
> I think there is nothing more for me to say about my political life. With regard to my imminent death, I await it without bravado, for it is never pleasant to die at my age, but without protest. May God Our Lord accept what it may have of sacrifice to compensate in part for what there has been of vanity and egotism in my life. I pardon with all my soul all those, without exception, who may have harmed or

offended me, and I ask pardon from all those to whom I owe reparation for any offense great or small.[50]

On the nineteenth José Antonio composed a dozen short letters to his closest friends and relatives, in language that was laconic, eloquent, dignified, and full of affection.[51] He also said good-bye to the members of his family still in Alicante.

The confirmation and execution of the death sentence subsequently became a matter of controversy not merely among Falangists and sympathizers but also among Republicans. On 18 November, only hours after the sentence was handed down, the civil governor, Valdés Casas, directed a questionnaire to the leaders of all the Popular Front groups in Alicante. He insisted that they state, no later than noon the following day, whether they believed the sentence should be carried out or commuted in order to make use of José Antonio's vigorous statements of opposition to the rightist forces.[52] There is no record of their reply, which must be presumed to have supported execution.

The sentence, as well as the telegrams of appeal by José Antonio and his relatives, was reviewed at some length on the nineteenth by Emilio Valldecabres, the juridical adviser of the minister of war (who happened to be Largo Caballero, the prime minister), who seems to have had the responsibility to review major sentences and appeals under the proceedings of the Code of Military Justice. His swift report to Largo Caballero found no grounds for further appeal or delay "unless there are greater political reasons for it," but concluded, "Your Excellency, nonetheless, will resolve what you conclude is most just and appropriate."[53] José María Mancisidor, who many years later published the text of the trial, has alleged that Largo Caballero personally added the words "Approved and proceed with the execution," and that the following telegram was dispatched: "To President Special Popular Tribunal of Alicante. Pursuant to terms decree 2 June 1931, Government informed of death penalty having been imposed on José Antonio Primo de Rivera y Sáenz de Heredia. Transmit."[54] In the absence of the original documentation, the validity of this allegation cannot be determined, though Juan García Oliver, the FAI–CNT justice minister of the Republican government, would later claim that Largo Caballero supported the execution when it was discussed in a cabinet meeting.[55] At any rate, the head of the Commission of Public Order of Alicante (half of whose members were representatives of the FAI–CNT) gave the order on the nineteenth that the execution of José Antonio and a number of other prisoners take place on the following day.

Francisco Largo Caballero would later emphatically deny in his memoirs that either he or the Republican government ever approved the execution. He wrote that in an effort to control the tens of thousands of political killings then taking place, he had shortly before established special review procedures that were never fully carried out in José Antonio's case. "The execution of Primo de Rivera was a source of profound disgust to me and, I think, to all the cabinet ministers," who, he claimed, were deliberating on the case when a telegram arrived from Alicante stating that the sentence had been carried out. "I refused to sign 'Approved' in order not to legalize a deed carried out in violation of the procedures just imposed by me to prevent executions being carried out by political passion."[56] He claimed that the sentence was executed precipitously precisely because of concern that the government might delay or commute it.

Though given to occasional bouts of depression, José Antonio was basically of an optimistic temperament. He was aware that Republican officials might find sound political reasons for sparing his life, and to the very last hoped to gain a reprieve. Moreover, though he could not have known of it, his friends and sympathizers continued until the final moment—and even beyond—to seek to mobilize intervention by foreign governments on his behalf. In Paris, Eugenio Montes had contacted a wide variety of émigré Spanish moderates, liberals, and conservatives, ranging from the former Republican prime minister Joaquín Chapaprieta to the monarchist conde de Romanones. Even the president of Argentina, Ramón Castillo, is said to have tried to intervene. According to one version, it was Santiago Alba (and according to another, Romanones) who was finally able to make contact with the French government leaders Blum and Delbos, who had at least a minor degree of influence with their fellow Popular Front government leaders in Valencia. According to such sources, the inquiry from the French government came only hours too late.[57]

The execution took place within the Alicante prison early on the morning of 20 November. José Antonio was shot by a firing squad together with four other political prisoners, two of whom were Falangists and two of whom were Carlist Requetés. There was no romantic flourish, only a laconic dignity[58]—common to many thousands of deaths in Spain that year. There was no formal burial; the corpses were simply thrown into a common grave, to be followed by the cadavers of ten other victims of political executions in Alicante later that same day.[59]

At that final moment, José Antonio could not have known that his martyr's image among Falangists and other Nationalists would later make him the most idolized of the three hundred thousand who fell in the Civil War. News of his death was completely silenced in the Nationalist zone for two years. Only as the second anniversary of the execution neared was the fact admitted, as on 16 November 1938 Franco officially hailed

José Antonio, declaring that the exemplary qualities of his life and death "make of him our National Hero and the symbol of the sacrifice of the youth of our times." His state decree established the initial terms of a massive martyr's cult without precedent in the history of modern western European politics. This cult would peak in the elaborate ceremonies of November 1939 attending the transfer of his remains for reburial before the high altar of the Church of San Lorenzo de El Escorial, very near the pantheon of Spain's kings; it waned slowly during the course of the long dictatorship.

In the years that followed, only Franco would be the subject of greater publication and adulation. Most of the vast outpouring of literature about José Antonio would be hagiographic and superficial, and more often than not misleading. One of the most convincing elegies was penned years later by his comrade and admirer Dionisio Ridruejo, in 1936 a twenty-three-year-old poet and provincial leader of the party:

> In 1935, outside of Falangist circles, I personally became acquainted with José Antonio Primo de Rivera, an appealing and intelligent man of great gallantry and dialectical elegance, possessed of sure personal honor, who added to these qualities a note of delicacy and timidity that was enormously attractive. He impressed me as has no other man since, and I seemed to see in him the model that every young man instinctively seeks to follow and to imitate; something like the older friend who guides the rebellious energies of adolescents when they feel the need to break with their immediate surroundings. . . .
>
> I never have ceased to feel for the figure of José Antonio the great respect and vivid affection that he inspired in me then, and I never shall, though many of his ideas now seem to me immature and others contradictory and mistaken. I still believe in his good faith, firmly demonstrated by the extraordinarily human behavior that preceded his death. In truth José Antonio did not possess that histrionic facility of fascist—and nonfascist—leaders and always seemed to be hiding a critical attitude toward himself, seeking something that he never succeeded in finding. In personal conversation—even with a very young person like myself, who showed him unconditional admiration—he did not hide his doubts about the quality of the small band that followed him. He tried to distinguish his movement from the fascist model, and did not renounce the hope of gaining an audience among the men of the left who might make his own political party superfluous by taking the [nationalist] direction that he sought. He believed in the threat of communist revolution, but he feared no less that the country might fall into the hands of the traditional right,

which he considered the surest means of guaranteeing that the revolution would be ultimately unavoidable and irremediable.[60]

Later Ridruejo added:

An element of perplexity had already entered José Antonio's mind about the nature of fascism. In one passage of his writings he noted the suspicion that these experiences are reducible to the formula of a strong personal power, and with regard to that, José Antonio's opinion was not constant and univocal. On occasion he exalted that formula as the most ideal, "superior to any complicated political machine," but other times the thought entered his mind that it was a formula in which chance might play too great a role. Who could guarantee that this power would fall into the hands of "the best," a benevolent rather than a cruel figure, a prudent man rather than an adventurer, a moral rather than a corrupt person, a wise leader rather than a schemer?[61]

What final assessment is to be made of José Antonio as a political leader? It should already be clear that the apologia developed after 1943 to the effect that his political goals and values were fundamentally non-fascist is a misrepresentation. His entire political life was strongly shaped by his family background, and his infatuation with authoritarian rule stemmed from the model of his own father, the Dictator, whom he saw as kindly, just, and benevolent. Subsequently, he extended an almost equivalent admiration to Mussolini. José Antonio and his colleagues founded the Falange in imitation of Italian Fascism, and privately he always recognized that the movement belonged to the same genus. At the same time, he struggled during the last two years of his life to give the Falange a more specifically Spanish identity and at least to some extent to differentiate it from Italian Fascism. It is difficult to see any particular success in the latter endeavor, even though he contradictorily always sought to associate the movement with Catholicism. Neither his eventual skepticism about such formulae as the "corporate state" and "totalitarianism" nor the increasing economic radicalism of Falangist national syndicalism distinguished Falangism from generic fascism in any clear way, for some of these same concerns could be found in German Nazism as well as in certain sectors of the pluriform Italian Fascist Party. At best, he succeeded only in differentiating Falangism as a Spanish subtype of generic fascism—more Catholic and culturally rather more traditionalist, less ultra-statist—within the broad spectrum of the fascist model. He did not propose any horrendous Nazi-type programs of mass liquidation, but neither did the majority of other fascist leaders. His more restrained, less murderous approach compared with Hitlerism merely identified Falangism with the more moderate, western European forms of fascism (Italian, French, British, and Dutch), as opposed to the extremely lethal and radical central and eastern European forms.

Fascism is often (no doubt correctly) seen as the most contradictory of all the radical ideologies of the twentieth century, and neither the Twenty-Seven Points nor the speeches and essays of José Antonio served to resolve these contradictions—between modernism and tradition, between secularism and religion, between capitalism and national syndicalism, between national weakness and imperialism, between centralized dictatorship and human and local liberties, between idealism and moral order as contrasted with mystical violence and armed coercion.

José Antonio was not unaware of these contradictions, as he was not unaware of the contradictions within his own personality and leadership. He never found any way to resolve them, probably because they were inherently irresolvable. He did not enjoy deadly force and violence for their own sake—in that sense his own personal instincts were not radically fascist. But he willingly and with increasing resolution embraced a political course that would inevitably involve increasing and ultimately massive amounts of violence, for by 1935 he had consciously and officially embraced a politics of civil war even more completely and explicitly than the revolutionary Socialists, who remained more ambivalent. To that extent he did overcome his own contradictions, but in the most destructive possible way and with the most disastrous possible results. By August 1936 he may indeed have been genuinely appalled by the character and extent of those results—mass death and a Spain more likely *roja* (red) or *rota* (broken) than "one, great and free." But by then it was much too late, for his exercise of political options came to a complete end on the eighteenth of July 1936, when the civil war that he had sought actually began. As the Bible says, those who live by the sword die by the sword.

In the postfascist era, much has been made by his admirers of José Antonio's "humanism," his ambiguous rejection of a pure "totalitarianism," his abstract invocation of the individual and of man "the bearer of eternal values," and his formalistic Catholicism.[62] Yet, as just indicated, not dissimilar usages might have been found in certain sectors of Italian Fascism. In 1934 he stopped using the term "fascista" in public and in 1936 once referred pejoratively to rightist conspirators as "fascist windbags," but he never renounced the basic fascist goals while a free man.

It would be pleasant to believe that his political observations of August 1936 represented a fundamental change in his thinking, but that is something that was never conclusively demonstrated and hence can never be known. Some of his more liberal admirers suggest that his execution constituted a fundamental political mistake for the Republic, as indeed it may have. But if José Antonio had been exchanged in 1937 as was the party secretary, Fernández Cuesta, would it have had a major impact on the government of Franco? This is of course the purest of counterfactual questions, about which nothing may be concluded with certitude. What happened in 1937 was that Franco adopted the political program of José Antonio and took control of his political movement with comparatively little resistance. Franco was the complete military dictator of a regime engaged in a desperate counterrevolutionary struggle in which it had become accustomed to adopting the most drastic policies, involving the deaths of tens of thousands of people. There is no a priori reason to assume that the mere physical presence of José Antonio would have made a profound difference, especially since he had devoted his entire career to preaching the need for a strong nationalist dictatorship. The point must therefore forever remain moot.

José Antonio Primo de Rivera failed to achieve significant political influence while he lived. His contribution was negative, merely accelerating and magnifying the Spanish disaster. His fame and apotheosis would come posthumously and probably could not have come any other way. The most likely presumption is that if he had survived he would ultimately have been totally discredited by the practical results of another disastrous fascist regime. Dead, however, he would become the subject of the most extraordinary martyr cult of contemporary Europe, which long guaranteed to him a status and a role that he could never have achieved in real life.

*Part III*

The Falange Española
Tradicionalista in the
Fascist Era, 1936–1945

# Francisco Franco and the Formation of the Falange Española Tradicionalista

On 1 October 1936 Francisco Franco assumed complete power as chief of state of Nationalist Spain. Within a matter of weeks he had moved from being one of the most respected figures in the military hierarchy and youngest of the major generals to holding the most extensive authority of any chief of state in Spanish history, a position that he would occupy for nearly four decades. There is no evidence that this was the result of any long-premeditated plan. Franco had never been a "political general" but had earned his rapid promotions by "combat merits" in the Moroccan campaigns between 1912 and 1926. He then served as the first director of the army's new General Military Academy from 1928 until its dissolution by the Republic in 1931. Despite this blow to his career, he had not initially conspired against the Republic, which soon restored him to active command and then promoted him to major general in 1934. He had served the Radical administration of Lerroux as special military adviser, supervising the repression of the revolutionary insurrection of 1934 in Asturias. Gil Robles made him chief of the General Staff in 1935, a position he held until the return of the left to power in February 1936.

He had refused to lead any military action against the Republican government; then, on the morrow of the last elections, he had urged higher constituted authority to declare martial law and annul the returns. Named military commander of the Canaries, he remained in relatively close touch with the military conspiracy, yet as late as 12 July, when a special plane was being readied to fly him to Spanish Morocco, he refused to agree to the revolt. He changed his mind the following day after hearing of the assassination of Calvo Sotelo. Unlike José Antonio Primo de Rivera, Franco had seen war and preferred to avoid the politics of catastrophe. Unlike the leader of Spanish fascism, he had sought to avoid, or at least delay, rather than to promote civil war. His final agreement came when he concluded that it was more dangerous not to participate in a revolt than to join it.

Franco held to certain basic political attitudes and values, formed no later than the 1920s, throughout his life. He was a Spanish nationalist who believed in a Regenerationist program to create a strong, unified, and influential Spain. He preferred an authoritarian political system above parliament and political parties. Franco was a firm if formalistic Catholic and a cultural traditionalist, opposed to what he viewed as the cultural and intellectual poisons of most aspects of modernity. The only sort of modernization that he sought was technological and economic, to create the necessary basis for a strong and prosperous Spain. Having built his reputation in Morocco, he was also a devout believer in empire, and was convinced that Spain should expand, if possible, its holdings in Africa. His chief political guide and inspiration had been the Primo de Rivera regime, which first revealed to him what an authoritarian government could accomplish, even if its lack of clear political content had inevitably resulted in its demise. Franco believed that it was important to learn from the failure of the Dictadura and thus to avoid what he termed "el error Primo de Rivera"—the lack of a real political system and doctrine. This was a major point of similarity between Franco and José Antonio, though the enormous differences in personality, temperament, experience, and background between the two men meant that while José Antonio was more radical and fascistic, Franco was more cautious and conservative. Franco had not so much disagreed with the longstanding conspiracy to restore the monarchy as he had doubted its feasibility, and during the first weeks of the Civil War he gave the appearance of accepting Mola's project of maintaining the Republic in a more rightist and authoritarian form.

Franco's role in the revolt was to take command of what became known as the Army of Africa, the military forces in the Protectorate who formed the only elite, battle-tested troops of the Nationalists. This gave him a position of special influence, reinforced by the fact that it was he rather than Mola who established the effective contacts with Rome and Berlin and was the main recipient of crucial Italian and German aid. This was made possible not merely by earlier monarchist contacts with Rome but even more by Franco's very effective relationship with the Italian consul in Tangier and with the head of the German Nazi Party in Morocco.[1] On 3 August Franco was made the ninth member of the rebel Junta de Defensa, as his elite units began their drive north from Seville to seize Madrid.

It was during the early phase of the final drive on the capital, in the second half of September, that pressure arose within the Junta de Defensa

General Francisco Franco and Colonel Juan Yagüe (the chief Falangist in the military), in the streets of Seville, August 1936

to have Franco recognized as commander-in-chief and also as acting head of the insurgent government. This goal stemmed from a peculiar alliance of monarchists (both inside and outside the military) and various individual military supporters of Franco. Since there was no rival candidate—not even the more self-effacing Mola—Franco was selected without any serious opposition. The monarchists counted on Franco's favorable attitude toward the monarchy as a guarantee of a restoration, but initially nothing was done to restrict or place a time limit on Franco's powers. Though the official decree named him "chief of the Government of the

State" rather than chief of state, any limitation was disclaimed by the additional words that he assumed "all the powers of the state." Thus Franco's assumption of unlimited authority gave him, at least in theory, broader personal powers than those held by Mussolini, Stalin, or Hitler, for even in Germany there remained a parliament, though shorn of authority.[2]

By this point Franco's own political thinking had become more specific, and he had firmly decided that there must be a drastically new system to replace the Republic, one based on the model of the new nationalist authoritarian states in Europe. To avoid "el error Primo de Rivera," such a state must possess clear doctrine and structure. While receiving a visit from the German ambassador to Lisbon on 6 October, he assured the latter that he would develop a firm program that would be accepted by all the forces supporting the Nationalists, whether Catholic rightist, Falangist, or monarchist. At that time, however, there was not yet any exact strategy for achieving this. During the final months of 1936, Franco was fully occupied with the effort to seize Madrid and could devote little attention to politics. During these weeks, what he most appreciated from the Falange was its military volunteers, whose militia guarded long stretches of inactive front, helped to police the rearguard, and formed battalions for the combat forces as well.

## THE FALANGIST MILITIA

The greater share of Falangist energy during the Civil War was directed toward military and paramilitary functions. From the first days of the revolt, the party became the chief source of paramilitary volunteers. The approximately 20,000 Carlist volunteers (Requetés) who flocked to the insurgent cause during the first weeks were in some cases better trained and prepared and often made better soldiers, providing an indispensable contribution to Mola's combat forces and to the later Nationalist Army (with unusually high casualty rates),[3] but the Falangists were much more numerous. By 7 September, 4,000 Falangist volunteers were said to be serving in Aragón with the Quinta Bandera de Aragón alone,[4] and by the following month all Falangist volunteers totaled more than 35,000. This amounted to at least 55 percent of all civilian volunteers with the forces of Franco,[5] and their number continued to grow rapidly.

José Antonio's orders for the revolt had stipulated that no more than one-third of the Falangist forces in any specific area would serve under regular army command. However, the acting jefe nacional of militia, Luis Aguilar, was killed in Madrid at the beginning of the conflict, and his successor, Agustín Aznar, devoted himself more to political affairs and

Falangist militia in Salamanca

the attempts to rescue José Antonio. The Nationalist zone was ruled by martial law, making all forces subject to military discipline, and though most Falangist units did not at first have regular army officers, they could not operate as independent forces, either.

The prospect of a longer civil war made it necessary to consider stronger organization and leadership. Falangist militia units had no real officers of their own (aside from their own Primera Línea leaders) other than those provided by the regular army, and no means to train any. The Junta de Mando did not initially act in this area but was soon persuaded to do so, and before the end of 1936 two small training schools for Falangist officers were formed, first at La Jarilla near Seville and later at Pedro Llen outside Salamanca. The latter, opened in February 1937, was directed by the experienced Finnish officer Carl von Haartman (a veteran of the Finnish civil war against communism)[6] and partly staffed by a small cadre of German instructors.[7]

These schools were not particularly successful. Many of the best candidates bypassed the Falangist rubric and entered the regular army's courses for "alféreces provisionales" (reserve lieutenants). The program at Seville was so short-lived that it never completed its first full course, its directors finally recommending that the Junta de Mando settle for a quota of the army assignments for the training of regular alféreces provisionales.[8]

The problem was partially solved on 22 December 1936, when Franco decreed the unification of all militia groups in the Nationalist zone under regular army command.[9] Henceforth all such forces would be fully subject to regular army discipline, and their senior commanders would normally be regular officers, though in fact veteran militia leaders were sometimes given temporary army rank. This decision—which made eminent military sense—had been partly provoked earlier that month by the announcement from the Carlist leader Fal Conde of plans to open a Royal Military Academy for Requetés. Franco saw this as a much more serious political challenge than the Falangist efforts because of its semiofficial character and use of the term "Royal," particularly in view of the fact that the Carlists had created their own parallel state administration under the Junta Nacional Carlista, which contained subsections equivalent in function to government ministries. Franco forced Fal Conde to choose between court-martial and exile; Fal selected the latter.[10]

Even after the nominal unification, many militia units remained poorly organized. The first Inspector nacional, Gen. José Monasterio, was appointed a full month later.[11] The Junta de Mando was permitted to go ahead with its own training school at Pedro Llen, even though on 28 January 1937 provision was officially made for officer candidates from the militias to enter the regular army courses for alféreces provisionales.[12] Variation in size and structure from battalion to battalion and from province to province remained extreme; some banderas (battalions) of the Falange included nearly two thousand volunteers, others only a few hundred. There was also more than a little difference in the rate of volunteering from province to province.

Aznar was himself not the most skilled organizer and administrator, but in the spring of 1937 he arranged to have a few of the better Falangist commanders recalled from the front to assist in organization and training. Before much was accomplished there occurred the crisis of political unification (described below) in which the entire upper class of officer candidates at Pedro Llen was temporarily placed under arrest and the facility completely taken over by the army.[13]

Falangist banderas varied considerably in combat ability. Draft dodgers sometimes joined to escape the full rigors of military discipline or to disguise a leftist political identity, and certain units were "regarded almost with derision by the various units of the army and by the 'Reds.'"[14] Furthermore, the military regularly preempted the ablest militia volunteers for the regular forces. Records of the Falange in Burgos show that 9,120 volunteers joined the militia in that province prior to 19 April 1937. Four hundred ninety were listed as casualties. Of the remainder, 4,252—presumably the more able half—were taken for the regular army.

Yet numerous Falangist banderas acquitted themselves well on a variety of fronts, and sometimes also served, like the Requetés, as shock troops. Aragonese Falangists, for example, served bravely in defensive positions against heavy Republican attacks during 1936 and 1937. Some banderas were included in a number of the elite divisions of the Nationalist Army during the decisive campaigns of 1937 and 1938.[15]

Full statistics are unavailable. Falangist recruiters sometimes labored to recruit volunteers for the regular army as well. After the Italian divisions began to withdraw following the defeat at Guadalajara in March 1937, Falangist volunteers helped in part to fill the Spanish contingents for the mixed units of the "Freccie Nere" (Black Arrows) and "Freccie Azzurre" (Blue Arrows). By the beginning of 1937, Falangist spokesmen referred to 100,000 Falangist militiamen, of whom half were said to be at the front, but this was an approximation and probably something of an exaggeration as well.[16] Years later, the Excombatientes organization circulated lists of 147 Falangist and Carlist banderas and tercios (including, of course, volunteers originally with other militia groups as well) with 244,077 volunteers and 95,000 total casualties.[17] Both the latter figures are doubtless exaggerations, based in part on duplicate memberships.

General Rafael Casas de la Vega, the principal historian of the militia, has found that by the end of the war, 96,376 militia volunteers were still on the "Estadillo de fuerzas" of the Nationalist Army, while some 32,000 others had become alféreces or sergeants. A total of 17,015 were listed as killed or dead of wounds—a rate that, if correct, would be twice as high as that of the regular army—while some 26,000 had been invalided out, for a grand total of 172,000.[18] Yet this total may in some ways be an underestimate, for it would not include all the volunteers drained off into the regular army.

There is no doubt that the militia volunteers were numerous and made an important contribution to the victory of the Nationalists. Their performance was uneven, as in the case of most sizable forces. As befit an organization dedicated to militancy and the priority of violence, the main Falangist contribution to the war was in combat—and also in repression.

## FALANGISTS IN THE REPRESSION

Though a systematic effort was made in the months before the Civil War to identify the Falange as the chief source of the political violence in Spain, no single aspect of the Falange's history has so blackened its reputation as its role—true and alleged—in the repression in the Nationalist zone, particularly during 1936–1937. Republican commentators found it easy to spotlight the role of the Falangists, since they were presumably the "most fascist," but other sectors among the Nationalists also preferred to blame the Falangists as much as possible, particularly after the Civil War was over.

The reality was, first of all, extremely bad. As soon as the fighting started, both sides began seizing political enemies and executing them, sometimes together with military prisoners, in horrendous numbers. This process started with the killing of dozens of military personnel and Falangists by revolutionary militia when the former tried to surrender in Madrid's Montaña barracks on 19 July 1936, and rapidly escalated on both sides. Large-scale political killings are a standard feature of twentieth-century revolutionary civil wars, and took place in Russia, Finland, eastern and central Europe, and east Asia. This century's revolutionary wars have demonized the adversary in apocalyptic and chiliastic terms, permitting him no quarter as the very incarnation of evil in a desperate struggle in which only the physical liquidation of the enemy can assure one's own salvation.

It is impossible reliably to quantify the repression during the Civil War. Guesswork with global demographic statistics by such commentators as Gabriel Jackson[19] and Elena de la Souchère[20] is completely illusory and unreliable. The only attempt to employ a systematic methodology to quantify the total number of deaths was the painstaking study by Ramón Salas Larrazábal,[21] by far the most detailed study that has ever been done, but its assumption that all deaths were eventually recorded in some fashion in the local or provincial district in which they occurred cannot be fully accepted. Thus his conclusion that there were approximately 72,500 executions in the Republican zone and only 35,500 in the Nationalist zone is probably in error—the figure is much too low for the latter and too high for the former. A number of provincial studies have attempted to quantify the repression in individual provinces or regions, but these seem often to be motivated politically to "expose" the repression by the Nationalists, often only study one side, and in most cases are also uncertain in methodology.[22] The most objective recent global analysis is that by Angel David Martín Prieto, which has concluded that repression in the Nationalist rearguard took approximately 55,000 lives, that repression in the Republican rearguard took approximately 60,000, and that there were approximately 25,000 to 30,000 executions in Spain during the years immediately following the war.[23] As many people were killed in the repression as in military combat.

There is no doubt that Falangists played a significant role in the brutal repression in the Nationalist zone and were guilty of many crimes, but it

is not clear that their role was so disproportionate or their general responsibility so great as was often alleged. Murder during the Spanish Civil War
bore many different political names. A judicial state of war was officially
decreed for the Nationalist zone by the Junta de Defensa on 28 July 1936,
and on 31 August all military and naval tribunals were ordered to proceed under "sumarísimo" (summary) rules.[24] The military command, on
both the national and the local levels, was responsible for the repression
from the beginning. Local army commanders and military governors thus
bore the overall responsibility for directing most of the repression during
the first six or seven months, and after February 1937 the system of military tribunals became more orderly and comprehensive.

Though the arrest and liquidation of political enemies was generally
supervised by military officials from the beginning, during the early
months various militia groups—as in the Republican zone—were permitted to operate to some extent on their own. In various provinces Falangist
groups therefore conducted widespread repression with a certain degree
of autonomy for several months, just as rightist militia groups did. Moreover, victims marked for killing by the military and police authorities in
the first months were often executed by civilians. Since soldiers were
needed at the front, the actual killings were carried out by the Civil
Guards, Assault Guards (in areas where they joined the rebels), Falangists, and other militia groups. It seems to be correct that Falangists—in
part simply because of their now greater numbers—played this role to a
greater extent than any other political group, but they frequently did so
as policemen and executioners for the military rather than as independent agents.

One of the better local studies of the structure of repression is the recent work on Zaragoza and its environs by Julia Cifuentes Checa and
Pilar Maluenda Pons. They found that, of the 3,117 killings they were
able to identify, no fewer than 2,578 took place in 1936. Few of these
first executions were directed by military courts, but by 1938 nearly all of
the much smaller total of 255 were so directed.[25] This is probably roughly
indicative of the situation in the Nationalist zone as a whole.

After the fighting began, most of the Falangist Primera Línea was assigned to military duty, while the older members or those in poorer physical condition of the Segunda Línea were assigned to security and "vigil-
ancia." In some areas the latter were disproportionately used for the
repression. The flood of new members sometimes gravitated toward such
tasks, while the "cantonalismo" under which local units functioned during the first months left provincial leaders somewhat greater autonomy
for a short period. During the first weeks in Logroño there functioned a

special tribunal for the repression composed of an army officer, a regular court judge, and one representative each from the Falange, the Carlists, and Renovacion Española.[26]

Falangists were guilty individually or collectively of thousands of killings, yet there was also a tendency on the part of their allies, as well as their opponents, to make them scapegoats for the entire repression. This was because their real role was bad enough and because they were fascists and, with the swagger and glorification of violence typical of the fascist style, sometimes boasted of their exploits. Unfortunately for the people of Spain, the real essence of "fascist style" was shared by many different groups on both sides: the military, monarchists, anarchists, Communists, Socialists, and sometimes even left Republicans.

The most notorious single killing of the many thousands in the Nationalist zone was that of the poet Federico García Lorca. This and several thousand other executions in Granada were directed by the local military governor and physically carried out by the Civil Guards, Assault Guards, and the "Escuadra Negra" (Black Squad), a mainly rightist militia group, as well as Falangists. The only people who attempted to save Lorca were in fact Falangists: Lorca was for some time sheltered in the family home of one of the principal Falangist leaders.[27] Antonio Ruiz Vilaplana, a jurist who escaped from the Nationalist zone, gave a somewhat similar report from a northern district, declaring that to his knowledge the Falangist leaders were the only ones who tried to restrain their members. He explained:

> The Falange . . . has been surrounded by a sinister fame, born of certain deeds, but exploited unjustly by elements who have exceeded it in the quantity and quality of repressive acts. . . .
> It was useful to the clerical and monarchist forces, jealous of the expansion of the Falange, to emphasize the repressive activities of the latter, thus diverting attention from their own direct participation in this work. In this respect the polemic sustained between the Falange and the Requeté–monarchist sector about this is interesting, because in the course of it the Falange, and most recently Radio F. E. of Valladolid, declared repeatedly that they had not acted as a repressive force on their own, but with the agreement of the military authorities.
> The Falange must take its share of the responsibility for vengeance and social repression, but ought not to bear the exclusive blame.[28]

Manuel Hedilla's radio address on Christmas Eve 1936 stressed the need to discipline the repression and to avoid injustice—a forlorn hope, at best, but still one of the very few occasions on which a leader in the Nationalist zone spoke publicly in favor of limiting the repression.[29]

The other side of the coin, of course, was that Falangists were prime targets of the repression in the Republican zone. Nearly all the hundreds held in prison in those provinces at the beginning of the war were executed. Along with military personnel, for example, Falangists formed one of the two prime categories of those slaughtered in the mass executions at Paracuellos del Jarama—the "Spanish Katyn"—and several other spots behind the Madrid front in November 1936, the largest single atrocity on either side. No other European fascist movement, not even the Legion of the Archangel Michael in Romania, lost such a large proportion of its membership in the struggle for power, yet another singularity of fascism in Spain.

## THE JUNTA DE MANDO AND THE EXPANSION OF THE FALANGE UNDER MANUEL HEDILLA

The purpose of the new Junta de Mando that had been organized in meetings held on 29 August and 2 September was to restore some form of central leadership and administration to the party, overcoming the confusion and "cantonalismo" of the first six weeks of the Civil War. Manuel Hedilla Larrey was selected as the jefe of the Junta largely because he was the highest-ranking party leader to survive, a national councillor and national inspector during the spring of 1936 who had helped provide what little cohesion the party retained during the months of clandestinity. Hedilla was a former naval mechanic from a lower-middle-class family in northeastern Santander province who had briefly operated a trucking service and at one time served as technical supervisor for the Sindicatos Agrícolas Montañeses in Santander, in connection with which he had formed one of the first Falangist syndicates. He had been away on an organizational visit to Galicia when the revolt began, and from that point had stepped forward to try to restore some leadership to a fragmented organization that by the late summer of 1936 was undergoing what was very possibly the most rapid growth of any political party in Spanish history.

Hedilla was honest, taciturn, and somewhat slow of speech, but a dedicated Falangist who recognized the need for leadership and administration. He faced a difficult internal political situation in addition to all the objective demands of rapid expansion and civil war, for the epigoni of José Antonio were divided and eagerly jockeying for power among themselves. Several general cliques formed. Hedilla was particularly supported by some of the other district leaders from the north and center, such as Jesús Muro in Aragon, José Moreno in Navarre, and José Sainz in Toledo. The tightest power bloc was made up of the "legitimists" from the Madrid leadership, headed by Agustín Aznar, the militia chief and coordinator of efforts to rescue José Antonio. Sancho Dávila was also important in this circle, as was José Antonio's former legal assistant Rafael Garcerán, who arrived in Salamanca on 8 September and was soon made territorial chief for the surrounding region of León. The legitimists were at first not particularly jealous of Hedilla, whose manner was modest; it was some of the more powerful regional leaders who were creating powerful fiefdoms who represented a problem. The ones who particularly aroused concern were Andrés Redondo in Valladolid, who had quickly succeeded his fallen brother there as provincial chief and also territorial chief for part of Old Castile, Ramón Cazañas in the insurgent base of Morocco, and Joaquín Miranda in the main southern power center of Seville, who was very influential in the Falange in the south.[30] There was some overlap between these sectors, as Redondo often leaned in the direction of the legitimists.

Hedilla completely lacked the qualities, charisma, and personal leadership of José Antonio. Many of the party bosses now affected an exaggerated fascist style with uniforms, confiscated fancy cars, and large, almost feudal, armed retinues. Hedilla, by comparison, lived modestly with his wife and three children and was comparatively unostentatious. He seemed relatively indifferent to the frequent opportunities for corruption and arrogance indulged in by many of his colleagues, but it was soon feared that he lacked the personality and political skill to impose leadership on a party whose character, he admitted, was one of "considerable disorder and great ambition."[31] Thus after a few months an Italian Fascist journalist wrote:

> One cannot say that his appearance reveals incontrovertible signs of a leader, and nothing would indicate that he could show himself tomorrow to be that statesman for whom Spain waits. I should rather call him an excellent lieutenant, an energetic and scrupulous executor of orders, indeed the man needed in this hour when all power is concentrated in the hands of the military. . . . The lack of a true leader constitutes the great handicap of Falangism.[32]

The German representative appointed to Franco's government in November, a Nazi Party member and sometime army general named Wilhelm Faupel, sought to influence and assist Hedilla politically, but eventually came to much the same conclusion: "Hedilla was a completely honest person, but by no means equal to the demand imposed on a leader of the Falange. He was surrounded by a whole crowd of ambitious young persons who influenced him instead of being influenced and led by him."[33]

Hedilla seemed at first reasonably successful in his relations with the military command. On 25 September, during the days of transition into

Manuel Hedilla Larrey, head of the Falangist Junta de Mando, 1936–1937

Franco's mando único (sole command), the insurgent Junta de Defensa had issued a decree that categorically prohibited "all worker and management political and syndical activities of a political character so long as the present circumstances continue . . . , eliminating, if necessary, every kind of political and syndical activities or partisanship of a party nature, even those activities involving the highest motives."[34] This decree was not, however, normally enforced against Falangists and Carlists, the semi-official auxiliaries of the insurgency.

Hedilla moved the office of the Junta de Mando to Salamanca after Franco established his headquarters there on 1 October. The Falangist leadership sought to cooperate very broadly with the military, announcing on 19 October that it had officially forbidden Falangist battalions to fly their own red-black-red flags at the front, though inevitably some points of friction arose. Hedilla spoke not infrequently with the new Generalissimo, who would occasionally ask his opinions and even go to the trouble of flattering him. But he did not readily give in to the Falangist's requests. Nothing was done, for example, to try to arrange the exchange of members of Hedilla's family trapped in the Republican zone.

Firm and clear leadership was all the more important because the literally scores of thousands of new party members and militia volunteers had little notion of Falangist national syndicalism and its ideology. An American correspondent sympathetic to the Nationalists wrote of the new Falangists:

> Actually I found there were very few of them who had even taken the trouble to inquire into the doctrines of the party. Many of the younger ones had joined up because the smart blue uniform gave them a decided advantage over Red youth in the matter of their girl friends. The greatest number had undoubtedly joined up as being the simplest way to help their country. I have questioned dozens of them here, there, and everywhere; I found them on duty on the roads, guarding post-offices, banks, etc., and none of them was clear about anything except that they were anti-Red. One of them told me quite simply that he "guessed it was a kind of Communism, only much better expressed."[35]

The development of propaganda and indoctrination was thus of prime importance. The opportunity was all the greater because, though Franco had an official propaganda chief in his government, the new military regime devoted much less proportionate energy to propaganda than the opposing Republican government did. The Falange's jefe nacional of press and propaganda was the very young journalist Vicente Cadenas, appointed by José Antonio under the stressful conditions of April 1936. He maintained his own office in San Sebastián (hardly the best arrangement, but then the administrative branches of Franco's own government were also geographically dispersed) and worked energetically with limited resources to expand facilities, opening a second office in Salamanca. The first Falangist daily, *Arriba España,* had been initiated in Pamplona on the first of August under the direction of the Falangist priest Fermín Yzurdiaga (also known as "el cura azul"—the blue priest), but the daily that Cadenas later initiated in San Sebastián, *Unidad,* was the nearest thing to an official, national Falangist daily.

Cadenas organized the Falange's first National Congress of Press and Propaganda, held in Salamanca on 25–27 February 1937. There he presented an elaborate "National Press Plan," accompanied by proposals for a new Falangist press agency, a national publishing house, a school of journalism, and a school of political studies.[36] By that time there were approximately forty Falangist publications, featuring, in addition to daily and weekly papers, the theoretical journal *F. E.,* a cultural journal called *Vértice, Flechas (Arrows)* for children, and the picture magazine *Fotos.* Falangist style was also propagated through a myriad of posters, calendars, uniforms, and ceremonies, and a small Falangist film company was formed in Morocco.[37]

Falangist demagogy was not a materialist demagogy of tangible economic promises but a fascist demagogy that preached unity and sacrifice as well as social justice and economic readjustment. In an interview for Italian correspondents on 11 March 1937, Hedilla outlined a broadly and militantly nationalist program. He declared that the Falange's goals were to capture the Red masses, to eliminate their leaders, and to organize Falangist volunteers serving at the front into a National Militia that would survive the war and create a unified, militarily strong Spain.[38]

The party press devoted considerable space to favorable reports on the Nazis, the Italian Fascists, and minor fascist movements. Periodic outbursts of anti-Semitism also occurred, despite the absence of Jews in Spain. The notorious forgery of the "Protocols of the Elders of Zion" was dusted off by several party publicists.[39]

Falangist spokesmen readily accepted their affinity with Italian Fascism and Nazism, admitting derivations from the former,[40] but they also sought to affirm the uniquely Spanish identity of the movement. In one of his first major interviews as head of the Junta de Mando, Hedilla declared to a correspondent of the official German news agency DNB: "We are and feel ourselves to be of the same blood as Italian Fascism and German National Socialism, and proclaim our most open sympathy with these revolutions. This does not and should not mean that our fascism is an imitation. It is a fascism born Spanish, that ought to and will continue to be Spanish."[41] Falangist propagandists also took some pains to distinguish their doctrine from racism and ultra-statism per se. In what would become a standard trope for them and for the government of the Nationalists generally, they preferred to compare their ideology to the policy of unity of the Reyes Católicos. Their propaganda did differ significantly from that of most European fascist groups in its emphasis on Catholicism, and religious themes swelled as the war progressed. As Hedilla declared in a newspaper interview in October: "The pagan sense of the cult of the Fatherland and subordination to race, force, and so forth, which one finds in some foreign movements of an analogous type, is replaced in ours by a strong current of spirituality very much in accord with our tradition."[42]

Church leaders would eventually characterize the struggle as a holy crusade, and Falangist spokesmen increasingly emphasized that all Spanish institutions must be imbued with a specifically Catholic spirit. Fermín Yzurdiaga, the Pamplona priest who directed *Arriba España* and was one of the party's most active propagandists, developed an ideological circle in the Navarrese capital and eventually rose to the post of chief of press and propaganda of the official new FET after April 1937. In a major address delivered by radio on Christmas Eve 1936, Hedilla declared that the doctrine of the Falange was "the expression of divine justice in this century," and that the party's mission was to "*sow love*."[43]

Despite this increasing religious emphasis, more than a little friction was created by the Falangists' opposition to the right and by their "leftist" economic pronouncements, to the point where rightists in the Nationalist zone occasionally called them "our Reds" and "FAIlangist" (Anarcho-langists). During the early months Falangists sometimes demonstrated antipathy toward readoption of the historic monarchist red-and-yellow flag, and showed even more hostility toward CEDA leaders. Gil Robles was virtually driven out of town by Falangists when he appeared briefly in Burgos in August, and the democratic CEDA leader Giménez Fernández was temporarily forced into hiding by them in Cádiz province.

Falangist propaganda was much more directed toward the working class than that of any other group among the Nationalists. The tone had been set by Onésimo Redondo in his only speech during the few days between his liberation from prison and his sudden death, as he declared over Radio Valladolid:

> The doctrine and program of the Falange is impregnated with the
> broadest and deepest concern: to redeem the proletariat. . . . Let us

give back to the workers the spiritual patrimony that they have lost, conquering for them, above all, the satisfaction and security of nourishment in their daily life.

The capitalists and the wealthy will be traitors to the Patria if, immersed in a facile euphoria . . . they continue as they have, with incorrigible egotism, concerned exclusively with their own interests, without looking to the side or rear to witness the wake of hunger, scarcity, and suffering that follows them and closes in on them.[44]

Hedilla closed his Christmas Eve radio address with the following peroration:

Open arms to the worker and to the peasant!
Let there be only one nobility, that of labor!
May the bosses of industry, the countryside, the bank, and the city disappear!
Let us extirpate the idle!
Work, well remunerated, for everyone!
The state must care for your children as for its own blood!
May none of the social gains obtained by workers remain on paper alone, without effect, but be converted into reality![45]

Falangist publications were subjected to censorship by the military government and sometimes suffered deletions. The censors were disturbed not so much by abstract demagogy, as in the passages above, as by any tendency to claim public authority or prescribe the specific outcomes of state policy in political or social matters.

Perhaps the most notable single conflict about propaganda during the autumn and winter of 1936–37 developed after the Junta de Mando insisted on reprinting on its first anniversary José Antonio's electoral campaign speech of 2 February 1936, which had proclaimed the need to "have the courage to dismantle capitalism." After the Junta de Mando had issued orders to all Falangist papers and to all provincial chiefs to reproduce this discourse, the Delegation of Press and Propaganda of Franco's government decided that the Falangists had gone too far. On 31 January 1937 it dispatched telegrams to Falangist officials and publishers categorically forbidding republication or distribution of the speech on the grounds that it violated the decree of 25 September. This was an almost unprecedented step in the Nationalist zone, and some of the provincial leaders ignored it. José Andino ordered 25,000 copies prepared for distribution in Burgos, and other copies were distributed in Salamanca, while the speech was also read over the radio in Burgos and Valladolid. For this action a number of Falangists were arrested, the most notable detainees being Dionisio Ridruejo, provincial chief of Valladolid, Antonio Tovar, José Antonio Girón, and Javier Martínez de Bedoya. Though all were released within four days, plans were made for prosecution (in most cases never carried out). In the name of Franco, the deputy chief of the General Staff of the army sent a message to Hedilla ordering that he purge the "undesirables infiltrated into the organization" and discharge the provincial leaders in Burgos, Valladolid, and Salamanca (though this order also seems to have been rescinded).[46]

Concern about Falangist radicalism was heightened by the influx of leftists trapped in rebel territory. By early 1937 in some districts of the western part of Seville province, up to 69 percent of the members were workers and farm laborers previously attracted to the left. After Málaga fell on 10 February, a thousand new members joined the Falange within twenty-four hours, many of them former leftists.[47] Similarly, in Logroño and Navarre liberals and leftists joined the party as a means of thwarting Carlists. In Andalusia and Extremadura Falangist organizers sometimes followed the military advance into worker and farm-laborer districts, registering leftists and incorporating them into the militia. After the occupation of the northern Republican zone, many leftist miners were brought into the Falange, if only on the most nominal basis.[48]

Party membership did not always save former leftists. They were often required to volunteer for the combat militia, where some were killed while others sometimes deserted to their former comrades. New party members with strong leftist records were not exempt from the repression; a number were executed.[49]

Nonetheless the party continued to welcome former liberals and leftists, though so many sometimes joined that it became temporarily necessary, as at Salamanca, to suspend such admissions.[50] Falangist posters read: "The past is not important to us. . . . There is room in our ranks as comrades for all who share our goals and the desire to redeem the Patria."[51] As late as six months after the war ended, so many of those arrested in the wholesale purges conducted by military tribunals were found to have enrolled in the Falange that a special order was finally published, on 9 September 1939, stipulating that everyone arrested in the future would have to be asked if he was a member of the movement. If the reply was affirmative, Falangist authorities would be notified immediately.[52]

Under the Junta de Mando progress was made in developing the party's auxiliary organizations. The military government's veto of 25 September on new politically affiliated syndical activities was soon overcome by Hedilla, and the Confederación de Obreros Nacional-Sindicalistas (CONS) was revived and expanded, though it would not become a major organization under wartime conditions. The SEU was also reconstituted.

A Falangist children's organization was created, at first called "Balillas" in imitation of Italian Fascism but soon changed to the more Spanish and independent-sounding "Flechas" (Arrows).

It soon developed, however, that after the militia the most important of the Falangist auxiliary organizations was the Sección Femenina, which quickly began to expand into a mass organization. The Sección's most important activity was its network of social welfare centers, first established in Valladolid in the winter of 1936–37 by Mercedes Sanz Bachiller, the widow of Onésimo Redondo. It was initially called Auxilio de Invierno in imitation of the Nazi Winterhilfe, but later hispanized as Auxilio Social. Originally created especially for the care of orphans and other needy children suffering under wartime conditions, the centers of Auxilio Social quickly expanded into maternity care and the large-scale provision of food and clothing for the needy. The Sección Femenina organized volunteer female labor for the war effort, particularly in military hospitals and laundries, counting 1,250 local centers by the beginning of 1938 and nearly 3,000 by 1939. This became the largest single welfare and assistance network in Spanish history to that date, and filled a very important role in the relief of suffering during the war.[53]

The third plenary meeting of the party's National Council was convened by Hedilla for 20 November. There was, of course, no anticipation that this would become the most fateful date in the history of the movement to that point. Word of José Antonio's execution reached the councillors by radio from the Republican zone that very evening. They were stunned, but there remained considerable doubt as to whether it was really true. Could this be more Republican propaganda to weaken Falangism? In view of the uncertainties and the potential effect on the movement, it was quickly decided that no announcement would be made regarding José Antonio's fate, though in the weeks to come his death would increasingly be accepted as a fact by most of the leaders.

This naturally raised the question once more of leadership and the succession, but for the time being everything continued as before, since no productive alternative was available. José Antonio himself had not been the best judge of personnel or leaders, and was as much influenced by cronyism as anything else, though he did have the critical sense to perceive that the party's secondary leadership structure was weak. A personal supporter would in turn later complain that Hedilla's "principal mistake . . . lay in respecting overmuch all the appointments made by José Antonio, or attributed to him, which had been made, in any event, in conditions absolutely different from those of the second half of 1936."[54]

By December 1936 it had become clear that the Falange had a leadership problem, related to both the succession to the regular Jefatura Nacional and the autonomy and centrifugal tendencies among the provincial leaders. According to one reading, the worst cases of excess among the latter might be found in Andalusia, where the legitimist Sancho Dávila had acquired extensive power, in Extremadura under José Luna, under Andrés Redondo in Valladolid, and under José Moreno in Navarre, Alava, and Guipuzcoa. None of these leaders challenged Hedilla directly, and most of them at one time or another had supported him as a necessary convenience, but all tended to act with a degree of independence, and the same might be said for a number of leaders in other provinces.

There was also a distinctive Falangist culture and propaganda center in Pamplona led by the "cura azul," Yzurdiaga, which featured the eminent Catalan philosopher and essayist Eugenio d'Ors and also included several other writers and intellectuals, of whom the most capable was the young Pedro Laín Entralgo. D'Ors had migrated from moderate Catalanism and cultural vanguardism to Spanish nationalism and his own style of "cultural fascism," with heavily classical overtones. As a strong supporter of Hedilla, Yzurdiaga obtained approval to begin a new cultural and intellectual review called *Jerarquía* (the name patterned directly on the leading Italian Fascist journal *Gerarchia*), subtitled "La revista negra de la Falange" ("The Black Journal of the Falange"—again featuring the prime color of Italian Fascism). *Jerarquía* was supported not only by Hedilla but also by other leading young Falangist writers such as Ridruejo and Agustín de Foxá, but was much resented by other sectors of the party for seeking to usurp an elite role and copying the Italians too directly.[55]

The worst immediate problem developed in Valladolid between Andrés Redondo and a dissident faction of young militants led by José Antonio Girón and Luis González Vicén. Girón eventually fled to Hedilla in Salamanca, declaring that Redondo wanted him killed. Redondo himself followed Girón to Hedilla's office and, according to the latter, burst in, with little regard for Hedilla, in order to punish Girón. In his most drastic act as head of the Junta de Mando, Hedilla discharged Redondo "explosively," replacing him with Ridruejo as the new provincial chief, Girón as territorial inspector, and Vicén as a national inspector of militias.[56]

In this tense and difficult situation, the meeting of the National Council on 20 November—though only a rump meeting, since the many missing councillors had not been replaced—officially ratified the leadership of the provisional Junta de Mando. Hedilla would later admit that the Junta "met rarely. We tried to have regular meetings, but in practice, and for reasons not under my control, it was hard to get the members to meet in Burgos or in Salamanca. Once we had a meeting in Seville."[57] The most active period, in fact, was the six weeks following the National Council, for the Junta de Mando met four times between 5 December and 8 January.

At the meeting on 5 December, the "legitimist" Garcerán was named secretary of the Junta, and one week later it was agreed that the auxiliary services that were being developed would be known henceforth as the Technical Services of the Falange. At the latter meeting it was also stressed that Hedilla should be known simply as the Jefe de la Junta de Mando Provisional, not as Jefe Nacional. On the seventeenth it was agreed to send delegations to Rome and Berlin to establish more formal relations with the Fascist and Nazi parties.[58]

The earlier removal of Andrés Redondo was ratified at the meeting on 8 January, which also approved the new statutes of the CONS and the new juvenile organization, the Flechas. The Junta agreed that Hedilla should approach Franco to ask for greater autonomy for the militia and the syndicates, topics that he had dealt with in the past, and took further measures to restructure the administration and territorial organization of the party. National delegates for press and propaganda were approved in the persons of José Antonio Giménez Arnau and Tito Menéndez Rubio.[59]

Relations with the Fascist and Nazi parties ought presumably to have been very important to the Falangist leaders, whose publications were full of the highest praise for the Italian and German regimes. Hedilla apparently received personal invitations to visit both Rome and Berlin, but declined them. Though he was not at all the illiterate that his enemies portrayed and had a strong enough grasp of the Falangist program, his lack of sophistication in dealing with foreign representatives and international affairs became a handicap, and he failed altogether to use the offered Italian and German contacts to strengthen the Falange or its position in the Nationalist zone. The small delegation headed by José Sainz was approved on 5 December and carried out a successful visit to Nazi organizations in Germany, but generally failed to broaden contacts with Italy, which would have been the most useful foreign ties.[60]

## THE UNIFICATION

It was clear to Franco from the very beginning of his rule that his new regime must develop a strong political base of its own, with a doctrine and capacity for mass mobilization. Whereas in October 1936, Franco's first month in power, the monarchist leader Goicoechea had talked of the need for a broad "patriotic front," that sounded too much like the limited Primo de Rivera regime. Similarly, Franco's older brother Nicolás, who was at first his chief adviser and head of his secretariat, played with the notion of creating a "Partido Franquista" (Francoist Party), but this was soon rejected as too shallow and personalistic, in the manner of a Caribbean banana republic.

The two movements that had semiofficially collaborated in what was now coming to be called the Movimiento Nacional were the Falange and the Carlists,[61] the various other rightist groups proving comparatively less effective in mobilizing military manpower and new members. In 1933, before founding the Falange, José Antonio had referred to the Carlists as the only existing political force with a sound national doctrine, but he believed that Carlism was too old-fashioned and inadequate in social and economic affairs.

Franco found brief moments to talk with leaders of the various anti-Republican forces and also looked at proposals for corporative reorganization of political and economic structures. After the arrival of the first German and Italian diplomatic representatives, Wilhelm Faupel and Roberto Cantalupo, he assured them that he was aware of the need for a modern new social program, later telling Faupel that if necessary Falangist doctrine could be incorporated without the Falange itself.[62] He also discussed the problem at least briefly with Hedilla, and before the end of November 1936 the two asked the head of the Falange's Servicio Exterior, Felipe Ximénez de Sandoval, to sketch out possible terms of unification of Falangists and Carlists.[63]

By the closing days of 1936, Franco's administration had become more rigorous, and propaganda efforts increased. The censorship tightened and the slogan "Una Patria Un Estado Un Caudillo" (an obvious imitation of "Ein Volk Ein Reich Ein Führer") began to be used.

The Carlists also began to undertake new political initiatives. More than a few individual members of the CEDA had joined the Carlists, and the conde de Rodezno, key political leader of the Carlists in Navarre, talked with certain CEDA figures about the possibility of a more general movement from the CEDA to Carlism. His thinking was that all the Catholic forces should form one large group to avoid Falangistization or fascistization, but the Carlist national jefe-delegado, Fal Conde, as usual opposed any concessions to other Catholic or rightist groups.

The strongest, and also most independent, group of Carlists, the Navarrese, were more willing at least to consider alternatives. Thus on 19 December 1936 the Carlist writer Román Oyarzun published an article in *El Pensamiento Navarro* (Pamplona) entitled "An Idea: Requeté and Fascio":

> There are things that I don't like about fascism, among other things its flag, whose colors are the same as those of the FAI, its

uniform, which can be confused with those of the Red militia (which can even give rise to dangerous incidents on the battlefield), its habit of calling members "comrades," a word that sounds bad (having been prostituted by Marxists, those same Marxists who have hunted down with gunshots so many valiant and noble Falangists in our cities), and other things possibly of more importance. But this should not prevent our realizing that we have many things in common, and that it might be useful to tighten the bonds of union, reducing the rough spots and rounding the corners . . . rather than deepening divisions or encouraging conflict.

. . . Both forces have their roots in the people, both fill their ranks from the masses; in neither of them do the big plutocratic interests have a place of privilege or positions of command. . . . Both forces are believers and confess to God. Between them exists no fundamental incompatibility.

. . . Reader: though you may oppose the idea, consider that the goal is noble and patriotic.

For his part, Hedilla declared in *Arriba España* on 6 January: "The tendency toward the formation of a single force is undeniable. We believe that this will come about by Falange Española assimilating . . . those points of traditionalism that are compatible with the needs of the moment. . . . In the religious field there is nothing to do, because everything is resolved." The Falange, he added "sought the re-Christianization of society according to evangelical norms," which distinguished it from foreign fascisms.

Two days later, on 8 January, the very small Partido Nacionalista Español of Dr. Albiñana officially merged with the Carlists, while in the Canaries the local sector of Renovación Española had also joined the local Carlists, producing a new hybrid uniform. Soon afterward, the Confederación Española de Sindicatos Obreros, the main Catholic syndical organization, joined the Carlist Obra Nacional Corporativa. The main leaders of the CEDA and of Renovación Española nonetheless remained aloof.

The first direct political cooperation between Falangists and Carlists took place at the close of October, when leaders of the two organizations made a detailed agreement concerning the division of political and press facilities and office space in the Madrid that they assumed was about to be conquered.[64] By January, some were thinking about more serious negotiations. On behalf of the "legitimist" sector of the Falange, Sancho Dávila had an inconclusive conversation with Rodezno in January.[65] Though that discussion had been covert, hidden even from Hedilla, the head of the Junta de Mando approved a trip by Dávila, José Luis Alfaro, and the twenty-three-year-old Pedro Gamero del Castillo to negotiate with Fal Conde in his Lisbon exile on 16–17 February. The Falangists proposed that the Carlists simply join the now-larger Falange, with the ultimate goal of a "traditional monarchy," whereas the representatives of the Comunión Tradicionalista proposed no more than a temporary alliance to restore the monarchy under Don Javier, the Carlist heir. All they could agree on was to leave open the possibility of new discussions, pledge no agreements with third parties, and oppose formation of any new government in which they would not play the leading roles.[66] Further conversations were then held in Salamanca on 23 and 27 February. On that occasion Gamero observed that "it could be said that Traditionalism represents predominantly doctrine and the Falange predominantly proselytism," a formulation that enraged Rodezno. The new Falangist proposal was that the Comunión Tradicionalista join the larger Falange, which would retain most Carlist symbols and would be ruled by a triumvirate in which the Carlist regent Don Javier would play a role. Such a proposal failed, however, to speak to the issue of establishing a Carlist monarchy and state, which were the basic Carlist goals.[67]

The Spanish conflict had awakened much keener interest among Italian Fascists than among German Nazis, for obvious reasons. The first major Fascist Party delegation to Spain was the fact-finding mission of Roberto Farinacci, former secretary of the party and still a leading Fascist, which arrived in Spain at the beginning of February. It was then and afterward alleged that Farinacci's mission was to encourage a new corporate state under the duke of Aosta, younger brother of Vittorio Emanuele, as king of Spain (a sort of Fascist variant of the nineteenth-century enterprise of D. Amadeo), but in fact it had no such rigid agenda. Cantalupo, the new Italian diplomatic representative, thought that the Falange was a sort of undeveloped fascist party lacking "organic doctrine." A common tendency among Italian Fascists, as among Nazis, was to express grave concern over the "reactionary" influence of the Church, the military, and the right in the new Spanish regime. Farinacci reported that his impressions of his meeting with Franco on 4 February were "not rosy." Though Franco was younger and less "ignorant" than most of the Spanish generals, he was "rather timid" and talked vaguely about the need for some sort of corporatism. Mola, he thought, was "much more astute and intelligent."[68]

If anything, Farinacci found the Falange less impressive than did Cantalupo. He worked to convince Franco and others of the need for a sort of "Partido Nacional Español" that would have a strong pro-worker social program. Farinacci spoke with both Hedilla and Rodezno, and floated the idea of a broader government in which Franco might be prime minister, with Mola and one or two other generals in the cabinet, together with some technocrats and the Falangist and Carlist leaders.

Whatever the effect of Farinacci's visit, from February on Franco showed more interest in political organization. The arrival in Salamanca of his brother-in-law, Ramon Serrano Súñer, also played a role. Serrano had been radicalized by the war and the executions of his brothers in Madrid and of José Antonio. He had the higher education, trained lawyer's skill, and direct political experience that Franco lacked, and soon became the Generalissimo's chief adviser, displacing the latter's brother Nicolás.

Serrano later wrote that by the time he had arrived in Salamanca Franco "was already considering the idea of reducing to a common denominator the various parties and ideologies of the Movement. He showed me some statutes of the Falange with his copious marginal annotations. He had also established comparisons between the speeches of José Antonio and those of the Carlist Pradera." The problem with Carlism, according to Serrano, was that "it suffered from a certain political anachronism. On the other hand, a good part of its doctrine was included in Falangist thought, and the latter had, moreover, the social, revolutionary content that should permit Nationalist Spain to absorb ideologically Red Spain, which was our great ambition and our great duty." Conversely, the problem with the Falange was that "it was full of masses of new members coming from the Republic and from anarchosyndicalism. . . . Its leaders were old provincial chiefs, generally little known, or excessively young activists, or even, in many cases, new improvisations."[69] A party sometimes referred to as the "FAIlange" and "our Reds" would require firm control, as well as combination with more conservative elements.

A speech by Franco on 18 February was more direct than anything he had said to that point. In the "Nationalist camp," he declared, "there is no question about a movement that could be called exclusively fascist. . . . If our Movement were exclusively fascist, I would have no reluctance in saying so, since I consider fascism a respectable form of government." He went on to emphasize the importance of a "national ideology," which he said was most evident in the Falange and the Comunión Tradicionalista.[70] Franco would nonetheless continue to mark time for well over a month, preoccupied by the military coordination of the last offensive against Republican Madrid.

At the Falange's first National Congress of Press and Propaganda, held at the end of February, Hedilla spoke of "the decided will to achieve power," though he was clearly aware of the need to "pact" in order to get there. When Tito Menéndez, the new national delegate for propaganda, met with Danzi, the Italian press attaché in Salamanca, he avowed that Spain should be "Italophile in a totalitarian way" and "should accept a spiritual paternity that can only be Mussolinian." Menéndez went on to assure him that "Franco is the today; we are the tomorrow," and that the Falange could absorb the Carlists as the Italian Fascists had absorbed the Italian Nationalist Association in 1923. Hedilla had much the same things to say when Danzi spoke with him a few days later.[71]

Cantalupo also met with the Falangist leaders during this period, and on 23 February Hedilla gave him a letter to transmit to Mussolini. He assured Cantalupo that the Falange would be "totalitarian," though at the moment it insisted only on full autonomy and not on control of the government, which should not include either "generals" or "priests." Whereas Cantalupo thought Franco and his brother were "unimpressive fellows," he found Hedilla "hardheaded, elementary, distrustful."[72]

Other Falangists thought that Hedilla was being increasingly influenced by personal advisers such as the journalist Victor de la Serna and the chemist José Antonio Serrallach, both of whom had the reputation of being strongly pro-Nazi.[73] They were accused of trying to develop a sort of "cult of personality" around Hedilla; a Falangist press article entitled "Hedilla at 120 kilometers an hour" much annoyed other party luminaries. Paradoxically, he was being accused of being both a weak and ineffective leader and also of trying to advance himself too much. Yet many of the other leading party figures—Aznar, Moreno, Muro, Arcadio Carrasco in Córdoba—made a poor impression through their exaggerated "fascist style," with big cars, large retinues of guards and subordinates, and abuse of power. There was still no alternative national leader. By the spring of 1937 the legitimists were finding a new focus in the home of Pilar Primo de Rivera, now directing the Sección Femenina from Salamanca. While some of the militia leaders talked of the need for a stern "Falangist general" like Juan Yagüe to run the party, and other malcontents simply wanted a change of leadership in general, without any candidates in mind, the legitimists continued to insist that no new Jefe Nacional be selected until José Antonio's death could be fully verified. In the meantime, they pushed for the exchange from the Republican zone of Raimundo Fernández Cuesta, the former secretary general; but when Hedilla presented this request to Serrano Súñer, the latter called it morally indefensible, since it had not yet been possible to arrange exchanges for people of greater rank and importance.[74]

The Carlist leadership was meanwhile dividing on the issue of a political compromise with Franco. The regent, Don Javier, sent a letter to Rodezno fully supporting Fal Conde's rejection of a fusion, which the regent insisted be given also to Franco, who was infuriated by it. Yet the political leadership of Carlism within the Nationalist zone was now dominated by the Navarrese, who obtained the resignation of the acting Junta Nacional Carlista, replaced by the formation in Burgos on 22 March of a new Council of Tradition led by Rodezno's Navarrese. Its president, José Martínez Berasain, then had a cordial meeting with Franco, who was assured of cooperation. Franco subsequently met with Rodezno on 9 April and with other Carlist leaders two days later, telling them that he would soon move toward a unification of political groups. When they pointed out that Salazar had not followed such a strategy in Portugal, Franco countered that this was why Salazar's government was weak.[75] Meanwhile, the Carlists' "alfonsino" counterpart, Renovación Española, had dissolved itself on 8 March, its leader declaring that all the rightist forces were in favor of a more advanced social policy and that the wartime emergency required "a totalitarian structure . . . in a purely organic system, in which all have a place to fill."[76]

Hedilla was apparently encouraged by agents from Franco's headquarters to believe that the main interests of the Falange would be upheld in any process of unification. The most important of the latter were the "captains from Mallorca": two Falangist army officers, Ladislao López Bassa and Vicente Sergio Orbaneja, from the main garrison in the Balearics. López Bassa was a Falangist veteran, one of the founders of the party on Mallorca, and Orbaneja a distant relative of José Antonio Primo de Rivera. They seem to have assured Hedilla that the core Falangist leaders would play the predominant roles in a united party.[77] Some observers noted that Hedilla now spoke publicly of Franco in the most glowing terms.

Hedilla also moved, somewhat belatedly, to rally more support from the Italians and Germans. The Italian ambassador and press attaché were assured that Franco was a reactionary while Falangists were revolutionary men of the left who would tolerate the portly Generalissimo only for the duration of the war. Though his supporters pictured Hedilla as a charismatic leader of working-class origins who could provide political leadership for a united fascist party that would be totally beyond the grasp of a general like Franco, Cantalupo in fact regarded the head of the Junta de Mando as poorly educated and essentially mediocre.[78] Only the German representative Faupel could have been considered a real foreign supporter of Hedilla. "According to Cantalupo, Faupel despised Franco and, immediately after the battle of Guadalajara, told him on two separate occasions that it was necessary to eliminate Franco in order to give power to the Falange, which, for the Germans, meant Hedilla."[79] Higher German officials, however, gave such thinking no endorsement.

Other Falangist leaders were more overtly belligerent than Hedilla, and at the last regular meeting of the Junta de Mando on 30 March they approved unanimously a very labored sentence that they instructed Hedilla to dispatch to Franco:

> In view of the attacks directed at our movement by the servants of the state, who are generally old politicians declared enemies of the Falange, and of the difficult circumstances undergone by the military situation, it is agreed to send a message to the Chief of State requesting for Falange the political task of governing the country, save for the Departments of War and Navy.[80]

Whether or not Hedilla supported this demand in the meeting, he clearly soon had second thoughts about it, explaining later that, since "I considered it in some respects inappropriate, I impugned it [sic] with another document that I strongly supported, and circumstances have shown that I was right, but I ended up resigning myself to the votes of the rest."[81] The "other document" prepared by Hedilla apparently softened the demand and made references to the greater support and representativeness of a unified movement based on the Falange. Nonetheless, pressure from the other party chiefs forced Hedilla within a matter of days to transmit the original demand without his more accommodating message. It undoubtedly irritated Franco but made not the slightest impression on him.

Franco apparently made his final decision on 11 April, when he asked Serrano Súñer to finish drafting the terms for a fusion of the Falangists and Carlists. That same day Nicolás Franco told the Italian press attaché that Franco must quickly seize control of the parties, for a dangerous dissidence was developing, and Franco said much the same to Faupel, observing that the Falangists, like the Nazi Brown Shirts in 1934, had to be firmly controlled.[82] Meanwhile, he obtained the agreement of Mola and the other top generals, including Yagüe, the senior Falangist officer, for his plans.

Hedilla finally began to react by the end of the first week of April, trying to assess the attitude of the party leaders, making direct contact with various militia leaders, and also discussing possible terms with the Carlists. He generally had the support of most (though not all) Falangist leaders in the northern provinces, while the "legitimists" and other dissidents were stronger in the south. The important leaders in Valladolid (Girón and Ridruejo) tended toward a discreet neutrality. On 12 April he told several Falangist leaders in San Sebastián that an agreement would soon be reached with the Carlists. Meanwhile, López Bassa and Orbaneja initiated their own unification process with the Mallorcan Carlists, and on the fourteenth, sixth anniversary of the founding of the Republic, the leaders of the JAP, the CEDA youth group, denounced "political parties" and declared their complete loyalty to Franco. At almost the same time Hedilla learned that the Carlists were too divided to deal directly with the Falangist leadership and would wait for Franco to act. He therefore asked subordinates to prepare a list of his political opponents within the party and moved on the fourteenth to ratify his position by scheduling a new meeting of the party's National Council in Burgos for the twenty-fifth.[83]

By April a Falangist "theater of the absurd" was developing. Agents of the Generalissimo were encouraging Hedilla to reaffirm his authority within the party while stimulating his opponents to challenge him directly. The goal was to create maximum conditions of internal turmoil and weakness that would facilitate and justify Franco's takeover. The main opposition to Hedilla continued to come from the legitimists, but they were also supported to some degree by others, such as José Moreno (transferred by Hedilla from the provincial jefatura in Navarre to the central Falangist administration in Salamanca) and Fernando González Vélez, a medical doctor who some months earlier had become provincial chief of León.

After informing Franco of their intentions and moving a squad of armed supporters into Salamanca, on mid-morning of 16 April the core legitimist leaders (Aznar, Dávila, and Garcerán) and Moreno went to the office of the Junta de Mando to present Hedilla with a series of grave charges of failure and malfeasance, attributed above all to what they called the "manifest ineptitude of comrade Manuel Hedilla, due to his illiteracy, which makes him fall into the hands of the most bankrupt assassins and of the men most dangerous for the movement, of whom he is the prisoner."[84] They accused him of replacing the Junta de Mando with his own personal clique. Basing themselves on a party statute that stipulated that if the Jefe Nacional had to be absent from Spanish territory for any length of time, a triumvirate would govern in his absence, they announced that they possessed a majority of the votes on the Junta and were now deposing Hedilla in favor of a new triumvirate composed of Aznar, Dávila, and Moreno, with Garcerán as secretary. The new triumvirs then took over. During the course of the day, both they and Hedilla presented themselves separately at Franco's headquarters to inform his staff of these developments. Both sides were cajoled into believing that they enjoyed the government's acceptance.

Hedilla thus felt free to initiate his counterattack. Late on the evening of the sixteenth, the Finnish officer Carl von Haartman, head of the Falangist officer training school at Pedro Llen just outside Salamanca, received orders to arm his cadets and move them into the city to secure the

Falangist headquarters. Von Haartman insisted on obtaining such orders in writing. When these arrived shortly after midnight, he moved his armed officer cadets into Salamanca, where the police made no effort to impede their entry. They seized control of the office of the Junta de Mando and several other Falangist sites about 1:30 A.M. on the seventeenth. Small detachments of armed Hedilla loyalists were then sent to the homes of the dissident triumvirs in the middle of the night. When they entered Dávila's quarters, the latter's bodyguard shot and killed José María Alonso Goya, the head of Hedilla's personal escort, and was then himself killed in turn. Dávila was arrested. The detachment sent to Garcerán's residence was held off by pistol fire.

At this point Franco's forces intervened, occupying the Falangist center and arresting von Haartman, Dávila, and Garcerán on the charge of provoking disorders. All the Falangist officer candidates were temporarily arrested as well, while the government dispatched orders to all Falangist provincial leaders, warning them against any further disorder.

That day, the seventeenth, Hedilla hurriedly accelerated plans for the National Council, which he convened in Salamanca on the eighteenth. In a somewhat macabre scene, with Goya's embalmed corpse in an adjoining room, Hedilla's candidacy for the vacant post of Jefe Nacional was presented in an effort to strengthen his position prior to Franco's impending unification. Hedilla received ten votes, while eight councillors abstained and four voted for other candidates. Despite the lack of a majority, Hedilla was proclaimed the new Jefe Nacional.[85]

About 9:30 that evening he presented himself once more at Franco's headquarters, where he was cordially received by the Generalissimo. Soon afterward, as Hedilla waited, Franco announced the unification in a radio address that he had written himself in order to present his concept of the new party. Franco assured listeners that unity had its starting point in the Reyes Católicos and would include "nothing inorganic, hasty, or transitory." He stressed the open and eclectic character of the process, for, just as the Carlists would be joined with the Falangists, "other forces" would also be added to achieve "an effective and not an ordinary democracy."

> The movement that we lead today is just that: a movement more than a program. And as such it is in the process of development, subject to constant revision and improvement, to the degree that reality requires. . . . When we have completed this enormous task of spiritual and material reconstruction, if patriotic needs and the sentiments of the country so advise, we do not close the horizon to the possibility of establishing in the nation the secular regime that forged its unity and historical greatness.[86]

Thus at the outset Franco emphasized the eclectic and open-ended quality both of the new partido único and of his regime, avoiding any clear-cut fascist identity and even announcing the eventual possibility of a monarchist restoration, to which the revolutionary Falangists were strongly opposed.

Hedilla was still left to believe that he would play the leading role within the party itself. When the National Council was convened for the second day on 19 April, the corpse had been removed but a Civil Guard captain at the entrance relieved all the councillors of their pistols. There was no gesture of rebellion against Franco's announcement. Hedilla informed his colleagues that the official name of the new party had not been determined but that its program would be based on the Twenty-Seven Points with no more than two or three changes.[87]

The official decree of unification was released by the government at 9 P.M. on the nineteenth, announcing that, "as in other countries of totalitarian regime," the old must be combined with the new. All members of the Falange and the Comunión Tradicionalista would henceforth be joined in an official new partido único called Falange Española Tradicionalista y de las J. O. N. S. "Other organizations and political parties are dissolved." The new party would be led by "the Chief of State, a Secretariat or Junta Política and a National Council."[88] Subsequent decrees named Franco the new Jefe Nacional, with Hedilla to be the first member of the new Junta Política and the organization to be directed by a new political secretariat under the captain of engineers and recent agent of Franco, Ladislao López Bassa. Membership in the FET would be open to all followers of the Movimiento Nacional, though new members would be subject to certain restrictions. The official program of the Falange was then adopted for the FET as the Twenty-Six Points (suppressing the final point, which had stated, "We shall make very few pacts"). On 24 April the raised arm was officially decreed to be "the national salute," and other Falangist slogans and insignia were similarly adopted, such as the blue shirt, the red-black-red banner, the symbol of the Yugo y flechas, the anthem "Cara al sol," the slogan "Arriba España," and the standard appellation of "camarada." That same day the military command ordered that the Falangist militia, the Requetés, and other militia units, which had just been nominally fused into a single organization, would be directly integrated into the regular army, though the Falangist and Requeté battalions would continue to form individual units.

Creation of the FET represented the triumph of the "fascistized" rightists, denounced by Ledesma two years earlier, over the core fascists of the old Falange, and was an absolutely logical measure for Franco to take

Table 8.1. Arrests after the unification

| | |
|---|---|
| F. E. members arrested | 43 |
| Requetés arrested | 41 |
| F. E. members sentenced | 75 |
| Requetés sentenced | 21 |
| FET members arrested | 581 |
| FET members tried | 568 |
| FET members sentenced | 192 |

Source: Fundación Nacional Francisco Franco, *Documentos inéditos para la historia del Generalísimo Franco*, 4 vols. (Madrid, 1992–94), I, 97–103.

in an all-out revolutionary civil war. The extent of the takeover was too complete and the subordination of the old leadership too great for some Falangists at first to accept. Hedilla found himself under pressure both from his closest supporters and from the rival legitimists not simply to hand the Falange over to Franco, though privately he acknowledged on various occasions that there was no way to resist effectively. He had, however, probably thought that he would be at least secretary general in charge of the new party and refused the proffered position on the Junta Política of the FET, though military headquarters cajoled him for several days. Representatives of the Axis powers sought to ease the tension by reviving the invitation for him to visit their countries, but Franco would not permit that. On 25 April Hedilla was arrested on charges of inciting disorder and rebellion.

There was no organized resistance among either Falangists or Carlists, though there were a number of cases of minor indiscipline and even small public demonstrations by Falangists in several cities.[89] As indicated in table 8.1, this led during the first days of the unification to 665 arrests and 288 condemnations, including 49 to life imprisonment, though all these sentences were eventually commuted.[90] The provinces in which the greatest number of arrests were made were Málaga (206), Salamanca (91), Seville (90), and Zaragoza (145).

The Carlists accepted the unification with skepticism but with even less resistance than the Falangists. Rodezno and the other Navarrese leaders managed to quiet the fears of the regent, Don Javier, for the moment, though in an interview with Franco shortly afterward they were shocked to hear him say that there was no real difference between the ideologies of the two forces.[91] All other political groups made haste to cooperate. From Lisbon, Gil Robles wrote on 25 April with directions for the dissolution of Acción Popular, the largest nucleus of the old CEDA.[92] There was no real challenge from any source.

Hedilla and more than twenty other Falangist leaders and militants were prosecuted for resisting the unification, and a number of them were also prosecuted on a second charge of being responsible for the disorder and violence of 17 April. Perhaps the major piece of documentary evidence on the first charge was a telegram sent from the Junta de Mando office on 22 April to all provincial leaders: "Given possible erroneous interpretations decree of unification, follow no orders other than those received from high authority." This was, according to the defense, simply dispatched to avoid confusion, but on the twenty-first Franco had ordered that all messages be sent from government offices only. Hedilla was condemned to death on both charges, while Daniel López Puertas (head of the group that went to Dávila's residence on the seventeenth) received a death sentence on the second charge. Nearly all the others indicted were sentenced to comparatively long prison terms, only Dávila and Garcerán being absolved. After a month and a half, following the intercession of Serrano Súñer and other Falangists, the death sentences were commuted. Within a period of several months to two years, nearly all of the several hundred sentences were commuted or completely rescinded. With few exceptions, Franco was not overly vindictive with dissident Falangists.

The principal exception was the luckless Hedilla, who was sent to solitary confinement in the Canaries for four years before being moved to more comfortable quarters on Mallorca in 1941. Only in 1946 was he completely freed and later permitted to establish himself comfortably in private business, where, using political contacts and his willingness to make some reparation, he was able to do quite well for himself.[93]

Despite or because of the injustices done to Hedilla and some of the Falangists, the operation was a major success for Franco. He had established a semifascist single party, based in large measure on the Italian model, but not slavishly imitative of foreign models. In an interview published in a pamphlet called *Ideario del Generalísimo*, released just before the unification, he had declared: "Our system will be based on a Portuguese or Italian model, though we will preserve our historic institutions." Later in an interview published by *ABC* (Seville) on 19 July, Franco would reiterate that the goal was a "totalitarian state." Yet the context in which he always placed this term, invoking the institutional structure of the Reyes Católicos, indicated that what Franco had in mind was not any system of total institutional control such as that of the Soviet Union or of the most radical fascists—a true functional totalitarianism—but simply a unitary and authoritarian state that permitted varying degrees of limited but traditional pluralism. As he put it in turning to one of his pet ideas in an interview for the *New York Times* in December 1937, "Spain has its own tradition, and the majority of the modern formulas that have been discovered in the totalitarian countries can be found already incorporated within our national past."[94] In February, prior to the unification, Franco had declared that the Falange could not be considered a strictly fascist movement: "The Falange does not call itself fascist; its founder said so personally." The custom, very common in the Nationalist zone during the first months of the war, of referring to Falangists as "fascists" had disappeared by 1937, even though some writers or ideologues, rightist or Falangist, occasionally invoked the term on their own, sometimes using sui generis concepts.[95] All that Franco had been willing to admit before the unification was that the supposedly nonfascist character of the Falange "does not mean that there are not individual fascists *within it*" (Franco's italics).[96] The function of the FET, in his words, was to incorporate the "great neutral mass of the unaffiliated," and ideological rigidity would not be allowed to impede that.

# Nine

# The FET during the Civil War
## 1937–1939

One of Franco's principal achievements as Caudillo of the Nationalists in the Civil War was to avoid the political conflict and disunity that often weakened the Republican zone. He accomplished this in part through the creation of the nominally unified partido único, and negatively through simply banning all ordinary political activity from the Nationalist zone. In an *ABC* interview on 19 July, Franco proclaimed once more that his goal was "a totalitarian state." He reiterated that the FET was to serve as a great political melting pot for such a state: "There exists, moreover, in Spain a great neutral mass, that has not wanted to join any party. That mass, which might feel too timid to join the victors, will find in the Falange Española Tradicionalista y de las JONS the adequate channel to fuse itself with Nationalist Spain."[1]

The FET was designed to incorporate all political activity and, at the same time, to limit political activity. Thus no rapid political development followed the unification decree, for the goal was as much negative in the short run as it was positive. The new organization began with limited funds[2] and the first task given it by the governor general of Salamanca was to organize nursing courses.[3] Incorporation of local auxiliary units under the party structure began on 11 May, and the growth in membership proceeded apace.

It would nonetheless be difficult to develop the new party without the active support of most of the surviving leaders of the old Falange. Though most had not resisted the unification, the main figures remained skeptical and unconvinced. A number of the most important—such as Aznar, Girón, and Ridruejo of Valladolid, and Fernando González Vélez, the provincial chief of León—clustered around the home of Pilar Primo de Rivera in the plazuela de San Julián in Salamanca. They wished to remain faithful to the spirit of José Antonio while determining on what terms they would collaborate with the new party.[4]

Franco's representative in the initial development of the FET was his brother-in-law, Serrano Súñer, who a few months later, in January 1938, would become his first regular minister of the interior and the second most powerful figure in the Nationalist zone. Born into a Catalan-Aragonese family in 1901, the handsome, dapper, blue-eyed Serrano had been educated in law at the University of Madrid, where he was a senior classmate of José Antonio Primo de Rivera. Both were intelligent and serious, and both had lost their mothers at a very young age. They became close friends, and Serrano, who studied for a year in Rome at the beginning of the Mussolini regime, may have been among the first to awaken José Antonio's interest in Italian Fascism. Serrano soon became an elite state lawyer, number four in his class, and was assigned in the late 1920s to Zaragoza, where he met Franco, then the head of the new General Military Academy. Serrano Súñer briefly ranked as the most eligible bachelor among the upper middle class in Zaragoza, where this handsome, polite, and highly intelligent young man became known to some as "Jamón Serrano" (Serrano ham), because of his attractiveness as potential bridegroom. The young woman who won his favor was Zita Polo, younger sister of Franco's wife, thus establishing his close relationship with the general.

Under the Republic Serrano rose to a degree of minor prominence as one of the younger leaders of the CEDA, revealing oratorical and political skill as a Cortes deputy. All the scorn that Falangist propaganda heaped on the CEDA and its youth group, the nonviolent JAP, does not seem to have weakened the friendship between Serrano and José Antonio, and indeed Serrano represented the sector of the CEDA most prone to radicalization and proto-fascistization, as he drew ever closer to the Falangist chief during the spring and early summer of 1936. Trapped in Madrid at the outbreak of fighting, he was later arrested but was eventually moved to a prison hospital from which the slight Serrano escaped to a friendly foreign legation dressed as a woman. His two brothers, to whom he was very close, were less fortunate and were executed in the mass killings in Madrid. The experience of revolutionary civil war and the violent deaths of his brothers completed Serrano's radicalization; he was now determined to help create a strongly authoritarian, fascist-type state. His blond hair, already graying, turned mostly gray after his harrowing experiences, even though he was only thirty-six years of age, nine years younger than his all-powerful brother-in-law.[5]

During the first six months of the conflict, Franco had relied politically above all on his brother Nicolás, head of his political secretariat, but Serrano soon superseded Nicolás because of his greater political experience and talent (and not least because of the close relationship between Zita and Carmen Polo). The Serrano family even lived intimately with the Francos, being installed in the same episcopal palace that housed the Generalissimo's wife and daughter.

Within months Serrano would become a close friend of the twenty-four-year-old provincial chief of Valladolid, Dionisio Ridruejo, who has described him at that time in the following terms:

> He was very slender and always dressed in black civilian clothing. His hair, which had been blond, was already gray but abundant. His features were delicate and his hands unusually fine and well-manicured. His gestures were free though measured. He was very thin and when relaxed slightly bent as though burdened by a great weight. His gestures were melancholy . . . and he exhibited unusual courtesy.

He was not then the arrogant, overweening foreign minister of World War II, as Ridruejo adds: "The image that I evoke corresponds to the months in Salamanca and was very different; a Serrano of modest attire, with the bodily delicacy of an artist, pained, devoted, patient, and ruled by an almost insufferable moral tension."[6]

If his earlier orientation had been toward what the left called "clerical fascism" (meaning politically authoritarian and corporative Catholicism), he would later declare that he had felt totally "benumbed" by the time he reached Salamanca and now inclined toward a Falangism strongly combined with Catholicism. He proposed to realize as many of José Antonio's original Falangist goals as possible within the structure of a new juridically defined and institutionalized system. Even more than Franco, he sought to have the new regime avoid "el error Primo de Rivera."

Franco delegated Serrano to carry out the transformation of the FET, and in fact preferred that his brother-in-law become its first secretary general,[7] but Serrano was shrewd enough to perceive that this would be resented by the "camisas viejas" (the old shirts, as the party veterans began to be called). Instead, during the following weeks he carried on negotiations with some of the old Falangist leaders, and a somewhat vague but effective understanding was reached. The Falangists would fully accept Franco's new hierarchy, an organized national political system and state would be developed, and after the war a sincere effort would be made to carry out the national syndicalist program.[8]

The majority of Falangists who had been arrested, most of them rank-and-file militants, were soon released. Some, such as José Luis de Arrese, a relative by marriage of José Antonio and provincial chief of Málaga (where the largest number of arrests had taken place), were kept in prison for six months or more, and Hedilla himself would not be completely freed from all restrictions for nine years. More than a few Falangists continued to harbor private reservations, while others, such as the national councillor and provincial chief of Seville, Martín Ruiz Arenado, were willing to be convinced of Franco's sincerity. At any rate, they had no choice. Almost all accepted Serrano's argument that it would be better to participate and have the new FET set up and administered primarily by Falangists rather than by an assortment of Carlists and diverse right-wing opportunists. Some resolved to build as large a core of dominant camisas viejas within the organization as they could. González Vélez was a strong advocate of boring from within, and he was given Hedilla's vacant seat on the new Junta Política.[9]

What was called in the decree of 22 April the political secretariat of the FET contained only one other civilian camisa vieja, Joaquín Miranda of Seville. It included one military camisa vieja, Ladislao López Bassa, the captain of engineers from Mallorca who had actively promoted the unification on behalf of Franco and who became secretary of the Junta, and one military "neo-Falangist" or wartime affiliate, Lt. Col. Darío Gazapo Valdés of the General Staff. The other members were the unclassifiable but slavishly franquista Giménez Caballero (who had earlier served briefly as Franco's chief of propaganda) and four Carlists: the conde de Rodezno, Luis Arellano, Tomás Dolz de Espejo, and José Ma. Mazón. Serrano managed to convince Rodezno that it was his duty to serve, though the Carlist leader was reluctant and soon decided that he had made a mistake, privately terming López Bassa "un bruto."[10]

On 11 May Franco officially assumed supreme command of what was henceforth called La Milicia Nacional, into which all the diverse militia formations from various groups had already been fused. Subsequently Pilar Primo de Rivera was ratified in her position as Delegada Nacional de la Sección Femenina, as were José Luis Escario for Technical Services and Aznar as national inspector of militia.

In establishing the network of FET leadership, the norm was to appoint a Carlist provincial secretary in provinces where a Falangist veteran or neo-Falangist was provincial chief, and vice versa. González Vélez and most other camisa vieja leaders, however, made no secret of their determination that the FET should be totally dominated by camisas viejas, rather than achieving an evenly fused leadership with Carlists and others. To a degree, Serrano Súñer agreed, and thus Carlists were only awarded nine jefaturas provinciales, compared with twenty-two for Falangists. Equally galling for the Carlists was the wholesale adoption of Falangist symbols and liturgy, whereas little more than the red beret of Carlism was introduced into the FET.

Rarely spoken but generally assumed was the centrality of the Italian model, with the goal of full fascistization of the FET—something already accepted as a matter of course by the camisas viejas—and also of the new state. As Tusell points out, during the first year of the Civil War Franco did not employ a particularly fascist vocabulary in his public speeches, but this would begin to change under Serrano's influence. Also of some minor rhetorical importance in 1937 was Giménez Caballero, who (though forbidden by the Junta de Mando in December 1936 to make public declarations on behalf of the Falange) was extremely active in public meetings and propaganda.[11]

What was not important was the Junta Política, whose powers remained vague. Perhaps induced by Serrano, Franco at first attended weekly meetings, but soon realized that he was wasting his time. The Junta was divided between two camisas viejas, two opportunistic military neo-Falangists, and the Carlists. Soon members began to disappear physically: Gazapo was transferred to Aragon, Mazón was seriously injured in a traffic accident, and López Bassa became gravely ill. By July at least two of the Carlists—Rodezno and Arellano—stopped attending altogether.[12]

Work on the new organization proceeded through the summer, and the first party statutes, released on 4 August, preserved much of the original structure but made the new party even more hierarchical and authoritarian. Articles 47 and 48 defined Franco's role in the following terms:

> The Jefe Nacional of F.E.T. y de las J. O. N. S., supreme Caudillo of the Movement, personifies all its values and honors. As author of the historical era in which Spain acquires the possibilities of realizing its destiny and with that the goals of the Movement, the Jefe assumes in its entire plenitude the most absolute authority. The Jefe is responsible before God and before history.
> . . . The Caudillo has the right to designate his successor, who will receive from him the same dignities and obligations.

The statutes went on to declare:

> Falange Española Tradicionalista y de las J. O. N. S. is the militant Movement that is the inspiration and base of the Spanish state, which in a communion of will and beliefs assumes the task of returning to Spain the profound sense of an indestructible unity of destiny and of resolute faith in its Catholic and imperial mission, as protagonist of history, to establish an economic regime transcending the interests of the individual, group, and class, for the increase of wealth, the service of the power of the state, of social justice, and of the Christian liberty of the person.
> Falange Española Tradicionalista y de las J. O. N. S. is the discipline by which the people, united and in order, ascend to the state and by which the state imbues in the people the virtues of service, brotherhood, and hierarchy.

Article 27 stressed the importance of the party's Militia:

> In war and in peace, the Militia represents the ardent spirit of
> Falange Española Tradicionalista y de las J. O. N. S., and its virile
> will to the service of the Patria as vigilant guard of its postulates
> against any internal enemy. More than a part of the Movement,
> the Militia is the Movement itself in a heroic attitude of military
> subordination.

Articles 29 and 30 defined the party's responsibility for the new Spanish syndical system:

> Falange Española Tradicionalista y de las J. O. N. S. will create
> and maintain the syndical organization to structure labor and the
> production and distribution of goods. At all times the leaders of this
> organization will be drawn from the ranks of the Movement and will
> be shaped and trained by the latter, to guarantee that the syndical
> organization will be subordinated to the national interest and imbued
> with the ideals of the state.
> The national leadership of the Syndicates will be conferred on
> a single militant, and its internal order will have a vertical and
> hierarchical structure, in the manner of a commanding, just, and
> ordered army.

The statutes provided that the Caudillo would designate his successor
secretly, to be proclaimed by the National Council only in the event of the
Caudillo's death or permanent incapacity. The Jefe Nacional held direct
authority to appoint provincial chiefs and members of the National
Council, though henceforth in theory half of the advisory Junta Política
would be chosen by the Jefe Nacional, half by the National Council. The
local chiefs and local secretaries of the party would be designated by the
provincial chiefs.

The Carlist component of the FET was defined as guaranteeing "historical continuity," and the representatives of the original Falange stood
for "national revolution." Two categories of members were established:
militants and adherents. The status of militants was reserved for those
affiliated with the Falange and the Comunión Tradicionalista before the
unification, for all military officers and NCOs (who automatically became members), and for those recognized for special service. Ordinary
new affiliates would henceforth be relegated to the status of "adherents"
and would be expected to "serve the FET without any of the rights"
of full militants, full membership being granted only after a period of
service.

Twelve National Services were created, mostly paralleling the state administration: foreign affairs, national education, press and propaganda,

feminine section, social work, syndicates, youth organization, justice and law, initiatives and orientation of the work of the state, communications and transport, treasury and administration, and information and investigation. This elaborate structure of service cadres was designed to compensate for the FET membership's lack of preparation by training elite cadres that could later help administer the one-party state.[13] During August the outline of the future youth organization was also drawn up, and in October the statutes of the new SEU were approved, though membership was not at that time made obligatory for all university students. Subsequently a decree of 30 October announced that any appointment to a position in local or provincial government would require approval by the local chiefs of the FET and Civil Guard; such double authorization was declared necessary until the "new totalitarian state" was completed.

The only people powerful enough to make direct criticisms of the new FET were some of the major military commanders, who sometimes complained privately if not in public. Thus Col. Juan Beigbeder, high commissioner of the Moroccan Protectorate, would write to Franco on 10 June:

> I should like again to point out the need to intensify work with the laboring masses, and to be implacable with the little bosses and petty syndicates of Falangist leaders who represent nothing. In the Spanish Protectorate the High Commissioner ought to have the power to recommend the dismissal of the leaders of the Falange and also that none be named without his approval.[14]

In practice Beigbeder seems to have been given much of the authority that he desired and would later be credited with building a stronger FET structure in the Protectorate during the remainder of the Civil War.

Opposition naturally lingered among camisas viejas but it was diffuse and without structure, organization, or leadership. The only kind of complaint that Franco heard was the one sent to him by José Antonio Girón on behalf of the Falangist militia leaders in Valladolid. Girón emphasized the importance of the Militia's having a real political identity and role, insisting that this could build a more direct power base for the Caudillo at the expense of the monarchists, who would seek to weaken Franco by downgrading the FET. Girón stressed that it was important for the Militia to have a genuine leader of its own, and not merely a general of the regular army who would treat it as an ordinary army corps.[15] There is no indication that this argument impressed Franco.

Later in 1937 there appeared a series of leaflets attacking the capture of the Falange by the military government, signed "Falange Española Auténtica" (FEA). These sheets were clearly printed abroad, probably in France, and had little effect. Rumors linked their appearance to Vicente

Cadenas, last National delegate of press and propaganda prior to the unification, who had fled to France after 19 April. Cadenas later disclaimed any such initiative and, so far as he was able to learn, the actual existence of any such organization as the "Falange Española Auténtica" at that time.[16] It was also suggested that the initiative was the brainchild of Indalecio Prieto, though he never subsequently acknowledged any such activity. Having failed in their purpose, the pamphlets soon dwindled and disappeared, but the "FEA" would continue to remain a concern for the FET leadership.[17]

The old Falange had been formally Catholic and its leader a champion of neotraditionalist religion, but the new FET would have to embrace "national Catholicism" much more completely than the somewhat anticlerical party of José Antonio, for neotraditionalist Catholicism was a spiritual and ideological mainstay of the new regime and of the whole franquista effort in the Civil War. Hence the new national delegate of press and propaganda was "the blue priest," Fermín Yzurdiaga, the extravagant Pamplona cleric who had founded the party's first daily newspaper. A supporter of Hedilla before unification, he easily adjusted and became the living incarnation of the purple rhetoric that became characteristic of the FET, invoking God and praising Franco in the same breath. During 1937 his *Arriba España* normally ran a front-page caption reading "Por Dios y el César" (For God and the Caesar—the "César" having first been Hedilla, but now Franco). His extravagant language led the Falangist wit Agustín de Foxá to remark, paraphrasing the Popular Front slogan from the defense of Madrid, "Yzurdiaga will be the tomb of fascism." Appointed in May, his chief lieutenants were Dionisio Ridruejo as chief of propaganda and a veteran Carlist, Eladio Esparza, as chief of press.

After some six months, Yzurdiaga was forced to resign by the Church hierarchy. He had helped to establish the ultra-baroque language characteristic of the new regime, but for the Church leaders his use of religious language for fascistic politics, his lack of respect for the hierarchy (Yzurdiaga liked to refer to a "Catholicism of the apostles"), and his praise of Hitler were simply too much.[18]

Even as a state party, the press and propaganda of the FET remained subject to state censorship and were occasionally curtailed. They were full of praise for the military and consistently condemned liberalism, parliamentarianism, and the left, while running numerous articles expressing great admiration for Italy and Germany. In a speech at Vigo on 28 November 1937, Yzurdiaga replied to murmurers in the party, admitting that there was some truth in the charge that the Falange was not as revolutionary as in the past, saying that many changes had already been accomplished and that one must tread the path to revolution carefully.[19] The party's propaganda participated to some extent in the rising tide of Catholic fundamentalism in the Nationalist zone, but Falangist papers sometimes criticized the more Franciscan and pacifist aspects of Catholicism and even asserted that papal policies were not infallible.[20] There were also occasional diatribes against the Jews[21] (then virtually nonexistent in Spain).

When the Junta Técnica that administered Franco's government declared 1 October 1937, anniversary of Franco's elevation to supreme power, to be henceforth the "Fiesta Nacional del Caudillo," it fell to the FET to organize the celebration. This assignment further emphasized its preeminent functions in liturgy, propaganda, and ceremony.

Meanwhile months passed and no secretary general was named for the FET. This function was to some extent being filled by Serrano Súñer, but he had no intention of settling for an ordinary bureaucratic position, nor were some of the camisas viejas willing to accept him. Party legitimists still talked of the possible exchange of Raimundo Fernández Cuesta, last regular secretary before the war, who remained imprisoned in the Republican zone. Franco at first had no particular interest in this, undesirous of augmenting the influence of the camisas viejas, but after some months Serrano became aware that he was being referred to with increasing frequency as *el cuñadísimo* (the "supreme brother-in-law" of the Generalissimo) and that there were few candidates for secretary.[22] He therefore persuaded Franco to undertake the exchange, arranged with the good offices of Indalecio Prieto, who still hoped to foment Falangist dissidence.[23] When Fernández Cuesta appeared in the Nationalist zone in October, he went immediately to thank the Caudillo, whom he soon convinced of his general reliability.[24] He also quickly established contact with the Italian embassy, to which he looked for guidance. Fernández Cuesta had always been more sympathetic to the monarchy than were most camisas viejas, and, declaring that "the Falange has lost in intensity what it has gained in breadth," he gave the impression of being a decidedly moderate rather than radical fascist. At his first public appearance in Seville on 29 October 1937, the fourth anniversary of the party, he made the usual remarks that Falangists were "revolutionary, profoundly revolutionary," but emphasized that national syndicalism was fully compatible with capitalism and added that the party would not object if "a specific form of symbolic representation" (the monarchy) were restored,[25] drawing praise from the non-Falangist right.

Though Franco was still somewhat uncomfortable with camisas viejas, Fernández Cuesta seemed adequately conformist, and on 2 December was appointed first secretary of the FET. He was flattered by the appointment and was strongly urged to take it, though he seems to have had personal misgivings and to have murmured "Yes, they appoint me so that I will fail."[26] Those legitimists who had first looked hopefully to him were already becoming disillusioned with his plodding habits and lack of initiative. In the words of Ridruejo, "We were completely wrong," for they soon realized that at best "he was a man of normal ability for a public responsibility of secondary rank."[27] A gulf quickly developed between the new secretary and the younger party radicals, which only deepened after he emphasized the syncretic character of the FET in a New Year's Day interview: "Sincerity and affection oblige me to say to the old guard that it must have an understanding spirit, without enclosing itself in exclusivism or adopting airs of repellent superiority, receiving with love and comradeship all those who come with good faith to Falange Española Tradicionalista."[28]

Fernández Cuesta was more moderate and more tolerant than many of the other Falangist chiefs and not unintelligent, but he lacked initiative and administrative talent. Moreover, as a camisa vieja he was not fully trusted by Franco, at least at first. Thus the principal director of domestic politics under Franco and the man who effectively pulled the strings in the Falange was still Serrano Súñer. Dressed in a well-tailored black business suit, he was practically the only important person in Salamanca who felt little compulsion to sport a uniform (a habit that would soon change). Serrano would later claim that "my work was mainly devoted to three tasks: helping to establish effectively the political leadership of Franco, saving and carrying out the political thought of José Antonio, and contributing to the structuring of the National Movement as a juridical regime, that is, instituting a state of law."[29]

A Falangist pedigree was quickly built up for Serrano, and his close relationship with José Antonio strongly emphasized.[30] By the close of 1937, he had completed the formation of a tacit pact between the new regime and most of the former leaders of the party. It was an arrangement relatively favorable to the latter, except for the fact that it eliminated their independence. For the most part, the FET would be led administratively and politically by the old Falangist leadership, with the Carlists increasingly marginalized. Falangists would lead a burgeoning media and propaganda network, as well as the new syndical system, and would be able to work for the implementation of all but the most radical of the remaining Twenty-Six Points.

During the final months of 1937, Serrano's bitterest opponents were monarchists, who blamed him for the development of a new fascistic partido único that might help Franco delay the possibility of restoration. Monarchists, together with Carlists, were the most active in spreading denunciations of the "cuñadísimo."[31]

Those complaints tended to overlook the fact that Serrano was executing Franco's policy. The new statutes described the Jefe Nacional as only "responsible before God and history," but despite his total authority it would be some time before the Caudillo felt fully comfortable with the party. He would never become a genuine Falangist and would never subscribe to the entire Falangist creed—particularly aspects of its social and economic radicalism—but he did accept the greater part of it, and later during 1938 his speeches would acquire a more fascistic, though never completely fascistic, tone.

Further demonstration of the character of the FET was provided through the function of the first National Council, whose fifty members were not announced by Franco until 19 October. Their ceremony of taking office was delayed until a special meeting at the monastery of Las Huelgas (Burgos) on 2 December, coinciding with the appointment of Fernández Cuesta. Nearly a third of this ceremony was spent swearing loyalty to Franco, who addressed his appointees as "my councillors." Fernández Cuesta was also made secretary of the National Council, and his first act was to give back to Franco the power to name six members of the Junta Política that the new statutes had initially accorded the Council.

The membership of the first National Council of the FET was eclectic. The first to be named was Pilar Primo de Rivera, followed by the conde de Rodezno, Gen. Queipo de Llano, and the alfonsino monarchist José María Pemán, in that order. Serrano Súñer was only listed twentieth. Of the fifty members, a maximum of twenty could be considered genuine Falangists (whether camisas viejas or serious neo-Falangists), while thirteen were Carlists, four were monarchists, and seven (later eight) were military commanders.[32]

According to Serrano, at the Council's first regular meeting its leading military member, Queipo de Llano—who had increasing difficulty adjusting to the full authoritarianism that he had helped bring about—complained that all appointments were being made by one man. Franco observed that this was not "a parliament" and soon ended the meeting.[33] Altogether, the first Council was convened only a few times, and it played no role of any significance.[34] Little more could be said for the new Junta Política. According to Serrano:

> Its labor was rather insignificant. It served, above all, to see to it that the party and the state not lose contact with each other. In some cases the meetings (let us not forget that both the official party and the National Movement in general were a conglomerate of forces) were tense and agitated. The political life of the regime lay primarily in the various ministries.[35]

The unification and the terms of development of the FET retained sufficient ambiguity and eclecticism to allow Franco to balance diverse political interests. Though Falangists predominated, the growth of the FET would still maintain a state of at least partial equilibrium with the various other factions supporting the National Movement—the several "ideological families" of the regime, as commentators would later term them. The responsibility for this balancing act always rested ultimately with Franco himself. As the German ambassador noted:

> Franco has very cleverly succeeded, with the advice of his brother-in-law, . . . in not making enemies of any of the parties represented in the United Party that were previously independent and hostile to one another . . . but, on the other hand, also in not favoring any one of them that might thus grow too strong. . . . It is therefore comprehensible that, depending on the party allegiance of the person concerned, one is just as apt to hear the opinion . . . that "Franco is entirely a creature of the Falange," as that "Franco has sold himself completely to the reaction," or "Franco is a proven monarchist," or "he is completely under the influence of the Church."[36]

All the while the shadow of "el Ausente" (the Absent One), as the slain José Antonio was referred to, still lay over the party and was much resented by Franco. He told Serrano and a few others that he preferred to believe variously that José Antonio had been sequestered and castrated [sic] by the Soviets or reduced to the most craven whimpering and pleading for his life prior to his execution.[37] Publicly he could only respect what was now the burgeoning cult of José Antonio, whose execution still had not been officially announced. Meanwhile, as Foxá liked to say, Franco found himself in the position of a man who had married a widow and then was forced to listen to her endlessly praise the virtues of her first husband.

Basically the FET did what Franco asked of it for the remainder of the conflict. It provided an official organization that all supporters of Franco could join, an official radical nationalist program (whether or not much of it was being fulfilled), and manpower in the form of military volunteers and politico-bureaucratic cadres. It continued to grow steadily, the rapid expansion of 1936–1937 proceeding with little slack, and by 1942 reached a nominal total of more than 900,000 affiliates in all its major sectors combined. This was not at all equal to the even more bloated membership of the Nazi Party in Germany or the Fascist Party in Italy (nominally well over three million), but nonetheless far and away the largest membership of any political group in Spanish history.

Yet membership in the FET came to have somewhat limited significance, and many nominal members remained inactive or soon became so. A subsequent law of 1 October 1938 further increased the cadres by giving automatic membership to anyone jailed in the Republican zone for political reasons. Beyond that, anyone who proposed to get ahead, hide a liberal or leftist past, or merely cooperate fully with the regime for the duration was likely to join, however marginal the resultant membership might be. Serrano Súñer later admitted that "a large number of party members never went beyond being merely nominal affiliates. They were, in reality, people with their own interests and representatives of more or less cautious currents of free opinion,"[38] little influenced by the official Twenty-Six Points. The FET's new Servicio Nacional de Información e Investigación was charged with a purge of undesirables, but the expulsion of 1,500 members for disciplinary and other reasons during 1937–1938[39] had little effect on the size or zeal of the party's following.

The eclecticism of the party and the partial definition of the new state left the "fascism" and the "totalitarian state" of the regime's propaganda somewhat indeterminate. The most interesting commentary would be found not in Falangist publications but in the Jesuit journal *Razón y Fe*. In October 1937 Constantino Bayle asked, "Is the genuine spirit of Falange Española Catholic?"—a question that in turn posed the issue of fascism. Bayle was certain that the National Movement in general was not fascist but pluralist, being composed of a wide variety of forces. If, conversely, by "fascism" one meant simply the resurrection of the Spanish spirit, a true Spanish culture, and the reestablishment of law and order, there was no problem with "fascism": "If by that they understand fascism, then we are in agreement. And, carefully examined, the party or organization for whom the term is least ill-suited [the Falange] stands for nothing else [no otra cosa es]."

Spain's leading Catholic theorist of corporatism, the Jesuit Joaquín Azpiazu, was less ingenuous and more to the point concerning the structure of the new state. In his article "The Traditional State and the Totalitarian State," published in the same number, he asked:

> What is the concept of the totalitarian state and what does it
> represent? Above all—in Spain more than anywhere else—it
> represents a strong and complete type of state, shorn of the
> weaknesses and hesitations of the liberal and socialist state, a power
> representing all the vital forces of the nation. . . . For many—though
> mistakenly, in our judgment—the totalitarian state means a state that
> takes into its hands the direction and control of all the affairs of the
> nation. Such a concept is totally false, and one must expunge it. If
> that were true, the totalitarian state would be equivalent to the
> socialist state or, at least, very similar to it.
>     . . . The state must assist the Church in achieving her most holy
> goal of the salvation of man to the greatest degree possible. This is

not different from the goal of the state but simply superior to it. So that if we should try to define the essence of the totalitarian state in a single phrase, we would say that the Spanish totalitarian state should not be totalitarian in the objective sense—that would be equivalent to a socialist one—but in the subjective sense of a total and sovereign power, strong and not limited, directive and not frustrated. . . . If it were thus, let us have the totalitarian state, for that would be equivalent to the total resurrection of the pure and authentically traditional Spain, without shadows of foreign systems or the mixture of non-Catholic doctrines.

Though himself perfectly ingenuous concerning the supposed benefits of authoritarian government, Azpiazu was the only theorist who grasped the full implications of "totalitarianism." If taken literally, in terms of the complete and total control of all institutions—from cultural and social affairs to the economy—this would be more descriptive of the Soviet Union than of Fascist Italy, and would literally imply total control of the Church as well. Thus "totalitarian state" was being used primarily to refer to the total concentration of political power, which could intervene in other institutions, but not a system of total control of all society, culture, religion, and institutions. The ambiguities surrounding the meaning of totalitarianism—and the question of how "total" is "total"—have lingered to the present day.[40]

## CARLISM AND THE FET

The greatest tension within the Nationalist zone vis-à-vis the FET would be found among their only official partners in the unification—the Carlists. Though an order of 30 April 1937 had stipulated equal representation for Falangists and Carlists on committees of fusion to integrate the activities of the FET in each province,[41] this had limited effect. In most provinces, the fusion was dominated de facto by Falangists, while Carlists continued to maintain their separate centers in each town until an order of 8 June declared that in towns with populations of less than 10,000 it was absolutely mandatory that Carlists and Falangists occupy the same quarters.[42] Plans were made to fuse the respective youth groups,[43] but these were never carried out, and some veteran Carlists simply refused FET membership cards. By the beginning of June, the Carlist members of the new Junta Política had sent a letter to Franco complaining about the wholesale adoption of the Twenty-Six Points and the almost complete predominance of Falangist symbolism in the FET.[44] There is no indication that Franco paid any particular attention to this complaint. The majority of camisas viejas reciprocated much the same sentiments about Carlism, and indeed about monarchism in general. One French journalist asked a camisa vieja leader what his local group would do if the monarchy was restored. "There would simply be another revolution," the latter replied, "and this time, I assure you, we would not be on the same side."[45] Young Carlists were occasionally heard in the streets of Salamanca shouting, "Franco and the King," to which young Falangists would respond "Franco and the Falange." In practice, the Falangists continued to wear their regular uniforms minus the red beret, which had been added by the unification, while most Carlists refused to wear the Falangist uniform at all. There was no official decree requiring that all members of the FET wear the proper uniform until January 1939, and even then it was not fully enforced.

The first large rally of students of the FET, held in Burgos on 12 October ("Día de la Raza"), dramatized the antagonism between the two forces. Reports claimed that between twelve and fifteen thousand SEU members participated, together with eight to nine thousand members of the Asociación de Estudiantes Tradicionalistas (AET). The AET leader José Ma. Zaldívar allegedly insisted that the AET members form in a completely separate area apart from the seuistas, while the latter generally monopolized the ceremony. Zaldívar was subsequently expelled from the FET, while two Carlist professors were temporarily suspended, being deprived of party rights for two years.[46] In compensation, to avoid alienating Carlists further, Franco made a personal appearance in Pamplona the following month to honor the signal contribution of Navarre to the Movement.

At the end of November, however, Fal Conde rejected Franco's olive branch and officially resigned his recent appointment to the party's National Council, the only councillor to do so. In consequence, when the Carlist regent Don Javier of Borbón-Parma made his first visit to the Nationalist zone the following month, he was after some days officially expelled. Even so, Fernández Cuesta did not give up and urged Fal to reconsider; he was not officially dropped from the membership list until March 1938.[47]

Fal Conde's letter of resignation of 28 November had affirmed his basic opposition to "*the idea of the party* as a means of national unity, base of the state and inspiration of the government, which I understand to be contrary to our traditionalist doctrine, to our antecedents and to our very racial temperament."[48] His associates prepared their own "Sketch of the Future Political Organization of Spain Inspired by Traditional Principles," which among other things emphasized "the rights of the human person" and the "rights" of "the family" and of "natural society," which are "prior to the state," as well as their aversion to lining up internationally with the fascist new order.[49]

By early 1938 there were physical incidents between Carlists and Falangists in the Basque Country. In this region Carlists predominated among Movement supporters, but Falangists insisted on having half of all party positions and perquisites, alleging that Basque nationalists were now masquerading as Carlists. Three Carlists were temporarily imprisoned for a strong statement demanding control of a contested newspaper in Guipuzcoa.[50]

By April 1938 even the conde de Rodezno, the most prominent advocate of Carlist collaborationism, called on Franco to protest that, as he put it, "My general, traditionalist doctrine is not that of fascism."[51] Franco put him off with his standard observation that the core Carlist doctrine was the best and the most Spanish of that of any political group, but that key aspects simply had to be brought up to date. Subsequently there circulated in Pamplona a pamphlet entitled *La gloriosa Comunión Tradicionalista a los pies de los caballos de unos advenedizos insolventes* (The Glorious Comunión Tradicionalista under the Horses' Hooves of a Group of Insolvent Upstarts), protesting that Falangists had taken over almost everything, suppressing the doctrines of monarchy and regional rights, and replacing Catholic corporatism with revolutionary national syndicalism. The pamphlet also alleged that Falangists exhibited "a purely decorative Catholicism," suppressed papal encyclicals, and sought to create "a nonconfessional state," while Franco "aimed to convert himself into a Spanish Hitler."[52] During the course of the year, Rodezno broke off personal relations with Serrano Súñer, whose power and increasing arrogance he detested, though he was forced to write to him in August 1938 to avoid further sanctions against Carlists in Navarre and against their official mouthpiece, the Pamplona newspaper *El Pensamiento Navarro*.[53]

## RELATIONS WITH GERMANY AND ITALY

Relations between the FET and the representatives of the two senior fascist regimes in Italy and Germany were very friendly but less than intimate. The German representative, General Faupel, who was an enthusiastic Nazi, had overcome his earlier exasperation with Franco and, on the eve of the unification, had accepted his leadership as indispensable:

> If in his attempt to bring the parties together Franco should meet opposition from the Falange, we and the Italians are agreed that,

in spite of all our inclination toward the Falange and its sound
tendencies, we must support Franco, who after all intends to make
the program of the Falange the basis of his internal policy. The
realization of the most urgently needed social reforms is possible only
with Franco, not in opposition to him.[54]

Moreover, Franco was very resistant to anything in the nature of German or Italian political pressure. Despite Faupel's partial understanding of this, Franco considered the German representative too officious and too ready to offer advice. During Yzurdiaga's term as chief of press and propaganda, Faupel tried to foist on the Pamplona priest a plan for a German-directed propaganda and cultural institute in association with the FET, to be named for Carlos V.[55] This was the last straw for Franco, who resented Faupel's arrogance as well as the price in mining concessions that Germany was demanding in return for continued military assistance. Faupel was soon replaced with a more restrained and professional career diplomat, Eberhard von Stohrer.

In keeping with Hitler's axiom that the Mediterranean was an Italian sphere, the Germans believed that Italian Fascists would be better tutors. As the German ambassador in Rome put it:

Anyone who knows the Spaniards and Spanish conditions will
regard with a great deal of skepticism and also concern for future
German–Spanish relations (perhaps even for German–Italian
relations) any attempt to transplant National Socialism to Spain with
German methods and German personnel. It will be easier with Latin
Fascism, which is politically more formalistic; a certain aversion to
the Italians on the part of the Spaniards, and their resentment of
foreign leadership in general, may prove to be a hindrance, but that is
a matter for the Italians to cope with.[56]

The Italians were happy to offer a certain amount of advice, but, as has been seen, they too maintained a certain distance, neither Ambassador Cantalupo nor special envoy Roberto Farinacci being overly impressed with the Falange. By this point, the brief interlude of Italian ambitions for "universal fascism" in 1933–1934 had ended, and after unification their attitude did not greatly change. A senior Italian diplomat sent to Nationalist Spain at the end of September 1937 found that the Falange had "a progressive and democratic character in the Italian manner," and that the new FET was dominated by genuine Falangists and a fascist rhetoric, but also found it a very complicated situation. Various sectors of rightists were also influential, and Nationalist Spain was not ipso facto a purely fraternal fascist state; it was better for Italy to avoid any deep internal political involvement.[57]

By February 1938 von Stohrer would similarly recommend avoiding "any interference in Spanish domestic affairs." He explained to his superiors in Berlin:

> We have thus far confined ourselves to indicating our particular sympathies for that movement in the Falange which is called the "original Falange," the "revolutionary Falange," or the "Camisas Viejas," which is closest to us ideologically and whose aims, in our opinion, also offer Spain the best guaranty for the establishment of a new and strong national state that could be useful to us. We have, therefore, readily placed our experience at the disposal of the Falange, have shown our party organizations, social institutions, etc., in Germany to picked representatives of the Falange, and have advised them upon request. We have thereby considerably lightened their task here, but we have naturally not been able to strengthen them to the extent that the victory of this element is assured.[58]

There was considerable exchange of propaganda, and the women leaders of Auxilio Social enjoyed particularly extensive orientation tours in Germany, but there was no very deep or elaborate interrelationship:

> On request, the Falange receives from the German press office a wealth of material on German conditions and the organization, etc., of the NSDAP [Nazi Party]. There is no importunate propaganda or "intervention in the internal affairs" of Spain. Any objection of this type formerly made can at most refer to the beginnings of the Falange (the Hedilla affair).[59]

By the spring of 1938 Ernst von Weizsäcker would observe in the Foreign Office in Berlin that it no longer seemed worthwhile to cultivate the Falange as an independent entity.[60] Dionisio Ridruejo would recall that the party was never mentioned in any serious way on either of the trips he made to Germany in 1937 and 1938.

## THE FET UNDER THE NEW GOVERNMENT OF 1938

Franco chose 30 January 1938, eighth anniversary of the downfall of the Primo de Rivera dictatorship, to announce a new administrative law establishing the structure of his government; the names of his first regular cabinet ministers appeared on the following day. Article 16 of the new decree on government and administrative structure officially affirmed the powers of dictatorship, stipulating that "the Chief of State holds supreme power to dictate juridical norms of a general character."[61] This law also stated that the office of President of the Government was "united to that of Chief of State," permanently reserving the position for Franco. Howcver, Serrano Súñer, who drafted the decree, also arranged to have its preamble declare: "In every case, the organization that is being carried out will be subject to the constant influence of the National Movement. . . . The administration of the new state must be infused with its spirit." Moreover, the law established certain procedural requirements for Franco's exercise of power when it declared that "the dispositions and resolutions of the Chief of State" must be made "at the proposal of the appropriate minister" and would be subject to "prior deliberation by the government" before becoming law.[62] This procedure was sometimes ignored, particularly during World War II.

The new cabinet, appointed on 31 January, replaced the Junta Técnica with regular government ministries and provided the first clear example of what would become Franco's typical balancing act, giving representation to all the main currents supporting the new regime. The senior position went to the able and respected Lt. Gen. Francisco Gómez Jordana, who was made vice president of government and foreign minister. He had served in the government of Primo de Rivera and most recently as head of the now-defunct Junta Técnica del Estado, where he had managed to bring greater order into domestic administration, so that his new role was an extension of his previous eminence. Jordana was a conservative monarchist and something of an Anglophile of the old school; his appointment greatly angered Falangists, who had hoped to see pro-Falangist generals in the cabinet. The Ministry of Justice went to the Carlist conde de Rodezno. Apart from Serrano, the only Falangists appointed were Fernández Cuesta, who was made minister of agriculture (a position for which he had no qualification, indicating how low a priority agriculture was for the regime, even though its strongest support came from the conservative agrarian north), and the neo-Falangist Pedro González Bueno, the new head of the inevitably Falangist Ministry of Syndical Action and Organization. Of eleven cabinet positions, three went to veteran generals who had served Primo de Rivera, two to right-wing alfonsino monarchists, one to a Carlist, two to relatively apolitical technicians, and three to Falangists, only one of whom was a camisa vieja.

Though the new government promised to begin construction of the "national syndicalist state," it represented primarily the military and the right, not the national syndicalists of the partido único. Subsecretaryships and other top administrative positions were filled in much the same proportions as the ministries, with a high ratio of state lawyers, civil engineers, and technicians, especially from Aragon, prewar home of Serrano Súñer. Technical personnel were of course more effective than Falangists in state administration, and it was the state apparatus (as in Italy), not the party, that dominated most affairs.

The most influential minister was not Gómez Jordana, the vice president of government and foreign minister, but Serrano Súñer. The *cuñadísimo* became the regime's first regular minister of the interior and also the new national delegate of press and propaganda for the FET.[63] These changes represented the definitive triumph of Serrano over Nicolás Franco, and he personally named many of the secondary personnel in various ministries. Even some of the nominal technicians were de facto *serranistas*. His own ministry had very broad scope, for Interior managed not only much of the domestic politics of the Nationalist zone but also local administration, health and welfare, and the "devastated regions." His own goal was clearly the construction of a formal and juridical authoritarian party-state, and he would later become increasingly outraged with Franco when the latter failed to move firmly and clearly in this direction.

From this point dated the development of Serrano's overweening arrogance. Totally elitist, believing himself the master craftsman of a firm new authoritarian regime, he made less and less effort to hide his sense of superiority. His manners became curt and arrogant, and his style increasingly unilateral, though its worse excesses would become manifest only after the end of the Civil War.

The principal functions of the FET would be social and propagandistic. All publishing activity was to be controlled by the new press law for Spain that Serrano introduced on 22 April. In presenting this measure—which would establish the norms of censorship in Spain for twenty-eight years[64]—Serrano declared that the FET constituted "the impetus and firm base of the state," whose goal was "carrying out the National Revolution" through "a state of war."[65] The law had actually been written by José Antonio Giménez Arnau, head of the Press Service in the ministry as well as FET national delegate for the press.[66] It declared that the press should "communicate to the nation the orders and directives of the state and its government" in order to build "the collective conscience," and thus it must be rescued "from capitalist servitude, and from reactionary or Marxist clienteles." The Press Law therefore established a rigid system of control and prior censorship, regulating the number and size of newspapers as well as the naming of their directors and the rules of journalistic and editorial procedure. In each provincial government there would be a censor from the Ministry of the Interior, with the power of complete confiscation of presses and enterprises, if necessary, to "punish governmentally any writing that directly or indirectly tends to diminish the prestige of the nation, hinder the work of government, or sow pernicious ideas among the intellectually weak." The only appeal was to the head of the government himself.

The young triad now in charge of Falangist propaganda and publications were Giménez Arnau, Antonio Tovar (head of Radio Nacional), and Ridruejo, the new national delegate of propaganda.[67] Ridruejo and Tovar, who were becoming close friends of Serrano, represented the most zealous elements within Falangism and burned to create a genuinely revolutionary and totalitarian system. Their empire grew rapidly; between 1936 and 1943 there developed a network of forty-five daily newspapers, numerous radio stations,[68] and many specialized publications.[69]

Ridruejo's goal was the development of a propaganda machine that would permeate and also help to regenerate Spanish culture. Still only twenty-five years old, he would be called by detractors the "Spanish Goebbels," partly in reference to his diminutive stature. A poet and writer of ability, he would also in later years earn a more serious place in Spanish letters than any other Falangist writer.

In practice, however, the new press and propaganda system was both more restrictive and more rightist than Ridruejo and Giménez Arnau intended, particularly at the local level. The censorship also restricted Falangist publications, discouraging elaborate denunciation of the "bourgeoisie" and "capitalism," though such denunciations would still be found not infrequently in the Falangist press.

Falangist leaders generally believed that the party had been slighted in the composition of the new government. They distrusted most of the military and all of the monarchists. On the one hand they feared that Jordana was too conservative to combat "the crime of Gibraltar" and resented the appointment of the very right-wing Gen. Severiano Martínez Anido to the Ministry of Public Order. Martínez Anido was resented not just because he was a military man, but above all because of the severity and, it was felt, the capriciousness of the repression of the left under his leadership. Some Falangists argued that his policies in the long run weakened rather than strengthened the regime. This feeling was given public utterance by Gen. Juan Yagüe, one of those responsible for elevating Franco to supreme power but also the nearest thing to a genuine Falangist among the senior generals. On 19 April 1938 Franco addressed a rather spectacular mass meeting in Zaragoza to mark the first anniversary of the unification.[70] Yagüe also spoke, attributing the war among other things to many years of social injustice. He suggested that greater leniency toward defeated Republicans could help overcome that, and also asked pardon "for the camisas viejas" who were still in prison, "soldiers of the old guard who have been mistaken, but who have been mistaken in good faith."[71] As Von Stohrer reported it:

> In particular it was felt that the parts of his speech in which he
> gave free recognition to the bravery of the Red Spanish opponents,
> defended the political prisoners—both the Reds and the "Blues,"

who were arrested because of too much political zeal—and severely attacked the partiality of justice, went beyond his authority and represented a lack of discipline: the answer was his recall from command, at least temporarily.[72]

After the Nationalist Army broke through to the sea in April 1938, some expected a quick end to the war, but rather than rolling up a semi-defenseless Catalonia, Franco committed his army to a slow, difficult advance southward down the coastal road toward Valencia. This was followed by the Republican Ebro offensive in July, and for the first time a certain degree of war weariness was being registered among the Nationalists—among both some of the military and some of the Falangists. This was pointed out in Von Stohrer's report to Berlin on 1 July, which explained that some elements among the Nationalists now wanted an end to the war:

> This is especially true also because in circles of the original Falange, already angered by the Church policy of Franco and Suner [sic], the opinion is being expressed more and more that the regime of General Martínez Anido is unbearable and that it is desirable to bring about a change in these methods, regarded by wide circles in National Spain as unendurable in the long run. In this connection it is not without interest that the Falange recently demanded of Franco that the Ministry of Public Order be given over to it and that a Ministry of Public Health be created by Martínez Anido.[73]

The general, in turn, reciprocated the deepest animosity against the "cuñadísimo." Someone close to Martínez Anido handed the Italian consul a "confidential report" petitioning Mussolini to intervene with Franco to obtain dismissal of Serrano, whom Anido described as "proud, malicious, all-encompassing, inattentive to his government colleagues." The minister of public order insisted that "no one can be found who speaks well of him," and that he was so destructive he would ruin "fascism" in Spain.[74]

One response to all this was Franco's speech in Burgos on 18 July 1938, the second anniversary of the rebellion, which was both extremely nationalist and unusually fascistic, proclaiming a "National Revolution" that would create a state which would be both "missionary and totalitarian." In a preliminary draft he had written the phrase "fascist Spain," but thought better of it and crossed it out.[75] This in turn was only slightly balanced by the standard invocation of religion, with a feeble reference to "the human fraternalism that has its deepest tradition in the precepts of the Holy Gospel."[76]

Serrano Súñer, if not the Falange, won the contest with Martínez Anido. The elderly general fell gravely ill in August (dying four months later), and Serrano added public order to his already extensive powers and responsibilities.

## SOCIAL POLICY

Demagogy was not a feature of Falangist rhetoric alone, for tough talk about "capitalism" and "bankers" was characteristic of the military leadership, particularly during the early phase of the war. Nationalist commanders had threatened stiff sanctions against employers who failed to honor the existing social legislation of the Republic,[77] and in an interview Franco had promised

> all possible reforms within the capacity of the nation's economy. We
> balk at nothing that the country's economy can stand. No use in
> giving poor land to poor peasants. It is not land alone that counts,
> but money to work it. Another twenty-five years will see the breakup
> of big estates into small properties and the creation of a bourgeois
> peasantry.[78]

In a subsequent interview he had emphasized that the goal of the Nationalist movement was not to "defend capitalism" but to save the national interest and the well-being of Spain. "We come for the middle class," he said, "we come for the humble class," not the wealthy. Franco promised state regulation of large concentrations of wealth and an agricultural development program featuring easier credit, the cultivation of unused land, reforestation, stimulation of the cattle industry, and special encouragement for such cash crops as tobacco, cotton, and flax.[79] Queipo de Llano, for his part, had declared, "We realize that the problem of class hatred can only be solved by the removal of extreme class distinctions. We realize, also, that the wealthy, by means of taxation, have to contribute toward a more equitable distribution of money."[80] Mola had early plumped for a "representative" kind of corporatism.[81] During the first months of the Civil War especially, the press in the Nationalist zone carried dire warnings addressed to "capitalists" demanding their conformity and financial contributions before it was too late.

During 1937 Franco had still tended to stress the roots in Catholic doctrine of the social policy of the new state, in a manner more Carlist than Falangist. He occasionally denounced "the dehumanized banker," as in his speech on the first anniversary of the rebellion on 18 July,[82] and later declared:

> We are carrying out a profound revolution in the social sense, which
> is inspired by the teachings of the Catholic Church. There will be

Women supporters of the Nationalists

fewer rich, but there will also be fewer poor. The new Spanish state will be a true democracy in which all citizens participate in the government through their professional activity and their specific employment.[83]

If its new role as state party somewhat inhibited national syndicalist demagogy, the main thrust of Falangist economics lay not in Catholic reform or pure corporatism but in a policy of statism and control—perhaps as close as one can come to defining the general policy of "fascist economics." Thus when late in 1937 a group of businessmen in the Nationalist zone organized themselves as a "Junta Directiva Provisional de Fuerzas Económicas" to press for a relatively liberal policy, the writer Gonzalo Torrente Ballester, one of the new FET intellectuals, emphasized instead the need for widespread state control and intervention.[84]

Despite repetition of the Falangist slogan "National Revolution," neither Franco nor the FET spokesmen offered any clear proposal for systemic change, but much was promised along the lines of populist and nationalist reform to regulate large property and finance, to stimulate development, to provide greater opportunity for small business and small property, and greater social justice for the lower classes.

In January 1938 the National Council of the FET formed a committee to study the development of a plan to be called "Corporative Bases of the Spanish State,"[85] and at approximately the same time there appeared a book entitled *Manual del fascismo*, published under a pseudonym by Alfonso García Valdecasas, who had returned to the party and was the government's new undersecretary of national education. The chief purveyor of information on social policy both to the government and to the FET seems to have been the Italian labor attaché, Marchiandi, a rather radical Fascist national syndicalist, who had been sent to Spain the preceding summer.[86]

The first regular government of Franco therefore approved early in 1938 a proposal that a "Fuero del Trabajo" be prepared to fulfill the same function as the Carta del Lavoro (Labor Charter) in Fascist Italy. This would in fact be the regime's only major institutional statement on domestic policy during the Civil War.

Two draft projects were prepared, one by Pedro González Bueno, the neo-Falangist minister of syndical organization, and a few associates,[87] the second by two of the more radical neo-Falangists with academic backgrounds, Joaquín Garrigues and Francisco Javier Conde, working together with Rodrigo Uría and receiving some collaboration from Fernández Cuesta. The last four worked out of the General Secretariat of the FET. Their draft was originally entitled "Carta del Trabajo," reflecting its Italian inspiration, and turned out to be quite radical, proposing to place the national economy under the control of the "National-Syndicalist State" and its future syndical system, with a program based on an anticapitalist concept of property.[88]

The Garrigues–Javier Conde project was championed by Fernandez Cuesta in a six-hour meeting of the Council of Ministers but rejected. It drew the opposition of all the rightist ministers and especially of Martínez Anido. The González Bueno project, conversely, was more moderate, though even here conservative amendments were desired, and the text was referred to the National Council of the FET for further polishing.[89]

Fernández Cuesta therefore convened a full meeting of the National Council in Burgos on 6 March. It was fully attended; both Franco and Serrano Súñer were present. Extensive discussion ensued, Carlists and other more conservative sectors seeking to make the Fuero more conservative and more Catholic, Falangists countering with amendments to make it more radical. Serrano tried to salvage the situation by recommending as the most acceptable outcome a general statement of aims and ideas, and Franco directed that a third draft be prepared by a special commission headed by Fernández Cuesta. It began work immediately. The Italian labor attaché Marchiandi remained in active contact with members of the commission, working particularly with three of the rightist members—José Yanguas Messía, the Carlist Esteban Bilbao, and Eduardo Aunós (Primo de Rivera's labor minister). It has been suggested that he worked more with the right because Marchiandi now saw radical Falangists as becoming increasingly influenced by Nazism.[90]

The resulting document, called the "Fuero del Trabajo," was approved unanimously by the National Council on 9 March. In its final redaction, it adopted much of the language of social Catholicism, while retaining the basic principles and ideas of the Italian Fascist Carta del Lavoro. The historic if anachronistic Castilian term "Fuero" was adopted in place of the mimetic Italian term in order to avoid the appearance of imitation and emphasize the traditional Spanish principles and identity of the regime. Thus the terminology of "young nations with a totalitarian sense," as initially reported,[91] was consciously rejected in favor of more traditional phrasing. The resulting compromise pleased most sectors—except for the most radical Falangists—drawing the approbation of Catholics[92] as well as the general approval of Italian Fascist authorities. It nonetheless marked a further step in the fascistization of the regime.

The document announced the goal of "renovating the Catholic tradition, social justice, and high human sentiment that informed the legislation of our Empire." It emphasized Catholic identity and the appeal to tradition, containing specific references to the family in a manner absent from the Italian Carta del Lavoro. At the same time, the Spanish state was declared a "totalitarian instrument in the service of the integrity of the Patria," repeating language from the official Falangist program. Strikes were condemned as "a crime against the Patria," and whereas the Carta del Lavoro referred to theoretically separate and semiautonomous worker and employer organizations joined in the corporations, the Fuero spoke of a "single and vertical" syndicate that would organize all "branches of production hierarchically under the direction of the state," again faithful to the original Falangist concept. As Tusell has observed, one might find greater theoretical semipluralism in the original Italian Fascist document.[93]

The Fuero proclaimed an economic middle way equidistant from "liberal capitalism" and "Marxist materialism," leading its defenders later to claim that the Fuero was not merely a statement of norms of labor relations but a proposal for a new structure for the economy. It declared labor both a duty and a right and defined capital as "an instrument of production." Private initiative and ownership was recognized as the most effective means of production, but owners and managers were given the responsibility of advancing that production for the common good. State protection was promised in limiting the work day and in guaranteeing Sunday rest, holidays, annual vacations, and the development of recreational facilities. The principle of a minimum wage was endorsed, together with family assistance and the goal of a "gradual, but inflexible" increase in the standard of living. Point 10 promised such basic social security measures as sickness, unemployment, and retirement insurance, while strikes and lockouts were both proscribed as "crimes against the supreme interest of the nation." Special labor tribunals were planned to adjudicate between capital and labor. Social justice within large industrial enterprises was made the special responsibility of an ambiguously defined "head of enterprise." The most radical provision was that which obligated the state to "try to give every peasant family a small parcel of land," while protecting long-term rent leases and working toward the ultimate goal that the land may belong eventually to him who works it.

At the same time, it was made clear that the economy would continue to rest on private property, whose protection was guaranteed. The state was envisioned as undertaking economic initiatives only when private enterprise failed or "the interests of the nation require it." The Fuero promised protection to artisans, as well as guaranteeing enough income to entrepreneurs to make it possible for them to increase wages. Point 9 promised regulation of credit to make it available for large and small loans.

Construction of national syndicalism nominally began with the formation of the Ministry of Syndical Organization and Action under Pedro González Bueno on 30 January 1938. It was to comprise five National Services: Syndicates, Jurisdiction and Harmony of Labor, Social Welfare, Emigration, and Statistics. A subsequent decree of 30 April elaborated the upper echelon of the syndical bureaucracy. A Central Syndical Council of Coordination was provided for, with national syndicalist centers to be established in each province.[94] On 13 May provisions were made for the establishment of magistracies of labor to adjudicate disputes.

Three months later Fernández Cuesta made the following distinctions between the nascent Spanish national syndicalism and Italian Fascist corporatism:

> Nor is the vertical syndicate a copy of the Italian corporation. In those countries in which the leaders have found on coming to power, as has happened in Italy, a class syndicalism they could not dismantle, they saw themselves forced, as a lesser evil, to convert it into a state syndicalism and to create afterwards supersyndical organs, first, for liaison, and later for self-discipline in defense of the totalitarian interest of production. And those organs are the corporations. The corporation, then, had a forced basis in class syndicalism. The vertical syndicate, on the other hand, is the point of both departure and arrival. It does not suppose the previous existence of other syndicates.

> Horizontal structures do not interfere with it. It is not an organ of the
> state, but an instrument at the service of its economic and utilitarian
> policy.[95]

The Falangist state, he said, would not be a national syndicalist state
per se.

> When we say "the national syndicalist state" we are referring to only
> one aspect of the state, the economic aspect. We mean that the state,
> to discipline the economy, employs the instrument of the syndicates,
> but we do not mean that the state is based exclusively on the
> syndicates nor that national sovereignty lies in the syndicates.[96]

In a public statement, González Bueno had agreed that "decisions in the
economic field" would be made by the state, but declared that "their
study will always be carried out by the Syndical Organization."[97]

González Bueno enjoyed little success. Wartime conditions were disturbed, and the authority of his ministry was in fact limited. A professional engineer, he seems to have lacked full capacity for the job. Three
small syndical organizations already existed in the Nationalist zone: the
Spanish Confederation of Worker Syndicates (CESO), the Catholic organization, which before the war had counted no more than 300,000 affiliates; the Carlist Obra Nacional Corporativa, formed after the start of
the war, with modest membership;[98] and the existing Falangist syndicates.
The latter consisted of the Confederation of National-Syndicalist Workers (CONS), dating from 1934, and the Confederation of Nationalist
Syndicalist Employers (CENS). The Carlist Obra Nacional Corporativa
had published its own *Plan* of corporative theory in May 1937, though a
series of steps had been taken at that time to bring together the Falangist
and Carlist groups, even if only on paper. Confusion so abounded prior
to the creation of the new ministry that Fernández Cuesta had dispatched
a public order to all local press and syndical leaders: "YOU WILL COM-
PLETELY ABSTAIN FROM PUBLISHING ANY WRITING WHICH
MAY PRETEND TO INTERPRET THE CONTENT OF THE CITED
POINT."[99] As it turned out, the ministry had such difficulty alleviating
this confusion that some provincial chiefs referred to the hapless González Bueno as the "minister of syndical disorganization," and a few even
resigned.

The first step began late in April 1938 with the beginning of the formation of a Central Nacional-Sindicalista for each province, to be headed
by a delegado provincial de sindicatos who was both a local official of
the FET and a state official. The Centrales did not so much organize syndicates as begin to create "syndical services" that dealt with particular
economic problems such as agricultural credit, fertilizers, rural coopera-

tives, and fishing and construction materials—branches of economic organization and assistance more than syndical organization. This was followed in July by the creation of "commissions for the regulation of production" for major economic sectors. Their function was to arrange allocation of imports and organization of exports, otherwise serving mainly an informational role.[100] Little was done actually to organize syndicates while the war lasted, and the first formal plan of syndical organization, drawn up late in 1938, was officially canceled in January 1939.[101]

In agriculture no more was accomplished. Though Fernández Cuesta might invoke in some detail variations of José Antonio's support for agrarian reform,[102] there was no intention of introducing even minor reforms so long as the war lasted (and afterward there would be no money). The Nationalist zone benefited from the fact that it included the greater share of Spain's agricultural production and could thus concentrate on obtaining steady, normal output from the existing structure of cultivation. It never faced the severe food shortages, eventually bordering on starvation, that afflicted the larger Republican cities in the winter of 1938–39.

The problems would begin to arise immediately after the war, with the full panoply of statist regulations and controls for agriculture under the national syndicalist system. This would create a nightmare of restrictions and allocations that would totally disrupt much of Spain's food production after 1938. In Paul Preston's view, "By means of the rigid imposition of a corrupt syndical administration in the countryside, Fernández Cuesta helped to turn the great wartime agricultural surpluses of the Francoist zone into the famine of the 1940s."[103]

## THE WOMEN'S AND YOUTH ORGANIZATIONS

The most effective social action of the FET was being achieved not by any of the standard pompous masculine organizations but by the Sección Femenina, whose membership expanded to approximately 580,000 by the end of the Civil War[104]—the largest women's organization in Spanish history. The Sección Femenina created a conservative social and moral framework for female activism that took hundreds of thousands of women out of their accustomed routine to a greater extent than any single organization on the Republican side. It provided practical assistance on an increasingly large scale in the form of nursing and family and children's welfare, as well as significant support for the Nationalist Army.[105]

Notable political divergence also developed within the female auxiliary leadership. After the unification, Carlist women's auxiliaries led by María Rosa Urraca Pastor were given direction of the Service of Fronts and Hospitals and did not fully cooperate with the national leadership headed by Pilar Primo de Rivera.

Pilar Primo de Rivera, head of the Sección Femenina

As indicated in the preceding chapter, the most important formation of the Sección Femenina was Auxilio Social, directed by Mercedes Sanz Bachiller, much influenced by the work of the National Socialist Frauenschaft in Germany. It became the regime's national social assistance agency, with woman power provided in part by a decree of 7 October 1937, which established an obligation of six months of "social service" for all unmarried women between seventeen and thirty-five. Though not made absolutely compulsory, this became a requirement for most young women who sought professional qualification or certain forms of employment.[106] Ultimately a severe personality conflict and power struggle developed between Mercedes Sanz and Pilar Primo de Rivera, and it was not fully resolved by a subsequent decree of 28 December 1939 that directly subordinated the welfare agency to the leadership of the Sección Femenina.[107]

Though the women's auxiliary of the FET never achieved the goal of politically educating and indoctrinating Spanish women as a whole, its far-flung social and cultural programs had a significant impact on the well-being of the less fortunate in the Nationalist zone, produced much more tangible and positive results than did the work of its male counterparts, and contributed more than a little to the generally good morale and social cohesion of the war effort.

The Falangist youth organization originated early in the Civil War, but the official Organización Juvenil (OJ) was established as a Technical Service only on 4 August 1937, and its official code of conduct, "The Twelve Points of the Flecha," was approved in the autumn of 1937. "The Twelve Points" created a strange amalgam of the Christian, military, and imperial, with such precepts as "1. Christian faith is the basis of my acts"; "8. Life is militia"; and "12. By land, sea, and air we will build the Empire." Three categories were formed: "Pelayos" for children from seven to ten years, "Flechas" for those aged ten to seventeen, and "Cadetes" for those seventeen to nineteen, with separate sections for girls. They were formed in a sui generis pseudo-military structure of "escuadras, pelotones, falanges, centurias, banderas y legiones."

Ridruejo gave considerable thought to the Organización Juvenil and prepared a fairly elaborate program, but it was decided that he was too young, too radical, and too much of a womanizer to serve as an example to youth. The first leaders received only temporary appointments until Sancho Dávila was finally named national delegate on 19 May 1938.[108]

Enthusiasm tended to decline during the final year of the war, but new sections were automatically formed as the eastern provinces were occupied during 1938 and 1939. Marches were a favorite activity, the most notable being a very large one in Seville on 29 October 1938, but the OJ could not be modeled on paramilitary activity alone, especially for the girls, and from the end of the war sports and culture began to play a larger and larger role.[109]

## THE FET IN THE LAST YEAR OF THE CIVIL WAR

Only two months after taking over the Secretariat of the FET, Fernández Cuesta had become minister of agriculture, leaving the work of the Secretariat to his assistants. They were a relatively able group, featuring such personalities as Joaquín Garrigues, Francisco Javier Conde, Rodrigo Uría, and Pedro Laín Entralgo. In decisive matters, however, Serrano Súñer's judgment usually remained uppermost.

Though Italian commentators continued to complain that the FET was far too eclectic and not a real party,[110] this in fact suited Franco. His concern was "not to let any portion of the Falange become too strong," as von Stohrer put it in February 1938.[111] He seems not to have been greatly pleased with the executive organs of the party, distrusting the National Council and its potential for either new initiatives or obstructionism. Similarly, the divisiveness and potential radicalism that had surfaced during the preparation of the Fuero de Trabajo had displeased him.

The FET's second Junta Política, selected in March 1938, comprised five Falangists, four reliably collaborationist Carlists, two monarchists (Eduardo Aunós and the education minister Sainz Rodríguez), and the pro-Falangist Gen. Carlos Asensio as the military member in place of the obstreperous and increasingly anti-Falangist Queipo de Llano.[112] Though he was somewhat suspicious of the Junta Política as well, Franco often presided over its meetings, which were rather more frequent than those of the National Council.

Since the role of the FET was still limited and partly undefined, in June 1938 the Junta Política appointed a commission of three—Dionisio Ridruejo, Gamero del Castillo, and the Carlist Juan José Pradera—to draw up a plan to reorganize the FET and its role within the state. Gamero and Pradera realized that no bold adjustment would be favored, but the young firebrand Ridruejo proposed a system for a totalitarian party-state. His two associates shied away from his proposals but suggested that he advance them on his own initiative. Presented at the next meeting of the Junta, these would have made the FET Militia autonomous and increased the party's power throughout the state.

Opposition was led by Sainz Rodríguez, whose ire had already been drawn by Ridruejo's criticism of the great influence that his ministry had granted the Church in education. He declared that the new proposal "breathed through all its pores lack of confidence in the government." Franco agreed and, in one of the rare occasions on which he seemed to lose his temper, cut in to add, "Yes, lack of confidence in the government and above all in the Caudillo." Ridruejo defended himself by saying that he had simply drawn up a proposal as requested by the Junta itself, and that there could be no "lack of confidence" when Franco himself was the Chief of the party whose powers would have been increased. Franco quickly regained control of himself, and Ridruejo escaped formal censure,[113] but the strong opposition in the Junta was further indication of the general rejection, most of all by Franco himself, of a genuine party-state. Franco had already lost interest in the National Council and henceforth would rarely preside over the Junta Política.

This incident only increased Franco's suspicion of camisas viejas, and he soon took action against two of the most prominent ones, Agustín Aznar and Fernando González Vélez, who were charged with political conspiracy. Vélez was known to be highly critical of the failure to go ahead with the development of a mass national syndicalism during the war and was alleged to want to lead a radical new "Frente de Trabajo" (Labor Front), whose name was derived from the Nazi Arbeitsfront. But as Serrano Súñer would later explain:

> From an anti-Franco viewpoint, the most dangerous Falangist in not accepting the unification was not Vélez but Agustín Aznar, because the latter, though a man of limited ideas, was firm, very brave, a fighter, intolerant. He was the real leader of the Falangist resistance. And with him there were many more, among them Vélez and Salvador Merino, who had some talent as an agitator and knew how to approach people.
> This group of irreducible Falangists maintained constant communication with those who were fighting at the front, whom they wanted to influence.[114]

It seems unlikely that there was any real conspiracy, but murmuring had continued among the camisas viejas, and Aznar certainly remained the most active of the former legitimists. He and González Vélez apparently approached Gen. Antonio Aranda, perhaps the most liberal (and one of the most politically minded) of the top commanders, about reviving an autonomous Falangist militia, and may also have taken the matter up with Yagüe. Aranda is said to have revealed the conversation to Franco, and the two were further denounced by someone in the party's General Secretariat. The phrase "Franco should be sent to command a division" was attributed to Aznar. Two days after Aznar and González Vélez had left the meeting of the Junta Política and returned to the front, they were arrested. With Ridruejo, they had constituted two of the three most authentic Falangists on the Junta, but Franco was taking no more chances: he replaced them with two loyal military men. Both Aznar and

González Vélez were prosecuted by military courts and sentenced to lengthy terms. Their expulsion from the FET was initiated by Antonio Luna, national delegate of justice and law, and Fernández Cuesta did little to defend them, a weakness which he later claimed to have regretted but which further reduced his prestige among the camisas viejas.[115] As usual, it was up to Serrano to mitigate Franco's wrath, and by the end of the war the sentence of Aznar (who, it must be remembered, was by this point married to a cousin of José Antonio) was commuted to one year of house arrest. Vélez, however, remained in prison several more years and died soon after his release.[116]

The Serrano core group directing the FET, composed partly of camisas viejas and partly of neo-Falangists, made it clear during 1938 that there must be an end to all dissonance within the party and that better coordination must be achieved. Franco personally ordered a judicial investigation of FET problems in the province of Toledo, though observing that the investigators were simply looking into "what must not be more than very modest rumors."[117] Giménez Caballero, still an important "cultural Falangist," prepared a "Report" for Franco to warn that the shadowy "FEA" was in fact dangerous and must be stamped out, and that it was also important to control dissident Carlists. "Gece" emphasized that "the Franco party should be made up of the combatants in this war" and that the Generalissimo "should do what you consider opportune for your victory." "Today Your Excellency should abandon patience, courtesy, and respect to prevent these people from ruining your work."[118] The "FEA," however, was so thin and distant a confabulation that few besides Giménez Caballero took it seriously. Nonetheless, in the police state that Franco had developed, measures were regularly taken against nominal dissidents, and a figure of the relative importance of Joaquín Garrigues had to spend several months in jail on charges stemming from rumors of "defeatist" statements.

As for the Carlists, their main achievement in 1938 was a set of new religious regulations introduced by Rodezno as minister of justice, which, flanked by the education policies of Sainz Rodríguez, began the "re-Catholicization of Spain." The Carlists had virtually ceased to vie for influence within the FET and left the initiative almost exclusively to the Falangists.

Alfonsino monarchists were also brought to heel. They had urged the political unification of the preceding year because they had calculated that, among other things, it would dilute and control the fascistic radicalism of the Falange, creating a more amorphous organization that might be dominated by the monarchist right. When they found that this was not to be the case, but that the dictatorship and the FET had dynamics of their own, a few monarchists became more confrontational. Chief among them was the national councillor Eugenio Vegas Latapié, who sought to encourage new leadership and a different orientation for both the FET and its Council. He was therefore expelled from the National Council in March 1938 and, when he tried to volunteer for the Legión, assigned to a form of internal exile in Ceuta instead. By November he had indicated to Serrano his willingness to work within the new system.[119] Similarly, no concessions were made to anti-Falangists within the military, such as Gen. Queipo de Llano in Seville.[120]

Thus by the final year of the Civil War the political unification could, from Franco's point of view, be judged a success. It had not succeeded in unifying all the diverse political tendencies or in creating a completely effective and monolithically fascist state party, for these had never been Franco's primary goals, but it had succeeded in unifying all the main political tendencies around the person and leadership of Franco, which was the most basic goal of all.

The man who might have been his only genuine rival within the Falange—a theoretical possibility that can never be tested—had now been dead for two years. José Antonio's age at the time of his execution—thirty-three years—was the same as that of Alexander the Great when he died or the imputed age of Jesus Christ at the time of his crucifixion (later, Evita Perón would die at thirty-three). As the figure of José Antonio assumed increasingly messianic proportions, the official cult was initiated by a government decree of 16 November 1938, which declared 20 November an annual day of mourning. Plaques commemorating José Antonio and other insurgent dead were to be placed permanently on the walls of churches. Chairs of political doctrine, named for José Antonio but appointed by Franco, were to be established at the universities of Madrid and Barcelona. Various press and propaganda initiatives were to be undertaken under the honorary patronage of the Founder. Projects were outlined for naming trade schools and special military units for the fallen leader. All centers of learning were directed to give a special lesson on his exemplary life and works.[121]

On 20 November 1938 Franco delivered a special address over Radio Nacional in honor of "El Ausente,"[122] who had become the secular patron saint of his regime. Franco did not object to the cult so long as it had no practical consequences directed against the Caudillo. A safely dead José Antonio—another of Franco's "providential dead"—could figure as proto-martyr of the cause, a symbol and metaphor for the "half-million deaths" that the Nacionalists claimed to have suffered in the war (the real figure was scarcely more than a quarter of that). He was a messianic example to the youth of Spain to follow the ideals of the Falange, but this increasingly would mean in practice serving the regime of Franco.

The ultimate apotheosis took place after the war ended, when José

Antonio's remains were removed from their original gravesite in Alicante. Between 10 and 20 November 1939, endless relays of young Falangists bore the bier of their vanished Jefe on a ten-day, torch-lit trek of 500 kilometers across Spain to a grand and solemn burial in front of the high altar in the church of San Lorenzo de El Escorial, which held the pantheon of the kings of Spain in a royal crypt below. Carefully and elaborately scripted every step of the way, with manifold brief ceremonies during the lengthy course of the funeral march,[123] this was perhaps the longest such funeral march in world history and was also the most endlessly elaborate ceremony in the contemporary history of Spain—a far cry from the "austere" and "plain" style that its subject had held should be characteristic of the Falange. It was certainly a fitting expression of the fascist cult of death and of the fallen, which up to a point could be made to coincide with ceremonial and theological aspects of the traditional Catholic culture, so resurgent during the Civil War. The cult of José Antonio would become, in fact, the most extraordinary death cult associated with any deceased political figure of western Europe in the mid-twentieth century, one that foreigners might look upon as "typically Spanish," though also typically fascist. It was only the most elaborate of the many new neobaroque styles and ceremonies of the FET and of the regime, as an extensive new calendar of national observances was created between 1938 and 1940.[124]

By the close of the Civil War, observers believed that the Falange had largely been domesticated and was a secondary factor compared with the power of the new state itself and of the military. The generally well-informed von Stohrer reported to Berlin on 19 February 1939:

> *The influence of the original Falange has decreased. What direction will the Falange take after the war?*
>
> As far as the Falange itself is concerned, its influence has probably declined vis-à-vis the victorious Army, and within the Falange proper the power of the original Falange has doubtless been considerably diminished by the skillful political measures of the Caudillo against the extreme Leftist (as well as Rightist) elements and by the lack of real leaders that has frequently been mentioned in the past. This goes so far that there is talk that some of the original Falangists who occupy the most important party and government positions, especially the Secretary General of the Party, Minister of Agriculture Fernández Cuesta, are supposedly attempting to retire to diplomatic posts abroad. It remains to be seen whether the "Camisas viejas" still at the front will be in a position to imbue the original Falange with new life at the end of the war. I consider it entirely possible.[125]

In fact, the future influence of the Falange would depend not so much on the end of the Civil War as on the course of the general European war that would break out five months later. Only a generally "fascist Europe" would guarantee the full fascistization of Spain. As it was, the FET developed in the first phase of the Franco regime as a kind of hybrid fascist party whose fascism was diluted primarily by its Catholic identity. More categorically yet than the original Falange, the FET took the official position that the religious teachings of the Catholic Church were correct and binding, and that the Spanish state must be a strongly Catholic state that would help to imbue Catholic teachings in the national society. There was of course a basic tension here between the fascist pretensions of the core Falange and the Church that would not be resolved until the victory of political Catholicism and the downgrading of the Falange that took place at the end of World War II.

But during the Civil War and afterward, the Church always accepted the FET as a Catholic institution, even though it would not categorically endorse fascism or every aspect of the FET. A situation of "double membership" existed for hundreds of thousands of Catholics who were simultaneously members of the FET or the Sección Femenina and of the major Catholic organizations. "Falangist anticlericalism"—which could never be formally anti-Catholic—had to do with areas of conflict in cultural and educational matters but never went beyond that.[126]

Similarly, the image and influence of Falangism abroad was felt primarily among radical nationalist forces that were also strongly Catholic. The Falange Socialista Boliviana that was formed in La Paz was not categorically fascist but a right-radical and Catholic authoritarian party.[127] Conversely, the Falanga organized in Poland by Boleslaw Piasecki was an attempt to marry extreme fascism (in this case, heavily influenced by Nazism) with Polish nationalist Catholicism.

The FET was modeled primarily but far from exclusively on the Partito Fascista Italiano, just as the original Falange had been. By 1939, however, the radical sector of the party was increasingly oriented toward and inspired by Nazi Germany. Nor was this radicalism merely a matter of the camisas viejas, most of whom had largely accommodated themselves to the compromises of the new regime. Radical Falangists, increasingly Naziphile, came from the youngest party members and also from the most radical sectors of the "camisas nuevas," as well as from the extremist sectors of camisas viejas. They would reach the height of their influence during the first three years after the close of the Civil War.

# Ten

# The FET during the Climax of European Fascism, 1939–1941

Franco's total victory in the Civil War determined two issues. The first was the complete defeat of liberalism and the left, whether in the form of the largely democratic Republic of 1931–1936 or the revolutionary regime of 1936–1939. The second was the certification of the personal power and authority of Franco himself, who now had the most extensive jurisdiction of any ruler in the history of Spain, and was at that moment the most formally or theoretically unchecked authority in Europe. Stalin had at least a nominal constitution and Hitler a nominal parliament; Franco had neither. Moreover, a new Law of the Leadership of the State, published on 9 August 1939, further expanded Franco's powers as originally defined by the decree of 29 January 1938. The new measure declared that Franco held "in a permanent manner the functions of government," and was categorically relieved of the need to submit new legislation or decrees to his cabinet "when urgent demands so require it."[1] In addition, revised statutes of the FET, issued a few days earlier, further extended his direct control over the party. Propaganda concerning Franco's personal role and leadership hit its full stride during the final year of the Civil War, with invocations of "Franco, Franco, Franco" in the Italian Fascist style of "Duce, Duce, Duce."

What were not solved were the conflicting political tensions and rival expectations from the diverse forces within the regime. These numbered at least five. Falangists themselves were potentially divided into two sectors: the large majority of the "acomodados" (accommodated), basically franquista and looking to Italy as their model, and the minority of Falangists, mostly younger but made up of both camisas viejas and camisas nuevas, who were revolutionary in outlook and strongly Naziphile. Then there were the alfonsino monarchists, looking toward an authoritarian "instauración," as well as the Carlists, still vigorous and not lacking in influence within the regime, who sought the establishment of their own system. A somewhat separate current yet was that of "political Catholicism," also rightist and authoritarian, which accepted the FET and Franco, but emphasized the role of Catholic tutelage and Catholic corporatism. By the same token, political Catholicism might be equally content with a right-wing monarchy. The most influential single force within the regime, the military, did not represent a single tendency, for the military had no specific program of their own. They supported Franco, though they would accept a monarchy. There were both Falangist and Carlist minorities within the military, but in general the officer corps after the war became increasingly hostile to the pretensions of the FET.

Thus victory began to accentuate the growing differences between Franco and Serrano on the one hand and varying alignments of high military officials, rightists, monarchists, and political Catholics on the other. At issue above all was whether the regime would become categorically fascist or evolve in the direction of a conservative Catholic and/or monarchist system. Serrano's ambition tended to grow rather than diminish, aiming at construction of a fully institutionalized and largely fascistic authoritarian system. During the final month of the war, he had been embroiled in intense controversy with Gen. Gómez Jordana, the senior general who served as foreign minister and vice president of government and who keenly resented the encroachment of the "cuñadísimo's" influence. It was Serrano, not the foreign minister, who in May led the sizable state delegation to Fascist Italy, the victorious regime's closest ally, in the first major state delegation abroad in peacetime. Serrano returned with a large collection of Fascist books for guidance in the further development of the Spanish system.

This trip was reciprocated two months later by Count Ciano, Mussolini's foreign minister and son-in-law. In their conversation of 19 July, Franco strongly praised the FET. This and other specimens of Falangist activism that he had been shown led Ciano to conclude that "the central factor in the country is now the Falange. It is a party which is still only beginning to build up its formation and activity, but it has already regrouped around it the youth, the most active elements, and in particular the women."[2] To Ciano, Spain was beginning to look more like Italy.

Franco clearly intended to build a strong nationalist and authoritarian system, though just how strong he wished the FET to become was not clear. He completely reorganized his cabinet on 8 August 1939, retaining only two incumbents, Serrano Súñer and Alfonso Peña Boeuf, the professional engineer in charge of public works. Five cabinet posts were given to Falangists and neo-Falangists, compared with three in the preceding government, reflecting an effort to approximate, at least symbolically, the new fascistic era that seemed to be dawning in Europe. Yet three of the five new Falangist ministers were army men, beginning with Col. Juan Beigbeder, the new foreign minister, who had earned neo-Falangist credentials during the Civil War. Whereas the military had held four of twelve cabinet posts in Franco's first regular government, they held five of fourteen in the second. Juan Yagüe, the nearest thing to a genuine Falangist general, was named Spain's minister of the air force. Yagüe had no particular competence in this area, but he had shown signs of political restiveness. The air ministry would deprive him of regular military command, busy him with new responsibilities, and help placate Falangist sentiment.

Though at first some dubbed this a Falangist government, it was obviously no such thing. The new cabinet represented what had become Franco's regular balancing act between the various politico-ideological "families" of the regime. The nearest thing to a true concentration of power lay in the military, yet even they held little direct corporate power, the individual military ministers being carefully selected in terms of personality, loyalty, and political identity (or lack of it) to fulfill what were primarily individual roles. One study has concluded that during the entire first phase of the regime through the end of the fascist era in 1945, military personnel would hold 45.9 percent of the ministerial appointments and 36.8 percent of the top government positions,[3] concentrated primarily in the armed forces ministries and in Interior, which directed the police. Falangists, by comparison, would hold 37.9 percent of the ministerial appointments and only 30.3 percent of all top administrative positions, concentrated above all in the party administration, in Labor, and in Agriculture.[4] An earlier study of the top administrative positions, however, found that of a grand total of 1,871 appointments to higher-level positions, military personnel provided only 25.1 percent of the personnel involved, compared with a total of 31.6 percent for all Falangists (the great bulk of whom were camisas viejas). Various categories of monarchists accounted for 21.6 percent of senior positions, political Catholics for 14.4 percent in this period, and Carlists for only 6.6 percent.[5]

Just a few days before forming the new government, Franco carried out his first postwar changes in the FET. The new secretary general, replacing Fernández Cuesta, was General Agustín Muñoz Grandes, a professional officer and military africanista who had played a major role in organizing the urban Assault Guards for the Republic in 1931–1932. For most of his career he had been a professional soldier and then police commander, avoiding involvement in politics. Thus he had refused originally to join the conspiracy and revolt of 1936. Though he was soon arrested by Republican authorities, in April 1937 a Republican court had completely absolved him of anti-Republican activities,[6] providing him with the free-

Falangist leaders in 1939: Raimundo Fernández Cuesta, Miguel Primo de Rivera, Pilar Primo de Rivera, General Agustín Muñoz Grandes (*foreground*), Rafael Sánchez Mazas, Pedro Gamero del Castillo, and Ramón Serrano Súñer

dom that he employed to leave Spain and subsequently enter the Nationalist zone. Franco gave Muñoz Grandes a divisional command during the war, and he rose rapidly, thanks to his professional talents and a rather unique combination of austerity and ambition. Franco gave him the surprising post of administrator of the FET, as well as a cabinet seat, because of Muñoz Grandes's professed neo-Falangism (something in which he had not shown the slightest interest before mid-1937), but even more to keep the organization under the authority of a military man.

Muñoz Grandes was similarly made chief of the militia, whose independence and future development had been a major concern of the camisas viejas ever since the unification. José Antonio Girón, a leading figure among the latter, was named the first head of a new Organización Nacional de Excombatientes on 21 August. This was to be a separate veterans' organization for all who had participated in the militia during the war and would be a fairly active group, but only as a comradely association, not a paramilitary force.

The other Falangist cabinet ministers were Serrano Súñer, Pedro Gamero del Castillo, and Rafael Sánchez Mazas. Serrano retained the Ministry of the Interior and was named head of the FET's new Junta Política. A new vice secretary general was appointed for the FET in the person of Gamero del Castillo, the young right-wing neo-Falangist from Seville, former president of the Catholic student association in Seville and a prime protégé of Serrano. Gamero was also made a minister without portfolio, as was the camisa vieja writer and new vice president of the Junta Política, Rafael Sánchez Mazas. Ramiro Ledesma had once dismissed Sánchez Mazas as "the provider of rhetoric for the Falange," but he was a talented novelist and a close friend of José Antonio, who had considered him the party's "first intellectual" (in itself an interesting commentary on the party). After spending the war in Republic prisons, however, Sánchez Mazas had little appetite or energy for new initiatives.[7]

If the FET did not hold the position ascribed to it by Ciano, Franco's new cabinet and policy priorities nonetheless assigned it a prominent place. While the balance of power in 1939 did not meet all of Serrano Súñer's goals, it created a kind of military/Falangist dyarchy that the military leaders would find increasingly irritating and threatening, generating major tensions and setting the stage for the ensuing internal conflicts of 1940–1942.

The new statutes of the FET of 4 August made the Junta Política a permanent organ of party government, and Serrano Súñer carefully selected the members of the new Junta to obtain personnel who would cooperate with him. The most independent camisa vieja member was Ridruejo, but he was also a close personal friend. The other camisas viejas chosen, Miguel Primo de Rivera and José María Alfaro, had spent the war in Republican prisons and showed every sign of cooperating. The two monarchist-Falangists selected were José María de Areilza and the conde de Mayalde, together with two other neo-Falangists, the law professor and jurist Blas Pérez González and the young businessman Demetrio Carceller.[8] There were also two Carlists and an army officer. Moreover, the new National Council was even less representative of the camisas viejas. Of 100 members, only 24 were party veterans, almost as many were monarchists, nearly 20 were army officers, and only 7 were Carlists.

In general, liberated former leaders and activists who had spent the war in Republican prisons seemed happy to rally to Serrano Súñer and the structure of the FET. These included such luminaries as Sánchez Mazas, now minister without portfolio, Alfaro as undersecretary of press and propaganda, as well as member of the Junta Política, Miguel Primo de Rivera as Junta member and also the new provincial chief of Madrid, and Manuel Valdés Larrañaga as the government's new undersecretary of

Falangist membership card, February 1939

labor. Some of them would, however, momentarily become more ambitious with the course of Axis victories in World War II.

The new statutes maintained the parallel system of Services and Delegations.[9] This achieved only the illusion of a parallel state structure, however, since nearly half the Technical Services dealt with the internal administration of the FET, and most of the national delegates had no governmental authority. One exception was the new syndical chief, Gerardo Salvador Merino, who was given explicit powers to construct the new system of national syndicates.

By 1939 the FET organizations claimed a nominal active male membership of 650,000,[10] the largest political agglomeration in Spanish history. Most younger men who hoped to get ahead in public affairs, obtain state employment, or flourish in various lines of professional or economic activity found it expedient to sign up, and FET membership would continue to increase with Germany's wartime victories, reaching 932,000 in 1942.[11] In February 1939 the two distinct membership categories of "militants" and "adherents" were made fully effective. An effort was later instituted—though never completed—to establish a complete network of party organization, with local FET district, section, and street delegates, and "jefes de bloque" in the larger cities in imitation of the "block chiefs" in Nazi Germany. This last effort largely failed, for the bulk of the male membership was relatively passive and rarely mobilized. The FET would never develop an organized mass activism equivalent to the totalitarian model of the Soviet Union or Nazi Germany. Hundreds of disillusioned camisas viejas, finding the new Spain not at all the dynamic system of revolutionary national syndicalism to which they aspired, were already dropping out of active participation. Most FET members would remain essentially passive and opportunistic. Though Serrano's speech to the first meeting of the new Junta Política on 31 October referred to the need for a purge of the opportunists in the party,[12] little came of this: the latter were far too numerous to weed out.

Where Falangists excelled was in public display, liturgy, and ceremony. In victorious Nationalist Spain, uniforms and public pomp of all kinds became de rigueur. This reached the point that before the end of 1939, Falangists in Madrid—where political spectacle was most frequent— were given orders *not* to wear their uniforms on ordinary occasions, such as going shopping or spending time in bars, but to save them for official functions, work, and ceremonies.

To overcome the intellectual limitations of the FET and its weakness in theory, an Instituto de Estudios Políticos was created on 9 September 1939. It was designed as a sort of brain trust for the regime and the party, combining features of an advanced training school for higher-level party leaders with those of a study institute for policy and theory. The kind of half-baked ideas served up during the Civil War—one Falangist pamphlet had declared that "fascism is no more than the nationalization of the theories of Marx"[13]—obviously would not do, but it would take the Instituto several years to make any contribution.

The most active doctrinal publicist in the immediate aftermath of the Civil War was the young Juan Beneyto Pérez. In *El Partido* (1939), *El nuevo Estado español* (1939), and *Genio y figura del Movimiento* (1940), he proclaimed the "totalitarian" character of the new state and its similarity to other one-party regimes,[14] while limning out a theory of *caudillaje:*

> The concept of the Caudillo is a synthesis of reason and ideal necessity. It is not only force, but spirit; it constitutes a new technique and is the incarnation of the national soul and even of the national physiognomy. As a technique, it is the natural consequence and organic necessity of a unitary, hierarchical, and total regime. As an incarnation it is the exaltation of a mystique. It becomes a new concept by which a man arises as rector of the community and personifies its spirit, a concept that proceeds directly from the

Revolution. It has a fully and typically revolutionary contexture, like the idea that nourishes it. . . .

In the totalitarian regimes the Party appears exalted in the precise function of selecting the Chief. . . .

. . . As a minority, it is to integrate whatever is healthy and robust into political life. Therefore the unification itself has a task of selection, since it seeks homogeneity even in the solvency of its elements. . . . The Party thus becomes the depository of a force that is continually renewed and knows how to orient each new generation in a revolutionary spirit. Thanks to the concept of the permanent revolution, and owing to the instrumentality of the Party, conflicts disappear and all energies are concentrated on the task of national affirmation.[15]

Perhaps the nearest thing to a serious philosophical work on Falangism during these first years was Laín Entralgo's *Los valores morales del nacional-sindicalismo,* which appeared in 1941. Laín classified Falangism as belonging to the new political genus of "the national-proletarian revolution," chief examples of which were "Fascism, National Socialism, and National Syndicalism." He recognized that one of the chief problems in "the revolutionary attitude" was "violence":

This avidity for violent action stems from the most hidden depths of human instinct: the instinct that Freud called aggression, for example. The problem lies in uniting this deep and vital urge to violent action with the normative and with justice. With this understood, just and normative violence has for the man who executes it the value of a purification, is almost a "catharsis" in the Hellenic sense of the word, and the supernatural equivalent and ultimate model of just violence will always be the violent action of Christ against the merchants in the temple. . . . There are occasions—aberrant parodies of this justified and even sanctified violence—in which pure violence, without possessing a justifying motive, appears to man as a means of salvation, a "vox Dei"; the latter may perhaps be the ultimate sense of the "fortiter" of Luther. Of course, violence appears in Sorel as something valuable in itself, with historic virtuality prior to its concretion in the class struggle.

. . . The National Syndicalist, without falling into pseudo-religious derivations, knows well the Christian value of just violence, and demands violent action in the service of social justice and of national justice. And, in the highest term, of Christian justice.[16]

Falangism thus shied away from any naturalistic "fascist theory of violence," and defined National Syndicalism in terms of a sort of hybrid fascism, what a later Spanish sociologist would call *el fascismo frailuno* (friar fascism). Laín emphasized, at least in part, the Christian sources of the doctrines of José Antonio, and the relation of Falangism to Catholic tradition. Even though he called "the immense and fecund national revolution of National Socialism" a project that was "like a brother to" National Syndicalism, in its specific mode the latter was also seen as distinct.

Though it first dated from 1936–1937, the official "Press of the Movement" was formally constituted on 13 June 1940, and was the largest publisher in Spain. By 1944 it operated 37 newspapers and 5 Monday papers, 8 weekly and 7 monthly magazines, and other publishing facilities. This was indeed the most public and the most tangible of all the FET's activities.[17]

The great bulk of Falangist writing was simply "press and propaganda," but the FET's literary elite also assumed a commanding role in cultural and literary affairs in the first years after the Civil War. If most novels and poems by party members were undistinguished,[18] the work by Laín Entralgo, Ridruejo, Foxá, and several others was of a higher order, and they, with some of the leading conservative writers such as Pemán, would dominate the literary and cultural scene during the years of World War II.[19]

At the height of the fascist era, when fascism seemed to be achieving a new order of nationalist modernity for Europe, the party succeeded in attracting an important group of intellectuals and professional scholars to its ranks. These included such diverse figures as Ridruejo, Foxá, Luis Rosales, José María Valverde, and Gonzalo Torrente Ballester in literature and criticism; Laín Entralgo, Eugenio d'Ors, and José Antonio Maravall in philosophy and history; Antonio Tovar in philology; and Joaquín Garrigues, Rodrigo de Uría, and Francisco Javier Conde in law. These intellectuals all achieved distinguished careers, sometimes at the very forefront of their disciplines, but in most cases would reach the pinnacle of success only in later years, after they had abandoned the fascist enterprise.

The main focus of Falangist high culture would be the new journal *Escorial*, founded by Ridruejo, Laín Entralgo, and others in December 1940, replacing the now defunct *Jerarquía* and *Vértice*. *Escorial* briefly established itself as the most liberal enterprise of the immediate postwar period. As Ridruejo has recalled:

> The journal quickly gained the collaboration of such men as
> Menéndez Pidal, Marañón, Zubiri, Baroja, Eugenio d'Ors, Marías,
> and in fact nearly all the writers and poets who had not gone into
> exile, whatever their political tendency. With the journal we were
> attempting to counter the climate of intellectual intolerance unleashed
> by the Civil War and develop a strategy of integration and greater
> understanding of the adversary. . . . It condemned the "excess of
> repentance" on the part of those who went from being leftists to

reactionaries, leaving us with no hope of equilibrium; it condemned, finally, in one way or another the idea of the intellectual monopoly of the winners and of converting their ideas into dogma.[20]

Though *Escorial* was, like all Spanish culture of that time, officially Catholic, on one occasion it briefly condemned—albeit "not without negative consequences"[21]—the pretentiousness of calling the Civil War simply a "crusade." For its founders, fascism represented the revolution of modernity, a modernity that, though politically authoritarian, was creating a "new civilization" that was dynamic and open to change.

There were also significant efforts to create a new national Falangist theater. Here, as in most other areas, significant works of theory were lacking, with the possible exception of Giménez Caballero's *Arte y Estado,* which had been published in 1935. The latter had called for a national theater grounded in "the new Catholicity"—though not in the old Catholicism—and invoked a new "Christian classicism," with the ultranativist Lope de Vega as a chief inspiration. This national theater was to incorporate a new sense of mystery and hierarchy, and would privilege the heroic.[22]

A major role was to be played by the Syndicate of the Cinematographic Industry and Public Spectacles, formed in the spring of 1939. It encouraged the revival of *autos sacramentales* (sacred plays) and dramas based on patriotic historical themes, as well as innovation in sets and designs. The most important new figure among Falangist writers and critics in this field was Gonzalo Torrente Ballester, though within only a few years he would move in a more liberal direction.

During the years of World War II there was also an emphasis on what might be called "Falangist spectacle," public ceremonies and rituals of strongly nationalist character in mass meetings of thousands. These "were organized according to liturgical principles and were used to present an image of order, discipline, cohesion, and harmony under the guidance of the Nationalist leadership."[23]

Nonetheless, the attempt to create a distinctively Falangist theater lost all its momentum by the final years of the war, exactly as and because the era of fascism was suddenly drawing to a close. This gave way to a general policy of state support for production of the Spanish classics, which were also encouraged in commercial theaters.

## THE YOUTH ORGANIZATIONS AND
## THE SECCIÓN FEMENINA

Like most radical new states, the Franco regime officially placed considerable emphasis on youth, giving it frequent attention in official propaganda, and Spanish youth were to remain an important part of Falangist mobilization, at least in theory. This was not a question of the state's school policy, for most of that was dominated by the Catholic right from January 1938 on. The FET's role lay in political indoctrination and in paramilitary and extracurricular activities.

The SEU, the Falangist student syndicate, had been officially revived in November 1937, and Falangist pressure had managed to block the rightist and ultra-Catholic Law of University Reform originally prepared by the monarchist minister of education in Franco's first government, even though the Falangists could not control general educational policy. *Haz*, the SEU journal, was revived in September 1938 and was initially published free of censorship. It would remain until 1945 the most radically and outspokenly fascist of all Falangist publications.

Even though José Miguel Guitarte, the first postwar chief of the student syndicate, was selected precisely because he was considered more moderate and manageable, the SEU leaders were outspokenly elitist and aspired to a major role in the new Spain. Thus the official booklet that they prepared and published at the end of the Civil War declared the SEU the "central nerve of the National Syndicalist Revolutionary Movement in Spain,"[24] and SEU spokesmen and writers were vociferous in their denunciations of "rightist" and "reactionary" influences in the new Spain. An Extraordinary Congress was held at El Escorial on 4–8 January 1940 to seal the unification of Carlist and Catholic groups within the SEU, and spokesmen expressed grave concern about the possible "miscarrying of the revolution."[25] Numerous ambitious "projects" were presented, and as Miguel A. Ruiz Carnicer has written, "It was intended that the SEU control all the activities of Spanish university and cultural life,"[26] even to the point of restoring an autonomous paramilitary "university militia" that would permanently militarize student life. All the while *Haz* vociferously denounced continuing efforts at "the counterrevolution" in Spain.

The SEU's Fifth National Congress, convened at Alcalá de Henares from 9 to 16 December 1941, continued to advance broad ambitions. It was addressed by key Falangist cultural and university luminaries such as Antonio Tovar[27] and Laín Entralgo, who endorsed the SEU's goal of leading a full "revolution" in the universities, controlling the ideological formation of science in Spain and of the professoriate generally.[28]

SEU membership at first expanded rapidly. Starting with 9,700 on the eve of the Civil War, the Syndicate registered 34,670 members in 1938 and grew to 52,886 three years later. Members were drawn not merely from the universities but from advanced technical and professional schools as well. Enrollment was greatest both absolutely and proportionately in Madrid, Valladolid, Seville, and Granada, though there was also a large proportionate membership in several other centers; it was weakest in Barcelona.[29] A significant minority of the members were female. Alarmingly, however, membership dropped to 50,170 in 1942, perhaps reflecting changes in the international context. SEU leaders were divided on the issue of obligatory enrollment, which would solve the membership problem but seriously dilute revolutionary zeal. Obligatory membership was officially decreed by the Law of University Organization (LOU) of 1943. Though the SEU leaders tried to describe the LOU as a victory for them, it was more nearly the opposite, for it denied the Syndicate and its radical goals the tutelary role over university life that they sought.

The leading firebrand in the SEU at the close of the Civil War was Enrique Sotomayor, who had become director of *Haz* at the age of nineteen in 1938. In consonance with the strong support for fascism by students in many parts of Europe, on 16 August 1938 Sotomayor and two other young turks from the SEU leadership had a personal interview with Franco to lobby for the creation of a radical nationalist youth front. Afterward Sotomayor claimed that on this occasion Franco had been moved to tears, declaring that all his hopes lay in the youth of Spain and that before long he would name Sotomayor head of the SEU. Sotomayor rapidly completed his law degree at the University of Seville, where he also temporarily directed the Falangist newspaper *F. E.* In the interim, however, more conservative advisers encouraged Franco to have second thoughts about the young activist, who among other things spoke of a revolutionary union of nationalist students and workers. Thus it was that the more moderate Guitarte, one of those gratefully liberated from the Republican zone and initially named national inspector of the Organización Juvenil (OJ) in May 1939, was made national chief of the SEU in his place on 20 August 1939.

Sotomayor was given the second place in the SEU hierarchy, as secretary general.[30] As Saez Marín has written: "From this point began the legend of the SEU revolutionary, whose speeches and declarations would form a mythical reference for generations of young Falangists later on. And almost exclusively because of activities developed in little more than three months."[31]

Against the advice of his most radical friends, Sotomayor accepted the appointment under Guitarte. His manner seems to have been charismatic, combining a youthful grace, informality, and energy with an air of engagement and authority. He used his new platform to propose creation of a broad, new, and totally inclusive Frente de Juventudes (Youth Front), to be composed of twelve different sections and categories.[32] In Sotomayor's version, revolutionary Falangism was to be distinguished from Italian Fascism by its greater radicalism and spiritual authenticity. Its revolu-

Assembly of leaders of the Frente de Juventudes

tion would be "morally barbarous" compared with the materialism of liberals and the left, but also "Catholically barbarous," recapturing the dynamism and commitment of "primitive Christianity." If necessary, children would even be taken from their families for a revolutionary education. These concepts were forcefully advanced in a major speech in Madrid's Teatro Calderón on 1 November, and also in a pamphlet distributed at the same time:

> I know that to excessively cautious spirits all this about a strong vanguard of youth must seem dangerous and extravagant.
> . . . For the very people who were interested in prolonging our war, the same reasons multiplied a hundred times make them today require a hungry, rancorous, and inert Spain. The same people who for centuries have been hemming us in and defeating us, who were counting coin after coin while we were losing man after man, today await us at the juncture of our discouragement to go on spewing out the corrosive negations of always.
> . . . The negative slogans reemerge again. Not this. Not that. But, once and for all, definitively: What do they offer? What does the Spanish reaction represent and propose today?
> . . . Perhaps nothing gives us such zeal as the rage with which they oppose us.
> . . . We feel the immense joy of being hated by them!

> Let those who so blithely join the chorus of murmurers consider
> the terrible responsibility which is theirs.
> . . . There is only one path open to us: revolution.
> . . . NOW OR NEVER!
> . . . All Spanish youths must band together. *Let all the impetus of
> the Revolution be united in a compact front of youth!*[33]

No one since Ramiro Ledesma himself had so captured Ledesma's rhetorical vein of frenetic revolutionism, and it was not surprising that Sotomayor suffered much the same fate as Ledesma. After the speech of 1 November, all his publications were censored, and he resigned within a month, to be replaced by the much more pliable Diego Salas Pombo.

Plans for a Frente de Juventudes were not abandoned but proceeded more slowly, and by February 1940 were nearly completed.[34] In April membership in the OJ became compulsory for all children of FET members. The full Frente de Juventudes, after some further delay to ensure discipline and subordination, was then officially announced on 6 December 1940. José Antonio Elola was made national delegate six months later, and during 1941 and 1942 a cadre of leaders and instructors was slowly developed. Though the goal was patriotic and cultural "formación" and political indoctrination, in the long run the Frente's most extensive activities would have to do with camping and sports.

The largest sector of the Frente was the Falanges Juveniles de Franco, defined by articles 13 and 14 of the official statutes as "voluntary units which, within the Frente de Juventudes, aspire to achieve, through the exercise of the greatest virtues of the race, primacy in all Falangist enterprises." Though the official goal was that all the young become "incorporated" into the Frente, there was never sufficient investment in youth organization to make it broadly encompassing, and the voluntary principle ensured limited enrollment.[35] According to their own statistics, the Falanges Juveniles—even at their height—at no time mobilized more than 18 percent of the boys and 9 percent of the girls in Spain between seven and eighteen years of age.[36] Membership remained voluntary, and members were primarily children of ardent Nationalists, but even many of these received only limited indoctrination.

As during the Civil War, the various functions of the Sección Femenina continued to outperform other auxiliary services of the FET—a remarkable situation for a fascist movement ardently devoted to the principle of masculine superiority. By 1940 a total of 1,189 youth centers (though mostly very small) were administered by the Sección Femenina. In addition to its health services, it increasingly turned its attention to cultural activities and even women's physical education. The tone, however, remained relentlessly conservative. Women were always taught that family

A parade of the Falanges Juveniles in 1940

and children were their "only goal to achieve in life," as the celibate and childless Pilar Primo de Rivera put it. The basic idea of all this was that "woman forms man," to whom she must remain absolutely subordinated. As Delegada Nacional, Pilar outdid even herself in a speech of February 1943, when she insisted: "Women never discover anything. They lack creative talent, reserved by God for virile intellects; we can do no more than interpret what men present to us."[37]

## THE CARLISTS IN 1939

As the Civil War ended, the only organized dissident force among the Nationalists were the Carlists. Most Carlists had not abandoned their principles, nor had they followed orders to dissolve their separate local groups. Carlism's important contribution to complete victory in the Civil War led some Carlist leaders to believe that the time had come to implement their program. They were not at all impressed by the Falangist faith in the "era of fascism" now expanding in Europe. Thus on 10 March 1939 Fal Conde had addressed a lengthy missive to Franco accompanied by a highly detailed "Outline for the Future Political Organization of Spain Based on Traditionalist Principles"—a plan for a sort of Carlist constitution to restore the traditional monarchy. Fal made it clear that such a monarchy would be based on a neotraditionalist state, regional and municipal autonomy, and corporative or "guild" social and economic organization. There would be no place in such a system for the FET, for Fal repeated that "the party, we have said, corrupts," whether fascist or liberal.[38] Franco sympathized with many Carlist principles, but he had not the slightest intention of restoring a genuine Carlist monarchy.

By this point the Carlists held only four provincial leadership positions in the FET in all Spain. Only in Navarre was their situation relatively secure, and even there not completely. In recently conquered Catalonia, they considerably outnumbered genuine Falangists, but held only one of the four Catalan provincial chief positions. Therefore on 1 March 1939 the Carlist leaders of Catalonia addressed a letter to Franco insisting on Carlist leadership and control of the partido único in the region.[39] This request also was largely ignored. In Catalonia the Carlists lost control of their principal newspaper and figured prominently only in the leadership of the Militia. A number of "token Carlists" were taken into the regional FET leadership for the sake of appearance, but they continued to be largely excluded from power.

On 5 April 1939, the prince regent Don Javier entered the British embassy in Paris to express to British representatives his concern over the course of the Spanish regime, its unbalanced autarchic economic policy, and its pro-Axis orientation. He declared that the Carlists were opposed to fascist autarchy and favored closer relations with Britain in particular, but drew little response from British diplomats, who dismissed the Carlists as "medieval reactionaries."[40]

Later, on 31 August 1939, a "Junta Suprema del Requeté" met privately in Pamplona, where twenty-four former Requeté officers signed a pledge to maintain the unity of Carlism and oppose all "treason" to Spain.[41] There had been physical altercations between Falangists and Carlists at the San Fermín festival in July, and incidents of this sort would continue for several years. In fact, however, the Carlists were even less able than the alfonsino monarchists to influence Spanish policy.

The Carlists were the more disarmed because their banner of traditional Spanish Catholicism had been raised and embraced by the regime itself. Both Falangist and non-Falangist elements within the FET accepted traditionalist Catholicism as basic,[42] and the genuinely anticlerical minority was almost without influence. In Rome Serrano Súñer explained to the Italian Fascist leaders that one of the main reasons Franco and the Falangists felt closer to them than to the Nazis was because of the importance of Catholicism. Franco indeed backed out of a close cultural agreement with Berlin signed at the close of the Civil War because of protests from the Vatican about the anti-Catholic content of Nazi culture. Cardinal Gomá, who was primate and archbishop of Toledo until his death in 1940, nonetheless regarded Serrano and the FET with suspicion because of their fascist tendencies, but agreed with most of his fellow prelates that Franco himself was a providential figure for Spain. In general, the leaders of the Spanish Church during the era of the Second World War continued to support the Spanish state strongly, and also accepted the special relationship with the Axis, though Catholic spokesmen normally tried to "translate" the special relationship with the fascist powers into terms compatible with right-wing Catholicism.

## THE FIRST YEARS OF WORLD WAR II

Though Franco never fully adopted the entire core fascist revolutionary ideology, there is no question that he identified his regime politically with the fascist powers and considered himself not merely an associate but virtually an ally of the Axis. Of all the years of his long dictatorship, the first three years after the Civil War, 1939 to 1942, were the period of greatest danger for Franco, for his regime, and for Spain, for these were the years when Franco was most inebriated with his total military victory, his sense of power and destiny, and his perception of being closely associated with the rising tide of new forces in European and world history. These were the years of the "fascist temptation" of Franco, and the period in which he felt most purely self-confident and most convinced of his own wisdom, even on matters about which he knew little or nothing. Thus the Portuguese ambassador Pedro Theotonio Pereira, who detested the Spanish dictator, observed of him in August 1939: "I find him besotted with state power and with personal power. Of everyone in the Spanish government, he is the one who says the strangest things to me and who speaks in the language closest to the Axis."[43]

In the closing days of the Civil War, Franco signed a treaty of friendship with Germany that required mutual consultation in the event of a military attack against either country. He also joined Hitler's Anti-Comintern Pact, though the latter was a gesture without concrete obligations. On 8 May 1939, the new Spanish government officially withdrew from the League of Nations. If the leaders of the regime clearly felt closer to and more at home with Italian Fascists than with German Nazis, they also recognized that the latter were taking the lead in forging the authoritarian, nationalist and anti-Communist new order with which the Spanish leaders identified, in opposition to the "capitalist plutocracies."

This did not mean that the regime was a satellite of either Axis power, for Franco's policy was based on pragmatism and his judgments of the best interests of Spain and of his regime.[44] Thus a ten-year treaty of mutual friendship had been signed with Portugal, largely at Madrid's request, just a few days before the German pacts, and this was harmonized with the traditional British alliance with Portugal. The state visit of Serrano Súñer to Rome immediately after the war ended[45] was designed to express in part the Spanish regime's closer sense of identity with Italy than with Germany, and was partly a response to the fact that Italy had made a more extensive contribution to the triumph of the Nationalists. As indicated earlier, Foreign Minister Ciano returned the visit in July.

Franco, in contrast, held at bay a proposed visit in May from Hermann Goering, arguably the highest-ranking Nazi leader after Hitler. To lead the Berlin counterpart to Serrano's visit to Rome, the Generalissimo selected the semiliberal and anti-Falangist General Antonio Aranda, one of his ablest commanders, who accompanied the returning Condor Legion to Germany. In Berlin Aranda stressed the importance of good relations with Britain and tended to downplay the role of the FET[46]—the latter, of course, a common attitude among the military.

Of all the regime's objectives, few were more important than the negotiation of a concordat with the Vatican, a proposal already broached before the end of the Civil War. For Franco this would be the culmination of his neotraditionalist religious policy, roofing the solid edifice of Catholic support for his new half-fascist, half-Catholic fundamentalist system—however uneasy the contradictions to which this gave rise. During the Civil War, the most radical and Nazi-influenced Falangists—going even farther than Ramiro Ledesma—had talked of the need for a Spanish national church, a real "national Catholicism" not unlike that which was being developed by the Nazi organization of "German Christians" in the Third Reich. But this had been a failure even under Hitler, and talk among Falangist anticlericals about a national church was quieted even before the war ended. *Arriba*, the new central FET organ in Madrid, underlined the desirability of a regular concordat, and Muñoz Grandes issued orders to all provincial chiefs on 25 October forbidding imitation of such Nazi styles as "Nazi uniforms, goose steps, fascist salutes, etc."[47] If the Vatican had been willing to sign a concordat with Germany during Hitler's first year as chancellor, Franco believed that it ought to be all the more interested in an accord with so ultra-Catholic a state as his.

The Vatican did not see matters so simply, despite the regime's resumption of the state ecclesiastical subsidy on 1 December 1939. It had been burned by dealings with Hitler and Mussolini, while the outbreak of war in Europe complicated the international outlook. Moreover, the demands of the regime, which insisted on the state's right to nominate bishops, further strained relations. At one point the Spanish representative to the Vatican was withdrawn briefly, and no progress was made in negotiations during the fall and winter of 1939–40.[48]

The key institution in the regime was neither the FET nor the Church but the army. Though the size of the peacetime army was soon cut by nearly 75 percent, Franco and his chief associates planned a state-led, intensely state-regulated economy that would privilege military production. A huge ten-year naval expansion program was announced on 8 September 1939, though it soon had to be cut drastically; not to be outdone, the new minister of the air force, the Falangist General Juan Yagüe, presented a ten-year program of his own that would involve nearly four thousand new combat planes. This, however, was sharply cut back to only 150 planes per year, involving little more than normal replacement of existing materiel.

The new economic policy announced in 1939 was based on autarchy, or the goal of relative self-sufficiency with greatly enhanced military production, a program derived from Italy and Germany. A decree of October 1939 announced the Law for the Protection and Development of National Industry, which featured a series of incentives, tax benefits, and special licensing arrangements for the creation of new factories. A subsequent Law for the Organization and Defense of National Industry of 24 November identified certain industries worthy of special assistance, and two years later in 1941 the regime created the Instituto Nacional de Industria (INI), a state investment and holding company to stimulate industrialization, modeled on the Italian Istituto per la Ricostruzione Industriale. The decree of 25 September 1941 announced that the purpose of the INI was to "stimulate and finance, in the service of the nation, the creation and resurgence of our industry, especially those whose principal contribution is to resolve the problems imposed by the requirements of the country's defense or that are directed toward the development of our economic autarchy."[49]

During 1939–41 the regime built a rigid system of state economic controls, regulations, and artificial incentives that in many cases restricted rather than encouraged new economic growth. This autarchist statist model of "fascist economics," together with a foreign trade and technology model heavily skewed toward Germany and Italy, had disastrous effects on the Spanish economy during World War II. The tight controls on grain marketing and pricing, together with other restrictions, discouraged agricultural production, so that part of Spanish society would soon teeter on the brink of famine, while the regime's overall policies made it impossible for Spain to exploit the economic opportunities of neutrality as did other neutral states. "Fascist" or autarchist economics, Spanish-style, heavily tilted toward the Axis, resulted in economic stagnation, failure to recover from the losses of the Civil War, and six years of extreme hardship for Spanish citizens.[50]

The new economic policies, which used the nascent national syndicates primarily as instruments of negative control, did not produce a system of national solidarity of the sort envisioned by José Antonio Primo de Rivera and the original Falangists or preached by the regime's own propaganda. Their terms favored the established industrial and financial powers to the detriment of the defeated and much of the rural population in general, part of which had fought for the Nationalists. The regime granted considerable autonomy to individual ministries and to major industrial and financial enterprises, which was not ipso facto wrong, but such activity was not exposed to either general market forces, broader international trade, or countervailing free trade union or other interests. Thus those who could afford to pay could buy nearly anything they needed, either at higher prices from legitimate enterprises or more frequently on the black market. To Franco, the suffering being endured by the people of Spain was in large measure a judgment elicited by the political and spiritual apostasy of half a nation. As he put it during a speech in Jaén on 18 March 1940, "The suffering which a nation undergoes at a certain point in its history is not a matter of chance; it is a spiritual punishment, a punishment which God imposes on a distorted life, on an unclean history."[51]

As international tensions heightened during the summer of 1939, Franco used the phrase "careful prudence" to describe Spain's foreign policy at a July meeting of the FET's National Council. The new foreign minister in the 1939 government was Col. Juan Beigbeder y Atienza, who had served as high commissioner of the Protectorate during much of the Civil War[52] and had earlier been attaché in Berlin. He was a somewhat odd choice, a tall and nervous eccentric who had in certain respects "gone native" in Morocco. According to Serrano, Franco at first thought the nomination was "madness," but accepted it in part because Beigbeder's appointment would be gratifying to the military. He had encouraged the expansion of the Falange in the Protectorate—though under military dominance—and had also taken the post of the FET's territorial chief, though his Falangism was much more a result of opportunism than of conviction. Nonetheless, this made him, along with Yagüe and Muñoz Grandes, one of the few nominally Falangist military commanders, and, like much of the top Spanish brass, he was relatively pro-German though not fanatically so.[53]

Hitler's signing of the Nazi–Soviet Pact only two weeks after the formation of the new Spanish government was a shock to Madrid, contradicting the basic orientation of Franco's policy. The Falangist organ *Arriba* could only headline it as "A Surprise, A Tremendous Surprise." Sudden outbreak of a general war created a difficult and dangerous situation. Though Franco provided some indication of still favoring German policy, the Spanish government had no reasonable option but to declare its neutrality.

In March 1940 the senior generals who made up the army's Superior Council approved a statement by the increasingly critical-minded monarchist Gen. Alfredo Kindelán that declared it impossible for Spain to enter the conflict because it lacked economic support and materiel. They also complained of the internal divisions within the FET and questioned its role as partido único, declaring that the army was "the only instrument available to orient Spanish politics."[54]

Hitler's startling conquest of France in the spring of 1940 drastically altered this attitude and the regime's policy. Germany's sudden ascendancy opened a new period of temptation combined with danger for both Spain and its government. The clear pro-German alignment that Franco now adopted nonetheless stopped short of immediate or outright belligerence. It also had implications for domestic politics, arguing for some the logic of a more strongly Falangist regime.

Thus by June 1940 most political and military opinion in Spain had swung sharply in the direction of Germany. The army was not at all prepared for a major war, but it was full of combat veterans and for the moment the mood of its officers was for the most part aggressive and pugnacious. As Ignacio Merino has written: "Its combat morale was still fresh. . . . The bodies of the veterans were still tense, while the very young were eager for military action. Going off to war was still a heroic gesture, macho and idealistic."[55]

Moreover, the goal of a new Spanish "empire" had always formed part of the Falangist program, even though it had usually been expressed in cautious and relatively nonaggressive, almost metaphysical, terms.[56] It was employed by Franco, by Falangists, by the military, and by other commentators in several different dimensions. The first dimension was the leadership of "Hispanidad"[57]—the restoration of a Spanish hegemony over the greater Spanish-speaking world that would be first of all cultural and religious, and politically might eventually aim at a kind of commonwealth or federation of Spanish-speaking states headed by Spain. Beyond that, there was the aspiration to reestablish Spain as a power in Europe, and even as a "world power,"[58] conceived in terms of its close association with the New Order in Europe, its leadership in Hispanidad, and its extended empire and influence in Africa and the Middle East, this last connection founded on a special relationship with Islamic countries. Beyond regaining Gibraltar from Britain, direct territorial expansion could probably take place in only northwest Africa, at the expense of France, and that would require the assistance of Germany and Italy. Only radical Falangists and a few other exceptionally ambitious imperialists spoke of reannexing Portugal. This was not a practical goal for the most immediate future, and would ultimately depend on a total victory of the New Order in Europe. The same might be said for any Pyrenean rectification with France, which was not for the moment an agenda item.[59]

Franco's new state proclaimed the mission of empire with vigor,[60] albeit in rather abstract formulae, and its social pronouncements during these years sometimes echoed the Italian Fascist emphasis on a high birth rate for future military manpower. After the fall of France, the attitude of most of the military hierarchy had changed in favor of getting into the war on the winning side, and Falangists became almost uniformly ardent in public expressions of Germanophilia.

Though radical Falangists had become increasingly oriented toward Nazi Germany even during the Civil War, from June 1940 might be dated the tendency of FET propaganda to endorse National Socialism in the most categorical terms. More and more it was to Berlin rather than to the original model of Rome that Falangists would look in the next several years,[61] and the fullest solidarity was pledged to the Axis.[62]

Franco was now firmly convinced of German victory and would remain so, though with diminishing conviction, until mid-1944. On 3 June 1940 he prepared the text of a letter to Hitler congratulating him on the incipient triumph over France and identifying Spain with the German cause, which he chose to define as a continuation of the struggle waged by the Nationalists in the Civil War. At the same time he detailed the economic and military weaknesses that made it difficult for Spain to enter the war at that time, and on the following day Beigbeder handed the German ambassador a list of Spanish claims in northwest Africa.[63]

On 9 June, the eve of Italy's attack on France, Mussolini urged Franco to join him, but the Caudillo, sensing the frustration that might attend Italian and Spanish participation as long as France and Britain were still resisting, politely declined in a cordial response.[64] Despite the German victories and the increasing Falangist orientation toward Nazism, the leaders of the Spanish regime continued to feel closer to Mussolini's government, which they regarded as their own representative within the Rome–Berlin Axis. Thus Ciano asked Serrano Súñer to convince Franco that even if Spain could not enter the war for the moment, it should demonstrate solidarity with the Axis by altering its position of neutrality to a declaration of nonbelligerence,[65] just as Italy had originally done after the German invasion of Poland. Franco agreed immediately, and Madrid declared its new policy of nonbelligerence—with an obvious tilt toward the Axis—on 12 June.

Two days later, on 14 June, Spanish troops occupied the international zone of Tangier, though this was cautiously announced as simply a temporary wartime measure to guarantee the continued neutrality of the zone. The move was accepted by Britain (which officially reserved full rights for the future), while Franco prudently ignored the crowd of pro-expansionist Falangists who gathered outside the presidency building. The rhetorical Sánchez Mazas, now minister without portfolio, was persuaded by young radicals to give an impromptu speech insisting that Tangier should always remain Spanish, an action that earned him a severe dressing-down from Serrano.[66]

General Juan Vigón, head of the Supreme General Staff, was dispatched to Berlin to discuss possible terms of Spain's entry into the war, while on 19 June the ambassador formally presented Spain's territorial claims: incorporation of all Morocco, annexation of the entire Oran district of western Algeria, extension of the Spanish Sahara southward to the twentieth parallel, and the addition of the French Cameroons to Spanish Guinea. At this time, however, Hitler, convinced that Britain was already defeated, had no interest in Spain's shopping list, which could only complicate German relations with the rump but independent regime of Vichy France as the German forces prepared for the invasion of the Soviet Union.

Franco nonetheless had no real doubts concerning his new international orientation, and at the celebrations attending the Movement's anniversary on 18 July he declared that the struggle of the Nationalists in Spain had been "the first battle of the New Order" in Europe, adding that "we have made a pause in our struggle, but only a pause, because our task has not yet ended," and boasting that Spain "has two million warriors ready for battle in defense of our rights."[67]

From about the end of July, Hitler slowly developed more interest in securing Spain's entry into the conflict. This was partly due to his eagerness to consummate the defeat of Britain by strangling its position in the Mediterranean. Even more important—since he considered the latter little more than a detail—was to align Spain fully with the Third Reich, not merely to conquer Gibraltar but to provide Germany with new strategic bases in northwest Africa and the Atlantic. By this point Hitler was actively accelerating his planning, looking ahead to the destruction of the Soviet Union in 1941 and to later strategic world war against the United States.

Both Franco and Serrano Súñer were firmly convinced of eventual German victory and realized that Spain could profit from the coming New Order only if it entered the war in time. Yet they were also apprehensive about involving their weak and unprepared country in the conflict as long as Britain retained dominance at sea. Whereas Germany for the time being had become almost self-sufficient, the Spanish economy could be devastated by a British naval blockade. To survive for even a brief period, it would require concrete guarantees of major assistance from Germany. Moreover, if a new Spanish empire was to be carved out of French northwest Africa (concerning which contingency plans had been under way in the Spanish General Staff since June), new acquisitions would have to be firmly recognized and guaranteed by Germany from the beginning, when Spanish assistance still had value in Hitler's eyes. To wait until the final victory would be too late.

As German interest grew, Serrano, even though not foreign minister, was deputed to head a special delegation to Berlin that departed on 13 September. On arriving, he gave an interview to the Nazi party organ *Völkischer Beobachter* in which he stressed that the Spanish conflict had been a struggle against "the capitalism of the great democracies" similar to the *Kampf* of National Socialism,[68] employing, as he sometimes did, the rhetoric of the radical sector of the Falange. Between 15 and 25 September, Serrano engaged in several lengthy conversations with Foreign Minister von Ribbentrop and two shorter ones with Hitler. In a personal communication of the twenty-fourth, Franco stressed to Serrano: "We must guarantee the future with a pact and, though there is no doubt about our decision, we have to consider the specificities of the agreement and the obligations of both sides."[69] Serrano was meanwhile dismayed to find that Hitler wanted Spain to enter the war immediately while merely trusting in German good will to provide a certain amount of economic assistance and military supplies; moreover, he refused to make any territorial commitments on northwest Africa in advance. Ribbentrop was even more aggressive, asking for the cession to Germany of one of the Canary Islands as a naval base, together with one or more ports in any southward expansion of Spanish Morocco. On Franco's orders, this was rejected with barely concealed indignation, and any agreement on entering the war now began to be postponed behind a screen of Spanish economic, military, and territorial requests.[70]

Clearly the simultaneous and contradictory requirements of retaining Germany's good will, winning a place for Spain in the New Order, and avoiding premature entry into the war on hazardous terms created the most difficult and dangerous challenge faced by the Franco regime in its long history. To deal with it, Franco needed the most capable and reliable assistance possible, and therefore on 15 October, immediately after Serrano's return, Franco appointed his brother-in-law foreign minister in place of the bohemian and somewhat unreliable Beigbeder. This was not a matter of replacing an Anglophile with a Germanophile, as was often said then and afterward. Serrano was no Germanophile in the strict sense but simply convinced, like most major figures in Madrid at that time, that Spain must come to terms with Germany in a way that would safeguard its interests. Beigbeder's work had become increasingly haphazard, for he tended to change his position according to his audience and had developed friendly relations with the British ambassador. Moreover, Beigbeder had a taste for "exotic" ladies, including, allegedly, a "Miss Fox" in the employ of the British Secret Service, and the Germans had become reluctant to deal with him.[71] Equally important was Franco's concern to have his most trusted collaborator in charge of foreign affairs during this crucial phase. Because he was president of the Junta Política and in some respects the key leader of the FET, and because of his entrance into the Foreign Ministry at the time when Spain's ties to Germany were closest, Serrano would often be called the "minister of the Axis," but this was never more than a half truth.

On 23 October there occurred the only personal encounter between Franco and Hitler, the famous meeting at Hendaye on the French border. Franco once more presented what had become the standard Spanish shopping list—territorial, economic, and military—and was evidently prepared to enter the war at that point if Hitler would promise Spain control of most of northwest Africa,[72] but Hitler refused all guarantees at that time. After enduring some seven hours of the polite, fawning, evasive, and loquacious conversation of the "Latin charlatan," as Hitler would soon term Franco, he later declared that he would prefer "having three or four teeth pulled" to going through such an experience again.[73]

Spain would never represent a high priority for Hitler. He sought Spanish entry into the war primarily to favor Germany's long-range geostrategic position, and also to help drive Britain to terms, but he was in no position to grant Franco's demands. About Spaniards themselves he was at best ambivalent. Though Hitler once remarked that Spaniards were "the only Latins willing to fight," he believed them inevitably compromised by their historical contacts with the Islamic world, and they could never rank high on his racial hierarchy.[74]

Up to this point Franco had apparently held the ingenuous conviction that Hitler was a great leader friendly to Spain, with any obstacles stemming from mediocre or ill-intentioned subordinates. Hitler and Ribbentrop now insisted on the signing of a secret protocol that would pledge Spanish war entry, though without fixing a specific deadline. Franco and Serrano quickly replaced the German draft with one of their own, and

Hitler and Franco at Hendaye, 23 October 1940

Franco signed this second document, which pledged Spain to join the Tripartite Pact (the alliance of Germany, Italy, and Japan) at some undetermined date to be mutually agreed on in the future, made at least vague references to Spanish territorial aggrandizement in Africa, and promised Spain's entry into the war against Britain at some unspecified date to be determined after future assistance and consultation.[75]

Though Hitler left Hendaye believing that he had gained most of what he wanted, his propaganda minister Goebbels would write in his diary:

> The Führer's opinion of Spain and Franco is not high. A lot of noise, but very little action. No substance. In any case, quite unprepared for war. . . .
>
> Landesgruppenleiter Thomsen of the AO [Nazi Party abroad] in Spain reports on conditions there simply unbelievable. Franco and Suner [sic] are completely the prisoners of the clerical faction, totally unpopular, no attempt made to deal with social problems, enormous confusion, the Falange totally without influence. All areas of the economy in ruins, a lot of grandiose posturing, but nothing behind it. Germany is looked upon with awe as a wonderland.[76]

Though Franco was still interested in joining Germany, Hitler's refusal of serious guarantees meant that the Spanish government would henceforth show increasing resistance to German demands, even though for some time it would hope to win the terms that might yet reconcile all differences. Hitler peremptorily summoned Serrano Súñer to Berchtesgaden in mid-November to insist that a date be fixed for Spain's entry into the war. Before Serrano's departure, a formal meeting was held in Madrid with Franco and the military ministers. England's recent success in the Battle of Britain had diminished the military hierarchy's ardor for the war. At this time the only major interventionist sentiment was fostered by the two principal Falangist generals, Muñoz Grandes and Yagüe,[77] but neither any longer held a cabinet position.

At Berchtesgaden on 18 November, Serrano complained to the Führer about Germany's apparent lack of interest in implementing the article of the recent secret protocol that vaguely referred to Spain's colonial aims in northwest Africa. Hitler candidly replied that under present circumstances Spain's acquisition of these territories could not be formally guaranteed, for it might lead to disputes with other powers. Serrano then detailed the disastrous state of Spain's economic and military production, compounded by severe shortages of all kinds, which made it impossible to enter the war at that moment.[78]

When Serrano returned to Madrid four days later, the National Council of the FET was in full session, a majority of its members favoring entry into the war. This, however, had little effect on Franco's policy, demonstrating the extent to which his emasculation of the partido único served the purposes of his regime. Before the end of the month, he assured Berlin that Spanish preparations to enter the war were about to begin, but still no date was set. Similar sparring continued through December.

By this point economic privation in Spain was becoming extremely severe. The winter of 1940–41 may have seen the worst shortages of food and other necessities during the entire course of the World War, as extreme hunger became a problem for millions of Spaniards. It became clear to Franco that amid such disastrous conditions Spain could not presently plan to enter the conflict, even though the government might still wish to do so at some future date. From the beginning of 1941, dilatoriness would become a studied technique for the Generalissimo, who would henceforth systematically delay Spanish compliance.

German pressures were resumed during January and February. After three ultimatums at diverse levels during late January produced no result, Hitler continued with a long, harsh letter to Franco on 6 February, telling him in no uncertain terms that in "a war to the death" no "presents" would be given to Spain, and warning that should Germany ever lose, the Franco regime itself would have no chance of survival. By this point Franco's enthusiastic appraisal of Hitler seems to have moderated considerably, and he resisted these pressures with his customary evasive tactics, accompanied by requests for large amounts of German supplies, without which Spain could not fight.

Hitler then turned the Spanish problem over to Mussolini, who had just met disaster in his effort to invade Greece the preceding October. The only personal meeting between the Spanish and Italian dictators took place at Bordighera on 12 February, but Mussolini—himself ambivalent about Spanish ambitions in Africa—made little effort to pressure or deceive Franco. He admitted that the initiative for the meeting had come from Hitler and that prospects now were for a long war, while some in his own retinue could scarcely hide their growing demoralization.[79]

Henceforth the German government desisted from overt pressure to force Spanish entry into the war, primarily because Hitler's priorities lay elsewhere and he did not judge Spanish participation to merit a high price. The attitude toward Franco in the German regime was now universally negative (Franco in turn had even denied to German officials that their aid was decisive in winning the Civil War), though ire was especially directed against the "clerical," "reactionary," and "Jesuitical" Serrano Súñer.[80] As usual, Franco ceded on minor points, signing an agreement for

Serrano Súñer, Franco, and Mussolini at Bordighera, 12 February 1941

German–Spanish cooperation on propaganda in Latin America in March 1941 and again renewing the supply facilities for German submarines that several Spanish ports provided for much of the war.

Support for entering the war nonetheless dominated among active Falangists (whether of the new or old varieties) and a small minority of the military leaders. This sentiment increased with the next successes of the Blitzkrieg in Greece and Yugoslavia during April. The most notorious expression of Spanish expansionist sentiment was the publication in April of the book *Reivindicaciones de España* by José María de Areilza and Fernando María Castiella. Though not bellicose in tone, this volume declared that the Spanish conflict had been but the first phase of an extended world war, blamed Britain and France for originating the war, and defined publicly what the Spanish government wanted: Gibraltar, a protectorate over all Morocco, the Oran district of northwestern Algeria, and expansion in equatorial Africa at the expense of British Nigeria and French possessions. The book's clear and vigorous style, with its reasoned historical and geopolitical analysis and lack of shrillness, made it probably the most influential and successful piece of wartime propaganda among the more nationalist sectors of Spanish society.[81]

Within the peninsula, tensions momentarily rose. On 26 February *Arriba* had published a strong attack on the Portuguese government for being too moderate, semiliberal, and pro-British. Two months later, just as *Reivindicaciones* was being published, General Aranda informed the German ambassador that he had been ordered to draw up secret plans for a possible invasion of Portugal.[82] It seemed as though Franco, lacking greater possibilities, toyed with the notion of making Portugal his Albania or Greece. There is no indication that such ideas went very far, for Franco was aware that Spain probably could not conquer Portugal any more easily than Italy had been able to conquer Greece, but they indicated the true feelings of the Spanish leaders. On 17 April Franco made one of his most bellicose speeches to the Superior War College, declaring peace to be no more than "a preparation for war," and "war the normal condition of humanity,"[83] as ultra-fascist a pronouncement as Franco ever made.

The most humorous note during these grim months was provided by a personal phone call to Serrano from his Italian counterpart Ciano, delivered in the stilted Spanish the latter had learned as a diplomat in Buenos Aires. The Italian foreign minister demanded the immediate recall of the first secretary of the Spanish embassy in Rome, the Falangist writer and noted wit Agustín de Foxá, on charges of being a subversive and a spy. Foxá's mordant and sometimes ingenious sarcasm had found ripe targets in the pretensions, pomposity, and failures of Italian Fascism, which he liked to refer to in conversation as a "burlesque of the Nazis." Mussolini, hailed as "Fondatore [Founder] dell'Impero," was termed by Foxá "Affondatore [Founderer, or Sinker] dell'Impero." The Spanish government withdrew Foxá for his wicked tongue but soberly rejected the insinuation of espionage.[84]

Relations were still closer with Rome than with any other foreign capital, and late in the spring of 1941 the Italian government made a new effort to draw the Spanish regime more publicly to the side of the Axis. On 9 June Serrano received a personal letter from Ciano urging him to convince Franco that the time had come to announce Spain's adherence to the Tripartite Pact, as pledged in the secret protocol of the preceding autumn. Serrano seems to have agreed and had a very long talk with his brother-in-law, whom he declared not averse to the step, but Serrano warned the Italian ambassador that it would be tantamount to a declaration of war by Spain. In such an event, the Spanish leaders expected Britain to seize at least one of the Canaries and blockade Spain, so that a pledge of economic assistance would be needed first. Yet a meeting between Ciano and Ribbentrop on the fifteenth indicated that Germany had no interest at that point in offering even minor enticements to bring Spain into the war.[85]

Germany's invasion of the Soviet Union one week later provoked a contradictory response in Madrid. On the one hand, the attack on the Communist heartland aroused a strong emotional response, particularly from Falangists, but it also steeply raised the stakes for any prospective ally of Germany. Thus, at Serrano's suggestion, within forty-eight hours the government requested an opportunity for Spanish participation in some form short of official entry into the war. Before a huge crowd in front of Falangist headquarters on the twenty-fourth, Serrano delivered his famous "Russia Is Guilty" speech, invoking Soviet responsibility for the Spanish war with its attendant destruction and loss of life, and declaring that "the extermination of Russia is required by the history and for the future of Europe." The anti-Soviet struggle was declared an extension of the Spanish Crusade, and Spain "a moral belligerent" in the new conflict.

Since Franco had no intention of declaring war on the Soviet Union at that point, Serrano suggested the formation of a "Blue Division" of FET volunteers to fight beside the Germans on the Russian front. This found acceptance among Franco and other cabinet members, and registration of volunteers began on 28 June, the seventh day of the German invasion. Falangist enthusiasm was intense; among the volunteers were six members of the National Council and seven provincial governors, as well as some of the most militant younger leaders such as Dionisio Ridruejo and Enrique Sotomayor, the latter soon to be killed in battle. Army commanders were rather less enthusiastic, and insisted on maintaining military control. All officers of the Blue Division were drawn from the regular army, as were nearly 70 percent of the volunteers; civilian Falangists ultimately comprised less than a third of the total manpower. Command was given to Muñoz Grandes, one of the best organizers among the few Falangist

Falangist demonstration in Madrid to support the German invasion of the Soviet Union, 24 June 1941

generals. The first units of an initial force of 18,694 officers and men began to leave Spain on 17 July for further training in Germany, followed by a volunteer contingent of combat aviators who formed an "Escuadrilla Azul" (Blue Squadron). The Division later formed as Wehrmacht Division 250, fighting in German uniforms on the northern sector just below Leningrad. It entered into combat on 4 October, under overall German command but always technically subordinate to the Ministry of the Army in Madrid.[86]

The genuine enthusiasm in the ranks of the Nationalists in Spain was undeniable. The summer of 1941 marked the last major peak in wartime feeling on behalf of Germany. This led Franco to present the most outspokenly pro-German public speech that he ever delivered in his annual address to the National Council on 17 July. He denounced the "eternal enemies" of Spain, with clear allusions to Britain and France, who still engaged in "intrigues and betrayal" against it. "Nor can the American continent dream of intervening in Europe without exposing itself to a catastrophe," Franco insisted. "To say that, in this situation, the outcome of the war could be affected by the entry of a third country is criminal madness. . . . The war was wrongly conceived and the Allies have lost it." His concluding sentence hailed Germany for leading "the battle sought by Europe and Christianity for so many years, and in which the blood of our youth will be united with that of our comrades of the Axis, as a living expression of solidarity."[87] Even the Axis ambassadors commented on the imprudence of these remarks.[88]

In the following month an agreement was signed with Germany to provide 100,000 workers for the increasingly strained German industrial force, though none left Spain for months. In the long run, fewer than 15,000 were sent, compared with approximately 10,000 Spanish workers who labored daily for the British in Gibraltar throughout the war. For that matter, Spanish consulates in France managed to recruit 40,000 unemployed Republican émigrés for German jobs,[89] whom Hitler later dreamed of converting into pro-German revolutionaries to overthrow the reactionary "Latin charlatan" Franco.[90]

## FALANGE EXTERIOR IN LATIN AMERICA

The Falange's Servicio Exterior had been created before the Civil War but began to develop, like the party itself, only after the war began. Felipe Ximénez de Sandoval, a member of the party and of the Spanish diplomatic corps since 1933, had been named national delegate of the Servicio Exterior by Hedilla in January 1937. Though there was significant membership in such regions as Spanish Morocco[91] and the Philippines,[92] as well as very modest memberships in a number of European countries,[93] the most important goal was to expand both the party and support for the Nationalists among the Spanish residents and pro-Spanish citizens of Latin America. According to Rosa Pardo Sanz:

> The first sections were created in Chile, Argentina, Cuba, Mexico, and Uruguay. Their beginnings were hesitant, with great autonomy vis-á-vis the peninsula and grave leadership problems. Their inexpert chiefs, who became involved in various scandals of corruption and of abuse of authority, recruited individuals of doubtful moral and ideological reputation and damaged the image of the nascent organization.[94]

After the unification, another professional diplomat, José del Castaño Cardona, was named national delegate and given broad responsibility to organize support among pro-Nacionalist elements in Latin America. The FET apparatus was expanded, with an effort to create accompanying Technical Services, particularly Latin American sections of Social Welfare, to generate money and other support. A wide range of conflicts developed between divergent elements within the FET, and there was friction with regular Spanish diplomats, who found the Falangists overweening and sometimes excessively radical. By the end of the Civil War, the Servicio Exterior had created sections in most Latin American countries and was given orders to develop the full structure of the FET organization in the western hemisphere, including syndicates and excluding only militias. The largest FET membership, approximately a thousand affiliates, was in Uruguay, whereas the combined membership in all the rest of Latin America was only about four thousand. Nonetheless, the name inspired admirers, leading to the formation of such separate Latin American parties as "Falange Nacional Chilena," "Falange Boliviana," and "Falange Socialista Boliviana."

As foreign minister, Gómez Jordana had theoretically been in a position to supervise and control the Servicio Exterior, since the national delegate was a diplomat under his command. The general did not favor any extended role for the party abroad, and political pressure in Latin America began to build with the first expulsions of members of Falange Exterior by hostile governments in Cuba and Mexico in April 1939. As a result, during the next three months all the regular offices of the Servicio Exterior in Latin America were closed, though a series of cover organizations were formed in those countries in which the FET was active, and the appointments of jefes for various countries continued officially until March 1940.

After Serrano Súñer took over the foreign ministry in October, Spanish policy became more ambitious. Serrano planned to use the Servicio Exterior as a major tool and made Ximénez de Sandoval national delegate once more. The budgets of both the Foreign Ministry and the Servicio Exterior increased, and a limited number of Falangists were brought into the diplomatic corps, much like the *ventottisti* in Italy in 1928. Activities abroad took on a more pronouncedly fascist tone, and in May 1941 Ximénez de Sandoval was made chief of Serrano's diplomatic cabinet. This coincided with the last Falangist offensive in Latin America, which had begun in April and by July resulted in the announcement of a plan to send "Missionaries of the Falange" to every Latin American country.

But the impoverished Spanish state totally lacked funding for a major cultural and political offensive, while opposition mounted rapidly from hostile liberals and leftists in Latin America and even more from the only great power in the western hemisphere. The artificiality of these pretensions was underscored by one of Serrano's press officials, Ramón Garriga, who claims that in July 1941:

> I told Serrano that the Germans did not understand why we talked so much about Empire when it turned out that Spain could not send a single typewriter or radio set to Buenos Aires or Mexico, but that today it was the Argentines or the Mexicans who could teach the Spaniards how to build a bridge or a highway rapidly and well.
> "We really have exaggerated too much, and I will give orders not to be so ridiculous," he replied, making an entry in his notebook.[95]

August 1941 would prove to be the point of inflexion. In the face of a concerted counterattack by North American diplomacy and pressure in every country where there had been any significant Falangist organization, all plans for expansion had to be abandoned even before Pearl Harbor. Apparently, no "Missionaries of the Falange" were ever sent.

There was nonetheless more concern about "Spanish fascism" in Latin America in 1942 than in 1941, due to a mounting hysteria in Washington[96] that was ably fomented by British intelligence and deliberate disinformation.[97] Nonetheless, the truth of the matter was that the problem had receded even before the United States entered the war.

## TENSIONS WITHIN THE FET AND THE SYNDICAL ORGANIZATION

During the first phases of World War II, the FET was involved in a series of sharp tensions and struggles that were not resolved until September 1942. This was in retrospect almost inevitable, given the prominent role of the Falange, the wide disparity between the political criteria of Franco and other sectors of the regime compared with those of Falangist radicals, and the encouragement given the latter by the German military victories.

Though the extremist sector of the party had criticized the governmental realignment of August 1939 for not giving more power to the Falange,[98] it had further increased the influence of Serrano Súñer, making him president of the Junta Política and naming two of his supporters (Gamero del Castillo and Sánchez Mazas) to the new cabinet. There seems to have been some notion on the part of Serrano and his closest colleagues that in the new alignment he would be responsible for new political ideas and initiatives, and that Franco, as victorious Caudillo, might wish to leave his laurels untarnished by ordinary politics and would therefore relinquish much of the political administration—though this was to underestimate Franco's insistence on personal control. The appointment of Muñoz Grandes as secretary general to some extent limited Serrano's power, but Serrano expected to take personal charge of policy and ideology, leaving Muñoz Grandes to deal only with the technical details of FET organization. As vice secretary, moreover, Gamero provided a certain check on Muñoz Grandes. Fernández Cuesta was shunted aside as ambassador to Brazil, but he would later be given the much more important post in Rome.

Muñoz Grandes abruptly resigned in March 1940, after only seven months in his post. Though known to possess skill in military organization and command, he had little political talent and limited personal authority in the new position, and found it almost impossible to deal with the sprawling, amorphous, and internally disharmonious structure of the FET. He found his relationship with Franco equally unsatisfactory, complaining that whenever he raised serious issues of abuse and corruption or party reorganization, the Caudillo simply diverted the conversation into his customary patter of small talk, evading all major issues.[99] For the time being, the FET was left under the administration of twenty-seven-year-old Vice Secretary General Gamero del Castillo, a basically conservative young man of sense and discretion whom Serrano trusted and who lacked the prestige, independence, or radical ambition to create a separate power base. Though nominal membership continued to increase, the FET organizational system would languish for the following year.

Its principal rival was the military. Though most army officers at least to some extent shared the Falangists' Germanophile attitude toward the European war, nearly all resented the bureaucratic quasi-monopoly of the FET, its ideological radicalism, and the elitist presumption of Falangist militants. Few took their ex officio membership in the FET very seriously, and almost all were gratified by the decree of 2 July 1940 that reconstituted the militia strictly under military command. The jefe nacional was the monarchist General Staff officer Col. Valentín Galarza, Franco's secretary of the presidency and essentially anti-Falangist. The militia comprised four distinct sections,[100] to which was added on 23 February a fifth section, the University Militia, charged with the task of maintaining patriotic order within the universities.[101] There would be no rivalry with a "Spanish SA" similar to that which had developed in Germany during 1933 and 1934: the Falangist militia was even more strictly subordinated to the military and given even less of a direct paramilitary role than the MVSN (Fascist militia) in Italy.[102]

Throughout the years of World War II, the most politically active figure in the military hierarchy was Gen. Antonio Aranda, who was overtly anti-Falangist, even though he occasionally tried to pretend otherwise. He had intervened several times as captain general of Valencia to moderate the repression there, and rumors had even circulated that he had two Falangists executed for trying to drag Republican prisoners from military jails to be killed privately,[103] though this seems unlikely. Aranda hoped to replace Gen. Juan Vigón as head of the new Supreme General Staff, a post for which he was qualified, but by 1940 Franco had begun to doubt his loyalty and made him instead director of the Superior War College, a less prestigious position that also deprived him of command of troops. Franco's suspicion was more than justified; British documents reveal that he was the centerpiece of the bribery operation in which no less than thirteen million dollars was paid out to a sizable number of Spanish generals through the Swiss Bank Corporation in New York in return for their efforts to maintain Spanish neutrality. Aranda himself seems to have netted at least two million of that.[104]

While Aranda and many others schemed pro and con, Serrano Súñer tried to work toward the juridical institutionalization of Franco's highly arbitrary regime. Under Serrano's leadership, in the summer of 1940 the Junta Política of the FET had begun to draft a set of constitutive laws to regularize the structure of government without particularly reducing the Caudillo's personal powers. The text of this Law of the Organization of the State was composed of five sections, dealing with the state, the powers of the Chief of State, a proposed new corporative Cortes, the Junta Política itself, and the scope of a new national economic council. Article 1, echoing the original Falangist program, declared the state to be "a totalitarian instrument at the service of the integrity of the Patria. All its power and all its institutions are devoted to this service, and are subject to law and to the political and moral principles of the National Movement." Twenty of the draft's thirty-seven articles were devoted to defining the scope and structure of a proposed new corporative Cortes, which was to be rather like that of Fascist Italy. The most controversial aspect was article 28, which declared: "The Junta Política is the supreme political council of the regime and the means of liaison between the state and the Movement." Article 31 went on to stipulate: "The Junta Política must be fully heard in matters which affect the constitution of power and the fundamental laws of the state, international political treaties and concordats, and the declaration of war and the conclusion of peace. The competence of the Junta Política includes those matters indicated by the Statutes of the Movement."[105]

This alarmed non- and anti-Falangists because it threatened to give the upper echelon of the party a constitutive place within the highest structure of state power, and it elicited a formal letter of protest from Esteban Bilbao, one of the few significant representatives of Carlism within the regime, against the "systematic interference of the party" in the organism of the state.[106] Franco evidently agreed and ordered the project shelved.

Less easily short-circuited was the secret conspiracy against Franco that had begun to gestate among a small core of camisas viejas. The aftermath of the Civil War had made it clear that the new regime was not so much a revolutionary fascist state as a rightist authoritarian system flavored with fascist rhetoric. In these circumstances one German diplomat replied to the question, "How do you find the new Spain?" by saying, "When I find it, I shall tell you."[107] A number of the most radical young camisas viejas refused to accept this, and determined to take action.

Quite aside from the shadowy and perhaps nonexistent "FEA," several attempts had been made to create clandestine Falangist opposition groups. During 1937 and 1938, Patricio González de Canales, a militant young camisa vieja from Seville who held posts in Falangist publications (and later in state commercial administration), had sought unsuccessfully to build a small network of a crypto-"Falange Autónoma." In 1939 the camisas viejas Narciso Perales, Tito Meléndez, and Eduardo Ezquer (a former provincial chief in Badojoz who had been expelled from the FET in November 1937) had been arrested on charges of trying to form their own "Falange Auténtica," though only Ezquer—an inveterate intriguer and conspirator—would remain in jail long.[108]

At the close of 1939, a small group met at the home of Col. Emilio Rodríguez Tarduchy, a veteran of Primo de Rivera's UP, the UME of 1933, and the original Falange. A clandestine junta política was formed, with Tarduchy as president and González de Canales, whose position in the FET enabled him to travel freely, as secretary. Seven or eight other camisas viejas, representing various other small sectors of party veterans in diverse parts of the country, formed the rest of the junta's fluctuating membership.[109] Their most coveted ally would have been General Juan Yagüe, who was close to José Antonio Girón and other elements of the Falangist

Excombatientes organization but refused to move directly against Franco, insisting that the Falange must change the regime from within. Though the conspirators later claimed to have gained the support of several thousand Falangists in various parts of Spain, most of this support was doubtless quite tenuous, and they completely lacked influence among key power holders.[110]

The clandestine junta then turned to outside support and especially to Hans Thomsen, Landesgruppenleiter for the Nazi organization among German residents in Spain. Thomsen, however, would or could offer German support only on terms that would have reduced a new Spanish government to the status of a satellite, while the conspirators were further discouraged by rumors that a clique of rightist dissidents was also intriguing for German assistance. The German government is said to have refused aid unless the Falangists would agree to place themselves under the direct orders of the Führer.[111]

Franco meanwhile was aware of Yagüe's personal contacts with the German embassy and his sometimes public criticism of cabinet ministers and anti-Falangists. His insistence on a greatly increased air force budget was a source of conflict within the government, while political foes complained that he was an inveterate intriguer who sheltered Masons and former Republicans within the air force officer corps. The results of an earlier investigation of Yagüe's conduct had been delivered to the Generalissimo on 8 February 1940, but Franco apparently found them inconclusive. On 15 March the air force minister sent him a note complaining that the military juridical commissions had been much less lenient in reducing sentences of former Republican officers in his branch of service than in the army and navy, but this lament only renewed suspicion that Yagüe was politically soft on Reds. What finally brought matters to a head was the new situation suddenly created by Hitler's triumph in the west in June 1940. This caused Franco to take much more seriously the rumors of German intrigue to provoke a change in his regime. When the military governor of San Sebastián invited the new German occupation authorities across the Spanish border to a reception at which he shouted, "Viva Hitler," Franco quickly had him replaced. Yagüe was called in for a final dressing down by Franco in the presence of Army Minister Varela on 27 June, in the course of which Yagüe was summarily dismissed as minister.[112]

The Falangist plotters nonetheless continued their meandering course. After toying with and rejecting the notion of assassinating Serrano Súñer, they finally faced up to their only direct alternative—the assassination of Franco himself. At a final meeting in Madrid near the end of March 1941, they concluded that there was no one with whom to replace him and that

Falangism lacked the strength to continue without him. Among the five conspirators, the vote was four to nothing, with one abstention, against attempting assassination.[113] The conspirators attributed their failure to gain more support to Vice Secretary Gamero del Castillo's success in attracting Falangists to bureaucratic positions within the regime.

The most important development within the Falangist sphere in the immediate postwar period was the elaboration of the national syndical system. In an effort to remain faithful to the original Falangist program of organizing the entire economy into a "gigantic syndicate of producers," the text of a proposed "Law of the Bases of National Syndicalist Organization" was prepared in the spring of 1939 by a special interministerial commission composed of the ministers and undersecretaries from the three ministries of Syndical Action and Organization, Industry, and Agriculture. The result was a rather radical document declaring that the economy of Spain would be "subordinated to the imperative of social justice that our revolution demands" and would reflect "the new moral style."[114] It was therefore "up to the party, as its genuine and primordial mission, to transfuse the National Syndicalist Organization with the emotion of its spirit and the intransigent dynamism of its youthful vigor." After this opening barrage of typically fascist rhetoric, the proposed law declared that the Organization would assume "with an exclusive character the representation of the various economic activities before the state," eliminating such intermediaries as chambers of commerce and professional bodies. Similarly, anyone lacking the Organization's "labor card" would be barred from employment.

The Organization was to be headed by a national director and an appointive national syndical council, with sweeping powers to impose economic sanctions. There were to be directors for each large "economic zone" of Spain and for each province, while on the local level there would be syndical juntas, syndical commissions, and commissions of juries, all their personnel appointed from above.[115]

This draft was sharply criticized by a report of the National Council of the FET for such fundamental defects as devoting nearly half its great length to vague rhetoric, leaving the impression that membership might be voluntary, making the syndicates organs of the party rather than of the state, appearing merely to incorporate existing economic institutions, and failing to define fully the "vertical" characteristics of the vaunted "vertical syndicate."[116]

The proposal was again strongly attacked when presented to the Council of Ministers on 2 June 1939. Juan Antonio Suanzes, then minister of industry and commerce, a naval officer, and boyhood friend of Franco, denounced it as "something absurd, crazy and confusing for the economic order, full of demagogic verbiage." Most ministers agreed, and Franco passed it on to the National Council for revision. There it met a further hail of criticism, even from some camisas viejas; in view of the general disapprobation, apparently not a single camisa vieja voted in favor of the text.[117] It became clear that the days in office of González Bueno, the first syndical minister, were numbered. Even Franco seems to have been taken aback by the extent of the criticism, and though the Council then helped to prepare a more moderate new law, Franco never again referred major matters to it for discussion.

The eventual Law of Syndical Unity, announced on 26 January 1940, lacked most of the original revolutionary rhetoric. It reaffirmed the principles of unity and hierarchy, subordinating the Syndical Organization to the state rather than to the party. Chambers of commerce and professional colleges were permitted to survive, though all private economic organizations would be subordinated to the new system.

In the government of 1939, the functions of the still nonexistent Ministry of Labor were attached to those of the Ministry of Agriculture, held by the right-wing engineer and neo-Falangist Joaquín Benjumea Burín. (This further indicated the limited importance attached to the latter ministry.) Gerardo Salvador Merino was named national delegate of syndicates of the FET, and was charged with the creation of the new syndical system. Since the new press and censorship powers that had been established in February 1938 were exercised through the Ministry of the Interior, Salvador Merino thus became the only high official of the party who was given a major administrative function in Franco's system without becoming a government minister. Conversely, separation of the Ministry of Labor from the syndical system would remain fundamental to Franco's mode of *divide et impera,* and would continue for many years.

Salvador Merino had come to the Falange from the Socialist Party[118] and had served as FET provincial chief of La Coruña during part of the Civil War, winning a reputation for worker organization and radical rhetoric. This, in fact, had originally cost him his post as provincial chief, but he was known for intelligence and organizational ability. He was, as it turned out, highly ambitious and by 1939–1940 an ardent Naziphile whose goal was to build a powerful and relatively autonomous syndical system as the decisive element in the new regime.[119] This aim was similar to that of Edmondo Rossoni for the Italian Fascist syndicates during the 1920s[120] and ultimately proved no more successful.

During his first year, Salvador Merino built a structure of three Sections and nine Services under the Syndical Organization. Though the syndicates were declared to be "vertical," employers and workers were organized in separate sections, which in practice was not very different from the system in Fascist Italy, and, as in Italy, the employers would enjoy greater autonomy, even though that autonomy was circumscribed during the first years of the system. Structure was hierarchical,[121] all appointments being made from the top down. Moreover, local worker sections were subdivided according to each major branch of industry in every district, fragmenting the worker network on the local level. While FET leaders often engaged in radical anticapitalist rhetoric, conservative Falangists and other government spokesmen were sometimes more frank in declaring that the state and the employers rather than the workers dominated the system.[122] Moreover, ultimate authority for national economic regulation lay primarily in the hands of central government ministries and agencies—just as in Italy at that time—not in those of the syndicates.

Salvador Merino nonetheless continued with his ambitious plans, drawing an increasing amount of attention to himself. On the Day of Victory, 31 March 1940, first anniversary of the end of the Civil War, he arranged for a large number of workers to participate in the gigantic Madrid parade, drawing the ire of right-wingers, especially in the military. Later, in a speech of 8 July, he warned:

> We have a strictly authoritarian and directive concept of our
> responsibility, and by the force of authority we shall either succeed in
> imposing our doctrines or the Revolution will be lost; and we add
> that if the National Syndicalist Revolution is lost the greatest loss will
> be of those who feared our demagogy and who failed to develop faith
> in our doctrines. . . . Only a period of weeks or at most of months is
> left to make them understand that through the complete achievements
> of the syndicalist conscience must be developed a new political
> concept of the Patria and of the duties of citizens with regard to it.[123]

At that point in mid-1940 he began the formation of a national Labor Service that could begin to provide employment for some of the masses of unemployed. He also began to create special elite worker "centurias of labor" to participate in and to discipline labor parades and other activities. Each centuria would be composed of 120 men, three units forming a "bandera" and three Banderas a "tercio." The new centurias played a major role in the massive labor participation in the huge public celebration of 18 July 1940 in Madrid, fourth anniversary of the beginning of the Movimiento Nacional. To the military and to the right, this looked suspiciously like the rebirth of a sort of workers' militia, all the more since Salvador Merino's speech that day referred to "the eternal enemies . . . on the left and on the right."[124]

Salvador Merino convened the First Syndical Congress in Madrid from 11 to 19 November, which was followed by the Law for the Constitution of Syndicates, promulgated on 6 December 1940. This defined syndical organization in fuller detail, replete with the standard rhetoric, in this case declaring the sindicatos "ordered in militia, under the command of FET de las JONS,"[125] which tended somewhat to confuse the terms of the earlier Law of Syndical Unity. Membership was obligatory for employers in the organs of economic control, but individual membership for workers theoretically was not.

In reality, the pace of organization was rather slow. Full national syndicates were declared to have been organized in ten sectors of the economy—the most important being textiles and metallurgy—by the close of 1940, yet the number of workers organized totaled only about 110,000 in Madrid, possibly 300,000 in Barcelona province, and approximately 197,000 in Asturias. A National Agrarian Council was set up for agriculture in June 1941, as the system slowly absorbed the functions of CONCA, the Catholic small farmer syndicate.[126]

It was the pomp and publicity attending Salvador Merino's activities, together with his evident ambition, that aroused the apprehensions of rightists and rivals in other branches of the state, particularly military leaders who considered him a dangerous fascist demagogue and subversive, a kind of crypto-Red. Merino sought to create strong syndical provincial delegations in each province and to begin a sizable series of new "social works" for workers, but in fact his more ambitious projects were usually blocked by other departments of government. Serrano eventually recognized that Salvador Merino might become unviable politically, and even suggested to him that he might be moved into the cabinet as the first real minister of labor. Since that would have required giving up control of Sindicatos, Merino refused. When asked what other position he would accept, he replied that he would only be willing to take the currently vacant post of secretary general of the FET, and then only if it was combined with the Ministry of the Interior. Serrano Súñer replied that Merino was hopelessly ambitious,[127] which was indeed the case.

Like the FET's vice secretary, Gamero del Castillo, Salvador Merino maintained extensive contacts with Nazi groups in Germany for information concerning their structure and organization. In defiance of the regular party procedures, these contacts were usually made directly, without going through the Servicio Exterior.[128] Thomsen, the Nazi leader in Madrid, thus made arrangements for a special trip to Germany in which Salvador Merino could inspect the German Labor Front (DAF), meet with selected officials, and discuss possible arrangements to provide Spanish workers for German industry.

At this point the German embassy in Madrid constituted the largest

German diplomatic delegation anywhere in the world, its personnel total-ing approximately five hundred, not including many others in various large German consulates. The Sicherheitsdienst (SD) of the Nazi SS also maintained two different intelligence networks of its own in Spain, rely-ing especially but by no means exclusively on Falangists. One SD report at the beginning of 1941 declared that "at the present time, three general lines, and about 20 to 30 different groups, coexist within the Spanish Unified Party, all of which openly call themselves followers of their own particular political ideas."[129]

This was something of an exaggeration, but certainly at that time Sal-vador Merino occupied the strongest radical position, even more pro-Nazi than the bulk of the FET. On 7 May 1941 he met with Goebbels in Berlin. Even though Thomsen would later claim that this had been set up so that Merino could elicit German support for pressuring Franco, eliminating Serrano, and raising the Falangist radicals to power in order to bring Spain into the war,[130] there is no corroboration of this in surviv-ing records. In his diary, Goebbels merely referred to Merino as "a clever and likable man, one of the few Spaniards that I have any time for."[131] The primary outcome of this trip was the initial signing of an agreement between the Syndical Organization and the DAF to recruit Spanish work-ers for labor in Germany.

In fact, the trip coincided with the outbreak of the first high-level polit-ical crisis in Madrid since the end of the Civil War, a crisis that in certain respects was the most difficult Franco would ever have to face. At its root lay the growing restiveness of many of the camisas viejas and Falangist radicals who had cooperated with Serrano Súñer in the FET. On the one hand they complained that Serrano had failed to give the Falange authen-tic leadership, and that Franco had failed to live up to his adoption of the Twenty-Six Points; on the other they claimed that Serrano had appointed too many of his former CEDA colleagues to positions in the FET and the state administration. Under Vice Secretary General Gamero del Castillo, the party leadership had often seemed restricted to the narrow internal issues of the FET bureaucracy, itself poorly developed. Gamero himself had lamented in *Arriba* on 19 January 1941:

> Our finest colleagues and many others in Spain are daily asking
> a basic question: the question about the relationships between the
> present problems of Spain and the possibilities of the party. For the
> truth is that the Falange neither rules a State of its own—which has
> not yet been built—nor combats an opposing state, which has been
> destroyed.

> At the present time the Falange has been called upon to perform
> a dangerous service of partial eclipse. It has to work in the most
> difficult circumstances, weakened by a deep substratum of political
> heterogeneity that at times reduces the visible result to zero.

A few days before the close of 1940, Ridruejo had told an SD agent
that a big political change was about to take place, and in January Gamero himself informed Hans Lazar, press attaché in the German embassy,
that Falangists were insisting that "an activist, homogeneous Serrano
Súñer government should be formed as soon as possible," asking that
Berlin indicate to Franco that it wished for Serrano to assume greater
power.[132]

Falangist ambitions were further fueled by developments in Romania,
which of all countries had a government structure most similar to that of
Spain. Since September 1940 power had been shared by the military dictator, Marshal Ion Antonescu, and the Iron Guard, Romania's fascist movement, though the autonomy of the latter was considerably greater than
that of the FET in Spain. The Iron Guard, demanding full power, rose in
revolt against Antonescu in late January 1941 and was soon crushed. A
Falangist demonstration in Madrid in support of the Iron Guard was
quickly prohibited by Spanish authorities.[133]

At this point certain Falangist leaders attempted to hand Serrano Súñer
a sort of ultimatum, demanding that he actively assume the real leadership of the FET and lead it to victory within the Spanish system or cast
off pretenses and admit that he was no more than a rightist reactionary.
Their goal was to limit Franco to the role of Chief of State, with Serrano
to hold the posts of president of the government and minister of foreign
affairs. Other Falangists would be given the ministries of the Interior and
of National Education, while Agriculture and Industry and Commerce
would be combined into a national syndical superministry of Economics,
to create an economic dictatorship. They also demanded that Serrano dismiss various rightists and neo-Falangist moderates from key posts around
him. Otherwise they threatened massive resignations by camisas viejas
and even a campaign of sabotage against the regime.[134]

Serrano of course realized that there was no way he could meet all
these demands. Franco had no intention whatsoever of allowing anyone
else to direct the government, and Serrano therefore sought a compromise
that would increase his influence as de facto leader of the FET and of the
party within the system.

Apart from Franco himself, the most serious obstacle to the Falangists'
ambitions was the military. German intelligence reported that in mid-
January three generals (the hyperactive Aranda and the more conservative

García Escámez and García Valiño) had protested to Franco about the corruption and maladministration that persisted amid acute economic shortages—corruption and maladministration that they insisted were most serious in the FET itself. They were said to have urged Franco to work toward a monarchist restoration.[135]

The major monarchists in the military hierarchy at this time were José Enrique Varela, who was minister of the army, and Alfredo Kindelán. Though Varela was married to a Carlist and was a nominal Carlist himself, he tended to agree with Kindelán that the restoration of the main branch of the dynasty was the most feasible alternative, combined with neutrality in the war and even greater cooperation with Great Britain.[136]

Conversely, from mid-1940 to mid-1941 the Spanish royal family and its closest advisers assumed, not unnaturally, that it would be necessary in some fashion to come to terms with a hegemonic Nazi Germany in order to guarantee a rapid restoration in Spain. For a decade the royal family had supported the doctrine of "instauracion" of a more authoritarian, neotraditionalist monarchy that might unify both branches of the dynasty behind Don Alfonso and his heir, Don Juan. In the first months of 1941, monarchist leaders believed it necessary to press for a restoration as soon as possible, for if Germany should win the war, such an outcome would be likely to reconfirm Franco's semifascist caudillaje. Thus immediate steps toward restoration must be taken at least to some degree "in agreement with the Wilhelmstrasse." One monarchist document declared that "our policy must be very cautious in the international field, but given his [the Pretender's] place of residence [Rome] and the geographic situation of the German army, we must endeavor confidentially, to the degree that we can, to win from the diplomacy of the Axis a sympathetic attitude." Though the goal must be continued Spanish neutrality, it was important that the restoration "in no way appear to be part of a political maneuver against the Reich."[137]

Thus between January and April someone who presented himself as a representative of the new Pretender, Don Juan, held brief conversations with a representative of the Wilhelmstrasse in Berlin, seeking German support for a monarchist restoration in Madrid that could avoid a potential military coup against Franco and the breakdown of the government.[138] As Tusell observes, "The contacts made with Germany were indirect, superficial, and of scant duration, and, moreover, enjoyed a very cold reception."[139] One effort at contact by means of a German journalist in Rome was communicated by the German authorities to Serrano Súñer,[140] while the Italian leaders in Rome correctly perceived the royal family as basically more Anglophile than pro-Axis.[141]

Meanwhile the gadfly Aranda met with the Nazi leader Thomsen and the key German businessman and diplomatic contact Johannes Bernhardt in Madrid on 20 April to propose a different scenario that he hoped might be more appealing to the Germans: German acceptance of a proposed Spanish military coup that would eliminate Serrano Súñer and reduce Franco's authority but still permit the FET to function, albeit with reduced influence.[142]

Though it was typical of Aranda to claim more influence than he actually possessed, the criticism of domestic policy among the military was sharper than ever. Military leaders generally agreed with Franco's increasing reluctance to enter the war, but they disagreed strongly with other aspects of state affairs. Criticism was fueled by increasingly severe shortages (the rationing of bread had been introduced in January 1941), the rapid growth of corruption, and the frequent inefficiency of the new state system, with its clumsy bureaucratic controls. Ever more intense hostility was focused on the pretensions of Falangists, and more concretely on Serrano Súñer, who was detested by the military and many others not simply because of his power but also because of the manner in which he exercised it. Serrano never wore his authority lightly; he became increasingly intemperate in speech and manner, arrogant and overweening, the object of constant attention in the official media. His pro-Axis statements, particularly those made to his favorite interlocutors of the Italian Fascist press, were more frequent and extreme than those of Franco. Army officers and anti-Falangists resented his pride, power, and quasi-leadership of Falangism; monarchists held him partly responsible for the regime's failure to recognize the monarchy; and malcontents and critics of diverse stripe detested him simply because he was the "cuñadísimo"—so that German intelligence could describe him in Berlin as "the most hated man in Spain."[143]

Franco and Serrano largely agreed on foreign policy, but Serrano backed a more coherent and integrated, and to that extent a more fully fascist, political system than Franco was willing to permit. The Generalissimo's extreme personalism, suspicion, relative caution, and refusal to commit himself to a systematic, juridically defined system—fascist or otherwise—all caused Serrano increasing frustration. He was also aware of the intense hostility, rumors, and gossip of which he was the object, and believed—not incorrectly—that he was the target of so much criticism because in large measure he served as a kind of scapegoat for Franco. Serrano's public arrogance partly masked the fact that he found his position increasingly uncomfortable.

Falangists finally seized the initiative at the close of April, when Gamero del Castillo abruptly threatened to resign his vice secretarial position within the party. On 1 May both Pilar and Miguel Primo de Rivera sent letters to Franco threatening their own resignations. Pilar's missive stated: "I in conscience cannot continue collaborating in this thing that we are making people believe is the Falange but which in reality is not it. . . . The Falange . . . for some time has been no more than a languid disorganization in which the only thing that remains upright is the Sección Femenina."[144]

The communication from Miguel Primo de Rivera was yet more explicit:

> My respected General: For some time we have clearly felt discontent, expressed to you on repeated occasions, and reiterated to the president of the Junta Política and to whatever superiors we have had, that the politics of Spain differ notably from the thought of the person who inspired all the men of the Falange to ardent service.
>
> . . . Though it is true that the complete fulfillment of the doctrine of José Antonio would be hard to carry out in the present circumstances, heavily burdened within and dangerous without, it is also true that the instrument created to make that doctrine effective some day, that is, the Party Falange Española Tradicionalista y de las J. O. N. S., absolutely lacks the means and minimal possibilities of carrying out its difficult mission.
>
> The National Council, proclaimed by Your Excellency to be the fundamental leadership organ of the Party, so completely lacks any authentic mission that it has only met once since its constitution more than a year and a half ago, and that was only to listen passively to the reading of the Syndical Law and that of the Frente de Juventudes.
>
> The Junta Política, the council that supposedly inspires the politics of the New State, is a disgraceful parody of what such an organism ought to be in the practice of a strong and renovative policy.
>
> The Militia of the Party . . . only exists in a law without articulation, so that in all our territory there are scarcely one hundred Spaniards who know what the Militia of the Party is, or who commands it directly.
>
> The Frente de Juventudes, proclaimed five months ago and called by Your Excellency the priority work of the regime, is without command, since no one has been named to that position, and makes of our hopeful youth . . . a large, perplexed body of lads who, if this continues, will one day come to doubt that our Crusade was anything more than a slaughter among Spaniards.
>
> . . . The reason for all the aforesaid is that, and very especially since General Muñoz Grandes left as Secretary General, the Party lacks direct leadership, a lack of leadership very keenly felt by the National Delegations, the provincial commands, and all those Services which ought to function under direct, clear, and constant leadership.

Nonetheless, the Primo de Rivera siblings expressed their "loyalty" to Franco, concluding in each case that they remained "at his orders."[145]

On the following day, Serrano delivered an unusually aggressive speech at a ceremony in Mota del Cuervo, denouncing the foes of Falangism, claiming that the party should dominate policy, and stressing that "those who lead this work can be none other than the minority moved by light and by faith." "The problem," Serrano insisted, "does not exactly lie in broadening the base—such is the depraved language of liberalism—but in tightening its coherence and employing it in its full and rigorous meaning by those who understand and love the Falange, . . . not by that eclecticist centipede requested by those who are too blind to see our paths and too disabled to follow them."[146] Two days later, on 4 May, José Antonio Maravall published an article in the same vein in *Arriba*, stressing that present contradictions could be overcome only by recognizing that "decisions must be made by the politicians and not by the technicians."

Similarly, on 4 May there was published a decree signed three days earlier in which Antonio Tovar, the Falangist press undersecretary in the Ministry of the Interior, stipulated that "political responsibility for and censorship of" all FET publications "will fall directly on the National Delegation of Press and Propaganda," technically freeing them from state censorship and thereby creating a politically autonomous fascist press in Spain.[147]

Franco's reply to all this was immediate. On 5 May he announced a series of major new military appointments. His trusted undersecretary (or chief executive assistant) of the presidency of the government, the monarchist General Staff colonel Valentín Galarza, was named minister of the interior, a crucial political post nominally vacant since Serrano had been moved to foreign affairs the preceding October. Thus a vital cabinet position, in a post that dominated domestic political affairs, was taken over by one of the leaders of military opposition to the FET. When José Lorente, a close associate of Serrano and the acting undersecretary of the interior who had in fact been overseeing the ministry, refused Franco's offer of the undersecretary of the presidency, the Generalissimo then appointed to this sensitive position a naval officer, Capt. Luis Carrero Blanco. Several days later two leading monarchist generals, Luis Orgaz and Alfredo Kindelán, received the key posts of high commissioner of Morocco and captain general of Barcelona, respectively.

All this brought a firestorm of criticism from the camisas viejas, who considered the administration of the Ministry of the Interior—which they considered "their" ministry—by what they called the "Casino Militar of Madrid" a supreme insult to their ambitions. Lorente made his vehement criticism publicly known and was said to be preparing the resignation en masse of the top personnel in the ministry. Franco quickly countered this by discharging Lorente and appointing in his place the Carlist Antonio Iturmendi—another enemy of the Falange—as undersecretary of the interior.

Falangist indignation reached its maximum. Primo de Rivera and eventually nine other provincial chiefs of the party turned in their resignations, and Serrano told Franco that he might do the same thing. On 8 May *Arriba* carried a prominent article entitled "The Dots over the 'I's: The Man and the Pipsqueak," with a clear allusion to Galarza as "the pipsqueak," while resignations within the party continued to mount. Tovar added his own, and Ridruejo, presumed author of the article, was soon dismissed, while Galarza quickly canceled the decree exempting FET publications from state censorship. On 9 May, however, the General Secretariat of the FET declared inoperative Galarza's new appointments of provincial governors, alleging technical deficiencies in the respective decrees. During the next few days there were street altercations in several cities between Falangists and military men and between Falangists and police. Two people were killed in León.

Franco had fundamentally miscalculated—for perhaps the first and last time in intra-regime affairs—and matters only became worse when the competent minister of finance, José Larraz, resigned for strictly personal reasons on 10 May. When Serrano indicated that he intended to add his own to the other resignations, the Generalissimo had to take action. He had not intended to push Serrano that far, and on the thirteenth wrote a gentle letter to his brother-in-law that succeeded in heading off the intended resignation.[148]

Franco had no intention of reducing his own authority by rescinding any of the new appointments, but he recognized the need to conciliate the Falangists. Serrano, Miguel Primo de Rivera, José Antonio Girón, and several other FET leaders met at the Madrid home of José Luis de Arrese, apparently on the fifteenth, to consider alternatives. Serrano proposed compensation by awarding Girón the still-unclaimed portfolio of labor.

Franco's resolution of the matter was announced in a further series of personnel changes on 18 and 19 May. The announcement of the eighteenth officially discharged Gamero del Castillo as vice secretary as well as Tovar and Ridruejo (the dismissal of the latter two being dated 1 May, before the crisis began). On the following day Franco announced the appointment of Girón to Labor and of Arrese to the long-vacant post of secretary general of the FET.[149] Moreover, the Falangist Carceller, who had headed the Ministry of Industry and Commerce since the preceding October, would retain his cabinet position, while the nominal Falangist Joaquín Benjumea had been moved from Agriculture to Finance.

The propaganda elite: Dionisio Ridruejo, Antonio Tovar, and Serrano Súñer

Franco badly needed a reliable leader for the FET who could control the radicals but would also be beholden only to the Caudillo and not to his brother-in-law. He had decided that his choice would be Arrese, the camisa vieja provincial chief of Málaga. Arrese was an architect from a prominent ultra-Catholic, right-wing Basque family and had married a first cousin of José Antonio. He had literary ambitions and, as noted earlier, had written a book-length attempt at an exposition of the Falangist social program.[150] Jailed for some months as a camisa vieja rebel in 1937, he had afterward demonstrated a full and sincere desire to collaborate. Franco had become acquainted with Arrese during an inspection tour of Málaga and had been impressed by his pleasant and servile manner, together with his achievements in local social administration.[151] Though Arrese was one of the provincial chiefs who had just resigned, Franco shrewdly decided to take the calculated risk that he could become a reliable subordinate independent of Serrano and of the Falangist ultras as well. Arrese snapped up Franco's offer of the post of secretary general, but suggested that the FET would require some further recognition. Franco countered by awarding the agriculture portfolio to Miguel Primo de Rivera, which was announced on the twenty-second.[152] In addition, control of censorship and propaganda was soon taken away from the Ministry of the Interior and placed under a newly created Vice Secretariat of Press and Propaganda of the FET. On these terms, together with a number of secondary appointments, ended the only real rebellion in the history of the FET.[153]

The full development of the crisis had taken Franco at least partially by surprise, and its duration of more than two weeks made it the longest cabinet crisis in the history of the regime. Existing divisions and tensions were at this point far too deep to be solved by any single reorganization, but the resolution of the crisis revealed Franco's growing skill in finding ways to balance off against each other the contending forces within his system. The outcome managed to meet the minimum demands of the military while conciliating their Falangist rivals.

Though the latter did not grasp it at this time, the crisis also recorded the high-water mark of Falangist pretensions within the Franquist state, coming at the moment when the prestige and military strength of Nazi Germany were at their highest levels, and the prospects for a more general fascistization of Europe unsurpassed. Indeed, as some of the new Falangist ministers assumed office, they would deliver further bombastic and revolutionary pronouncements indicative of their general expectations. Similarly, military leaders were rather chagrined by the way in which the whole process had played out, for the initial expansion of military influence that had initiated the crisis had, in typically franquista fashion, become considerably counterweighted by the time the new changes were concluded.

The calculated risks that Franco took in the appointments of Arrese and Girón were nonetheless very shrewdly conceived, amounting to genuine masterstrokes of political calculation that would have the effect of further dividing the Falangist leaders internally and greatly augmenting Franco's dominance over the FET. The new Falangist leaders would be in a position to work directly with the Caudillo as his immediate government subordinates, rather than having to proceed in large measure through Serrano Súñer, as had most of their predecessors. The new working relationships would consequently subordinate Falangism more personally and directly to Franco than ever before.

This would also mark the beginning of the decline of the political influence of Serrano Súñer. He was immediately aware that, despite the new appointments of Falangists, the outcome of the crisis was not at all the "compact government" of Falangists under a more powerful government-dominating Serrano that many of them had hoped for in recent months. Nonetheless, Serrano still hoped and at first assumed that he would maintain the same preeminence over the FET while Arrese was its secretary general as during the earlier administrations of Fernández Cuesta, Muñoz

Grandes, and Gamero del Castillo. Only a few months would be necessary to demonstrate that this was not to be. On the basis of his personal relationship with and direct subordination to Franco, Arrese would quickly prove much more adroit than his predecessors in gaining more direct control over the FET. Years later Serrano would ruefully observe: "The important thing about these developments was that I had ceased to be the mediator between the Chief of State and the authentic leaders of the Falange. . . . From that moment the FET y de las JONS was above all the party of Franco. After the crisis of May 1941 the Falangists who had fought by my side lost faith in our political enterprise."[154] This final sentence generalizes overmuch: all that would not become fully clear until after the following government crisis of September 1942. Yet the new conditions were being initiated in May 1941.

Exactly how these changes would work out was by no means predetermined, and would depend not merely on the evolution of domestic affairs in Spain but also to a significant extent on the fortunes of Germany's military effort. The combined results of these two sets of circumstances during the following year would not merely begin to bring the FET more completely under control than ever before, but also chart the very beginning of a slow but progressive process of defascistization within the Spanish state. The years 1939–1941 marked the apogee—limited though that was—of the FET. From that time forward its subordination would steadily increase, though all this would not become fully clear for another year or more.

# Eleven

# The First Phase of a Long Defascistization, 1941–1945

The FET had been designed as a hybrid fascist-type state party, combining the Falange with the Carlists and to some extent with other rightist forces. For at least four years after the unification, the camisas viejas had expected to predominate, brushing aside Carlists and others. They had designed the crisis of May 1941 to force this issue, and although the terms of the settlement did not in any way give them a clear-cut victory, the appointment of activist camisas viejas to the position of secretary general and two new ministries gratified them as an apparent step in the right direction.

This was not really the case. Franco had resolved the crisis on terms that proved more satisfactory to himself and his personal authority than the situation that existed during 1939–1941. It would soon become clear that the influence of Serrano Súñer and his Falangist colleagues, as well as of activist camisas viejas in general, was waning rather than waxing.

Though it could not have been known in 1941, Franco had also appointed Serrano Súñer's eventual replacement in the person of an aspiring naval officer, Capt. Luis Carrero Blanco. One of Franco's most pressing needs had been to find another military man to replace Galarza as undersecretary to his presidency of the government. In selecting Carrero Blanco for this post, he chose the man who would become his own political alter ego for more than three decades, soon to become his most influential and trusted counselor, playing a more decisive role than Serrano in the direction and evolution of the Franquist system.

Luis Carrero Blanco was a career naval officer who prior to the Civil War had been a professor in the Naval War College in Madrid. He managed to escape the bloody purge that killed 40 percent of the naval officer corps in the Republican zone, thanks to his lack of previous political involvement and the fact that he had no active command. The slaughter of naval officers by the revolutionaries only hardened his extreme right-wing convictions. He gained asylum in the Mexican embassy and then fled to the Nationalist zone, where during the last phases of the war he commanded first a destroyer and then a submarine. He was later made chief of operations for the Naval General Staff.

Politically, Carrero Blanco was at first a discovery of Serrano Súñer and Gamero del Castillo, who had searched for reliable and interested military men to add to the National Council of the FET. There Carrero had come to the attention of Franco, who had had some marginal contact with him before the Civil War.[1] In November 1940 Carrero had prepared a report on the naval aspects of entry into the war, which accepted as obvious ("claro está") that any entry would be on the side of the Axis, but warned that it should be delayed, from the naval point of view, until the Axis had first taken Suez, crippling British power in the Mediterranean.[2] Carrero Blanco had some ability as a writer, and his principal work, *España en el mar*, was published by the Editora Nacional at the beginning of 1941. It was devoted to the importance of naval power in Spain's past and future and expressed the author's personal convictions, which were ultra-Catholic as well as strongly anti-Semitic.[3]

Ironically, as the crisis began to develop in May, Franco first offered the undersecretary position to Lorente, the current undersecretary of the interior, who sought to resign that position in solidarity with Serrano and the Falangists. Though he had been a Serrano appointee, Franco had been pleased with his work as de facto head of the Ministry of the Interior during the winter of 1940–41. When Lorente immediately rejected the offer, Franco did not hesitate long in making what would prove to be the much surer appointment of Carrero Blanco. In this beetle-browed, devoutly Catholic and conservative naval officer, Franco would find an ideal, devoted, and almost sycophantic executive assistant and adviser, more suitable for his purposes than his brother-in-law and someone with whom he could be more comfortable. Carrero was genuinely self-effacing and thus the very opposite of the lofty and arrogant Serrano. While aspiring to become the Caudillo's dominant "privado" in a personal sense, he had no desire ever to hold the limelight directly. His own ideas were closer to Franco's than Serrano's thinking was. Whereas the latter was more of a modernist and a Europeanizing fascist, Carrero was more conservative, more military-oriented, and semimonarchist in his convictions. The notion that subsequently developed to the effect that Carrero had no ideas of his own was exaggerated, but Carrero quickly became attuned to Franco's wishes and was extremely discreet in proffering advice. Differences of principle between the two turned out to be surprisingly few, and Carrero became the nearest thing to an alter ego that Franco would ever have. As this relationship began to develop during 1941–1942, Serrano Súñer would become more and more expendable—indeed, counterproductive. Carrero was also pro-Axis in foreign policy, but he lacked any ideological fascist commitment and so could be somewhat more detached. As executive and administrative secretary, he set much of Franco's agenda, filtering a large part of the information and advice that he received.

Carrero's first major memorandum to Franco on the principles and structure of his state was a lengthy missive dated 25 August 1941.[4] It started from the premise that sound policy must have a basis and a goal, residing in "an absolute truth," and the latter can only have been enunciated by God. Carrero thus began at the opposite pole from fascist activism-relativism (though one that might have been congenial to the more nuanced thinking of José Antonio Primo de Rivera), and went on to observe that "if we analyze history, it is necessary to realize, without any fear of succumbing to the sin of national vanity, that there has never been any nation whose trajectory has been so clearly marked in this sense as Spain."

He pointed out that while the regime had to base political activity on a new unitary party, the FET had become too inclusive and eclectic. Party policy "tended toward the ingenuous" and had admitted "a great mass of semi-Reds, or clear-cut Reds though not of significant political personality, of Masons, of the amoral, and simply of opportunists." "To our absolutely real misfortune, one reaches the conclusion that the Party has grown without direction, that, in a word, it has slipped through our hands. . . . It is certain that Your Excellency did not desire this." It had reached the point where "the Party, which could have been the solution, has complicated problems even more," for

> it has constituted a duplicate state organization, maintaining a marked parallelism and a troublesome doubling of function and dependency in certain positions. Facing a Council of Ministers there is a Junta Política; facing a provincial governor there is a provincial chief, often combined in the same person, but answering at one and the same time to both the minister of the interior and the minister-secretary of the party; facing the police, there is an information service of the party; the syndicates have to answer both to the minister of industry and commerce and to the National Delegation of Syndicates; facing state welfare, the Delegation of Social Welfare; abroad, delegations in a certain way bearing a diplomatic function of the party, and, finally even the militia wants to be a copy of the army.

Therefore "the state organism requires a profound reform." "A divorce exists between the Army and Party, and disunity and disagreement within the latter; a divorce from the Party, equally, of good Spaniards that remain outside it, either because they do not want to join or are not allowed." "In a totalitarian regime, like the present one, there can be only one political doctrine . . . , but this partido único, which is no longer any single one of its components, has no definite policy at all."

Carrero concluded that "the organic scheme of a totalitarian state" was based on five components:

a) A Caudillo
b) A Party
c) An administrative organism functioning with maximum simplicity, dynamic, active, and coordinated, with a minimal number of functionaries
d) A National Plan
e) A People who obeys

The FET must therefore be unified under a clear "doctrine or credo" announced by Franco. It must become a dedicated elite, preferably led by "200 men" of "Catholic ideas," "sound moral constitution," and full loyalty to the Caudillo. A streamlined and efficient state must be created, dedicated to a National Plan that would develop strong armed forces, a productive economy, justice, and sound education. Fascism was not mentioned, for Carrero's obvious goal was a Catholic and semitraditional authoritarianism designed to achieve strength, prosperity, and national pedagogy. This outline pointed toward the future of the Francoist state, mutatis mutandis, beyond the fascist era.

DISCIPLINING THE FET

In fact, the instrument for the fuller unification and subordination of the FET was already at hand in José Luis de Arrese, whose appointment as secretary general would soon prove to be one of Franco's masterstrokes, one of the most useful appointments he ever made. Between 1941 and 1943, Arrese would largely complete the task of bureaucratizing and domesticating the Falange that Serrano had never been able to complete.

This was not, however, clear during the late spring and summer of 1941, for Arrese's power over the FET apparatus was at first carefully circumscribed. The initial arrangement seems to have been that Arrese was to handle appointments and administration within the FET organization itself, while Serrano Súñer would continue to deal with ideology and general policy as president of the Junta Política. This arrangement suited Franco, who in the first weeks was not entirely sure how much he could trust Arrese. The new secretary general found, however, that, in practice,

this arrangement gave Serrano the power to initiate and review all significant policy decisions, leaving Arrese with no more than the bureaucratic
paperwork formerly handled by Gamero del Castillo. Arrese soon complained to Franco, who indicated initial surprise, saying that he thought
that the new secretary general had agreed to this modus operandi. Franco
then took the second step of deciding to place fuller confidence in Arrese
and gave him full control over party appointments and activities, reducing
Serrano's sphere to ideology and doctrine.[5]

This relationship developed because an understanding was quickly
reached between Franco and Arrese that the latter's task was to render the
party more completely obedient to the Generalissimo himself. As Manuel
Valdés has put it, "It can be stated that Arrese set for himself, as his main
task, to unite the political framework of the party with Generalissimo
Franco, both directly and indirectly, and to guarantee that the latter's Jefatura Nacional was not merely nominal but could be effectively exercised."[6] While maintaining a purely verbal radicalism that was pleasing
to the old guard, Arrese did all he could to expedite the buying off and
domestication of the core Falangists.

A very few had to be directly removed, beginning with the national
delegate of syndicates, who had returned from Berlin during the gestation
of the crisis. For several months Salvador Merino had been a marked man
for certain military and rightist enemies, and the initiative in hunting for
his head had been taken by the elderly Andrés Saliquet, captain general
of Valladolid. Saliquet was an unconditional franquista and one of the
small group who had originally elected Franco to the jefatura única. He
was thoroughly outraged by Merino's revolutionary fascism and demagogic ambitions. Probably with the assistance of the military courts, he
was able to present evidence that Merino had been a Mason in the early
years of the Republic, and Masons, just as much as leftist revolutionaries,
had been targeted as principal enemies of the new regime.

The swan song of Salvador Merino was sung at the Second Syndical
Congress, which convened in Madrid in June 1941. Unaware that the end
was at hand, Merino's rhetoric was at its radical best, grandiloquent and
completely inaccurate:

> The decision is very near for the integration under the discipline
> of the Movement of all the official and semiofficial entities that have
> had an established mission of channeling or directing the country's
> commercial or economic activity, dissolving all the inefficient
> groups. . . . You all know what I am talking about. The days of the
> chambers of commerce and industry and agriculture, and similar
> entities, are numbered.[7]

Soon afterward, on 7 July, a still-unsuspecting Salvador Merino was married and departed on his honeymoon. Not long after his return, he was relieved of his post and sent into internal exile in the Balearics,[8] and thus one of the most demagogic Falangists, as well as one of the most radically pro-Nazi, suddenly vanished from public life. In October he was officially expelled from the FET, along with a lesser figure named Alvarez Sotomayor,[9] who in July had publicly called for "all power to the Falange."

On 13 September the new undersecretary of labor, Manuel Valdés Larrañaga, was named national delegate of syndicates. Valdés had been a personal friend of José Antonio and was a core camisa vieja leader who, after spending the war in a Republican prison, had become a thorough accommodationist.[10] During the next four months he carried out an extensive purge of Sindicatos leaders down to the provincial level, declaring that he was facing a rebellion from Merino's appointees. He has also claimed that Salvador Merino had run up a debt of more than fifty million pesetas within the Syndical Organization, which Valdés managed to rectify through financial reforms and the establishment of "syndical dues," to be paid by employers on all workers.[11]

What is incontestable is that the syndical system became increasingly docile and conservative, a process completed after Valdés was replaced in 1942 by the Navarrese Sanz Orrio. Over a period of a year or two, all the distinctively radical syndical leaders and administrators were dismissed, their places sometimes taken by right-wing figures from employer associations.

The reduction of the syndical system during 1941 and 1942 to a safely controlled bureaucracy removed the most important single source of tension within the system—save for the FET itself—and may be compared in its effects to the "Sbloccamento" of the original Italian Fascist national syndicalism under Edmondo Rossoni in 1928. Mussolini's action has been seen correctly as a further step of the Italian regime toward the right. This was even more true of the purge of the syndical leadership in Spain, though it is doubtful that Falangist national syndicalism ever had the radical impetus of its Italian Fascist counterpart.

In a maneuver similar to the appointment of Valdés and Sanz Orrio to the Syndical Organization, Arrese found docile appointees with camisa vieja credentials for major posts in the FET apparatus, beginning with José Luna Meléndez to replace Gamero as vice secretary. The new leadership in the party and Sindicatos was further complemented by the work of José Antonio Girón as the regime's first regular minister of labor. Like Arrese, Girón could be rhetorically demagogic, but he was equally bureaucratic and loyal to Franco, devoting himself to the development of

Falangist mass assembly

practical labor benefits and welfare supplements to the extent that the meager economy permitted.[12]

None of the new appointees, however, was more symptomatic than Gabriel Arias Salgado, named in September 1941 to the newly created Vice Secretariat of Popular Education within the FET. (This replaced the old Undersecretariat of Press and Propaganda, which had been part of the Ministry of the Interior rather than the party.) This was the second most important FET post after the secretary generalship, for it simultaneously controlled state censorship, press, and propaganda. Arias Salgado, a relative of Franco's first cousin and military aide Salgado Araujo, was of uncertain Falangist identity but very much an ultra-right-wing Catholic from the hard core of Catholic Action and the Asociación Católica Nacional de Propagandistas (ACNP), who had once studied to become a Jesuit. His career had been patronized by Franco, and he was appointed to Popular Education by Arrese to help undermine Serrano Súñer's allies and reinforce a policy even more attuned to Catholic norms. Though Arias was strongly pro-Axis, the main thrust of his long-term censorship of Spanish cultural life would be more specifically the propagation of right-wing Catholicism. Arias came to enjoy virtual ministerial status and would soon be dealing directly with Franco; indeed, after World War II his position would be elevated to cabinet rank. Arias Salgado came to represent the quintessence of what has been called the "fascismo frailuno" of the Spanish regime, for his personal orientation was more that of Catholic Integrism than fascism.[13]

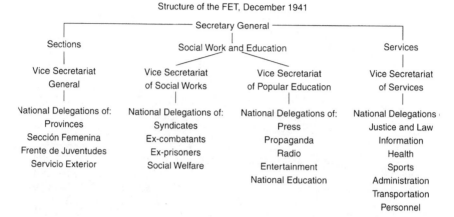

Figure 11.1. Source: *BMFET*, 1 Dec. 1941, arranged in R. Chueca, *El fascismo en los comienzos del regimen de Franco* (Madrid, 1983), 229.

Under Arrese the FET reached its highest membership, with more than 900,000 registered in the various categories of affiliation. In November 1941 the secretary general announced the beginning of the second and last purge in the party's history, designed to eliminate crypto-leftists, former Masons, those guilty of "immoral" activity or simply activity "incompatible" with the party.[14] For this purpose a new Purge Inspectorate was created under a colonel from the Military Juridical Corps, and during the next five years nearly six thousand were expelled from the FET.[15] This was not a very large number, yet it helped to bring the party closer to heel. Cheerleading became an even more important function under Arrese than before, and during 1942 a series of major marches and mass meetings were held in various parts of the country. Restiveness and conspiracy among radical Falangists would not come to a complete end until after the close of World War II, but the appointment of Arrese and his companions marked a major step in the final domestication of the party.

Some elements of party structure were also realigned (figure 11.1). On 28 November 1941, the echelon of twelve National Services parallel to the state that had been created in 1938 was abolished, as recommended in Carrero's memorandum. It was replaced by four vice secretariats: that of the Movement (the party apparatus), Social Works (including the Syndical Organization and Ex-combatants), Popular Education (for press and propaganda), and Services (a miscellaneous grouping, including other aspects of communications and health and recreation groups). For the first time, however, the post of provincial chief of the FET was made synonymous with that of provincial governor in the state structure. The pattern of syncretism continued to prevail in the next renewal of the National Council, as Franco awarded only about 40 of the 106 seats to genuine Falangists of any sort, while 20 went to army officers and only half a dozen to Carlists.

Internal security was meanwhile being tightened, as economic conditions remained desperate and the "Estraperlo" or black market thrived. Serious black market offenses had been officially subject to the death penalty for more than a year, and in March 1941 a number of "crimes of treason" were given the same penalty under the jurisdiction of military courts. In November two black marketeers were executed in Alicante, one of them the camisa vieja José Pérez de Cabo, author of the first pre–Civil War attempt at a book on Falangist doctrine.[16] He had been involved in the anti-Franco conspiracy of the clandestine junta política (see chapter 10), and friends later defended his honor by claiming that the deals for which he was prosecuted and condemned had been designed to finance the Falangist plot.[17]

The disastrous economic conditions, the continuing conflicts within the new system, and the widespread corruption all combined to weaken the regime itself and led more than a few army generals to conclude that it might be necessary not merely to eliminate Serrano Súñer but also to replace Franco himself. On 15 January 1941, only two weeks before his own death, the exiled Alfonso XIII had abdicated on behalf of his third son and official heir, Don Juan (soon to be known as the conde de Barcelona). He was the main candidate of potentially dissident generals to succeed Franco, yet the military found it impossible to agree among themselves. By October Aranda was using the completely inflated term "junta of generals" to describe these murmurings to British representatives, fundamentally distorting the situation.[18] A few of the monarchist generals were Anglophile or at least neutralist, but throughout 1941 and perhaps even the first months of 1942, the prevailing orientation was to seek a potential restoration within some sort of framework of cooperation with Germany. Various monarchist representatives were inevitably involved in a double game, some talking to British officials about a restoration aimed toward neutrality, though initially maintaining good relations with Germany.[19]

Anti-Serrano, pro-monarchist pressure by the military began to mount as early as August and September 1941, as the German invasion of the Soviet Union first threatened to stall. There is some evidence that Serrano made another offer to resign, which was rejected by Franco, though the latter now moved to strengthen his relations with the Pretender in a personal letter that stressed that the monarchy would eventually become the "coronation" of the regime.[20]

As rapid conquest of the Soviet Union came to seem less certain, Serrano began to wish that he had some of the approximately six thousand Falangist enthusiasts in the Blue Division back in Spain for political support. On the occasion of the renewal in Berlin of Spain's membership in the Anti-Comintern Pact on 29 November, he personally asked Hitler for the selective transfer of certain Falangists back to Madrid, to be replaced by new volunteers. Hitler did not refuse, but tense combat conditions did not make this practicable for some time. Meanwhile, several monarchist generals made contact with Muñoz Grandes, the division's commander, for the opposite purpose, asking him to lobby the German leadership to support a monarchist restoration in Spain.[21]

Entry of the United States into the war in December 1941 made the outlook more complex and uncertain. Franco used the occasion of a state visit to Catalonia in January 1942 both to appear slightly more conciliatory and to refer to a monarchist restoration at some undetermined time in the future, when proper conditions had been prepared; at the same time, he lavishly praised the political role of the FET. Serrano Súñer was growing increasingly discouraged by the weakness and internal divisions of the FET and had begun to despair that the Franco regime would develop along the lines he sought. He began to consider the possibility of resigning in order to become ambassador to Rome (the city that politically had become his second home) and also began to develop more personal contact with Don Juan.[22]

Serrano's new rival Arrese tacked according to the same winds, indicating to German officials that a monarchist restoration should be the ultimate goal in Spain, but that it could be adequately prepared only through Franco and the Falange.[23] On 10 March FET leaders in the Basque Country even ended one public ceremony with the cry "¡Viva Cristo Rey!" (Long Live Christ the King—a Carlist-Integrist slogan), to which the public allegedly responded "¡Viva el Rey!" (Long Live the King).[24] Even the "Falangist general" Yagüe now admitted that only the monarchy could guarantee Spain's political future and sought to encourage a meeting between Don Juan and German government figures.[25]

Franco himself dispatched a letter to the Pretender in mid-May 1942, explaining that only the Caudillo would be able to introduce the "revolutionary, totalitarian Monarchy" (allegedly in the tradition of the Reyes Católicos) that Spain required, but that Don Juan should in the meantime identify himself fully with the FET and wait for the Generalissimo to complete his task.[26] At this point plans were being completed for a visit to Berlin by Gen. Juan Vigón, Yagüe's replacement as minister of the air force. Since Vigón was a moderate monarchist, some of the pro-monarchist generals hoped that this occasion might be used to clarify the

German attitude toward a restoration. Though Vigón had always been loyal to him, this was a risk that Franco did not care to take, and the trip was abruptly canceled on 4 June.[27] There followed a trip by Serrano to Rome on 14 June—his last major initiative as foreign minister—to gain support in Italy, where he suggested to Mussolini and Ciano that they show more interest in Don Juan to offset the influence of Germany.

Hitler and Ribbentrop nonetheless maintained their reluctance to be overly involved in Spanish affairs, despite the active German propaganda and intelligence networks in the peninsula. The German dictator had become increasingly disgusted with his Spanish counterpart, whom he considered incapable of leading a Nazi-type revolution in Spain. In his after-dinner conversation with subordinates on 19 February, he lamented that the Communist menace had forced him to intervene in Spain, where "the clergy ought to have been exterminated" in the best interests of the country. Later, on 5 June, he declared himself stupefied by Franco's religious obscurantism, adding: "I am following the evolution of Spain with the greatest skepticism, and have already made the decision that, though I may eventually visit any other European country, I shall never go to Spain." "Conflict between the Church and Franco's regime was inevitable, and so possibly was a new revolution." Informed a few minutes later that only a few Falangist leaders had been permitted to wear blue shirts during the last Corpus Christi procession in Barcelona, he added: "Something like that clearly shows that the Spanish state is headed toward disaster. . . . If a new civil war breaks out, I wouldn't be surprised to see the Falangists having to make common cause with the Reds to free themselves from the clerical-monarchist trash."[28] There would obviously be no German encouragement for Don Juan, even though Hitler was beginning to think that Franco was only slightly better.

The Führer did not pay enough attention to Spain to realize that the FET's current secretary general in fact maneuvered adroitly and relatively comfortably with the varied currents of the regime, and was personally at least as Catholic as Franco. Whereas Serrano had become a lightning rod, Arrese tried to act more like a conduit, discreetly identifying the FET or sectors thereof with diverse options, while trying to avoid the formation of opposition elements.

Despite the secretary general's relative success, a clandestine dissident "Falange Auténtica" (FA) distributed leaflets in the spring of 1942. The FA declared that it stood for the authentic national syndicalist revolution, which would only be effectively carried out with German support for a Falangist government that would bring Spain into the war on the side of the Axis. Though this sounded like a new outburst of fascist radicalism, it was more likely a "tolerated" Falangist opposition group, partly manipulated by Arrese and others to frustrate the monarchists. The rumors that alleged the involvement of Girón, Miguel Primo de Rivera, and Valdés Larrañaga in the FA were most implausible. Arrese was apparently able to monitor the situation, and only later, on 2 November, was the imputed leader of the FA, the architect Juan Muñoz Mates, finally arrested in San Sebastián.[29]

The core members of the FA were supposedly radical veterans of the Blue Division, mustered out for medical reasons and now back in Spain. More serious was the fact that the division's commander, Muñoz Grandes, seemed to share the opinion that a more radical government needed to be established in Madrid with German help to bring Spain into the war. Franco therefore relieved Muñoz Grandes of command in mid-May, innocently blaming the decision on the hostility of Serrano and the anti-Falangist army minister, Varela. At Hitler's insistence, he nervously agreed to let Muñoz Grandes remain a little longer.

During the after-dinner conversation at his headquarters on 7 July, the Führer observed:

> One must take care not to place the regime of Franco on a level with National Socialism or Fascism. Todt, who employs many of the so-called Spanish "Reds" in his factories, tells me repeatedly that these Reds are not Reds in our sense of the word. They see themselves as revolutionaries in their own way and have greatly distinguished themselves as able and industrious workers. The best thing we can do is get as many of them as we can, beginning with the forty thousand that we already have in our camps, and keep them as a reserve in case of the outbreak of a second civil war. Together with the survivors of the old Falange, they would be the force at our disposal most worthy of confidence.[30]

Field Marshal Keitel, one of Hitler's chief sycophants, added that before the Hendaye conference he had been warned that he would be disappointed by Franco's physical appearance, that "he was not a hero, but an insignificant little fellow." Hitler concluded:

> Whether there exists a Spanish general with the intelligence to succeed is something that only time will tell. But in any case, we have to promote as much as we can the popularity of General Muñoz Grandes, who is an energetic man and, as such, seems the most adequate to dominate the situation. I am delighted that the intrigues of Serrano Súñer to withdraw this general from command of the Blue Division were frustrated at the last moment, because the Blue Division, at the right time, could play a decisive role when the time comes to overthrow this regime controlled by priests.[31]

Hitler apparently planned to give Muñoz Grandes a prominent place in the anticipated conquest of Leningrad during the summer of 1942, thus endowing him with the prestige to play a more prominent role in Spanish affairs. At a subsequent meeting with Hitler on 12 July, Muñoz Grandes was allegedly captivated by the Führer's charm, readily agreeing that Spain needed a totally pro-German government. He is said to have declared that after the next victory on the eastern front, his ambition was to return to Spain and become president of government under a somewhat weakened Franco, eliminating Serrano Súñer altogether. Just how far Muñoz Grandes was prepared to go, and whether he really told Hitler any more than what the latter wanted to hear while directing his animus against Serrano and Varela rather than Franco, is not clear, but what Franco knew of this situation was enough to give the Generalissimo pause. There seemed all the more reason for alarm in Madrid when only a few days later the German military attaché visited Muñoz Grande's friend and sometime associate Yagüe at the latter's provincial home.[32]

Though the military situation of the Tripartite Powers seemed in some respects more favorable by July 1942 than at the beginning of the year, Franco was becoming increasingly cautious. His last outspokenly pro-Axis speech had taken place in February, and his speech on 17 July, the anniversary of the Nationalist rebellion, was so cautiously worded that it even pleased the American ambassador.[33] Returning Falangist veterans of the Blue Division were isolated as much as possible from positions of influence. At the same time, Arrese maintained regular contact with Thomsen, the Nazi Party leader in Spain, and with Gardemann, the counselor of the German embassy, giving them to understand that he and the FET were strongly in the German camp and that Serrano's elimination would be required for an even closer relationship between Madrid and Berlin.

Rivalry between the military and the Falangists remained intense. Strong pressure from senior military commanders in January led Falangist spokesmen to become more circumspect. Arrese strove to moderate this conflict, issuing public statements concerning the need for unity between the party and the armed forces. Nonetheless, the return of mild weather in March and April produced a series of incidents between young Falangist militants and monarchists and Carlists, and between Falangists and army officers.

Arrese complained to Franco on 25 March that two Falangists had been arrested by the military when attempting to carry out an assignment that he had given them. Arrese rather grandiloquently offered his resignation—which was not accepted—so that he could testify on their behalf before a military court, or even in order to "take their place in prison."[34]

He was also feeling frustrated because the growth in membership had not added to the strength or solidity of the FET. A report of the Dirección General de Seguridad on 7 April calculated that only 10 percent of the party members in Vigo were "sincere militants."[35] A subsequent report one month later described the sabotaging of certain FET activities in La Coruña, ascribing part of this to "Reds" but another part of it to partisans of the disgraced Salvador Merino, who were "fairly numerous" there.[36] Yet another report from Vizcaya declared, "The F. E. T. y de las J. O. N. S. in effect does not exist in this province. It has thousands of affiliates who do no more than pay their dues, since this is all that is required of them."[37]

Despite the weakness and internal division of the party, radicals within the FET remained sporadically aggressive, convinced that the historical and international situation favored them. Thus the spring and summer of 1942 registered continuing public altercations between radical young Falangists on the one hand and the military, Carlists, and juanista monarchists on the other. A scandal developed in March involving the key Falangist diplomat Felipe Ximénez de Sandoval, who was chief of cabinet for Serrano in foreign affairs, director of Falange Exterior, supervisor of foreign news coverage by the Spanish press, and the principal biographer of José Antonio Primo de Rivera. After being involved in a fistfight with monarchists who took umbrage at his negative remarks about Calvo Sotelo in the biography, he was reported by the Italian chargé to have engaged two Falangist gunmen to assault the principal monarchist in this altercation. The latter nonetheless mastered one Falangist assailant and turned him over to the police. In the following month, the highly pro-German Gen. Espinosa de los Monteros (recently ambassador in Berlin) was named captain general of Burgos and immediately made a public denunciation of Serrano Súñer. Both Espinosa and Ximénez de Sandoval were dismissed from their posts, but the latter was also charged with homosexuality and expelled from the diplomatic corps—a decided blow to Serrano. According to a common version, the exposé had been carefully orchestrated by Arrese.

Even within the Italian government, doubt began to develop as to the stability of the Spanish regime, and for the first time Ciano showed interest in courting the monarchist pretender, inviting Don Juan to a special hunting party in Albania during April.[38] As public insults from and incidents with Falangists increased, the commanders of the Madrid military garrison even issued instructions in mid-April that officers carry sidearms when off duty. The minister of the army, Varela, then had a serious talk with Franco, not as minister but as the political representative of the armed forces, insisting that the present uncertain balance could not continue. Either the FET should become the genuine amalgam of Falangists, Carlists, and others that had been announced in 1937, which would require relative defascistization and awarding half the positions in the party to Carlists and other non-Falangists, or it should simply be dissolved. "The governing of the country with the Falange is disastrous, with checas and private police, kidnappings . . . etc., by Falangists with no control from the state; it is shameful," Varela insisted. "The millions carried off by the party are considered out of control by honest people." He added that the minister of labor, Girón, went about accompanied by "a floozie from a house of ill repute."[39] He outlined two different schemes of cabinet reorganization, either of which would drastically downgrade Falangist influence. When the need for a new effort to achieve unity between Falangists and the military was introduced at a cabinet meeting on 4 May, the discussion broke down into violent verbal recriminations between the two sides.[40]

Carrero Blanco analyzed the situation in a memorandum to Franco dated 12 May and entitled "Notes about the Political Situation." The principal problem was, he said, the FET itself. Even its own leaders were strongly dissatisfied with the present state of the party, but "among the Falangists there is a wide variety of opinions, and they do not agree within themselves, with a blind struggle going on between groups formed around different leaders." Various cliques supported Arrese, Serrano, or Girón "without it being possible, however much honest effort one puts into it, to define what are the differences between various sectors." Thus the reality was that "the Party does not exist" as such, even though there was "a complex organism that absorbs a copious bureaucracy and that constitutes a duplicate of the state organization, which acts in a disordered manner and lacks either true doctrine or positive discipline." The FET included "more than a few undesirables of every kind, whose excesses and bad example set the tone for the group"; "far from attracting people, it repels them, acting rude and despotic toward everyone else."

> The authoritarian lexicon of its writings, the inappropriate *tuteo* to everyone, and a general air of hoodlumism that is not readily accepted by the innate dignity of Spaniards, and the fact that such behavior is practiced by individuals who do not through their ability, antecedents, or conduct inspire the least confidence, make the Party antipathetic, so that rather than attracting people it repels them, detracting from positive values, so that if it gains a member, it is only from someone looking for a job, a means of livelihood.[41]

For Carrero, the only solution was "to step back and repair the damage rapidly," with Franco intervening to take personal command of the Junta

Política, and reconstituting the party with new leaders drawn from the military and the Carlists. Thus it could achieve a genuinely Spanish nationalist ideology and build strength and unity. Franco, however, failed to respond directly, for so drastic a change seemed out of the question.

He did restate his position in a speech before the Sección Femenina at their national center in the Castillo de la Mota on 29 May, invoking the "totalitarian monarchy" of the Reyes Católicos as the inspiration of the regime. He denounced as the historic internal foes of the Reyes Católicos the selfish and sectarian aristocracy, a scarcely veiled allusion to his own critics among the monarchist elite. Lauding the "totalitarian" character of the fifteenth-century monarchy, he also applauded its "racist" and anti-Jewish policies, in terminology unusual for Franco.[42]

A new series of brawls then erupted between young Falangists and Carlist and monarchist youth in Madrid, Pamplona, Burgos, and Santiago de Compostela. Encouraged by Varela, Carlists showed increasing signs of dissidence. By July their leaders in Navarre and the Basque Country were said to be discussing the desirability of having their remaining representatives within the regime resign one at a time. At a Carlist parade in Bilbao on 18 July, cries of "Death to Franco!" were allegedly heard.[43] Street affrays between Falangists and their rivals also took place in other cities.[44]

Though Franco stubbornly denied the military hierarchy the satisfaction of eliminating Serrano Súñer, the foreign minister's influence was clearly on the wane. If Arrese had not yet been able to bring the Falange totally under control, he was increasingly successful in making the FET more pliable than Serrano and his predecessors ever had, and his continuingly loyal collaboration gave Franco a reliable support he had not possessed so far.[45] Serrano in turn grew increasingly exasperated. During his June trip to Rome he had complained bitterly of the constant maneuvering and petty conspiracies within the regime that Franco seemed to have little interest in eliminating.[46] Meanwhile, one of Serrano's closest friends and collaborators within the FET, the poet and activist Dionisio Ridruejo, had become severely disillusioned. He renounced all his positions in the party in August.[47]

Serrano mounted a counteroffensive, preparing new legislation to regain control of the censorship of foreign news, which he had lost to the Vice Secretariat of Popular Culture of the FET (under Arrese's ally Arias Salgado) after the expulsion of his key aide Ximénez de Sandoval. Such control was declared necessary for the proper conduct of foreign affairs, fully aligning the press with official policy, but it lacked the neutralist overtones that Serrano has alleged in his several memoirs.[48] This was demonstrated by the appearance in the Spanish press early in August of his article "Spain and the World War," reprinted from a Nazi journal in Germany. It reaffirmed the Spanish government's solidarity with the Axis and against "democracy and communism," the two foes in the west and east. At that moment German and Japanese expansion was reaching its farthest points in the Soviet Union, North Africa, and the southwest Pacific, and Serrano seemed determined to justify his sobriquet of "minister of the Axis" while attempting to recoup lost prestige in Berlin.[49]

In Madrid, however, the voices of Carrero Blanco and Arrese gained Franco's ear with increasing frequency. Thus when Franco announced to the National Council on 18 July that a corporative Cortes would later be introduced (a proposal first advanced two years earlier by Serrano and a subcommittee of the Junta Política), he first charged Arrese with drafting the project, though it was later polished a bit by Serrano.[50]

These rivalries came to a head after a bloody incident in the outskirts of Bilbao that turned into the most notorious cause célèbre of the 1940s in Spain. Carlists were active in public ceremonies in Navarre and the Basque Country that honored their war dead and occasionally were accompanied by expressions of hostility against the FET and the present structure of the regime. Antagonism once more erupted at the annual memorial mass held on 16 August in the sanctuary of the Virgen de Begoña in memory of Requetés fallen in the Civil War. A handful of Falangists had positioned themselves just outside the sanctuary, and later alleged that they were taunted by Carlists, a few of whom even supposedly shouted, "Death to Franco!" However that may have been, the Falangists tossed two hand grenades into the crowd of Carlists emerging from the church. Only one exploded, and it may or may not have caused fatalities (Carlist sources claim there were ultimately two deaths); between 30 and 117, depending on the account, were injured.[51]

Gen. Varela happened to be inside the sanctuary at the time of the incident. He immediately seized on it as evidence of a Falangist attack on the military (possibly even an assassination attempt), sending telegrams in this vein to all district captains general of the army and protesting vehemently to Franco. He was seconded by the minister of the interior, Col. Galarza, who dispatched similar messages to provincial governors throughout Spain. Six Falangists arrested at Begoña were then prosecuted before military tribunals.

Franco was greatly displeased by the initiatives of Varela and Galarza, which he considered excessive, imprudent, and even potentially insubordinate. Yet Varela succeeded in mobilizing the sympathies of much of the military hierarchy, and despite some Falangist pressure (though not from the Arrese leadership), Franco hesitated to intervene in the military justice system, even though he deeply resented the tone of the Carlist ceremony and the cries of "Long live the King!" that had accompanied it. Several of the Falangists under indictment were veterans of the Blue Division who sought a fully Falangist regime and entry into the war on the side of Germany. All six were convicted, two received the death penalty; one of these, Juan Domínguez (national sports inspector of the SEU and the person allegedly responsible for throwing the one grenade that exploded) was executed at the beginning of September.[52]

The principal divisions within the FET during the summer of 1942 were between the associates and followers of Arrese on the one hand and of Serrano Súñer on the other,[53] though there were various subfactions as well. A small constellation had also formed around the labor minister Girón; its interests in some respects paralleled those of the Arrese group but were far from identical with them. When the Begoña crisis developed, Serrano called a special meeting of the Junta Política to rally support, but this was stymied by the refusal of other factions to attend.[54]

Varela demanded of Franco direct political satisfaction against the Falange. According to one version,[55] their conversation became so hostile that Franco realized he would have to dismiss his army minister. He also decided to remove Galarza, whom he blamed for having run a slack ship and for having withheld information on the incident, as well as the FET's vice secretary general, José Luna, who had been sent to Bilbao to collect information but was also accused of involvement in the affair. No action, however, was taken against the principal FET leaders—Arrese and his chief colleagues (with the exception of the "serranista" Luna)—who had demonstrated complete obsequiousness to Franco and had disassociated themselves from the defense of the Falangists who were prosecuted and convicted.

When Franco communicated these personnel decisions to his undersecretary, Carrero Blanco (who had for some time been conniving with Arrese to eliminate Serrano), Carrero pointed out that firing two army ministers without also discharging someone on the other side could create serious complications. Serrano had done much more than Arrese to try to save Domínguez, and Carrero warned that if Serrano was allowed to remain in the government, the military and all other non- and anti-Falangists would say that Serrano and the FET had won a complete victory and that Franco was no longer in full control.[56] Franco seems to have required little convincing, for he had become increasingly impatient with his brother-in-law, who tended to contradict and criticize him more and more, and who had already suggested resigning.[57] Equally important, he now had trusted and reliable personnel in Carrero and Arrese to fill the roles earlier held by Serrano.

The cabinet reorganization carried out on 3 September 1942 sought to achieve a more fully pragmatic equilibrium than those of 1939 and 1941. The conservative and practical Gómez Jordana returned to Foreign Affairs, while Varela was replaced with General Carlos Asensio, one of the more capable figures in the military hierarchy, generally pro-German and much less hostile to the FET than Varela, a trusted and disciplined subordinate whom Franco nonetheless had to press vigorously to accept the appointment.[58] Galarza was replaced by Blas Pérez Gonzalez, a prewar University of Barcelona law professor who was a neo-Falangist but also a member of the Military Juridical Corps. Pérez was an astute jurist and an administrator of unusual ability and self-control. He had already developed an outstanding career in the juridical and administrative system of the new regime[59] and was a friend of Girón. Within the FET, José Luna was replaced as vice secretary general, and during the next few weeks a number of the more radical remaining provincial chiefs (Almería, León, Valladolid, and Vizcaya) were also cashiered.

These changes proved quite effective, giving Franco the best combination of ministers he had enjoyed to this point. None of the major political contestants—the military, Falangists, mainline monarchists, or Carlists[60]—were fully satisfied, though the military gained rather more than the others. This by no means stilled military criticism of the FET,[61] but it ended the crisis and generally relaxed the state of domestic tension among supporters of the regime.

One of the most important consequences was the return of Gómez Jordana, who slowly but steadily altered Serrano's approach in foreign policy and soon began to steer Spanish policy toward something nearer neutrality than before, still friendly to the Axis but more genuinely prudent and increasingly more even-handed in foreign affairs.[62] This was not, however, Franco's primary intention in appointing him, and Jordana was well aware of that, so that the change in Spanish foreign policy occurred gradually, by degrees.

During the summer of 1942, German leaders had still toyed with the notion of sending Muñoz Grandes back to Spain to try to force Franco into entering the war, but this remained a very secondary consideration for Hitler, who was fixated on winning the decisive victory on the eastern front in a few months. At the very least, he had wanted to wait until the Blue Division participated in the final victorious offensive against Leningrad at the end of August, but the entire operation was preempted by a powerful Soviet offensive. Moreover, Muñoz Grandes also wanted major colonial compensation from Germany, though he required for this no more than "a word" from Hitler, and he assured the Germans that he had refused to respond to purported overtures from Don Juan. When the cabinet change of 3 September occurred in Madrid, Franco used the contacts of Arrese and other FET leaders with German embassy officials to assure the latter that this would in no way result in a change of policy. The result was that Berlin tended to view the change as essentially favorable to its own interests, hitherto supposedly thwarted by the "Jesuitical" Serrano Súñer. On 5 September Muñoz Grandes reiterated his enthusiasm for a revolutionary fascist change in Madrid, but there is no real evidence that he would have been willing to try to lead this as a mere "quisling" of Hitler.[63]

On 26 September the embassy counselor Gardemann arrived in Berlin with word that Arrese, with the agreement of Franco, sought an invitation to visit Germany in order to tighten relations, since Arrese was said to recognize Hitler as "the leading opportunity for a new ordering of Europe."[64] Manuel Valdés Larrañaga, his closest collaborator in the FET leadership, had declared to Gardemann that Spain would enter the war as soon as Germany could provide adequate supplies, stressing that "when you arrive in Batum, we shall enter into action."[65]

Captain Hans Hoffmann, German liaison officer with the Blue Division, reported that Muñoz Grandes had announced that at the time of the recent cabinet change he had been offered the post of minister of a possible new ministry of food procurement, or, alternatively, the ambassadorship in Berlin, but had rejected them as lacking decisive importance. At any rate, rather than send Muñoz Grandes back to Madrid, Hitler agreed on 7 October to invite Arrese to Berlin. Three days later Hoffmann was sent to Spain to interview Yagüe, in provincial exile for more than two years. Yagüe declared that Franco had rejected his plan to use every opportunity—even including closer economic relations with Great Britain—to supply Spain in order to enter the war on Germany's side. Yagüe urged that Muñoz Grandes return immediately to Spain, where he might be able to oust Arrese and once more assume the secretary generalship of the FET. Together with the army minister, Asensio, he could then develop a more decisive pro-German orientation within the Spanish government, so that, once Germany had provided large-scale economic assistance, the three of them (Muñoz Grandes, Asensio, and Yagüe) could force Franco to enter the war. This was not, however, a convincing scenario for the Germans, who had become aware that Asensio was very hostile to the proposed Arrese visit, viewing it as a ploy by the latter to help restore the primacy of the FET. Moreover, both Yagüe and Asensio were convinced that it was very important to prepare for the restoration of the monarchy under Don Juan as the only viable long-range successor to Franco. Yagüe, in fact, claimed that he had written to urge the Pretender to work more closely with Germany to that end. On 5 November, however, Ribbentrop vetoed any German effort to foster the latter connection.[66]

General Agustín Muñoz Grandes as commander of the Blue Division

The Allied invasion of northwest Africa on 8 November altered the international perspective. Though Franco received personal guarantees from Roosevelt and Churchill that the Allied offensive was in no way aimed at Spain or the Spanish regime, the Falangist and pro-German ministers in the Madrid government (Asensio, Arrese, Girón, Primo de Rivera, Blas Pérez Gonzalez, and Demetrio Carceller in Commerce) urged closer alignment with Germany. Conservative and Catholic ministers opposed them. Both Asensio and Yagüe soon informed Counselor Gardemann that in so critical a situation they would not support any "political experiments" in Spain.[67] Franco then neutralized Yagüe even further by reactivating him and giving him command of the Twelfth Army Corps in Melilla, a region in which the high commissioner (Orgaz) and several other top military staff were considered rather Anglophile and where the only adjacent military contacts were with the Allies. Four days later, following a report that Hitler might soon request the passage of troops across Spanish territory, the majority of the cabinet agreed that the entry of any German troops must be resisted. Franco ordered a partial mobilization. On 15 November, for the first time, the Spanish press was directed not to favor Germany and Italy in war reporting but to present the news in a somewhat more objective manner.

Nonetheless, during the final weeks of 1942, Franco made it clear that the Anglo-American offensive had not changed his basic orientation, engaging in what would be the last general round of publicly fascistic remarks. On the first anniversary of the Japanese attack against the United States at Pearl Harbor, he declared to the National Council: "We are witnessing the end of an era and the beginning of another. The liberal world is going under, victim of the cancer of its own errors, and with it collapse commercial imperialism, finance capitalism, and their millions of unemployed." After praising Fascist Italy and Nazi Germany, he insisted: "The historic destiny of our era will be realized either by the barbarous formula of Bolshevist totalitarianism, or by the spiritual patriotic one that Spain offers, or by any other of the fascist peoples. . . . Those who dream of the establishment of demoliberal systems in western Europe delude themselves."[68]

Yet this language may have been designed merely to reassure the Germans and to hold at bay the interventionist impulses of Falangists. The Germanophilia of core militants had not abated, and several groups apparently attempted to circulate petitions to encourage Spanish entry into the war. Franco indicated that he might agree to let Arrese make the trip to Berlin, but in return insisted that Muñoz Grandes—whose departure Hitler had delayed for six months—come back to Spain at once, ostensibly to serve as further liaison between Madrid and Berlin. Muñoz Grandes was only the second foreign officer ever to be decorated with the Eichenlaub zum Ritterkreuz of the Iron Cross, but when Hitler said good-bye to the hard-bitten Blue Division commander, whom he admired, he realistically requested no more than that Muñoz Grandes try to obtain Franco's pledge that Spain would defend itself vigorously against any Allied incursion. When Muñoz Grandes arrived in Madrid on 17 December, he was met by the entire government (except Franco). He was subsequently awarded the Palma de Plata, the Falange's highest decoration (and the first such award since the death of José Antonio), and promoted to lieutenant general, highest rank under Franco in the Spanish army. But on 3 January Franco placed him without active assignment under the orders of the army minister, Asensio, keeping him under closer control. Franco did not provide the explicit assurance that Hitler wanted, merely declaring to the Superior War College on 19 December that "the destiny and future of Spain are closely tied to a German victory,"[69] which Franco still thought likely, if far from certain. He later came to a sort of understanding with Muñoz Grandes, naming him head of his personal military staff on 3 March 1943. This kept him away from command of troops and directly under Franco's thumb. Though the former commander of the Blue Division would continue to correspond with Berlin, his pro-German ardor had cooled, while German maneuvering with Spanish generals and politicians, always lacking in coherence, had come to a virtual standstill.

Franco gave his final approval to the Arrese visit on 7 January 1943, but before the departure of the secretary general held a six-hour conversation with him to be sure that he would not overstep himself. Accompanied by Valdés Larrañaga and Arias Salgado, his two chief henchmen, Arrese arrived in Berlin on 17 January. During the next six days, he met a variety of party and government officials, and visited various Nazi organizations and social agencies. There is no indication that he showed the slightest willingness to engage in any serious political, diplomatic, or military conversation, having been thoroughly coached by the Generalissimo. During his meeting with Ribbentrop, "Arrese became inaccessible. Any attempt to engage in a political discussion was blocked, ending in mutual assurances of anticommunism and phrases without concrete meaning."

> The conversation between Hitler and Arrese, which was also attended by Arias Salgado and Valdés, was sustained by Hitler with a degree of excitement. Just as in his earlier meeting with Ribbentrop, Arrese did not show, along with his courtesy, the slightest interest in carrying on a dialogue of a political character.[70]

Later, when he met with Goebbels, the conversation descended to bull-fights. From Franco's point of view, the trip was a great success; from the

Arrese meets Hitler, January 1943

German viewpoint, virtually a disaster. Though in the early months of 1943 Asensio and Muñoz Grandes would continue to meet with German embassy personnel and assure them that they were still working to persuade Franco to enter the war, after January 1943 the Germans gave up all hope of stimulating any domestic political change or overtly altering Spanish policy.

Even so, the new foreign minister, Jordana, bitterly resented the special relationship between FET leaders and German officials. In a memorandum to Franco soon after Arrese's return from Berlin, he complained that his efforts to achieve "a position of neutrality" were not being supported, declaring, "I have had to fight for this and I continue having to struggle with the Party, which still, and certainly without the least instinct of self-preservation, has not assimilated such a policy." He judged Arrese's trip to have been useless. Moreover, "Arrese himself on returning published a pamphlet in which he talked of the policy of Arrese and of the Party in complete conflict with that defined by the government," or at least by Jordana. The foreign minister was absolutely correct: at the beginning of

1943 most FET activity in press and propaganda continued to align Spain fully with the Axis, while, he went on, "they make the maximum amount of propaganda against me." Yet Jordana observed that this had only limited effect because most Spaniards in fact supported Jordana's policy, which was probably a correct evaluation. The fact that Falangist activists continued to carry out all sorts of pro-German escapades only complicated his diplomatic task.[71]

Occasional propaganda leaflets labeled "Falange Auténtica" still appeared. On 2 November 1942 the San Sebastián architect Juan Muñoz Mates was indicted in Madrid as the organizer of the FA. A camisa vieja, he denied that to his knowledge any such organization existed, saying only that some members of the "old guard" got together from time to time to discuss problems. He was eventually released for lack of evidence.[72] Another mimeographed leaflet of the alleged FA nonetheless appeared early in 1943, pledging loyalty to Franco but calling for the National Syndicalist revolution, less influence from the clergy, more opposition to Great Britain, and more support for Germany, "to move Spain decisively toward the course of those peoples who have made their decision in favor of the revolutionary orbit of the New Order."[73] A subsequent report by the DGS on 20 February concluded that the FA was in fact almost completely inactive, and divided between two currents: moderates on the one hand and the radicals on the other who wanted to push Spain into the war on Germany's side.[74]

The most determined Falangist dissident, not a member of the shadowy FA, was Eduardo Ezquer Gabaldón, former provincial chief of Badajoz in 1935, who enjoyed the dubious distinction of having been the Falangist most frequently arrested by Franco's police. He had first been imprisoned at the time of the unification in 1937, and then again when a member of the clandestine junta política of 1939. Confined to Gerona, in 1940 he began to organize a tiny dissident group known by the acronym ORNS (rendered variously as the Ofensiva de Recobro Nacional Sindicalista or the Ofensiva Revolucionaria Nacional Sindicalista), which had allegedly even tried to blow up a power station in Valencia. Imprisoned yet again, his pugnacity was undiminished, even earning him a term in solitary confinement. When this was lifted in June 1943, he boasted that a sector of the FET had begun to rally behind him[75]—yet another Falangist exaggeration.

## POLITICAL REDEFINITIONS

The altered balance of the war during 1942 and 1943 was slowly reflected in fundamental changes in political nuances. Franco's chief appeal was never to fascist doctrine in general or Falangism in particular, but to a modernized version of the traditional Spanish ideology of Catholic unity, authority, traditional culture, and spiritual mission. He never had difficulty restating his basic principles independently of an explicit fascist context, and he had mastered the art of altering his appeal to fit the audience. As early as January 1942, in a series of short speeches delivered during his brief tour of Catalonia—then the opposition region par excellence—he had refashioned some of his main themes. Though his most important discourse emphasized the central role of the Falange,[76] in Catalonia he also invoked an idealized traditional society—not a fascist culture of "new men"—composed of middle-class hidalgos who lamentably had been turned into "proletarians" by "liberal democracy" and its accompanying liberal capitalism. Only a modernized Catholic traditionalism as represented by the institutions and culture of his regime could redeem the situation, but this also required technical ability and should reflect an integrated eclecticism. "We need ministerial leadership, based on the competence of administrative collaborators and technical elements, to lift the nation out of the peril in which it finds itself." In this enterprise there was room for all, and especially for "the Catalan entrepreneurs and producers whose sensibility is greater than that of the rest of the nation."[77]

One of the more careful spokesmen for the regime was Alfonso García Valdecasas, the onetime orteguista intellectual and co-founder of the original Falange who became the first director of the Instituto de Estudios Políticos. He had always been wary of the imitation of foreign fascism, and during the Civil War had stressed José Antonio's occasional denial of the fascist character of the Falange. García Valdecasas began to redefine the regime's ambiguous use of the term "totalitarian" early in 1942, in an article entitled "The Totalitarian States and the Spanish State":

> In the original Points of the Falange, the state is defined as a "totalitarian instrument at the service of the integrity of the Patria." It is, then, deliberately expressed that ours is an instrumental concept of the state. Every instrument is characterized by being a medium for something, by a task that it serves.
> No instrument is justified as an end in itself. It is worthwhile insofar as it fulfills the end for which it is destined. Therefore, the state is not for us an end in itself, nor can it find its justification in itself.
> . . . The state ought not to pursue ends nor undertake tasks that are not justified as a function of the integrity of the Patria. On the contrary, its forces are dispersed and wasted in improper enterprises,

which, when attempted, aggravate the process of bureaucratization to which we have previously referred.

... In order to justify itself in a positive sense, the state must act as an instrument for the achievement of ultimate moral values.

... Genuine Spanish thought refuses to recognize the state as the supreme value. This is the meaning of the polemical attitude of all classical Spanish thought against the *razón de Estado* enunciated by Machiavelli.[78]

At the First Congress of European Youth, organized by the Nazis in Vienna for 14–18 September 1942, the sizable Spanish delegation, led by the Falangists José Antonio Elola and Pilar Primo de Rivera, energetically defended similar concepts. It deflected Nazism's pagan, racist, and anti-Semitic themes, asking that the official record be modified in order to recognize traditional Catholic morality. Elola underlined José Antonio's insistence that Spain had always exercised "leadership in the universal enterprises of the spirit."[79] The Spanish delegation won passage of a resolution affirming "faith in God and the values of the family, the nation, and the Patria: Honor, work, and liberty,"[80] and achieved the formation of a special commission for Youth and Family, whose members were subsequently invited to Spain for the Feast of the Immaculate Conception, converted by the Frente de Juventudes into the Day of the Mother.[81] Three Falangist writers—Giménez Caballero, José María Alfaro, and Gonzalo Torrente Ballester—propounded equally strong Catholic statements the following month when they attended the second congress of the Nazi-organized European Writers' Federation in Germany, though Giménez Caballero declared that "a tragic destiny unites us" with the common European struggle being led by the Germans.[82]

As this slow and very limited distancing of Spanish institutions from the Axis developed, the chief institutional innovation accompanying it in the Franco regime was the introduction of a corporative parliament, plans for which were first announced on 17 July 1942. In this, as in all other institutional changes, Franco made haste slowly. As indicated earlier, Arrese drew up the original project, which was further polished by Serrano Súñer just before his ouster. The new chamber was not per se a move toward defascistization, for it was modeled to a large degree on Mussolini's Chamber of Fasces and Corporations. The advantage it offered Franco, as Mussolini had pointed out to Primo de Rivera fifteen years earlier, was that it provided an appearance of representation within the regime, even though it was not directly elected and had no power to introduce legislation.

Convening of the new Cortes was not announced until 7 February 1943, exactly one week after the disaster at Stalingrad, when for the first time the possibility of Germany's defeat loomed on the horizon. Of 424 seats in the first Cortes, 126 were allotted to members of the National Council of the FET and other Falangist appointees (as in Fascist Italy), 141 to officials of the syndical system (also Falangist, and also as in Italy), and 102 to mayors of the leading cities. Ex officio members included all cabinet ministers, the heads of leading state institutions such as the Tribunal Supremo, and rectors of all universities. Despite the relative predominance of FET members among the "procuradores" of the new Cortes, the distribution of seats "produced discouragement among Falangists," according to a DGS report of 20 February, for it was felt that too many clergy, aristocrats, and generals had also been appointed.[83]

The third National Council of the FET, with its usual mixed membership, was appointed by Franco in November 1942, and its official statutes were finally issued the following month.[84] A new Junta Política was then selected, based largely on Arrese's recommendations. By the beginning of 1943, with the waning of German power, the relative enthusiasm of the preceding three years for a strongly fascist alignment was beginning to diminish somewhat among the FET rank-and-file, and even the Sección Femenina began to lose support. An informer for the DGS commented on the "coldness" of participants at the Seventh Congress of the Sección Femenina in January 1943, noting that they were all Sección officials.[85] Similarly, it noted, "the Falangist mobilization" for a visit by Arrese to Seville on 9 February "has generated little enthusiasm. The means adopted to ensure the presence of a large crowd, which did not turn out, have failed."[86]

Several of the most moderate and nonfascist figures in the National Council were now moving toward the monarchist opposition. When in June twenty-seven procuradores of the new Cortes signed a petition urging restoration of the monarchy, Franco punished most notably six of the signatories who also happened to be members of the National Council (such as Gamero del Castillo and García Valdecasas), expelling them from the Council on 26 June.

Tension persisted between the continuing pro-Axis line of Franco and the FET on the one hand and the patient efforts of Jordana to move Spain toward neutrality on the other. In April the FET prepared a statement that was published throughout the Spanish press, affirming that "the war of Spain, like that of today, was a civil war in the European and universal sense, a war between fascism and antifascism. On one side Jews, Masons, democrats, liberals, communists, and anarchists; on the other side Spain,

Italy, and Germany. On a much vaster scale this situation is repeated today."[87]

In a new publication that year, so measured a Falangist intellectual as Laín Entralgo would insist that "there is much discussion of cultural unity within the New Order, and this European culture, at once old and renewed, is justly that which is defended with the assault against the Marxist materialism of the East and against the capitalist materialism of the West. . . . Our duty as Spaniards is without doubt within the ranks of that proclaimed, newborn New Order."[88] As late as 19 June, the FET's illustrated magazine *Fotos* published an article emphasizing the unity between Nazi institutions and those of Spain.

Franco delivered a ringing endorsement of the FET at the annual 17 July meeting of the National Council. He continued to use the fascist salute and denounced those who failed to understand "our revolution," which he promised to lead to complete victory.[89]

Only eight days later Mussolini was overthrown by the Grand Council of his Fascist Party, and the whole Italian regime began to collapse. The senior fascist system that had provided a sort of model for Franco's government was suddenly ceasing to exist, and this had greater impact in Madrid than anything since the fall of France. Many Falangists were simply stunned. The effect was compounded soon afterward by a lengthy letter from the personal secretary of Fernández Cuesta, the ambassador in Rome, to friends in Spain. In it he described scenes of disorder in the Italian capital, including attacks on Fascists and on party headquarters; he concluded with an allusion to potentially similar consequences in Madrid. This missive was widely copied and circulated throughout the capital among Falangists and government personnel. The reaction was summarized in a DGS report of 17 August for Franco:

> It produced great disillusionment in the Party, and at first there
> was not an energetic reaction or any effort to overcome it, but rather
> symptoms of withdrawal. In the office of the secretary general of the
> Movement, some people were frankly frightened and did not want to
> leave their papers there, or even wanted to destroy them; others talked
> about how hard it was at the present to find refuge in neighboring
> countries, etc., and all this in an atmosphere of worry and defeat
> expressing itself as though similar and immediate repercussions were
> expected in Spain. . . .
> After the first moments they began to react and, to be ready for
> any contingency, agreed to prepare a sort of guard by forming groups
> of twenty men each in the districts of the capital, with Falangists
> organized in district organization blocs under the political leadership

of each area, and with everyone ready to appear whenever the time might come.

Moreover, several Carlists indicated to Arrese and Valdés Larrañaga their willingness to cooperate with the FET in this time of peril if they were allowed to work toward a Carlist restoration. The accommodationist Valdés was said to have indicated his willingness to cooperate with them, as well. "In conclusion," the report stated, "the impression is that neither Sr. Arrese nor Larrañaga seems to have great influence in the Party, nor does it seem that the members of the latter would for the most part obey them in a decisive moment"; conversely, "the working class is full of satisfaction because of the fall of Fascism."[90]

To Jordana's exasperation, the FET leadership responded during the first days with a kind of bewildered stubbornness, indicating continued support for Mussolini and ignoring the post-Fascist royalist regime currently in power in Rome. Just when Jordana had succeeded in obtaining the beginning of a more factual and prudent treatment of international news, the FET chieftains seemed determined to wrap themselves in the banner of the fallen Duce. In a memorandum to Franco, Jordana lamented: "This tactic and the lack of understanding by our party, determined to do all it can to appear *without any physiognomy of its own and tied only to fallen Fascism and to no other,* seem to me suicidal."[91] Even Pilar Primo de Rivera aligned herself with the core Falangists in opposing any change in foreign policy.[92] Ironically, on 26 July, the day after the overthrow of Mussolini, she departed for Berlin on a major visit of Sección Femenina leaders to Nazi Party authorities and agencies in Germany.[93]

Franco was, as usual, slow to respond, but respond he did, drawing some of the logical conclusions. The following month, August 1943, was the time he and the principal FET leaders began to decide that they must initiate a redefinition to differentiate the regime and the party from generic fascism. The formal defascistization of the FET then commenced, on orders from the top downward, though it was a maneuver that would require considerable time to achieve any effect.

In this new vein, Franco described the party to the British ambassador on 20 August as an instrument for social programs, not a fascistic state party to govern the country.[94] Jordana, who had felt that he was butting his head against a wall, now began to discern victory and was greatly relieved by the incipient change in line. Exaggerating somewhat, he told the duque de Alba, the ambassador in London, that the FET "has changed totally," insisting that "it has undergone an enormous change, naturally obeying orders from above."[95]

Mussolini's post-Fascist successors in Rome under Marshal Badoglio sought to make use of Spain's good offices and diplomatic contacts to expedite negotiations with the Allies, but Franco and Jordana largely refused assistance, fearing to have Spain in any way involved in the Italian debacle. Mussolini's subsequent Italian Social Republic, organized as little more than a German puppet in occupied northern Italy, was denied official recognition. Franco merely dispatched a personal representative, similar in status to the Spanish representative attached to De Gaulle's Free French government in London, and major Italian Fascist figures who sought Spanish passports and the opportunity to flee to Spain were usually denied assistance.[96]

In a major speech at Burgos on 8 September, Arrese gave voice to the new line, stressing that Falangism was a strictly indigenous movement. The ultimate goal of the FET and the Franco regime was no longer held to be the construction of a totalitarian state, for "Falangism is the submission of the state to the supreme end of man," with the goal of integrating mankind into a universal community free of Bolshevism.[97] On 23 September, official instructions were issued forbidding anyone thenceforward to refer to the FET as a "party"; it was to be exclusively termed a "movement," the "National Movement." Later, on 27 December, the National Delegation of Press and Propaganda dispatched categorical instructions to the party's press:

> The following must be kept in mind as a general norm: in no case and under no pretext shall foreign texts, doctrines, or examples be used to refer to the characteristics and political principles of our movement, whether in collaborative articles or editorial commentaries on other newspapers. The Spanish state is exclusively based on national political norms, principles, and philosophy. In no case will the comparison of our state with others that might appear similar be tolerated, and particularly the drawing of consequences from supposed foreign ideological adaptations for our Patria. The basis of our state must always be identified in the original texts of its founders and in the doctrine established by the Caudillo.[98]

The late summer and autumn of 1943 were for Franco not merely a period of renewed international challenge but also the moment of the greatest internal political danger, due to the pressure of his senior military colleagues. The much milder equivalent of the challenge to Mussolini in the Italian Fascist Grand Council came in the form of a letter of 8 September signed by a majority of the lieutenant generals. It was highly respectful in tone, a more confrontational draft having been rejected,[99] but directly raised the issue of an early restoration of the monarchy. Though not explicitly stated, what the signatories seem to have had in mind was a Badoglio style of government to complete the initial movement away from fascism, disbanding the FET and preparing for local elections, to be followed soon after by a restoration. Avoiding any collective meeting with the senior generals, Franco astutely surmounted this potential crisis through clever manipulation of the military hierarchy, making maximum use of the most pro-franquista elements. He sought to solidify the armed forces around him by accelerating promotion of some of the younger officers and generals who had risen during the Civil War, and by promoting several antimonarchist major generals to the rank of lieutenant general, thereby creating a new majority of nonmonarchists at the highest echelon. Younger commanders tended to be more ardent supporters of Franco and his regime and were less influenced by the monarchism of some senior generals. In addition, Franco would rely more on certain pro-German generals such as Asensio, Yagüe, and Muñoz Grandes, though they would not be allowed to influence foreign policy.[100]

In October the regime officially abandoned its policy of "nonbelligerence" in international affairs to return to "neutrality," and the Blue Division was disbanded, ending Franco's major collaboration with Nazi Germany. Altogether, 47,000 Spanish officers and men had served on the eastern front, suffering 22,000 casualties; approximately 4,500 died.[101] Some volunteered to remain, but Franco limited these to three small battalions (2,133 officers and men), so that this residual Legión Azul (Blue Legion), as it was informally known, would be relatively inconspicuous. It in turn was dissolved on 15 March 1944, the remaining troops being directly incorporated into other units of the Waffen SS or new, hastily formed foreign units of the regular Wehrmacht. Some of them helped to defend Berlin during Hitler's final days at the close of April 1945.[102]

The relative "defascistization" of the FET would be slower and more difficult. The most militant were reluctant to lose their fascist identity, and on 29 October 1943, the tenth anniversary of the party's founding, the provincial leadership in Madrid announced the formation of new "banderas de choque" (shock units), to be formed in collusion with the Organization of Ex-combatants to repress subversives who might threaten the regime. This helped to explain why Franco, as Aranda lamented to the monarchists, still "believes that the Falange is something serious."[103]

During the autumn and winter of 1943–44, Falangist leaders publicly expressed support for Mussolini's new puppet Italian Social Republic (RSI). They participated in RSI propaganda ceremonies and permitted the printing of RSI propaganda on FET presses, Arriba and several other major publications being outspoken in this regard. The Falangist journalist

Ismael Herraiz enjoyed great success when he published his account of Mussolini's downfall, *Italia fuera de combate* (*Italy Out of Combat*), early in 1944. He praised the Duce but criticized his regime for having been inadequately fascist and forceful, holding up revolutionary and totalitarian Germany as the superior model. *F. E.* in Seville devoted a conspicuous part of its edition of 1 January to similar sentiments, and altogether several hundred Falangists volunteered to fight with Mussolini's neo-Fascist units in northern Italy.[104] FET publications continued to express solidarity with the Axis and with what they continued to call "New Europe" or "United Europe," and to indulge in anti-Semitic sentiments (despite the regime's own assistance to Jewish refugees).[105] Falangist activists were still involved in incidents directed particularly against British consular offices and pro-British Spaniards, and as late as March 1944 Jordana continued to complain that Arrese still made personal dinner dates directly with the German ambassador.[106]

From the fall of 1943 onward, nonetheless, Arrese continued to try to move the FET into a mode of postfascism, and by mid-1944 public statements generally, though not completely, reflected the new orientation. At a national meeting of Falangist chiefs in mid-December 1943, he recommended some liberalization of censorship and a reduction in certain government controls. He also urged a rapid end to prosecutions for political actions dating from the Civil War, so as to achieve "national brotherhood" in "constructive tasks of profound community."[107]

Arrese made his major theoretical effort at redefinition in a brief work published in 1944 entitled *El Estado totalitario en el pensamiento de José Antonio* (*The Totalitarian State in the Thought of José Antonio*), which stressed the grounding of Falangist doctrine in Spanish history, tradition, and even theology. The term "totalitarian" had been used persistently in the early years of the party and during the first six years of the regime, though primarily with respect to the goal of complete unity and the concentration of political power, not to advocate total control over all institutions.[108] Arrese did not dare attempt a complete exegesis, since the term had also been used to identify Spain with Italy and Germany. Instead, he emphasized that the term had appeared infrequently in the political vocabulary of José Antonio and on those occasions had been used to mean not a state of total control, but one of total involvement and service to the national interest. He also noted that it had been largely dropped by 1935.

The new line was reflected by an article appearing in the SEU journal *Juventud* on 1 February 1944. Entitled "Liberalism, Communism, and Fascism, Superannuated Systems for the Postwar Period," it criticized Italian Fascism for its "minoritarian mentality" and insisted that "the Spanish Falangist state" had achieved complete "unity." Similarly, a piece in the March number of *Haz* declared that "Fascism has collapsed" because it failed to convince "the agnostic majority of the Italian people." It announced that, by contrast, "we want the cordial and unanimous assent of the Spanish. Which does not mean that we have a majoritarian concept of power. But we are certain that the dictatorial minority does not serve us as a form of government."[109] Despite such unconvincing efforts at theoretical differentiation, it was totally impossible to eliminate all the rhetoric of fascist propaganda, and *Haz*, for example, would repeat once more in May the standard fascist definition of the war as a conflict between "capitalist nations and proletarian nations."

During 1944, the watchword in the FET leadership was "realism," which made radical Falangists furious. They persisted in minor demonstrations and street altercations, with continuing insults for those who might be found reading British or American newspapers in public. There was little planning or organization behind such outbursts, which eventually died away. To expedite the new orientation, Arrese ordered the dissolution of the FET militia on 27 July 1944, though this did not affect paramilitary youth formations. The incumbent vice secretary general, Manuel Mora Figueroa, failed to fall completely in line, however, and authorized the distribution of leaflets threatening violence against anyone who tried to displace the Movement.[110] In September he was replaced by Rodrigo Vivar Téllez, a lawyer and former judge who was a reasonable and reliable neo-Falangist, and not an ideological fascist.

During the last two years of the war, the Catholic press came more to the fore. Beginning in 1943, it had taken an increasingly antifascist position, and Catholicism increasingly would become the new first line of defense for the regime. During 1944 the leaders and spokesmen of the FET sought more and more to wrap the Movement in a Catholic banner. Thus when rumors circulated in mid-1944 of new negotiations between Germany and the Soviet Union, Arrese observed with seeming innocence to the German embassy counselor that he could understand how that might be possible, declaring that National Socialism was altogether different from Catholic Falangism, being more like a west European nationalist form of Bolshevism.[111]

Minor collaboration with Germany nonetheless continued, at least through the first part of 1945. Though Franco was forced to come to terms with the Allies on key issues in May 1944, various Spanish agencies and individuals continued to provide certain kinds of intelligence facilities to the Germans and made possible the first transfer of the wonder drug penicillin from the west to Germany in October. Though the FET press obeyed instructions and ceased to identify Falangism with Fascism and

Nazism, its publications continued to present highly positive and sympathetic accounts of Nazi institutions and the German war effort. After the liberation of Paris, Jesús Suevos, a camisa vieja member of the FET's National Council and ardent Naziphile, remained in the French capital apparently to try to serve—ineffectively, as it turned out—as liaison with Jacques Doriot's Parti Populaire Français (PPF), the leading French fascist party, which hoped to mount resistance to the new French government.[112] In February 1945, immediately after the Yalta Conference, the Nazi SS Reichsführer Heinrich Himmler used the Madrid embassy counselor Gardemann as a channel to contact Valdés Larrañaga and Arrese in order to ask the Spanish Foreign Ministry to open contact with the Anglo-American Allies concerning the possibility of a separate peace for Germany with the west. The Falangist leaders initiated the effort, but results were immediately negative.[113]

All this has led more than one observer to conclude that Franco tried to hedge his bets as long as possible. That is probably correct, for, though Franco and his closest collaborators had realized in 1943 that Germany could probably not achieve victory, they still believed that Hitler would somehow at least avoid total defeat. Moreover, the minor assistance that continued to be lent to Germany throughout 1944 and the favorable commentary in the FET press even into 1945 may also be seen simply as the continuation of the undeniable pro-German sympathies felt by so many Spanish government, military, and political personnel.

The success of the Allied invasion of France during the summer of 1944 marked a turning point. Franco began to realize that he must prepare to deal primarily with Britain and the United States as power factors in the future. The regime's fumbling efforts to do so during the final months of the war achieved, however, only the most limited results. When the patient, practical Jordana died as a result of a hunting accident in August 1944, to the surprise of many Franco replaced him as foreign minister with the cynical and slippery José Félix de Lequerica, for five years the regime's ambassador in Paris. Lequerica came from the españolista radical right in Bilbao, where he had once helped raise money for Ledesma and José Antonio, though he had never joined the party prior to the Civil War. He had served as intermediary for the armistice after the fall of France, and his relations with German authorities in occupied Paris had been so close that at one point he had been nicknamed the "ambassador of the Gestapo." Though he could not instantaneously manufacture a new image for the regime, he was chosen for his diplomatic skill, amoral pragmatism, and the certainty that he would be loyal to Franco, having burnt all bridges with the opposition. Lequerica had no illusions about the FET, which he had once called "una casa de locos" (a house of madmen).[114]

The new line under Lequerica was that the Spanish regime was a purely Catholic state that had nothing to do with fascism, since its vocation was "Atlanticist" and "American" and sought only peace and brotherhood. As the Third Reich finally collapsed in defeat, the vice secretary general of the Movement (né Falange) dispatched instructions on 18 April 1945 to all provincial chiefs of the party that the end of the war should be presented only as a triumph for the regime and the Movement, which had always sought peace and had preserved Spain from war. It underlined the conclusion that *"to celebrate peace is to celebrate the triumph of the Falange and of the Caudillo."*

Yet in the short run nothing could be done to rehabilitate the foreign relations of the regime, often termed abroad "the last remaining fascist regime in Europe." The Allies' Potsdam Conference of July 1945 formally recommended to the new United Nations that relations with the present Spanish government be broken and that recognition be transferred to "democratic forces" so that Spain might have a regime of its own choice.[115] Beginning on 30 June, Panama broke relations with Madrid, the first of a series of actions that by the end of the following year would leave the Spanish regime isolated amid general diplomatic ostracism.

The "era of fascism" had ended with the most total and devastating defeat ever experienced by any major modern political force. Franco and his regime would now have to undergo a sort of political metamorphosis to survive in the postfascist era, and that would be true for the FET–Movement as well.

# Part IV

The Movimiento Nacional during
the Postfascist Era, 1945–1977

# Partial Eclipse and Frustrated Resurgence, 1945–1958

As the war drew to a close, Franco developed a fairly clear design for the future course of his regime. Calling a meeting of the Junta Política del Movimiento early in May 1945, he explained, as one camisa vieja remembers it, that "when a ship tries to stay on course, if it is necessary to lower some of the sails, they are temporarily lowered, which doesn't mean they are going to be thrown overboard."[1] So it would be with the Movement. The image of fascism must be totally discarded and a new identity found in Catholic corporatism, to make the Spanish system "the most Catholic in the world." Fundamental new laws would have to be introduced to give the regime more objective juridical content and provide some basic civil guarantees. A major effort would be made to attract new Catholic political personnel in order to win the support of the Vatican and reduce the hostility of the democracies. The FET would be de-emphasized but not abolished, for it was still useful, and no rival political organizations would be tolerated, though censorship might be eased somewhat. A municipal government reform law would be promulgated, and ultimately a new statute to legitimize the regime as a monarchy under Franco's regency would be submitted to popular plebiscite.[2]

In other words, there would be a formal metamorphosis of the regime from a completely arbitrary, semifascist caudillaje to a Catholic monarchy or, (technically, a regency), but no drastic change in the regime itself. The FET, now commonly called the Movimiento Nacional, would remain, though less prominent and even more subordinate than before. Thus when on 3 September Franco received a letter from Serrano Súñer (whose political thinking was now greatly altered) urging a complete change of government to include representation of "all non-Red Spaniards," with the addition of liberals like Ortega and Marañón to the cabinet and total dissolution of the Falange, Franco merely wrote "je, je, je" in the margin.[3]

The first step was to develop a "Fuero de los Españoles," or set of civil guarantees. This task had at first been assigned to Arrese but was transferred to the Instituto de Estudios Políticos, where Arrese had earlier placed in charge Fernando María de Castiella, the professor of international law who had once co-authored the now embarrassing *Reivindicaciones de España*. With origins in the Confederación Nacional de Estudiantes Católicos and the elite ACNP, Castiella represented the ultra-Catholic rather than the fascist sector of the Movement. Though a veteran of the Blue Division, he was flexible and imaginative. Assisted by several intellectuals of the Instituto, he elaborated the terms of a new Fuero that was strongly opposed by Arrese and some of the core Falangists but largely accepted by Franco.[4]

Promulgation of the Fuero on 17 July 1945 was accompanied the following day by major cabinet changes, the primary features of which were the downgrading of the Movement and the installation of a leading Catholic layman and relative moderate, Alberto Martín Artajo, as foreign minister. The faithful Arrese would have to go, even though he had managed to domesticate the Falange and moderate its fascism,[5] and for the time being the office of secretary general was left vacant. However, the Falangist Girón, whose pliant demagogy was quite useful, remained as minister of labor (a post that he would hold for a total of sixteen years, until 1957, making him Franco's most durable minister after Carrero Blanco). The Carlist Esteban Bilbao was replaced as minister of justice by Fernández Cuesta, and Miguel Primo de Rivera, the outgoing agriculture minister, was replaced by a camisa vieja, an agronomist engineer from Arrese's circle, Carlos Rein Segura. Franco's childhood friend Juan Antonio Suanzes, a naval officer and head of the state industrial corporation, INI, had already replaced the too-independent and conniving neo-Falangist Demetrio Carceller as minister of commerce and industry in the preceding partial reorganization of 1944.[6]

Most of the changes that followed were purely cosmetic. The Movement was not at all eliminated but, for the time being, relegated to the background, and thus the annual Day of Victory, 1 April 1945, marked the last of the Civil War victory parades at which members of the Falange and its auxiliary organizations would march together with the military.[7] One week after the Cabinet changes, the Vice Secretariat of Popular Education, which controlled press and censorship, was taken away from the Movement and placed under the Ministry of Education, a Catholic fief held by José Ibáñez Martín. The raised arm, declared the regime's "national salute" in April 1937, was officially abolished on 11 September 1945 over the objections of the remaining Falangist ministers, though the core members of the Movement would continue to employ it from time to time. The party organization, without a secretary general, was left under the administration of the vice secretary general, the magistrate Rodrigo Vivar Téllez, whose honesty was generally respected. Vivar Téllez was not a fascist, and privately indicated that he doubted the wisdom or need of maintaining the Movement as an organization.

Franco, however, was clear in his own mind regarding its value. In an earlier conversation with Martín Artajo, he had observed that the Falange was important in maintaining the spirit and ideals of the original Movement of 1936 and in educating political opinion. As a mass organization, it had the potential to incorporate all kinds of people, and it organized the popular support for the regime that Franco insisted he saw on his travels. It also provided the content and the administrative cadres for the regime's social policies and served as a "bulwark against subversion," for after 1945 Falangists like Muñoz Grandes had no alternative but to support the regime to the very end. Finally, the Caudillo observed somewhat cynically, Falangists functioned as a kind of lightning rod, for "they are blamed for the mistakes of the government," relieving pressure on the latter.[8] Franco declared that it was a sort of "instrument of national unification" rather than a party, and could not be dispensed with.

Falangist leaders had alternative ploys to advance. The vice secretary of syndical organization, José María de Olazábal, suggested to Franco in a report of 29 August 1945 that one way to meet the objections of the democracies would be to liberalize the syndical system, converting it into a corporation operating under the public law governing free associations, partly on the basis of the preceding syndical elections, which had taken place at the lowest level for "enlaces sindicales" (shop stewards of a sort) in 1944. There would be no obligatory membership, but such syndicalism might take the place of political parties. This was too liberal for Franco, who, after carefully annotating the report, dismissed it altogether.[9]

A totally different maneuver was initiated by the camisa vieja and Guardias de Franco leader Luis González Vicén, who began negotiations that summer with the new clandestine secretary general of the CNT, José Leiva, in Madrid. His goal was to rescue the Falange by gaining the support of opposition anarchosyndicalists for a broader, stronger, and more popular national syndicalism. Franco eventually rejected the CNT's demands,[10] and negotiations foundered the following year. Repression of the CNT, which had never ceased, was renewed more vigorously.

A limited number of Falangist true believers began to participate in a group called the "Círculo Nosotros" (the Circle Ourselves), formed under the patronage of the SEU's chief, Carlos María Rodríguez de Valcárcel. Their unofficial slogan was "never surrender," and one sympathizer has observed that their brief activity sufficed "to show the extent to which despair had seized many hearts that wished to die with the conquered of

Europe."[11] The Círculo ceased to operate early in 1946, but even this group to some extent looked toward the possibility of educating Don Juan's heir, the young Prince Juan Carlos, in Spain in order to achieve the "instauración" of a truly nationalist monarchy.[12]

Dissident Falangists attempted their own version of an independent and revolutionary "Alianza Sindicalista," formed by thirty or so activists led by such veteran camisa viejas as Narciso Perales and Patricio González de Canales, who had a long record of dissident activities (even though Canales had held a major post in the Vice Secretariat of Popular Culture). They endeavored to conduct their own negotiations with CNT leaders, in jail and out; long after these maneuvers collapsed, and even into the 1950s, they continued to meet secretly (occasionally with the attendance of Dionisio Ridruejo) to discuss the possibilities of a renewed and independent Falangist syndicalism.[13] A tiny dissident fringe of this sort could, as usual, be ignored.

The official Movement apparatus under Vivar Téllez adjusted to all the cosmetic changes of the regime and helped to organize large crowds in support of Franco during the crucial period of international ostracism in 1946–1947. It also played an important role in preparing for the approval of the Law of Succession, which sought to legitimize the regime in 1947 by transforming the Spanish state into a monarchy once more, with Franco as regent for life. For the national referendum scheduled on 6 July 1947, the Movement's National Delegation of Provinces reported that of the fifty provinces of Spain, only two—Vizcaya and Guipuzcoa—were clearly "enemies" of the regime, with six others "doubtful."[14] Various means of suasion were employed to guarantee a high turnout for the referendum, and the results were manipulated as well, producing something of a public relations victory for the regime.

Members of the Movement were also mobilized in certain districts to repress the guerrilla offensive of the leftist opposition, which had begun in October 1944 and continued with waning vigor for the remainder of the decade. Even though Mora Figueroa had been dismissed as vice secretary general in 1944 partly for identifying the Falange with the repression and drawing attention to its role, Falangists continued to play a minor role in overtly combating the opposition. Though the anti-insurgency campaign was waged primarily by the Civil Guards and secondarily by the regular army, selected members of the Movement were occasionally issued firearms in a few high-risk districts and were occasionally employed in secondary tasks of repression.

Thus Franco weathered the period of ostracism following World War II, together with the guerrilla struggle of the opposition, by a combination of strict repression (when necessary mobilizing large numbers of troops), active support from the Movement, and passive support from conservative and also moderate sectors of society who feared a return to civil war. From 1947 the onset of the Cold War in international relations produced a slow but steady process of rehabilitation of the regime abroad accompanied by restoration of diplomatic and other contacts, even though the dictatorship itself would always remain persona non grata to the social democratic governments of western Europe. The Law of Succession was also of undeniable political benefit, the least significant aspect of which was that it gave Franco "regential" prerogatives to create new titles of nobility. Three of the first recipients of dukedoms in 1948 were the heirs of Primo de Rivera, Mola, and Calvo Sotelo, while the status of count was awarded to the heirs of the Carlist Pradera and the Falangist Redondo. Altogether, however, seventeen of the new titles, or nearly half, went to the military, and only three to veteran Falangist families.[15]

Though the Movement largely lacked a role in political administration on the national level after 1945, its leading figures continued to be important in the administration of labor and social programs. In his rare speeches to workers, such as the one at the inauguration of the new SEAT automobile factory at Barcelona in June 1949, Franco liked to reassure them by saying that the regime rejected capitalism as much as Marxism.[16] What was meant by rejection of capitalism, however, was the rejection of liberal economics in favor of state regulation and the arbitration of the Syndical Organization. The national syndical structure was completed during the 1940s, though many workers, particularly in small towns and in the countryside, were still not included.[17] One of the four vice secretariats created under the FET in 1941, the Vice Secretariat of Social Works, included the Syndical Organization of the Movement, the National Delegation of Ex-combatants and Ex-prisoners, and Social Welfare (Auxilio Social). The first vice secretary of Social Works was Fermín Sanz Orrio, a Navarrese Falangist of quite different stripe from Salvador Merino. Under Sanz Orrio the Syndical Organization abandoned any ambition to direct the economy, limiting itself to the technical and social functions assigned by the state. A total of sixteen national syndicates had been officially formed in the major branches of the economy by 1945,[18] though the ones dealing with agriculture were still not fully organized, and a National Congress of Workers was then held in Madrid in 1946 as part of the regime's new show of representative rights.[19]

Sanz Orrio attempted to give at least a minimal consistency to syndical doctrine, which generally followed a theory of Catholic state corporatism whose goal was to harmonize class conflict and carry out Catholic social principles. He was concerned that the syndicates play a real role, and under autarchy they held some power to regulate certain conditions of production and to allocate imports and raw materials. For this reason, and because they were concerned about working conditions and made frequent demands for statistics on business operations, they were unpopular with business and management from the start.

Sanz Orrio sought to assuage this friction, and was not reluctant to stress the hierarchical nature of the system and the prerogatives of entrepreneurs within it. In 1943 he had declared that the function of entrepreneurs and their profit was of such legitimacy and importance that syndicates should when necessary undertake to protect industrial enterprises from undue state control or interference.[20] He had declared:

> It is also said that uniting workers and owners in one total syndicate is equivalent to ending the authority of the entrepreneur. In reality it is quite the contrary, since in the National Syndicalist system the entrepreneur is . . . the fundamental pivot of the entire system, for to his role of business manager . . . are added those of syndical representative of a group of producers and delegate of the authority of the state and the Movement in that sector . . . exercising on his subordinates authority directly protected by the strength of the state and the Movement.[21]

This was a remarkably frank declaration of the way in which the system really worked, though Sanz Orrio added the usual verbal guarantees about the role of the syndicates in seeing to it that such authority was not abused.

Sanz Orrio would thus never support any form of syndical radicalism, whether aiming at a degree of collectivism or simply at syndical dominance within the system. At the same time he was eager to develop somewhat greater influence and initiative for the Syndical Organization in order to give it a more coordinated policy, but he never found the exact place that he sought.[22] In concept and function his administration essentially paralleled that of Arrese and Girón in domesticating post-Falangist institutions and fitting them into the new system.

Workers' benefits and general social welfare were divided between the Syndical Organization and the Ministry of Labor, which further limited the former's influence. Whereas syndical organization was not completed for many years, general welfare benefits such as medical services were steadily developed by the labor ministry for the broader population and were not limited to syndical members. Thus it was Girón, the labor minister, and not Sanz Orrio, who directed the major share of the regime's social policy, an arrangement apparently preferred by Franco himself. The Generalissimo was confident of Girón's loyalty, however demagogic his public utterances, but maintained strict limits on the power of the Syndical Organization. This delimitation—compared, for example, with the greater power of syndicates in Peronist Argentina or some other systems—actually discouraged deeper social penetration by the Spanish regime, which in certain respects would never complete the full institutionalization of its own syndical structure.

In his memoirs, Girón details his pride in the social accomplishments of his ministry, all the while, as he puts it, "disdaining the vulgarity with which the National Delegation of Syndicates operated under the direction of Sanz Orrio."[23] He has claimed that from the beginning he stood apart from the FET apparatus, first under Arrese and then under Vivar Téllez, as well as from most of the other cabinet ministers, relying on his direct relationship with Franco.[24]

Girón's ministry created a series of Regional Labor Delegations apart from the syndicates in 1941, though the chief powers of labor inspection were ultimately vested in the provincial delegations of the syndicates, whose initial organization dated from 1940. By the close of 1942, new labor regulations for all the main branches of industry had been worked out and promulgated. Organization then began of a series of labor tribunals to adjudicate disputes, the magistracies of labor. Their structure and functions were defined by a law of 17 October 1944, after which the creation of the tribunals was completed.

The only representative elements were bottom-level enlaces sindicales, delegates of the smallest local subgroups or shops of workers, though without the authority of regular shop stewards in a free syndical system. The first elections by workers of a total of 210,000 enlaces had taken place on 22 October 1944, at the beginning of the cosmeticization of the regime.[25] Though this process was by no means entirely free, and many workers either did not take part or cast derisory ballots, neither were the elections a complete fraud, for from that point on the enlaces sindicales did play a very limited role as worker representatives at the lowest level of the system. Three years later, in August 1947, the formation of new advisory factory juries (jurados de empresa) was announced, though they would not actually function for six years.[26] Greater freedom was permitted for the election of enlaces in 1950, and this was used by the left to elect more crypto-oppositionists.

In general the syndicates were able to dominate the workers but not to generate much in the way of support. The influence of the syndical system was particularly weak in such areas as Barcelona, Vizcaya, and Asturias, where organized labor had previously been strongest. The civil governor of Barcelona from 1945 to 1947 would write a year later with surprising frankness:

> That the masses of workers do not always find themselves represented
> in their syndicates is evident. Many times the workers do not

recognize moral authority in their own delegates, saying that they
are servants of boss so-and-so. Other times they even claim that
leadership has been arranged, through political influence, for persons
who hold their positions not to benefit the workers, but for their own
personal or party interests, or to make possible their private profit.[27]

Some of the more imaginative syndical leaders hoped to coopt part of
the opposition and remained interested in the clandestine CNT, which
still had significant labor support in Barcelona and a few other regions,
but further efforts to negotiate some sort of pact with members of the
CNT leadership were unsuccessful.[28] Thus Franco's cousin Salgado Araujo would write privately eight years later: "What is sad is that the mass
of workers turn their backs on the Syndical Organization, since its bosses
are not popular leaders in contact with the workers, but gentlemen of
leisure who exploit their position."[29] Whatever strength the Syndical Organization enjoyed was derived from its status as a state bureaucratic organization, not from direct worker support.

The situation was undoubtedly alleviated by the steady economic
expansion and rise in living standards that began in the late 1940s. This
process would continue and accelerate throughout the remaining years of
the regime, ultimately producing a broadly transformed society in Spain.
Authoritarian government and top-down labor organization were made
much more endurable by rising employment and greatly improved economic conditions. By the end of 1945, some of the economic leaders of
the regime had realized that the "fascist economics" of statism, regulation, and control under autarchy could no longer function as originally
conceived at the height of the fascist era in 1939–1940. The ambition to
create a major military-industrial complex for aggressive warfare[30] had
to be relinquished long before the war ended, and by 1945 the regime's
economic leaders recognized the need to liberalize at least certain aspects
of their policy and to associate Spain somewhat more with the international economy. The alteration of the regime's economic policy took place
in three different phases, the first in 1945–1946, the second in 1951, and
the third and most extensive and decisive in 1958–1959. Each step took
Spain farther and farther from the original "fascist model" of economics
and was opposed—always relatively unsuccessfully—by remaining Falangist leaders.

## THE FAILED REVIVAL OF FALANGISM, 1948–1957

By the end of the 1940s, Franco's regime had taken mature form. It did
not so much resemble the original fascist formulae and "National Syndi-

calist revolution" of the Falange as it did the blueprint laid down by Calvo Sotelo and the *Acción Española* theorists for the "instauración" of an authoritarian monarchy. All the main points of *Acción Española* theory had been met: the legislation of 1947 had converted the system into an authoritarian monarchist state; a controlled corporative parliamentary system had been in place since 1943; economic policy was based on state-directed neocapitalism; labor relations were administered through state corporative syndicalism; the system relied on the ultimate political support of the military, who had initiated it; and religious, cultural, and educational policy had developed an elaborate structure of "national Catholicism" that provided more effective support than did any remaining fervor for the Falangist program. Thus for several years after the end of World War II it was possible for monarchists and reformist Catholics to think that Franco would soon proceed to the complete dissolution of the Movement en route to further reforms and a monarchist restoration.

Yet the Movement remained a significant part of the system, for—despite its profound limitations—in Franco's thinking it was still indispensable as a means of propaganda, limited mobilization, and political and social support. First, it provided a necessary cadre of loyal leaders and manpower to help staff certain portions of the regime. Second, it provided a social doctrine, was largely responsible for administering the syndical system, and had developed most of the regime's social welfare program. Third, with the Movement's large nominal membership, Franco could tell Don Juan at their first personal meeting in August 1948 that an immediate restoration of the monarchy was not needed to reconcile the "two Spains," since the Movement had already incorporated much of the left. It also continued to staff much of the press and propaganda apparatus and was responsible for the youth program. Its National Delegation of Information and Investigation still functioned effectively in certain areas, and to some extent Franco relied on it for intelligence concerning monarchist and opposition activities.[31] Finally, the Movement was the most loyal of franquista institutions save for the military because it had no other basis for its existence after 1945. As Franco had observed earlier, it could even serve as a scapegoat whose ostensible downgrading would then be further evidence of reform and liberalization.[32]

Thus as external pressure against "fascist Spain" began to diminish, in November 1948 he appointed a regular secretary general for the first time in more than three years, giving the post to the unimaginative and reliable Fernández Cuesta, in addition to his regular portfolio as minister of justice. When the next government of Franco was announced on 19 July 1951, the Movement gained slightly greater status. Girón remained as minister of labor, while Fernández Cuesta retained cabinet rank when the

Table 12.1. Budget of the FET/Movimiento, 1940–1974

| Year | Total pesetas | Constant pesetas | % of state budget |
|------|---------------|------------------|-------------------|
| 1940 | 32,307,071 | 32,307,071 | 0.54 |
| 1941 | 36,802,271 | 31,134,721 | 0.54 |
| 1942 | 141,490,427 | 108,806,138 | 1.80 |
| 1943 | 179,561,041 | 123,717,557 | 1.90 |
| 1944 | 181,371,827 | 116,259,341 | 1.73 |
| 1945 | 204,374,581 | 117,924,133 | 1.92 |
| 1946 | 43,449,922 | 20,913,842 | 0.38 |
| 1947 | 41,414,779 | 16,980,039 | 0.29 |
| 1948 | 41,214,103 | 15,785,001 | 0.27 |
| 1949 | 44,476,899 | 15,922,730 | 0.28 |
| 1950 | 50,000,000 | 15,150,000 | 0.28 |
| 1952 | 61,242,125 | 14,330,657 | 0.27 |
| 1954 | 71,684,705 | 15,555,581 | 0.28 |
| 1956 | 81,770,396 | 15,699,916 | 0.23 |
| 1958 | 102,174,652 | 15,326,198 | 0.21 |
| 1960 | 154,799,850 | 22,291,178 | 0.28 |
| 1962 | 317,000,000 | 42,161,000 | 0.29 |
| 1964 | 404,800,000 | 50,195,200 | 0.33 |
| 1966 | 544,900,000 | 59,939,000 | 0.32 |
| 1968 | 603,300,000 | 64,553,100 | 0.25 |
| 1970 | 1,349,500,000 | 137,649,000 | 0.44 |
| 1972 | 1,693,265,000 | 152,393,850 | 0.40 |
| 1974 | 2,467,700,000 | 172,739,000 | 0.42 |

Source: Presupuestos Generales del Estado, compiled in R. Chueca, *El fascismo en los comienzos del regimen de Franco* (Madrid, 1983), 203.

position of secretary general of the Movement was upgraded to ministerial rank, as in the days of Arrese. The Movement bureaucrat and agricultural engineer Carlos Rein Segura was replaced in Agriculture by Rafael Cavestany, a relatively apolitical neo-Falangist with stronger technical credentials. Arias Salgado, not a true Falangist but a veteran functionary of the Movement, became the regime's first minister of information and tourism (the department to which the Vice Secretariat of Popular Education was now attached), and Muñoz Grandes, the most respected of the few "Falangist generals," was named minister of the army, still on ceremonial occasions wearing the Iron Cross awarded him by Hitler. More than 900,000 names were still on the membership lists of the various organizations of the Movement—active membership was a different story—and Franco would publicly declare from time to time, as he did in Granada on 13 October 1952, that the Falange was necessary for the life of Spain.[33]

The Movement's organizational budget had been cut drastically by more than 75 percent in 1946. As indicated in table 12.1, Franco was at

Table 12.2. Uniforms worn by Franco and his ministers in the first six months of 1940, 1945, and 1950

| Type of uniform | 1940 Franco | 1940 Ministers | 1945 Franco | 1945 Ministers | 1950 Franco | 1950 Ministers |
|---|---|---|---|---|---|---|
| Falangist blue | 44% | 44% | 35% | 25% | — | 2% |
| Falangist white (summer) | 3 | 9 | 3 | 7.5 | — | 8 |
| Military | 50 | 12 | 40 | 25 | 87 | 6 |
| Civilian | 3 | 35 | 5 | 55 | 4 | 71 |
| Other (Diplomat, admiral, etc.) | — | — | 19 | 2 | 9 | 12 |
| N | (32) | (75) | (37) | (132) | (46) | (49) |

Source: Photographs from *ABC* (Madrid), analyzed in J. J. Linz, "From Falange to Movimiento-Organization," in *Authoritarian Politics in Modern Society*, ed. S. Huntington and C. Moore (New York, 1970), 151.

first unwilling to spend much money on the party, allotting it only a half of one percent of the state budget in the first two years after the Civil War. Once Arrese took over, this was more than tripled for the four years between 1942 and 1945. After that, the party would never again claim as much as a half of one percent of the state budget, and sometimes only received a quarter of one percent. The party's reduced status was further indicated by the fact that by 1950, if not before, Franco had generally ceased to appear in Falangist uniform (save for the annual party rally), though certain government ministers prominent in the Movement occasionally did so (table 12.2).

A minor degree of dissidence had been endemic in the eclectic Movement throughout its brief history, and after resuming office as secretary general, Fernández Cuesta discharged certain officials in March 1949 in an effort to improve discipline. When the second national congress of provincial chiefs of the party met on 10 July of that year, there was considerable criticism of government policy on price controls, rationing, the censorship even of the Movement press, and the holding of double offices under the regime. There was no evidence, however, that Fernández Cuesta's administrative vigor had increased since his first tour of duty, and his leadership proved anodyne in the extreme.[34] Moreover, there would be no real increase in the budget until 1960. Unable to give direction to the more active elements or provide a true focus for the Movement, he eventually lost a good deal of whatever support he had retained among the membership.

The character and limits of Movement activity were illustrated by two incidents that occurred between 1950 and 1952. A small circle of reformist elements in the party was allowed briefly to publish a journal called *Sí*, but this was suspended in 1950 for having supported an illegal strike by bank employees. Conversely, the regime's more liberal cultural and education policy (to be discussed below) enabled a cleverly written new satirical journal, *La Codorniz*, to become more daring.[35] Early in 1952 it satirized one of the most cherished Falangist slogans by publishing a piece entitled "Abajo" (Downward), after which the regime allowed its offices to be sacked by Falangist toughs.

During these years Franco repeatedly reaffirmed that the Movement was indispensable to the regime,[36] and thus the only National Congress in the entire history of the FET/Movement was convened in Madrid late in October 1953. Its primary function was simply to ratify the regime's postfascist policies and counterbalance the pressure of the monarchists. The opening address was presented by the camisa vieja writer Eugenio Montes, a personal friend of José Antonio, who reminded the Congress that the founder had rejected the appellation "fascist" for the Falange. No significant new initiatives were undertaken, though some subsequent speeches and reports revealed continuing dissension within the party between radicals and bureaucratic moderates, the former still urging drastic economic measures. Wearing a now unaccustomed black Falangist uniform, Franco presented the closing address on 29 October, beginning at exactly the time of José Antonio's founding speech in the Comedia twenty years earlier. Speaking to an audience described officially as numbering more than 150,000 (though other observers suggested half that), he denounced "traitors" who advocated "a third force," in an obvious reference to the monarchists.[37] The Congress proved a disappointment to serious Falangists—Girón would later write that "it was not equal to its great opportunity"[38]—for it failed to chart any new course for the Movement.

The party had always served the function of forming on public occasions what Franco himself would privately call his "claque," and under his new scheme of "cosmetic constitutionalism" the task of electoral mobilization had been added, as shown at the time of the referendum in 1947. A second part of the new scheme was to hold carefully controlled elections in the larger cities, in which, starting in 1954, one-third of the new municipal councillors would be chosen individually by the direct "inorganic" vote of heads of families and married women. For the balloting in Madrid on 24 November 1954, the official "candidacy of the Movement" was challenged by a monarchist slate—the only opposition permitted—for the four seats to be chosen. The monarchist candidates were frequently harassed by young activists from the Frente de Juventudes and Guardias de Franco, with the government exerting heavy pressure. It was then announced that the "candidacy of the Movement" had won by

220,000 as against approximately 50,000 for the monarchist independents, but the blatant coercion underscored the regime's fear of independent opinion, and amounted to something of a public relations defeat.[39]

Some Movement leaders were becoming increasingly restive because of the growing prominence of monarchists and Catholic reformists. At the beginning of 1955, leaders of the Vieja Guardia del Movimiento (Old Guard of the Movement) called on Fernández Cuesta in the secretary general's office to insist that he speak with Franco about the political definition of the monarchist succession. This seems to have led to a statement by the Generalissimo in *Arriba* on 23 January that the monarchy of the future would be based on the institutions of the regime, and that "the succession to the National Movement is the National Movement itself, without mystifications." The Pretender, Don Juan, was much more willing to cooperate than he had been at the close of World War II, and indicated from his residence in Estoril that he supported the "ideals of the National Movement" and might be willing to reach an agreement with the Falangists.[40] Nonetheless, only a few days later the Junta Política sent Franco a report warning against concessions, whether to the monarchists or to Catholic reformists.[41]

During the late 1940s and early 1950s, Movement cultural figures and writers had increasingly lost the initiative in culture and education to Catholic conservatives and reformists. The leading Falangist intellectuals of a decade earlier had largely withdrawn from political engagement. Ridruejo would slowly emerge as a dissident against the regime, Tovar largely concentrated on university affairs, and Laín Entralgo had devoted himself to a series of major scholarly works on Spanish culture and identity, such as *Menéndez Pelayo* (1944) and *La Generación del Noventa y Ocho* (1945), climaxing in *España como problema* (1949). This important study sought to reexamine Spanish identity from a broad perspective that had comparatively little to do with Falangism but tried to reincorporate the concerns of the noventayochistas and the liberal intellectuals of the nineteenth and early twentieth centuries. Its publication touched off a lengthy running debate and polemic in the pages of *Arriba* and other journals that continued until the end of 1950. The discussion of Spanish history and institutions was being led increasingly by right-wing Catholics, including figures associated with the new secular institute Opus Dei, and even in *Arriba* itself they played a role in the criticism of the "liberal" Laín.

Cultural differentiation had been slowly developing in Spain ever since the beginning of the ideological shift of the regime in 1943. This was first noticeable in some of the "critical" or "semicritical" new journals that had appeared during the second half of the world war, as the classic Falangist cultural journals faded. The SEU of Barcelona, probably more "Europeanist" and critical than its Madrid counterpart, had published *Alerta* from 1942 to 1944 and *Estilo* from 1944 to 1946. The new Catholic semicritical orientation had produced *Cisneros* from 1943 to 1946 and, more significantly, *Alférez* from 1947 to 1949. These journals, published by students and young intellectuals and writers, had functioned within a broadly conceived franquista orthodoxy but tended increasingly to introduce critical ideas. In 1946 *La Hora* appeared, sometimes described as a journal of "heterodox Falangism," which was finally suspended altogether in 1950.[42]

The new, more progressive Catholic minister of education in 1951, Joaquín Ruiz Giménez, was fully loyal to Franco but sought to expand educational facilities, reform and modernize procedures, and incorporate important sectors of modern Spanish culture that had previously been ostracized. Formally, he was a member of the Movement and would occasionally wear a blue shirt in public ceremonies, and he appointed some of the more liberal and modernist young (now mostly nominal) Falangists to key posts in his ministry and in the university system, in the hope of projecting a new synthesis of the best (not particularly fascist) ideals of the Movement and a more open-minded Catholic progressivism. Laín Entralgo was made rector of the University of Madrid, and Tovar took up the rectorship of Salamanca.

While Ruiz Giménez and the new initiatives of his ministry were combated by the Catholic extreme right and the bureaucratic right of the Movement, younger Movement elements supported them. This was especially the case with the new SEU journal *Alcalá* (financed, in fact, by the Ministry of Education). Though in some ways reminiscent of earlier semiprogressivist SEU publications such as *Juventud* and *La Hora*, *Alcalá* defined itself in the postfascist era as a "militant organ of intellectual Catholicism" and adopted an increasingly reformist position. Early in 1952 Ridruejo returned to the public scene by playing a leading role in *Revista*, a new journal published in Barcelona that adopted a rather parallel position, gaining the adherence of a number of more liberal intellectuals and trying to reassert the more progressivist aspects of Falangism, minus the overtly fascist politics.[43]

Strong criticism and pressure from the extreme right and from core Movement leaders by 1954 largely curtailed Ruiz Giménez's freedom of action, so that the general "apertura" in educational affairs momentarily came to an end. The Spanish cultural panorama nonetheless continued to broaden, pulled by the expansion of the university system and the growth of the economy, stimulated by new international and cultural relations. Thus the cultural debate continued to widen at the university levels.

As indicated in the preceding chapter, SEU membership had been made compulsory for all university students in 1943–1944, even though the educational system had been broadly taken over by the Catholic right. In April 1944 the SEU was incorporated into the general Frente de Juventudes, supposedly as an elite, guiding sector. Carlos María Rodríguez de Valcárcel, the Falangist true believer who was head of the Sindicato during the last years of the world war, had been discharged in 1946, to be replaced finally in February 1947 by the pliant bureaucrat José María del Moral, a much more appropriate leader for the postfascist era. Under del Moral, the SEU abandoned many of its earlier political aspirations and concentrated on practical student concerns, recreation, and cultural activities (the latter reflected in the various new journals that appeared).[44]

The SEU was nonetheless still assigned responsibility for helping to form the political education of Spain's new elite. In November 1951 the General Secretariat of the Movement promulgated a new "Plan of Action and Political Formation of the SEU," even though its proposal to create a new political vanguard under the fascistic rubric of a new university "Primera Línea" ran contrary to the spirit of the times. Subsequently, a special National Congress of Students, convened in Madrid in April 1953, sought to reaffirm political orthodoxy and the special role of the Syndicate, but the danger that youth activities might revive some of the old Falangist radicalism was demonstrated in the unusually strong remarks of the rector of the University of Salamanca, Tovar, which had appeared in *Alcalá* the month before.[45]

As the country's educational and cultural horizon expanded, students became increasingly active and critical-minded. Dissident ideas, even though not overtly expressed, became more and more common, whether from a reformist Falangist, independent Catholic, liberal, or leftist perspective.[46] By the mid-1950s the enforced consensus of Spanish cultural life was beginning to show its first cracks.

In 1953 direct opposition among university students led to the first attempt to contest SEU elections as a new circle called Juventud Universitaria (University Youth) tried indirectly to resurrect the essence of the old Republican Federación Universitaria Española. Though this was not successful, a turning point of sorts was reached on 27 January 1954, when the SEU mobilized a student crowd, as it did from time to time, to protest against British control of Gibraltar. The demonstration took place in front of the British embassy on the occasion of a visit by Queen Elizabeth to the colony. For reasons that are not clear, the armed police charged the student crowd near the end of the protest, breaking it up violently. This led to a direct clash between students and police, followed by a spontaneous new counterdemonstration in the Puerta del Sol demanding the

SEU student demonstration in Madrid to protest continued British rule over Gibraltar, 27 January 1954

ouster of the director general de seguridad.[47] The authorities' apparent betrayal of an organized patriotic protest helped to destroy the remaining legitimacy of the SEU. This was the last student mob ever mobilized by a government agency, and from that time political opposition in the country's largest university became more overt.

A few days later, on 2 February 1954, new workplace elections for enlaces sindicales resulted in the selection of a larger number of oppositional crypto-leftists, indicating that labor activities were not as thoroughly controlled as in the past, even though the syndical system was not formally challenged. Near the close of that year, a minor attack came from a totally unexpected source, when Bishop Pildain of Las Palmas attacked the syndical system in a pastoral letter, charging that its state-dominated structure violated papal teachings on social organization. This caused little excitement in Spain, where the news was censored, but sparked considerable comment abroad. During the next few weeks, Spanish diplomats in several other Catholic countries labored to reduce the negative impression created.[48]

The hollowness of the regime's institutions was even noted by Franco's cousin Salgado Araujo several months later in his diary:

> On hearing these brilliant speeches I think often of Hamlet when he said, "Words, words, words." There is too much talk about the Movement, the syndicates, and so forth, but the truth is that the whole business is only sustained by Franco and by the Army. . . . The rest . . . Movement, syndicates, Falange, and other political contraptions have not taken root in the country nineteen years after the rebellion; it is sad to recognize this, but it is the pure truth."[49]

Salgado Araujo might have agreed with the *New York Times* correspondent Herbert L. Matthews, who would soon write that "the Falange, Spain's only authorized political organization, is a shadow, a scarecrow that Franco picks up and waves threateningly now and then. It has no power in itself. Its original Falangist doctrines have gone with the wind. . . . The Falange is dead on its feet, and it is surprising how many authorities admit it."[50] Privately, many of the camisas viejas agreed with this assessment.

The resentment of writers in the Movement press was sometimes directed against the monarchy. Though the nephew of José Antonio, Miguel Primo de Rivera, was among the companions of the young Prince Juan Carlos in Madrid, Franco played his usual double game to keep the monarchists on the defensive. A pamphlet would appear, bearing the yoke and arrows, declaring, "We don't want a king!" and denouncing various alleged iniquities of the Bourbon monarchy. Such gestures were nonetheless sharply limited by the authorities, and two new attempts to form dissident, semiclandestine Falangist groups between 1952 and 1954 were soon repressed by the police.[51]

At the same time, Franco encouraged the strengthening and reactivation of the youth organizations,[52] which he thought important for the future of the regime; thus they were the only sectors of the Movement that had continued to grow after the end of the fascist era. The masculine sections of the Frente de Juventudes, which numbered only 316,402 members in 1943, had jumped to 680,098 by the following year and to 839,893 by 1946. They passed the one million mark in 1955, before reaching their maximum level of approximately one and a half million by 1959, at which point they included a significant minority of all Spanish boys. The Falanges Juveniles de Franco, composed of the older boys, had numbered 155,000 in 1945 and nearly 180,000 four years later, eventually reaching 300,000. It was the Falanges Juveniles who provided the "pase al Movimiento" of young adult affiliates, but in 1953 this resulted in only 6,699 new members,[53] probably not equal to the number who had dropped out.

Moreover, any effort to make the youth groups more active politically ran the risk of radicalization and a revival of the old militancy. This was hardly desired by Franco—even though it would not be possible to energize young people with the bland goal of becoming passive supporters and bureaucrats of an aging military dictator. Thus a small minority of ardent young Falangists were once more growing more radical. During the course of 1954, there had been a number of SEU disorders at various universities, and at the ceremonies on 9 February 1955 ("The Day of the Fallen Student," the commemoration of the death in 1934 of Matías Montero), the elite Primera Línea of the Madrid SEU abruptly withdrew, and Fernando Elena, the secretary of Centuria 20, its most combative group, shouted insults at the tepid Fernández Cuesta, denouncing him as "traitor."[54] When Elena was discharged from his post and expelled from the university, SEU comrades organized a brief protest strike against the party leadership, and later the current jefe nacional of the Syndicate, Jorge Jordana, resigned. Insubordinate gestures continued throughout the year, and there was also a disturbance at the University of Valencia, where SEU militants shouted insults at monarchists. At a camp of the Falanges Juveniles de Franco in July, some of the young people displayed public rudeness to Prince Juan Carlos,[55] making his normally awkward situation even more difficult.

The unrest extended beyond the SEU and the Frente de Juventudes into an activist sector of the Movement itself, which in the latter months of 1955 agitated "against the bourgeois and capitalist monarchy." The political leadership of the Central District of Madrid released a manifesto demanding that "the Falange conquer the syndicates, that a purge be carried out in its ranks, that the nationalization of the bank be carried out, and that in future elections there be closed lists of exclusively Falangist candidates."[56] The slogan "We don't want idiot kings!" was being painted on walls, and among young Falangist radicals

> a little ditty quickly became popular: "We don't want idiot kings that do not know how to govern." The words claimed to be against capital, in favor of the syndical state, and of the Falange. It concluded with "Down with the king!" On the 19th of November a centuria of the Frente de Juventudes that was marching toward El Escorial, passing by the Puerta de Hierro, intoned stanzas to the tune of a well-known Pepsi-Cola advertisement, satirizing Franco himself: "With granddaughters by the hand, he inaugurates dams. In salmon-fishing, he is a great champion. Pa.co" [short for Francisco].[57]

It was evident that the effort to revitalize the youth movement was becoming counterproductive, since Franco had not the slightest intention of meeting radical demands. As usual, at first he tried to ignore the situation. His only change in the Movement during the balance of 1955 was to appoint personally another fifty members of the National Council, naming a new member from each province. The intention was not so much to change the composition of the Council (which had not met since 1943) as to give the bureaucratic leadership of the Movement 150 of the 510 places in the Cortes instead of 100 out of 460.

Worse incidents followed. At the annual commemoration of the death of José Antonio, held on 20 November of each year at El Escorial, one young Falangist shouted, "We don't want idiot kings!" and there was a generalized protest in the presence of Franco himself.[58] For some time there had been extreme tension between Fernández Cuesta and José Antonio Elola, for fifteen years the national delegate for youth, whom the former thought had gone too far and had let the older youth slip out of control. Elola was discharged before the end of the month, as was Luis González Vicén, the head of the Guardias de Franco.[59]

In December Laín Entralgo, who had tried to resign as rector of the University of Madrid,[60] completed a report based on a sample of questionnaires. It concluded that university youth were basically disaffected and that the university system was in need of drastic reform. Published as a pamphlet,[61] this report dealt more with problems of moral and religious rebelliousness than with politics, and, though it apparently reached his desk, it made scant impression on Franco. There were now at least four small, dissident student sectors in Madrid, in addition to the remaining core Falangist minority within the SEU. There was a clandestine Communist sector, a small Socialist group, a number of students who followed Dionisio Ridruejo[62] in seeking the drastic reform, though not necessarily the overthrow, of the system, and a dissident SEU group that simply wanted to reform the existing SEU.[63]

Free student elections were a prime goal, and on 1 February 1956 an oppositionist student manifesto was distributed calling for an elected national assembly of students. Official SEU candidates were then defeated for the first time in elections for the minor office of sports delegates in the Faculty of Law, a principal hotbed of dissent. A group from the Guardias de Franco physically assaulted anti-SEU students there, and a number of violent incidents ensued. The climax came on 9 February, when student protesters ran into a column of Falangist youth returning from the annual ceremony of the "Day of the Fallen Student." By the time the melee had been broken up by police, a seventeen-year-old Falangist lay severely wounded by a bullet in the back of the neck, apparently fired errantly by a fellow Falangist.[64] In the ensuing crackdown, about fifty dissident students or their associates were arrested. Falangist leaders demanded more action, and the party press immediately launched a heated campaign about the danger to the Movement and the regime. As reports spread of a list prepared by SEU and Guardias de Franco activists for a "night of the long knives," the captain general of Madrid made it clear that the army would brook no further violence, and even placed the headquarters of Falangist activists under surveillance to keep them in line. As in the 1930s, the authoritarian right suppressed any outbreak of a more radical neofascism.

Franco was, as usual, slow to respond,[65] spending the tenth on a hunting trip, to the disgust of his cousin Salgado Araujo.[66] Not until one day later did the government decree for the first time the suspension of articles 14 and 18 of the Fuero de los Españoles, followed by closure of the University of Madrid. The Generalissimo could not ignore the tensions between various sectors of the regime or the disarray in the Movement, where the loyal Girón reported that there was considerable anti-Franco sentiment.[67] It was obvious that Fernández Cuesta had been unable to maintain order, but the chief innovator within the existing government, Ruiz Giménez, had drawn intense opposition and eventually the hostility of Franco himself. Conversely, the extreme right within the government, as represented by Information Minister Arias Salgado or the Carlist minister of justice, Antonio Iturmendi, could not offer new support. One alternative might be to bring in more technical experts, something favored by Carrero Blanco, but in the winter of 1956 Franco was not willing to consider any major change.

After one week, on 16 February, Franco carried out a very limited cabinet realignment to replace the two ministers whose authority had been most directly challenged. The Caudillo's most trusted Falangist, Arrese, was brought back to replace Fernández Cuesta as secretary general, and the portfolio of Ruiz Giménez in Education was given to Jesús Rubio García-Mina, a university professor, veteran Falangist, and former undersecretary of education. Ruiz Giménez's reformists within the ministry and the university system were replaced by more orthodox personnel, though the key appointees remained: Torcuato Fernández Miranda became director general of university instruction and the young Manuel Fraga Iribarne took over the Instituto de Estudios Políticos.

Girón has written that Arrese initially declined the appointment, referring to the very poor health of his wife, and Franco then turned to his minister of labor. Girón, however, alleged that he was somewhat compromised by the work of his ministry, and certainly he had never played a major role in the main Movement apparatus. Arrese then accepted the appointment, but insisted that Girón take over the Vice Secretariat of Social Works of the Movement, a post that Girón occupied in addition to his ministry. Girón's greatest frustration was that he could not achieve the appointment of the veteran Ismael Herraiz, director of *Arriba,* as National delegate of press and propaganda. The veteran Falangists were completely incapable of presenting a vigorous united front; as Girón put it, "We Falangists were not equal to the circumstances."[68]

There is no indication that Franco had any major changes in mind other than tighter administration. The new secretary general, however, realized that the malaise of the Movement could not be resolved merely through bureaucratic manipulation. He had opposed the entire direction, monarchist and reformist, of the Fundamental Laws of 1945–1947[69] and since then he and other camisa vieja leaders had sought a new opportunity for a stronger institutionalization of the Movement within the system, monarchist or not. Arrese believed that his new appointment as secretary general might be one of the last opportunities; he was surprised and delighted to receive Franco's approval when he proposed to assemble a new Falangist commission and prepare the text of new laws to redefine and advance the role of the Movement.[70]

Even though on at least one occasion Franco privately gave his opinion that the Movement was little more than a "propaganda claque,"[71] he still hoped to stabilize its place, for he continued to believe that it fulfilled certain indispensable functions. Arrese accompanied him on a number of public trips in which Franco spoke very highly of the Movement, insisting, for example, on 29 April that "the Falange can live without the Monarchy; what could not survive would be a Monarchy without the Falange."[72] Addressing 25,000 Movement members in Seville on 1 May, he declared that "in politics you cannot remain stationary; you must renovate, for failing to renovate would be to begin to die. Therefore we cannot remain static in the past, neither in old things nor in old formulas." Franco invoked the old Falangist rhetoric—"We are making a revolution"—but added, "We shall revise whatever is necessary."[73]

He had been aware for some time of the Communist Party's policy of encouraging infiltration of the Movement and the Syndical Organization. Franco was convinced that Masons were doing the same and prepared a new warning for Movement leaders.

> It is important to warn comrades and especially the youth that they need to be on guard against infiltration in our ranks of the enemies of Spain and of the Falange. Recently the leaders of the Movement have been alerted about these attempts at infiltration decreed by the policies of the Masonic lodges. To undermine the Falange, to sow disunion and discord, to lessen its prestige in order to deprive the state of its political base. . . . The Falange is the minority impervious to discouragement that must not allow itself to be influenced by any opposing influence. To be convinced of the superiority of our doctrine and to be champions of it. So many advantages are derived from it that its small defects can be easily forgiven.[74]

A meeting of the Junta Política on 17 May approved creation of a commission under Arrese to prepare drafts of new fundamental laws to redefine the Movement, its principles, and its role in the system. This was seen by party leaders as perhaps the last opportunity to renew and strengthen the Falangist sector of the regime. The commission was made up of such party notables as Fernández Cuesta, Sánchez Mazas, and Francisco Javier Conde, in addition to cabinet ministers Carrero Blanco and Iturmendi. There was at first considerable disparity of opinion. The most radical proposal was made by the national councillor Luis González Vicén, who presented a draft in June that would not only have given the National Council a dominant institutional position but would also have reorganized the Cortes on a partially direct elective basis. Offices within the Movement would have been made directly elective on the local level and indirectly elective on the higher levels. Such extensive loosening of control was obviously unacceptable, and after a stormy argument González Vicén resigned.[75]

By autumn three "anteproyectos" (drafts) had been prepared dealing with the Principles of the National Movement, a new Organic Law of the National Movement itself, and a proposed Law for the Structure of Government. The first seemed to provoke little controversy, for it carried out a drastic defascistization of the original Twenty-Six Points. Its four articles dropped all references to empire or any other radical goal, stressing instead the principles of Catholicism, the family, state syndicalism, integrity of the individual, national unity, and international cooperation. The National Movement was defined as an intermediate organization between society and the state and a means of integrating public opinion.

The proposed Organic Law of the Movement was much more drastic, for its terms would have made the Movement absolutely autonomous to the point of independence after the death of Franco, with great power concentrated in the hands of its secretary general and National Council. The chief of state after Franco would hold no direct position of leadership in the Movement, though members of the National Council would be partly appointed by him and partly elected by the Movement. Future secretaries general would be elected by the National Council and then named (in effect, ratified) by the chief of state, and would be responsible only to the Council. The Council would hold the power of a tribunal of constitutional review and could declare invalid any legislation under consideration by the Cortes. It would also be empowered to transmit its recommendations on policy, legislation, and administration to the government.

The proposed Law for the Structure of Government was intended to give the Movement a dominant role in the functioning of the government. It provided for the chief of state to appoint a separate president of government after consulting with the president of the Cortes and the secretary general of the Movement. The latter would automatically become vice president at the time of Franco's death, should the latter office then be vacant. The president and his cabinet would serve for five years, removable at the order of the chief of state or three adverse votes by the National

Council. The secretary general was endowed with a perpetual legislative veto as a member of cabinet, for his abstention or negative vote on any issue would trigger a vote of confidence in the government by the National Council. The Cortes, by contrast, was only empowered to censure individual ministers, and its vote could be negated through an expression of confidence by the National Council. The latter would thus become an executive senate with veto power over a future president of government and all subsequent legislation. Moreover, none of these documents ever referred to either the monarchy or the king.

In this fashion Arrese and the old-guard Falangists hoped to perpetuate the power of the party after Franco's death. The new ambition that Arrese injected into the Movement resulted in a flurry of new adherents; approximately 35,000 new members joined in 1956, the party's last significant increase. Arrese hoped that a defascistized neo-Falangist doctrine, though totally repudiated by western Europe, might still exert influence in the Middle East,[76] where the Spanish regime enjoyed friendly relations with Arab states.

Most members of the regime desired a formula that could maintain basic features of the system after Franco's death, but none save core Falangists would support a proposal to give such permanent power to the secretary general and to the National Council of the Movement. Monarchists objected particularly to the exclusion of any mention of the crown, and the more reform-minded also objected to the power granted a future chief of state.[77] While Carrero Blanco at first recommended revision, all the other cabinet ministers, even including the Falangist minister of education, opposed the proposals in varying degrees. Iturmendi, the minister of justice, had already presented to Franco a completely different project for a non-Falangist set of new laws to complete the construction of an authoritarian Spanish Rechtstaat or state of law, based on detailed proposals from a new adviser, a thirty-six-year-old professor of administrative law at Santiago de Compostela named Laureano López Rodó.[78] Though not a word appeared in the press, copies of the "anteproyectos" circulated widely among the regime's elite, and opposition mounted from all sides. Some of the top military commanders expressed objections, and the monarchist minister of public works, the seventy-year-old conde de Vallellano, distributed two documents during October denouncing what he termed introduction of a "totalitarian state" and a "politburo in the oriental style," emphasizing that to declare dogmatically in a state document that the political ideas of the Falange represent in a permanent manner the political will of the Spanish people was objectively absurd.[79]

The coup de grâce was delivered by the three cardinals of the Spanish Church, who called on Franco on 12 December to present a document that declared that the proposals "are in disagreement with pontifical doctrines." It went on to say, "The projects of the Organic Law of the National Movement and the Law for the Structure of Government have no roots in Spanish tradition, but rather in the totalitarian regimes of certain peoples after the First World War, whose doctrines and practices received serious admonitions from the Roman pontiffs." The cardinals declared that they did not defend "the liberalism of an inorganic democracy"— that is, a directly elected parliamentary system—but they urged the Generalissimo to promote "truly organic representation and proceeding," rather than "a dictatorship by one party."[80]

Arrese at first refused to give in. For the twentieth anniversary of the execution of José Antonio, he sent the following communication to all sections of the Movement:

> José Antonio, . . . are you satisfied with us?
> I think not.
> . . . José Antonio, you cannot be satisfied with us. You must be
> looking at us, from your site, from your Twentieth of November, with
> a profound sense of displeasure and melancholy.
> You cannot be satisfied with this mediocre and sensual life.

The statement concluded "But do not fear," as Arrese assured the affiliates that the Movement would yet rise to the occasion and carry out José Antonio's ideals.[81]

To underscore the absence of any Falangist domination or even very broad influence under the regime, he prepared data for a report to the National Council on 29 December. It concluded that in the current Spanish political structure, camisas viejas of the party had only the following representation:

> 2 of 16 ministers
> 1 of 17 undersecretaries
> 8 of 102 directors general of ministries
> 18 of 50 provincial chiefs
> 8 of 50 mayors of provincial capitals
> 6 of 50 presidents of provincial assemblies
> 65 of 151 national councillors
> 137 of 575 procuradores in the Cortes
> 776 of 9,155 mayors
> 2,226 of 55,960 municipal councilmen

"That is to say," commented Arrese, "that the original Falange occupies approximately five percent of all the positions of leadership and representation in Spain."[82]

Since Franco had instructed him to revise the proposals over Christmas vacation, Arrese tried to interest the Caudillo in watered-down versions of the two principal "anteproyectos." In a revised draft, the National Council would merely form a part of a new Court of Constitutional Guarantees, sharing power equally with Franco's appointed Council of the Realm. To assuage the cardinals' wrath, a faint proposal for greater representation was advanced in the form of new "Hermandades" (Brotherhoods) that could be organized within the Movement to correspond to the various groups that had originally composed it in 1937. As it turned out, Franco found none of this acceptable.

Ever since the preceding summer, there had been talk of a general government change, and Arrese had been working toward expanding Falangist influence in the cabinet. By the first weeks of 1957, however, Franco was more concerned about the economy's continued high inflation and heavy balance of payments deficit, which was becoming a severe problem. The regime needed better economic leadership, while any accentuation of Falangism had become futile and anachronistic and was clearly unacceptable to the major institutions and currents of opinion in the country. A more detailed and complete elaboration of new fundamental laws might be desirable, but that would have to be postponed until they could be prepared under different terms and more acceptable patronage than that of the Movement. The present climate of Spain and of international opinion instead required efficient technical administration, something that the Movement itself was unprepared to provide. In February 1957 Franco decided to shelve the Falangist proposals sine die and carry out a broad new cabinet renovation.

Girón has faulted Arrese for "not having provoked the crisis in time,"[83] but in fact Arrese was in no position to do so. The collapse of the Falangist initiative nonetheless provoked a militant response from young activists of the Frente de Juventudes. Since Arrese had physically withdrawn, they harassed the vice secretary general, Diego Salas Pombo, in his own office, and on the following day organized an illegal demonstration in the Plaza de Salamanca to march on Arrese's residence and demand more vigorous leadership. This led to arrests and more altercations between demonstrators and Movement leaders,[84] and at that point all the national delegates threatened to resign en masse. This Salas Pombo, in the absence of Arrese, managed to stave off, but it was all for naught.

The Arrese initiative never really had any chance of success. It attempted to seize an opportunity stemming from the mini-crisis of February 1956, encouraged by the general strength of the regime during those years. But that strength and security had been purchased at the cost, among other things, of relative defascistization, and all the changes since the end of World War II were leading Spain in a different direction.

Carrero Blanco realized that the regime was at another turning point, and encouraged Franco to move away from the Movement, at least in part. This was advice that the Generalissmo decided to accept, completing reorganization of his cabinet in February 1957.

## THE SECOND METAMORPHOSIS OF THE FRANCO REGIME: TECHNOCRACY AND ECONOMIC LIBERALIZATION

There is no evidence of any specific grand design in the new government of 1957. Franco had decided months earlier that he would have to replace a number of key ministers but typically procrastinated over the alternatives. A memo from Carrero Blanco on 26 January emphasized the need to reinforce Franco's personal authority after the events of the past year: strikes, student disorders, the loss of the Moroccan Protectorate, and the frustrated institutional reform. Rather than stemming from the preponderance of any particular sector, new policy changes and institutional laws should be developed by the joint efforts of a cabinet that could work together as a team with the chief of state.[85] Franco's new choices thus revealed a further downgrading of Falangists and renewed emphasis on technical expertise, yet he had always used experts freely, usually civil or military engineers or elite state lawyers. Privately he described the new cabinet as simply a renewed effort to give balanced representation to the forces behind the regime, adjusted to the realities of the late 1950s.[86]

The key new appointees were mostly professionals with university or technical backgrounds. Carrero Blanco exerted rather more influence than before, anxious to short-circuit the remaining Falangist influence and bring in experts capable of reorganizing state administration and carrying out a more efficient economic policy. Arrese may also have played a role in bringing one or two of the new people to Franco's attention.

The three key technicians in economic affairs and state administration were all members of the Catholic secular institute Opus Dei; all were resolute enemies of the Falange and had the direct backing of the undersecretary of the presidency. The first was López Rodó, already the general technical secretary for Carrero's ministry and later to be named chief of the Secretariat of the Government and of the Office of Economic Coordination and Programming. The other two were Alberto Ullastres and Mariano Navarro Rubio, respectively ministers of commerce and of finance. The last two would be responsible for conceiving and executing crucial changes in economic policy during the next two years, changes that would dismantle much of what was left of the original program of "fascist economics." The dramatic success of economic liberalization would eventually bring in its wake further liberalization of the regime and, even more important, decisive change and modernization in society and culture. The subsequent changes within the regime would in certain respects further marginalize the Movement, though it is more than doubtful that Franco had alterations of such magnitude in mind when he assembled the new government.

He saw to it that the Movement retained four cabinet posts—the Movement itself, Labor, Education, and the newly created Ministry of Housing for Arrese—to which might be added the retention of Arias Salgado in Information and Tourism. The turn away from any re-Falangization meant the replacement of his two favorite Falangists, Arrese in the Secretariat of the Movement and Girón in Labor. To date the latter had been the regime's only minister of labor, still only forty-five after sixteen years in office, a man whom Franco esteemed as "very good" and extremely loyal but also "too impetuous"[87] and compromised politically by his long tenure in office, as well as having been severely criticized by other sectors of government for his inflationary wage hikes.

Girón felt that he was being made a scapegoat for current economic problems and was particularly galled by the prospect of being replaced by the bland and innocuous Sanz Orrio, whose earlier administration of the Syndical Organization he would later characterize as one of "vulgarity." According to his description: "Fermín Sanz Orrio's taking possession of the Ministry of Labor was tense and on the verge of being violent. In the same way that young Falangists rebelled in the General Secretariat, older Falangists did not accept my departure. There were pamphlets, meetings, and very delicate situations."[88] Girón's farewell speech in the ministry hailed the "revolution of the Falange" that had been accomplished and proclaimed absolute fidelity to Franco, though in his final leavetaking of Franco himself he claims to have observed, "My general, you have had very bad luck. My substitute is inadequate."[89]

Arrese was replaced in the General Secretariat by José Solís Ruiz, a suave and accommodating syndical boss who had labored to catch Franco's eye. The Generalissimo was so convinced of the reliability of this veteran bureaucrat that Solís became the first minister to hold the posts of secretary general of the Movement and national delegate of syndicates simultaneously. He had helped organize the first elections of enlaces sindicales in 1944 and had been active in giving the syndical system a more representative appearance at the close of World War II, having been in charge of the First National Congress of Workers in 1946. After appointments as civil governor of two different provinces, he became national delegate of syndicates in 1951 before being given direction of the Movement as well six years later.

Solís, the father of thirteen children, was cordial and effusive in manner and fluent in speech. He cultivated a popular style that attempted the common touch and was known to kiss babies on certain public occasions; in the following decade he would sometimes be termed "the smile of the regime."[90] If Franco had seen Arrese as the right man to take over the FET in 1941, this "public relations bureaucrat" and glad-hander was equally appropriate for the increasingly bland and defascistized leadership of 1957. Girón would later insist that Solís

> had never been a Falangist and I think that he died . . . without ever knowing exactly what the Falange was. All Falangists nonetheless learned from the very first instant that with Solís began the saddest and darkest phase of Falange Española. After some time had passed, Franco defined him . . . with a rigorously exact phrase: "Light in the street and the house in darkness."[91]

Solís Ruiz would spend the next twelve years announcing successive reforms of the syndical system, none of which changed its essential structure but some of which did loosen its mode of functioning and allow slightly more representation. This stemmed in part from his perception that the Movement as an organized party was little more than moribund, whereas a more active syndical system could provide a stronger political base during a period of rapid economic expansion. Thus the elections for enlaces sindicales in the autumn of 1957 were freer than ever before, resulting in the election of more crypto-oppositionists than ever before, though Franco did not seem to be fully aware of what was taking place.[92]

Under Solís Ruiz there occurred the final and definitive defascistization of the Frente de Juventudes and the SEU. The more open and pragmatic Jesús López-Cancio Fernández had become national delegate of the Frente de Juventudes at the close of 1955, replacing the camisa vieja José Antonio Elola, who had held the position for nearly fifteen years. He directed the subsequent conversion of the fascist-sounding Frente de Juventudes into the more neutral-sounding Organización Juvenil Española, the original name prior to 1940, and its depoliticization became virtually complete.[93]

The SEU in turn was withdrawn from the Frente de Juventudes and placed under the aegis of the National Delegation of Associations of the Movement, a new department created under Arrese to take advantage of new forms of postfascist civil or professional mobilization. The SEU was also generally depoliticized, and an extensive effort was made to convert it into a student professional and recreational organization. Elected representatives were introduced at various levels, the structure of the SEU being elaborately reorganized during 1957–1958 in a process not fully completed until 1961. The depoliticization of the "new" SEU largely defascistized it, but increasingly deprived it of any political function or utility.[94]

Arrese's retention in the new government was not a consolation prize for a loyal minister—Franco was not very sentimental about such things—but simply the result of shrewd calculation by the Caudillo, who did not wish to permit him to become a martyr-figure for Falangist militants. As he remarked to Carrero Blanco: "It is not convenient to have him leave now when he can still wave the flag of his proposed fundamental laws. I need to have him cool down first in the Ministry of Housing."[95]

Once more, things worked out more or less as Franco planned and hoped. As an architect and promoter of social works, Arrese was an appropriate choice for the regime's first minister of housing, but he found that the new government limited his budget. Eventually, on 27 February 1960, he presented his master plan for the construction of no fewer than one million units of housing in only five years, and his accompanying public remarks indulged in the passionate ideological rhetoric that was now out of favor—very possibly an index of his frustration and a final effort to reclaim the old Falangism.[96] The following month, after the government had rejected his plan, Arrese resigned, putting an end to his long political career.

The only one of Arrese's anteproyectos enacted into law, in somewhat altered form, was the new defascistized program of the Movement. Promulgated on 29 May 1958, the new Principles of the Movement completely replaced the Twenty-Six Points and were different in concept and style. They affirmed patriotism, unity, peace, Catholicism, individual personality, the family, representation through local institutions and syndicates, and international harmony. All this reflected Carlist and right-wing Catholic concepts and terminology more than those of the Falange, and the Carlist term "Communion" was used for the Movement itself, while the regime was defined as "a Catholic, traditional, social, and representative monarchy." Veteran Falangists were further irritated by the fact that Franco's speech to the Cortes introducing the Principles on 17 May had failed to mention even once either the name of José Antonio Primo de Rivera or the original fascistic Twenty-Six Points.[97]

Franco's pharaonic tomb and pantheon, the Valle de los Caídos (Valley of the Fallen), was officially inaugurated on 1 April 1959, twentieth anniversary of the end of the Civil War. Two days earlier, on 29–30 March, the coffin of José Antonio had been exhumed and then reburied in the place of second-highest honor (after the future resting place of the Caudillo) in the basilica at the Valle de los Caídos. During the exhumation in El Escorial on the twenty-ninth, small groups of Falangists chanted, "We don't want idiot kings," and gave various shouts of "Falange sí, Movimiento no," "We won't swallow either the Fundamental Principles or the monarchy," and even "The Falange, at the side of the people, demands revolution." There were few if any arrests because such gestures had been rendered perfectly harmless. Radicals of the old guard or the dissident youth might be convinced that the regime had completely sold out to monarchism and capitalism, but their last hope had disappeared two years earlier.

During the next year, the government's main concern would be the new liberalizing reforms in economic policy, which within two years set off the greatest single spurt of economic development in all Spanish history. This would be accompanied by ever-growing depoliticization, as the regime endeavored to assume a more technocratic form, becoming a variant of development dictatorship resting on little more than a sort of "bureaucratic authoritarianism,"[98] rather than a classic fascist regime or even a corporatist system relying primarily on Catholicism. As this second metamorphosis was somewhat ambiguously completed during the 1960s, the Franco regime would assume its third and final form.

# Thirteen

# The Last Phase of the Movimiento, 1959–1977

The success of the liberalized economic policy of the "technocrats" at first relieved the buildup of political pressure from the opposition, though in the long run it may have had the opposite effect. Franco came to support the new economic program more fully after he had the opportunity to observe its productive consequences, but it provided more reason to limit political changes. At the meeting of the National Council of the Movement on 1 October 1961, held in honor of the twenty-fifth anniversary of his ascension to power, Franco reaffirmed the doctrinal basis of his regime:

> The great weakness of modern states lies in their lack of doctrinal content, in having renounced a firm concept of man, life, and history. The major error of liberalism is its negation of any permanent category of truth—its absolute and radical relativism—an error that, in a different form, was apparent in those other European currents [of Fascism and Nazism] that made "action" their only demand and the supreme norm of their conduct. . . . When the juridical order does not proceed from a system of principles, ideas, and values recognized as superior and prior to the state, it ends in an omnipresent juridical voluntarism, whether its primary organ be the so-called majority, purely numerical and inorganically expressed, or the supreme organs of power.[1]

Later, amid a wave of new industrial strikes in May 1962, Franco addressed an outdoor rally of former alféreces provisionales, and aware of their criticism of the regime's new leniency, preempted it with a hard-line speech pledging to maintain undiminished the principles and institutions for which they had fought.

Foremost among the changes in the partially new government of 10 July 1962 was the appointment for the first time of a vice president of government and lieutenant to Franco himself in the person of the veteran

431

Muñoz Grandes, who also retained his post as head of the Supreme General Staff and was the only army commander save Franco himself to hold the rank of full captain general. Even though Muñoz Grandes would not play a very active political role, his new eminence was not only a guarantee of support for Franco but also a minor sop for the Movement, with which Muñoz Grandes was still more identified than were most generals.

In fact, the influence of the technocrats and reformers was in several ways increased. Another member of Opus Dei was appointed to an economics ministry (Gregorio López Bravo in Industry), and two other ministers were appointed who were considered "afectos" (attached) to the Opus Dei ministers.[2] Arias Salgado, in poor health and the target of increasing criticism for the rigidity of his censorship, was finally discharged after more than twenty years in high office. The new minister of information and tourism was the forty-year-old Manuel Fraga Iribarne, holder of the most impressive credentials of any younger official of the regime, a product of what its publicists liked to call the "bureaucracy of competence." An outstanding student and youthful winner of a chair of political science, Fraga had already occupied a wide variety of university, Movement, and government positions. He was identified with Movement reformists but had carefully dissociated himself from any antiregime position. Extraordinarily energetic and concerned to bring the regime abreast of new currents in society and culture, Fraga soon became known at home and abroad as a reformer who would encourage further transformation of the system.

This new cabinet, which with minor changes would last for seven years, harbored two different sets of rivalries. One was between the technocrat-monarchists (supported and to some extent led by Carrero Blanco) and the so-called regentialists or at least lukewarm monarchists (to some extent led by Muñoz Grandes and including Solís Ruiz and the new navy minister, Pedro Nieto Antúnez). The regentialists' posture represented the post-Falangist stance of those who still sought more of a role for the Movement or other regime institutions. Thus Fraga, though basically a supporter of the monarchist succession, tended to be allied with the regentialists.

The second rivalry was between political reformists and those who preferred to avoid major immediate political change, instead concentrating first on economic development and second on the monarchist succession. The reformists were thus led by ministers from the Movement, such as Castiella, the foreign minister, Fraga, and Solís (though these three did not agree among themselves as to the character and content of political reform), who were "frequently supported by Romeo Gorría and sometimes by López Bravo."[3] They also drew some support from Muñoz Grandes and Nieto Antúnez, while Iturmendi (Justice) and Navarro Rubio (finance) fluctuated. For the most part on the other side were Carrero Blanco, Gen. Alonso Vega (interior), Gen. Jorge Vigón (public works), and to a lesser degree Gen. Martín Alonso (army), who were more concerned with the succession than with internal reform.

The role of Muñoz Grandes was in fact very limited, basically that of Franco's watchdog and guarantee insurance policy, and a check on the more ardent monarchists. Had Franco suddenly died at any point between 1962 and 1967, Muñoz Grandes would at least temporarily have been his successor, possibly with some opportunity to try to undo the working of the Law of Succession, had he been so inclined. From Franco's point of view, he played his role all the more effectively because of his lack of a broader constituency.

The reformists took the position that economic development must be accompanied by new political development, not mere immobilization. This would involve reform of the Syndical Organization to achieve greater representation, flexibility, and responsiveness, and a reorganization of the Movement that would allow it to incorporate new political tendencies of broader participation. The concept of maintaining the Falangist core while expanding the Movement more broadly had originated in 1945 with Castiella (then director of the Instituto de Estudios Políticos) and several other leaders. The general concept was that core Falangism as an organized force would always remain the Movement's base, but that the latter would be made broader and more representative by also incorporating (and controlling) political expression from the other sectors that had supported the Nationalists in the Civil War.[4] All this was to be accompanied by further social reforms to increase well-being and balance the disequilibria created by rapid industrial expansion.

The initial champion of reform had been the affable and oily glad-handing Solís Ruiz, "the smile of the regime." After replacing Arrese in 1957, he had dropped Arrese's talk of institutionalizing the existing Movement in favor of broadening it to include "the complete incorporation of the activities of the people."[5] Within the Movement he had organized a new National Delegation of Associations to try to generate new organs of association or limited representation within the existing system and to attract new members to the Movement. Such ploys might lend at least modest substance to the regime's prating about "organic democracy" and give the impression that the Spanish system was approximating the practices of contemporary western states.

During 1964 Solís made increasing use of the term "political development,"[6] and that summer the new National Delegation of Associations moved ahead with a vague project concerning the "hermandades" proposed in the Arrese anteproyectos of 1956, beginning to sketch drafts for some sort of "asociaciones políticas" within the Movement. Such associations were not to be political parties but simply expressions of several diverse elements in the Movement. They would remain under the control of the National Council and make the Movement more pluralistic and representative while expanding its role within the system. Solís thus obtained the approval of the National Council to prepare means by which "the Movement would promote the associative process within its institutional structure, pluralizing, if possible, the means for constant fulfillment of its fundamental principles."[7]

A partial cabinet reorganization on 7 July 1965 replaced six ministers without changing the overall balance and raised López Rodó to full cabinet rank for the first time, increasing somewhat further the influence of the technocrats. The first major change of the 1960s was nonetheless Fraga Iribarne's new and distinctly liberalized press law, ratified by the Cortes on 15 March 1966. This had a decisive effect on the future of Spain, for, though it did not by any means end censorship, it greatly reduced its extent. After 1966 the scope and volume of publishing in Spain on contemporary history and current affairs increased, creating within a few years a much better informed public and a much more active elite, and resulting in what by the early 1970s would be termed "a parliament of paper" in place of a freely elected parliament. This change commenced slowly but soon accelerated, though there were still sharp limits: the regime itself and Franco personally could never be questioned, but individual policies were increasingly brought under public review.

Fraga's notoriety came to rival or exceed that of any other minister. In constant motion and generating new publicity on every hand, he was associated with new glamour projects in the massive expansion of the tourist industry, while the press law made him appear the focus of reformism. Franco himself regarded Fraga with some uncertainty, apprehensive that his reformism might go too far, while Carrero Blanco saw him as a distinct danger and determined to cut him down.[8]

Earlier, in October 1963, Fraga had presented to Franco his own version of a "Draft Project for a Constitution of the Spanish State," intended to structure a political and parliamentary system of authoritarian government that would nonetheless be more inclusive and representative. It proposed a bicameral legislature composed of a Chamber of Procuradores based on electoral suffrage but without political parties; all those standing for election would belong to groups or associations within or approved by the Movement. The National Council, partly appointive and partly elected within the Movement, would serve as Senate or upper house. It would initiate all political and constitutional legislation, while the lower house would initiate legislation dealing with social and economic affairs. The National Movement would be governed by a new statute declaring that it included all groups who had formed part of the Crusade of 1936 or supported its Principles, and these would enjoy a certain amount of autonomy. It would still take charge of youth organization, "popular education" (meaning primarily political education), physical education, and various aspects of social services.[9]

This was much too liberal for Franco, and the eventual Organic Law of the State instituted in 1966 would prove a disappointment for reformists, being no more than a codification, clarification, and very slight reform of already existing practices. It was intended to complete the process of institutionalization and round out the "open constitution" of the regime, giving more precise expression to its so-called organic democracy without notable alterations.

The Organic Law reconciled various inconsistencies among the six Fundamental Laws (the Fuero de Trabajo, the Law of the Cortes, the Fuero de los Españoles, the Law of the Referendum, the Law of Succession, and the Fundamental Principles of the National Movement) and eliminated or altered certain lingering vestiges of fascist terminology. The membership of the National Council was expanded to 108 (40 appointed by the Caudillo, 50 elected by the provincial sections of the Movement, 12 elected by the Cortes, and 6 appointed by the president of the Cortes), with the presidency to be held by the president of the Cortes. The appeal of "contrafuero" was established, which provided that either the National Council or the permanent commission of the Cortes might present an appeal against any new legislation or government measure held to contradict the Fundamental Principles. A decision would be rendered by a special committee reporting to the state's Council of the Realm, which would thus become a decisive institution, while the new power given to the National Council of the Movement was much more limited. Some changes were also introduced in the organization of the Cortes, expanding its membership to 565, of whom 307 would be chosen through indirect corporate representation and 108 chosen directly for the first time by the vote of "family representatives."

Amendments to the Fuero de Trabajo did away with the old fascistic designations of national syndicalism and the unitary "vertical syndicate" (which Franco claimed never to have understood). Somewhat greater flexibility was introduced, together with division of local syndicates into management and labor components. The Syndical Organization was declared to be autonomous and to provide a channel for the "participation" of all, though no structural or procedural reforms were introduced to make that possible.

Rather than being the real opening sought by reformists, the Organic Law represented the final partial readjustment of the system during the phase of Franco's life when he was rapidly losing physical and political energy. No basic changes were introduced, though Franco described the measure to the Cortes on 22 November as "a broad democratization of the political process."[10] The referendum of 14 December registered a 96 percent majority, the kind of tally typical of Communist states, voter mobilization being one of the Movement's last major efforts.

The Organic Law also ratified the fact that the last attempt at institutional revival of the Movement had ended ten years earlier. On ceremonial occasions Franco still reiterated to members of the Movement that he was with them and that the organization was still essential, insisting that "the Movement is a system and there is a place in it for everyone."[11] In 1967 he would avow that "if the Movement did not exist, our most important task would be to invent it."[12] Franco was fully aware that camisas viejas had criticized him for years for never having desired a strong party (which was, of course, essentially correct), yet he would insist privately that he had always wanted to strengthen the Movement. Franco laid the blame for its weakness on the intransigence of the camisas viejas themselves, their insistence on maintaining the original fascistic doctrines and the predominance of the early leaders, and their failure to adjust their postulates and personnel to attract a broad and diverse new membership.[13]

The Pretender, Don Juan, treated the Movement in an even more opportunistic fashion. Playing from weakness, he felt it necessary to tell each political audience whatever it wanted to hear. At his residence in Estoril on 28 January 1959, he had told visitors from Spain that the restored monarchy would establish a parliamentary system of political parties, and that it would be simple to abolish the Movement by decree, because of its lack of support.[14] This was probably a fairly honest statement of his real intentions, and predicted with considerable accuracy what his son would do nearly twenty years later. In the late 1950s and early 1960s, however, Franco's position remained strong and that of the conde de Barcelona remained weak. Thus the latter continued publicly to acknowledge his support for the regime and its Fundamental Laws, which of course included the Movement. Moreover, in his effort to play all sides, the conde de Barcelona had earlier announced his adherence to the traditionalist principles of Carlism.[15] There were limits to this sort of thing, even for Don Juan, and thus he had refused to make the public announcement of support for the new Principles of the Movement and for Carlist doctrines that some had desired at the time of the opening of the Valle de los Caídos in 1959; yet he had also privately assured one Falangist, "I support what is national and social, if I support anything. That is the Falangist formula, of the old Falange. . . . What must be maintained are the ideas, the principles, and the banners held high. Consider how I have been concerned from afar for the Falange, for the old Falange."[16] In a letter to Franco of February 1960, he had reiterated his support for the "Law of the Principles of the National Movement,"[17] and this was restated in a letter of 10 July 1961[18] and even in the public press. Such formalistic rallying to the regime and the Movement did not, however, reduce the Movement's general hostility toward the monarchy, which was correctly seen as inclined toward more serious liberalization and the final end of the Movement.[19]

For many years the Secretariat of the Movement had refused to recognize any appreciable decline in membership.[20] The 1963 report of the National Delegation of the Provinces declared a total membership of 931,802, but this was made up of the following components:

    372,069 Ex-combatants
     43,419 Ex-prisoners
     47,043 Members of the Servicio Español de Magisterio
            (teachers)
      2,351 Members of the Servicio Español de Profesorado
            (professors)
     37,534 Members of the Old Guard
     80,037 Members of the Guardia de Franco
    173,588 Militants below eighteen years of age
      3,310 University students[21]

The grand total was deceiving, first because it apparently registered the same affiliates in more than one category, and second because the number of ordinary Movement affiliates was apparently no more than 172,451, of whom an indeterminate number had become totally inactive. A special report of 19 May 1958 that had apparently reached Franco analyzed the organization of the Movement in fourteen northern provinces (including some such as Valladolid in which it had once been very strong) and found the infrastructure uniformly weak.[22]

The Sección Femenina had reported only 207,021 members for 1959,[23] scarcely more than a third of the total of two decades earlier; the nominal figure for 1963 was 294,931.[24] These statistics were equivalent to the number of women affiliated with Catholic Action, though the latter's data may have been more reliable.

Secretary General Solís Ruiz represented the logical evolution of the style of leadership sought by Franco. Arrese had been an authentic camisa vieja and party veteran, however docile, who represented a large number of his original comrades. Though technically also a camisa vieja, Solís had developed his career as a military juridical officer and an administrator of the syndical bureaucracy, and had little experience with the original fascist movement. Jovial, garrulous, and histrionic, he realized that the old-style party was dead and could not be revived. He is quoted as having observed privately, "Arrese had the totalitarian concept of the partido único guarding the state. In the Council of Ministers, he kept watch. He negotiated his political plans directly with the Caudillo, excluding any participation by the other ministers."[25] Solís also complained that Arrese had tried to use the Syndical Organization as a sort of bank account from which to draw further funding for the General Secretariat. For Solís, the syndicates remained of prime value in and of themselves, as well as a centerpiece for demagogy. Emilio Romero has recounted an occasion on which Solís received a group of visiting British trade union leaders: "José Solís gave them a description of Spanish syndicalism that left the British trade union leaders fascinated. When they had gone and we were left alone, I said to Solís: 'All this that you have told the British in large part is not true.' Then Solís burst out laughing and replied: 'But doesn't it sound great?' "[26]

All this does not mean that he was without plans and ambitions. Solís hoped to develop a larger and stronger Syndical Organization by creating new structures of pseudo-representation that would enable it to play a greater role in the future. Moreover, he hoped to overcome what he called "the duality between the state and the Movement" through a new Organic Law of the Movement that would achieve some of Arrese's goals in more modest form, also including new structures of limited representation to attract new members. Through concentrating on the syndicates and the Movement's political or pseudo-political role, he aspired to transcend the confusing and sometimes useless array of secondary structures that the Movement still anachronistically maintained. López Rodó has quoted Solís as observing at the beginning of 1962:

> The present number of Movement organizations is excessive: Old
> Guard, Servicio Español de Magisterio, Delegation of Health,
> Delegation of Justice and Law, and so forth. They are duplicates and
> create interference. The Movement should rely on the representative
> channel of the Movement and of the Syndical Organization, without
> maintaining bureaucratic organs that collide with those of the state.[27]

López Rodó and some of the other anti-Falangist ministers logically believed that this arrangement harbored residues of the partido único, even if in attenuated form.

The original vice secretary general under Solís was Alfredo Jiménez Millas, a true camisa vieja in the Arrese tradition and proud of it. Friction

José Solís Ruiz and Torcuato Fernández de Miranda

eventually mounted between the two, as Jiménez Millas complained of the disordered and rhetorical administrative style of the secretary, who perpetually traveled and talked but showed no interest in reconstituting anything resembling the old structure of the party. Solís was solicitous in maintaining good relations with the most diverse sectors, and especially with the collaborationist elements among the Carlists. After a series of personal snubs, Jiménez Millas resigned early in 1961.

He was replaced by a protégé of Solís who had formerly been number three in the Movement (national delegate of the provinces), Fernando Herrero Tejedor. The new vice secretary general was a total contrast to the old, for he was a suave and subtle politician who happened to be both a high official of the Movement and a member of Opus Dei. Thus even more than Solís he represented the prefect blend of qualities for the bland bureaucratic era of the 1960s. Herrero Tejedor showed a pronounced ability to catch Franco's eye, directing the staging of the Asamblea Internacional de Excombatientes at the Valle de los Caídos in October 1963. This was the first and only international military assembly ever held in Spain in support of the regime, bringing in ex-fascist and pro-Axis veterans from all over western Europe. Herrero was no fascist himself, but he correctly judged that this tribute from military veterans would be greatly appreciated by the Caudillo, and he managed to seize much of the limelight himself. Herrero also launched the career of a young Movement bureaucrat named Adolfo Suárez, who would later play a decisive role in the ultimate fate of the Movement.[28]

Symptomatic of the Movement's current direction was the appointment of three Opus Dei members as provincial governors and provincial chiefs: Hermenegildo Altozano Moraleda in Seville, Santiago Galindo Herrero in Tenerife, and Juan Alfaro in Huelva. At that point new provincial governors were named through mutual agreement between the secretary general of the Movement and the minister of the interior. López Rodó had managed to win appointment of a number of Opus Dei members while director general of local administration in the ministry, facilitating the appointment of three governors who were not only at best indifferent to the Movement's Falangist past (that might have been said of most) but overtly anti-Falangist in their attitudes. The most outspoken was Altozano in Seville, who gained a reputation for having been the first provincial chief of the Movement to refuse ever to wear the blue shirt under any circumstances; he also ignored or suppressed other emblems. His independence was so extreme that even the supple Herrero Tejedor was said to find it impossible to deal with him.[29]

The most severely eroded of all Movement institutions was the SEU, its university student syndicate. The jefe nacional of the SEU appointed in 1957 following the crisis of the preceding year was a moderate, Jesús Aparicio Bernal, of Catholic reformist leanings. He had introduced changes to try to make the Sindicato more representative and to introduce more elected positions, but the consequence was to favor the infiltration of opposition students who turned sections of the SEU into antagonistic political forums. Thus a reorganization imposed by the Movement by decree in September 1961 further restricted its functions and activities. This had the desired effect of eliminating student oppositionists from the SEU but also reduced it to little more than a shell, directly combated by student activists. The hapless Aparicio was then replaced in February 1962 by an aggressive young "duro" (hard-liner), Rodolfo Martín Villa, who proposed to restore the SEU's energy and neutralize the student opposition.

Martín Villa failed almost completely in this enterprise, caught between the rising tide of leftist students on the one hand and the increasing influence of antagonistic students and professors of Opus Dei on the other. Any effort to restore strength and dynamism to the SEU would involve greater independence and internal democratization, for which there was no sympathy among the Movement leaders. Martín Villa in turn gave way to Daniel Regalado in September 1964, who was no more successful in trying to square this circle, and who was fired by a decision of the Council of Ministers within two months. The hopeless task finally devolved onto José Miguel Ortí Bordás, young neo-Falangist leader of the SEU "left," who proposed to recapture some of the old social radicalism. It was much too late for this, and the political situation, particularly at the University of Madrid, continued to deteriorate. The SEU was consequently dissolved by a decree of 5 April 1965, to be replaced by Asociaciones Profesionales de Estudiantes, though the administrative superstructure that served as the official intermediary between the Asociaciones and the Movement would be known as the Comisaría para el SEU for five years more. The old Falangist organization had thus come to a dead end by 1965, and the government largely accepted the fact that the Movement could no longer deal politically or organizationally with Spanish students.[30] The Movement's elite political youth group, the Guardias de Franco, was also in decline, but as an expression of the hard core it managed to sustain itself somewhat more effectively.[31]

During the 1960s the remaining ultras in the Movement probably looked more to José Antonio Girón than to any other figure. Solís Ruiz "kept the Falange," as he put it, "in a state of complete abandonment,"[32] and he did not believe that the Movement press was in much better state, for "it had fallen into the government's orbit of power,"[33] rather than maintaining opposition to the current non-Movement orientation. Especially annoying to Girón and the ultras in this regard was that

> Solís had his "own" newspaper, *Pueblo,* whose director had been
> Emilio Romero since the crisis of 1957. *Pueblo,* in theory, was the
> newspaper of the Syndicates, but in practice was an organ of power
> for Solís and for Emilio Romero, who intelligently played the
> chessboard of politics with extraordinary ability. The old glories of
> *Arriba* had disappeared.[34]

Girón was overgeneralizing, for the press of the Movement was not quite so completely servile as he described, expressing frequent hostility to the technocratic leadership of the 1960s. Rodrigo Royo, the director of *Arriba,* wrote an editorial that appeared on 30 January 1962, invoking once more the original Falangist leadership of José Antonio, Ledesma, and Redondo and denouncing by contrast the "planning projects of the triumvirate" who were in charge of economic affairs. Royo was fired immediately but eventually gained a measure of revenge through his novel *El Establishment* (1974), an unflattering portrayal of the government leadership. For camisas viejas, the "Opus ministers" represented a "new right" who were selling the birthright of the Nationalists of the Civil War for a mess of foreign investment, and at one Movement meeting in Madrid in June 1964 they accused the technocratic government of killing the spirit of the Eighteenth of July. In April 1966 Franco complained of these criticisms, lamenting that "the only newspapers who do not say what their owners want are those of the Movement."[35] Verbal assaults on Opus Dei, however veiled, became so persistent that on 28 October Monsignor Escrivá de Balaguer, the institute's founder and director, wrote directly to Solís to protest against "the campaign against Opus Dei that is carried on so unjustly by the press of the Falange, dependent on Your Excellency."[36] So little satisfaction was gained that the matter was carried to the pages of the French daily Le Monde. It was typical of Franco that he did not bring the Movement press fully to heel, for its hostility to the technocrats maintained a certain pressure against them, as well as something of the counterbalance that he always sought within the system. Complaints against government ministers also provided an opportunity for the Falangists who still remained to release some of their general political resentment, which they were always careful never to direct against Franco or the regime in public.

Falangists had originally constituted the "left" of the regime, and they still occupied a nominally leftist, "anticapitalist" position in social and economic affairs, but politically since 1945 they had formed the "extreme right" of the system. Major leaders of the old guard, especially Girón, wrote directly to Franco from time to time during the 1960s to complain about the danger of liberalizing reforms and the weakness of the party. Franco usually ignored laments about the latter, but warnings about the threat of excessive liberalization occasionally stirred him to take a harder line against certain reformist policies.

## DISSIDENT FALANGISM

No secretary general had ever generated so much resentment among camisas viejas and younger devotees of the party as Solís Ruiz. As one resentful young Arriba journalist is supposed to have remarked to Girón: "Solís flees the Falange as though it were the plague and every year approaches the anniversaries of the Twenty-Ninth of October and Twentieth of November with genuine fear, for when the ceremony begins someone may yell, 'Bastard!' at him and then a brawl breaks out."[37] The most dramatic outburst—directed against the Caudillo rather than Solís—took place at the annual commemoration for José Antonio, now held at his new resting place in the Valle de los Caídos. On 20 November 1960 a young militant shouted, "Franco, you're a traitor!"—bringing his immediate arrest and five years in prison.[38]

The 1960s produced new currents of dissident Falangism, which may be divided into two general sectors: the semiloyal and officially permitted, and the oppositionist and clandestine. Chief expression of the former was the Círculos Doctrinales José Antonio, organized by a mixed group of camisas viejas, militants of the Sección Femenina, and young Falangist radicals at the close of 1959. The goal was to form discussion groups to recapture and propagate the pristine Falangist doctrines of José Antonio, breaking decisively with the new technocratic right. From the first Círculo in Madrid, a total of at least twenty had been organized in various parts of the country by the end of 1961, now under the leadership of Luis González Vicén. Party intellectuals and theorists presented a series of lectures in Madrid, and a monthly publication, *Es así (The Right Way)* appeared irregularly from the beginning of 1963 until it was suppressed by the authorities in May 1964. In the year preceding, González Vicén had sent a strong letter to Solís denouncing his leadership and proclaiming support for a protest letter against police brutality that had been signed by many leading Spanish intellectuals. Pressure against Vicén steadily increased until he resigned in mid-1965, but he was replaced as leader of the Círculos Doctrinales by Diego Márquez Horrillo, the most active and prominent of the young radicals. Márquez revitalized the Círculos, expanding their program and activities and initiating small new "youth sections of workers and university students." By 1970 some seventy local círculos had been organized in diverse parts of the country. They strongly supported the efforts toward reform and liberalization, not, as Sheelagh Ellwood correctly points out, because their doctrines were democratic, but because only thus could they gain greater freedom of action.[39]

Chief leader of the more clandestine and more directly oppositionist dissidents was the camisa vieja physician Narciso Perales. An idealist of the original movement, Perales, despite poor health, took the lead in forming a tiny clandestine Frente Nacional de Trabajadores (FNT—National Workers Front) to recapture revolutionary anticapitalist national syndicalism. A related Frente de Estudiantes Sindicalistas (FES) was led by his son, Jorge Perales Rodríguez, Sigfrido Hillers de Luque, and several others. As the highly authoritarian Hillers came more and more to dominate the FES, Perales and his comrades abandoned the FNT in favor of a new Frente Sindicalista Revolucionario (FSR), which held a semiclandestine assembly in Madrid in 1966. This marked the return to active politics of Manuel Hedilla for the first time in twenty-nine years, as he was elected president and Perales first vice president of the new FSR. The organization was quickly declared illegal, but strove to develop contacts with leftist worker opposition elements, supported a number of illegal strikes, and even discussed strategies for a coup d'état as it progressively lost contact with reality.[40]

A parallel initiative was launched on the semiofficial level when the Secretariat of the Movement permitted the opening in 1964 of the Centro Social Manuel Mateo in Madrid. Named for the original head of the Falangist CONS, this was designed to be an educational and social center for workers of the Syndical Organization. It soon drew the participation of Perales, the Falangist dissident Cerefino Maestú (himself engaged in a variety of semiclandestine activities), and other oppositionists, and published a radical journal, *Orden Nuevo*, whose name was fully reminiscent of fascism. It eventually developed contacts with Marcelino Camacho and other clandestine Communist leaders, who used the Center's premises for meetings of the opposition Communist/Catholic Worker Commissions. The government finally ordered Solís to close all this down in 1966.[41]

Manuel Hedilla was uncomfortable as leader at an advanced age of a "revolutionary" semiclandestine organization, and in 1968, while Perales was in Latin America, abandoned it to form a new Frente Nacional de Alianza Libre (FNAL) with such extreme rightists as Blas Piñar and the army generals García Rebull and Pérez Viñeta. After Hedilla died in 1970, the ultra-rightists left this new group, some of its remnants going back to the FSR of Perales, who was generally recognized as the main leader of dissident Falangism. By that time, however, a number of other tiny groups had been formed.[42]

By 1970 the only groups that sustained any real activity were the FSR, the FNAL, and the Círculos Doctrinales José Antonio. While the Círculos were permitted a certain degree of freedom more or less within the Movement, functioning as a kind of safety valve, the FSR continued its efforts at semiclandestine appeals to workers. The FSR finally disintegrated in 1975 as one set of members tried to create a Partido Sindicalista Autogestionario (Self-Managing Syndicalist Party) and Perales formed yet another little group.[43]

## THE FINAL PLOY: "ASOCIACIONES POLITICAS"

By the late 1960s only two possibilities remained to the bureaucratic leaders of the Movement: one was to enhance the role of the Syndical Organization, as Solís Ruiz attempted to do, and the other was to try to revive the Movement by acquiring for it some sort of new representative function, its days as partido único being obviously numbered. Latin American models were vaguely invoked, for an expanded state syndicalism suggested a parallel to Peronism, whereas a more open and representative hegemonic party that encouraged semipluralism within unity raised the specter of the Mexican Partido Revolucionario Institucional. In fact, neither alternative was feasible. Regarding the Syndical Organization, Solís observed privately in September 1967 that "Franco had told him more than once that if the syndicates were given too much power they might turn against us."[44] The Fourth Syndical Congress, held at Tarragona in May 1968, was to have reflected the development of a more powerful and influential Syndical Organization, but by that time it had become painfully clear that the system could never achieve authenticity or even maintain the control that it had once possessed. Not only did it not determine workers' opinions, but it was becoming increasingly unable to contain their collective action. The recognition of limited collective bargaining four years earlier and the broadening of representation within the syndicates at the level of enlaces sindicales and jurados de empresa created opportunities that industrial workers were not slow to seize, but the results overflowed the syndical structure. From 1967 on, strike actions were no longer sporadic but were comparatively regular and had little or nothing to do with the official syndicates. The Syndical Organization lacked the strength and support to develop into a "Spanish Peronism," an outcome that had really been decided when Salvador Merino was cut down in 1941. It did constitute a center of antagonism to Carrero Blanco and the economics ministers, but its criticisms had comparatively little effect on policy,[45] and its attempt to broaden its base ended in failure.[46]

Solís still sought to maintain the official place of the Movement and find some way to give it greater standing and more members. At a meeting of the national council of the Sección Femenina in Ponteveda in January 1964, the major officeholders of the Movement all spoke. The most curious intervention was that of the camisa vieja Luis González Vicén, who seemed to blame Franco for having once "fascistized" the Falange, when the truth of the matter was more the other way around. Without directly referring to the Caudillo himself, Vicén declared that the Falange had been converted into a partido único in order to win support from Germany and Italy, whereas the original Falange had never sought to become a fascist movement. He also claimed that recruitment for the Blue Division had originally been carried out from the offices of the secretary general in order to be able to cast the blame on the Falange if the Axis lost the war, adding the usual laments about the changes and loss of influence after 1945, and concluding with the usual absurd warning that "the people" were opposed to the current liberal economic policies.[47]

Solís closed the proceedings with a widely publicized speech that was, by his standards, fairly hard-line. He warned that when reformists within the regime "try to create something to substitute for what is established, all they do is to copy it totally, but nonetheless with a different meaning, completely changing our emblems."[48] He concluded that "we must revise and reestablish our old laws, completing our institutionalization, and we are working on that now." He insisted that this could only be carried out by "the combat generation" and demanded that membership in the Movement be required of all those who held public employment.

During 1964 the National Council prepared its own "Project for the Structure of the National Council," which would have reestablished part of Arrese's proposals. It recommended converting the Council into a kind of senate, with significant political, legislative, and constitutional powers. Several government ministers, and some of the councillors themselves, objected that this created duplication and conflict with existing institutions,[49] and in the final form of the Organic Law of the State that was approved two years later, the powers of the Council remained much more circumscribed, though, as noted, it did gain the right of appeal of "contrafuero," or unconstitutional legislation. The other change was that the Tenth National Council, constituted in June 1964, included a not insignificant number of new reformist councillors,[50] even though it retained an eclectic mix of people from diverse political backgrounds.

There remained the intermittent debate that had gone on since 1957 over whether the old form of Movement as "organization" should give way to a new form as a broader "communion" of Spanish society that would guarantee its future not as a strict old-style partido único but as a broader multicurrent channel for participation and representation. This was essentially the meaning of "political development" as the term was used in the Movement during the 1960s. During his term as vice secretary general, Herrero Tejedor prepared the draft of a proposal to redefine the function of the Movement through the formation within its ranks of associations of heads of families and married women. This gained initial support but had to be withdrawn at the beginning of 1965 after a firestorm of disapproval in the Cortes from the Church hierarchy, reformist Catholics, and Carlists.[51] A second, broader project drawn up by Herrero and other Movement leaders was vetoed directly by Franco. As López Rodó later observed:

> Herrero Tejedor was a "rara avis" in Spanish politics; he had no sharp edges, offended no one, was motivated by a truly conciliatory spirit, and had a great capacity to bring together people of good will. Perhaps because of that, he was the object of keen vigilance by certain elements in the General Secretariat of the Movement who accused him of "deviationism."[52]

He first tried to resign in 1965 in disgust over the failure to make the SEU more representative. Though his resignation was not at first accepted, within a few months he left the Vice Secretariat to become chief prosecutor of the Tribunal Supremo. Later that year even the bland Fernández Cuesta admitted publicly that the Falange was "in a gaseous state,"[53] so unusually frank a statement from him that it attracted considerable attention. The proposals that Herrero Tejedor had helped to prepare were not included in the Organic Law of 1966, which made no mention of the National Movement as such. Its only relevant section dealt with the aforementioned right of contrafuero that was granted to the National Council, as though the state functions of the Movement were reduced to limited actions of its Council alone.

The technocrats' attitude toward the Movement was reflected in a discussion between López Rodó and Franco on 31 May 1966, which the former has reported as follows:

> "It is an artificial assemblage," I told him, "and from its ranks have come many of the present opponents of the regime. The only jeers which Your Excellency has ever heard," I dared tell him, "have come from uniformed militants at special political convocations. Those militants believe that they have a charismatic right that permits them to confront the Chief of State." (I was referring to the incident that occurred in the Valle de los Caídos on the day of the commemoration for José Antonio Primo de Rivera on 20 November 1960, when a Falangist shouted: "Franco, you're a traitor!")
>
> Franco replied that just as the Church had to have a clergy, so the state needed a number of men devoted to its service. I responded that no such analogy existed, reminding him that the partido único had been condemned in various encyclicals and in the recent documents of the Vatican Council, and that, if political pluralism was not permitted, it could not be said that the Movement is not a partido único.[54]

To recover some of the ground lost, Solís Ruiz and his new vice secretary general, Alejandro Rodríguez Valcárcel prepared a draft "Organic Law of the Movement and Its National Council," first presented in March 1968. Rodríguez Valcárcel, who had joined the Falange at the beginning of the Civil War, was one of the last determined leaders of the Movement, insisting that "the Movement must be the principal driver of the task of achieving the progress and growth of Spain."[55] During the next three months this new proposal became the center of debate in the Cortes, the press, and the government. It would ratify once more the position of minister secretary general of the Movement, redefine the functioning of provincial and local councils, and safeguard the party's institutional structure, though it did not claim the special powers that had been advanced in the Arrese anteproyectos. Movement procuradores presented several amendments in the Cortes to recapture some of the latter features, but other political sectors strongly criticized the proposed law, alleging that it contradicted the recent Organic Law of the State and was a partial return to the old concept of partido único.[56] Nonetheless, the Organic Law of the Movement was approved on 26 June, as Franco privately dismissed complaints about its conflict with legislation of the preceding year on the grounds that this new Organic Law was mere ordinary legislation that could be altered at any time, whereas the preceding Organic Law of the State was a Fundamental Law that took precedence and could only be modified by a national referendum.[57] Thus he indicated once more his lack of concern about contradictions so long as they served his purposes, as well as his determination to maintain the Movement as a political organization, even if it was without significant power.

Celebration of the party's anniversary in the following year, held at the Teatro de la Comedia on 29 October 1968, occasioned perhaps the most outspoken incidents and the worst heckling of Solís in recent times. The newspaper *Pueblo* published two days later the results of a questionnaire that asked, "What is happening in the Falange?" Arrese and Fernández Cuesta made their customary anodyne remarks, and Solís merely observed that "the Falange maintains continuity within the Movement." Some of the leaders from earlier years were more frank. Hedilla declared that "the Falange no longer amounts to anything. It slipped out of our hands and is finished." Serrano Súñer simply repeated his advice of 1945 to Franco:

> The Falange was never the basic force of the state. It struggled long ago to make a place for itself. After that it did no more than protect its permanence in the government in any form. . . . Today the Falange ought to be honorably discharged. . . . A democratic and pro-Allied Falange cannot simply be invented at the present time. . . . The Falange should be either dissolved or removed from power.[58]

Since Franco would never permit that, the leadership had no alternative but to return again and again to the concept of "associationism," the ploy that had been toyed with for more than a decade. The Organic Law of the State had paid it no more than lip service, declaring vaguely that one of the goals of the National Council was to "stimulate authentic and effective participation in national entities" and "the legitimate exchange of opinion." To try for the first time to induce new associative features, therefore, a new Organic Statute of the Movement was drawn up during the final months of 1968, terming the organization "the communion of the Spanish in the Principles of the Movement" in order to imply the possibility of a broader membership. Rodríguez Valcárcel's proposal to grant the Movement control over propaganda and ordinary state employment as well as a massive budgetary increase for political and organizational work—easily affordable amid the current record prosperity in Spain—was vetoed, perhaps by Franco himself. Attention focused on the proposed article 15, which raised the possibility of "associations" that might be legalized "within the Movement" for the "legitimate exchange of ideas."

A small group in the old guard, led by Fernández Cuesta, opposed any sort of "associations" as opening the door to the return of political parties, but the statute was approved by the National Council in December 1968 in terms that recognized the possibility of "constituting associations for the development of family representation in public life and promoting and defending the interests of the family," presumably an acceptably conservative goal. In addition, it was stipulated that associations might be formed within the Movement for other goals, such as defending professional interests not represented by the Syndical Organization, promoting national culture, and studying and implementing the doctrines of the Movement itself, as well as for any other purpose that might be specifically approved by the National Council.[59] Yet none of these options would actually materialize until the latter also prepared yet another law to define more specifically these terms of association and until all this was officially ratified by Franco. The only measure that would be put into effect by the statute itself was one that provided for the direct election of "local councillors," to be chosen by universal suffrage of all Spaniards over eighteen years of age—a much broader suffrage than that permitted for the election of "family representatives" to the Cortes under the Organic Law. This was to be the party's equivalent of the enlaces sindicales chosen within the syndicates since 1944, and the councillors would have no more authority than their syndical counterparts. During the debate on the new statute in the Cortes during the first months of 1969, there was for the first time public criticism of the "monopoly" of the Movement. For Fernández Cuesta and Girón, all this was simply "the cancellation of Falange Española."[60]

As ultras asked aloud, "What is the difference between a political association and a political party?" a new "Draft Project of Bases for the Associative Juridical Regime of the Movement," prepared during the spring of 1969, seemed to bring that danger well under control. The new statute on associations that was approved unanimously by the National Council on 3 July defined them as "associations of opinion" whose organizers would have to collect 25,000 signatures in order to register them legally. The National Council would have complete control over their legal authorization, and the goals or functions of such associations (should any ever be authorized) were not specified. Once more a step toward apertura

The party's national headquarters on Madrid's calle de Alcalá, during the final years

(openness) and greater participation was being made so limited in practice as to frustrate any serious reform. Moreover, the draft project was never approved by Franco, who had serious doubts about going even that far.[61]

While these deliberations continued, the phrase "Organo de FET y de las JONS" finally disappeared from the front page of *Arriba* on 5 January 1969. Awareness of the Movement's decline produced a number of serious evaluations in the now semifree Spanish press during the year that followed.[62] With each passing year the membership simultaneously aged and shrank. A check of records indicated that in Lérida province in 1965, 85 percent of the affiliates were more than forty-five years of age, while in 1974 the average age among members in Madrid would be at least fifty-five. Though a few new members were gained every year (27,806, for example, in 1969), they did not compensate in numbers for those who dropped out or died, and came mostly from the semirural Catholic and conservative provinces of the north.[63]

On 23 November 1969 a middle-aged camisa vieja, Francisco Herranz, shot himself fatally in front of the large church in Madrid's Plaza de Santa Bárbara to protest against the marginalization of the Falange. It was to no avail. A subsequent law of 3 April 1970 ratified the definitive abolition of the name Falange Española Tradicionalista y de las JONS in favor of Movimiento Nacional; the earlier decree of 1945 had been inadequately worded and had failed to achieve complete derogation of the nomenclature that had been established in April 1937. Henceforth the name Falange would belong only to various dissident grouplets organized semiclandestinely.

A non-Falangist political future was determined by the official recognition in July 1969 of Prince Juan Carlos as heir to Franco and future king of Spain.[64] The "Operación Príncipe" (Operation Prince) had been above all the work of the non- and anti-Falangists in the present government, but some of the latter in turn were seriously embarrassed by the outbreak of the "asunto MATESA" (MATESA Affair), the greatest official scandal in the history of the regime, which became public immediately afterward. This involved false export credits for Maquinaria Textil, S. A. (MATESA), a Pamplona firm directed from Barcelona that claimed to be the first industrial multinational company developed by Spanish citizens. The false credits were formally denounced by the director general of customs on the symbolic date of 17 July 1969, perhaps partly in an effort to embarrass the economics ministers connected with Opus Dei. Leaders of the Movement quickly seized on the issue, and Movement newspapers were among the most active in denouncing the fraud.

Negative publicity soon reached such proportions that only a change in government ministers could resolve the matter. The ministers of finance and commerce would have to go, but that would be balanced by the elimination of several Movement ministers, such as Castiella, the "dangerous liberal" Fraga Iribarne, and even the oily Solís, who was painted as a dangerous intriguer with many enemies, a veritable new Salvador Merino of the Syndical Organization who sought to establish the dominance of the Syndical bureaucracy. The resulting new cabinet of October 1969 was quickly labeled the "monocolor government" because virtually all its key members were either members of Opus Dei or the ACNP, associates of those members, or otherwise known to be identified with their policies.

The new minister secretary general of the Movement was the veteran university professor and bureaucratic politician Torcuato Fernández Miranda, master of the rhetorical double-talk of the system.[65] A law professor, he had held positions in the Ministry of Education and the Ministry of Labor, and in 1966 had become the Movement's first national delegate of culture. Earlier he had played a key role in the university education of Prince Juan Carlos. As his tutor in law, Fernández Miranda had explained to the young prince how the regime really worked and had also helped resolve his doubts on the eve of his recognition as Franco's successor, describing how the laws and institutions of the system could be legally used to change those very laws and institutions.[66]

Fernández Miranda was a politician of the Movement, but neither a fascist nor a Falangist in the original sense. Joaquín Bardavío has written that "when Carrero told him that the Chief of State had decided to designate him minister secretary general of the Movement, Fernández Miranda could not contain his astonishment: 'Movement? But I am not a Falangist!'"[67] Fernández Miranda nonetheless reflected the thinking about the Movement of Carrero Blanco, who dominated the new government, and even of Franco himself. He had been selected to complete the final phase of its defascistization and to render it more flexible, though always within the limits of the regime. As secretary general, he immediately exchanged the blue shirt for a white bureaucrat's shirt—the first minister secretary general to do so—and later abolished the blue shirt altogether as official dress, eliminating yet another fascist residue.

He had also been selected to eliminate the opposition within the Movement to Juan Carlos and the monarchist restoration. In the mid-1960s, Solís Ruiz and some of his associates had hoped to be able to influence the monarchist candidate[68] if a restoration proved unavoidable, and had even made gestures to promote the candidacy of the cousin of Juan Carlos, Alfonso de Borbón-Dampierre. Such maneuvers, never more than half-hearted, would come to an end under Fernández Miranda.[69]

The other main task of the new secretary general was to cope with the problem of the proposed political associations. Here Fernández Miranda had to try to conciliate the reformists while being careful to conform to the expectations of Franco and Carrero Blanco. After initial approval was given to the Statute of Associations on 3 July 1969, four distinct groups began to take the initiative in forming associations. The first, called Acción Política, was led by moderates like Pío Cabanillas and José García Hernández, together with well-connected newcomers such as the civil engineer Leopoldo Calvo Sotelo. A second, composed of reformist veterans of the Frente de Juventudes, proposed to form an association called Reforma Social Española, led by the "left" Falangist reformist Manuel Cantarero del Castillo.[70] Another handful of Movement members, led by a national councillor, had announced their intention to form an association called Democracia Social, while the ultra-rightists of Blas Piñar and the journal *Fuerza Nueva* declared that "against their own will" they would assume the responsibility of forming an association to defend franquista orthodoxy. As of late 1969, however, all this was beside the point, since Franco had not ratified the Statute of Associations.

Neither Franco nor Carrero Blanco approved of the idea of associations, yet they did not move to quash the concept directly, probably for lack of any other reformist alternative. A loyal servant, Fernández Miranda grasped that his assignment was to make haste slowly. He thus began with a meeting of the National Council on 15 December 1969, in which he presented a new proposal for the reorganization of the General Secretariat and its relationship to the National Council. This would increase the powers of the Secretariat, which would in fact take over some of the functions of the National Council, and abolish the National Delegation of Associations, replacing it with the new National Delegation of the Family and the National Delegation of Political Action and Participation. He insisted that the aim was not to prevent the development of associations but to make better preparation for them. Fraga Iribarne, now looking toward a political career in the post-Franco era, protested that despite such verbal reassurances, the Delegation of Associations was being abolished and that the word "asociaciones" never appeared once in the new proposal. He also observed that the text of the Organic Statute of the Movement passed in 1968 had still not been officially published, but emphasized that a golden opportunity lay at hand to transform the Movement behind a great national "centrist policy." Fernández Miranda's changes were finally approved, though against the unusual opposition of twelve negative votes and four abstentions.[71]

Fernández Miranda held that the "pluralism" of political parties could never be accepted, but that the "pluriformism" within unity of the Movement could still provide opportunity for participation in some form of associationism.[72] It was important, he stressed, that "power not be something tied to a person or a group, but tied to society, tied to the people"[73] and he insisted that "the Spanish national state has never been a corporative state. The political representation that it attempts to achieve is not the political representation of entities or corporations. It is the political representation of the national community."[74]

At the meeting in Valladolid on 4 March 1971, which commemorated the original fusion of the Falange and the JONS, however, he tried to sound the call of Falangist radicalism:

> The only authentically true attitude in face of Marxism is a deep and radical national socialism that carries to its ultimate consequences the national revolution, the revolution of the Movement, the realization of social justice. . . . There is, beyond doubt, an integrating national socialism, born from the sources of our doctrine, of the doctrine that constitutes the essence of the JONS and of the Falange, which unites with authentic Spanish traditionalism, which emerges and overflows in the doctrine of our Movement. All that is needed is to define it with rigor and precision both in its postulates and in its action.[75]

This was criticized by reformists as sounding too "national socialist" or even "Nazi," and by other Movement figures as treacherous leftist rhetoric, though it was probably no more than a verbal effort to connect the original Falangist social radicalism with the concerns of the 1970s.

Fernández Miranda did manage to carry out one sudden initiative, obtaining approval of a decree-law of 3 April 1970 that declared that the Movement's "norms and internal resolutions of a statutory character" would henceforth be published in the *Boletín Oficial del Estado* (article 4) and that "the decisions of the National Council that, by their content, have the character of general dispositions, will be invested with the force of laws, decrees, or ministerial directives" (article 5). This abrupt decree, personally dictated by Franco on the basis of his authority as head of state as originally defined in 1938–1939, was not the result of any ministerial or legislative reform project but was an executive order that suddenly enlarged the power of the Movement's leadership, approved by Franco no doubt to increase official authority in a time of change. Its effect was confusion and widespread criticism, since it contradicted the reforms of 1966–1968,[76] and these powers were in fact never exercised in any significant way.

On the issue of associations, "the position of Torcuato . . . had been extremely cautious, waiting to see which way the wind would blow."[77] At the beginning of 1970, a small number of reformist members of the National Council, led by Herrero Tejedor, presented to the secretary general a petition urging that arrangements for political associations be speedily brought into effect, and a month later the small minority of directly elected procuradores en Cortes ("family delegates") prepared their own proposal, denying the jurisdiction of the National Council and insisting that the right of association be legislated by the Cortes.[78]

Finally, on 21 May Fernández Miranda presented to the permanent commission of the National Council a new draft outline for associations of political action. This stipulated that any proposed political association must consist of no fewer than 10,000 signed affiliates. The members of the organizing commission of each association would be required to sign a notarized document stating that they respected the Principles of the Movement and the Fundamental Laws, and in addition they would have to obtain the signed agreement of three members of the National Council who pledged themselves to supervise and guarantee the reliability of the association. It would then have to be approved by a special committee of associations to be created by the Council, by the new national delegate of political action, by the secretary general, and by a full meeting of the National Council. Thus the bureaucracy of the Movement would hold full authority over any associations, and no provisions were made either for elections or for any representative or legislative authority, leaving the terms of any future elections to be taken up by subsequent legislation.[79]

There the project remained for the next three years. Franco and Carrero Blanco drew back before even such a carefully controlled scheme, and the associations project was buried. A "Note to the Second Edition" of the pamphlet *Concurrencia de pareceres: Coincidencias y discrepancias en el Movimiento*, published by the General Secretariat in August 1971, stated that the proposal for associations "has not succeeded in being formulated in a manner sufficiently distinct from parties, and, therefore, the conclusion has been reached that it is inviable, since, not being differentiated from the reality of parties, it remains incompatible with the existing institutional system."

One further effort was made by reformists to air the issue in the press and other forums during the spring of 1972, but by that time Fernández Miranda had received clear instructions. Echoing Franco's terminology, he declared publicly that any action that attempted to reintroduce political parties would be a mere "dialectical trick," and in November 1972 he informed the Cortes: "To say yes or no to political associations is simply a Sadducean trap. The question is to see if by saying yes to political associations we also say yes or no, or do not say yes or no, to political parties." [80]

Immobilism was accentuated in April 1971 with the dismissal of the active young vice secretary general, Miguel Ortí Bordás. Once one of the hard-line young radicals of the Movement and author of a notorious article urging nationalization of the banking system, Ortí Bordás was an energetic young politician who favored apertura and had gained the enmity of the old guard. He was replaced by a camisa vieja literally twice his age, the docile and immobile Manuel Valdés Larrañaga, a companion of José Antonio and a veteran figure in the Movement. Valdés "publicly declared that not a single one of the supporters of political associations would be renewed in the new membership of the National Council." [81] His appointment, however, had been a sop to the old guard that would protect Fernández Miranda's right flank; Valdés was given little authority or responsibility within the administration of the Movement, which Fernández Miranda had tightened considerably.

The new secretary general had established himself firmly in the good graces of Carrero Blanco and of Juan Carlos (the latter having told him privately that in his view the Movement "had no future whatsoever"),[82] though Franco regarded him with greater skepticism. Fernández Miranda understood full well that so long as Franco ruled, the status quo would be maintained, and this meant a mere holding action. As a consequence, on 5 May 1971 Rodríguez Valcárcel complained to López Rodó that "four or five provincial governors have been to see him complaining that they receive no political instructions. The General Secretariat of the Movement is lacking in imagination and initiative. Torcuato Fernández

Miranda may be a fine thinker, but he is no man of action, and in his hands the path of the Movement is not clear." [83]

Even part of the Falangist old guard now seemed willing to demonstrate some greater degree of flexibility. Though Girón, its most categorical spokesman, had expressed to Franco a sense of hopelessness in 1970, on 4 May 1972 he delivered a speech in which he suggested that in the Spanish state of the future three different "tendencies" might be expressed within loyalty to the franquista "Constitution": a left, center, and right. [84] On orders from above, all the Movement press attacked Girón's declaration, [85] and two months later Franco gave explicit orders to Carrero Blanco to put an end to further discussion of "tendencies" and associations. [86] Girón returned to his more accustomed vein in a speech before the National Council on 29 October, thirty-ninth anniversary of the founding of the party, as he insisted that Spain was much more capable of achieving the Falangist "National Revolution" in its present state of prosperity than it had been during the grim 1930s. [87]

A minority of young reformists remained active within the Movement, organizing themselves as the Group of Thirty-Nine at the beginning of 1973. Led by Ortí Bordás and Rodolfo Martín Villa, who had been one of the last SEU chiefs, they continued to try to turn the Movement toward political associations and a semirepresentative system.

## DISSIDENT FALANGISM IN THE 1970S

During the final years of the regime, the main group of "dissident" or "alternative" young Falangists were those participating in the Círculos Doctrinales José Antonio. In their effort to recapture pure and radical Falangism, theoretically without contamination from the regime, they increased meetings and discussions during 1969, planning a major demonstration to be held in Alicante on 22 November 1970 to commemorate the thirty-fourth anniversary of the death of José Antonio. Under strict injunctions from the government, however, the leaders of the Círculos submitted, limiting their activities to the participation of 4,000 followers in a public mass for the founder. In June 1973 the Círculos Doctrinales held their fourth national assembly in Toledo, which abruptly ended when a disturbance broke out during a speech by Vice Secretary General Valdés Larrañaga. As punishment, Fernández Miranda ordered all Círculos Doctrinales closed throughout Spain for the next three months. The most radical dissident Falangists then rejected the Círculos, claiming (correctly) that the Círculos drew funding and indirect support from the Movement. The number of local Círculos nonetheless continued to expand, reaching a total of 231 by 1976.

The "alphabet soup" of tiny neo-Falangist dissident grouplets continued to expand, with half a dozen new ones being formed during the first half of the 1970s.[88] The most active was the Frente de Estudiantes Sindicalistas, led by Sigfrido Hillers de Luque, which by 1970 was virtually the only publicly active nonleftist student political group at the University of Madrid.

Dissident neo-Falangism equaled or surpassed the revolutionary left in its divisiveness and internal schisms. This of course reflected the normal sectarian factionalism and exclusiveness of the twentieth-century political religions of whatever stripe, but in this case also seemed to express an unusually high degree of anarchic personalism and voluntarism, qualities most salient in the neofascist culture. This divisiveness might have been partially overcome if any of the grouplets had generated any support.[89] None did, however, and post-Franco elections would show that all the neofascist elements combined could not muster 2 percent of the popular vote, though of course the original movement of José Antonio had done even worse in 1936.

Violent street action during the final years of the regime rarely came from the ranks of the regular Movement youth, but more often from dissident Falangists, and more yet from new cliques of neofascists and neo-Nazis inspired by developments in other parts of western Europe, and especially from the "Fuerza Nueva" of the radical-right ultra Blas Piñar, a noisy feature of Spanish life in the 1970s, even though lacking in popular support.[90]

## THE FINAL PHASE

Soon after reaching the age of eighty, Franco finally accepted the fact that someone else should serve as president of government. On 8 June 1973 he appointed to that office Carrero Blanco, who seemed to represent the best guarantee for the maintenance of the regime's institutions under the future monarchy. Franco did not understand that the admiral would promise Prince Juan Carlos that he would offer his resignation whenever Franco died.[91] The new ministers were chosen primarily by Carrero and were in every case veteran loyalists of the regime. At the first cabinet meeting six days later, the new president expressed his loyalty to the basic principles of the present system, which he described as "the common denominator of traditionalist and Falangist ideologies."[92]

The basic goal of the new government was to strengthen the regime, which would mean in some fashion strengthening the Movement. Both Franco and Carrero Blanco therefore now finally accepted the need to proceed with some sort of arrangement for political associations, since no other scheme was at hand. Thus Fernández Miranda, whose intellect and ability Carrero respected, not only retained his post as minister secretary general but was also made vice president of government. On the one hand he had kept the Movement under control and tightened its administration, while expediting its further defascistization; on the other, he was the leader most qualified to try to expand it in the future through the ploy of associations.

A new mixed commission representing the cabinet and the National Council of the Movement began once more to study the issue. Given a green light, Fernández Miranda quickly did a "Copernican revolution,"[93] something in which he would henceforth specialize. The commission submitted a document "on the convenience and opportunity of presenting to the Cortes a project of general law on the political participation of the Spanish." The secretary general directly posed the question of "whether the Movement is today capable of attracting members," declaring that "whatever contributes to winning popular support is politically desirable" and stressing that "it is necessary to run the risks that freedom permits."[94]

The matter was discussed at a cabinet meeting on 14 November, at which Fernández Miranda stated emphatically:

> Some flatterers of the Prince talk to him about the strength of "pure monarchy" by itself. They set a trap for the king, encouraging him to get rid of the Movement after a prudent interval. But a monarchy without a Movement would collapse, and therefore, with a concern for tomorrow, we must renovate the Movement. We must organize the "Movement of the king," which is a Francoist Movement in its origins but tomorrow will be the king's. I do not want to see the Movement end up in a one-way street. In 1974, the only means of gaining support for the Movement is "from liberty." There must be free associations within the Movement open to all Spaniards.[95]

The issue was scheduled for further debate when the regime was thrown into its most severe crisis since the end of World War II by the assassination of the president by Basque terrorists on 20 December.

The problem of a successor to Carrero Blanco was most difficult, for there was no one of equivalent stature in the regime. Franco would have preferred a personal friend from the military, such as the seventy-five-year-old Admiral Nieto Antúnez, or the current president of the Cortes (and former vice secretary of the Movement) Rodríguez Valcárcel, or even possibly a hard-liner like Girón (though more as vice president than as president). For the first time, Franco was unable directly to impose his will, for members of the Council of the Realm, who would prepare the list of possible candidates, proved unwilling to cooperate, and resistance appeared in other quarters as well. A strange alliance of members of Franco's family and personal entourage, together with other government leaders, finally managed to promote the candidacy of Carlos Arias Navarro, a veteran regime administrator and bureaucrat, currently minister of the interior.

The Arias Navarro government that was announced on 3 January 1974 was the first all-civilian government in the regime's history. It was largely composed of remnants of the bureaucratic inner core of the regime, but it eliminated all the remaining cabinet members who were associated directly or indirectly with Opus Dei and was influenced by two key aperturistas, Antonio Carro Martínez and Pío Cabanillas, who became minister undersecretary of the presidency and minister of information and tourism, respectively. The first speech of the new president, on 12 February, proved a major surprise. It promised a new, more liberal local government law, "immediate acceleration" of a more liberal syndical law, and approval of a new system of political associations. All this created what became known immediately as the "spirit of the twelfth of February," to the surprise and consternation of many, and to the delight of the press, reformists, and the opposition.

Girón promised to cooperate with Arias, but demanded the appointment as minister secretary general of a real Falangist who still believed in the system. Fernández Miranda was thus replaced by the comparatively young José Utrera Molina, an ardent activist of the postwar generation who expressed pride in the fact that he had become the first secretary general who had entered the Movement as a juvenile "flecha" and passed almost his entire life in it. He had served as governor and provincial chief of three provinces, as undersecretary of labor, and most recently as minister of housing.[96] His appointment was, however, a severe annoyance to Arias, who feared that Utrera might hamper his plans for a limited aperturismo.

Utrera insisted on the relative vitality of the Movement, citing statistics given by Fernández Miranda in an interview in *Pueblo* soon after Carrero Blanco's assassination. The preceding secretary general had indicated that total membership in all Movement organizations in 1973 had reached 980,054, one of the highest figures ever, though, given Spain's increased population, proportionately much less than under Arrese in the early 1940s. The Organización Juvenil numbered more than 300,000 (proportionately its lowest figure ever), the Sección Femenina 279,697 (also proportionately the lowest), and the Guardias de Franco approximately 50,000, about the same figure as the Vieja Guardia.[97] The problem, as ever, was active membership, for actual participation was much lower than nominal membership among the adult sectors. The organization was not totally moribund, but signs of life had been steadily weakening, and it was weakest of all among young adults. The general dynamics of political activism, media expression, and public opinion in Spain all militated against it.

Utrera Molina thus became the last real leader of the Movement, generating plans to revive its popular base and expand the provincial cadres and youth groups. In this he apparently achieved a modest degree of success, since the Movement registered 36,000 new members between the ages of eighteen and thirty in less than a year[98]—a higher rate than usual—though this was balanced by the increasing volume of deaths of older members and accelerating defections.

Utrera has written that he faced extreme hostility from most other ministers, and that the government restricted funding for the Movement and denied other forms of cooperation. Before long he came to believe that Arias and his chief advisers wished to abolish the General Secretariat of the Movement, reducing it to the Secretariat of the National Council and depriving the Movement of central leadership.[99]

Both Utrera and Girón favored going ahead with the associations project so long as it could be kept under the control of the National Council, whereas Carro Martínez, Cabanillas, and other reformists in the government sought a more liberal structure that would come under the jurisdiction of the Ministry of the Interior. Conflict became so intense and Utrera so outnumbered within the government that after some months he adopted the practice of speaking directly with Franco. When Arias tried to put a stop to this, Franco—who greatly trusted and appreciated Utrera—gave the latter full authorization to speak with him directly. In fact, it was apparently Utrera who first urged Franco to resume the powers of Chief of State as soon as possible after his recovery from thrombophlebitis during the summer of 1974.[100]

On 11 September Arias spoke about the Movement in negative terms to the Agencia EFE, declaring that "the organization of the Movement was historically variable," with a view to the further change and reduction of its structure, and adding that it was a mistake to try to mobilize young people "with dubious attributions of a representation more or less controlled and digested."[101] Girón and Utrera were livid, and at a meeting in the General Secretariat it was decided that the latter must resign in protest, though Arias talked him out of it.[102]

During October ultras in the Movement launched an all-out attack on Cabanillas, the main leader of reformism in the government. Directors of leading Movement newspapers prepared for Franco an elaborate dossier of the extensive soft-core pornography appearing in Spanish publications.

Franco required Cabanillas's resignation but agreed to let the associations project go forward.

The deliberations on this project constituted the chief drama of the late autumn. Two different versions had been prepared, one by Utrera and a commission of the National Council along the lines of previous limited and controlled proposals, and quite a different one under the aegis of a young aperturista, Juan Ortega Díaz-Ambrona, whom Carro had appointed director of the Instituto de Estudios Administrativos. The latter had formed a committee within his institute of young reformers such as Gabriel Cisneros and Rafael Arias Salgado, son of the former information minister. Their project would open the right of political association to all citizens, not restricting it to membership in or the control of the Movement. When the initial draft was ready in August, it was edited by Carro and passed on to Arias Navarro. The president eventually transmitted it to Franco for his approval on 14 November, but Franco quickly gutted the project to bring it back under the Movement's control once more.[103]

This opened the way for Utrera's project, which was to involve reform of the Movement's organizational structure as well, stimulating local activities and the role of the local and provincial councils of the Movement. Another major goal was to encourage the ideological rearmament of the regime by reanimating the Instituto de Estudios Políticos under Jesús Fueyo and creating new cultural and recreational centers for the Movement on the local level. Yet another goal was revival of the youth organizations, and to that end Utrera had visited most of the remaining youth camps during the preceding summer to whip up enthusiasm.[104] All this aroused the opposition of the president, who had sought to eliminate Utrera during the October crisis, but Franco protected him. Thus Utrera and his associates transmitted to Franco the essence of their own draft project, whose main points were superimposed by the Caudillo in place of the government's draft. This cleared the way for its adoption by the National Council on 16 December.[105] The measure was promulgated by Franco by decree four days later and subsequently ratified by the Cortes in January.

The new Juridical Statute of the Right to Political Association still restricted associations to the ideological orbit and organizational control of the Movement, but unlike the earlier proposal by Fernández Miranda, it did not technically require members of proposed associations also to be members of the Movement. It authorized formation of political associations that were in accord with the Principles of the Movement, subject in each case to final approval by the National Council. Each association would have to achieve a minimum membership of 25,000, distributed through at least fifteen provinces. In thinly inhabited provinces containing fewer than 500,000, a minimum of 2 percent of the population would have to be registered with the party in order for that province to qualify, a figure reduced to 1.5 percent for provinces with a population between 500,000 and a million, and to 1 percent in those with more than a million. The Movement was to contribute toward the financing of each qualifying association, which would be authorized to participate in whatever electoral processes might subsequently be established by law. Three categories of fines were set up to punish associations that might infringe the terms of these regulations.[106]

Fernández Miranda declared in an interview that "the associationism of our system does not derive its main rationale from ideological pluralism, the basis of a party system, but rather its true basis lies in the pluriformism essential to our Movement from its origin."[107] One critic wryly observed that "it gives the impression that the decree-law favors above all the association of those who previously have not let us associate,"[108] and the sociologist Salustiano del Campo succinctly defined it as "a typical Spanish invention." A cabinet minister declared the following May that "the government is trying to carry out the great political operation of [transforming] the established system from within the system itself,"[109] while Ricardo de la Cierva wrote that during the biennium since Carrero Blanco first became president, "what we are perhaps achieving is the difficult task of combining together all the disadvantages of both authoritarian and democratic regimes, without the clear advantages of the one or the other."[110]

Yet Franco himself stalled the apertura during his final months, fearing to see the whole system unravel. The Caudillo remained convinced that the only hope of an authoritarian "monarquía instaurada" lay in maintenance of the institutions of his regime, observing privately in December 1974 that if a plebiscite were held, the monarchy on its own would gain less than 10 percent of the vote.[111]

The second crisis of the Arias Navarro government erupted on 20 February, when its third vice president and minister of labor, the Movement veteran Licinio de la Fuente, resigned under fire from other cabinet members. For months he had sought to develop a new law of labor relations that would liberalize existing provisions. After this was blocked, he concentrated on a new law that under certain conditions would legalize a strike within a single firm, while opposing other legislation from the Syndical Organization and the Ministry of the Interior that would completely invalidate a contract in the case of an illegal strike by individual workers.[112]

Arias became determined to use this opportunity to carry out the kind of government reorganization that he would have preferred the preceding October. While replacing La Fuente in Labor, he also insisted on relieving the other two orthodox Movement ministers, Utrera Molina and Francisco Ruiz Jarabo in Justice. Franco was at first opposed, placing great value on Utrera's loyalty. Arias's insistence marked another "first" in regime annals, for he stood fast, even at the risk of his resignation, calculating correctly that a feeble and aged Caudillo lacked the strength to force a general government crisis at that time. The last orthodox minister secretary general was thus released on 4 March 1975.[113]

His replacement was Fernando Herrero Tejedor, who had been a loyal, agreeable, and somewhat imaginative vice secretary under Solís and more recently prosecutor of the Tribunal Supremo. As mentioned, he was the only top leader of the Movement who was also a member of Opus Dei. An aperturista, he was, together with Fernández Miranda, one of the two most trusted contacts of Prince Juan Carlos in the Movement leadership. His skill, liberality, and ability to deal smoothly with all sectors had made him Arias's first choice when the government had originally been formed, but Girón and the old guard had intervened. Herrero Tejedor brought in as vice secretary his forty-year-old protégé Adolfo Suárez, an adroit young leader with a knack for dealing with people, who had developed some pedigree in the Movement as provincial leader and later, as director of state television, had shown himself to be a strong supporter of Juan Carlos. Thus a unique reversal of political relations developed after March 1975: the prince now enjoyed greater backing from the new leaders of the Movement than from any other part of the government. Juan Carlos so appreciated Herrero's loyalty and talent that the latter was at that time apparently the prince's first choice for the new president of government after Franco's death,[114] and late in 1974 Herrero and Suárez were among several aperturista figures who were asked to submit outlines for a possible fundamental reform or transformation of the system.[115]

There is no indication that Franco resisted the appointment of Herrero Tejedor, who had proven his loyalty and whose ability he respected.[116] Moreover, the Caudillo was steadily losing confidence in Arias and knew that Herrero was no special crony of the president. Similarly, he did not resist the appointment of Suárez, though he observed that the latter was "very audacious."[117]

As minister Herrero continued to repeat that there was no place in Spain for political parties, but he presided over the permanent commission of the National Council, which held the power to approve all new associations, and immediately began to use his vice secretary for a wide range of direct political contacts, not merely with the leaders of proposed associations but also with the opposition. Suárez dealt with domestic leaders of the Socialist Party and with Enrique Tierno Galván—among many others—and also apparently established correspondence with so inveterate a foe of Franco as Salvador de Madariaga.[118]

Herrero planned to exploit fully the possibility of "associationism," with an eye toward the post-Franco transition. The centerpiece was to be a new center-right Unión del Pueblo Español (whose acronym was UDPE, to distinguish it from the old UPE of Primo de Rivera), led by either Herrero or Suárez, or possibly both. Herrero seemed convinced that a system of associations could become the vehicle for a transition to a reformed regime under the monarchy,[119] though it is not clear how far or fast this would go.[120] Conversely, he vetoed the proposal by Girón and Fernández Cuesta to form an association called Falange Española de las JONS,[121] and by September only eight associations had been formally registered. Of these only the UDPE had gained the requisite 25,000 members. Six of the eight originated from various segments of the Movement, and at most only three or four stood for serious reform.[122]

The most widely publicized politician in the country at that point was Fraga Iribarne, and one survey of political opinion in mid-January had found that those thought to have the best chance of leading a political association were Fraga, Cabanillas, and Solís, in that order.[123] Yet Fraga decided not to participate and was rumored to have rejected Herrero's offer of the leadership of the UDPE. The whole associationist ploy began to appear doomed, for the bulk of the opposition and even many moderate reformists refused to participate.

A general scramble had already begun among those currently or previously associated with the regime to define new identities for themselves. This was true for many in the Movement, as well. Franco was not unaware of this exodus, and his rumored anxiety and worry over it may have been a factor in the definitive decline of his health in the summer and autumn of 1975. Such a stampede was developing that the monarchist journalist Luis María Anson wrote an article entitled "Moral Cowardice," which appeared in *ABC* on 20 May 1975:

> In political Spain one now hears with greater frequency each day the interminable call of sheep and the loud cackle of hens. There is also the sound of rats abandoning the ship of the regime. Each day moral cowardice takes hold of greater and greater sectors of our political class. Such a spectacle of fear and desertion gives one a vicarious sense of shame.
>
> . . . Without sharing their ideas, I nonetheless must proclaim my admiration for those franquistas and Falangists who still defend, within the logical evolution of time, those principles for which they

earlier fought bravely in war and peace. And shame rises to my face for those other franquistas and Falangists, for those men of the regime, for those chickens of the system, who sometimes dissimulate what they used to be, at other times deny their own convictions, and besmirch the principles and symbols with which they formerly enriched themselves in order now to align themselves with the change and continue to fill both cheeks in the future. There are some ready to proclaim the most humiliating repentance so long as they can gain a single sentence of praise from those new leftist journals who hand out democratic credentials or impart Red blessings according to their own caprice.

Government plans suffered another severe blow when Herrero Tejedor was suddenly killed in a highway accident in Avila province on 12 June. Though even Herrero could not have made the associations project function for very long, there was no successor in view with his skill, for Franco was extremely wary of Suárez, his vice secretary, whom the Caudillo considered too ambitious and unscrupulous[124] (certainly a correct judgment from Franco's point of view). Suárez's farewell speech in the General Secretariat on 3 July was audacious and outspoken, directly invoking Juan Carlos and "democracy"[125] (though there had been so much double-talk in Spanish government for the past thirty years that the full import of his meaning was doubtless lost on most). Franco selected as the new secretary general the tried and true Solís, who at least would not attempt anything dangerously new. Solís then canceled his predecessor's veto of the new political association to be called Falange Española de las JONS, but he also rejected the old guard's opposition to Suárez as leader of the new UDPE, of which he became "coordinating president" when it was officially constituted on 17 July.

Some time after this, Suárez visited the aged Caudillo to report on the progress of the new association. According to Suárez's own testimony, Franco remained alert and questioned him privately about whether he believed that the Movement would be able to survive "the death of General Franco," referring in the third person to his own demise. Suárez replied negatively and, when next asked if he thought that Spain faced "an inevitably democratic future," this time responded in the affirmative, after which the aged dictator turned on his heel and ended the interview.[126]

Solís remained more loyal to his Jefe Nacional than most. It was Solís rather than the foreign minister who was dispatched to Rabat on 21 October, as Franco lay on his deathbed, to arrange for bilateral negotiations in the tense dispute over the future of the Spanish Sahara, which played its own role in Franco's final decline. And on the night of his death, "the only minister who remained at the hospital after midnight was the secre-

The last public demonstration on behalf of Franco, October 1975

tary of the Movement, José Solís Ruiz. He spent most of the time weep-ing."[127] To that extent, Franco's insistence on maintaining this artificial organization was repaid in his final hours. The Generalissimo finally died about 3:20 A.M. on 20 November 1975, just a few hours before the thirty-ninth anniversary of the execution at dawn of José Antonio Primo de Rivera.

According to Suárez, even Franco had come to realize in his final weeks that the Movement could not survive his passing. Only he had sustained it for the past three decades. With the reorganization of the Arias govern-ment in a much more aperturista direction under the monarchy of Juan Carlos, the young but nonetheless veteran Movement politician now took over the ministry. This was the beginning of the end: the last year and a half of the Movement belongs to the history of the democratic transition. With the formation of the first Suárez government in July 1976, the Secre-tary Generalship passed to another veteran of middling years, the pliable Ignacio García López. The function of both the Suárez and the García López administrations as secretary was first to keep the Movement under control during the initial phases of the transition, to use its facilities to a certain extent to facilitate aspects of the democratization process, and later to prepare for its rapid and total dissolution.

All these goals were substantially achieved. The Movement bureaucracy did not serve the democratization as loyally as it had the dictatorship, but aside from a certain amount of criticism in the press did not substantially hamper that process. Franco's absence disarmed members of the state party from more than token opposition. Small minorities of ultras had voted in the Cortes first against the recognition of Juan Carlos as heir and then—in somewhat greater numbers—against the crucial Law for Political Reform in November 1976. In both cases, however, most members of the Movement followed the government's initiative, aware of the complete absence of any practical alternative. The Movement even served the cause of democracy to the extent that it was used in the electoral campaign of March 1977 to hamper the extreme right and assist Suárez's new jerry-built Unión de Centro Democrático, when the UCD suddenly became a much broader and much more democratic version of the UDPE.

The order for the dissolution of the Movement, a useless and contradictory relic under a multiparty democracy, came on 1 April 1977. The great emblematic Yugo y flechas were taken down from the facade of the headquarters building on the calle de Alcalá, and the partido único ceased to exist. Most of the regular functionaries in the General Secretariat were then transferred to other branches of state employment. The Sección Femenina, which filled more useful functions, survived only slightly longer, and Pilar Primo de Rivera was finally replaced as the head of the organization.[128]

The last direct vestiges of the Movement were its publications, many of which continued until they were finally liquidated or sold off in 1982 and 1983, though *Arriba* was terminated in 1979.[129] Moreover, the neo-Falangist and various neofascist or neo-Nazi parties and grouplets fared no better under democracy than had the original Falange in the elections of 1933 or 1936. All combined were never able to reach the 2 percent threshold in direct elections.[130]

In a vague and general sense, neofascism forms a permanent, if absolutely insignificant, political subculture that is expressed at least to a very small degree in almost every country in the world and will probably persist into the next millennium as well. Yet categorical neofascism completely lacks popular appeal, and of itself will never be a decisive force in any modern society of the twenty-first century. Within Spain neofascism has been distinctly weaker than in Italy, the western country with the largest neofascist movement. The weakness of neofascism in Spain is perhaps due in part to the fact that the original fascism was less popular there and in part to the fact that the dictatorship lasted much longer and later there, enduring into a later cultural epoch that had eroded its basis to a large degree even before the dictator died. Thus nostalgic myth has been rather less attractive than in the case of Italy. Residues of franquismo have in minor ways endured in Spain into the 1990s,[131] but the politics of generic neofascism have had extremely little appeal.

# Conclusion

The fascist party in Spain was the longest-lived political organization of its type, surviving in one form or another for forty-six years, from the formation of the JONS in 1931 to the dissolution of the Movement in 1977. By comparison, the Italian party survived for only twenty-six years, and the German party a total of twenty-seven. This longevity stands in inverse proportion to the original strength of the movement, however, for under conditions of normal electoral politics the Italian and German parties became mass movements, and in the German case, particularly, generated a huge following, whereas the Falange was insignificant. In Austria, Hungary, and Romania, fascist parties also gained a large share of the popular vote during the 1930s, whereas the original Falange registered only 0.7 percent of the ballots in Spain in February 1936. Even in neighboring Portugal the National Syndicalist movement enjoyed higher support: given the size of the respective national populations, the Portuguese party at one point in the early 1930s was proportionately nearly eight times as large as its Spanish counterpart.[1] Conditions of mere political crisis, however, were inadequate to win a significant following for the Falange in Spain, where only the incipient collapse of the political system—a collapse that the Falange itself at least in small measure helped to bring about—followed immediately by an intensively mobilized revolutionary civil war, sufficed to expand the Falange into a mass movement.

Some of the reasons for the weakness of fascism in Spain—a weakness that at first persisted even under conditions of crisis—are fairly obvious, being similar to those which underlay the general weakness of nationalism in the country, and were analyzed by Marxist writers such as Luis Araquistain and Joaquín Maurín in 1934 and 1935. In his article in *Foreign Affairs* in April 1934, Araquistain referred to a series of factors missing in Spain: a demobilized mass army, large-scale urban unemployment, a Jewish question, or a recent history of nationalist resentment or imperial ambitions. This analysis was accurate enough as far as it went, though Araquistain himself was disingenuous, for it would be he and his colleagues in the violent, revolutionary sector of socialism who would soon be providing much of the rationale for a Spanish fascism.

His Marxist-Leninist rival Joaquín Maurín would be even more explicit in the following year. Despite having committed the egregious errors inevitable in any form of orthodox Marxist-Leninist analysis, Maurín has continued to hold a deserved reputation as the outstanding Marxist theorist in Spain during the Republican years. In his book *Hacia la segunda revolución* published in Barcelona in 1935,[2] he expressed doubt that any genuine fascism was possible in Spain. Maurín pointed out that the recent experience of the Primo de Rivera dictatorship had inoculated much of the country against any new form of rightist authoritarianism, that in Spain a large part of the lower middle class was politically democratic, that Spanish workers (unlike their counterparts in Italy and Germany) were generally impervious to such appeals, and that the small industrial bourgeoisie seemed to be oriented toward the conventional rightist forces rather than toward a radical fascism. The tiny fascistic elements were themselves somewhat divided, whereas the only mass party of the right, the CEDA, was Catholic and not really fascist (despite all the leftist propaganda about the CEDA's representing "fascism on the march"), and its leader, Gil Robles, was in fact frightened by fascism. Thus in Spain, as in eastern Europe, the counterrevolution would be rightist and military, not fascist, in character.

With the benefit of comparative historical hindsight, it is possible to extend these contemporary analyses. Elsewhere I have suggested that any "retrodictive theory" seeking to account for the relative strength or weakness of fascism in any given country or milieu must consider a series of fundamental cultural, political, social, economic, and international variables.[3] In the case of Spain, for example, none of the cultural factors that would inform a retrodictive theory of fascism was particularly strong or influential. The cultural elites had not experienced a comparatively strong influence from the cultural crisis of the end of the century, which was rather weaker in Spain than in central Europe, France, and Italy; nor were there preexisting, comparatively strong currents of nationalism. The artistic world in Spain provided very little assistance to fascism; whereas in Italy avant-garde culture had nourished nationalism and proto-fascism, in Spain Giménez Caballero was left virtually isolated by the close of the 1920s.

A certain perceived crisis of values existed, but before it would become predominant in Spain there quickly developed a tendency toward polarization between the new values of leftist materialism and the old values of Catholic neotraditionalism, leaving less space in Spain than in some other countries for an alternative radical modernism. Secularization was a strong force by the 1930s, but the sectors who experienced this were largely monopolized by the left, once more leaving little space for a radical, non- or anticlerical fascism of the sort originally preached by Ramiro Ledesma. The dominant historical role of religion had always presented an obstacle to any form of modern secular nationalism in Spain, and when fascism belatedly achieved significance, it would inevitably be mutated and syncretized into a more hybrid "fascismo frailuno" a la española.

Strictly political factors at first seemed more favorable, at least in the abstract, even though the Spanish state was not one of the inexperienced "new states" of central and eastern Europe. In Spain, however, as in most of the latter countries, political democracy was a novel experience, totally unconsolidated, and under the Republic there existed a system of parties that was at one and the same time badly fragmented and, increasingly, gravely polarized. Though the prospects for fascism were weakened by the absence of any previous strongly developed form of nationalism, the threat from the revolutionary left was more real than in most other countries. Conversely, fascist leadership in Spain failed to find new ways to generate support and was unable to find political allies. Ultimately, the party was simply suppressed by a government that no longer maintained civil rights. One of the paradoxes of the historic fascist movements was that their broad cross-class nationalism could only be developed in European countries that had undergone considerable political development, and by the same token they required the relative maintenance of civil liberties in order to become strong enough to gain the strength to triumph. They could not come to power independently in countries that failed to guarantee them civil liberties, either because of a sectarian government of the left (as in Spain on the eve of the Civil War) or because of a rightist or military authoritarianism (as in Austria, Hungary, and Romania, or in Spain after the Civil War began).

One of the main social factors specified by any retrodictive theory of fascism—the existence of grave social tensions—certainly existed in Spain by 1934. Yet other key social factors were lacking. There was, for example, little opportunity for mobilization of workers, who had become strongly organized by leftist groups, and there was scarcely any greater opening among the middle classes as a whole, already mobilized by the liberal and Catholic parties. Neither of these large social sectors substantially altered their political orientation until after the Republic had begun to break down, but the breakdown would produce the imminent onset of civil war, rather than the rise of a dominant fascist movement. Contrary to the situations in Italy, Germany, Hungary, or Romania, prior to the Civil War no new social or political space was available for the mobilization of a broader fascist force. The left remained strong, while the middle classes felt little need to move beyond the established left-liberal, liberal, and Catholic parties. Thus the Spanish party system—however fragmented and ultimately destructive—was nonetheless more sophisticated and developed than in many other European countries and yielded no new space; in Spain the political system broke down, but up to that point the party system proved relatively impervious.

Even the peculiarly intermediate structure of the Spanish economy had an effect, for a system not heavily linked to exports softened the impact of the Depression of 1930, limiting urban unemployment and reducing the pressure on both the middle classes and urban workers. Another factor that reduced the potential of fascist demagogy in Spain was the fact that even though the Depression caused stress and suffering, there was little sense that its causes were purely "exogenous" or that it was a national rather than a class problem. No "proletarian national" theory thus proved attractive in Spain. It was fairly clear that Spain's problems had not been brought on by foreign defeat or even especially by foreign discrimination, and a nationalistic discourse for economic solutions had less appeal than in central or east-central Europe.

Even Spain's modern "pretorian tradition" played a role. Though the Republic had hoped to overcome it altogether, its effect was to create expectations in many quarters that an authoritarian nationalism, to be effective, would almost inevitably have to be led by the military (as indeed proved to be the case in July 1936). Conversely, in countries such as Italy and Germany, the combined level of development was such that the military had generally been superseded as a major variable, and certainly as an independent variable. The situation in Spain was therefore more analogous to that in eastern Europe and in Portugal, where the military remained a significant political power factor, ultimately helping to limit the possibilities of any independent fascist mobilization.

Nothing was more important, as Araquistain pointed out, than neutrality in World War I, which had obviated any wartime mobilization of nationalism as well as such postwar problems as unemployed veterans, prolonged economic costs, or national frustration and irredentism. Given the absence of international and military competition, there could be little in the way of a perceived foreign threat or menace, and no sense that Spain had been overtly humiliated or exploited during the past generation. Resentments about foreign relations certainly existed but never became a predominant factor in political competition. Given the combination of all these factors, no lever existed with which to "nationalize" part of the left. The predominant sense of nationalism that did begin to emerge on the right was not a revolutionary fascist nationalism (in which, by definition, the right would not be interested) but a rightist reaction against the internal threat of the left to the established Spanish structure of nation and society, and against the perceived threat of what was generally called "communism." This strengthened the right and made polarization more acute, but provided no independent opening to fascism until the right finally fell into disarray in the spring of 1936 and civil war loomed on the horizon. But that situation in turn increasingly placed all initiative and power in the hands of the military.

Fascism came to Spain as an import. It was initially embraced by members of the radical intelligentsia, as in other countries, but lacked the cultural and social support to develop. Giménez Caballero made the first major effort to affirm a Spanish fascism, and responded not simply to the original revolutionary national syndicalism of Italian Fascism but to the tentative Italian synthesis of 1928–1932, with its rightist and semi-Catholic compromises, which he tried to Hispanize as the "new Catholicity." "Gece" did not focus on pristine revolutionary fascism, in which he had comparatively little interest. What he did intuit was the greater appropriateness of a hybrid fascism merged with rightism and religion, and to that extent he became the initial prophet not of the more revolutionary Falange but of the hybrid "fascismo frailuno" of the Franco regime.

A full or genuine fascism was thus first articulated by Ramiro Ledesma Ramos, who may be considered a paradigm of the radical intellectual. For Ledesma, fascism was *only* revolutionary, and he sought to draw out the fullest logical consequence of fascist ideas, all the easier for him in that he never had to lead a significant political force of any size. Ledesma recognized that the ideal type of generic fascism existed, abstracted from the common features of the new European revolutionary anticommunist movements, but he also quickly grasped the danger of mimicry, and the need to avoid simply imitating the Italians.

By contrast, the point of departure of José Antonio Primo de Rivera was different, as he sought to vindicate the work of his father and develop the formula for an effective modern nationalist and authoritarian regime. In his case, fascism was less the motivation than the solution, and thus his initial mimetism of 1933 and 1934 became logical and obvious, though ultimately embarrassing. By 1935 he was trying to create a sort of "differentiated fascism" that was less dependent on the Italian model, but while a free man José Antonio never renounced the fundamental fascist principles of extremist nationalism, an authoritarian state, radical national syndicalism, and the three fascist negations—opposition to the collectivist left, the liberal center, and the conservative or reactionary right; nor did he reject fascistic militarism and the preferred orientation toward violence, even though in practice he had sometimes resisted the latter.[4]

The differentiation of or from fascism in the later thinking of José Antonio Primo de Rivera involved the increasing avoidance of the term or concept of totalitarianism and the corporate state as a slogan or formula, though the state remained a "totalitarian instrument" in the Falangist program. Cynics might point out that Adolf Hitler avoided the term "totalitarian" more scrupulously than did José Antonio. Moreover, the attempt to create a sort of fascist humanism with an abstract stress on "man the bearer of eternal values" and the recognition of human personality might have been more promising had this vein of rhetoric enjoyed the slightest development in political theory. But like nearly all of José Antonio's concepts, these remained vague, abstract, and merely formulaic, and were never developed concretely in conjunction with a precise political program or theory. The few scattered critical or negative references to fascism found in his writings expressed little concern over the tyrannical aspects of fascism, but much more over the danger of its being "false" or "inauthentic" as a revolution or transformation.

The main differentiation—incomplete and disconnected—lay in the areas of religion and traditional culture. There was a natural need for fascists everywhere to come to terms with national culture and tradition, but the incorporation of traditional religion and culture was in some sense important for José Antonio, for Redondo, and for many other Falangists, even though largely rejected by the uncompromising revolutionary Ledesma.[5] Yet if José Antonio had been primarily a traditionalist, he would have been a Carlist, whereas in fact he rejected Carlism as inadequate for the twentieth century. Neither was he any sort of neo-Thomist. José Antonio's vaguely invoked concepts never developed into a clear doctrine in which religion and traditional moral and cultural values specifically differentiated Falangism from generic fascism; although he may have wished to do so, this effort remained inchoate and formless, a potential idea, not a developed doctrine. He rejected Giménez Caballero's notion of "the new Catholicity" because its formulation was too rightist, too reminiscent of the compromises and limitations of the Mussolini regime. This orientation nonetheless became very strongly developed under the Franco regime. What José Antonio would have rejected about *franquismo* was not its religiosity so much as its lack of revolutionary content, but he would also probably have been uncomfortable with the extreme clerical quality of its cultural and educational policies as well. There is no doubt that religion and cultural traditionalism were important to him, but he failed to integrate them clearly into political doctrine, or to use the former to control or differentiate the latter in any specific manner.

Since fascist movements so strongly emphasized the roles of elites and of leadership—characteristics fully reflected in the Falange—one must ask whether the leadership of fascism in Spain was inherently deficient. By 1935 José Antonio had established almost uncontested personal dominance within the Falange, but he was never able to exert that leadership effectively in Spanish politics. Given, however, the limited number of "fascistogenic" factors affecting Spanish affairs prior to the outbreak of the Civil War, it is doubtful that a more skilled leadership would have accomplished very much more. The most serious breakdown in José Antonio's political leadership occurred in the negotiations for the elections of 1936, when he proved unable to persuade the other leaders of the party to accept the very limited terms of alliance offered by the CEDA. The resultant Falangist electoral strategy of total independence appealed to revolutionary fascist intransigence and a certain kind of political romanticism dear to the hearts of José Antonio and his associates, but it proved disastrous. It deprived José Antonio of the parliamentary immunity that might have made possible a more effective and continuous leadership of the movement, and that might have guaranteed his own physical survival (though it is likely that, had he not been in prison, José Antonio would have been the primary target of the insubordinate Assault Guards on the night of 12 July).

The poor quality of Falangist leadership during the first year of the Civil War is something about which nearly all commentators agree, and yet again it is not clear that more able directors would have accomplished a great deal more, given the basic realities of total civil war and the complete military and political dictatorship of Franco. The character of Spanish public affairs did not permit a fascist movement the space for mobilization and independent action that would have been required to develop earlier or to triumph politically later. With regard to the possibilities for fascist politics, Spain was more similar to Romania than to Italy or Germany, but even this comparison is inadequate, for by 1937–1938 the Legion of the Archangel Michael had developed a mass following and become the second-largest popular force in the country, something of which the Falange had been totally incapable during peacetime. Its expansion was due exclusively to complete national political breakdown, not to the inherent mobilizing potential of Falangism in other circumstances. Though Falangism was dependent on total crisis, only the military could act decisively to resolve the crisis, and thus the Falange could be subordinated much more easily and effectively under the Franco regime than the

Legionnaire movement under Antonescu in Romania, where direct violent conflict was required. At first a weak fascism in a land of weak nationalism, Falangism always remained a dependent, rather than an independent, variable—dependent first on external financing, second on total external crisis to accelerate mobilization, third on the Franco regime, and fourth and finally on the course of World War II.

At first glance this would seem to substantiate Azaña's observations in his diary on 6 October 1937:

> When they talked of fascism in Spain, my opinion was this: in Spain there are or can be all the fascisms you want. But a fascist regime there will not be. If a movement of force should triumph against the Republic, we would fall into a military and ecclesiastical dictatorship of a traditional type. However many slogans might be translated and however many mottoes might be used. Sabers, chasubles, military parades, and homages to the Virgen del Pilar. In that direction, this country does not offer anything else. Now they are seeing it. Late. And with a difficult adjustment.[6]

But Azaña's political analyses, though superficially plausible, were usually mistaken in one or more major respects. In this case, he seems to be defining the Franco regime as "a military and ecclesiastical dictatorship of a traditional type." To exactly what "traditional type" would this refer? The only possible candidate would be the Primo de Rivera regime. Franco certainly drew inspiration from the first Spanish dictatorship, but to conceive of Franco as a second Primo de Rivera is profoundly mistaken. Franco was much more radical, much more sanguinary, and much more authoritarian, determined to create a lasting regime of the twentieth century. He incarnated a new Spanish radical right that was more innovative and vigorous than Azaña gave it credit for. The Franco regime would not seek to embrace tradition fully until after a gigantic world war had been fought and lost by its preferred allies.

This does not mean that Franco was ever a generic fascist *sensu strictu*. More than twenty years after his death, Franco has still eluded precise definition save in the vague and general categories of "dictator" and "authoritarian." Thus scarcely any of the serious historians and analysts of Franco consider the Generalissimo to have been a core fascist. Paul Preston, never known to give Franco the benefit of the doubt, once observed at a scholarly conference in Madrid, "Franco no era un fascista sino algo mucho peor" (Franco was not a fascist but something much worse). Compared, for example, with paradigmatic Italian Fascism, the Franco of the first ten years of the regime, having come to power by means of a ruthless civil war, was much more violent, autocratic, and repressive in every respect—politically, culturally, socially, and economically.

Franco's political style, though always retaining fundamental principles of authoritarianism, nationalism, traditionalism, and Catholicism, was always eclectic. He demonstrated no interest in Falangism before the Civil War, but devoted his political attention to the CEDA and was raised to the highest military posts by Radicals and the CEDA. Soon after the beginning of the Civil War, he picked up the language of "totalitarianism" and an ad hoc model of charismatic leadership to develop an authoritarian new system with its own *partido único*. The nearest thing to a paradigm was Mussolini's Italy; but while retaining the Twenty-Six Points as the doctrine of the FET in 1937, he explicitly recognized the goal of a more broadly syncretistic amalgam of Falangism and other doctrines of the right, flanked by and to a completely ambiguous degree mediated by a strongly traditional and authoritarian form of Catholicism. In comparative political analysis, all this was no more than "semifascist."[7]

Somewhat paradoxically, the weakness and subordination of Falangism, with the peculiar syncretism and compromises decreed by Franco—those very factors most vituperated by radical *camisas viejas*—were the qualities required for its longevity. A truly revolutionary and independent fascism might have undermined Franco's war effort, producing the triumph of the Republic and the end of fascism in Spain,[8] or else it could have resulted in a subsequent rebellion that might have required the total suppression of the movement by Franco, much as Antonescu had to eliminate the Legion in Romania completely after its armed revolt of January 1941.

The one FET institution that became better developed than its Italian counterpart was the Sección Femenina. Though the girls' organization was never as extensive as its counterpart in Italy, the adult Sección Femenina was more extensive and more active. Thus it merits the attention it has received from historians in recent years, generating more new bibliography than any other Falangist institution. Yet the relative success of the Sección Femenina was not due to its fascism, for ideologically and politically it was distinctly less fascist than either the Italian Fasci Femminili or the much larger National Socialist Frauenschaft. More than the male party, the Sección Femenina exhibited a culture of Catholic traditionalism even though expressed in original forms of mobilization.

Franco was never a "core fascist" or a genuine Falangist, and never personally espoused or gave any priority to all the goals of the Falangists and their Twenty-Six Points, but his political orientation was definitely pro-fascist. During the second half of the Civil War, perhaps partly under the influence of Serrano Súñer, his thinking and language moved farther in the direction of fascism,[9] a trend only encouraged by the outcome of the first phases of World War II and also by the tensions and frustrations encountered in negotiations with the Papacy between 1939 and 1941. A process had thus been begun whose result would be determined not merely by the outcome of the Spanish conflict but also by the results of the world war in Europe.

Moreover, the core Falangists largely dominated the FET, and the chief opportunity for the triumph of Falangism came not during the Civil War but during the three years that followed—the high water mark of fascist domination in Europe. Nearly all the activist Falangists during World War II were fully identified with the Axis powers, even though many of them sought in certain respects to differentiate Falangism from National Socialism. Though the regime did not go beyond nonbelligerence, its basic position was, in Tusell's words, "much more for the Axis than was Finland,"[10] a country that had openly entered the war on the German side against the Soviet Union. Even during this period, however, Franco's personal authority and power were so great that any complete Falangist takeover per se remained only the most remote of possibilities, for the anti-Falangist military always remained loyal to Franco. Thus only the basically exogenous factor of a complete triumph by the Axis in World War II could have brought about a more genuine and thorough process of fascistization in Spain.

The creation of the FET in 1937 had first established the inherently contradictory goal of syncretism between a form of fascism and Catholic traditionalism, though the complete transition to a watered-down fascismo frailuno was only carried forward in the later phases of the world war. For the remainder of the long history of the FET, the latent contradiction within the doctrines of founders such as José Antonio and Onésimo Redondo was resolved—to the extent that it could be resolved—more and more in favor of an authoritarian form of Catholic corporatism and cultural neotraditionalism.

The National Movement that survived for more than three decades after the end of the world war is most accurately described as an increasingly postfascist partido único. It kept one foot anchored in historic fascism, did not receive a fully postfascist program until 1958, and scarcely completed its full defascistization until the very last years of Franco's life, if then. Yet it had been forced by the unalterable consequences of world history to abandon any effort to realize a genuinely fascist program after 1943, and served merely the political and bureaucratic convenience of an aging dictator, determined to avoid "el error Primo de Rivera" (perhaps the main root similarity between José Antonio and Franco), and ever hoping to leave a structured system behind him. Falangism lived on as no more than an ambiguous residue, a consequence of the idiosyncrasies of national history, as contrasted with world history, and of the longevity of a dictator from an increasingly distant era. Even more than the regime itself, the Movement had lost its cultural and social basis long before the physical death of Franco. All this has tended historically and historiographically to obscure the fact that native fascism was extremely weak in Spain, whose political culture and historical development prior to the Civil War had generated fewer fascistogenic qualities than most other European countries.

*Notes*

*Index*

# Notes

PREFACE

1. Particularly interesting are the private remarks the leading Falangist intellectual Antonio Tovar expressed in a letter to Pilar Primo de Rivera of 20 January 1962, published in the latter's *Recuerdos de una vida* (Madrid, 1983), 388–89.

CHAPTER ONE

1. The best study is J. A. Maravall, *El concepto de España en la Edad Media* (Madrid, 1954).

2. To use the words of M. Díaz-Andreu, "The Past in the Present: The Search for Roots in Cultural Nationalism. The Spanish Case," in *Nationalism in Europe: Past and Present*, ed. J. G. Beramendi et al., 2 vols. (Santiago de Compostela, 1994), I, 199–218.

3. B. de Riquer and E. Ucelay Da Cal, "An Analysis of Nationalisms in Spain: A Proposal for an Integrated Historical Model," ibid., II, 275–301.

4. In my *Spanish Catholicism* (Madison, 1984).

5. See, for example, J. Mercader i Riba, *Felip V i Catalunya* (Barcelona, 1968).

6. B. J. Feijóo, *Teatro crítico universal* (Madrid, 1986), 235.

7. See J. Demerson, "Cadalso y la política," in *Historia y pensamiento: Homenaje a Luis Díez del Corral*, 2 vols. (Madrid, 1987), I, 203; and J. A. Maravall, "El sentimiento de nación en el siglo XVIII: La obra de Forner," in his *Estudios de la historia del pensamiento español (Siglo XVIII)* (Madrid, 1991), 31–55.

8. In the work of Martínez Marina and Sempere y Guarinos.

9. See the observations by J. P. Fusi Aizpurúa, "Centralismo y localismo: La formación del Estado español," in *Nación y Estado en la España liberal*, ed. G. Gortázar (Madrid, 1994), 77–90.

10. The literature is, of course, enormous. A good recent summary and analysis may be found in T. Mitchell, *Blood Sport: A Social History of Spanish Bullfighting* (Philadelphia, 1991), 47–81.

11. At the level of political philosophy see J. Herrero, *Los orígenes del pensamiento reaccionario español* (Madrid, 1982).

12. Cf. L. Roure i Aulinas, *Guerra gran a la ratlla de França* (Barcelona, 1993).

13. B. de Riquer and E. Ucelay da Cal, "An Analysis of Nationalisms in Spain: A Proposal for an Integrated Historical Model," in Beramendi et al., *Nationalism in Europe: Past and Present*, III, 275–301, and also B. de Riquer, "L'espanyolisme durant el segle XIX," in *IIIes Jornades de Debat: Origens i formació dels nacionalismes a Espanya* (Reus, 1994), 245–61. See also J. L. Abellán, *Historia crítica del pensamiento español*, IV: *Liberalismo y romanticismo* (Madrid, 1984).

14. The best study is C. P. Boyd, *Historia Patria: Politics, History, and National Identity in Spain 1875–1975* (Princeton, 1997).

15. Cf. J. M. Jover, "Caracteres del nacionalismo español 1854–1874," *Zona Abierta* 31 (1984), 1–22.

16. These shortcomings are discussed in J. Alvarez Junco, "El nacionalismo español" (manuscript).

17. This is clearly brought out in J. Fernández Sebastián, *La genesis del fuerismo: Prensa e ideas políticas en la crisis del Antiguo Régimen (País Vasco, 1750–1840)* (Madrid, 1991).

18. Cf. L. Alier y Sala, *El partido carlista y la revolución española* (Barcelona, 1872).

19. As in *La Reconquista,* 16 Jan. 1873, cited in V. Garmendia, "Carlismo y nacionalismo(s) en la época de la ultima guerra carlista," in *Las guerras carlistas,* ed. A. Bullón de Mendoza (Madrid, 1993), 103–12.

20. F. Pi y Margall, *Las nacionalidades* (Madrid, 1877), 322–23.

21. See G. Trujillo, *Introducción al federalismo español* (Madrid, 1967); and J. M. Jover Zamora, "Federalismo en España: Cara y cruz de una experiencia histórica," in Gortázar, *Nación y Estado en la España liberal,* 105–67. The relationship of subsequent republican thought to nationalism is treated in A. de Blas Guerrero, *Tradición republicana y nacionalismo español* (Madrid, 1991).

22. J. A. Rocamora, *El nacionalismo ibérico* (Valladolid, 1994).

23. Cf. E. Yllán Calderón, *Cánovas del Castillo: Entre la historia y la política* (Madrid, 1985), and "Historia y nación en Cánovas del Castillo," in *Estudios históricos: Homenaje a los profesores José María Jover Zamora y Vicente Palacio Atard* (Madrid, 1990), I, 137–59.

24. C. Dardé, "Cánovas y el nacionalismo liberal español," in Gortázar, *Nación y Estado en la España liberal,* 209–38.

25. See A. Santovena Setién, *Marcelino Menéndez Pelayo: Revisión crítico-biográfica de un pensador católico* (Santander, 1994); and P. Laín Entralgo, *Menéndez Pelayo: Historia de sus problemas intelectuales* (Madrid, 1944).

26. In Stendhal's *Mémoires d'un touriste* (1838), quoted in T. Mitchell, *Flamenco Deep Song* (New Haven, 1994), 112. This latter work provides one of the best brief treatments of the myth of romantic Spain.

27. L.-F. Hoffmann, *Romantique Espagne: L'Image de l'Espagne en France entre 1800 et 1850* (Paris, 1961); M. Bernal Rodríguez, *La Andalucía de los libros de viajes del siglo XIX* (Seville, 1985); A. González Troyano, *La desventura de Carmen: Una divagación sobre Andalucía* (Madrid, 1991). For a good brief summary, Mitchell, *Flamenco Deep Song,* 111–25.

28. See the quotation in the classic study by P. Laín Entralgo, *La Generación del Noventa y Ocho* (Madrid, 1945), 196.

29. J. Ortega y Gasset, *España invertebrada* (Madrid, 1922), 32–33.

30. *Obras completas* (Madrid, 1983), I, 299.

31. See the excellent brief discussion of Ortega and nationalism in A. de Blas Guerrero, *Sobre el nacionalismo español* (Madrid, 1989), 59–75.

32. For a general discussion of attitudes in the early twentieth century, J. Marías, "La identidad de España," in *La Edad de Plata de la cultura española*, ed. P. Laín Entralgo, 2 vols. (Madrid, 1993), I, 57–128, is very useful.

33. See V. Garmendia, *La ideología carlista (1868–1876): En los orígenes del nacionalismo vasco* (San Sebastián, 1984).

34. I. Molas, *Lliga Catalana*, 2 vols. (Barcelona, 1972), is the principal study, but for the early years see B. de Riquer, *Lliga Regionalista (1898–1904)* (Barcelona, 1977).

35. See Prat's classic *La nacionalitat catalana* (Barcelona, 1906), and the study by J. Solé Tura, *Catalanisme i revolució burgesa: La síntesi de Prat de la Riba* (Barcelona, 1967).

36. Of the many works on Cambó, the most thorough is J. Pabón, *Cambó*, 3 vols. (Barcelona, 1952–69). Later, during the crisis of 1930, the concept of a federal imperialism was advanced once more by Joaquim Pellicena in his lecture *El nostre imperialisme (la idea imperial de Prat de la Riba)* (Barcelona, 1930).

CHAPTER TWO

1. This aspect of the Regenerationist literature has been brought out most strongly in E. Tierno Galván, *Costa y el Regeneracionismo* (Barcelona, 1961).

2. As Vasco Pulido Valente has written:

> Both D. Luis and D. Carlos were besieged by candidates to be dictator. In the decade of the 1880s by the group of Oliveira Martins, which claimed to represent "New Life." In the decade of the 1890s by the "rectifiers" of Franco and Lopo d'Avila, so called because they proposed to "rectify" matters. Later by the would-be "hero of Chamite" and the "africanist" officers, in Mouzinho de Albuquerque. And even the head of the Republican Party, José Falcão, at a certain point encouraged D. Carlos to carry out a revolution "from above" in order to "save" the Fatherland."

*O poder e o povo* (Lisbon, 1982), 20. Among the Republicans, perhaps the most insistent was Basilio Teles, as in his *Do Ultimatum ao 31 de Janeiro* (Porto, 1905).

3. J. M. Sardica, *A dupla face do franquismo na crise da monarquia portuguesa* (Lisbon, 1994).

4. See Carlos Ferrão, *O Integralismo e a Republica*, 3 vols. (Lisbon, 1964–65).

5. M. Braga da Cruz, *As origens da democracia cristã e o salazarismo* (Lisbon, 1980).

6. On these groups, see A. J. Telo, *Decadência e queda da I Republica*, 2 vols. (Lisbon, 1980), I, 49–103, 249–55. In this book "Fascism" will be capitalized

when referring to the Italian Fascist Party or regime, while "fascist" and "fascism" are used in a broader and more generic sense.

7. J. Canal, "Republicanos y carlistas contra el Estado: Violencia política en la España finisecular," in *Violencia y política en España,* ed. J. Aróstegui (Madrid, 1994), summarizes what little there was of organized efforts at political violence in Spain outside of the anarchist left during the latter part of the century.

8. On both the theorists and the citizens' groups, see E. González Calleja and F. Del Rey Reguillo, *La defensa armada contra la revolución: Una historia de las "guardias cívicas" en la España del siglo XX* (Madrid, 1995); and González Calleja's "La defensa armada del 'orden social' durante la Dictadura de Primo de Rivera 1923–1930," in *España entre dos siglos (1875–1931),* ed. J. L. García Delgado (Madrid, 1991), 61–108.

9. The scholarly literature on this is generally weak, but see J. León-Ignacio, *Los años del pistolerismo* (Barcelona, 1981).

10. The definitive study is C. Winston, *Workers and the Right in Spain, 1900–1936* (Princeton, 1985).

11. There are numerous works on Maura. The best accounts are J. Tusell and J. Avilés, *La derecha española contemporánea. Sus orígenes: El maurismo* (Madrid, 1986); C. Robles, *Antonio Maura* (Madrid, 1995); and, for Maura's ideas, Tusell, *Antonio Maura: Una biografía política* (Madrid, 1994).

12. E. Ucelay da Cal, "Estat Català: The Strategies of Separation and Revolution of Catalan Radical Nationalism (1919–1933)" (Ph.D. diss., Columbia University, 1979), 98–102.

13. On the Liga Monárquica, see I. De Loyola Arana Pérez, *El monarquismo en Vizcaya durante la crisis del reinado de Alfonso XIII (1917–1931)* (Pamplona, 1982); and J. de Ybarra, *Política nacional en Vizcaya* (Madrid, 1948), 541–72.

14. It might also be mentioned that a few individual voices in the Cortes, such as that of the independent Conservative Joaquín Sanchez de Toca, spoke of the need for extrademocratic measures, stronger discipline, and a nationalist program in both politics and economics.

15. Quoted in E. Ucelay da Cal, "Vanguardia, fascismo y la interacción entre nacionalismo español y catalán," in *Los nacionalismos en la España de la II República,* ed. J. Beramendi and R. Maíz (Madrid, 1991), 39–95.

16. V. Panyella, *J. V. Foix: 1918 i la Idea Catalana* (Barcelona, 1989), 108–9.

17. Panyella, who has provided the best study of Foix's political ideas, points out that the legend of "el foixista feix" [*sic*] persisted well into the 1930s. Foix's subsequent distinguished achievement in Catalan poetry was of course much more important than his brief foray into politics. See M. Guerrero, *J. V. Foix, investigador en poesía* (Barcelona, 1996).

18. Ucelay da Cal, "Estat Català," 1–473; K.-J. Nagel, *Arbeiterschaft und nationale Frage in Katalonien zwischen 1898 und 1923* (Saarbrücken, 1991), 450–556.

19. See A. Joaniquet, *Alfonso Sala* (Madrid, 1955).

20. See S. Bengoechea Echaondo and F. Del Rey Reguillo, "En vísperas de un golpe de Estado: Radicalización patronal e imagen del fascismo en España," in

*Estudios sobre la derecha española contemporánea,* ed. J. Tusell et al. (Madrid, 1993), 301–26; and J. Del Castillo and S. Alvarez, *Barcelona: Objetivo cubierto* (Barcelona, 1958), 115–22.

21. The best general treatment of the politics of the modern military is C. Seco Serrano, *Militarismo y civilismo en la España contemporánea* (Madrid, 1984). See also G. Cardona, *El poder militar en la Espana contemporánea hasta la Guerra Civil* (Madrid, 1983).

22. This is well treated in R. Núñez Florencio, *Utopistas y revolucionarios en 1900* (Madrid, 1994).

23. For the early twentieth century, see C. Boyd, *Pretorian Politics in Liberal Spain* (Chapel Hill, 1979).

24. D. Woolman, *Rebels in the Riff* (Stanford, 1968).

25. T. Trice, *Spanish Liberalism in Crisis: A Study of the Liberal Party during Spain's Parliamentary Collapse, 1919–1923* (New York, 1991).

26. Gen. M. Primo de Rivera y Orbaneja, *Cuestión del día: Gibraltar y Africa* (Cádiz, 1917), is an earlier discourse that helps to explain Primo's reputation as an "abandonista."

27. There is no satisfactory biography of Miguel Primo de Rivera. The best succinct sketch of the immediate Primo de Rivera family will be found in J. Gil Pecharromán's biography of his more famous son, *José Antonio Primo de Rivera: Retrato de un visionario* (Madrid, 1996), 17–60. The best account of his personality is J. Capella, *La verdad de Primo de Rivera* (Madrid, 1933). Other sketches are admiring apologias: E. R. Tarduchy, *Psicología del Dictador* (Madrid, 1930); E. Aunós, *Primo de Rivera, soldado y gobernante* (Madrid, 1944); F. Cimadevilla, *El general Primo de Rivera* (Madrid, 1944); M. Herrero García, *El general D. Miguel Primo de Rivera* (Madrid, 1947); C. González Ruano, *El general D. Miguel Primo de Rivera* (Madrid, 1954); and A. De Sagrera, *Miguel Primo de Rivera: El hombre, el soldado y el político* (Jerez, 1973), which concentrates on his earlier years. Most of his writings and pronouncements as dictator are collected in *El pensamiento de Primo de Rivera: Sus notas, artículos y discursos* (Madrid, 1929).

28. According to Primo de Rivera's own account in his *La obra de la Dictadura* (Madrid, 1930), 12–13.

29. The key study of the background of the pronunciamiento is J. Tusell, *Radiografía de un golpe de Estado: El ascenso al poder del General Primo de Rivera* (Madrid, 1987).

30. This and other basic documents may be found in M. C. García-Nieto et al., eds., *Bases documentales de la España contemporánea,* VII: *La Dictadura, 1923–1930* (Madrid, 1973).

31. The membership of 250,000 that it eventually claimed is open to some doubt. See González Calleja, "Defensa armada."

32. The chief political history of the Dictadura is J. Tusell, "La Dictadura regeneracionista," in *Historia de España,* ed. R. Menéndez Pidal (Madrid, 1995), XXXVIII:2, 131–623, while S. Ben Ami, *Fascism from Above: The Dictatorship of Primo de Rivera in Spain* (Oxford, 1983), is an excellent general account. J. L. Gómez-Navarro, *El régimen de Primo de Rivera* (Madrid, 1991), presents a useful

political, institutional, and comparative analysis. For the Military Directory, see M. T. González Calbet, *La Dictadura de Primo de Rivera: El Directorio Militar* (Madrid, 1987).

33. S. E. Fleming, *Primo de Rivera and Abd-el-Krim: The Struggle in Spanish Morocco, 1923–1927* (New York, 1991).

34. S. Sueiro Seoane, *España en el Mediterráneo: Primo de Rivera y la "Cuestión Marroquí,"* *1923–1930* (Madrid, 1992).

35. Quoted in *Dos años de Directorio Militar,* ed. Marqués de Cáceres (Madrid, 1926), 2–5.

36. G. Maura Gamazo, *Bosquejo histórico de la Dictadura* (Madrid, 1930), 51–52.

37. Quoted in F. Duarte, *España: Miguel Primo de Rivera* (Madrid, 1923), 197–98; cited in Ben Ami, *Fascism from Above,* 132.

38. Quoted in Capella, *Verdad de Primo de Rivera,* 19.

39. *El Debate,* 1 Dec. 1923, quoted in González Calbet, *La Dictadura,* 131.

40. N. González Ruiz and I. Martín Martínez, *Seglares en la historia del catolicismo español* (Madrid, 1968), 111–33.

41. *Pensamiento de Primo de Rivera,* 109.

42. González Ruiz and Martín Martínez, *Seglares en la historia,* 133.

43. The best accounts of the UP will be found in Ben Ami, *Fascism from Above,* 126–68; and in Gómez-Navarro, *El régimen,* 207–60. See also articles by G. Alvarez Chillida, F. J. Cabrera Rayo, A. M. Cervera Sánchez, F. F. Pérez Ortiz, and M. Requena Gallego in Tusell, *Estudios sobre la derecha española contemporánea,* 327–92.

44. Here see once more the analysis in Gómez-Navarro, *El régimen,* 207–60.

45. The most extensive exposition of the UP's ideas will be found in J. M. Pemán, *El hecho y la idea de la Unión Patriótica* (Madrid, 1929).

46. *La Nación,* 9 Aug. 1928, cited in Ben Ami, *Fascism from Above,* 192.

47. *La Nación,* 11 Aug. 1928, cited ibid.

48. *La Nación,* 6 Dec. 1928, cited ibid.

49. G. Palomares Lerma, *Mussolini y Primo de Rivera: Política exterior de dos dictadores* (Madrid, 1989); and J. Tusell and I. Saz, "Mussolini y Primo de Rivera: Las relaciones politicas y diplomáticas de dos dictaduras mediterráneas," *Boletín de la Real Academia de la Historia* 179 (1982), 413–83.

50. See G. Redondo, *Las empresas políticas de José Ortega y Gasset* (Madrid, 1970), vol. II.

51. Cf. C. Navajas Zubeldía, "La ideología corporativa de Miguel Primo de Rivera," *Hispania* 53 (1993), 617–49.

52. Pemán, *El hecho,* 113.

53. Cf. J. Pemartín, *Los valores históricos en la Dictadura* (Madrid, 1929), 637.

54. J. Calvo Sotelo, *Mis servicios al Estado* (Madrid, 1931), 331.

55. *La Nación,* 6 Aug. 1927.

56. Ibid.

57. Quoted in J. Pabón, *Cambó,* 3 vols. (Barcelona, 1952–69), II, 548.

58. Ben Ami, *Fascism from Above,* 202.

59. J. Velarde Fuertes, *Política económica de la Dictadura*, rev. ed. (Madrid, 1973).

60. Ben Ami, *Fascism from Above*, 242.

61. Ibid., 286.

62. For further discussion of social and economic policies, see J. H. Rial, *Revolution from Above: The Primo de Rivera Dictatorship in Spain, 1923–1930* (Fairfax, Va., 1986), 133–234.

63. E. Aunós, *La política social de la Dictadura* (Madrid, 1944), 58–59.

64. The text of the decree and Aunós's own explanation are given in his booklet *Organisation corporative nationale* (Madrid, 1927).

65. Aunós, *Política social*, 64. He elaborated his concepts further in his *La organizaación corporativa del trabajo* (Madrid, 1928); *Las corporaciones del trabajo en el estado moderno* (Madrid, 1928); and *El Estado corporativo* (Madrid, 1929).

66. See J. Andrés-Gallego, *El socialismo durante la Dictadura (1923–1930)* (Madrid, 1976).

67. According to figures given by Aunós in a speech of 3 May 1929, published in his *La organización corporativa y su posible desenvolvimiento* (Madrid, 1929).

68. Aunós, *Política social*, 86–89.

69. Calvo Sotelo, *Mis servicios*, 336.

70. See M. Gómez, *La reforma constitucional en la España de la Dictadura* (Valencia, 1930); and M. García Canales, *El problema constitucional de la Dictadura* (Madrid, 1980).

71. On the failure of Primo de Rivera's efforts at new political institutionalization, see Ben Ami, *Fascism from Above*, 209–39; and Tusell, "La Dictadura regeneracionista," 523–53.

72. Quoted in Tusell, "La Dictadura regeneracionista," 536.

73. Ibid.

74. Quoted ibid., 537.

75. Ibid., 352–53.

76. Tusell and Saz, "Mussolini y Primo de Rivera," 482–83.

77. Quoted in C. Fernández, *El general Franco* (Barcelona, 1983), 43.

78. E. Aunós, *Semblanza política del general Primo de Rivera* (Madrid, n.d.), 28–29.

79. Ben Ami, *Fascism from Above*, 402.

80. On the military under the Dictatorship, see C. Navajas Zubeldía, *Ejército, Estado y sociedad en España (1923–1930)* (Logroño, 1991).

81. Gómez-Navarro, *El régimen*, 531.

82. Cf. R. De Felice, *Mussolini il Duce* (Turin, 1974), I, 131.

83. These distinctions were clearly seen by the author of the only near-contemporary study that I have found, Wolfgang Scholz's *Die Lage des spanischen Staates vor der Revolution (unter Berucksichtigung ihres Verhältnisses zum italienischen Fascismus)* [sic] (Dresden, 1932). Scholz correctly noted that although both countries were underdeveloped, Spain was distinctly more so and had a tradition of military pretorianism to which Primo could be related. He further observed that the equivalent "idea world" of Fascism was lacking in Spain.

There existed in Italy a broader Fascist culture that enjoyed considerable support from the intelligentsia. In Spain, practically the entire intelligentsia had turned against the Dictatorship by the late 1920s.

Probably the only sophisticated commentary on Italian Fascism written in Spain under the Dictatorship is in two works by the Catalan statesman Francesc Cambó: *Entorn del feixisme italià* (Barcelona, 1925), originally a series of newspaper articles published in *La Veu de Catalunya* in mid–1924, followed by a broader and more comparative book-length essay, *Las Dictaduras* (Barcelona, 1929). In his 1924 articles, Cambó shrewdly observed that what was beginning to develop as the ideology of Fascism was produced at least partly ex post facto, organized in a more conservative context and often in sharp contrast to some of Mussolini's own pre-1922 ideas. Writing at the time of the Matteotti crisis in Italy and soon after a personal interview with Mussolini, Cambó expressed doubt that Fascism would be more than a temporary counterrevolutionary force. In his subsequent book, Cambó put forward a theory of dictatorship as a consequence of relative backwardness and as a strictly transitory response to current problems. Finally, he emphasized one of the worst dilemmas caused by temporary dictatorships created to deal with specific crises: the difficulty of finding simple and inexpensive means of bringing them to an end and completing the transition back to representative government. There is further commentary by P. V. Cannistraro and J. W. Cortada, "Francisco Cambó and the Modernization of Spain: The Technocratic Possibilities of Fascism," *Review of Politics* 37 (Jan. 1975), 66–82. "El Capitan Centellas," in *Las Dictaduras y el senor Cambó* (Madrid, 1929), presented a reply from the regime's viewpoint.

The two principal Spanish Marxist critiques of the regime were by Andrés Nin, *Las dictaduras de nuestro tiempo* (Madrid, 1930); and Joaquín Maurín, *Los hombres de la Dictadura* (Madrid, 1930).

84. S. Ben Ami, "The Forerunners of Spanish Fascism: Unión Patriótica and Unión Monárquica," *Journal of Contemporary History* 9 (Jan. 1979), 49–79.

85. The PNE was more committed to the fascist style than was the UMN, engaging in several street disturbances in Madrid by the spring of 1931. Its membership was mainly lower-middle-class. "Of the first three hundred affiliates, 82 were white-collar employees, 20 were small businessmen, and 26 skilled workers, compared with 17 industrialists, 8 lawyers, and 5 professors. Many of the members were veterans of the Spanish Legion in Morocco." J. Gil Pecharromán, "Albiñana, el rey de los ultras," *Historia 16* 45 (Jan. 1980), 32.

On the PNE, see M. Pastor, *Los orígenes del fascismo en España* (Madrid, 1975), 38–61; J. J. Jiménez Campo, *El fascismo en la crisis de la Segunda República española* (Madrid, 1979), 78–83; Gil Pecharromán, *Conservadores subversivos: La derecha autoritaria alfonsina (1931–1936)* (Madrid, 1994), 67–73, 105–7; and L. Palacios Buñuelos, *Elecciones en Burgos, 1931–1936: El Partido Nacionalista Español* (Madrid, 1981).

86. J. Estelrich, *La qüestió de les minories nacionals* (Barcelona, 1929).

87. J. M. Gil Robles, *No fue posible la paz* (Barcelona, 1968), 79.

88. The most thorough study is J. R. Montero, *La CEDA*, 2 vols. (Madrid, 1977). R. A. H. Robinson has presented the most scholarly positive evaluation of

the CEDA in *The Origins of Franco's Spain* (London, 1970); and Paul Preston the most searing indictment in *The Coming of the Spanish Civil War,* rev. ed. (London, 1995).

89. Quoted in Robinson, *The Origins,* 118, 124.

90. Ibid., 115.

91. *ABC* (Madrid), 17 Oct. 1933. See also Montero, *CEDA,* II, 249–55.

92. See O. Alzaga, *La primera democracia cristiana en España* (Barcelona, 1973).

93. P. C. González Cuevas, *Acción Española: Teología política y nacionalismo autoritario en España (1913–1936)* (Madrid, 1998), is the most thorough ideological study; but see R. Morodo, *Orígenes ideológicos del franquismo* (Madrid, 1985).

94. An inventory of backers is presented in Morodo, *Orígenes,* 65–73.

95. One of the first statements of this critique was Victor Pradera's *Al servicio de la Patria: Las ocasiones perdidas* (Madrid, 1930).

96. *Obra de Ramiro de Maeztu* (Madrid, 1974), and, more concretely, *Frente a la República* (Madrid, 1955), an anthology of his writings from these years. The principal studies are Vicente Marrero, *Maeztu* (Madrid, 1955), and, more briefly, Ricardo Landeira, *Ramiro de Maeztu* (Boston, 1978). Douglas Foard presents a lucid overview in "Ramiro de Maeztu y el fascismo," *Historia 16* (May 1979), 106–16.

97. The principal account is Gil Pecharromán, *Conservadores subversivos,* 91–126.

98. The basic study for this period is M. Blinkhorn, *Carlism and Crisis in Spain, 1931–1939* (London, 1975), 1–206. A Carlist narrative will be found in L. Redondo and J. Zavala, *El Requeté* (Barcelona, 1957), 225–310.

99. A. Madureira, *O 28 de maio* (Lisbon, 1978).

100. A. Costa Pinto, "The Radical Right and the Military Dictatorship in Portugal: The National May 28 League (1928–1933)," *Luso-Brazilian Review* 23:1 (1986), 1–16.

101. D. Wheeler, *A ditadura militar portuguesa (1926–1933)* (Lisbon, 1986).

102. M. Braga da Cruz, *O partido e o estado no salarismo* (Lisbon, 1988).

103. The phrase is derived in part from Marcello Caetano, last leader of the regime, and is developed in M. Braga da Cruz, "Notas para uma caracterização política do salazarismo," *Análise Social 72* (1982), 897–926. The principal history of the Salazar regime is *O Estado Novo (1926–1974)* by Fernando Rosas, which constitutes volume 7 of the *História de Portugal* edited by J. Mattoso (Lisbon, 1994). Good brief accounts will be found in T. Gallagher, *Portugal: A Twentieth-Century Interpretation* (Manchester, 1983), 38–190; and R. A. H. Robinson, *Contemporary Portugal* (London, 1979), 32–193. The two broadest treatments of Portuguese corporatism are M. De Lucena, *A evolução do sistema corporativo português,* 2 vols. (Lisbon, 1976); and H. J. Wiarda, *Corporatism and Development: The Portuguese Experience* (Amherst, 1977); but see P. C. Schmitter, *Corporatism and Public Policy in Authoritarian Portugal* (Beverly Hills, 1975). The best collection of recent studies will be found in *O Estado Novo,* 2 vols. (Lisbon, 1987). Antonio Costa Pinto provides an excellent analysis

of the diverse interpretations of the Portuguese regime in O *salazarismo e o fascismo europeu: Problemas de interpretação nas ciencias sociais* (Lisbon, 1992).

CHAPTER THREE

1. J.-C. Mainer, *La Edad de Plata (1902–1939)* (Madrid, 1987), 245–46.
2. The only critical biography that deals with the political aspects of his career is D. W. Foard, *The Revolt of the Aesthetes: Ernesto Giménez Caballero and the Origins of Spanish Fascism* (New York, 1989). (The Spanish edition, translated by Giménez Caballero himself, is less complete and less trustworthy.) See also E. Selva Roca de Togores, "Giménez Caballero en los orígenes ideológicos del fascismo español," in *Estudis d'història contemporània del País Valencià* (Valencia, 1982), 183–213.

   On *La Gaceta Literaria*, see the works of M. A. Hernando, *La Gaceta Literaria (1927–1932)* (Valladolid, 1974), and *La prosa vanguardista en la generación del 27 (Gece y La Gaceta Literaria)* (Madrid, 1975); C. Bassols, *La ideología de los escritores: Literatura y política en la Gaceta Literaria (1927–1932)* (Barcelona, 1975); studies by L. Tandy and M. Sferazza in *Giménez Caballero y la Gaceta Literaria* (Madrid, 1977); and M. L. López-Vidriero, *Bibliografía de E. Giménez Caballero* (Madrid, 1982).
3. E. Giménez Caballero, *Cartas marruecas* (Barcelona, 1983), 187.
4. E. Giménez Caballero, *Circuito imperial* (Madrid, 1929), 48–49.
5. *ABC*, 30 Aug. 1923, quoted in Selva Roca de Togores, "Giménez Caballero," 196.
6. For the transition of 1929–1930, see Foard, *The Revolt*, 133–58. The influence of Italian Fascist culture on Giménez Caballero personally and in Spain generally during the 1920s and 1930s is examined in V. Peña Sánchez, *Intelectuales y fascismo: La cultura italiana del "ventennio fascista" y su repercusión en España* (Granada, 1995).
7. There are two biographies, both entitled *Ramiro Ledesma Ramos*, by Tomás Borrás (Madrid, 1971), and J. M. Sánchez Diana (Madrid, 1975). Both provide sketches of his early years.
8. His leading philosophical writings were collected posthumously in book form as *Los escritos filosóficos de Ramiro Ledesma* (Madrid, 1941).
9. Quoted in Sánchez Diana, *Ramiro Ledesma*, 58.
10. According to Borrás, *Ramiro Ledesma*, 45.
11. Juan Aparicio, in the preface to his reprint edition of *La Conquista del Estado* (Barcelona, 1939), xi. Cf. S. Montero, *La Universidad y los orígenes del nacionalsindicalismo* (Murcia, 1939). In his memoir *¿Fascismo en España?* (Madrid, 1935), 78–81, Ledesma gives a brief profile of the founding group.
12. According to an interview with Aparicio in Selva Roca de Togores, "Giménez Caballero." Aparicio also referred to this subsidy on other occasions.
13. E. Aguado, *Ramiro Ledesma en la crisis de España* (Madrid, 1943), 13.
14. E. Hughes, *Report from Spain* (New York, 1947), 23–24.
15. *La Conquista del Estado*, 11 April 1931.

16. According to Sánchez Diana, *Ramiro Ledesma,* 96.

17. Cf. F. Miró, *Cataluña, los trabajadores y el problema de las nacionalidades* (Mexico City, 1967), 54–55.

18. Ledesma managed to purchase a motorcycle on credit, using it for weekend excursions and an occasional trip to Bilbao to seek further support and to pay a rare visit to the circle of Pedro Eguillor, a doctrinaire proponent in Bilbao of authoritarian Spanish nationalism. On the coterie of right-radical Spanish nationalists in that city, see G. Plata Parga, *La derecha vasca y la crisis de la democracia española (1931–1936)* (Bilbao, 1991), 28–40; and I. De Loyola Arana Pérez, *El monarquismo en Vizcaya durante la crisis del reinado de Alfonso XIII (1917–1931)* (Pamplona, 1982) 111–19.

19. J. M. de Areilza, *Así los he visto* (Barcelona, 1974), 89.

20. C. Winston, *Workers and the Right in Spain, 1900–1936* (Princeton, 1985), 226–330.

21. The only study is J. L. Mínguez Goyanes, *Onésimo Redondo (1905–1936): Precursor sindicalista* (Madrid, 1990). See also *Onésimo Redondo, caudillo de Castilla* (Valladolid, 1937); and *Onésimo Redondo: Vida, pensamiento, obra* (Valladolid, 1941).

22. It would be the longest-lived of all national syndicalist publications. See R. M. Martín de la Guardia, *Información y propaganda en la Prensa del Movimiento: "Libertad" de Valladolid, 1931–1979* (Valladolid, 1994).

23. *Libertad,* 5 Oct. 1931.

24. For a comparison of the characteristics of Redondo's group with those of generic fascism, see J. L. Pérez-Riesco, *La Falange, partido fascista* (Barcelona, 1977), 57–79.

25. A modern use for the emblem had perhaps first been suggested by the Socialist Fernando de los Ríos, professor of law at the University of Granada, in a class attended by Juan Aparicio. The device was also on the municipal shield of Guadix, Aparicio's hometown. M. Fernández Almagro, *Historia de la Segunda República española* (Madrid, 1940), 212; F. Guillén Salaya, *Los que nacimos con el siglo* (Madrid, 1953), 96.

It seems, however, that the symbol had also been recommended by such nationalist writers as Giménez Caballero and Rafael Sánchez Mazas in speeches and articles dating from 1927 and 1928. The latter had declared in Santander in January 1927: "We never had a better emblem. Let's restore the yoke and the bundle of arrows." *Boletín de la Biblioteca Menéndez y Pelayo* 9:1 (Jan.–March 1927), cited in I. Gibson, *En busca de José Antonio* (Barcelona, 1980), 39; D. Jato, *La rebelión de los estudiantes* (Madrid, 1967), 104.

26. Cf. R. Ledesma Ramos, *Discurso a las juventudes de España* (Madrid, 1935), 14.

27. Ledesma, *¿Fascismo?* 97.

28. In *El Estado Nacional,* 20 Feb. 1932. *El Estado Nacional* was a review for the discussion of political doctrine, directed by Redondo.

29. *Libertad,* 15 Feb. 1932.

30. Ledesma, *¿Fascismo?* 78.

31. V. Fragoso del Toro, *La España de ayer,* 2 vols. (Madrid, 1973), I, 168–70.

32. For an attempt to systematize Ledesma's sketchy ideas, see M. Moreno Hernández, *El nacional-sindicalismo de Ramiro Ledesma Ramos* (Madrid, 1963).

CHAPTER FOUR

1. After Franco, more has been written about José Antonio Primo de Rivera than about any other figure of twentieth-century Spain, and yet in all this vast bibliography, there is only one scholarly and objective biography: J. Gil Pecharromán, *José Antonio Primo de Rivera: Retrato de un visionario* (Madrid, 1996). Otherwise, the vast bulk of this literature is remarkably uninformative. Nearly all the other nominal biographies or biographical writings are hagiographic and lack even a trace of critical analysis, while works that deal with his thought are, with a few exceptions, largely uncritical repetitions of simple ideas.

For many years the semiofficial biography was *José Antonio (Biografía)* by the veteran Falangist, diplomat, and personal friend Felipe Ximénez de Sandoval, first published in Barcelona in 1941. Its original subtitle of "Biografía apasionada" became an embarrassment when the author was stripped of political and professional position the following spring on charges of homosexuality, and its subtitle was dropped from subsequent editions.

Other so-called biographies appeared over the years, some mere propaganda sketches, others more ambitious. Probably the best informed of the later hagiographies is A. Gibello, *José Antonio, ese desconocido*, rev. ed. (Madrid, 1985). See also C. De Arce, *José Antonio: Biografía* (Barcelona, 1983). Some of the typical earlier works are M. Barilli, *José Antonio Primo de Rivera, precursore ed eroe* (Rome, 1940); G. Mauger, *José Antonio: Chef et martyr* (Paris, 1955); L. Santa Marina, *Hacia José Antonio* (Barcelona, 1958); E. Villoria, *José Antonio, veinticinco años después* (Madrid, 1962); J. Alarcão Júdice, *José Antonio Primo de Rivera* (Coimbra, 1972); and J. Pemartín, *José Antonio* (Madrid, 1974).

Though not a conventional biography in format, the first critical work to be published in Spain was I. Gibson, *En busca de José Antonio* (Barcelona, 1980). More recently there has appeared the acerbic and revisionist work of C. Vidal, *José Antonio: La biografía no autorizada* (Madrid, 1996). V. Cerezo, *En defensa de José Antonio: Contestación a Ian Gibson* (Madrid, 1983), is a reply by an admirer. Brief critical sketches may be found in C. Rojas, *Prieto y José Antonio: Socialismo y Falange ante la tragedia civil* (Barcelona, 1977); and B. Nellessen, *José Antonio Primo de Rivera: Der Troubador der spanischen Falange* (Stuttgart, 1965). A. Imatz, *José Antonio et la Phalange Espagnole* (Paris, 1981), combines a biography and an account of the party.

There are numerous presentations of José Antonio's political ideas. The best critical study is N. Meuser, "Nation, Staat und Politik bei José Antonio Primo de Rivera" (Ph.D. diss., University of Mainz, 1993). The best treatments by admirers are A. Muñoz Alonso, *Un pensador para un pueblo* (Madrid, 1969); and J. Nin de Cardona, *José Antonio: La posibilidad política truncada* (Madrid, 1973).

The original incomplete edition of the *Obras completas* of José Antonio, edited by A. Del Río Cisneros and E. Conde Gargollo, was published in three volumes in Barcelona in 1939 and 1940, and later augmented and republished various times as a single volume. It was later supplemented by the *Textos inéditos y epistolario* (Madrid, 1956) and several minor collections such as *Ultimos hallazgos de escritos y cartas de José Antonio Primo de Rivera* (Madrid, 1962). Various anthologies have been published in other languages, such as *José Antonio Primo de Rivera: Sämtliche Werke* (Berlin, 1941); and *José Antonio Primo de Rivera: Selected Writings*, ed. H. Thomas (London, 1972). Two anthologies that seek to systematize his thoughts are *Revolución nacional (Puntos de Falange)*, ed. A. Del Río Cisneros (Madrid, 1957), and *Textos revolucionarios: José Antonio* (Barcelona, 1984).

Guides to the vast literature concerning José Antonio may be found in L. Alvarez Gutiérrez, "Ensayo bibliográfico sobre José Antonio Primo de Rivera," in *Estudios de historia contemporánea*, ed. V. Palacio Atard, 2 vols. (Madrid, 1976), I, 441–95; and J. Onrubia Revuelta, *Bibliografía sobre el Nacional-Sindicalismo* (Madrid, 1987).

2. Ximénez de Sandoval, *Biografía*, 33.

3. The best account of his early years will be found in Gil Pecharromán, *José Antonio Primo de Rivera* (hereafter cited as *JAPdR*), 28–85. Other material may be found in Ximénez de Sandoval, *Biografía*, 1–56; Gibello, *José Antonio*, 1–65; in articles by personal friends in *Dolor y memoria de España en el segundo aniversario de la muerte de José Antonio* (Barcelona, 1939), 174–200; and in R. Serrano Súñer, *Semblanza de José Antonio, joven* (Madrid, 1959). S. De Brocá, *Falange y filosofía* (Salou, 1976), discusses some of the intellectual sources common to José Antonio and Ledesma.

4. In his sometimes novelistic *Mis almuerzos con gente importante* (Barcelona, 1971), 48–49, José María Pemán recalled a speech on the maladies of dictatorship that he heard José Antonio deliver one evening in the Primo de Rivera home.

5. Gil Pecharromán, *JAPdR*, 96.

6. *La Nación* (Madrid), 18 Feb. 1930, reprinted from the *Diario de Albacete*.

7. *La Nación*, 12 Feb. 1930; *Boletín de la Unión Patriótica*, 18 Feb. 1930.

8. *Diario de Jerez*, 1 July 1930, quoted in *Textos inéditos y epistolario* (Madrid, 1956), 25–26 (hereafter cited as *Textos*).

9. *Textos*, 37.

10. Ibid., 49.

11. *La Nación*, 17 Jan. 1931, in *José Antonio, íntimo*, ed. A. Del Río Cisneros and E. Pavón Pereyra (Madrid, 1964), 103–6. As Gibello points out, this speech was not included in the original editions of the *Obras completas*, either through oversight or because it seemed too liberal for the early years of the Franco regime.

12. *La Nación*, 12 June 1931.

13. *Textos de doctrina política: Obras completas* (Madrid, 1952), 6–7 (hereafter cited as *Obras*.)

14. *La Nación*, 30 Sept. 1931.

15. On his legal practice, see A. Del Río Cisneros and E. Pavón Pereyra, eds., *José Antonio, abogado* (Madrid, 1963), which is perhaps less misleading than other works.

16. Gibello, *José Antonio*, 90–103.

17. J. M. de Areilza, *Así los he visto* (Barcelona, 1974), 153.

18. Ibid., 99–101.

19. The best discussion of *El Fascio* will be found in Gibson, *En busca*, 43–52.

20. *ABC*, 22 March 1933, in *Obras*, 43–45.

21. *ABC*, 22 March 1933.

22. On the influence of Italian Fascism and Italian culture generally in Spain during these years, see V. Peña Sánchez, *Intelectuales y fascismo: La cultura italiana del ventennio fascista y su repercusión en España* (Granada, 1993).

23. This frustrated relationship is best described in Gibson, *En busca*, 228–32.

24. Quoted in S. Dávila and J. Pemartín, *Hacia la historia de la Falange: Primera contribución de Sevilla* (Jerez, 1938), 24.

25. Quoted in Ximénez de Sandoval, *Biografía*, 127.

26. Prieto touches on this rejection in an article in *El Socialista*, 19 May 1949. The best of several biographies of the Socialist leader is J. C. Gibaja Velázquez, *Indalecio Prieto y el socialismo español* (Madrid, 1995).

27. Cf. J. A. Ansaldo, *¿Para que? (De Alfonso XIII a Juan III)* (Buenos Aires, 1953), 89. Some details were added by Josep Pla in an interview at Mas Pla, Llofriu (Gerona), 28 April 1959.

28. *JONS*, 1 May 1933.

29. R. Franco and J. Ruiz de Alda, *De Palos al Plata* (Madrid, 1927).

30. "Prólogo" to J. Ruiz de Alda, *Obras completas* (Barcelona, 1939), 13–21.

31. Ibid., 21–28.

32. Ibid., 205–9.

33. Ramiro Ledesma, *¿Fascismo en España?* (Madrid, 1935), 109.

34. Ledesma's articles in this journal have been collected and published as *Ramiro Ledesma Ramos, Escritos políticos: JONS 1933–1934*, ed. T. Ledesma Ramos (Madrid, 1985).

35. On the expansion of the JONS organization, see Ledesma, *¿Fascismo?* 110–33; F. Guillén Salaya, *Anecdotario de las JONS* (San Sebastián, 1938), 88; F. Guillén Salaya, *Los que nacimos con el siglo* (Madrid, 1953), 128–30; and D. Jato, *La rebelión de los estudiantes* (Madrid, 1967), 109–23.

36. Cf. T. Borrás, *Ramiro Ledesma Ramos* (Madrid, 1971), 317.

37. According to Areilza, well acquainted with both, in his *Así los he visto*, 156.

38. A copy of this document was given to me by Sainz Rodríguez in Lisbon on 1 May 1959, and it has been printed in Gibson, *En busca*, 101–3. Copies were, however, undated, and the agreement has variously been dated to November 1933 and June 1934. Italian documentation discovered by Ismael Saz would appear to indicate that it was signed in the late summer of 1933. Saz, "Falange e Italia: Aspectos poco conocidos del fascismo español," in *Estudis d'Història Contemporània del País Valencià* 3 (1982), 241–54.

39. Quoted in Gil Pecharromán, *JAPdR*, 189–90.

40. A. Ossorio y Gallardo, *Mis memorias* (Buenos Aires, 1946), 217–18.

41. *La Nación*, 26 Aug. 1933.

42. Ibid., 13 Sept. 1933.

43. Quoted in I. Saz, *Mussolini contra la II República (1931–1936)* (Valencia, 1986), 115.

44. Barilli, *José Antonio,* 23, quoted in Saz, *Mussolini,* 115.

45. The visit has best been reconstructed in Saz, *Mussolini,* 114–16.

46. As observed by an interviewer in *Blanco y Negro,* 11 Nov. 1934.

47. *Obras,* 63–69.

48. Quoted in G. Díaz, *Cómo llegó Falange al poder* (Buenos Aires, 1940), 15.

49. Quoted in Gibson, *En busca,* 71.

50. *El Sol,* 1 Nov. 1933.

51. See the discussion in Gibson, *En busca,* 64–70; Gibello, *José Antonio,* 119–21; and Gil Pecharromán, *JAPdR,* 205–7.

52. Part of the reason for this may have been the fact that the monarchist leader Pedro Sainz Rodríguez helped to edit the Puntos Iniciales, or so he claims in his *Testimonio y recuerdos* (Barcelona, 1978), 220.

53. Interview with Alfonso García Valdecasas, Madrid, 18 November 1958.

54. *ABC,* 23 Nov. 1933.

55. *Textos,* 79–80. On this and other incidents, see *El Sol,* 14, 16, 18 Nov. and 2 Dec. 1933; Dávila and Premartín, *Hacia la historia,* 36–38, 43–50; and Maugher, *José Antonio,* 61–66.

56. The best account of the electoral campaign in Cádiz will be found in Gil Pecharromán, *JAPdR,* 207–15.

57. Interview with Pedro Sainz Rodríguez, Lisbon, 1 May 1959. Cf. S. Cánovas Cervantes, *Apuntes históricos de "Solidaridad Obrera"* (Barcelona, 1937), 68–69.

58. J. Miquelarena in *Dolor y memoria,* 239–41; and C. Foltz, *The Masquerade in Spain* (Boston, 1948), 68–69.

59. E. Giménez Caballero, *La nueva catolicidad* (Madrid, 1933), 198–99.

60. There is a content analysis by J.-M. Desvois, "Le contenu de F. E., hebdomadaire de la Phalange," in "Presse et Société," no. 14 of *Etudes Hispaniques et Hispano-Américaines* (1979), 102–21.

61. Quoted in A. Viñas, *La Alemania nazi y el 18 de julio* (Madrid, 1977), 122–23.

62. Quoted in Saz, *Mussolini,* 120.

63. According to Ledesma, *¿Fascismo?* 143.

64. According to Ledesma, the JONS had less than 12,000 pesetas in financial support between May and February, while the Falange received 150,000 pesetas during its first three months. Ibid., 123.

65. Ibid., 145.

66. Ledesma to Francisco Bravo (JONS leader in Salamanca), 14 November 1933, quoted in Bravo Martínez, *José Antonio: El hombre, el jefe, el camarada* (Madrid, 1939), 63–64.

67. Ledesma, *¿Fascismo?* 143.

68. Ibid., 145–46.

69. The nine organized local groups were located in Madrid, Barcelona, Valencia, Bilbao, Zaragoza, Valladolid, Granada, Santiago de Compostela, and Zafra.

70. Ximénez de Sandoval, *Biografía*, 228–29.

71. Ibid., 222.

72. Montero Díaz to Ledesma, 14 March 1934, in Ledesma, *¿Fascismo?* 149. At that point the Falangists numbered more than 2,000, whereas the jonsistas—not counting underage students—may have numbered no more than 300, according to Ledesma, ibid., 178.

73. F. Guillén Salaya, *Historia del sindicalismo español* (Madrid, 1943), 62.

74. Such a possibility had even been mentioned by José Antonio in an article in *La Nación* on 17 Jan. 1934, as pointed out by Gil Pecharromán, *JAPdR*, 264.

75. F. Bravo Martínez, *Historia de Falange Española de las JONS* (Madrid, 1943), 26–27. The fullest account is in V. Fragoso del Toro, *La España de ayer*, 2 vols. (Madrid, 1973), II, 40–52.

76. *Obras*, 194–95, 197.

77. *El Sol*, 6, 8 March 1934.

78. Bravo Martínez, *Historia*, 29.

79. He was apparently first referred to in print simply as "José Antonio" in an article in *La Nación*, 25 Aug. 1933.

80. Jato, *La rebelión*, is the principal Falangist account of the early SEU.

81. Ruiz de Alda, *Obras*, 217–18.

82. Articles dealing with the roles of political militias and violence in six organizations appear in the special section under that title in *Historia Contemporánea* 11 (1994), 13–179. See particularly E. G. Calleja, "Camisas de fuerza: Fascismo y paramilitarización," 55–81.

83. For an overview, see my *Spain's First Democracy: The Second Republic 1931–1936* (Madison, 1993), 359–64.

84. *Obras*, 49.

85. E. Aguado, *Ramiro Ledesma, fundador de las JONS* (Madrid, 1941), quoted in Borrás, *Ramiro Ledesma*, 514–17.

86. *JONS* 3 (Aug. 1933), 107–9.

87. *Libertad*, 20 June 1931.

88. Ibid., 11 April 1932.

89. Ibid., 4 Dec. 1933.

90. Ibid., 8 Jan. 1934.

91. Ibid., 15 Jan. 1934.

92. Jato, *La rebelión*, 165.

93. For the purported "confessions" of a Socialist pistolero, see V. Reguengo, *Guerra sin frentes* (Madrid, 1954), 24–68.

94. *El Sol*, 3–4 Nov. 1933. The jonsista youth, José Ruiz de la Hermosa, was slain by a Socialist of the very same name, an ironic symbol of Spain's descent into extreme fratricidal strife.

95. Ibid., 5 Dec. 1933.

96. On these two killings, see M. Ramos González, *La violencia en Falange Española* (Oviedo, 1993), 64; and Borrás, *Ramiro Ledesma*, 451.

97. According to F. Bravo Martínez, *José Antonio*, 45.

98. *El Sol*, 4 Jan. 1934.

99. Ibid., 12 Jan., 3 May 1934.

100. Ibid., 19–21 Jan. 1934; Bravo Martínez, *José Antonio*, 40.

101. *Textos de doctrina política* (Madrid, 1970), 139–41.

102. Ledesma, *¿Fascismo?* 98.

103. Quoted in Gil Pecharromán, *JAPdR*, 240–42.

104. When only seventeen, he had written to Ledesma a month before the appearance of *La Conquista del Estado:* "Sincerely convinced that your ideology can open a path to salvation in the existing politico-social confusion, I naturally send you my support and ask that you send me material that fully explains what the party will be. I am a medical student seventeen years old, but will be eighteen very soon." Montero Rodríguez to Ledesma, 9 February 1931, quoted in Jato, *La rebelión*, 96–97.

105. *Obras*, 157.

106. The convicted assassin was disavowed by the Socialist Youth but when detained was carrying a list of persons marked as "dangerous" for socialism. *El Sol*, 20 Feb. 1934. He was apparently a member of the special UGT group "Vindication." Cf. M. Tagüeña Lacorte, *Testimonio de dos guerras* (Barcelona, 1978), 44.

107. *ABC*, 13 Feb. 1934.

108. Ximénez de Sandoval, *José Antonio*, 203.

109. *ABC*, 13 Feb. 1934.

110. Ledesma, *¿Fascismo?* 138–40.

111. Bravo Martínez, *Historia*, 29; Ramos González, *La violencia*, 69–70.

112. *F. E.*, 19 April 1934.

113. *El Sol*, 11 April 1934.

114. Ramos González, *La violencia*, 70.

115. J. L. Bolín, *Los años vitales* (Madrid, 1967), 84, cited in Gil Pecharromán, *JAPdR*, 273.

116. E. Vegas Latapié, *Memorias políticas* (Barcelona, 1983), 194–97.

117. Ansaldo, *¿Para qué?* 71–78. The Falange would also follow the example of the CNT and other radical groups in hiring paid pistoleros for some of the most lethal assaults, as Ansaldo admitted. The British journalist Henry Buckley recorded a brief interview with one such Falangist pistolero in the *Life and Death of the Spanish Republic* (London, 1940), 129. Nonetheless, the vast majority of those involved in violence would simply be youthful members of the party or the SEU, like their leftist counterparts.

118. This colloquialism stemmed from the refrain of one of their favorite songs: "Ay, chíbiri, chíbiri, chíbiri; ay, chíbiri, chíbiri, cha."

119. As he confessed to Vegas Latapié, in the latter's *Memorias*, 203.

120. *El Sol*, 11 June 1934.

121. Cf. *Mundo Obrero* (Madrid), 18 Jan. 1936; *Claridad* (Madrid), 20 June 1936.

122. See the version by the marqués de Valdeiglesias in *Dolor y memoria*, 249–51.

123. *El Sol*, 24 June 1934.

124. Ledesma, *¿Fascismo?* 169; M. García Venero, *Historia de la Unificación* (Madrid, 1970), 31.

125. Ledesma, ¿Fascismo? 170.

126. Ahora, 12 June 1934, quoted in Gil Pecharromán, JAPdR, 282.

127. H. Saña, Indice, no. 259, quoted in Ramos González, La violencia, 77.

128. Cf. S. Dávila, José Antonio, Salamanca y otras cosas (Madrid, 1967), 47.


CHAPTER FIVE

1. J. M. Gil Robles, "Epílogo" to his Discursos parlamentarios (Madrid–Barcelona, 1971), 680, quoted in Gil Pecharromán, JAPdR, 228.

2. R. Serrano Súñer, Entre el silencio y la propaganda, la Historia como fue: Memorias (Barcelona, 1977), 477.

3. La Nación, 21 Dec. 1933.

4. J. A. Ansaldo, ¿Para qué? (De Alfonso XIII a Juan III) (Buenos Aires, 1953), 81–92.

5. El Sol, 7 June, 4 July, 13 July 1934.

6. One Falangist guard at party headquarters had already died of a self-inflicted gunshot wound caused by accident while on sentinel duty. Ibid., 17 June 1934; R. Ibáñez Hernández, Estudio y acción: La Falange fundacional a la luz del "Diario" de Alejandro Salazar (1934–1936) (Madrid, 1993), 70–72.

7. A. Gibello, José Antonio, ese desconocido, rev. ed. (Madrid, 1985), 167–69; Gil Pecharromán, JAPdR, 290–91. Prieto has referred to this incident in his Convulsiones de España, 2 vols. (Mexico City, 1967), I, 130.

8. F. Ximénez de Sandoval, José Antonio, Biografía (Barcelona, 1941), 378–79; Gil Pecharromán, JAPdR, 287–88; and Ansaldo, ¿Para qué? 56.

9. Ansaldo later observed of his excitable young associates: "Then one lived a good deal on external exhibition, so that for a more showy uniform or emblem the young people, eager for adventure, changed parties the way they changed shirts." ¿Para qué? 95.

10. For Ansaldo's version see ibid., 85–95, but the best brief account is in Gil Pecharromán, JAPdR, 292–94. See also R. Ledesma, ¿Fascismo en España? (Madrid, 1935), 179–89; and El Sol, 10 Aug., 1 Sept. 1934.

11. The full text was originally given to me by Pedro Sainz Rodríguez in Lisbon on 1 May 1959 and was subsequently published in his Testimonio y recuerdos (Barcelona, 1978), 375–76.

12. As related to E. Hughes, Report from Spain (New York, 1947), 32–33.

13. Sainz Rodríguez, Testimonio, 222.

14. Cf. the remarks of Gil Pecharromán, JAPdR, 300–301.

15. This is drawn from materials in the files of José Andino (in the early years provincial chief of the Falange in Burgos), seen by the author in Madrid in 1958 through the courtesy of Sr. Andino. For further treatment of the CONS, see J. Onrubia Revuelta, Manuel Mateo y las C. O. N. S. (Oviedo, 1985); and E. Gutiérrez Palma, Sindicatos y agitadores nacional-sindicalistas 1931–1936 (Valladolid, 1938).

16. El Sol, 4–5 Sept. 1934.

17. V. Fragoso del Toro, La España de ayer, 2 vols. (Madrid, 1973), II, 81;

Marqués de Zayas, *Historia de la Vieja Guardia de Baleares* (Madrid, 1955), 51–56; and F. Meleiro, *Anecdotario de la Falange de Orense* (Madrid, 1958), 114–20.

18. *La Nación,* 1 Nov. 1934.

19. Ledesma, *¿Fascismo?* 168.

20. Prologue to J. Ruiz de Alda, *Obras completas* (Barcelona, 1939), 36.

21. L. de Araquistain, "The Struggle in Spain," *Foreign Affairs Quarterly* (April 1934), 461–71.

22. *Obras,* 293–96.

23. F. Bravo Martínez, *José Antonio: El hombre, el jefe, el camarada* (Madrid, 1939), 183–85. A secondary problem was the ample evidence of infiltration within the Falangist organization in Madrid. A series of articles had appeared in *Mundo Obrero,* the Communist organ, entitled "Falange Española de las J. O. N. S., a criminal organization in the service of capitalism." Though some of the information was false, confidential data also appeared. The informant, a CONS secretary, fled before he was discovered. Ledesma, *¿Fascismo?* 194–97.

24. Quoted in Gil Pecharromán, *JAPdR,* 321–22.

25. Interviews with Felipe Sanz Paracuellos (council member from the Basque Country), Bilbao, 10 December 1958, and Jesús Suevos, Madrid, 8 February 1959.

26. J. M. de Areilza, *Así los he visto* (Barcelona, 1974), 162.

27. Bravo Martínez, *José Antonio,* 60. It should be noted that the principle of elective leadership was not uncommon in the early years of fascist parties. Mussolini had originally been elected, as had Hitler in 1921; the latter would later refer to the elective principle in the first edition of *Mein Kampf* (1925), though this passage was deleted from later printings.

28. F. Bravo Martínez, *Historia de Falange Española de las JONS* (Madrid, 1943), 77–79; and I. Núñez, *La revolución de octubre de 1934,* 2 vols. (Barcelona, 1935), I, 128.

29. See the discussion of the debate on fascism by left Catalanists presented in J. B. Culla Clarà, *El catalanisme d'esquerra (1928–1936)* (Barcelona, 1977), 111–210.

30. Quoted by J. Miravitlles, *Crítica del 6 d'octubre* (Barcelona, 1935), 117, cited in E. Ucelay da Cal, "Estat Català: The Strategies of Separation and Revolution of Catalan Radical Nationalism (1919–1933)" (Ph.D. diss., Columbia University, 1979), 541–42. This unpublished study remains the best work on extremist Catalanism prior to the Civil War.

31. José Antonio to F. Bravo Martínez, 3 November 1934, in Bravo Martínez, *José Antonio,* 81.

32. *Obras,* 326.

33. According to Ledesma, the draft "was then modified by Primo de Rivera in the triple sense of improving the form, making the expressions more abstract, and softening and deradicalizing certain points." *¿Fascismo?* 213.

34. Quoted in S. Galindo Herrero, *Los partidos monárquicos bajo la Segunda República* (Madrid, 1956), 358.

35. *Arriba,* 21 March 1935.

36. *La Época,* 29 Nov. 1934, cited in Gil Pecharromán, *JAPdR,* 342.

37. Cf. Bravo Martínez, *José Antonio,* 70.

38. Two priests who were prominent were Manuel Gutiérrez in Oviedo and Fermín Yzurdiaga (who later became Falangist chief of press and propaganda in 1937) in Pamplona.

39. The events surrounding Eliseda's departure are discussed in Bravo Martínez, *Historia* 76–77; and Ximénez de Sandoval, *Biografía* 361–62. Eliseda later developed his own ideas about a nonfascist Catholic political system in his *Autoridad y libertad* (Madrid, 1945).

40. There is a considerable literature on Calvo Sotelo but no adequate study. The best general account of the alfonsino radical right is J. Gil Pecharromán, *Conservadores subversivos: La derecha autoritaria alfonsina (1913–1936)* (Madrid, 1994). See also J. L. Rodríguez Jiménez, *La extrema derecha española en el siglo XX* (Madrid, 1997), 118–33; and R. Morodo, *Orígenes ideológicas del franquismo: Acción Española* (Madrid, 1985). Calvo Sotelo published two collections of his writings: *En defensa propia* (Madrid, 1933) and *La voz de un perseguido,* 2 vols. (Madrid, 1933); he outlined some of his economic concepts in *El capitalismo contemporáneo y su evolución* (Madrid, 1935). Aspects of his career are studied in M. Pi y Navarro, *Los primeros veinticinco años de Calvo Sotelo* (Zaragoza, 1961); and J. Soriano Flores de Lemus, *Calvo Sotelo ante la Segunda República* (Madrid, 1975). As was long the case with José Antonio Primo de Rivera, all biographical accounts have been written by admirers, such as A. Joaniquet (1939), E. Aunós (1941), and Gen. F. Acedo Colunga (1957). Eugenio Vegas Latapié, the real leader of *Acción Española,* published *El pensamiento político de Calvo Sotelo* (Madrid, 1941), as well as his own *Escritos políticos* (Madrid, 1940) and subsequent *Memorias políticas* (Madrid, 1983).

Beginning in 1933 quite a number of books on corporative doctrine appeared in Spain. Perhaps the most notable were E. Aunós, *La reforma corporativa del Estado* (Madrid, 1935); and Joaquín Azpiazu, *El Estado corporativo* (Madrid, 1936), which also appeared in an English translation, *The Corporate State* (St. Louis, 1951).

41. As quoted in *La Nación,* 3 June 1935.

42. The basic study for these years is M. Blinkhorn, *Carlism and Crisis in Spain, 1931–1939* (London, 1976), 1–206. A Carlist narrative will be found in L. Redondo and J. Zavala, *El Requeté* (Barcelona, 1957), 225–310.

43. Prologue to Ruiz de Alda, *Obras,* 36–38.

44. Bravo Martínez, *Historia,* 85; V. Marcotte, *L'Espagne nationale-syndicaliste* (Brussels, 1943), 74–75.

45. Cf. J. M. Sánchez Diana, *Ramiro Ledesma Ramos* (Madrid, 1975), 202–3.

46. *Obras,* 313–21. Eloy Vaquero, minister of the interior at this time, later recalled that he had received reports of Falangist contacts among the military. Interview in New York, 17 May 1958. Cf. his article in *Mensaje,* 2:4, p. 4.

47. Quoted by Serrano's friend Carlo Rojas in his *Prieto y José Antonio* (Barcelona, 1977), 145.

48. José Antonio was embittered by the sudden end of support and demanded the return of the original document of agreement. Reprisals were threatened, even

against Sainz Rodríguez. The latter, one of the great Spanish wits of the century, satirized the Falangist weakness in direct action: "This permitted Sainz Rodríguez to wax ironic about a supposed clause that he intended to insert into his will indicating that, should there be an attempt on his life, no one should be charged with his death, which would be exclusively due to his surprise at ever seeing the Falangists commit a violent act." Vegas Latapié, *Memorias*, I, 218.

49. Ledesma, *¿Fascismo?* 216–17.

50. Ibid., 201.

51. Ledesma obtained an interview with *El Heraldo de Madrid* on 17 January to present his own account, which also appeared in his *¿Fascismo?* 191–217.

52. *Informaciones* (Madrid), 18 Jan. 1935.

53. Ledesma, *¿Fascismo?* 5.

54. Ibid., 11.

55. Ibid., 14–15.

56. Ibid., 11.

57. Ibid., 21–22.

58. Ibid., 28.

59. Ibid., 29–30.

60. *Discurso a las juventudes de España* (Barcelona, 1968), 245.

61. Ibid., 263.

62. Ibid., 263, 271. Manuel Villares, a priest who shared imprisonment with him in the last days of his life, has reported that Ledesma was in one sense a typical Enlightenment-era modern intellectual who seemed to believe in a religion of science and learning. T. Borrás, *Ramiro Ledesma Ramos* (Madrid, 1971), 715–17.

63. *¿Fascismo?* 292–306.

64. Ibid., 306.

65. On Ledesma's last days, see Borrás, *Ramiro Ledesma*, 622–782; and Sánchez Diana, *Ramiro Ledesma*, 233–36.

66. H. R. Southworth, *Antifalange* (Paris, 1967), 64.

67. E. Aguado, *Ramiro Ledesma en la crisis de España* (Madrid, 1943), 114.

68. Ibid., 115.

69. For example, in *Haz* (the SEU journal), no. 12 (5 Dec. 1935), reprinted in *Textos*, 745.

70. A good illustration was provided by the liberal American ambassador, who strongly supported the Republic but penned the following portrait: "José Antonio Primo de Rivera . . . was young and darkly handsome. His coal-black hair shone glossily. His face was slender and of an Andalusian hue. His manner was courtly, modest, deferential. The passion of his life was the vindication of his father . . . a good speaker, his speeches rich in substance, well-phrased, but with an irresistible Andalusian weakness for floridity. . . . [In parliament] he would become a thorn in the side of many hypocrites with whom he was allied. Incapable of dissimulation, with a gift for the barbed phrase, he was to arouse the bitter enmity of many, and to live dangerously, going about with a reckless abandon that was the despair of his friends. He loved the crowds and refused to shun them. One night riding in Madrid he was fired upon from the shadows. Stopping his

car, he sprang out in pursuit, alone, unarmed, heedless of possible enemies lurking in the dark. A little later he appeared smiling and jubilant at the Bakanik, where fashion went for cocktails, and those to whom he told the story found him delighted as a child. He was of the breed of Dumas' Musketeers. I shall always remember him as I saw him first, young, boyish, courteous, smiling and dancing that afternoon in the villa in San Sebastián." C. G. Bowers, *My Mission to Spain* (New York, 1954), 28–29.

71. Prieto and Azaña are the best examples, but the Socialist José Antonio Balbontín later wrote, "There is no doubt that José Antonio Primo de Rivera bore a dream in his mind, a dream dangerous for him and for our people . . . but a dream, nonetheless, that it would be wrong to confuse with the bastard avarice of those 'new' Falangists whom we see today in the Spain of Franco." *La España de mi experiencia* (Mexico City, 1952), 306–7.

72. To friends, he lamented that "for a long time to the masses I will continue being a señorito, the son of the Dictator." R. Serrano Súñer, *Semblanza de José Antonio, joven* (Madrid, 1959), 54.

Falangist students never wavered in their attachment, but even they could be disturbed by the picture his enemies painted of him as a señorito. Once when a stylish, overly aristocratic portrait of the Jefe Nacional was exhibited in the show window of a photography shop, they decided it would be necessary to smash it, but the Young Socialists beat them to it. D. Jato, *La rebelión de los estudiantes* (Madrid, 1967), 213.

73. He devoted some time during his final imprisonment to a novel tentatively entitled "El navegante solitario."

74. Ansaldo, *¿Para qué?* 89.

75. Ledesma, *¿Fascismo?* 129. Sánchez Mazas had at one point been the correspondent of *ABC* in Rome, where he had refined his estheticism and developed an interest in Fascism. Like Giménez Caballero, he had married an Italian woman. His political writings during the first two years of the Falange were later collected in *Fundación, hermandad y destino* (Madrid, 1957).

76. J. M. Mancisidor, *Frente a frente: José Antonio frente al Tribunal Popular, Alicante, noviembre 1936* (Madrid, 1963), 61.

77. Ximénez de Sandoval has admitted that much of *F. E.* read like an "intellectual review for students of philosophy." *Biografía*, 231. Later, even in the violent weeks preceding the outbreak of the Civil War, when the party had been outlawed and its leaders imprisoned, José Antonio admonished those responsible for the clandestine Falangist sheet *No importa* that they would have to suspend publication if they could not improve its format. Bravo Martínez, *José Antonio*, 194–201.

78. Bravo Martínez, *José Antonio*, 11, 31–32; and *Historia*, 87. Unamuno thought that the proper rendering of "fascismo" in Spanish should be "fajismo."

79. "Gu" and Tellaeche have received comparatively little attention. According to two Basque art historians:

> The ideological scope of the first Basque vanguardism was broad and
> flexible. Emulating the alliance of Italian Futurists with Fascism, some artists

joined Falangism. . . . The philofascist sector in 1934 founded the art society called "Gu," which, in its two years of life proved to be the most lively, open, and innovative artistic institution in the Basque Country until the Civil War converted it into a factory of Francoist propaganda.

A few young artists who had already experienced the adventure of Paris— Cabanas, Olasagasti, and Kaperotxipi—visited Italy in 1933 and 1934. Olasagasti and Cabanas, who initially seemed to sympathize with Basque nationalism, were dazzled by Italy and the esthetics of Fascism. . . . Perhaps Fascism gave them an identity that was impossible for a Basque Nationalist Party that rejected any sort of vanguardism. At any rate, their philofascism had less to do with learned philosophical disquisitions than with the search for ideological support in a superpoliticized epoch. The political sympathies of the San Sebastián vanguard appeared more simple and elemental than anything else. The breadth of views of Julián Tellaeche, the fundamental artist of "Gu," might be typical: he collaborated indiscriminately with the Basque Nationalist Party, the Popular Front, and the Falange until shortly before the Civil War.

. . . Cabanas . . . ended up being one of the leading San Sebastián Falangists. He was without doubt one of the best-informed about surrealism, metaphysical painting, and Futurism. During the war he designed Francoist imperial symbolism, but the crass sordidness of the new regime eventually depressed him so much that, like other early Falangists, in 1945 he exiled himself to Argentina.

C. Martínez Gorriarán and I. Agirre Arriaga, *Estética de la diferencia: El arte vasco y el problema de la identidad 1882–1966* (San Sebastián, 1995), 224–25.

80. "But don't forget that the chief responsibility is yours, and that at this point, with the memory of our martyrs, it's too late to turn back." Bravo Martínez to José Antonio, 18 January 1935, in Bravo Martínez, *José Antonio,* 255. (In moments of disillusionment, José Antonio would always respond positively to the example of the "fallen" of the Falange, and the need to be faithful to their trust.)

81. *El Sol,* 22 May 1935.

82. H. Buckley, *Life and Death of the Spanish Republic* (London, 1940), 128.

83. *Ahora,* 19 April 1935, in Gil Pecharromán, *JAPdR,* 360.

84. Bravo Martínez to José Antonio, 12 October 1934, in Bravo Martínez, *José Antonio,* 218; for the latter's reply, see ibid., 104.

85. Interview in *La Voz* (Madrid), 14 Feb. 1935.

86. Ledesma, *¿Fascismo?* 186–88.

87. These concepts were thinly outlined in his speech of 3 March 1935, entitled "España y la barbarie," *Obras,* 417–23, and also taken up in a brief sketch prepared during his final days in prison in Alicante, published in *Razón Española* 58 (1993), 193–97.

88. *Obras,* 570–71.

89. For the original concept in Ortega y Gasset, see the latter's *Obras completas,* 8 vols. (Madrid, 1946), I, 265–308.

90. *Obras,* 716.

91. Interview in *La Rambla* (Barcelona), 13 Aug. 1934, quoted in I. Gibson, *En busca de José Antonio* (Barcelona, 1980), 291–92.

92. *Obras,* 569.

93. Ibid., 488.

94. Ibid., 364.

95. Ibid., 566.

96. On the religious aspects of his thought, see C. De Miguel Molina, *La personalidad religiosa de José Antonio* (Madrid, 1975).

97. *Obras*, 499.

98. *Textos*, 283.

99. *Obras*, 550.

100. Ibid., 483.

101. *José Antonio, íntimo*, ed. A. Del Río Cisneros and E. Pavón Pereyra (Madrid, 1964), 248.

102. *Obras*, 494.

103. *Ibid.*, 521.

104. *José Antonio, íntimo*, 391.

105. *Obras*, 501.

106. Ibid., 177–78.

107. "Ensayo sobre el nacionalismo," in *JONS* 16 (16 April 1934), reprinted ibid., 211–16.

108. Ibid., 42.

109. Ibid., 930.

110. Ibid., 943.

111. *José Antonio, íntimo*, 179.

112. *Obras*, 556.

113. Ibid., 663–64.

114. Ibid., 466.

115. Ibid., 17.

116. Ibid., 180.

117. Ibid., 188.

118. *José Antonio, íntimo*, 183.

119. *Obras*, 757.

120. Ibid., 320.

121. Ibid., 747.

122. Ibid., 186.

123. Ibid., 505.

124. Ibid., 492.

125. Ibid., 422.

126. Ibid., 505.

127. Ibid., 506.

128. Ibid., 409–12, 483–508. The principal attempt to synthesize José Antonio's economic ideas is M. Fuentes Irurozqui, *El pensamiento económico de José Antonio Primo de Rivera* (Madrid, 1957).

129. *Obras*, 556.

130. Ibid., 415.

131. The agronomist Florense, according to J. Pla, *Historia de la Segunda República española*, 4 vols. (Barcelona, 1940), IV, 140.

132. *Obras*, 560.

133. *José Antonio, íntimo,* 317–18.

134. *Libertad,* 31 August 1931.

135. *Obras,* 488.

136. Ibid., 139.

137. Ibid., 165.

138. Quoted in Ximénez de Sandoval, *Biografía,* 457.

139. *Obras,* 647–55.

140. Ibid., 882.

141. Quoted in *El Día Gráfico* (Barcelona), 28 Jan. 1934, from an interview published in *Luz.*

142. *Obras,* 265–66.

143. Ibid., 420.

144. *Textos,* 222–24.

145. *Textos,* 281.

146. Ibid., 282.

147. *José Antonio, íntimo,* 424–25.

148. Here I am following I. Saz, *Mussolini contra la II Republica (1931–1936)* (Valencia, 1986), 135–36.

149. *Obras,* 236.

150. Buckley, *Life and Death,* 127.

151. *Obras,* 555.

152. This has been pointed out most recently by M. Argaya Roca, *Entre lo espontáneo y lo difícil* (Oviedo, 1996), and in Gil Pecharromán, *JAPdR.*

153. This was most clearly expressed in the interview published in *Ahora,* 16 Feb. 1934: "There is one group, the traditionalist, which has a positive Spanish lifeblood and an authentic warlike tradition, but on the other hand it lacks modern sensitivity and technique, and, probably, the ability to adapt socially. Its social vision is not that of our times, though it has a very good guild background. I think, therefore, that it would not be a force adequate to stop a revolution, even though it is the rightist force with the most spirit." *Obras,* 163–64.

154. As indicated in the preceding chapter, the best single study of José Antonio's thought is N. Meuser, "Nation, Staat und Politik bei José Antonio Primo de Rivera" (Ph.D. diss., University of Mainz, 1993). Two different approaches may be found in A. Muñoz Alonso, *Un pensador para un pueblo* (Madrid, 1969); and V. Rodríguez Carro, "Die philosophischen Grundlagen des politischen Denkens José Antonio Primo de Rivera" (Ph.D. diss., University of Munster, 1978), both of the latter rather one-sided.

155. *Ahora,* 16 Feb. 1934, in *Obras,* 165.

156. Quoted in A. Viñas, *La Alemania nazi y el 18 de julio* (Madrid, 1977), 124.

157. The relevant German documentation has been studied ibid., 143–60.

158. Cf. Ansaldo, *¿Para qué?* 78.

159. *La Rambla* (Barcelona), quoted in *Luz,* 14 Aug. 1934.

160. *Textos de doctrina política,* ed. A. Del Río Cisneros (Madrid, 1971), 424.

161. This had been initiated by an earlier visit of Calvo Sotelo and Ansaldo

in December 1933. Fuller details may be found in Saz, *Mussolini*, 69–82; M. Mazzetti, "I contatti del governo italiano con i cospiratori militari spagnoli," *Storia Contemporanea* 8 (1977), 1178–99; J. F. Coverdale, *Italian Intervention in the Spanish Civil War* (Princeton, 1975), 49–54; and A. Lizarza Iribarren, *Memorias de la conspiración* (Madrid, 1969), 48–49.

162. Quoted in Saz, *Mussolini*, 127.

163. Ibid., 128.

164. Ibid.

165. Ibid., 131.

166. *Obras*, 391–92.

167. *Textos*, 270–71.

168. Saz, *Mussolini*, 138–39. José Antonio made regular trips to Paris to collect the subsidy.

169. The only study is A. Deniel, *Bucard et le Francisme: Les seuls fascistes français* (Paris, 1979).

170. Saz, *Mussolini*, 140–43.

171. Quoted in C. Vidal, *José Antonio: La biografía no autorizada* (Madrid, 1996), 149.

172. Quoted in Saz, *Mussolini*, 137.

173. The full text may be found in A. Viñas, "José Antonio analiza las fuerzas políticas," *Actualidad Económica* (23 Nov. 1974), 69–73; and in Viñas, *Alemania nazi*, 420–25.

174. Redondo had written in mid-1933, before the founding of the Falange: "Nor do we care to accept the dialectic—which can be better called the dialectic than the doctrine of Mussolini—about the relations between the state and individuals: what is called in this regard *fascist doctrine* is, in our judgment, transitory tactics, incongruous as a permanent policy, which the combative and constructive talent of Mussolini has progressively adopted in pursuit of his concrete and very personal aspirations to govern Italy in recent years. . . . What does not properly exist is a doctrine of public law, no matter how it seems: *Fascism* changes its course, as the calendar changes during the course of a year. We cannot even be certain that the 'doctrine' that appears to be characteristic and fundamental, that of the semi-pantheist supremacy of the state over everything else, will be maintained by Mussolini until his death." *El Estado Nacional*, 15 May 1933.

175. According to Dionisio Ridruejo, interview in Madrid, 17 November 1958.

176. Manuel Hedilla, in 1935 the provincial chief in Santander, later insisted that the membership in Santander province as a whole was almost as large as the possible total of 1,200 Falangists in Extremadura. Interview in Madrid, 4 January 1959.

There is a body of literature on Falangism in the provinces composed both of memoirs and of brief historical studies or sketches, such as L. Alvarez Rey and J. Ortiz Villalba, "Falange en Sevilla (1933–1936)," in *Los nuevos historiadores ante la guerra civil española*, ed. O. Ruiz-Manjón Cabeza and M. Gómez Oliver, 2 vols. (Granada, 1990), I, 187–205; M. Suárez Cortina, *El fascismo en Asturias (1931–1937)* (Gijón, 1981), 151–83; Marqués de Zayas, *Vieja Guardia de Ba-*

*leares;* Meleiro, *Anecdotario de la Falange de Orense;* and M. F. De la Mora Villar, *Las sangrientas cinco rosas: Recuerdos para la historia de la Falange de Santander* (Santander, 1971).

177. Mariano García, in 1935–1936 the administrative secretary of the Falange, was later inclined to raise the estimated total of all sectors combined to about 25,000. (Interview in Madrid, 8 January 1959.) José Luis de Arrese, provincial chief in Granada in 1935, recalled that the number of regular cardholders before the 1936 elections was no more than 8,000. (Interview of Prof. Juan J. Linz with Arrese, Madrid, January 1960.) The secretary general in 1934–1936, Raimundo Fernández Cuesta, has estimated that there were no more than 5,000 in the Primera Línea in February 1936. (Interview in Madrid, 13 February 1959.)

178. It was much the same elsewhere. In the province of Orense, 51 percent of all those in Falangist organizations of one sort or another were students. X.-M. Núñez Seixas, "Oral History and Fascism in Galicia, 1931–1936" (manuscript, European University Institute, n.d.).

179. Bravo Martínez, *Historia,* 87. Dionisio Ridruejo later calculated that less than 10 percent of the early members had any notion of ideology. Interview in Madrid, 4 November 1958.

180. Ximénez de Sandoval, *Biografía,* 340–41. One may speculate that José Antonio was thinking of some of his more sophisticated, better-educated rightist friends, such as Ramón Serrano Súñer.

181. José Antonio Girón and Luis González Vicén, the leaders of the Valladolid schism, played prominent roles in the party in later years. My information on this dissidence is drawn from interviews with González Vicén (Madrid, 27 February 1959) and Anselmo de la Iglesia (Madrid, 26 May 1959), the latter a strong supporter of Redondo.

182. Violence was said to have been narrowly averted in Santander. G. Montes Agudo, *Vieja Guardia* (Madrid, 1939), 134–39, and the "Diario" for 1935 of Florentino Torre Bolado (later provincial chief of press and propaganda for Santander).

183. Frank Jellinek, who later studied the CNT, concluded: "It is certain there was close cooperation between some irresponsible individuals and the Falange Española. . . . It is equally certain that these individuals were completely disapproved by the responsible committees." *The Civil War in Spain* (London, 1938), 259–60.

The cenetista writer and leader Diego Abad de Santillán later reported: "On diverse occasions we were approached by people from the Falange who wanted to arrange a meeting with Primo de Rivera, and we were sent letters and manifestos in which there were many common objectives." Quoted in Gibello, *José Antonio,* 216.

184. For example, a later headline in *Solidaridad Obrera* (the CNT daily in Barcelona) of 25 June 1936 declared: "To the purely materialist conception, which converts peoples into flocks of sheep solely interested in satisfying their physiological necessities, we must oppose the force of the spirit, the dynamic potency of the ideal."

185. J. Del Castillo and S. Alvarez, *Barcelona: Objectivo cubierto* (Barcelona,

1958), 132–34; interview with Luys Santa Marina in Barcelona, 20 December 1958.

186. In a letter to Sancho Dávila, in S. Dávila and J. Pemartín *Hacia la historia de la Falange: Primera contribución de Sevilla* (Jerez, 1938), 80–81.

187. On the campaign for a daily newspaper, see Gil Pecharromán, *JAPdR*, 373–76.

188. *Arriba*, 30 May 1935.

189. *Obras*, 647–55.

190. According to Vidal, *José Antonio*, 154–55.

191. *Obras*, 689–92. L. Alvarez Rey, *La Derecha en La República: Sevilla, 1931–1936* (Seville, 1993), 391, observed of the Falange that "in Seville, nonetheless, its gunmen would take charge of settling accounts so that the final balance of killings would be positive for the Falange." This may be correct, but he fails to provide any concrete data in support of such a conclusion.

192. Ximénez de Sandoval, *Biografía*, 635–36. The Jefe Nacional continued to plead with local leaders to encourage members to pay dues. *Textos*, 271, 311–12.

193. Hughes, *Report from Spain*, 31–32; E. Pavón Pereyra, *De la vida de José Antonio* (Madrid, 1949), 77.

194. A. Cacho Zabalza, *La Unión Militar Española* (Alicante, 1940), provides some details.

195. According to Ansaldo, *¿Para qué?* 81.

196. *Obras*, 313–21.

197. Ximénez de Sandoval, *Biografía*, 327; Gibson, *En busca*, 229.

198. *Textos*, 305.

199. Ibáñez Hernández, *Estudio y acción*, 36.

200. Among the sources providing extremely limited accounts of this abortive project are Bravo Martínez, *José Antonio*, 162–64; and his "Early Days of the Spanish Phalanx," *Spain* 1 (Oct. 1938), 6–7; M. Aznar, *Historia militar de la guerra de España (1936–1939)* (Madrid, 1940), 20; J. Arrarás, ed., *Historia de la Cruzada española* 8 vols. (Madrid, 1940), VIII, 358–59; *José Antonio Primo de Rivera (Antología)*, ed. G. Torrente Ballester (Madrid, 1940), 32, which refers to this as "la locura [madness] de José Antonio"; R. de la Cierva, *Historia de la Guerra Civil española, I: Antecedentes: Monarquía y República 1898–1936* (Madrid, 1969), 570–72; and Gibello, *José Antonio*, 221–22.

201. *Textos*, 199.

202. Cacho Zabalza, *La Unión*, 23–25.

203. This document is quoted in Viñas, *Alemania nazi*, 420–25.

204. On this initiative, see R. Fernández Cuesta, *Testimonio, recuerdos y reflexiones* (Madrid, 1985), 52–53; Comandante B. Gómez Oliveros, with General Moscardó, *General Moscardó* (Barcelona, 1956), 104; M. García Venero, *Falange en la guerra de España* (Paris, 1967), 66, 104; Southworth, *Antifalange*, 91–94; and Gibson, *En busca*, 137–40.

205. The only first-hand account is that of Serrano Súñer, *Memorias*, 56. This conversation has usually been dated to the early part of March, when Franco

engaged in his final political conversations in Madrid prior to taking up his new command in the Canaries. Gil Pecharromán, *JAPdR*, 410–11, much more convincingly dates it to January or the beginning of February, before the elections. It is much more likely that José Antonio went to Franco not long after the cancellation of the plan at the end of December, while Franco still enjoyed the decisive power and influence of Chief of the General Staff. Conversely, as we shall see, the Falangist leaders did not immediately return to their plans for insurrection in the first days after the Popular Front victory of February.

206. A. Costa Pinto, "A Direita Radical e a Ditadura Militar: A Liga Nacional 28 de Maio (1928–1933)," in *Conflict and Change in Portugal*, ed. E. De Sousa Ferreira and W. C. Opello, Jr. (London, 1985), 23–39; and M. Braga de Cruz, *O partido e o estado no salazarismo* (Lisbon, 1988).

207. J. Medina, *Salazar e os fascistas* (Lisbon, 1979), 239.

208. A. Costa Pinto, *Os camisas azuis* (Lisbon, 1994), 215. This is the fundamental study.

209. Ibid., 215–23.

210. Ibid., 260–303.

211. Quoted in A. Ferro, *Salazar* (Lisbon, 1933), 148.

212. A. Costa Pinto and A. Ribeiro, *A Accão Escolar Vanguarda* (Lisbon, 1980).

213. *Diario de Noticias* (Lisbon), 29 July 1934, quoted in Costa Pinto, *Camisas azuis*, 361; and in J. Ploncard d'Assac, *Salazar* (Paris, 1967), 107.

214. S. Kuin, "O Braço Longo de Mussolini: Os 'Comitati d'Azione per l'Universalità di Roma' em Portugal (1933–1937)," *Penélope* 11 (1993), 7–20.

215. Costa Pinto, *Camisas azuis*, 276–82.

216. *Obras*, 661.

217. According to Salazar, in Ibáñez Hernández, *Estudio y acción*, 37.

218. Bravo Martínez, *Historia*, 111.

219. *Obras*, 711–13.

220. See the account in Bravo Martínez, *Historia*, 123–27.

221. Ximénez de Sandoval, *Biografía*, 413.

222. M. Gil Robles, *No fue posible la paz* (Barcelona, 1968), 434–35; interview in Madrid, 14 May 1959.

223. *Ahora*, 8 Feb. 1936, in Gil Pecharromán, *JAPdR*, 418, 420.

224. Ibid., 420; J. Andino, "Diario" (unpublished), 31–32.

225. Meleiro, *Anecdotario*, 141–65; Bravo Martinez, *Historia*, 150; R. Gutiérrez, *Memorias de un azul* (Salamanca, 1937), 93.

226. M. García Venero, *Testimonio de Manuel Hedilla* (Barcelona, 1977), 63.

227. *Obras*, 861–72.

228. Ibid., 420.

229. Ibid., 831–32.

230. Ibid., 840.

231. *ABC*, 14 Feb. 1936. This sentiment was echoed the same day by *Informaciones* and *La Nación*, hitherto the only Madrid dailies somewhat friendly to the Falange.

232. *Obras*, 872.

233. The definitive study is J. Tusell et al., *Las elecciones del Frente Popular,* 2 vols. (Madrid, 1969).

234. According to the "Diario" of SEU chief Alejandro Salazar. Ibáñez Hernández, *Estudio y accion*, 41.


CHAPTER SIX

1. Patricio González de Canales in a questionnaire prepared for the author, 24 January 1959, 5.

2. R. Ibáñez Hernández, *Estudio y acción: La Falange fundacional a la luz del "Diario" de Alejandro Salazar* (1934–1936) (Madrid, 1993), 40.

3. *Obras*, 886.

4. J. Zugazagoitia, *Historia de la guerra de España* (Buenos Aires, 1940), 7–8; R. Llopis, "Spain Awaits Her Hour," part 3, *Iberica* 5:7 (1957), 4–6.

5. González de Canales, questionnaire, 3.

6. M. Ramos González, *La violencia en Falange Española* (Oviedo, 1993), 132.

7. D. Jato, *La rebelión de los estudiantes* (Madrid, 1967), narrates these incidents from the Falangist viewpoint, while J. A. Ansaldo, *¿Para qué? (De Alfonso XIII a Juan III)* (Buenos Aires, 1953), 119, describes the escape of the Falangist gunmen, whom he personally flew to France.

8. The only historian of the Republic to present a fully objective account of these events is Luis Romero, *Por qué y cómo mataron a Calvo Sotelo* (Barcelona, 1982), 40–42.

9. Quoted in Gil Pecharromán, *JAPdR*, 442.

10. The best account of this incident will be found in the memoirs of Raimundo Fernández Cuesta, who witnessed the scene. *Testimonio, recuerdos y reflexiones* (Madrid, 1985), 60.

11. As Luis Romero has written of Socialists engaged in violence and disorder, "The police never arrested them." "El fracaso de la República," *Historia 16* 100 (Aug. 1984), 55.

12. *El Sol,* 17 April 1936.

13. F. Bravo Martínez, *Historia de Falange Española de las JONS* (Madrid, 1943), 164–65.

14. According to the administrative secretary Mariano García, who kept the party records. Interview in Madrid, 8 January 1959.

15. For a broader discussion of the violence in the spring of 1936, see R. Cibrían, "Violencia política y crisis democrática: España en 1936," *Revista de Estudios Políticos* (Nov.–Dec. 1978), 81–115, and my *Spain's First Democracy: The Second Republic 1931–1936* (Madison, 1993), 359–64.

16. José Antonio logically feared that all the new contributions were not being used for constructive purposes. José Antonio to Onésimo Redondo, 17 June 1936, in *Textos*, 502–3.

17. Gil Pecharromán, *JAPdR*, 460.

18. *Textos,* 358.

19. J. Ruiz de Alda, *Obras completas* (Barcelona, 1939), 261–63. The title of *¡No Importa!* invoked the battlecry of the patriotic guerrilleros of the War of Independence against Napoleon, who refused to be intimidated by massive French terrorism against Spanish civilians.

20. The most thorough account is A. Del Río Cisneros and E. Pavón Pereyra, *Los procesos de José Antonio* (Madrid, 1963), 13–15 (hereafter cited as *Los procesos*).

21. Ibid., 19–24.

22. Ibid., 27–55. Though this trial was attended by numerous journalists, censorship forbade publication of the results. The only contemporary account appeared in *La Gaceta del Norte* (Bilbao), 1 May 1936.

23. *Los procesos,* 55–90. Varying accounts of aspects of these judicial processes may be found in *El Sol,* 5 April, 29 May 1936; *Claridad* (Madrid), 8 May 1936; *The Times* (London), 29 May 1936; *Obras,* 911–18; Gil Pecharromán, *JAPdR,* 446–53; A. Gibello, *José Antonio, ese desconocido,* rev. ed. (Madrid, 1985) 257–58; and F. Ximénez de Sandoval, *José Antonio (Biografía)* (Barcelona, 1941), 747–48.

24. The best account of this maneuver will be found in R. Serrano Súñer, *Entre el silencio y la propaganda, la Historia como fue: Memorias* (Barcelona, 1977), 56–58. See also J. M. Gil Robles, *No fue posible la paz* (Barcelona, 1968), 544–50; and E. Vegas Latapié, *Memorias políticas,* 2 vols. (Madrid, 1983), I, 290.

25. *El Sol,* 5 May 1936.

26. I. Prieto, *Cartas a un escultor* (Buenos Aires, 1961), 94.

27. The research of A. L. López Villaverde, "Cuenca durante la II República: Elecciones, partidos y vida política, 1931–1936" (Ph.D. diss., University of Castilla–La Mancha, 1993), has found that José Antonio received 47,283 votes, which would have placed him third on the rightist list and in any case would have been insufficient to win him a seat. (Cited in Gil Pecharromán, *JAPdR,* 457–58.) It should be kept in mind, however, that because of the government's announced refusal to accept the validity of his candidacy, the rightist "useful vote" was less likely to vote for him.

28. *El Sol,* 12 May 1936; *¡No Importa!* 2 (6 June 1936); Serrano Súñer, *Memorias,* 116; and A. Alcázar de Velasco, *Serrano Súñer en la Falange* (Madrid, 1941), 81.

29. Romero, *Por qué y cómo mataron,* 100.

30. In *Aquí estamos* (Palma de Mallorca), no. 1 (23 May 1936), in *Obras,* 927–32.

31. Quoted in I. Saz, *Mussolini contra la II República (1931–1936)* (Valencia, 1986), 164.

32. According to Ansaldo, "In those days a basic change in orientation occurred in the political line of José Antonio and the Falange. Until then the basic lines of his thought and activities had been ruled by an innate lack of confidence in the possibility of a military coup, together with a deep aversion for what might be its result." *¿Para qué?* 121.

33. *Obras,* 919–23.

34. P. Sainz Rodríguez, *Testimonio y recuerdos* (Barcelona, 1978), 222.

35. M. García Venero, *Falange en la guerra de España* (Paris, 1967), 197; B. Félix Maíz, *Mola, aquel hombre* (Barcelona, 1976), 129; and Manuel Valdés Larrañaga in M. García Venero, *Testimonio de Manuel Hedilla* (Barcelona, 1977), 125–26.

There are numerous accounts of the military conspiracy of 1936. See especially R. de la Cierva, *Historia de la Guerra Civil española*, I: *Antecedentes: Monarquía y República 1898–1936* (Madrid, 1969), 735–816; and F. Olaya Morales, *La conspiración contra la Republica* (Barcelona, 1979), 309–81; as well as Maíz's above-cited book on Mola; I. Bernard, *Mola* (Granada, 1938); and H. R. Wilson, *The Man Who Created Franco* (Ilfracombe, Devon, 1972).

36. Ximénez de Sandoval, *Biografía*, 496. José Antonio's hagiographer was seldom reluctant to record his hero's physical assaults on and verbal abuse of other people, apparently considering it appropriate macho behavior.

37. This is explained by Miguel Primo de Rivera in his unfinished manuscript, "José Antonio," in *Papeles póstumos de José Antonio*, ed. M. Primo de Rivera (Barcelona, 1996), 218–21 (hereafter cited as *Papeles póstumos*).

38. According to F. Bravo Martínez, *José Antonio ante la justicia roja* (Madrid, 1941), 39, 60.

39. *Ultimos hallazgos de escritos y cartas de José Antonio Primo de Rivera*, ed. A. Del Rio Cisneros and E. Pavón Pereya (Madrid, 1962), 127–30. Later, during his final trial in Alicante, he would refer to a total of approximately one hundred thousand members on the eve of the Civil War.

40. Serrano Súñer, *Memorias*, 60.

41. The only direct reference to this, however, is in Miguel Primo de Rivera, "José Antonio," *Papeles póstumos*, 221.

42. Quoted in Gil Pecharromán, *JAPdR*, 481–82.

43. Ansaldo, *¿Para qué?* 122.

44. Quoted in Gil Pecharromán, *JAPdR*, 481–82.

45. The text was later found among his prison papers. *Papeles póstumos*, 139.

46. As in the case of Ramón Castaños, provincial chief of Alava, who was involved in a conspiracy with local Carlists when he was arrested. *El Pensamiento Alavés* (Vitoria), 17 May 1936.

47. There are references to a vague agreement between José Antonio and the national Carlist leadership, but this is quite unclear. *La Unión* (Seville), 18 July 1937; F. Beltrán Güell, *Preparación y desarrollo del Alzamiento Nacional* (Valladolid, 1937), 130; interviews with José Martínez Berasain and Desiderio Jiménez, Pamplona, 16 December 1958.

48. According to Ansaldo, *¿Para qué?* 121.

49. Andino, "Diario" (unpublished), 49, 52. Mariano García, the organizational secretary, agreed that relations with the military were "very bad." Interview in Madrid, 8 January 1959.

50. *Obras*, 935–37.

51. From the files of Miguel Maura in Barcelona, seen by the author on 23 December 1958.

52. The sketch that Mola had drawn up on 5 June had nothing to do with a fascist regime, but outlined the structure of a more conservative, authoritarian Republic that would maintain separation of church and state and some form of parliamentary system, though with certain restrictions such as a required and restrictive "electoral card" for all voters. Quoted in J. Arrarás, ed., *Historia de la Cruzada española*, 8 vols. (Madrid, 1940), III, 449.

53. Maíz, *Mola*, 88; F. Bravo Morata, *Franco y los muertos providenciales* (Madrid, 1979), 121.

54. Cf. Gil Robles, *No fue posible*, 718.

55. Jato, *La rebelión*, 353; E. Pavón Pereyra, *De la vida de José Antonio* (Madrid, 1949), 165.

56. *Obras*, 941–42.

57. Quoted in Maíz, *Mola*, 224.

58. Ramos González, *La violencia*, 149.

59. The first objective account of these events was presented by Luis Romero, *Por qué y cómo mataron*, 167–70.

60. Ibid.; Ramos González, *La violencia*, 149–50; and F. Rivas, *El Frente Popular* (Madrid, 1976), 350–51.

61. The principal studies of this assassination are I. Gibson, *La noche en que mataron a Calvo Sotelo* (Madrid, 1983); and Romero, *Por qué y cómo mataron*.

62. According to Hedilla in García Venero, *Testimonio*, 136.

63. *Obras* (1976), II, 1182–83.

64. José Andino, provincial chief of one of the nearest fairly large sectors of the Falange in Burgos, had informed Mola that he could have 6,000 men ready in four hours, but this is doubtful, and Mola was skeptical. Andino, "Diario," 64–65.

65. The best account is A. de Lizarza Iribarren, *Memorias de la conspiración 1931–1936* (Madrid, 1969).

66. According to Mayalde's testimony in I. Gibson, *En busca de José Antonio* (Barcelona, 1980), 154–55.

67. *Obras*, 945–46.

68. For Germany, the basic study is A. Viñas, *La Alemania nazi y el 18 de Julio* (Madrid, 1977). For Italy, see Saz, *Mussolini contra la II República*, 163–240; J. F. Coverdale, *Italian Intervention in the Spanish Civil War* (Princeton, 1975), 66–84; and AA. VV., *Italia y la guerra civil española* (Madrid, 1986), 9–32.

69. *El Heraldo de Aragón* (Zaragoza), 25 July 1936.

70. Interview with Ricardo Nieto (provincial chief of Zamora in 1936), Madrid, 17 January 1959.

71. *Documents on German Foreign Policy 1918–1945*, Series D, 1937–1945, vol. III: *Germany and the Spanish Civil War 1936–1939* (Washington, D.C., 1950), 84–89 (hereafter cited as *DGFP*).

72. M. Fórmica, *Visto y vivido, 1931–1937* (Barcelona, 1982), 236.

73. *Hoy* (Badajoz), 30 Aug. 1936; *La Unión* (Seville), 30 Aug. 1936.

74. There is an account in García Venero, *Falange en la guerra*, 185–92.

CHAPTER SEVEN

1. Marqués de Zayas, *Historia de la Vieja Guardia de Baleares* (Madrid, 1955), 139.

2. Gil Pecharromán, *JAPdR*, 494–95.

3. According to the conde de Mayalde, quoted in I. Gibson, *En busca de José Antonio* (Barcelona, 1980), 299.

4. In his unfinished essay "José Antonio," in *Papeles póstumos*, 223.

5. Ibid., 224.

6. G. Sánchez Recio, "La trama de la rebelión en Alicante," in *Guerra civil y franquismo en Alicante* (Alicante, 1990), 27, cited in Gil Pecharromán, *JAPdR*, 496.

7. *Papeles póstumos*, 224. This writing by Miguel Primo de Rivera is also emphatic on the point that the brothers were first told to expect the revolt to begin on 16 July, but this is uncorroborated by other evidence, and may be due to faulty memory on his part.

8. F. Bravo Martínez, *José Antonio ante la justicia roja* (Madrid, 1941), 32.

9. On the failure of the revolt in Alicante, see V. Ramos, *La Guerra Civil (1936–1939) en la provincia de Alicante* (Alicante, 1972), 85–111.

10. According to Miguel Primo de Rivera, "José Antonio," in *Papeles póstumos*, 229.

11. According to A. Gibello, *José Antonio, ese desconocido*, rev. ed. (Madrid, 1985), 284.

12. For what it is worth, the *Causa General* would later report that Falangists comprised 35 percent of 904 people executed in the province of Alicante, 6 percent of approximately 1,200 in Castellón, and 11 percent of 2,637 in Valencia. Throughout the Levant the bulk of those killed were members of the Derecha Regional Valenciana, the large CEDA group in the region, as cited in R. Valls, *La Derecha Regional Valenciana (1930–1936)* (Valencia, 1992), 238.

13. Gil Pecharromán, *JAPdR*, 502–3.

14. Published with the text of a lecture by D. Martínez Barrio, "Episodio de Alicante: Sobre José Antonio Primo de Rivera" (Mexico City, 1941), in *Homenaje a Diego Martínez Barrio* (Paris, 1978), 183–89.

15. The account by Martínez Barrio and the version presented by José Antonio during his subsequent trial substantially coincide. For the latter, J. M. Mancisidor, *Frente a frente: José Antonio frente al Tribunal Popular, Alicante, noviembre 1936* (Madrid, 1963), 211–12.

16. Indalecio Prieto later gained possession of José Antonio's prison papers. The above document was published in the Socialist Party pamphlet *El Testamento de Primo de Rivera*, prepared by Prieto in Mexico (no date), and was subsequently reproduced in whole or in part in various writings by Prieto and Rodolfo Llopis, for many years secretary of the Socialist Party. A photocopy was kept in the party archives in Toulouse, where Llopis personally gave me a copy in October 1958. It has appeared most recently in the *Papeles póstumos*, 142–45.

17. Mancisidor, *Frente a frente*, 211–12.

18. Gil Pecharromán, *JAPdR*, 505–6.

19. M. García Venero, *Falange en la guerra de España* (Paris, 1967), 200; Gibello, *José Antonio,* 288. (Guzmán el Bueno was a famous figure of medieval Spanish history who permitted Moorish besiegers to slay his son rather than surrender the fortress he was commanding.)

20. P. Primo de Rivera, *Recuerdos de una vida* (Madrid, 1983), 78–79.

21. This is based on an undated six-page memorandum about the enterprise prepared by Agustín Aznar.

22. The "German connection" in these operations has been well summarized in A. Viñas, "Berlín: Salvad a José Antonio," *Historia 16* 1 (May 1976), 41–56; and A. Viñas, "Intentos de salvar a José Antonio," in *Guerra, dinero, dictadura* (Barcelona, 1984), 60–97.

23. González de Canales, questionnaire prepared for the author, 24 January 1959, 12.

24. P. Preston, *Franco* (London, 1993), 194.

25. F. Ximénez de Sandoval, *José Antonio (Biografía)* (Barcelona, 1941), 784–85, 828; the conde de Romanones in *Dolor y memoria de España en el segundo aniversario de la muerte de José Antonio* (Barcelona, 1939), 307–8.

26. Interviews with Manuel Hedilla, Madrid, 20 January 1959; Narciso Perales, Madrid, 12 February 1959; Luis González Vicén, Madrid, 23 February 1959; and Anselmo de la Iglesia, Madrid, 26 May 1959.

27. *DGFP,* Series D, III, 114–16.

28. S. Ellwood, *Prietas las filas: Historia de Falange Española, 1933–1983* (Barcelona, 1984), 88.

29. *DGFP,* Series D, III, 120.

30. C. Vidal, *José Antonio: La biografía no autorizada* (Madrid, 1996), 230.

31. Viñas, *Guerra,* 178–97; García Venero, *Falange en la guerra,* 203–7; Preston, *Franco,* 195.

32. According to R. Garriga, *La España de Franco* (Puebla, Mex., 1970), 18–19.

33. According to P. Sainz Rodríguez, *Un reinado en la sombra* (Barcelona, 1981), 278; and L. M. Anson, *Don Juan* (Barcelona, 1994), 137–38.

34. There are a variety of references to the attitudes of Republican leaders in I. Prieto, *Palabras al viento* (Mexico City, 1969), 229–38; J. Zugazagoitia, *Historia de la guerra de España* (Buenos Aires, 1940), 176; Garriga, *La España de Franco,* 529; and García Venero, *Falange en la guerra,* 200.

35. D. Abad de Santillán, *Por qué perdimos la guerra* (Buenos Aires, 1940), 41.

36. *Papeles póstumos,* 160–66. This is the only prison essay that can be dated exactly, since the title page was dated by José Antonio himself.

37. Ibid., 178–83.

38. Ibid., 168–75.

39. This is taken from the article by Allen that appeared in the London *News Chronicle* on 24 October 1936. The earlier text in the *Chicago Daily Tribune* of 9 October differs slightly. Both are given in full in Gibson, *En busca,* 300–313.

40. See the references in Gibson, *En busca,* 170–73. Gibson points out that in his autobiography *My Life* (London, 1968), 421, Mosley declares that he re-

ceived a visit from José Antonio in the headquarters of the British Union of Fascists at some unspecified time "in the 1930s."

41. These maneuvers are ably analyzed by Gibson, ibid., 173–84.

42. Zugazagoitia, *Historia*, 246.

43. On the structure of justice in the Republican zone, see the studies in *Justicia en guerra* (Madrid, 1990), 24–437.

44. The principal studies are C. Fernández, *Paracuellos del Jarama: ¿Carrillo culpable?* (Barcelona, 1983); I. Gibson, *Paracuellos, como fue* (Barcelona, 1983); and R. Casas de la Vega, *El terror: Madrid 1936* (Madridejos, 1994).

45. Quoted in I. Covarrubias Arriazu, "¿Quién ordenó el fusilamiento de José Antonio?" *Nueva Historia* 22 (Nov. 1978), 67–70.

In his earliest Civil War memoir, *Cómo y por qué salí del Ministerio de Defensa Nacional* (Mexico City, 1940), Indalecio Prieto charged the Communist civil governor, Jesús Monzón, with playing a sinister role in expediting José Antonio's prosecution and execution, a charge sometimes repeated directly or indirectly by Falangists. In this intensely anti-Communist memoir, however, Prieto confused the identity and role of the civil governor. The Communist Monzón in fact was not appointed until July 1937, and the governor from February 1936 until that date was Francisco Valdés Casas of Izquierda Republicana. In my first book on the Falange, published in 1961, I repeated Prieto's error, as did nearly all other students of the affair until the correction was published by Covarrubias in 1978.

46. In a declaration on the twelfth anniversary of José Antonio's execution to *Arriba* (Madrid), 20 November 1948, cited in Gibello, *José Antonio*, 294–95.

47. From the trial record, a typescript copy of which was originally given to me by Dionisio Ridruejo in 1959, 23, reprinted in Mancisidor, *Frente a frente*, 78.

48. Quoted in Ximénez de Sandoval, *Biografía*, 800–802. Other accounts may be found in *Solidaridad Obrera* (Barcelona), 17–18 Nov. 1936, and in E. Pavón Pereyra, *De la vida de José Antonio* (Madrid, 1949), 185–201.

49. There is no indication that Indalecio Prieto, the Republican minister most favorably disposed to José Antonio, made any effort to save his life during these final days, though he did make a special effort after his death to obtain possession of the papers left behind, and was impressed by them. Prieto later wrote: "The philosophical affirmation that there is some truth in all ideas has a long history. This comes to my mind on account of the documents that José Antonio Primo de Rivera left behind in the Alicante jail. Perhaps in Spain we have not examined with serenity our respective ideologies to discover the coincidences, which were perhaps fundamental, and measure the divergences, probably secondary, in order to determine if the latter deserved to be aired on the field of battle." Prologue to Prieto's *Palabras de ayer y de hoy* (Santiago de Chile, 1938), 17.

These materials were subsequently kept in a suitcase of José Antonio's that was stored in a bank vault in Mexico City until 1977, at which time, following the democratization of Spain, the executor of Prieto's estate turned the keys over to the heir of the Primo de Rivera brothers, Miguel Primo de Rivera (the son of Fernando), who had himself just played a not insignificant role in encouraging the new democratization process. Miguel Primo de Rivera eventually published the papers in 1996.

50. *Obras,* 947–49.

51. These have been published in various collections, first in *Textos,* 517–30, and in Mancisidor, *Frente a frente,* 235–37.

52. Manicisidor, *Frente a frente,* 235–37.

53. Ibid., 237–40.

54. Ibid., 240.

55. J. García Oliver, *El eco de los pasos* (Madrid, 1978), 342–43.

56. F. Largo Caballero, *Mis recuerdos* (Mexico City, 1954), 208–9.

57. According to Gibello, *José Antonio,* 293.

58. The standard accounts are in Ximénez de Sandoval, *Biografía,* 809–25, and Pavón Pereyra, *De la vida,* 217–18. There is also a pamphlet by A. R. Antigüedad, *José Antonio en la cárcel de Alicante* (n.p., n.d.), based on an interview with his brother Miguel.

59. All the other members of his family in Alicante survived. Carmen Primo de Rivera and Margarita Larios were exchanged in the autumn of 1937; Miguel Primo de Rivera, only in March 1939.

60. D. Ridruejo, *Escrito en España* (Buenos Aires, 1962), 13.

61. D. Ridruejo, *Casi unas memorias* (Barcelona, 1976), 54.

62. The most systematic exposition along these lines is A. Muñoz Alonso, *Un pensador para un pueblo* (Madrid, 1969), but see also C. de Miguel Molina, *La personalidad religiosa de José Antonio* (Madrid, 1975).

CHAPTER EIGHT

1. I. Saz, *Mussolini contra la II República (1931–1936)* (Valencia, 1986), 171–240; A. Viñas, *La Alemania nazi y el 18 de julio* (Madrid, 1977), 357–450.

2. See P. Preston, *Franco* (London, 1993), 144–98; and J. Tusell, *Franco en la Guerra Civil: Una biografía política* (Barcelona, 1992), 9–56.

3. Complete statistics for all Carlist volunteers are not available, but eventually they amounted to more than 60,000, or at least 6 percent of all Nationalist troops. Total casualties amounted to approximately 34,000, or some 56 percent, with approximately 6,000 being killed, for a death rate of about 10 percent, nearly twice as high as that of the Nationalist Army as a whole. See J. Aróstegui, *Los combatientes carlistas en la guerra civil española,* 2 vols. (Madrid, 1989), and for an excellent brief summary, F. J. De Lizarza, "Los combatientes carlistas en la Guerra de España (1936–1939)," in *Identidad y nacionalismo en la España contemporánea: El Carlismo 1833–1975,* ed. S. Payne (Madrid, 1996), 123–38.

The province of Navarre had the highest mobilization both proportionally and in absolute numbers. Altogether it provided 11,443 volunteers for the Requetés, 7,068 for the Falangist units, and 21,950 volunteers and recruits for the regular army. This amounted to 40,461 volunteers and recruits from a provincial population of 345,883—nearly 12 percent of the total population, the highest percentage in Spain. Of these, 4,552 died in combat or of wounds and injuries (the Navarrese often formed part of the shock units), a percentage of 13.2, much more than double the rate of 5.69 for all Nationalist units. R. Salas Larrazábal, *Cómo ganó Navarra la Gran Cruz Laureada de San Fernando* (Madrid, 1980).

4. According to J. M. Iribarren, *Con el general Mola* (Zaragoza, 1937), 344.

5. R. Casas de la Vega, *Las milicias nacionales en la Guerra de España*, 2 vols. (Madrid, 1977), reports a total of 36,809 Falangist volunteers by October 1936, amounting to 56 percent of total volunteers, while S. Ellwood, *Prietas las filas: Historia de Falange Española, 1933–1983* (Barcelona, 1984), 73–74, corrects this to 35,549 Falangist volunteers, 54 percent of the total.

6. Carl von Haartman, memorandum, n.d.

7. In a report of 10 December 1936, Gen. Wilhelm Faupel, the official German representative to Franco, expressed concern over the lack of training of the Falangist militia. *DGFP*, Series D, III, 159–62.

8. According to Patricio González de Canales, questionnaire, 13–14.

9. *Boletín Oficial de Estado* (hereafter *BOE*), 22 Dec. 1936.

10. The fullest account is J. Del Burgo, "Un episodio poco conocido de la guerra civil española: La Real Academia Militar de Requetés y el destierro de Fal Conde," *Príncipe de Viana* 53 (May–Aug. 1992), 482–506.

11. *BOE*, 24 Jan. 1937.

12. *BOE*, 28 Jan. and 1 Feb. 1937.

13. Interviews with José María Valdés, Bilbao, 13 December 1936, and with Luis González Vicén, Madrid, 6 May 1959.

14. According to the volunteer British officer Peter Kemp (who served with the Legion), *Mine Were of Trouble* (London, 1957), 21.

15. This process began even during the original drive on Madrid in 1936. For example, the first Falangist bandera from the Canaries shipped out on 5 September 1936. The regular army quickly converted some 300 of its ablest members into shock troops. *Hoy* (Las Palmas), 6 Sept. 1936; P. Doreste Morales, *Ocho meses de campaña* (Las Palmas, 1941).

16. *Arriba España* (Pamplona), 6 Jan. 1937.

17. These lists have been published in my *Politics and the Military in Modern Spain* (Stanford, 1967), 458–62.

18. *Las milicias nacionales*, vol. II.

19. G. Jackson, *The Spanish Republic and Civil War, 1931–1939* (Princeton, 1965), 526–40. Jackson overestimates the total number of fatalities in the Civil War by possibly as much as 80 percent, and the statistics of the repression in the Nationalist zone are greatly exaggerated, though his estimates for military deaths are not far off.

20. Elena de la Souchère, *Explication de l'Espagne* (Paris, 1962), 229–33. The most recent work to offer highly inflated statistics is an otherwise perspicacious work by C. Vidal, *La guerra de Franco* (Barcelona, 1996), 445–50.

21. R. Salas Larrazábal, *Pérdidas de la guerra* (Barcelona, 1977).

22. The best of the regional studies are J. M. Solé i Sabaté, *La repressió franquista a Catalunya 1938–1953* (Barcelona, 1985), which finds Salas Larrazábal's statistics for the franquista repression in Catalonia to have been generally correct; and J. M. Solé i Sabaté and J. Villarroya i Font, *La repressió a la reraguarda de*

*Catalunya (1936–1939),* 2 vols. (Barcelona, 1989), which finds Salas Larrazábal's figures in this case to be excessive. The best of the provincial studies, M. Ortiz Heras, *Violencia política en la II República y el primer franquismo: Albacete, 1936–1950* (Madrid, 1950), also finds Salas Larrazábal's figures incorrect, though A. D. Martín Prieto, *La represión roja en Badajoz* (n.p., n.d.), finds the latter's statistics substantially correct, though slightly underestimated.

Other regional and provincial studies include G. Herrero Balsa and A. Hernández García, *La represión en Soria durante la Guerra Civil,* 2 vols. (Soria, 1982); "Altaffaylla Kultur Tadea," *Navarra 1936: De la esperanza al terror* (Tafalla, 1986); F. Moreno Gómez, *La Guerra Civil en Córdoba (1936–1939),* rev. ed. (Madrid, 1986); J. Casanova et al., *El pasado oculto: Fascismo y violencia en Aragón (1936–1939)* (Madrid, 1992); M. C. Riviero Noval, *La ruptura de la paz civil: Represión en La Rioja (1936–1939)* (Logroño, 1992); V. Gabarda, *Els afusellaments al País Valencià (1938–1956)* (Valencia, 1993); and F. Alía Miranda, *La Guerra Civil en retaguardia, Ciudad Real (1936–1939)* (Ciudad Real, 1994).

23. A. D. Martín Rubio, *Paz, piedad, perdón . . . y verdad. La Represión en la guerra civil: Una síntesis definitiva* (Madridejos, 1997).

24. *Boletín de la Junta de Defensa Nacional,* 29 July, 1 and 8 September 1936; *Legislación del Gobierno nacional: Segunda semestre 1936* (Avila, 1937), 88–92.

25. J. Cifuentes Checa and P. Maluenda Pons, *El asalto a la Republica: Los origenes del franquismo en Zaragoza (1936–1939)* (Zaragoza, 1995), 44–61. Their macro statistics compare reasonably well with those of Salas Larrazábal.

26. According to the provincial chief, Rafael Herreros de Tejada y Azcona, in M. García Venero, *Falange en la guerra de España* (Paris, 1967), 232.

27. I. Gibson, *The Death of Lorca* (Chicago, 1973).

28. A. Ruiz Vilaplana, *Doy fe: Un año de actuación en la España nacionalista* (Paris, n.d.), 54, 138. See also pp. 168–69.

29. On that occasion, Hedilla declared:

> I direct myself to the Falangists in charge of police and political investigations in the cities and, above all, in the small towns. Your mission must be to purge the leaders and murderers. But use all your energy to prevent anyone from indulging personal hatreds or from punishing or humiliating anyone who merely voted for the left out of hunger or desperation.
>
> We all know that in many towns there were—and are—rightists who are worse than the Reds. I insist that these kinds of arrests must stop and, where they have taken place, you must become the support of those unjustly persecuted.

*Arriba España,* 6 Jan. 1937.

30. Interviews with Pedro Gamero del Castillo, Madrid, 6 December 1958, and Luis González Vicén, Madrid, 18 May 1959.

31. Interview with Manuel Hedilla, Madrid, 20 January 1959.

32. S. Volta, *Spagna a ferro e fuoco* (Florence, 1937), 87–88.

33. Report to Berlin, 14 April 1937, in *DGFP,* Series D, III, 267–70.

34. *Boletín de la Junta de Defensa Nacional,* 28 Sept. 1936.

35. C. Gerahty, *The Road to Madrid* (London, 1937), 17–18.

36. V. Cadenas, *Actas del ultimo Consejo Nacional de Falange Española de las J. O. N. S. (Salamanca, 18–19 – IV – 1937) y algunas noticias referentes a la Jefatura Nacional de Prensa y Propaganda* (Madrid, 1975), 27–62.

37. García Venero, *Falange en la guerra*, 263–77.

38. Quoted in Duca di Bergamo, *Legionari di Roma in terra iberica (1936 xiv–1939 xvii)* (Rome, 1940), 40–41.

39. For example, in *F. E.* (Seville), 15 Jan. 1937; *Arriba España*, 28 Jan., 2 Feb. 1937.

40. Even by Hedilla himself. *Arriba España*, 16 April 1937.

41. Quoted in A. Luchino, ed., *I Falangisti spagnoli, cosa vogliono, perchè si battono* (Florence, 1936), 15, cited in R. Southworth, *Antifalange* (Paris, 1967), 155.

42. Reprinted in *Arriba España*, 6 Jan. 1937.

43. Ibid.

44. Quoted in F. Beltrán Güell, *Preparación y desarrollo del alzamiento nacional* (Valladolid, 1937), 221.

45. *Arriba España*, 6 Jan. 1937. Later, the last independent interview with Hedilla would be published under the title, echoing José Antonio, "Spain Will Become a Gigantic Syndicate of Producers." Ibid., 16 Apr. 1937.

46. The only study of this episode is J. L. Rodríguez Jiménez, "Incidentes entre Falange y Ejército, 1936–1939," *Historia 16* 12 (Feb. 1987), 19–22.

47. A. Lazo, *Retrato de fascismo rural en Sevilla* (Seville, 1997), 37–38. A. Gollonet Morales and J. Morales López, *Sangre y fuego – Málaga* (Granada, 1937), 165. The United Press correspondent Charles Foltz watched Communists and anarchists tear up their former party cards as they crossed the threshold of the Falangist recruiting office. C. J. Foltz, Jr., *The Masquerade in Spain* (Boston, 1948), 77.

48. Interview with Ignacio González de Migoya, of the Asturian Falange, in Oviedo, 25 January 1959. Dionisio Ridruejo has estimated that some 20 percent of the new members came from the left. Interview in Madrid, 17 November 1958. In Seville a prosperous and conservative publisher was warned by a friend, "Don't get involved with the Falange. A flood is pouring in there. Since they set no requirements, a large percentage are Marxists." A. Bahamonde y Sánchez de Castro, *Un año con Queipo de Llano* (Mexico City, 1938), 5–6.

49. According to Bahamonde, *Queipo de Llano*, 15.

50. *La Gaceta Regional* (Salamanca), 9 Aug. 1950.

51. *Arriba España*, 2 Feb. 1937.

52. C. L. Clark, "The Evolution of the Franco Regime," 3 vols. (Washington, D.C., n.d.), I, 653.

53. The most extensive account of the Sección is L. Suárez Fernández, *Crónica de la Sección Femenina* (Madrid, 1993).

54. Quoted in García Venero, *Falange en la guerra*, 211.

55. According to García Venero, *Falange en la guerra*, 276–77. In fact, *Jeraquía* only published four numbers.

56. This, at least, is the version presented ibid., 290–91.

57. Quoted ibid., 209.

58. J. M. Thomás, "Actas de las reuniones de la Junta de Mando Provisional de Falange Española de las J. O. N. S., celebradas durante el periodo 5 de diciembre de 1936–30 de marzo de 1937," *Historia Contemporánea* 7 (1992), 335–51.

59. Ibid.

60. Cf. the remarks by Cadenas, *Actas*, 154–55.

61. The most recent general history of Carlism is G. Alférez, *Historia del Carlismo* (Madrid, 1995), while the best-informed treatment of Carlist politics during the Civil War will be found in Tusell, *Franco en la Guerra Civil.*

62. According to a report by Faupel, 18 January 1937, *DGFP*, Series, D, III, 229.

63. According to an interview with Sandoval, S. Ellwood, "La unificación," *Historia 16* 12 (April 1987), 11–26. García Venero, *Falange en la guerra*, 308–9, declares that the first initiative came from Nicolás Franco, who had been monitoring the Falange for some time and allegedly used the police agent Mauricio Carlavilla to observe it and help draft alternative schemes.

64. The full text may be found in Cadenas, *Actas*, 21–24.

65. García Venero, *Falange en la guerra*, 333.

66. Ibid., 323–30; Tusell, *Franco en la Guerra Civil*, 105–7; "Acta" of the Junta de Mando meeting of 5 March 1937, in Thomás, "Actas."

67. Tusell, *Franco en la Guerra Civil*, 107–9.

68. Ibid., 111–12. The nature of Farinacci's mission and his conclusions were confirmed to me by the military adviser who accompanied him, Gen. Emilio Canevari. Interview in Rome, 6 April 1959.

69. R. Serrano Súñer, *Entre Hendaya y Gibraltar* (Mexico City, 1947), 25–26, 32, 33.

70. *ABC* (Seville), 19 Feb. 1937.

71. These references and quotations are taken from Tusell, *Franco en la Guerra Civil*, 121.

72. Ibid., 121–22.

73. This is more or less admitted in García Venero's pro-Hedilla version; see his *Falange en la guerra*, 288.

74. Interview with Hedilla, Madrid, 8 January 1959.

75. Tusell, *Franco en la Guerra Civil*, 116–20.

76. *ABC*, 9 March 1937.

77. Interview with Hedilla, Madrid, 8 January 1959.

78. This is well summarized in Preston, *Franco*, 259.

79. Ibid., 259–60.

80. Thomás, "Actas," 351.

81. Cadenas, *Actas*, 113.

82. Tusell, *Franco en la Guerra Civil*, 124.

83. Ibid., 123.

84. The text was first published in A. Alcázar de Velasco, *Serrano Súñer en la Falange* (Barcelona, 1941), 64–66, and later in Cadenas, *Actas*, 93–95.

85. The events of 16–18 April 1937 in Salamanca were perhaps the most confused and controversial in the entire history of the Falange, and full and incontrovertible details of all aspects will probably never become available. This account

is based on interviews with Hedilla, Madrid, 8 January 1959, and with Daniel López Puertas (head of the detachment sent to arrest Dávila), Madrid, 5 January 1959; Hedilla's polemical pamphlet *Cartas entrecruzadas entre el Sr. D. Manuel Hedilla Larrey y el Sr. D. Ramón Serrano Súñer* (Madrid, 1947); García Venero, *Falange en la guerra*, 358–89, and the latter's subsequent rectification in his *Historia de la unificación* (Madrid, 1970), 189–212; Cadenas, *Actas*, 70–107; Alcázar de Velasco, *Serrano Súñer*, 64–71; A. Alcázar de Velasco, *Los siete días de Salamanca* (Madrid, 1976); S. Dávila, *José Antonio, Salamanca . . . y otras cosas* (Madrid, 1967); D. Ridruejo, *Casi unas memorias* (Barcelona, 1976), 87–96; E Vegas Latapié, *Memorias políticas*, 2 vols. (Madrid, 1983), II, 208–18; Tusell, *Franco en la Guerra Civil*, 124–29; and Preston, *Franco*, 262–64.

86. F. Franco, *Palabras del Caudillo* (Madrid, 1943), 9–17.

87. Cadenas, *Actas*, 110–31.

88. F. Díaz-Plaja, ed., *La España política del siglo XX*, 4 vols. (Barcelona, 1972), III, 287–90.

89. See the documentation in L. Suárez Fernández, *Francisco Franco y su tiempo*, 8 vols. (Madrid, 1984), II, 200–209 (hereafter cited as *FF.*).

90. The figure of 49 condemned to life imprisonment is cited by José Luis Fernando from "a document that Franco kept among his personal papers," in Fernando's *Los enigmas del Caudillo* (Madrid, 1992), 111.

91. Tusell, *Franco y la Guerra Civil*, 134.

92. Later published in J. Gutiérrez Ravé, *Gil Robles, caudillo frustrado* (Madrid, 1967), 198–99.

93. No one has ever impugned Hedilla's personal honesty in connection with these events; his political judgment or skill is another matter. His first apologia appeared in a series of letters published in the semiclandestine pamphlet cited above: *Cartas entrecruzadas entre el Sr. D. Manuel Hedilla Larrey y el Sr. D. Ramón Serrano Súñer*. These missives revealed that Hedilla tended to blame Serrano and others in the Generalissimo's entourage for what had happened to him more than he did Franco himself.

The case for Hedilla was first presented in detail in García Venero's *Falange en la guerra*, 287–427. (This project was contracted for and subsidized by Hedilla, whose business interests made him an affluent man in the 1950s and 1960s.) After Hedilla and García Venero quarreled, most of that work was revised from Hedilla's personal point of view and republished as *Testimonio de Manuel Hedilla* (Madrid, 1970), while García Venero published his own "rectification" of the preceding book in his *Historia de la unificación*. There is a critique of García Venero's work in Southworth, *Antifalange* (Paris, 1967), 176–240.

94. *Palabras del Caudillo*, 406.

95. For example, in the last number of the right-radical journal *Acción Española* (Feb. 1937), José Pemartín had called for a "Catholic-Spanish-Fascist-Nation-State," declaring that "in Spain we can be more fascist than Fascism itself. . . . Fascism is a religious concept, Mussolini has written. Spanish fascism will be, then, the religion of religion" (p. 401).

96. *Palabras del Caudillo*, 167.

CHAPTER NINE

1. F. Franco, *Palabras del Caudillo* (Madrid, 1943), 167.

2. As of 30 April 1937, the financial resources of the two groups forming the state party were as follows:

> Falangists: cash on hand, 5,157.40 pesetas; in the Banco de España, 4,064.30 pesetas; in the Banco de Bilbao, 50,000 pesetas. Total: 59,221.70 pesetas.
> Requetés: cash on hand, 1,439.70 pesetas; in the Banco Español de Crédito, 30,500 pesetas; other funds, 520.19 pesetas. Total: 32,459.89 pesetas.

Data from a receipt signed by Pablo de Legarreta, treasurer of the Falange, in the files of José Andino in 1959.

3. *BOE*, 22 April 1937.

4. According to Ridruejo. Multiple interviews in Madrid, November–December 1958.

5. With the possible exceptions of Indalecio Prieto and José María de Areilza, Serrano has generated more memoir literature than any other public figure of twentieth-century Spain. In addition to *Entre Hendaya y Gibraltar* (Mexico City, 1947), after Franco's death he produced a much more outspoken and extensive *La historia como fue: Memorias* (Barcelona, 1977), and at the age of ninety-four published the tape of a marathon lecture at the Cursos de Verano de la Universidad Complutense, *Política de España 1936–1975* (Madrid, 1995). Heleno Saña prepared *El franquismo sin mitos: Conversaciones con Serrano Súñer* (Barcelona, 1982), which was followed by a sort of authorized biography by R. García Lahiguera, *Ramón Serrano Súñer: Un documento para la historia* (Barcelona, 1983). A new level of panegyric is reached by I. Merino's superficial *Serrano Súñer: Historia de una conducta* (Barcelona, 1996).

6. D. Ridruejo, *Casi unas memorias* (Barcelona, 1976), 96, 108.

7. According to Serrano as quoted in Saña, *El franquismo*, 69.

8. Serrano Súñer, *Entre Hendaya*, 42.

9. *BOE*, 13 May 1937.

10. J. Tusell, *Franco en la Guerra Civil: Una biografía política* (Barcelona, 1992), 139.

11. "Gece" immediately whipped out the most obsequiously franquista of all the new pamphlets, entitled *La Falange — hecha hombre — ¡conquista el Estado!*

12. Tusell, *Franco y la Guerra Civil*, 142–43.

13. The limited functions of most of the Technical Services are treated in R. Chueca, *El fascismo en los comienzos del régimen de Franco: Un estudio sobre FET–JONS* (Madrid, 1983), 233–64.

14. Fundación Nacional Francisco Franco, *Documentos inéditos para la historia del Generalísimo Franco*, 4 vols. (Madrid, 1992–94), I, 133–41 (hereafter cited as *Documentos inéditos*).

15. Ibid., I, 156–59.

16. Interview in Madrid, 21 May 1959.

17. For further references on the FEA, see S. Ellwood, *Prietas las filas: Historia de Falange Española, 1933–1983* (Barcelona, 1984), 203–6.

18. Cf. Tusell, *Franco en la Guerra Civil*, 151.

19. *Unidad* (Santander), 30 Nov. 1937.

20. *Unidad*, 23 May 1937; *Sur* (Málaga), 12 Dec. 1937; *F. E.* (Seville), 1 Jan. 1938; *Hierro* (Bilbao), 7 March 1938.

21. Even quoting Pío Baroja in this connection. *F. E.*, 8 Jan. 1938.

22. According to Serrano, "In the first months there was really no viable candidate in the Falange, whether because of extreme youth, lack of importance in the history of the party, or the jealousies excited in the command." When the possibility of the exchange for Fernández Cuesta developed, "his candidacy was immediately presented for that post not only by the Falangists but also, with great determination, by other groups and sectors who maintained the most passionate opposition to myself." *Entre Hendaya*, 59.

23. Prieto had seen to it that copies of José Antonio's testament and extracts from his prison papers were sent into the Nationalist zone, hoping to incite the rebelliousness of camisas viejas. Before leaving Republican territory, Fernández Cuesta was urged by Prieto to join the shadow "Falange Española Auténtica." Fernández Cuesta has said privately that he never doubted the good faith of a few legitimists who may have promoted the FEA, but that amid the Civil War he had no desire to question Franco's leadership. Interview in Madrid, 13 February 1959.

24. R. Fernández Cuesta, *Testimonio, recuerdos y reflexiones* (Madrid, 1985), 109–36.

25. R. Fernández Cuesta, *Intemperie, victoria y servicio: Discursos y escritos* (Madrid, 1951), 51–57.

26. R. Serrano Súñer, *Entre el silencio y la propaganda, la Historia como fue: Memorias* (Barcelona, 1977), 256.

27. Ridruejo, *Casi unas memorias*, 119.

28. Quoted from *La Voz de Galicia* (La Coruña) in *F. E.*, 4 Jan. 1938.

29. Serrano Súñer, *Entre Hendaya*, 31.

30. The most extensive statement would eventually be A. Alcázar de Velasco, *Serrano Súñer en la Falange* (Barcelona, 1941). It was also pointed out that Serrano's brother Fernando had been provincial secretary of the Falange in the Balearics before the war. Marqués de Zayas, *Historia de la Vieja Guardia de Baleares* (Madrid, 1955), 29–31.

31. Serrano has said that before the end of 1937 he sought to allay such opposition by writing directly to Don Juan, then in Estoril, asking for the royal family's support for the duration of the war, and pledging that the question of the monarchy would be taken up afterward. Don Juan promised his support. Serrano Súñer, *Memorias*, 164.

32. Cf. Ridruejo, *Casi unas memorias*, 121.

33. Saña, *El franquismo*, 148.

34. Serrano observed wryly, "Its life was not exactly intense." *Entre Hendaya*, 65.

35. Ibid., 66.

36. Report from Eberhard von Stohrer, 19 May 1938. *DGFP*, Series D, III, 657–63.

37. Serrano Súñer, *Memorias*, 169–72. The only published account of José Antonio's execution by an eyewitness is that presented by Diego Molina, a member of the firing squad that carried it out. Though it does not directly confirm all the details of the standard Falangist accounts, it substantially agrees with them. This testimony, dictated by the illiterate Molina in 1940, has been published in H. R. Southworth, *Antifalange* (Paris, 1967) 163, together with a photocopy of the original manuscript.

38. Serrano Súñer, *Entre Hendaya*, 60.

39. The principal purge of those guilty of disciplinary infractions and common crimes was carried out during the second half of 1938. *Boletín del Movimiento Falange Española Tradicionalista* (hereafter *BMFET*), 15 June and 10 Oct. 1938. According to Chueca, *El fascismo*, 192–93, the number of expulsions during the next fourteen years varied as follows:

| | | | | | |
|------|-------|------|-----|------|-----|
| 1937 | 204   | 1942 | 777 | 1947 | 145 |
| 1938 | 1,303 | 1943 | 437 | 1948 | 85  |
| 1939 | 556   | 1944 | 519 | 1949 | 143 |
| 1940 | 685   | 1945 | 270 | 1950 | 178 |
| 1941 | 825   | 1946 | 198 |      |     |

40. The best, most recent discussions of the uses of the term are A. Gleason, *Totalitarianism: The Inner History of the Cold War* (New York, 1995); and A. Söllner, R. Walkenhaus, and K. Wieland, eds., *Totalitarismus: Eine Ideengeschichte des 20. Jahrhunderts* (Berlin, 1997).

41. *BMFET*, 15 Aug. 1937.

42. Ibid.

43. Circular of the Secretaría Política, no. 1, 5 July 1937.

44. Tusell, *Franco en la Guerra Civil*, 155.

45. G. Oudard, *Chemises noires, brunes, vertes en Espagne* (Paris, 1939), 251.

46. *BMFET*, 1 Nov. 1937; Tusell, *Franco en la Guerra Civil*, 150–51.

47. Tusell, *Franco en la Guerra Civil*, 155.

48. Quoted in M. Ferrer, "El General Franco y la Comunión Tradicionalista" (manuscript), 38–41. Fal Conde was allowed to return to Spain only after the Civil War was over, and subsequently placed under house arrest. In 1942 he was sent for a time into internal exile in Mallorca.

49. Quoted in Tusell, *Franco en la Guerra Civil*, 296.

50. Ibid., 297.

51. From Rodezno's unpublished memoir, "Veinte meses en el gobierno," 38–39, cited ibid., 298.

52. Quoted ibid., 298–99.

53. The threatened sanctions were lifted though the newspaper was fined in 1938. Ibid., 299–300.

54. *DGFP*, Series D, III, 267–70.

55. Interview with Fermín Yzurdiaga in Pamplona, 12 December 1958.

56. *DGFP*, Series D, III, 170–73.

57. Tusell, *Franco en la Guerra Civil*, 152–53.

58. *DGFP*, Series D, III, 590–99.

59. Ibid., 480–84.

60. Ibid., 640.

61. A subsequent decree of 22 April 1938 reiterated that the Chief of State would assume "the absolute powers of the state" in order to realize its "totalitarian aspirations."

62. These aspects are examined by Serrano's biographer, García Lahiguera, *Ramón Serrano Súñer*, 124.

63. Serrano Súñer's speeches during this phase were published as *Siete discursos* (Bilbao, 1938).

64. General studies of the regime's press policy include M. Fernández Areal, *La libertad de prensa en España (1938–1971)* (Madrid, 1971); M. L. Abellán, *Censura y creación en España (1939–1976)* (Barcelona, 1980); J. Terrón Montero, *La prensa en España durante el régimen de Franco* (Madrid, 1981); and J. Sinova, *La censura de prensa durante el franquismo (1936–1951)* (Madrid, 1989).

65. *ABC* (Seville), 24 April 1938, in Tusell, *Franco en la Guerra Civil*, 265–66.

66. Giménez Arnau includes a few remarks about his work during 1938 and 1939 in his extremely superficial autobiography, *Memorias de memoria* (Barcelona, 1978), 95–106.

67. Serrano Súñer was also FET national delegate of press and propaganda, while Giménez Arnau and Ridruejo were the heads of the corresponding branches of the Ministry of the Interior and FET national delegates of press and of propaganda, respectively.

68. On radio in the Nationalist zone, see J. García Jiménez, *Radiotelevisión y política cultural en el franquismo* (Madrid, 1980), 1–77.

69. A full list of FET publications will be found in Chueca, *El fascismo*, 461–70. For more information on the party's role in press and propaganda during the early years of the regime, see 276–94.

70. *Palabras del Caudillo*, 45–57.

71. Quoted in Tusell, *Franco en la Guerra Civil*, 293.

72. DGFP, Series D, III, 657–63.

73. Ibid., 709–11.

74. Quoted in Tusell, *Franco en la Guerra Civil*, 308.

75. Ibid., 253–54.

76. *Palabras del Caudillo*, 307–18.

77. One of the earliest pronouncements by Franco and a proclamation by the military commander of Zaragoza to this effect are reprinted in G. Orizana and J. M. Liébana, *El Movimiento Nacional* (Valladolid, 1937), 55–57.

78. *Chicago Daily Tribune*, 27 July 1936.

79. All this was reflected in the first agricultural program distributed by the FET, *El futuro de la agricultura nacional-sindicalista* (Valladolid, n.d. [1938?]).

80. *The Times* (London), 18 April 1937.

81. Ibid., 8 March 1937.

82. He repeated the theme in a United Press interview the same month. Franco, *Palabras del Caudillo,* 28, 149.

83. Ibid., 196.

84. *Amanecer* (Zaragoza), 14 Dec. 1937.

85. Tusell, *Franco en la Guerra Civil,* 257.

86. Ibid.

87. Fernández Cuesta and one other cabinet minister also participated to some extent in the preparation of this draft. Fernández Cuesta, *Testimonio,* 194–95.

88. Tusell, *Franco en la Guerra Civil,* 258.

89. This account is also based on interviews with Dionisio Ridruejo in Madrid, 10 and 19 January 1959, and his description in *Casi unas memorias,* 195; and in Suárez Fernández, *FF,* II, 288–89. A different kind of commentary was published by J. Garrigues in his *Tres conferencias en Italia sobre el Fuero del Trabajo* (Madrid, 1939).

90. Tusell, *Franco en la Guerra Civil,* 259–60, based partly on Italian documentation; and Fernández Cuesta, *Testimonio,* 194–95.

91. Tusell, *Franco en la Guerra Civil,* 261.

92. Cf. the commentary of Spain's leading theorist of Catholic corporatism, J. J. Azpiazu Zulaica, *Orientaciones cristianas del Fuero del Trabajo* (Burgos, 1939).

93. Tusell, *Franco en la Guerra Civil,* 262.

94. See the discussion in M. A. Aparicio, *El sindicalismo vertical y la formación del Estado franquista* (Barcelona, 1980), 53–80.

95. Fernández Cuesta, *Intemperie,* 91.

96. Ibid., 101–2.

97. *ABC,* 5 May 1938, quoted in Tusell, *Franco en la Guerra Civil,* 263.

98. J. M. Arauz de Robles, *Obra Nacional Corporativa* (Burgos, 1937).

99. *BMFET,* 1 Jan. 1938.

100. Cf. Aparicio, *Sindicalismo vertical,* 39–51.

101. Chueca, *El fascismo,* 348–49, 473–77.

102. "Syndical cultivation of large dry cultivation units, allotment of irrigated land in family units, immediate start of irrigation in those districts where the work was completed some time ago, the kind of cultivation in every zone to be determined by the conditions of exploitation, transfer of farming population from lands on which it is not possible to live, because of the sterility of the soil . . . , to other lands more fit for production." R. Fernández Cuesta, *Discursos* (Madrid, 1942), 104. There was, of course, no explanation of where the new land and capital were to be found, other than the implication that somehow it would come from state assistance and from requiring large owners to play a more socially constructive role.

103. Preston, *Franco,* 297.

104. *La Sección Femenina: Historia y organización* (Madrid, 1952), 20.

105. In addition to the detailed account by L. Suárez Fernández, *Crónica de la Sección Femenina* (Madrid, 1993), there are various shorter studies: M. T. Gallego Méndez, *Mujer, Falange y franquismo* (Madrid, 1983); R. Sánchez López, *Mujer española, una sombra de destino en lo universal: Trayectoria histórica de*

*la Sección Femenina de Falange (1934–1937)* (Murcia, 1990); M. García Basauri, "La Sección Femenina en la Guerra Civil española," *Historia 16* 5 (June 1980), 45–56; V. L. Enders, "Women's Political History: The 'Sección Femenina' in 1937," in *La mistica spagnola*, ed. G. Massa (1989), 129–39; and V. L. Enders, "Nationalism and Feminism: The Sección Femenina of the Falange," *History of European Ideas* 15 (1992), 673–80.

106. *Fundamentos del Nuevo Estado* (Madrid, 1943), 126–29.

107. This power struggle is treated in Gallego Méndez, *Mujer, Falange,* 59–66.

108. Dávila soon published a brief memoir, *De la O. J. al Frente de Juventudes* (Madrid, 1941).

109. The principal study is J. Sáez Marín, *El Frente de Juventudes: Política de juventud en la España de la postguerra (1937–1960)* (Madrid, 1988), 30–53.

110. Tusell, *Franco en la Guerra Civil,* 292.

111. *DGFP*, Series D, III, 590–99.

112. Neither of the works on Queipo—M. Barrios, *El último virrey: Queipo de Llano* (Seville, 1978), or I. Gibson, *Queipo de Llano* (Barcelona, 1986)—is fully satisfactory.

113. This is based on interviews with Ridruejo in Madrid, 27 November and 4 December 1958; his *Casi unas memorias,* 195–96; and Serrano Súñer, *Memorias,* 262. Cf. J. Lago, *Las contramemorias de Franco* (Barcelona, 1976), 119.

114. Quoted in Saña, *El franquismo,* 153.

115. Fernández Cuesta, *Testimonio,* 150–51.

116. *BMFET*, 1 July 1938; Ridruejo, *Casi unas memorias,* 126–27, 195–96; Serrano Súñer, *Memorias,* 262–64; Saña, *El franquismo,* 152–54; Tusell, *Franco en la Guerra Civil,* 304–5.

117. Quoted in Tusell, *Franco en la Guerra Civil,* 304.

118. Ibid., 302.

119. Ibid., 284–87. Vegas Latapié has described part of the background to this in his *Los caminos del desengaño: Memorias políticas 2, 1936–1948* (Madrid, 1987), 412–67.

120. Queipo had complained about the FET and various of its appointees and representatives on several occasions. In November 1938 he traveled by airplane to Salamanca to insist that Serrano's appointee as civil governor of Seville, the young neo-Falangist Pedro Gamero del Castillo, be removed. Serrano refused to budge, and Franco backed him up in a letter to Queipo. *Documentos inéditos,* I, 202–4. The most extensive of Serrano's several accounts of this is in his *Memorias,* 214–19.

121. *BOE*, 17 Nov. 1938. See also *Dolor y memoria de España en el segundo aniversario de la muerte de José Antonio* (Barcelona, 1939).

122. *Palabras del Caudillo,* 77–79.

123. S. Ros and A. Bouthelier, *A hombros de la Falange: Historia del traslado de los restos de José Antonio* (Madrid and Barcelona, 1940). Cf. the evocation a half-century later in the memoirs of J. A. Girón Velasco, *Si la memoria no me falla* (Barcelona, 1994), 62–69.

Years later the Pretender, Don Juan, is said to have complained to Franco about the burial of José Antonio at the site of the royal pantheon, to which the Generalissimo is said to have replied, "Your Highness is badly informed: José Antonio is not in the royal pantheon but in the central nave before the high altar, which is a much more important site." *Si la memoria,* 68.

124. The major political holidays and special occasions are listed in F. Moret Messerli, *Conmemoraciones y fechas de la España nacionalsindicalista* (Madrid, 1942).

125. *DGFP,* Series D, III, 843–51.

126. An occasional incident, such as the brawl in Seville in the autumn of 1938 between a Falangist youth demonstration and a religious procession, was quickly controlled and hushed up. See the report by von Stohrer, ibid., 796–801.

127. On the influence of European fascism in Bolivia, see F. Gallego and A. Viola, "Populisme i feixisme a Bolivia: Falange Socialista Boliviana i el Movimiento Nacionalista Revolucionario," *L'Avenç* 177 (Jan. 1994), 6–11.

CHAPTER TEN

1. Cf. the remarks of R. García Lahiguera, *Ramón Serrano Súñer: Un documento para la historia* (Barcelona, 1983), 142; and R. Tamames, *La Repúblicá: La Era de Franco* (Madrid, 1973), 498.

2. *Ciano's Diplomatic Papers,* ed. M. Muggeridge (London, 1948), 294–95.

3. M. Jerez Mir, *Elites políticas y centros de extracción en España 1938–1957* (Madrid, 1982), 230.

4. Ibid., 121.

5. These percentages are derived from data in C. Viver Pi-Sunyer, *El personal político de Franco (1936–1945)* (Barcelona, 1978), 157, which finds that the new government elite stemmed from the following backgrounds:

| | Number of individuals | Number of positions |
|---|---|---|
| Military and UME | 232 | 469 |
| F. E. before 18 July with leadership rank | 82 | 226 |
| F. E. before 18 July without leadership rank | 89 | 186 |
| F. E. after 18 July but before unification | 41 | 116 |
| JONS | 26 | 63 |
| Alfonsine monarchists | 87 | 184 |
| Acción Española | 34 | 103 |
| Bloque Nacional | 28 | 82 |
| Renovación Española | 13 | 30 |
| Carlists | 55 | 123 |
| Catholics | 39 | 83 |
| ACNP (Catholic propagandists) | 30 | 65 |
| CEDA | 72 | 122 |
| Republican moderate liberals | 7 | 13 |
| Unión Monárquica Nacional (1930) | 2 | 6 |

6. *Gaceta de la República*, no. 112, 22 April 1937. Though somewhat crude and lacking in advanced technical training, Muñoz Grandes was well regarded for his professional competence and enjoyed considerable esteem among his fellow officers. The initial left Republican government of 1936 had reassigned him as a colonel of Moroccan troops. After he refused to join the conspiracy, his old comrades asked him to resign his post so as not to create an obstacle to the revolt. Muñoz Grandes agreed to this, but after the war began was arrested and at first sentenced by the Republic to nine years imprisonment, leaving him embittered and eager to join the Nationalists.

7. Perhaps the most objective sketch of the background of Sánchez Mazas will be found in G. Morán, *Los españoles que dejaron de serlo: Euskadi, 1937–1981* (Barcelona, 1981), 134–48.

8. Though Carceller attempted to establish camisa vieja credentials, before the war he had in fact been a darling of the Catalan monarchist radical right; he had dealings with the Falange, but more as a "fellow traveler" than as a party member. Cf. M. Valdés Larrañaga, *De la Falange al Movimiento (1936–1952)* (Madrid, 1994), 181–83. Because of his background in business, he would be named minister of industry and commerce in October 1940, a position in which he would engage in slippery and opportunist dealings with both the Axis and the Allies.

9. *Fundamentos del Nuevo Estado* (Madrid, 1943), 22–37; *Recopilación sistemática de la legislación del Movimiento: Mayo 1937 a diciembre 1943* (Madrid, 1944).

10. According to a report by the vice secretary general to a meeting of the National Council in March 1963, cited in J. Bardavío, *La estructura del poder en España* (Madrid, 1969), 117.

11. Ibid.

12. R. Serrano Súñer, *De la victoria y la postguerra (Discursos)* (Madrid, 1941), 78.

13. R. Gutiérrez, *Memorias de un azul* (Salamanca, 1937), 62.

14. Especially in *El nuevo Estado español* (Madrid, 1939), 39, 59–68.

15. J. Beneyto and J. M. Costa Serrano, *El Partido* (Zaragoza, 1939), 150, 156, 169. Four decades later, after Franco's death, an elderly Beneyto would publish a very different book, *La identidad del franquismo* (Madrid, 1979), which would interpret the regime and its institutions at least somewhat more accurately as a kind of absolute monarchy and neotraditionalist system.

16. P. Laín Entralgo, *Los valores morales del nacional-sindicalismo* (Madrid, 1941), 7–8.

17. Aspects of press opinion during World War II, Falangist and otherwise, are presented in C. García Alix, *La prensa española ante la Segunda Guerra Mundial* (Madrid, 1974); and A. Lazo, *La Iglesia, la Falange y el fascismo (un estudio sobre la prensa española de postguerra)* (Seville, 1995).

18. For a good, brief study of Falangist novels dealing with the Civil War, see G. Thomas, *The Novel of the Spanish Civil War* (Cambridge, 1990), 65–93. The best of these was Foxá's *Madrid de corte a checa*, republished in Barcelona in 1993.

19. See J. C. Mainer, *Falange y literatura* (Madrid, 1985). For an extensive anthology of writings by Falangists and rightists, see the somewhat eclectic compilation of J. Rodríguez Puértolas, *Literatura fascista española,* 2 vols. (Madrid, 1986).

20. Ridruejo, *Casi unas memorias* (Barcelona, 1976), 224.

21. Ibid.

22. See S. Wahnón, "The Theatre Aesthetics of the Falange," in *Fascism and Theatre,* ed. G. Berghaus (Providence and Oxford, 1996), 191–209.

23. F. Linares, "Theatre and Falangism at the Beginning of the Franco Regime," ibid., 202–28.

24. *El SEU: Sentido de las falanges universitarias* (Madrid, 1939), 41, cited in M. A. Ruiz Carnicer, *El Sindicato Español Universitario (SEU) 1939–1965* (Madrid, 1996), 123. This excellent work is the key study of the SEU.

25. Ruiz Carnicer, *El Sindicato,* 131.

26. Ibid., 132.

27. The North American Hispanist Thomas Mermall has concluded that of all Falangist intellectuals, "It is perhaps Antonio Tovar who best reveals the pagan, modernist and distinctly secular-totalitarian strain in the Falangist ideology." "Falangist Esthetics and Politics," in T. Mermall, *The Rhetoric of Humanism: Spanish Culture after Ortega y Gasset* (New York, 1976), 21.

28. Ruiz Carnicer, *El Sindicato,* 147–56.

29. See ibid., 107–20, for a detailed analysis of SEU membership.

30. *BMFET,* 20 Aug. 1939.

31. J. Saez Marín, *El Frente de Juventudes (1937–1960)* (Madrid, 1988), 61.

32. Cf. FET, *Falange ante la universidad* (Madrid, 1942).

33. From the published text in the files of Sotomayor's comrade, Carlos Juan Ruiz de la Fuente. Sotomayor's emphasis.

34. According to S. Dávila, *De la O. J. al Frente de Juventudes* (Madrid, 1941), 22–25.

35. For the early development of the Frente de Juventudes, see Saez Marín, *Frente de Juventudes,* 86–151.

36. The Frente de Juventudes was composed of five categories: Labor Centers for adolescent and teenaged workers; Teaching Centers for secondary school students in the cities; Rural Centers; the SEU; and the Falanges Juveniles de Franco. Only the last two were directly political, and even the Falanges Juveniles spent most of their funds on sports and outings. The Falanges Juveniles were divided into three age groups, and their membership was reported by *Arriba* on 31 December 1941 as follows:

| Age | Males | | Females | |
|-----|-------|------|---------|------|
| 7–10 | Pelayos | 162,738 | Margaritas | 94,484 |
| 10–14 | Flechas | 251,797 | Flechas Femeninas | 126,590 |
| 14–18 | Cadetes | 150,464 | Flechas Azules | 57,878 |
| | | 564,999 | | 278,952 |

This amounted to only about 17.5 percent and 8.5 percent, respectively, of the male and female population of approximately six and a half million for these age groups in Spain. It may be compared with the figures for Fascist Italy, where approximately 65 percent of Italian juvenile males and 44 percent of females were at least nominal members of Fascist youth organizations in 1939. See R. Chueca, *El fascismo en los comienzos del regimen de Franco: Un estudio sobre FET–JONS* (Madrid, 1983), 311; and J. J. Linz, "From Falange to Movimiento-Organización," in *Authoritarian Politics in Modern Society,* ed. S. P. Huntington and C. H. Moore (New Haven, 1970), 167.

Moreover, by 1943 membership was already in decline, though according to the statistics of the Falanges Juveniles the peak of their camping activity came in 1942–1945.

37. *ABC,* 6 Feb. 1943, quoted in A. Mayordomo and J. M. Fernández Soria, *Vencer y convencer: Educación y política en España 1936–1945* (Valencia, 1993), 137.

38. M. De Santa Cruz (pseud.), *Apuntes y documentos para la historia del tradicionalismo español 1939–1966,* 2 vols. (Zamora, 1984), I, 21–100.

39. Quoted in J. M. Thomàs, *Falange, guerra civil, franquisme: F. E. T. y de las J. O. N. S. de Barcelona en els primers anys del règim franquista* (Barcelona, 1992), 362–64. This is the best local or regional study of any section of the FET.

A brief investigation of the FET in a much smaller Catalan town—Josep Sánchez, "La Falange de Flix: Aspectes socio-económics i polítics (1938–1965)," in *Franquisme a les comarques tarragonines* (Tarragona, 1993), 75–104—reveals the FET's active role in local government and affairs. In Flix membership quotas were divided into three categories according to ability to pay, and the membership included "many affiliates from the Republican Left of Catalonia (ERC)."

As Thomàs explains, greater harmony was achieved within the FET of Barcelona only after Antonio Correa Veglison was named civil governor and provincial chief at the close of 1940 (pp. 434–36).

40. Quoted in J. Tusell, *Franco en la Guerra Civil: Una biografía política* (Barcelona, 1992), 359–60.

41. Ibid., 360.

42. In his *El sentido fascista del Movimiento Nacional* (Santander, 1939), the right-wing marqués de la Eliseda averred, "Our National Movement is undoubtedly the translation of fascism which, for having been produced in Spain, will be the most positive fascism of all . . . , a fascism that will implant the Spanish Catholic state, which will be none other than the modern translation of the Old Spanish State of the Reyes Católicos."

A representative camisa vieja, José Luis de Arrese, who had suffered several months imprisonment at the time of the unification, published the first full book on the Falangist social program, *La revolución social del Nacional Sindicalismo* (Madrid, 1940), in which he insisted: "Spain—and hear this loud and clear, some who wear the blue shirt to hide the red shirt—Spain will be nothing if it is not Catholic. . . . Those who talk of a neutral Spain, of the Patria above everything else, of a Church without clergy, are neither Falangists nor do they know what they are talking about" (p. 4).

43. Pereira to Salazar, 31 August 1939, in *Dez anos de política exterior,* 12 vols. (Lisbon, 1978), II, 518–23, quoted in P. Preston, *Franco* (London, 1993), 341.

44. This was stressed in C. Barcia Trelles, *Puntos cardinales de la política exterior española,* published in Madrid that summer. Two reliable general treatments of Franco's foreign policy are J. M. Armero, *La política exterior de Franco* (Barcelona, 1978); and M. Espadas Burgos, *Franquismo y política exterior* (Madrid, 1987).

45. Serrano's speeches in Italy are collected in his *De la victoria,* and he has commented on this trip in H. Saña, *El franquismo sin mitos: Conversaciones con Serrano Súñer* (Barcelona, 1982), 135–39.

46. *Documents secrets du Ministère des Affaires Etrangères d'Allemagne,* 4 vols. (Brussels, 1946), III, 66–68; *Daily Express* (London), 19 June 1939; *O Diario de Norte* (Porto), 24 June 1939. There is a more extensive treatment in R. H. Whealey, "German–Spanish Relations, January–August 1939" (Ph.D. diss., University of Michigan, 1963), 177–92.

47. Quoted in R. de la Cierva, *Historia del franquismo,* 2 vols. (Barcelona, 1976), I, 164.

48. A. Marquina Barrio, *La diplomacia vaticana y la España de Franco (1936–1945)* (Madrid, 1983), 155–242.

49. Quoted in P. Schwartz and M. J. González, *Una historia del Instituto Nacional de Industria* (Madrid, 1978), 1.

50. See J. Catalán, *La economía española y la segunda guerra mundial* (Barcelona, 1995); *El primer franquismo: España durante la segunda guerra mundial,* ed. J. L. García Delgado (Madrid, 1989); and M. J. González, *La política económica del franquismo (1940–1970)* (Madrid, 1979).

51. F. Franco, *Palabras del Caudillo* (Madrid, 1943), 157.

52. C. R. Halstead, "A 'Somewhat Machiavellian' Face: Colonel Juan Beigbeder as High Commissioner in Spanish Morocco 1937–1939," *The Historian* 37 (Nov. 1974), 74–93.

53. On Beigbeder as foreign minister, see C. R. Halstead, "Un 'Africain' méconnu: Le Colonel Juan Beigbeder," *Revue d'Histoire de la Deuxième Guerre Mondiale* 83 (July 1971), 31–60.

54. Diario 16, *Historia del franquismo* (Madrid, 1976), 164.

55. I. Merino, *Serrano Súñer: Historia de una conducta* (Barcelona, 1996), 77.

56. The official declaration of the FET, *El imperio de España* (Valladolid, 1938), had announced that "our imperialism is not going to be an imperialism of petroleum or rubber." Its task was to restore and lead a pan-Hispanic unity, achieving a "new Catholicity. . . . Spain aspires to exercise effectively the rights of defense and of tutelage, . . . not of a protectorate . . . but to defend Spanish civilization in the world."

57. The classic expression of this orientation prior to the Civil War had been

made by the non-Falangist, right-radical intellectual Ramiro de Maeztu, *Defensa de la Hispanidad* (Madrid, 1934).

58. Cf. J. M. Doussinague, *España tenía razón, 1939–1945* (Madrid, 1950), 42.

59. Though Hitler seems to have indicated to the Italian leaders that Serrano Súñer mentioned it at the Hendaye meeting in October 1940. *Ciano's Diplomatic Papers,* 402.

60. A standard slogan of the period, "Por el Imperio hacia Dios" (For the Empire toward God), was said to have been coined by Victor de la Serna and was first employed extensively in the Organización Juvenil. P. Muro de Izcar, *Victor de la Serna, compañero* (Madrid, 1972), cited in Saez Marín, *Frente de Juventudes,* 39.

Given the tendency in Spain, as elsewhere, toward sardonic jokes, this could also generate mirth, as in the apocryphal case of the member of the Casino de Jerez who, on hearing the slogan over the radio, is supposed to have asked: "Empire? Have we taken Cangas de Onís?"—referring to the first defensive stronghold against the Muslims in the eighth century. Quoted from José María Pemán in P. Laín Entralgo, *Descargo de conciencia, 1930–1960* (Madrid, 1976), 231.

61. Though the exact month of publication is not clear, the new book by the law professor Luis del Valle, *El Estado nacionalista, totalitario, autoritario* (Zaragoza, 1940), identified the Nazi regime as the perfect state model.

62. Arrese, *La revolución social del Nacional Sindicalismo,* 35, put it this way: "Fascism, National Socialism and National Syndicalism are sons of the same mother . . . , therefore brothers, and twin brothers, if you wish, not Siamese."

A sample of this wartime propaganda for one FET newspaper may be found in R. M. Martín de la Guardia, *Información y propaganda en la Prensa del Movimiento: "Libertad" de Valladolid, 1931–1979* (Valladolid, 1994), 76–85.

63. See D. S. Detwiler, *Hitler, Franco und Gibraltar: Die Frage des spanischen Eintritts in den Zweiten Weltkrieg* (Wiesbaden, 1962), 22–23.

64. *Documenti Diplomatici Italiani* (Rome, 1963), Series P, IV, 620–30.

65. J. Tusell and G. García Queipo de Llano, *Franco y Mussolini* (Barcelona, 1985), 74–78. On this, as well as on all other major episodes of Spanish diplomacy during World War II, the reader should consult the major study by J. Tusell, *Franco, España y la II Guerra Mundial* (Madrid, 1995).

66. Serrano has related that he became so outraged at Sánchez Maza's attempts to justify his speech that he attempted to punch Sánchez in the face. The Falangist writer managed to dodge the blow but fell to the floor in a state of collapse. Saña, *El franquismo,* 169–70.

67. Quoted in R. Garriga, *El general Juan Yagüe* (Barcelona, 1985), 185. This imprudent speech was later excluded from the 1943 edition of *Palabras del Caudillo.*

68. Quoted in D. Sueiro and B. Díaz Nosty, *Historia del franquismo,* 2 vols. (Madrid, 1977), I, 194.

69. From the full text in R. Serrano Súñer, *Entre el silencio y la propaganda, la Historia como fue: Memorias,* (Barcelona 1977), 342–48.

70. There are various accounts by Serrano, as well as an interesting one in

Ridruejo's *Casi unas memorias*, 215–23, but the most complete and objective treatment will be found in Tusell, *Franco, España*, 131–46.

71. See *FF*, III, 188; and F. Franco Salgado Araujo, *Mis conversaciones privadas con Franco* (Barcelona, 1979), 12.

72. Serrano's categorical insistence on this point may be found in Saña, *El franquismo*, 193. He candidly admitted to Charles Favrel of *Paris-Presse*, 26 Oct. 1945, that in 1940 he had little doubt of final German victory and that "his intention was to enter the war at the very end, at the moment of the final victory, exactly as Russia did against Japan."

73. Serrano has presented his reminiscences in *Memorias*, 283–324; in Saña, *El franquismo*, 190–98; and in García Lahiguera, *Serrano Súñer*, 165–75. See, however, Tusell, *Franco, España*, 146–64.

74. See C. Vidal, *Intrépidos y sucios (Los españoles vistos por Hitler)* (Barcelona, 1996).

75. This document has been published most recently ibid., 153–54.

76. J. Goebbels, *The Goebbels Diaries, 1939–1941* (New York, 1983), 103.

77. Ibid., 203–6.

78. Ibid.

79. Tusell and García Queipo de Llano, *Franco y Mussolini*, 120–21.

80. Various references in the Nazi literature have been collected by Saña, *El franquismo*, 211–20, to which may be added the remarks of Ciano. Like many foreigners, Hitler was obsessed with the notion of the power of the Spanish Church, whose representative he made Serrano out to be.

81. A. Tovar, *El imperio de España* (Madrid, 1941), was more extreme. For more scholarly treatments, see J. Vicens Vives, *España: Geopolítica del Estado y del Imperio* (Barcelona, 1940); and J. M. Cordero Torres, *Misión africana de España* (Madrid, 1941) and *Aspectos de la misión universal de España* (Madrid, 1942).

82. Von Stohrer to the Wilhelmstrasse, 7 May 1941, in *Documents secrets du Ministère des Affaires Etrangères d'Allemagne: Espagne* (Paris, 1946), 72–78.

83. Quoted in Preston, *Franco*, 429.

84. Merino, *Serrano Súñer*, 267–68.

85. Tusell, *Franco España*, 223–24; Tusell and García Queipo de Llano, *Franco y Mussolini*, 139–40.

86. There are numerous accounts of the Blue Division. The most complete bibliography is C. Caballero and R. Ibáñez, *Escritores en las trincheras: La División Azul en sus libros, publicaciones periódicas y filmografía (1941–1988)* (Madrid, 1989). The best overall treatment is G. R. Kleinfeld and L. A. Tambs, *Hitler's Spanish Legion: The Blue Division in Russia* (Carbondale, Ill., 1979). For a Soviet presentation, see S. P. Pozharskaya, *Tainiya diplomatiya Madrida* (Moscow, 1971). For the Blue Division in films, S. Alegre, *El cine cambia la historia: Las imágenes de la División Azul* (Barcelona, 1994).

87. *Arriba*, 18 July 1941.

88. Von Stohrer reported that Serrano Súñer called the speech premature, because, in Stohrer's words, "It suddenly opened the eyes of the English and the Americans about the position of Spain. Previously the English government espe-

cially kept on believing that only he [Serrano] . . . was pushing for war, while the 'wise and thoughtful' Caudillo would preserve neutrality unconditionally. That illusion has now been taken from them. They had come to realize that Spain, in understanding with the German government, would enter the war at a suitable moment." *DGFP*, Series D, XIII, 233.

89. According to J. W. D. Trythall, *El Caudillo* (New York, 1970), 179.

90. H. R. Trevor-Roper, ed., *Hitler's Table Talk, 1941–1944* (London, 1953), 568.

91. Native Moroccan Muslims were in several parts of the Protectorate enrolled in the party in not insignificant numbers, though no precise statistics are available, and the Falangist Bandera de Marruecos enrolled both Spanish and Muslim military volunteers. See E. Martín Corrales, "La Bandera del Marroc i els 'Camaradas Moros': La participació marroquina a les files falangistas," *L'Avenç* 109 (1987), 25–30.

92. There were 800 members in the Philippines at the high point during the Civil War, but United States authorities virtually shut down the organization in September 1940. The Falange Exterior collaborated with the subsequent Japanese occupation and was involved in deep conflict with the established conservative Spanish community. F. Rodao, "Spanish Falange in the Philippines, 1936–1945," *Philippine Studies* 43 (1995), 3–26.

93. E.g., F. Veiga, "La guerra de les ambaixades: La Falange Exterior a Romania i l'Orient Mitjà, 1936–1944," *L'Avenç* 109 (1987), 10–18.

94. R. Pardo Sanz, *¡Con Franco hacia el Imperio! La política exterior española en América Latina, 1939–1945* (Madrid, 1994), 69. Most of the above section is based on this excellent study. See also L. Delgado Gómez-Escalonilla, *Imperio de papel: Acción cultural y política exterior durante el primer franquismo* (Madrid, 1992), 130–42; and, concerning Falange Exterior in Mexico, R. Pérez Montfort, *Hispanismo y Falange* (Mexico City, 1992), 134–70. The Consejo de la Hispanidad, designed as an agency of cultural imperialism and in existence from 1940 to 1945, is treated in M. A. Escudero, *El Instituto de Cultura Hispánica* (Madrid, 1994), 41–106.

95. R. Garriga, *La España de Franco*, 2 vols. (Puebla, Mex., 1970), I, 347, cited in Pardo Sanz, *Con Franco*, 234.

96. The major literary exposé of a virtually nonexistent "phantom Falangism" was the hysterical publication by A. Chase, *Falange: The Axis Secret Army in the Americas* (New York, 1943), an extreme example of wartime hyperbole.

97. R. C. Newton, *The "Nazi Menace" in Argentina, 1931–1947* (Stanford, 1992), details the buildup of hysteria in Washington concerning German penetration of Argentina, as fostered in part by British disinformation.

98. Criticism was perhaps most vehement among the camisas viejas of Valladolid. José Antonio Girón, as the Valladolid leader most loyal to Serrano, tried to mediate by arranging for the twenty-four-year-old Javier Martínez de Bedoya, National Delegate of social welfare (and the new husband of Mercedes Sanz, Redondo's widow) to assume a potentially powerful position as minister of labor and national delegate of syndicates, but this was too extreme and was quickly

vetoed by the military, according to Girón, *Si la memoria no me falla* (Barcelona, 1994), 52–59.

99. See the remarks of his acquaintance J. M. Taboada Lago, *Por una España mejor* (Madrid, 1977), 182–92.

100. These were: (1) a permanent cadre charged with maintaining order within the FET, with premilitary instruction of youth and with commanding the units of the Primera Línea; (2) the premilitary militia of members from the age of eighteen until they entered regular military service; (3) the Primera Línea of affiliates who had completed regular military service, up to the age at which all responsibility for military service ceased; and (4) the Segunda Línea of older affiliates no longer liable for military service, up to the age of fifty-five. All sections would be commanded by regular army officers. *BMFET,* 15 July 1940.

101. Ibid., 6 March 1941.

102. In Italy the MVSN maintained a partially autonomous structure, and provided about 25 percent of the 600,000 troops who had participated in the conquest of Ethiopia. Similarly, the MVSN provided nearly half of the Italian troops supporting the Nationalists in Spain during the Civil War—approximately 30,000 out of a total of 72,000. J. Coverdale, *La intervención fascista en la guerra civil española* (Madrid, 1979); and J. L. de Mesa, *El regreso de las Legiones* (Granada, 1994).

103. According to a British diplomatic document cited by A. Marquina Barrio, "Conspiración contra Franco: El Ejército y la injerencia extranjera en España: El papel de Aranda," *Historia 16* 7 (April 1982), 21–30. There is no confirmation from any primary Spanish source.

104. According to the data presented by D. Smyth, " 'Les Chevaliers de Saint-George': La Grande-Bretagne et la corruption des généraux espagnols (1940–1942)," *Guerres mondiales,* no. 162 (1991), 29–54.

105. The text is from L. López Rodó, *La larga marcha hacia la Monarquía* (Barcelona, 1978), 30–31.

106. Quoted in López Rodó, *Política y desarrollo* (Madrid, 1970), 18–19.

107. Report of von Stohrer, 19 February 1939, *DGFP,* Series D, III, 843–51.

108. This is treated briefly in S. Ellwood, *Prietas las filas: Historia de Falange Española, 1933–1983* (Barcelona, 1984), 204–5; and in R. Ibáñez, "La oposición falangista al régimen de Franco (1939–1975)," in Congreso de Jóvenes Historiadores y Geógrafos, *Actas,* 2 vols. (Madrid, 1990), II, 625–37.

109. Interviews with González de Canales and Luis de Caralt (a member of the clandestine junta from Barcelona) in Madrid and Barcelona during the first months of 1959. See A. Romero Cuesta, *Objetivo: Matar a Franco* (Madrid, 1976), 65–68, which seems to consist primarily of the recollections of González de Canales.

110. Ibid., 78–98.

111. Ibid., 98–111.

112. The memo prepared by Franco for this confrontation is quoted in Suárez Fernández, *FF,* III, 146–47. It emphasized Yagüe's political dissidence more than his German contacts.

113. Ibid., III, 111–18. For further discussion of clandestine Falangist activism during this period, see Elwood, *Prietas las filas,* 206–10.

114. This weirdly estheticizing language, terming morality "a style," was of course typical of Falangist rhetoric and of fascist rhetoric generally.

115. The full text of this extremely lengthy document may be found in *Documentos inéditos,* I, 378–412.

116. Ibid., I, 462–514.

117. The best discussion of the draft's reception by the Council of Ministers and the National Council will be found in J. Tusell, *Franco en la Guerra Civil,* 334–36.

118. According to Serrano Súñer, he had left the Socialist Party under the Republic because some of its activists had tried to assassinate Merino's father, a militant of the CEDA, but only succeeded in killing his mother instead. Saña, *El franquismo,* 154. This is corroborated by Tomás Garicano Goñi in *Franco visto por sus ministros,* ed. A. Bayod (Barcelona, 1981), 198.

119. Interview with Salvador Merino, Barcelona, 2 April 1959.

120. On the career of Rossoni, see J. J. Tinghino, *Edmondo Rossoni* (New York, 1991).

121. See the outline of syndical development during the immediate postwar period in M. A. Aparicio, *El sindicalismo vertical y la formación del Estado franquista* (Barcelona, 1980), 117–50.

122. One of the frankest was the able right-wing camisa vieja José María de Areilza, closely associated with the Bilbao elite, who after serving as the first mayor of reconquered Bilbao in 1937 later held the position of director general of industry in the Ministry of Industry and Commerce. He declared in one speech in 1940 that "the syndicate as conceived by the Falange is an instrument to discipline production and is used by the state for its goals in political economy," as quoted in Valdés Larrañaga, *De la Falange al Movimiento,* 174.

Areilza gave the following description of the "vertical syndicate" from the employers' viewpoint: "The Spanish syndicate will thus be composed by integrating all employers in a specific branch or zone of production, grouped as employers, that is, bearing the representation of factories as a productive unit. No classist [workerist] entity as such is accepted in our structure, because it was not accepted in the original [Falangist] doctrine and also because the character of the War of Liberation, in which the immense majority of the proletarian organizations bore arms as organizations against the Nationalist Army, would have proscribed the resurrection of such organisms—even if they had Spanish labels and goals at the present time—as completely inopportune and contrary to national feeling. All the enterprises of Spain dedicated to the manufacture of a particular product or group of products are thus grouped together under the orientation, guidance, and vigilance of the state. This great entity—whose deliberations will include a great variety of common problems, primarily economic, and which will serve as advisory organs to the economic ministries, directly bringing to them the voices and concerns of the producers—is what we term the Syndicates." *Problemas técnicos de importancia económica en la nueva organización de España* (Barcelona, 1940), 496, quoted in A. de Miguel, *Herencia del franquismo* (Madrid, 1976), 96–97.

123. Quoted in Aparicio, *El sindicalismo vertical,* 171.

124. W. H. Bowen, "Spaniards and Nazi Germany" (Ph.D. diss., Northwestern University, 1997), 119–21.

125. *BMFET,* 7 Dec. 1940.

126. For further data and details concerning the theory and structure of the initial syndical system, see Aparicio, *El sindicalismo vertical,* 79–169; and also Chueca, *El fascismo,* 341–91.

127. Interview with Salvador Merino in Barcelona, 2 April 1959.

128. Bowen, "Spaniards," 141–43.

129. Quoted in K.-J. Ruhl, *Franco, Falange y III Reich* (Madrid, 1986), 317.

130. Ibid., 68.

131. *Goebbels Diaries,* 353–54.

132. *DGFP,* Series D, XI, 1069–70. Just at that point, in January 1941, Alcázar de Velasco's *Serrano Súñer en la Falange* was published, portraying the "cuñadísimo" as the closest friend and direct political heir of José Antonio, and thus the natural leader of the Falange.

133. On the Iron Guard in Romania, see A. Heinen, *Die Legion "Erzengel Michael" in Rumänien* (Munich, 1986).

134. Ruhl, *Franco, Falange,* 64–65.

135. Ibid., 66.

136. Ibid.

137. Quoted in J. Tusell, *Juan Carlos I* (Madrid, 1995), 53. The first part of this outstanding study presents the best summary and analysis of the politics and diplomacy of the royal family during World War II.

138. Ruhl, *Franco, Falange,* 67.

139. Tusell, *Juan Carlos I,* 53–54.

140. *DGFP,* Series D, XII, 569–70.

141. *Documenti Diplomatici Italiani,* Series P, IX, 225–26.

142. Ruhl, *Franco, Falange,* 68.

143. Quoted in Detwiler, *Hitler,* 71. One of the more telling satirical jingles made up by his critics ran:

| | |
|---|---|
| Miradle por donde viene, | Behold whence he comes, |
| el Señor del Gran Poder, | the Lord of Great Power, |
| antes se llamaba Cristo | who once was called Christ |
| y ahora Serrano Súñer. | and now Serrano Súñer. |

144. *Documentos inéditos,* II:2, 139–41.

145. Ibid., II:2, 141–44.

146. Serrano Súñer, *De la victoria,* 186–87.

147. *BMFET,* 4 May 1941.

148. Serrano Súñer, *Memorias,* 180.

149. *BOE,* 18–19 May 1941.

150. *La revolución social del Nacional Sindicalismo.*

151. Arrese summarized some of this in his pamphlet, *Málaga desde el punto de vista urbanístico* (Málaga, 1941). For a darker view of the FET in Málaga

during the Arrese period, see M. Eiroa San Francisco, *Viva Franco: Hambre, racionamiento, falangismo. Málaga, 1939–1942* (Málaga, 1995), 155–211.

152. *BOE*, 22 May 1941.

153. There are numerous accounts of this crisis in the memoir and secondary literature. See particularly A. Ferrary, *El franquismo: Minorías políticas y conflictos ideológicos (1936–1956)* (Pamplona, 1993), 164–72; Tusell and García Queipo de Llano, *Franco y Mussolini*, 129–35; La Cierva, *Franquismo*, I, 203–17; and Serrano's version in Saña, *El franquismo*, 158–62.

154. Serrano Súñer, *Memorias*, 198. More recently he declared, with only slight exaggeration: "*After the crisis of 5 May 1941 there remained no more than 'franquismo'* " (Serrano's italics). R. Serrano Súñer, *Política de España (1936–1975)* (Madrid, 1995), 32.


CHAPTER ELEVEN

1. The basic political biography is J. Tusell, *Carrero: La eminencia gris del régimen de Franco* (Madrid, 1993). Also of use are C. Fernández, *El Almirante Carrero* (Barcelona, 1985); and the portrait in R. Garriga, *Los validos de Franco* (Barcelona, 1981), 214–368.

2. Tusell, *Carrero*, 40–42.

3. Spain's ideal would always be "the Civilization which is based on the doctrines of Christ"; conversely, the Civil War was but one aspect of the continual "struggle of Christianity against Judaism." L. Carrero Blanco, *España en el mar* (Madrid, 1949), 7, 9.

4. *Documentos inéditos*, II:2, 316–31.

5. Interviews with Arrese, Madrid, 10 January and 9 February 1959.

6. M. Valdés Larrañaga, *De la Falange al Movimiento (1936–1952)* (Madrid, 1994), 221.

7. *Boletín de la Delegación Provincial de Sindicatos de Barcelona* 12 (July–Sept. 1941), 16, quoted in G. Ramos i Ramos, "El Sindicat Vertical: Mecanisme de control social i instrument de poder," in *Franquisme: Sobre resistència i consens a Catalunya (1938–1959)* (Barcelona, 1990), 142–50.

8. See the remarks of Serrano Súñer in H. Saña, *El franquismo, sin mitos: Conversaciones con Serrano Súñer* (Barcelona, 1982), 154–57.

9. Not to be confused with Nicasio Alvarez de Sotomayor, the cenetista leader recruited by Ledesma for the JONS who subsequently passed to the Socialist Party and was executed during the Civil War.

10. There was considerable antagonism in the nascent Ministry of Labor between the newly appointed José Antonio Girón and his undersecretary, Valdés, but because of the latter's connections at the national level of the FET, Girón at first had trouble securing his dismissal from the ministry. Girón, *Si la memoria no me falla* (Barcelona, 1994), 95–96.

11. Valdés Larrañaga, *De la Falange al Movimiento*, 213–14.

12. Girón has presented a brief version of his entry into the ministry and his first activities in his *Si la memoria no me falla*, 75–89. His early speeches and

articles as minister were collected in his *Dos años de actuación al frente del Ministerio de Trabajo mayo 1941–1943* (Madrid, 1943).

13. See B. Bermejo Sánchez, "Vicesecretaría de Educación Popular (1941–1945): Un 'ministerio' de la propaganda en manos de Falange," *Espacio, Tiempo y Forma* 4 (1991), 73–96; and, more broadly, A. Ferrary, *El franquismo: Minorías políticas y conflictos ideológicos (1936–1956)* (Pamplona, 1993), 178–231.

14. This is treated by S. Ellwood, *Prietas las filas: Historia de Falange Española, 1933–1983* (Barcelona, 1984), 128–30.

15. R. Chueca, *El fascismo en los comienzos del régimen de Franco: Un estudio sobre FET-JONS* (Madrid, 1983), 198, gives the following figures for those expelled in all categories combined:

| | |
|---|---|
| 1942 | 631 |
| 1943 | 1,962 |
| 1944 | 2,087 |
| 1945 | 1,003 |
| 1946 | 20 |

Total 5,703

16. J. Pérez de Cabo, *¡Arriba España!* (Madrid, 1935).

17. Cf. A. Romero Cuesta, *Objetivo: Matar a Franco* (Madrid, 1976), 72–74.

18. Cited in A. Marquina Barrio, "Conspiración contra Franco: El Ejército y la injerencia extranjera en España: El papel de Aranda," *Historia 16* 7 (April 1982), 21–30. Aranda and certain other generals, who accepted enormous bribes from the British, engaged in notorious exaggerations about these discussions among the military. Tusell correctly observes that the generals "did not conspire, but simply talked about conspiracies." *Franco, España,* 652.

19. The extensive hagiographic literature on the conde de Barcelona, allegedly a democrat "all his life," tends to overlook these contradictions, partly inevitable under the circumstances. Two differing approaches may be found in R. Borrás, *El Rey de los rojos* (Barcelona, 1996), and J. Toquero, *Don Juan de Borbón, el Rey Padre* (Barcelona, 1992), but see especially the research synthesis in J. Tusell, *Juan Carlos I* (Madrid, 1995), the first 500 pages of which are largely devoted to the politics of Don Juan.

20. Quoted in P. Sainz Rodríguez, *Un reinado en la sombra* (Barcelona, 1981), 349–50.

21. K.-J. Ruhl, *Franco, Falange y III Reich* (Madrid, 1986), 99.

22. J. Tusell and G. García Queipo de Llano, *Franco y Mussolini* (Barcelona, 1985), 154–56.

23. Ruhl, *Franco, Falange,* 336.

24. According to the German consul in Bilbao, ibid., 336.

25. Ibid., 104–5.

26. Quoted in Tusell, *Juan Carlos I,* 63.

27. Ruhl, *Franco, Falange,* 106.

28. These quotations are drawn from C. Vidal, *Intrépidos y sucios (Los españoles vistos por Hitler)* (Barcelona, 1996), 185–92.

29. Suárez Fernández, *FF,* III, 359.
30. Quoted in Vidal, *Intrépidos y sucios,* 194–95.
31. Ibid., 195–97.
32. On these contacts, see Ruhl, *Franco, Falange,* 111–123; and G. R. Kleinfeld and L. A. Tambs, *Hitler's Spanish Legion: The Blue Division in Russia* (Carbondale, Ill., 1979), 192–97.
33. C. J. H. Hayes, *Wartime Mission in Spain* (New York, 1946), 54.
34. *Documentos inéditos,* III, 310–12.
35. Ibid., III, 326–27.
36. Ibid., III, 428.
37. Ibid., III, 555.
38. Tusell and García Queipo de Llano, *Franco y Mussolini,* 156–57.
39. Ibid., 158–59. The ultra-Catholic Arrese also sharply criticized Girón's loose private life, possibly finding this a useful issue in intraparty rivalry. In his memoirs Girón has claimed that he sharply rebuked Arrese, insisting that his personal life was his own affair and demanding that Arrese's criticisms cease. *Si la memoria no me falla,* 87–88.
40. Tusell and García Queipo de Llano, *Franco y Mussolini,* 159. The anger of the military had produced a satiric verse:

| | |
|---|---|
| La Falange a un militar | The Falange attacked |
| a traición apaleó | an officer from the back |
| y . . . nada ocurrió. | But . . . nothing happened. |
| Puede el baile continuar! | The dance can continue! |
| Ejército: has de aguantar | Army: you have to swallow it |
| si es Falange quien te pisa | if the Falange walks all over you, |
| y poner cara de risa | and pretend to smile |
| si algún día esos cabrones | if one day those bastards |
| te bajan los pantalones | pull down your trousers |
| y te suben la camisa. . . . | And pull up your shirt. . . . |

41. Quoted in J. Tusell, *Carrero,* 73–74.
42. F. Franco, *Palabras del Caudillo* (Madrid, 1943), 211–16.
43. Ruhl, *Franco, Falange,* 114–15.
44. Cf. Hayes, *Wartime Mission,* 56.
45. Arrese further ingratiated himself through such feats as turning out large crowds for Franco's visit to Catalonia in January 1942, after the Caudillo had been coolly received in Vizcaya. The applause in Barcelona was allegedly achieved by offering workers the day off at double wages to line the streets. Arrese's cheerleading was so much appreciated that he was frequently included in Franco's entourage during provincial tours.
46. *Ciano's Diplomatic Papers,* ed. M. Muggeridge (London, 1948), 460–65.
47. In a letter to Franco of 7 July 1942, Ridruejo described "the reality of the regime" as follows:

1. Failure of the government's plan and its authority in economic affairs. Triumph of the black market. Disproportionate hunger among the people.

2. Weakness of the state on the one hand, which suffers the most intolerable interference in matters that affect its own political texture, while on the other, popular will is alienated by an exclusive policy of conservative style.

3. Abandonment of a military policy based on efficient foresight and, in exchange, permanence of the Army as the active watchdog of political life, something that is justified by the instability of the regime, in the interventionist tradition stemming from a century of civil wars that has still not been overcome.

4. Confusion and arbitrariness in the affairs of justice, with a sharpening of leftist resentment among extensive sectors of the people.

5. Incessant conspiracy among the reactionary elements, Anglophiles by opportunism, inviting intrigue by those who defend privilege and adopt positions opposing the regime and more concretely the Falange.

6. Complete forgetfulness of the original Falangist doctrine. A Movement inert and without program. Leaders of scant authenticity but great vulgarity. The crowd at the expense of demagogues.

D. Ridruejo, *Casi unas memorias* (Barcelona, 1976), 236–40. These judgments were developed more fully in the letter of resignation that Ridruejo sent to Serrano Súñer on 29 August 1942, quoted in R. García Lahiguera, *Ramón Serrano Súñer: Un documento para la historia* (Barcelona, 1983), 229–32.

After being fired as director of propaganda in May 1941, Ridruejo had volunteered for the Blue Division, and his diary of the eastern front was later published as *Los cuadernos de Rusia* (Barcelona, 1978). Serrano wrote an account of Ridruejo's withdrawal from the FET and the regime, which appears in J. Benet et al., *Dionisio Ridruejo de la Falange a la oposición* (Madrid, 1976). Ridruejo's first memoir, representing the perspective he formed during the 1940s and 1950s, was *Escrito en España* (Buenos Aires, 1964).

48. Cf. R. Garriga, *La España de Franco*, 2 vols. (Puebla, Mex., 1970) I, 234.

49. Cf. Tusell and García Queipo de Llano, *Franco y Mussolini*, 165.

50. According to Serrano Súñer in Saña, *El franquismo*, 262–63.

51. Reconstructions of this incident vary considerably. The most detailed treatment is by A. Marquina Barrio, "El atentado de Begoña," *Historia 16* 4 (April 1980), 11–19, though some of his data may be inaccurate. See also R. Serrano Súñer, *Entre el silencio y la propaganda, la Historia Como fue: Memorias,* 364–73; Saña, *El franquismo*, 263–69; García Lahiguera, *Serrano Súñer,* 215–34; Garriga, *La España de Franco,* I, 428–30; and Ellwood, *Prietas las filas,* 145–54. The Carlists launched their own version in a semiclandestine pamphlet, *El crimen de la Falange en Begoña: Un régimen al descubierto.*

As indicated in Marquina Barrio and Garriga, it was rumored that the whole incident was part of a Falangist plot intended to discredit either the Carlists or Serrano Súñer. The conspiracy theory hinges on the motives for the presence of Juan Domínguez and his five fellow Falangists at the Carlist ceremony. Another version, defended by Narciso Perales and accepted by Serrano, has the Falangist group meeting at the French border a veteran returning from the Blue Division and then stopping at the latter's home in Bilbao, where they learned of the Carlist commemoration. The grenades employed, according to this explanation, were souvenirs brought from the eastern front by the returning veteran. Yet details of this theory are in turn contradicted by the testimony of the military governor of Bilbao, presented by Javier Tusell in Diario 16, *Historia del franquismo* (Madrid, 1977), 224.

52. The other death sentence was commuted, and all five surviving Falangists were finally pardoned and released in 1945.

German authorities made a futile effort to intervene on behalf of Domínguez, Hitler even awarding him the Cross of the Order of the German Eagle for his service in Russia. To counter this, the FET National Delegation of Information presented a report accusing Domínguez of having been in the pay of the British intelligence service. Two reports of the DGS on 20 and 28 August reported that Domínguez lived unusually well and traveled a great deal (though that may have been because of his responsibilities in the SEU), and concluded that it was likely that he was on the British payroll. *Documentos inéditos*, III, 585–86. Some radical Falangists believed that Domínguez was being made a scapegoat, but it is of course by no means impossible that the pro-Nazi Domínguez also took money on the side from the British, who were then spending such enormous amounts in Spain.

53. In *De Falange al Movimiento*, 229, Valdés Larrañaga refers to the "leaders of the Falange" as "divided into two groups, those of Serrano, led by Dionisio Ridruejo and José Luna, and those of Arrese by Sánchez Mazas, Arias Salgado, and Blas Pérez Gonzalez."

54. See ibid., 230.

55. Marquina Barrio, "El atentado de Begoña." The transcript of a telephone conversation between Franco and Varela during the crisis is presented in L. López Rodó, *La larga marcha hacia la Monarquía* (Barcelona, 1978), 503–7.

56. According to the version that Carrero gave years later to López Rodó, in the latter's *Larga marcha*, 29–30.

57. Saña, *El franquismo*, 271–74. A further source of personal and family tension was Serrano's extramarital affair with the wife of an aristocratic lieutenant colonel of cavalry, which became the gossip of Madrid and was even mentioned in diplomatic reports. Cf. D. W. Pike, "Aspects nouveaux du rôle de l'Espagne dans la Seconde Guerre Mondiale," *Revue d'Histoire Moderne et Contemporaine* 19 (1972), 516n; D. W. Pike, "Franco and the Axis Stigma," *Journal of Contemporary History* 17 (1983), 369–407; and C. Fernández, *Tensiones militares bajo el franquismo* (Barcelona, 1985), 41–43.

58. Varela bitterly resented his ouster and lobbied among his fellow lieutenant generals to dissuade any of them from replacing him, probably alleging that the honor of the military hierarchy was at stake. Franco therefore turned to Asensio, one of the best major generals and chief of the General Staff under Varela. According to Serrano, in the face of an initial reluctance by Asensio to accept the post, Franco railed in exasperation, "What is it you want? For me to be carried out of here feet first?" Saña, *El franquismo*, 267.

59. The only study of Blas Pérez is in Garriga, *Los validos de Franco*, 126–213.

60. A report of the DGS of 30 September 1942 indicated that extreme tension still existed between Falangists and Carlists in Barcelona (where in fact genuine

Carlists probably still outnumbered genuine Falangists). *Documentos inéditos,* III, 612. The same could probably still be said of other areas where the Carlists remained strong. The extreme hostility of Carlists to the FET, and by extension to the entire system, did not rapidly abate. A general circular of the Comunión Tradicionalista (which still maintained its separate existence) recommended that Carlists withdraw from all positions within the FET, Sindicatos, or other state agencies. Quoted in full in J. C. Clemente, *El Carlismo en la España de Franco* (Madrid, 1994), 373.

61. One anonymous military pamphlet soon afterward urged direct action to eliminate the FET altogether, likening the beneficial effects of this move to Antonescu's suppression of the Iron Guard in Romania: "A military action by the Army in Spain would have the same benefit for Germany as did that of the Army in Romania when it faced up to the gang of crazies in the party." Quoted in Tusell and García Queipo de Llano, *Franco y Mussolini,* 170.

62. The best account of Jordana's foreign policy will be found in Tusell, *Franco, España,* 331–537.

63. Ibid.; Ruhl, *Franco, Falange,* 167–73.

64. Ibid., 175.

65. Ibid., 176.

66. Ibid., 178–82.

67. Ibid., 182.

68. *Palabras del Caudillo,* 523–27. Franco's officially published version obviously aligned Spain with the "pueblos fascistas," but the phrase concerning the Spanish formula "o por cualquiera otra de los pueblos fascistas" has sometimes been rendered in secondary works as "España y cualquier otro de los pueblos fascistas" (Spain and any other of the fascist peoples).

69. *Informaciones* (Madrid), 19 Dec. 1942.

70. Ruhl, *Franco, Falange,* 206–7.

71. *Documentos inéditos,* IV, 95–99.

72. Ibid., III, 668–72.

73. Ibid., IV, 5–10.

74. Ibid., IV, 143. DGS reports on the FA continued through the winter and spring of 1943.

75. According to a report from the DGS:

> Ezquer thinks that when he is prosecuted for the organization O. R. N. S. (Ofensiva Revolucionaria Nacional-Sindicalista) will be the time when this organization acquires historical significance and a broader life, and that the current of sympathy which it now enjoys in part of one sector of the Falange is because some of the latter's leaders realize that they are losing ground, while his organization is gaining. He considers it certain that within a short period of time he will gain liberty and power for his movement.
>
> Among the numerous visits that he received last Sunday, 20 June 1943, was one from the Director General of Prisons, Bernardo Sanz Nougués, who spent more than an hour talking with him.

Ibid., IV, 317.

76. Arrese's overreaction to Franco's remarks of 28 January 1942 bordered

on the comical. On 2 February he dispatched a long letter to Franco hailing his verbal recognition of the FET and proclaiming that the "authentic Spanish revolution" would now begin, interpreting this particular passage in Franco's standard rhetorical shell-game as a sort of pledge that the long-awaited "National Syndicalist Revolution" would finally commence. This document from the Franco archive is quoted in full in chap. 5 of Jesús Palacios, *La España totalitaria* (Barcelona, 1999). Franco's reference was later deleted from the published book of his speeches.

77. *Palabras del Caudillo*, 189–90. Cf. La Cierva's comments on this visit in R. de la Cierva, *Historia del franquismo*, 2 vols. (Barcelona, 1976), II, 307–9.

78. *Revista de Estudios Políticos* 2 (Jan. 1942), 5–32.

79. Consejo Superior de Misiones, *Función espiritual de España en el Congreso de las Juventudes Europeas* (Madrid, 1943), 21.

80. Quoted in W. H. Bowen, "Spaniards and Nazi Germany" (Ph.D. diss., Northwestern University, 1997), 213.

81. According to A. De Miguel, *Herencia del franquismo* (Madrid, 1976), 131–32.

82. Quoted in Bowen, "Spaniards and Nazi Germany," 214–15.

83. *Documentos inéditos*, IV, 144.

84. *Fundamentos del Nuevo Estado* (Madrid, 1943), 37–46; *Recopilación sistemática de la legislación del Movimiento mayo 1937 — diciembre 1943* (Madrid, 1944).

85. *Documentos inéditos*, IV, 73.

86. Ibid., IV, 147.

87. Quoted in A. Lazo, *La Iglesia, la Falange y el fascismo (un estudio sobre la prensa española de postguerra)* (Seville, 1943), 296.

88. P. Laín Entralgo, *Sobre cultura española: Confesiones de este tiempo* (Madrid, 1943), 105–6.

89. *Arriba*, 18 July 1943.

90. *Documentos inéditos*, IV, 366–70.

91. Ibid., IV, 41 (Jordana's emphasis).

92. Cf. L. Suárez Fernández, *Crónica de la Sección Femenina* (Madrid, 1993), 157–61.

93. This is recounted in Bowen, "Spaniards and Nazi Germany," 254–56.

94. Tusell, *Franco, España*, 442.

95. Ibid., 444. As Lazo has put it, "Until the fall of Mussolini the majority of the militants and adherents of Falange considered themselves fascists and proclaimed themselves to be so. A good many of them were nonetheless mere reactionaries who, in parallel with what the clerical publicists had been doing, 'accommodated' themselves and manipulated fascism; thus, in fact, only the radical Falangists were true fascists. But after the fall of Serrano Súñer, the FET was led by reactionary pseudo-fascists, who . . . after the end of Mussolini received orders to defascistize the Falange." *La Iglesia*, 299.

96. The principal treatment will be found in Tusell and García Queipo de Llano, *Franco y Mussolini*, 209–40. Fernández Cuesta presents his own rather

anodyne account in his *Testimonio, recuerdos y reflexiones* (Madrid, 1985), 205–29.

97. J. L. de Arrese, *Escritos y discursos* (Madrid, 1943), 219.

98. F. Díaz-Plaja, ed., *La España franquista en sus documentos* (Barcelona, 1976), 139–40.

99. The rejected version declared, "The political regime installed in Spain by personal decision of Your Excellency has been officially declared and defined as totalitarian in essence at the service of the Falangist ideology," and insisted on its "ABSOLUTE SUPPRESSION." Quoted in Tusell and García Queipo de Llano, *Franco y Mussolini*, 223.

100. On these maneuvers, see P. Preston, *Franco* (London, 1993), 482–505.

101. Kleinfeld and Tambs, *Hitler's Spanish Legion*, 346. The enlistment and casualty statistics both include more than one enlistment and more than one casualty in the cases of certain individual soldiers, and may balance out statistically.

102. M. Ezquerra, *Berlín a vida o muerte* (Granada, 1994), is the perhaps partially fanciful memoir of one such diehard. It could not be published in Spain after the war and first appeared in a Portuguese edition in Lisbon in 1947.

103. Quoted in Tusell, *Juan Carlos I*, 83.

104. Bowen, "Spaniards and Nazi Germany," 238. In addition, Bowen calculates that between the disbanding of the Blue Division in November 1943 and the Allied invasion of France on 6 June 1944, the Germans managed to recruit another 450 Spanish military volunteers (pp. 292–93).

105. Despite the frequent frothings of anti-Semitic propaganda in the Falangist press, the policy of the Spanish government and its diplomatic representatives toward Jews was relatively positive. Altogether, during the first part of the war some 30,000 Jews from occupied Europe had received safe passage through Spain, and there is no evidence that any Jew who reached Spanish soil was turned back to German authorities. Approximately 7,500 more may have passed through between 1942 and 1944. During the later phases of the SS roundup in Hungary and the Balkans, Spanish consular officials managed to provide protection (through citizen passports) to more than 3,200 additional Jews, many of the latter Sephardic. The principal studies are A. Marquina Barrio and G. I. Ospina, *España y los judíos en el siglo XX* (Madrid, 1987); and H. Avni, *España, Franco y los judíos* (Madrid, 1982).

In addition, the 14,000 Jews residing in the Spanish Protectorate of Morocco were not only protected but received reaffirmation of Spanish nationality, so that a number of Sephardic Jews in French Morocco emigrated to the Spanish zone. There is a brief evaluation in B. Bennassar, *Franco* (Madrid, 1996), 150–53.

106. *Documentos inéditos*, IV, 482.

107. J. L. de Arrese, *Treinta años de política* (Madrid, 1966), 470–72. The foreign minister's chief of cabinet, José Luis Doussinague, told the American embassy counselor that Franco had required Arrese to use such terms. Kleinfeld and Tambs, *Hitler's Spanish Legion*, 339.

108. The FET's *Notas sobre la Falange como partido único (Cuadernos de orientación política)* (Madrid, n.d.), correctly distinguished between the Italian,

German, and Soviet regimes respectively in terms of the subordination of the party to the state, identification of the party with the state, and subordination of the state to the party. It emphasized that the Spanish system was totalitarian with respect to the political power of the state, but by implication suggested that no broader structural totalitarianism was aimed at. It also declared that the Spanish system was based on "military unity" but had no "warlike objectives," which again distinguished it from the other systems.

109. These two references are drawn from M. A. Ruiz Carnicer, *El Sindicato Española Universitario (SEU) 1939–1965* (Madrid, 1996), 175.

110. Bowen, "Spaniards and Nazi Germany," 317.

111. Ruhl, *Franco, Falange,* 248–380.

112. Suevos finally returned to Spain in December 1945. Bowen, "Spaniards and Nazi Germany," 330. Of all European sectors of Falange Exterior, the most active was the ardently pro-Nazi group in Berlin, though inevitably weakened during the aerial destruction of the German capital. Perhaps the weirdest of the Naziphile Spaniards there was Martín Arrizubieta, a defrocked Basque priest and former captain in the Republican People's Army during the Civil War. In wartime Berlin he sought to combine National Socialism, racism, and Basque separatism in a sort of revolutionary alliance, publishing a sheet called *Enlace,* which encouraged the mobilization of Spanish workers in Germany to help overthrow the "reactionary" Franco after Germany won the war (ibid., 325–26). Interestingly, Hitler came to share much the same sentiments and plans regarding the Spanish regime.

113. Valdés Larrañaga, *De Falange al Movimiento,* 299.

114. Quoted in Tusell, *España, Franco,* 543. For a somewhat "sanitized" biography of the new foreign minister, see M. J. Cava Mesa, *Los diplomáticos de Franco: J. F. de Lequerica (1890–1963)* (Deusto, 1989).

Lequerica's description of the Falange may be compared with the remarks of the monarchist leader Sainz Rodríguez, who characterized the Falangists' activities as "a perpetual incoherent paroxysm." Quoted in Tusell, *Juan Carlos I,* 99.

115. See A. J. Lleonart and F. J. Castiella y Maiz et al., eds., *España y ONU (1945–1946): La "cuestión española." Documentación básica, sistemática y anotada* (Madrid, 1978), 42–45.

CHAPTER TWELVE

1. M. Valdés Larrañaga, *De la Falange al Movimiento (1936–1952)* (Madrid, 1994), 308.

2. He explained most of this in a prolix interview with Alberto Martín Artajo (soon to become foreign minister) on 1 May 1945. J. Tusell, *Franco y los católicos: La política interior española entre 1945 y 1957* (Madrid, 1984), 50–51.

3. J. Palacios, *Los papeles secretos de Franco* (Madrid, 1996), 109. For Serrano's version, see R. García Lahiguera, *Ramón Serrano Súñer: Un documento para la historia* (Barcelona, 1983), 260–67; and also R. Garriga, *La España de Franco,* 2 vols. (Puebla, Mex., 1970), I, 437–40.

4. Tusell, *Franco y los católicos*, 51.

5. Arrese retained his seat in the Cortes and his place in the Caudillo's good graces. Two years later he published a new book, *Capitalismo, comunismo, cristianismo* (Madrid, 1947), which declared that "fascism is not a complete formula" because of its materialism and lack of religiosity, and pointed toward Catholic syndicalism as the proper solution.

6. In his memoirs, Girón records the disgust and contempt he experienced in the summer of 1945 when Carceller informed him that if Girón could provide "six men of confidence, ready for anything," Carceller would complete arrangements for them to flee across the border to Portugal. *Si la memoria no me falla*, (Barcelona, 1994), 107–8.

7. One year later, Pilar Primo de Rivera dispatched a long, stiff letter of protest to the director of Radio Nacional after its commemorative broadcast of 30 March 1946 failed to mention the name of José Antonio or the contributions of the Falange in the Civil War. P. Primo de Rivera, *Recuerdos de una vida* (Madrid, 1983), 294–96.

8. Tusell, *Franco y los católicos*, 58.

9. Suárez Fernández, *FF*, IV, 57–58.

10. According to a report presented to Franco in May 1946, the CNT leadership offered a policy of cooperation, proposing to withdraw from José Giral's Republican government-in-exile and accept three Falangists on their national committee, but in return insisted on freedom to proselytize. Ibid., IV, 116–22.

11. D. Jato, *La rebelión de los estudiantes* (Madrid, 1967), 472.

12. Ibid.; and M. A. Ruiz Carnicer, *El Sindicato Español Universitario (SEU) 1939–1965* (Madrid, 1996), 183–85.

13. See S. Ellwood, *Prietas las filas: Historia de Falange Española, 1933–1983* (Barcelona, 1984), 210–12.

14. These included the Carlist province of Navarre, the third Basque province of Alava, one Catalan province (Lérida), Teruel, and two populous leftist provinces in Andalusia (Seville and Málaga). Tusell, *Franco y los católicos*, 163–64.

15. Cf. the analysis by C. Viver Pi-Sunyer, *El personal político de Franco (1936–1945)* (Barcelona, 1978), 130–33.

16. A. del Río Cisneros, *Pensamiento político de Franco*, 2 vols. (Madrid, 1975), I, 90.

17. On the basis of the syndicates' own records, Chueca estimates that by July 1949 only 48.41 percent of Spanish workers were enrolled. R. Chueca, *El fascismo en los comienzos del regimen de Franco: Un estudio sobre FET–JONS* (Madrid, 1983), 385–86.

18. On the development of the syndical system in this period, see M. A. Aparicio, *El sindicalismo vertical y la formación del Estado franquista* (Barcelona, 1980), 179–203.

19. Congreso Nacional de Trabajadores, *Conclusiones* (Madrid, 1946).

20. F. Sanz Orrio, *Los sindicatos españoles: Una creación para el mundo* (Madrid, 1948), 206, 228–29.

21. Ibid., 105.

22. In a speech of 1945, for example, he tried to affirm a role for the syndi-

cates in the supervision of monopolies to ensure distributive justice. Ibid., 227. Cf his *Teoría y soluciones del sindicalismo nacional* (Madrid, 1948).

23. Girón, *Si la memoria no me falla,* 113.

24. Ibid., 113–30.

25. The official functions of the enlaces were detailed in the official *Representación y enlaces sindicales* (Madrid, 1963); and in E. Martín and J. Salvador, *Los enlaces sindicales* (Barcelona, 1976). Their number was later reduced to 163,000 for an expanded labor force.

26. The juries began to function in 1953. Though the head of each individual firm automatically became the head of a jury, election of worker members was partially free and to some extent representative. Experience in the juries may have contributed to the first independent Worker Commissions, which began to appear in Asturias and elsewhere as early as 1954–1955.

27. B. Barba Hernández, *Dos años al frente del Gobierno Civil de Barcelona* (Madrid, 1948), 58, quoted in Chueca, *El fascismo,* 102.

28. M. Ludevid, *Cuarenta años de sindicalismo vertical* (Barcelona, 1977), 32–35; L. Ferri, J. Muixi, and E. Sanjuan, *Las huelgas contra Franco (1939–1956)* (Barcelona, 1978); and C. Damiano González, *La resistencia libertaria (1939–1970)* (Barcelona, 1978), 286–315. In 1948 there apparently existed a temporary working agreement between CNT moderates in Barcelona and Falange Joven, a dissident neo-Falangist group, but their cooperation soon ended, along with the very existence of the latter.

29. F. Franco Salgado Araujo, *Mis conversaciones privadas con Franco* (Barcelona, 1979), 142.

30. This aspect is partly brought out in R. García Perez, *Franquismo y Tercer Reich* (Madrid, 1994).

31. Cf. Palacios, *Los papeles secretos,* 39, 51, 102.

32. Franco was not above mocking Falangist ideology in private, as on the occasion in 1954 when he playfully asked the young administrative specialist López Rodó whether he understood the concept of the "vertical syndicate," adding sardonically that he himself had never been able to figure it out. A. Bayod, ed., *Franco visto por sus ministros* (Barcelona, 1981), 165.

33. F. Franco Bahamonde, *Discursos y mensajes del Jefe del Estado 1951–1954* (Madrid, 1955), 234.

34. Cf. his bland collected speeches for 1950–1953: *El Movimiento político español* (Madrid, 1952), and *Afirmación falangista* (Madrid, 1953), the latter restoring the adjective "falangista" in 1953 as the regime signed key new agreements with the United States and the Vatican.

35. A. de Laiglesia, *La Codorniz sin jaula* (Barcelona, 1981), is a memoir by its founder and director.

36. As in a speech of September 1953 in which he declared that "the Falange is above all contingencies, . . . supporting the constituent force of our Army." Quoted in R. Gómez Pérez, *Política y religión en el régimen de Franco* (Barcelona, 1976), 71.

37. Quoted in R. de la Cierva, *Historia del franquismo,* 2 vols. (Barcelona, 1976), II, 115–16; and in Suárez Fernández, *FF,* V, 143–44.

38. Girón, *Si la memoria no me falla,* 154.

39. Suárez Fernández is of this opinion. *FF,* IV, 159.

40. Palacios, *Los papeles secretos,* 137.

41. Ibid., 139.

42. For a brief history, critique, and anthology of these short-lived journals, see J. Gracia, *Crónica de una deserción: Ideología y literatura en la prensa universitaria del franquismo (1940–1960)* (Barcelona, 1994).

43. See the discussion in A. Ferrary, *El franquismo: Minorías políticas y conflictos ideológicos (1936–1956)* (Pamplona, 1993), 298–364.

44. These years are treated in detail in Ruiz Carnicer, *El Sindicato,* 185–285.

45. "Tovar denounced the regime as a personal state, the destruction of the Falangist program, and the nonexistence of revolutionary goals, lamenting especially the deception practiced on young people: "Ay! If this had been said before, we could have spared ourselves incommensurate effort, and we would not have wandered—the path entirely mistaken—through the dream of a revolutionary utopia, through the dream of a revolution that no one intends to carry out. . . . Though an effort is still made to pretend that the political process of the new state . . . constitutes a revolution, we have to protest that this is not so. . . . Consequently our youth does not understand anything." Ibid., 312–13.

46. On the attitudes of the new university generation of the 1950s, see J. F. Marsal et al., *Pensar bajo el franquismo* (Barcelona, 1979).

47. P. Lizcano, *La generación del 56: La universidad contra Franco* (Barcelona, 1981), 95–97.

48. Tusell, *Franco y los católicos,* 363–66.

49. The entry is for 28 October 1955, in *Conversaciones privadas,* 142.

50. H. L. Matthews, *The Yoke and the Arrows* (New York, 1956), 73.

51. The clandestine Juntas de Acción Nacional Sindicalista, formed in 1952, were quickly broken up. During these years dissident Falangism sometimes looked to the partially rehabilitated Manuel Hedilla, last jefe nacional before Franco, now a private businessman without any role in the Movement. In 1954 another minor dissident initiative revived the name of the Juntas de Ofensiva Nacional Sindicalista, only to have its leaders soon arrested, though for several years the slogan "Hedilla-JONS" would appear from time to time on walls in Madrid.

52. As reported by Girón, in *Si la memoria no me falla,* 161–62.

53. These data are from J. Saez Marín, *El Frente de Juventudes, 1937–1960* (Madrid, 1988), 440–69. The only provinces where the rate of entry into the Movement proper was of significant proportion were Valladolid and Santander. For further discussion of the tensions in the Frente during these years, see J. L. Alcocer, *Radiografía de un fraude: Notas para una historia del Frente de Juventudes* (Barcelona, 1978).

54. Lizcano, *La generación,* 101–3; Ruiz Carnicer, *El Sindicato,* 285–89. The weak, defensive posture of Fernández Cuesta is apparent in some of his collected speeches of 1953 to 1955, despite their occasional criticism of "capitalism"; see *Continuidad falangista al servicio de España* (Madrid, 1955).

55. This incident is described in J. L. Alcocer, "Covaleda, 1955: La Falange desaira a Juan Carlos," *Nueva Historia* 2 (April 1978), 95–100.

56. Quoted in Palacios, *Los papeles secretos,* 146.

57. Ibid.

58. Girón, *Si la memoria no me falla,* 162.

59. A prime demand of Falangist dissidents was, as usual, a return to pristine radicalism, invoking the examples of Ramiro Ledesma and José Antonio, as well as the prefranquista leadership of Manuel Hedilla. To quash devotion to the last of these, Tomás Romojaro, the vice Secretary general, revealed that Hedilla was currently receiving a monthly subsidy from the government. Suárez Fernández, *FF,* V, 243.

60. Laín Entralgo has given an account of this period in his memoir, *Descargo de conciencia (1930–1960)* (Madrid, 1989).

61. P. Laín Entralgo, *Reflexiones sobre la situación espiritual de la juventud universitaria* (Madrid, 1955).

62. Ridruejo apparently had not yet incurred the total displeasure of Franco, who was said to have intervened personally in 1954 to ensure that Ridruejo was awarded a literary prize of which he might have been deprived. Ridruejo's letter of gratitude is reproduced in Suárez Fernández, *FF,* V, 164–66.

Ridruejo had worked as the correspondent of *Arriba* in Rome from 1948 to 1951, and direct experience with political democracy in the homeland of paradigmatic fascism was an important factor in his definitive defascistization. After the events of 1956 he became a co-leader of a tiny social democratic opposition group.

63. See the analysis in La Cierva, *Franquismo,* II, 137–40.

64. The fullest collection of materials on these incidents and their background will be found in R. Mesa, ed., *Jaraneros y alborotadores: Documentos sobre los sucesos estudiantiles de febrero de 1956 en la Universidad Complutense de Madrid* (Madrid, 1982). See also Lizcano, *La generación,* 123–53; and D. Ridruejo, *Casi unas memorias* (Barcelona, 1976), 335–55. The official report to Franco is cited in Palacios, *Los papeles secretos,* 149–50.

65. Girón claims that it was he who broke the news of the incident of 9 February to Franco, who was initially confused and perplexed:

—My general, they have just shot a student.
—Is he one of ours?
—Yes, he is a Falangist.
—That's not as bad. . . .

*Si la memoria no me falla,* 163.

66. *Conversaciones privadas,* 164.

67. Ibid., 159.

68. Girón, *Si la memoria no me falla,* 168.

69. Ellwood, *Prietas las filas,* 158–59, refers to a critique of the 1947 Law of Succession that he prepared for his fellow Cortes members.

70. Arrese's memoir, *Una etapa constituyente* (Barcelona, 1982), gives his account of the entire process that followed.

71. According to a memorandum of Antonio Garrigues to Martín Artajo, 8 January 1957, Franco had once told Garrigues: "Well, you must understand that

for me the Movement is like a claque. Have you not observed that when there is a large audience it is necessary for a few to begin to applaud so that the rest will join in and follow them? Well, that is more or less how I understand the purpose of the Movement." Quoted in Tusell, *Franco y los católicos,* 402–3.

72. Del Río Cisneros, *Pensamiento político,* I, 251.

73. Franco, *Discursos y mensajes del Jefe del Estado,* 183–89.

74. Quoted in Palacios, *Los papeles secretos,* 159.

75. For a full discussion of Vicén's proposals, see my *Falange* (Paris, 1964; Madrid, 1983), 204–10.

76. Arrese, *Una etapa constituyente.*

77. Franco later slyly observed to Salgado Araujo that the "anteproyectos" had to be rejected because they would have given the next chief of state enough power to place a future king in an awkward position.

78. López Rodó proposed a new law on the principles of the Movement, a new Fuero of the Crown that would define the future power of the monarchy, a basic national administrative reform law, a new Fuero of Justice, and a more moderate organic law on the National Council. L. López Rodó, *La Larga marcha hacia la Monarquía* (Barcelona, 1978), 129. Most aspects of these proposals were subsequently adopted to a greater or lesser degree in the decade that followed.

79. Créac'h, *Le Coeur et l'épée* (Paris, 1959), 386. Detailed accounts of the reactions of regime notables will be found in López Rodó, *Larga marcha;* and in Suárez Fernández, *FF,* V, 306–16.

80. Quoted in Tusell, *Franco y los católicos,* 421–22. See also the discussions in L. López Rodó, *Memorias,* 3 vols. (Barcelona, 1990), I, 53–76; and in Palacios, *Los papeles secretos,* 160–65.

81. J. L. de Arrese, *Hacia una meta institucional* (Madrid, 1957), 191–92.

82. J. L. de Arrese, *Treinta años de política* (Madrid, 1966), 1146–65.

83. Girón, *Si la memoria no me falla,* 170.

84. Ibid., 170–73.

85. Suárez Fernández, *FF,* V, 320–21.

86. According to Salgado Araujo, *Conversaciones privadas,* 206–8.

87. As quoted ibid., 182.

88. Girón, *Si la memoria no me falla,* 174.

89. Ibid., 183.

90. The career of Solís Ruiz is briefly described in the Equipo Mundo's *Los noventa ministros de Franco* (Barcelona, 1970), 299–310.

91. Girón, *Si la memoria no me falla,* 173.

92. The syndical changes between 1957 and 1962 are summarized by W. Bernecker, "Die Arbeiterbewegung unter dem Franquismus," in *Die geheime Dynamik autoritärer Diktaturen* (Munich, 1982), 108–12.

93. On this phase, see Saez Marín, *El Frente de Juventudes,* 223–39.

94. For the transformation, see Ruiz Carnicer, *El Sindicato Español Universitario,* 305–40.

95. Quoted in López Rodó, *Memorias,* I, 93.

96. Arrese departed public life with such expressions as, "It is not surprising that we let cautious folks call us crazy, because, amid everything, if our madness

led us to failure, it is also good to imagine oneself shut up in an asylum for having dreamed of eliminating misery with a single stroke of the pen." Ibid., I, 217. Though Arrese's career was generally characterized by considerable caution, it was perhaps not totally inappropriate that his final departure was occasioned by an extravagant action that recalled utopian fascism.

97. López Rodó was of the opinion that it was partly to make up for this slight that on 6 January 1959 Franco bestowed the title of condesa del Castillo de la Mota on Pilar Primo de Rivera. Ibid., I, 206. (The Castillo de la Mota was the national headquarters of the Sección Femenina.)

98. For the classic analysis of "bureaucratic authoritarianism" in Latin America, see G. O'Donnell, *Modernization and Bureaucratic-Authoritarianism: Studies in South American Politics* (Berkeley, 1973).

CHAPTER THIRTEEN

1. F. Franco Bahamonde, *Discursos y mensajes del Jefe del Estado (1960–1963)* (Madrid, 1964), 320–21.

2. These were Manuel Lora Tamayo, a member of Catholic Action, as minister of education and Jesus Romeo Gorría in the Ministry of Labor. Romeo Gorría was a Falangist camisa vieja but had made his career as an elite jurist.

3. M. Fraga Iribarne, *Memoria breve de una vida pública* (Barcelona, 1980), 41.

4. See M. Valdés Larrañaga, *De la Falange al Movimiento (1936–1952)* (Madrid, 1994), 366–72.

5. J. Solís Ruiz, *Nueva convivencia política* (Madrid, 1960), 13–39.

6. Cf. J. Fueyo Alvarez, *Desarrollo político y orden constitucional* (Madrid, 1964).

7. J. Solís Ruiz, *España: Su Monarquía y el futuro* (Madrid, 1975), 300.

8. Two flattering portraits of Fraga as minister may be found in M. Millán Mestre, *Fraga Iribarne: Retrato en tres tiempos* (Barcelona, 1975), 103–251; and O. Cabezas, *Manuel Fraga: Semblanza de un hombre de Estado* (Madrid, 1976), 101–242.

9. The full proposal may be found in L. López Rodó, *Memorias*, 4 vols. (Barcelona, 1990), I, 397–400.

10. F. Franco Bahamonde, *Discursos y mensajes del Jefe del Estado (1964–1967)* (Madrid, 1968), 317.

11. Franco, *Discursos y mensajes (1960–1963)*, 324.

12. Quoted in C. Fernández, *El general Franco* (Barcelona, 1983), 214.

13. F. Franco Salgado Araujo, *Mis conversaciones privadas con Franco* (Barcelona, 1979), 344.

14. "Let us not deceive ourselves, for they are very few." Quoted in J. Palacios, *Los papeles secretos de Franco* (Madrid, 1996), 231.

15. Ibid., 181–92; R. Borràs, *El Rey de los rojos,* (Barcelona, 1996), 212–21.

16. Quoted in Palacios, *Los papeles secretos,* 234–35.

17. Ibid., 266–68.

18. Ibid., 305–7.

19. As noted earlier, this occasionally led to public insults, though on one occasion in 1960 the Falanges Universitarias at the University of Madrid had refused to join a group of anti-juanista Carlists who harassed Prince Juan Carlos. Ibid., 290–91.

20. The chief decline officially registered was from a grand total of 922,000 in 1944 to 908,000 in the year following; membership rose to 934,000 in 1946. J. Bardavío, *La estructura del poder en España* (Madrid, 1960), 117–18.

21. Ibid.

22. Suárez Fernández, *FF,* VI, 49.

23. J. J. Linz, "From Falange to Movimiento-Organización," in *Authoritarian Politics in Modern Society,* ed. S. P. Huntington and C. H. Moore (New Haven, 1970), 167.

24. Bardavío, *La estructura,* 117.

25. Quoted in López Rodó, *Memorias,* I, 303.

26. E. Romero, *Tragicomedia de España* (Barcelona, 1985), 93, cited ibid., I, 303–4.

27. Quoted ibid., I, 302.

28. See G. Morán, *Adolfo Suárez: Historia de una ambición* (Barcelona, 1979).

29. Ibid., 110–18.

30. These final phases are described in greater detail in M. A. Ruiz Carnicer, *El Sindicato Español Universitario (SEU) 1939–1965* (Madrid, 1996), 332–86. See also J. L. Alcocer, *Radiografía de un fraude: Notas para una historia del Frente de Juventudes* (Barcelona, 1978), 153–66; P. Lizcano, *La generación del 56: La universidad contra Franco* (Barcelona, 1981), 227–34; and Morán, *Adolfo Suárez,* 147–64.

31. The membership of 225,000 reported for the Organización Juvenil (formerly Frente de Juventudes) in 1963 was a very modest figure for a country of more than 30 million. *Informe: Sesión de Pleno del IX Consejo Nacional* (Madrid, 1963). This figure had declined to 211,626 by 1969, and by that time the organization provided only 3,867 new adult members for the annual "pase al Movimiento." J. Saez Marín, *El Frente de Juventudes, 1937–1960* (Madrid, 1988), 469–72.

32. J. A. Girón, *Si la memoria no me falla* (Barcelona, 1994), 197.

33. Ibid.

34. Ibid., 197–98.

35. According to the new minister of finance, Juan José Espinosa San Martín, in A. Bayod, ed., *Franco visto por sus ministros* (Barcelona, 1981), 154.

36. Quoted in *España perspectiva 1974* (Madrid, 1974), 70–71.

37. Girón, *Si la memoria no me falla,* 200.

38. D. Sueiro, *La verdadera historia del Valle de los Caídos* (Madrid, 1976); Alcocer, *Radiografía,* 74–76.

39. The best summary will be found in S. Ellwood, *Prietas las filas: Historia*

*de Falange Española, 1933–1983* (Barcelona, 1984), 226–34. See also J. L. Rodríguez Jiménez, *La extrema derecha española en el siglo XX* (Madrid, 1997), 322–25.

40. Ellwood, *Prietas las filas*, 234–37.

41. Ibid., 237–39.

42. Ellwood notes the Unión de Trabajadores Sindicalistas, Acción Sindicalista Revolucionaria, Frente Sindicalista Unificado, Frente de Trabajadores Nacional Sindicalistas, and even an attempt to revive the CONS. To these might be added a number of others, such as the Juventudes Falangistas de España, who edited their own miniature version of *Haz*. None of these tiny groups, however, enjoyed the leadership of Falangist veterans, as the little organizations listed above did.

43. Ibid., 240–42. For varied documents of the dissident groups during the long span of the regime, see J. Onrubia Revuelta, *Historia de la oposición falangista al régimen de Franco en sus documentos* (Madrid, 1989).

44. López Rodó, *Memorias*, II, 217.

45. Dionisio Martín Sanz of the Syndical Organization was possibly the most outspoken critic in the Cortes of López Rodó and of the new Development Plans, which he attacked for lacking a national ideology, for relying too much on foreign capital and the emigration of labor, and for abandoning agriculture. Martín Sanz, *En las Cortes españolas: Crítica del Segundo Plan de Desarrollo* (Madrid, 1969), and *La planificación española la Olimpíada de las ideologías: Crítica del Tercer Plan de Desarrollo* (Madrid, 1972).

46. The last effort—apart from those of the semiclandestine dissident Falangists—to negotiate with elements of the clandestine CNT in Catalonia was apparently made in 1965, while there were also ongoing efforts to negotiate with opposition elements at the lower level of the Syndical Organization itself. Cf. Suárez Fernández, *FF*, VIII, 223–25.

47. López Rodó, *Memorias*, I, 432.

48. Quoted ibid., I, 433.

49. Ibid., I, 443–44.

50. One of the more outspoken young reformists in the Movement was Miguel Primo de Rivera, the nephew of José Antonio and now the popular new mayor of Jerez. He told López Rodó that when received by Franco on 24 March 1965 he had told the Caudillo that

> the blue shirt has become a disguise and a source of division. In 1933 it was justified, but thirty years later had lost its meaning.
>
> In municipal government we are under the dual discipline of the Ministry of the Interior and the General Secretariat of the Movement. One cannot serve two masters. City governments should represent the municipality, not the party.
>
> No one is joining the FET. The "azules" are an unpopular, obstructive little group. What Pilar has had to suffer from Pepe Solís!

He claimed that Franco listened attentively but made no response. Ibid., I, 512.

51. This is discussed in Suárez Fernández, *FF*, VII, 181–82.

52. López Rodó, *Memorias*, I, 514.

53. Quoted in J. M. Martínez Val, *¿Por qué no fue posible la Falange?* (Barcelona, 1975), 11.

54. López Rodó, *Memorias*, II, 42–43.

55. A. Rodríguez Valcárcel, *Una etapa política* (Madrid, 1969), 67.

56. There is a lengthy résumé of the debate in López Rodó, *Memorias*, II, 157–66, 180–203.

57. López Rodó, *La Larga marcha hacia la Monarquía* (Barcelona, 1978), 263.

58. All this, as usual, was somewhat obscured by the continuing barrage of propaganda from the Ediciones del Movimiento and allied organs: *Nueva etapa política* (Madrid, 1966); *Ley Orgánica, Movimiento y democracia* (Madrid, 1967); *Tiempo nuevo y Movimiento Nacional* (Madrid, 1967); and *Nuevo horizonte del Movimiento* (Madrid, 1970). The Servicio Informativo Español began its *Crónica de un año de España* for 1968–69 by declaring: "The movement toward the institutionalization and reform of the National Movement has been one of the fundamental concerns of the period from July 1968 to July 1969."

59. On the effort to begin the development of associationism during 1968, see J. Fernando Badía, *El régimen de Franco* (Madrid, 1984), 165–72.

60. Girón, *Si la memoria no me falla*, 204. It is doubtful that more than a very few of those involved in the associationist ploy during the final years of the Spanish regime were aware that a somewhat similar tactic had been suggested by the philosopher Giovanni Gentile for Mussolini's puppet "Italian Social Republic" in northern Italy after the overthrow of the regime in Rome. In an article entitled "Riconstruire" in *Il Corriere della Sera* (Milan), 28 Dec. 1943, Gentile advanced the notion of the expression of distinct "opinions" within the Fascist Party to represent diversity while maintaining a single state party. Cf. G. E. Rusconi, *Resistenza e postfascismo* (Bologna, 1995), 57–58.

61. J. A. González Casanova, "Asociaciones políticas y Monarquía moderada," in *España perspectiva 1974* (Madrid, 1974), 101–22.

62. Martínez Val has noted the following: "La verdad sobre la Falange," *Mundo* 1500–1501 (Feb. 1969); "¿Ha mandado la Falange en España?" *Informaciones*, 16 May 1969; three articles by Pedro Peñalva in *El Noticiero Universal* (Barcelona), Sept. 1969; the survey "Falange Española," ibid., 21 Nov. 1969; and Heleno Saña, "La Falange a examen," *Indice*, Nov.–Dec. 1969 and Jan. 1970.

63. Zamora, for example, provided 6,210 of the new members for 1969. A total of 2,485 more were registered in Orense, while Lérida, which at that time had a zealous provincial governor and provincial chief, acquired 1,819. The lowest enrollments were in Gerona and Guipuzcoa, with only 25 new members each. Formerly Carlist Navarre, changing rapidly under the impact of accelerating industrialization, ranked fourth from the bottom with 47. A total of only 28,513 young people entered the Organización Juvenil that year, scarcely 1 percent of their national age cohort, while the Sección Femenina gained only 2,193 new members. Martínez Val, *¿Por qué?* 148–59.

64. Juan Carlos had earlier privately assured several leaders of the Movement that he considered it important to maintain their organization and its Principles, as indeed he swore to do in declaring allegiance to the Fundamental Laws. Cf. Palacios, *Papeles secretos*, 432. The old-guard Falangist leaders, of course, feared the worst, and they were absolutely correct.

65. His general manual on "organic democracy," *El hombre y la sociedad*, was reissued in a new edition in 1969.

66. Cf. Palacios, *Los papeles secretos*, 499–500. As Adolfo Suárez has said of the tutor and pupil, "Fernández Miranda explained many things to him." Testimony at the "Simposio sobre la Transición," Fundación Ortega y Gasset, Toledo, 12–13 May 1984.

There are two works on Fernández Miranda, but both concentrate on the final climatic phase of his career, when he helped to guide the democratic transition: P. and A. Fernández Miranda, *Lo que el Rey me ha pedido: Torcuato Fernández-Miranda y la reforma política* (Barcelona, 1995); and J. L. Alcocer, *Fernández-Miranda: Agonía de un Estado* (Barcelona, 1986).

67. J. Bardavío, *Políticos para una crisis* (Madrid, 1974), 35.

68. The most public expression of this hopeless tactic took the form of two books by Emilio Romero, *Cartas a un Príncipe* (Madrid, 1964), and *Cartas al pueblo soberano* (Madrid, 1965).

69. Alfonso was the elder son of Don Juan's older brother, who had renounced his right to the succession very early because he was a deaf-mute. The matter attained momentary importance after Don Alfonso's father attempted to renounce his renunciation, and especially after Alfonso's marriage to Franco's eldest granddaughter in 1972. At that time Franco's wife and others of his family circle sought briefly to advance the candidacy of Alfonso to the throne. The Generalissimo, however, had made his choice and remained firm.

70. Cantarero del Castillo later published a volume entitled *Falange y socialismo* (Barcelona, 1973).

71. On this session and Fraga's speech, see Fernando Badía, *El régimen*, 174–79; and the *Anuario Político Español 1969* (Madrid, 1970), 409–38.

72. In a series of newspaper interviews and in Fernández Miranda's *El Movimiento y el asociacionismo* (Madrid, 1970).

73. Quoted in Alcocer, *Fernández-Miranda*, 41.

74. Ibid., 42.

75. Ibid., 44–45.

76. Cf. López Rodó, *Memorias*, III, 31.

77. Ibid., 174.

78. Fernando Badía, *El régimen*, 220–22.

79. Ibid., 194–97, 231–32.

80. Quoted in R. Carr and J. P. Fusi, *Spain: Dictatorship to Democracy* (London, 1979), 190. On Fernández Miranda's handling of the problem of associations, see J. Meliá, *El largo camino de la apertura* (Barcelona, 1975), 169–200.

81. López Rodó, *Memorias*, III, 175.

82. J. Tusell, *Juan Carlos I* (Madrid, 1995), 524.

83. López Rodó, *Memorias*, III, 180. This uncertainty was reflected in the ambiguous rhetoric of the official publications of the period: *Balances y rumbos nacionales: Plataforma 1972. Realidades y perspectivas 1973* (Madrid, 1973), and *El Movimiento Nacional, las Leyes Fundamentales y el sistema de instituciones* (Madrid, 1973). A more coherent and reflective discussion by a veteran was J. Velarde Fuertes, *El nacionalsindicalismo cuarenta años después (Análisis crítico)* (Madrid, 1972).

84. López Rodó, *Memorias*, III, 272–73.

85. Girón, *Si la memoria no me falla*, 219–24.

86. López Rodó, *Memorias*, III, 274–75.

87. Quoted in E. de Aguinaga, *Informe sobre la Falange de José Antonio* (La Coruña, 1973), 56. Girón's last major statement on the eve of Franco's death was his small book, *Reflexiones sobre España* (Madrid, 1975).

88. These minigroups appeared and disappeared in dizzying succession. The Acción Sindicalista Revolucionaria and Frente Sindicalista Unificado, Juntas de Oposición Falangistas and Frente de Estudiantes Sindicalistas were followed in 1970 by the Confederación de Obreros Nacional Sindicalistas (reviving the old Falangist syndical name) and the Frente Sindicalista Universitario, then by the Falange Española Nacional Sindicalista (1971), Unión Falangista (1972), Alianza Revolucionaria Sindicalista (1973), Juventudes Obreras Falangistas (1974), and the Juventudes Falangistas Universitarias (1973). Membership sometimes overlapped, particularly between the nominally syndicalist and student groups.

Of the first neo-Falangist organizations of the 1960s, the Frente de Estudiantes Sindicalistas, Frente Nacional de Alianza Libre, and Frente Sindicalista Revolucionario still survived. The latter split in two in 1975, one section forming a new Partido Sindicalista Autogestionario (employing the fashionable "autogestionaria" socialist terminology of those years).

During the final political associations phase of the regime in 1974–75, Hillers tried alternately to revive the old name of Falange Española de las JONS—which instead was appropriated by sectors of the old guard that formed around Fernández Cuesta—and then to create a Falange Española Independiente. Other groups would follow after Franco's death.

See R. Ibáñez Hernández, "La Oposición falangista al régimen de Franco (1937–1975): Consideraciones sobre una cuestion inédita," in *Actas: Congreso de Jóvenes Historiadores y Geógrafos* (Madrid, 1990), 625–37; Ellwood, *Prietas las filas*, 241–46; E. Cadena, *La ofensiva neo-fascista* (Barcelona, 1978); D. Márquez, *Círculos "José Antonio"* (Bilbao, 1977); S. Hillers de Luque, *Estilo y ética falangistas* (Madrid, 1974); and S. Hillers de Luque, *España: una revolución pendiente* (Madrid, 1975).

89. M. Veyrat and J. L. Navas-Migueloa, eds., *Falange, hoy* (Madrid, 1973), presents the attitudes of a sizable group of Falangist (mostly neo-Falangist) leaders and spokesmen during the final phase of the regime.

90. On the new neofascist, neo-Nazi, and violent right-radical groups in Spain during the final phase and immediate aftermath of the regime, and their relations with dissident Falangists, see J. L. Rodríguez Jiménez, *Reaccionarios y golpistas:*

*La extrema derecha en España del tardofranquismo a la consolidación de la democracia (1967–1982)* (Madrid, 1994), 97–109, 115–79; X. Canals, *Neonazis en España* (Barcelona, 1995), 37–116; and X. Canals, "Neofeixisme a Espanya (1975–1982): L'invenció d'una tradició," *Afers* 25 (1996), 639–49.

91. This is attested by various sources, including Juan Carlos himself and López Rodó. J. L. de Villalonga, *El Rey* (Barcelona, 1993), 210–11; López Rodó, *Memorias*, III, 14; and J. Utrera Molina, *Sin cambiar de bandera* (Barcelona, 1989), 73.

92. Tusell, *Carrero: La eminencia gris del régimen de Franco* (Madrid, 1993), 416.

93. López Rodó, *Memorias*, III, 366.

94. Quoted by J. M. López de Letona in Bayod, ed., *Franco visto por sus ministros*, 215–16. This proposal also insisted on its own absolute loyalty and orthodoxy, stressing that "this system of associations rejects political parties and . . . ideological party groups. It functions within the doctrinal framework of the National Movement. It rejects any parallel representation as contrary to Point VIII of our Principles." Quoted in Suárez Fernánez, *FF*, VIII, 342.

95. Quoted in López Rodó, *Larga marcha*, 456–57. There is further treatment of this cabinet discussion in López Rodó, *Memorias*, III, 478–83. It was on this occasion that Fernández Miranda is said to have declared: "My master has been Machiavelli, who was a creative politician."

96. Utrera summarizes his political biography in his *Sin cambiar de bandera*, 17–65.

97. Ibid., 241–42.

98. Ibid., 150.

99. Ibid., 154.

100. Ibid., 159.

101. Ibid., 167.

102. According to Gíron, *Si la memoria no me falla*, 235–36.

103. Ortega Díaz-Ambrona has given one version in Diario 16, *Historia de la transición* (Madrid, 1984), 117–18. See also J. A. González Casanova, "Asociaciones políticas y Monarquía moderada," *España perspectiva 1974* (Madrid, 1974), 101–22; and J. Amodia, "El asociacionismo político en España: Aborto inevitable," *Iberian Studies* 3 (Spring 1974), 9–14.

104. Utrera Molina, in Bayod, ed., *Franco visto por sus ministeros*, 322–2.

105. Utrera describes the discussion in the National Council in *Sin cambiar de bandera*, 201–6.

106. Fernando Badía, *El régimen*, 246–56.

107. *ABC*, 11 Jan. 1975.

108. Juan Antonio Ortega in *Tele-Exprés* (Barcelona), 11 Jan. 1975.

109. Quoted in *Mundo* (Barcelona), 17 May 1975.

110. R. de la Cierva, *Crónicas de la transición* (Barcelona, 1975), 29.

111. V. Pozuelo Escudero, *Los últimos 476 días de Franco* (Barcelona, 1980), 122.

112. Utrera presents his version in *Sin cambiar de bandera*, 248–50.

113. Utrera describes this in some detail, ibid., 253–61, while Antonio Carro Martínez presents a version favorable to Arias in Bayod, ed., *Franco visto por sus ministros*, 356–59.

114. Cf. L. M. Anson, *Don Juan* (Barcelona, 1994), 403.

115. According to the testimony of Suárez at the "Simposio sobre la Transición" (Toledo), 13 May 1984. Cf. R. Graham, *Spain: A Nation Comes of Age* (New York, 1984), 150; and Tusell, *Juan Carlos I*, 557.

116. Franco had apparently been impressed by the report on Carrero Blanco's assassination that Herrero had prepared as prosecutor of the Tribunal Supremo, as cited in L. Herrero, *El ocaso del régimen* (Madrid, 1995), 14.

117. Ibid., 188.

118. Ibid., 190–92.

119. Herrero's alleged plans have been presented in Morán, *Adolfo Suárez*, 285–96; and in M. Campo Vidal, *Información y servicios secretos en el atentado al Presidente Carrero Blanco* (Barcelona, 1983), 90–98. Cf. the sketch presented to Franco by Nieto Antúnez in February 1975, in Suárez Fernández, *FF*, VIII, 381–82.

120. Fraga Iribarne says that he drew the impression from a conversation with Herrero Tejedor on 27 April 1975 that "the definitive plan is to build the great continuist, more than reformist, association." Fraga, *Memoria breve de una vida pública*, 355.

121. Herrero Tejedor to Girón, 9 April 1975, in Herrero, *El ocaso*, 196.

122. J. Conte Barrera, *Las asociaciones políticas* (Barcelona, 1976), is a survey of the proposed groups.

123. *La Vanguardia* (Barcelona), 21 Jan. 1975.

124. Herrero, *El ocaso*, 195. Franco may have been well-informed about the political outlines that Suárez and others prepared for the prince. Cf. J. Figuero and I. Herrero, *La muerte de Franco jamás contada* (Barcelona, 1985), 14.

125. Herrero, *El ocaso*, 196–98.

126. Suárez has presented slightly different versions of this meeting, one at the symposium of the Fundación Ortega y Gasset in Toledo on 13 May 1984, and another repeated in Herrero, *El ocaso*, 199–200.

127. Herrero, *El ocaso*, 278.

128. Pilar Primo de Rivera has briefly narrated this final phase down to the time of her replacement in her *Recuerdos de una vida* (Madrid, 1983), 333–39.

129. On the transition in the world of the press, see C. Barrera, *Sin mordaza: Veinte años de prensa en democracia* (Madrid, 1995), 15–61.

130. There is a growing literature on neofascism in Spain. In addition to the key works by Casals and Rodríguez Jiménez—X. Casals, *Neonazis en España;* and Rodríguez Jiménez, *Reaccionarios y golpistas*—see Cadena, *La ofensiva neofascista*, 163–75; M. Sánchez Soler, *Los hijos del 20-N: Historia violenta del fascismo español* (Madrid, 1993); and M. Florentín, *Guía de la Europa negra* (Madrid, 1994), 289–307.

131. For a discussion, see F. Jáuregui and M. A. Menéndez, *Lo que nos queda de Franco* (Madrid, 1996).

CONCLUSION

1. See the statistics in A. Costa Pinto, *Os Camisas Azuis: Ideologias, elites e movimentos fascistas em Portugal 1914–1945* (Lisbon, 1994).

2. This work was reprinted much later as *Revolución y contrarevolución en España* (Paris, 1966).

3. In my *A History of Fascism* (Madison, 1995), 487–95.

4. The most recent attempt to deal with José Antonio's "fascisticity" is M. Argaya Roca, *Entre lo espontáneo y lo difícil* (Oviedo, 1996), especially 107–29. On this problem, see also J. L. Jerez-Riesco, *La Falange, partido fascista* (Barcelona, 1997); and the final chapter of J. del Aguila Tejerina, *Ideología y fascismo* (Madrid, 1982), even though the ideal types used in these works leave something to be desired.

5. Ledesma was quite firm on religion. While admitting on occasion that it could not be altogether avoided in a Spanish nationalist movement, he insisted that "the enterprise of building a national doctrine, a plan of historical resurgence, a strategy of combat, effective political institutions, etc. . . . is something that can be done without appealing to the Catholic emblem of the Spanish." *Discurso a las juventudes de España* (Barcelona, 1935 ed.), 94.

6. *Obras completas* (Mexico City, 1968), IV, 813.

7. On the comparative analysis of the Franco regime, together with its similarities to and differences from Fascist Italy, see J. Tusell, *La dictadura de Franco* (Madrid, 1988); E. Ucelay da Cal, "Problemas en la comparación de las dictaduras española e italiana en los años treinta y cuarenta," in *El Estado moderno en Italia y España,* ed. E. D'Auria and J. Casassas (Barcelona, 1993), 155–74; and the final chapter of my *The Franco Regime 1936–1975* (Madison, 1987).

8. This was, of course, the opportunity, however tenuous, that the Republican authorities had foregone with the execution of José Antonio.

9. This is brought out most clearly in J. Tusell, *Franco en la Guerra Civil: Una biografía política* (Barcelona, 1992).

10. Tusell, *Franco, España y la II Guerra Mundial* (Madrid 1995), 648.

# Index

ABC (monarchist newspaper): Anson article in, 464–65; and elections, 94, 182–83; on fascism, 78–79; Franco interview in, 271, 273; José Antonio's views in, 130, 131, 159; on violence, 108–9
Accão Escolar Vanguarda (AEV), 176, 177
Acció Catalana, 21, 22, 43
Acción Ciudadana, 19
Acción Española, 18, 46, 47, 110, 131, 132, 133, 409
Acción Nacional, 44, 75
Acción Nobiliaria, 42
Acción Política, 452
Acción Popular, 44, 270
ACNP. See Asociación Católica Nacional de Propagandistas
Action Française, 18, 21, 47, 117
Africa: in World War II, 334, 336, 337, 339, 384. See also Algeria; Morocco
Agencia EFE, 460
agriculture: and "definitive program" for Falange, 128–29; and FET, 295, 301, 352; José Antonio's views about, 152, 179, 213, 301; and Movimiento in postfascist era, 405; in Portugal, 178; and syndicalism, 301, 405. See also Ministry of Agriculture
Aguado, Emiliano, 103, 139
air force, Spanish, 206, 328, 342
Aizpurúa, Manuel, 142
Alava: Falange in, 258
Alba, duque de, 392
Alba, Santiago, 211–12, 232
Albiñana, José María, 42, 43, 77–78, 94, 96, 106, 130, 261
Alcalá Galiano, Alvaro, 107, 108
Alcalá Zamora, Niceto, 178–79, 194

Alcalá (SEU journal), 414, 415
Alerta (SEU journal), 414
Alfaro, José María, 141, 174, 314, 389
Alférez (Catholic journal), 414
alfonsino monarchism, 48, 132–33, 164, 183, 201, 291, 306–7, 310, 325
Alfonso Carlos (pretender), 48
Alfonso de Borbón-Dampierre, 452
Alfonso XIII (king of Spain): abdication of, 371; and Dictatorship (Primo de Rivera), 24, 25, 27–28, 33, 35, 37, 41; Primo de Rivera family's loyalty to, 74; and restoration of monarchy, 355
Algeria, 332, 339
Alianza Sindicalista, 404
Alicante: air attacks on, 227; demonstration on anniversary of José Antonio's death at, 456. See also Alicante prison
Alicante prison: Allen's interview of José Antonio in, 225–26, 230; anarchists as administrators of, 216; death of José Antonio at, 232, 235–36; and exchange of prisoners, 216, 220, 236, 264; executions at, 211, 232, 235–36; José Antonio as prisoner in, 198–208, 209–10, 214–35; Primo de Rivera family members in, 209–10, 212, 214, 231; rescue of José Antonio from, 209–10, 214–21, 228, 236, 242–43, 249–50; special treatment for prisoners in, 198–99, 210–11; and trial of José Antonio, 140–41, 215, 225, 226–30
Allen, Jay, 225–26, 230
Allies. See France; Great Britain; United States
Altamira, Rafael, 12
Altozano Moraleda, Hermenegildo, 440

Alvarez de Sotomayor, Nicasio, 60, 135, 368
Alvargonzález, Emilio, 82
Amadeo, D., 262
anarchists, 60, 61, 86, 102, 177, 183, 216, 224, 248
Andalusia: and authoritarian nationalism, 21; Falange in, 256, 258; Hispano-Berbers of, 221; and military revolt of 1936, 206; Primo de Rivera family roots in, 70; and problem of Spanish nationalism, 10
Ansaldo, Juan Antonio: and aviation, 83; and Calvo Sotelo, 130; expulsion of, 118, 122, 136; and Guerrillas de España, 130; and JONS, 87–88; and José Antonio, 116, 118, 140, 209; as monarchist, 83; and Ruiz de Alda, 122; and violence, 109, 111, 114. *See also* Falange de la Sangre
Anson, Luis María, 464
anteproyectos (Arrese), 422–25, 429, 433, 434, 446, 447
Anti-Comintern Pact, 326, 372
anti-Semitism, 54, 62, 63, 96, 253, 364, 378, 389, 395
Antonescu, Ion, 354, 476, 477
Antunia, Graciano, 220
Aosta, duke of, 262
Aparicio, Juan, 58
Aparicio Bernal, Jesús, 440
appeal of "contrafuero," 435, 446
appointments. *See* cabinet; *specific person or position*
Aragon: Falange in, 242, 245; historical development of, 3; and problem of Spanish nationalism, 3, 4, 5
Arana Goiri, Sabino de, 15
Aranda, Antonio, 305, 327, 339, 346, 354–56, 371, 394
Araquistain, Luis, 123–24, 469–70, 472
Areilza, José María de, 60–61, 77, 86, 125, 314, 339
Arellano, Luis, 276, 277
Argentina, 221, 232, 343, 407
Arias Navarro, Carlos, 459, 460, 461, 462–63, 466
Arias Salgado, Gabriel, 369, 378, 385, 410, 420, 427, 432
Arias Salgado, Rafael, 461

Arija: violence in, 169
aristocracy: José Antonio's views about, 222. *See also* elites
Army of Africa, 206, 240
army officers: as alfonsino monarchists, 164; British payment of, 346; as Carlists, 164; and defascistization, 375; and early years of World War II, 330; and Falange internal conflict, 134–35; and Falange plans for armed revolt, 170, 171–72; and FET, 311, 330, 371, 375; and José Antonio, 82, 134, 170; and military revolt of 1936, 207; and Portugese syndicalism, 176
Arredondo, Luis, 107, 109, 118, 164, 170
Arrese, José Luis de: achievements of, 402, 406; anteproyectos of, 421–25, 429, 433, 434, 446, 447; arrest of, 275; and cabinet of 1957, 426; as camisa vieja, 437; and Catholicism, 373; and civil guarantees, 402; criticisms of, 377, 425; and defascistization, 366–67, 369, 373–76, 378, 380, 382, 389, 390, 392, 393, 395, 396, 397; and disciplining FET, 366–67, 369, 373–76, 378, 380, 382; dismissal/resignation of, 402, 429; and FET between 1939–1941, 359, 360–62; as FET secretary general, 359, 360–62, 368–70, 410, 411; and foreign relations, 382, 395, 397; Franco's relationship with, 367, 379, 380, 429; German visit of, 382, 384, 385–87; as housing minister, 427, 429; and Junta Política, 390; and last phase of Movimiento, 448; as martyr-figure, 429; and monarchism, 374; and Movimiento in post-fascist era, 402, 428; as Movimiento secretary general, 420, 421; and new parliament, 389; and political redefinitions, 395; report about Falangist influence in regime by, 424; return to cabinet of, 420; and second metamorphosis of Franco regime, 426, 428; Serrano compared with, 373; and Serrano conspiracies, 375, 376, 380; Solís Ruiz's views about, 438; and syndicalism/labor, 368, 407; and totalitarianism, 438; and World War II, 384, 396
*Arriba* (Falangist daily, Madrid 1939–1979): and collapse of Italian Fascism,

394; decline of, 441; and early years of World War II, 330, 339; and FET between 1939–1941, 327, 330, 339, 353–54, 358, 359; and foreign policy, 394; and last phase of Movimiento, 441, 450; and monarchy in future, 413; and Movimiento in post-fascist era, 413; on Nazi–Soviet Pact, 330; termination of, 467

*Arriba* (Falangist weekly): and elections of 1936, 180; first publication of, 167; government closing of, 167; José Antonio's writings in, 185–86, 228; last issue of, 187; and National Front proposal, 180; and Right, 168, 186

*Arriba España* (Pamplona), 253, 254, 261, 280

*¡Arriba España!* (Pérez de Cabo book), 167–68

Arrow Cross, 176

artists, 141–42, 470

Asamblea Internacional de Excombatientes, 439–40

Asensio, Carlos, 381, 382, 384, 385, 386, 394

Asociación Católica Nacional de Propagandistas (ACNP), 28, 369, 402, 451

Asociación de Estudiantes Católicos, 70, 102

Asociación de Estudiantes Tradicionalistas (AET), 287

Asociación Oficial de Estudiantes, 70

asociaciones políticas. See associations; *specific association*

Asociaciones Profesionales de Estudiantes, 441

Assault Guards: and Aznar, 218; and Barcelona riot, 65; F. E. de las JONS as, 101; and José Antonio, 188, 209, 210, 218, 475; and military revolt of 1936, 206; organization of, 312; and repression during Civil War, 247, 248; and special elections of 1936, 194; and violence, 111, 113, 204

associations, 434, 444–56, 457–58, 459, 461–62, 463–64, 465

Associazione Nazionalista Italiana, 17

Asturias: historical development of, 3; insurrections in, 124, 126, 134, 239; syndicalism in, 352, 407

Asúa, Luis Jiménez de, 187, 189

Aunós, Eduardo, 30, 32, 33–34, 38, 172, 298, 304

authoritarian nationalism: and Barcelona, 20–23; and fascism, 472, 473; and FET between 1939–1941, 326; and Franco, 242, 311, 477; in Italy, 16–17; José Antonio's views about, 473; and legacy of Primo de Rivera dictatorship, 37–41; and monarchism, 46–48; origins of Spanish, 16–50; in Portugal, 21, 45, 48–50; and Primo de Rivera dictatorship (1923–1930), 23–37; and Right (1930–1933), 41–46

authoritarianism: bureaucratic, 430; Carrero's views about, 366, 377; and economy, 408; and FET, 285–86, 478; Franco's views about, 240, 271, 388, 477; José Antonio's views about, 146–47, 149, 150, 152; and last phase of Movimiento, 462; and Movimiento in post-fascist era, 408, 409, 430; and second metamorphosis of Franco regime, 430; and weakness of Spanish fascism, 470. *See also* authoritarian nationalism

auxiliary services, 256–57, 402. *See also* Technical Services; *specific service*

Auxilio de Invierno. *See* Auxilio Social

Auxilio Social, 257, 290, 303

aviation: and fascism, 83

Axis. *See* Germany; Italy

Azaña, Manuel: and authoritarian nationalism, 44, 45; and Catholicism, 44; criticisms of, 45; early career of, 56; and fascism of intellectuals, 54; and José Antonio in prison, 211; José Antonio's views about, 171, 185–86, 187, 199, 215; Mussolini's views about, 54; replacement of, 191; and Second Republic, 44, 45; and special elections of 1936, 194; violence during government of, 187–88, 189–90; and weakness of Spanish fascism, 476

Azlor de Aragón, Pilar, 80–81, 171

Aznalcóllar: violence in, 169

Aznar, Agustín: arrest and prosecution of, 305–6; and Falange funding, 219; and Falange internal politics, 249–50, 267; and Falange–Carlist fusion, 267; and FET, 273, 306; and José Antonio in prison, 216, 218–19, 242–43, 249–50;

Aznar, Agustín (*continued*)
  as Junta de Mando member, 208; as militia leader, 164, 207–8, 244; as national inspector of militia, 276; style of, 264; and violence, 107
*Azor* (culture review), 166
Azpiazu, Joaquín, 285–86

Badajoz: Falange in, 164; violence in, 105, 169
Badoglio, Marshal, 393, 394
Balbo, Italo, 160
Balillas (Falangist children's organization), 257
Balmes, Jaime, 18
Barba Hernández, Bartolomé, 170, 172, 210
Barcelona: and authoritarian nationalism, 19, 20–23; captain general of, 358; Carlists in, 20; class struggle in, 19; Dencàs's organization in, 127; Falange in, 373; and fascism of intellectuals, 52; Italian Fascism in, 127; JONS in, 86; labor and social programs in, 405; as Ledesma base, 136; nationalism in, 15; Primo de Rivera family in, 71; and Socialist insurrection, 126; syndicalism in, 352, 407–8; Treintistas in, 166, 167
Barcelona, conde de. *See* Juan (monarchy heir)
Barrera, Emilio, 160
Basque Country: artistic elite of, 141; assassination of Carrero Blanco in, 458; and authoritarian nationalism, 20, 21, 33, 45; Carlists in, 288, 378, 379; Falange in, 164, 288, 372; and military revolt of 1936, 207; nationalism of, 145, 152, 207; and problem of Spanish nationalism, 3, 4, 5, 6, 15
Bayle, Constantino, 285
Begoña crisis, 379–80
Beigbeder y Atienza, Juan, 279, 312, 329, 331, 334
Benavente, Jacinto, 160–61
Beneyto Pérez, Juan, 316–17
Benjumea Burín, Joaquín, 350, 359
Berbers, 221–22
Bermúdez Cañete, Antonio, 59
Bernhardt, Johannes, 356
Bilbao, Esteban, 298, 347, 402

Bilbao: artistic elite in, 141; and authoritarian nationalism, 21; Carlists in, 378, 379–80; executions in, 227; JONS in, 86; and monarchism, 47; nationalism in, 81–82; as source of funds, 47, 86, 87; violence in, 379–80
Black Arrows, 245
Black Legend, 10, 157
Bloque Nacional, 130, 131, 133, 135
Blue Arrows, 245
Blue Division, 340–41, 372, 374, 375, 380, 381, 382, 385, 394, 402, 445
Blue Legion, 394
blue shirts (Falange symbol), 269, 373, 414, 452
Blue Shirts (Portuguese syndicalists), 175–78
Blue Squadron, 342
Blum, Léon, 220, 232
Bolivia: Falange in, 309, 343
Bolshevism, 202, 384, 393, 396
Borbón, Juan de, 220–21
Bordighera: Mussolini–Franco meeting at, 337
Bottai, Giuseppe, 32
Bourbon dynasty, 5, 14, 417. *See also specific person*
bourgeoisie, 151, 189, 293, 470
Bravo Martínez, Francisco, 101, 142, 179
Bravo Murillo, Francisco, 18
Brown Shirts, 266
Buckley, Henry, 142, 157
bureaucratic authoritarianism, 430
Burgos: Arrese speech in, 393; captain general of, 376; Carlists in, 265; Falange in, 164, 201, 244, 254, 256; FET student rally in, 287; Franco's speech in, 294; and military revolt of 1936, 207; proposed Falange meeting in, 90; violence in, 378

Cabalzar, Guido, 160
Cabanas Erauskin, 141
Cabanillas, Pío, 452, 459, 460, 461, 464
cabinet: of 1938, 290, 291; of 1939, 311–14; of 1942, 380–82; of 1944, 402; of 1945, 402; of 1951, 409–10; of 1956, 420; of 1957, 425, 426, 427; of 1962, 431–32; of 1965, 434; of 1969, 451–52; of 1973, 457; of 1974, 459; of 1975, 463; and criticisms of FET, 358–61; and

defascistization, 380–82, 394; and German troops in Spanish territory, 384; and last phase of Movimiento, 431–32, 434; and Movimiento in post-fascist era, 402, 409–10, 420, 425, 426, 427; rivalries in, 432–33. *See also specific person or position*

Cáceres: Falange in, 164

Cadalso, José, 5

Cadenas, Vicente, 252–53, 279–80

Cádiz: elections in, 93–94, 181, 183; Falange in, 254; and military revolt of 1936, 206

Calderón, E. Yllán, 8

Calvo Sotelo, José: and alternatives to republicanism, 132–33; arrest and execution of, 133, 188, 204, 205, 239; as Cortes member, 117; criticisms of, 376; and Dictatorship, 31, 33–34; and elections, 94, 194; and fascism, 132; and Franco regime, 132; ideology of, 131–33; and Italian Fascism, 117; José Antonio's views about, 117, 200; and militarism, 131–32, 133; as monarchist leader, 117, 131–32, 197; as Right leader, 117, 129–30, 131–32, 200; satire about, 95; title of nobility for, 405

Calvo Sotelo, Leopoldo, 452

Cambó, Francesc, 15, 31

camisas nuevas, 309, 338–39

camisas viejas (old shirts): and Aznar matter, 306; and Carlists, 287; criticisms of Franco regime by, 347–49, 353–54, 358–59, 436, 442–44; decline of, 437–38; and defascistization, 363; and early years of World War II, 338–39; and FET between 1939–1941, 308, 310, 313, 314, 316, 338–39, 360; and FET during Civil War, 275–77, 279, 281, 282, 283, 284, 309; and Franco's cabinet appointments, 291; Franco's relationship with, 281, 282, 305, 359; and last phase of Movimiento, 436, 437–38, 442–44; and Movimiento in post-fascist era, 417, 421, 424; and National Council (FET), 314; and Nazism, 290, 310; pardons for, 293; resignations of, 354, 359; and syndicalism, 275, 305, 350; and weakness of Spanish fascism, 477. *See also specific person*

CAMPSA (state petroleum monopoly), 32

Canary Islands, 206, 239, 261, 271, 333, 340

Cánovas del Castillo, Antonio, 8, 9

Cantalupo, Roberto, 260, 262, 264, 265, 289

Cantarero del Castillo, Manuel, 452

capitalism: and defascistization, 388, 391; and Falange doctrine, 127–28, 255, 256; and FET, 295, 326; and Franco regime, 293, 430; Franco's views about, 388, 405; José Antonio's views about, 149, 151, 179–80, 182, 213, 225; and Movimiento in post-fascist era, 405, 430; and Portugese syndicalism, 175

"Cara al Sol" ("Face to the Sun"), 180, 269

Carañas, Ramón, 250

Carbonell, Josép, 21

Cárcel Modelo. *See* Modelo prison

Carceller, Demetrio, 82, 172, 314, 359, 384, 402

Carlists: achievements of, 306; and authoritarian nationalism, 16, 18, 19, 20, 23, 46, 47–48; and British relations, 325; and Catholicism, 261, 288, 325; and CEDA, 260, 261; characteristics of, 48; and corporatism, 30, 288; and defascistization, 363, 375, 376, 377, 378, 379–80, 381, 392; and disciplining FET, 375, 376, 377, 378, 379–80, 381; and elections of 1936, 181, 183; and Falange plans for armed revolt, 172; Falange unification with, 259–72; and fascism, 134; and FET between 1939–1941, 310–11, 312, 314, 320, 324–26, 347; and FET during Civil War, 276, 277, 278, 282, 283, 286–88, 304, 306; and Franco regime, 133–34, 158, 252, 291, 429; Franco's relationship with, 265, 270, 286, 287, 288, 325; Franco's study of speeches of, 263; and Franco's unification of all militia, 244, 245; Goicoechea's agreement with, 160; internal conflicts among, 264–65, 267; José Antonio's views about, 158, 201, 213, 260, 474; Juan announces adherence to principles of, 436; in Junta Política, 304; and last phase of Movimiento, 436, 439, 446; and liberalism, 48; and MES, 86;

Carlists *(continued)*
  military officers as, 164; and military revolt of 1936, 202, 203, 205; and monarchism, 46, 47–48, 160; and Movimiento
  in post-fascist era, 429; and National
  Council (FET), 283, 314; and problem
  of Spanish nationalism, 7–8, 9, 14–15;
  and proposed FET constitution, 347;
  and religion, 306; and repression during
  Civil War, 248; revival of, 133; and Second Republic, 47–48; slogan of, 29; and
  social policy, 295, 297, 300; and syndicalism, 288; and violence, 187, 204,
  378; and women's organizations, 301;
  and youth organizations, 320
Carlos (king of Portugal), 17
Carlos V, 289
Carls, Rolf, 219, 220
Carranza, Ramón, 94
Carrasco, Arcadio, 264
Carrero Blanco, Luis: assassination of,
  458; and associations, 452–53, 455,
  456, 457–58; and cabinet rivalries, 432,
  433; and defascistization, 377–78, 380;
  and disciplining FET, 377–78, 380; and
  fascism, 365; and Fernández Miranda,
  452; and FET restructuring, 370; and
  foreign policy, 365; on Fraga, 434; Franco's relationship with, 363, 364, 379,
  380; and fundamental laws for redefinition of Movimiento, 422, 423; goals of,
  457–58; and last phase of Movimiento,
  432, 433, 434–35, 445, 452–53, 455,
  456, 457–58, 459; length of public service of, 402; and Movimiento in post-
  fascist era, 420, 422, 423, 425–26;
  power and influence of, 364–65, 426; as
  president of government, 457; on principles and structure of state, 365–66; professional background of, 363–64; and
  second metamorphosis of Franco regime,
  426; and Serrano, 364, 380; style of,
  364; successor to, 458–59; and syndicalism, 445; as undersecretary of presidency, 358; writings of, 364, 365–66
Carretero, José María, 92
Carro Martínez, Antonio, 459, 460, 461
Carta del Lavoro (Labor Charter), 297,
  298

"Carta a un militar español" (José Antonio
  letter), 134, 170, 197
Casares Quiroga, Santiago, 191, 199, 213
Casas de la Vega, Rafael, 245
Casaus, Manuel Andrés, 122
Castaño Cardona, José del, 343
Castiella, Fernando María de, 339, 402,
  432, 433, 451
Castile: and authoritarian nationalism, 28;
  Falange in, 208; and fascism of intellectuals, 62; historical development of, 3,
  141; and problem of Spanish nationalism, 3, 4, 5, 7, 8, 10, 12, 14; and Spanish archetypes, 10
Castillo, José del, 204
Catalonia: and authoritarian nationalism,
  20, 21, 22, 24, 25, 28, 43, 51; Carlists
  in, 325; Falange in, 97, 164; and fascism
  of intellectuals, 52, 53, 60, 61, 65; and
  FET between 1939–1941, 325; Franco's
  speeches in, 372, 388; historical development of, 3; Italian Fascism in, 126–27;
  José Antonio's views about, 154; nationalism in, 3, 152; and problem of Spanish
  nationalism, 3, 4, 5, 6, 15; violence in,
  65
Catholic Action, 62, 369, 437
Catholicism: and authoritarian nationalism, 18, 19, 28–30, 31, 33, 44–45, 46–
  47, 48; and Carlists, 261, 288, 325; and
  censorship, 369; and culture, 319; and
  defascistization, 369, 384, 388, 389,
  396, 398; and "definitive program" for
  Falange, 130; and disciplining FET, 366,
  369; and early Falange, 92–93; and early
  years of World War II, 327–28; and elections of 1936, 183–84; and Falange in
  1935, 168; and fascism of intellectuals,
  53, 54, 61, 62–63; and FET between
  1939–1941, 311, 318, 319, 320, 325,
  326, 327–28; and FET during Civil War,
  253, 277, 280, 281, 285–86, 294, 295–
  96, 298, 304, 309, 478; and Franco regime, 132, 401, 402, 426, 429, 430;
  Franco's views about, 240, 326, 327,
  388, 477; and fundamental laws for redefinition of Movimiento, 422, 423–24,
  425; and Germany, 327; and Italian Fascism, 30, 89; and Italy, 327; José Anto-

nio's views about, 89, 90, 130–31, 146, 221–22, 223–24, 225, 234, 235; and last phase of Movimiento, 446; and monarchism, 42, 43, 46–47; and Movimiento in post-fascist era, 401, 409, 413, 414, 415, 422, 423–24, 425, 429, 430; and Nazism, 326, 327; as part of Falange propaganda, 253; political, 311, 312; and political redefinitions, 389; in Portugal, 18, 175, 176, 178; and problem of Spanish nationalism, 4, 9, 14; revival of, 9; and social policy, 295–96, 298; in Spanish history, 221–22; and syndicalism, 120, 318, 405; and weakness of Spanish fascism, 470–71, 472, 473; and women, 44; and Women's Section, 309, 477; and World War II, 384; and youth organizations, 102, 320. *See also specific person or organization*

Caudillo: and authoritarian nationalism, 16; Beneyto Pérez's theory of, 316–17; as component of totalitarianism, 366; FET views about, 278, 346. *See also* Franco, Francisco

CAUR (Comitati d'Azione per la Universalità di Roma), 160–61, 162, 177

Cavestany, Rafael, 410

Cazañas, Ramón, 220, 250

CEDA (Confederación Española de Derechas Autonómas): aim of, 45; and armed revolt against Azaña, 189; and Carlists, 260, 261; and Catholicism, 178; and early Falange, 94, 100; and elections, 94, 178, 179, 181, 183, 185, 194, 195, 475; and Falange in 1935, 168; Falange views about, 254; and Falange–Carlist fusion, 98; and fascism, 45–46, 54, 89, 123–24, 134, 470; formation of, 44; Franco's views about, 477; and JONS, 98; José Antonio's views about, 89; and outlawing of Falange, 189; power and influence of, 123; precursors of, 75; radicalization of, 274; and Socialist insurrection, 124–25; and violence, 113, 194. *See also* Juventudes de Acción Popular; *specific person, especially* Gil Robles, José María

Celesia, Geissler, 97

censorship: and Bishop Pildain's attack on

syndicalism, 416; and Catholicism, 369; and defascistization, 378–79, 395; and Falange–Carlist fusion, 260; and FET, 280, 320, 323, 350, 358, 359, 360–61, 369, 378–79; and foreign relations, 378–79; and Franco regime, 255–56, 292, 293; and Movimiento, 401, 402, 416, 432, 434; in Second Republic, 78, 95

Central Nacional-Sindicalista, 300–301

Central Syndical Council of Coordination, 299

Centro Académico da Democracia Cristã, 18

"centurias of labor" (elite workers), 351

Cervantes, Miguel y, 4, 5

CESO (Spanish Confederation of Worker Syndicates), 300

Chamber of Fasces and Corporations (Italy), 389

Chapaprieta, Joaquín, 232

Chíbiris (Young Socialists), 111

children: in Falange, 257, 259, 323, 417, 418. *See also* youth; *specific organization*

Chile: Falange in, 343

Churchill, Winston, 384

Ciano, Count Galeazzo, 311, 314, 327, 331–32, 339, 340, 373, 376

Cierva, Ricardo de la, 462

Cine Madrid: José Antonio's speech at, 151, 179–80

Círculo Mercantil (Madrid): José Antonio's speech at, 151

Círculo Nosotros (Circle Ourselves), 403–4

Círculos Doctrinales José Antonio, 443, 444, 456

Cisneros, Gabriel, 461

*Cisneros* (Catholic journal), 414

civil guarantees and rights, 195, 401–2, 420, 471

Civil Guards, 173, 189, 206, 247, 248, 269, 279, 404

Civil War: and Allen's interview of José Antonio, 225; anniversaries of end of, 351, 375, 402, 429; Calvo Sotelo murder as precipitation of, 204; as crusade, 319; Dictatorship as first step toward, 38; exe-

Civil War (*continued*)
cutions during, 211, 226–27, 246–47, 249, 256; first phase of, 215–16; Franco's total victory in, 310; Franco's views about, 239–40; German role in, 337; and imprisonment of Falange members, 191; and José Antonio's mediation offer, 212–14, 220; José Antonio's views about, 198, 211, 235; last victory parade of, 402; military in, 39; repression of Falange during, 245–49; weariness with, 294. *See also specific person or organization*

CNT (National Confederation of Labor): and authoritarian nationalism, 19, 20, 33; and camisas viejas, 403, 404, 408; dissolution of, 33; and execution of José Antonio, 231; FAI takeover of, 104; Falange similarity to, 166; and fascism of intellectuals, 60, 61; and José Antonio in prison, 221; José Antonio's views about, 151–52; and Popular Front justice system, 226; power and influence of, 121; Sindicatos Libres' battle with, 61, 120; and violence, 20, 61, 104. *See also specific person*

Code of Military Justice, 227–29, 231

*La Codorniz* (journal), 412

Cohen, Hermann, 55

Coimbra University, 18, 49

Cold War, 405

colonialism, 152–54, 168–69, 240, 330–31, 336

comedia. *See* Teatro de la Comedia

Comisaría Regia del Turismo (Royal Council of Tourism), 58

Comitati d'Azione per la Universalità di Roma. *See* CAUR

Communist/Catholic Worker Commissions, 444

communists: call for death of José Antonio by, 190; and early years of World War II, 340; and fascism of intellectuals, 53, 54; and FET between 1939–1941, 326, 340; Hitler's views about, 373; José Antonio's views about, 182; Ledesma's views about, 138; and Movimiento, 421, 444; and repression during Civil War, 248; and students, 419; and violence, 102,

104, 122, 169, 187, 190; and weakness of Spanish fascism, 473

Comunión Tradicionalista, 47, 262, 263, 269, 278

CONCA (Catholic small farmer syndicate), 352

Condés, Fernando, 204

Condor Legion, 327

Confederació Llatino-Occidental, 21

Confederación Española de Sindicatos Obreros (CESO), 261, 300

Confederación Nacional de Estudiantes Católicos, 402

Confederation of Autonomous Rightist Groups. *See* CEDA

Confederation of Nationalist Syndicalist Employers (CENS), 300

Confederation of National-Syndicalist Workers. *See* CONS

Conferencia Nacional de Catalunya, 21

Congo, 135

Congress of European Youth, 389

*La Conquista del Estado* (Ledesma publication), 58–60, 62, 63, 75, 92

CONS (Confederación de Obreros Nacional-Sindicalistas), 120–22, 135, 136, 163, 172, 187, 256, 259, 300

Consejo Nacional. *See entries for* National Council

conservatism: and authoritarian nationalism, 19, 20, 44; and elections, 94, 182–83; José Antonio's views about, 213, 474; and Movimiento in postfascist era, 405, 413; and syndicalism, 351; and weakness of Spanish fascism, 474; and World War II, 384. *See also* monarchism/monarchists

constitution: FET's proposed, 346–47; Fraga's proposed, 434; of 1929, 34–35, 37; in Portugal, 49; of Second Republic, 45

Córdoba: and military revolt of 1936, 206

corporatism: and authoritarian nationalism, 30–31, 34, 35, 39, 45, 49, 50; and Carlists, 30, 288; and "definitive program" for Falange, 127–28; and Dictatorship (Primo de Rivera), 30–31, 34, 35, 39, 45; and FET, 285, 295, 296, 299–300, 311, 478; and Franco, 260, 401, 430; José Antonio's views about,

130, 151, 156, 224, 234, 474; and monarchism, 132; and Movimiento, 401, 405, 430; in Portugal, 45, 49, 50; and social policy, 295, 296; and syndicalism/workers, 61, 405

Cortes: and armed revolt against Azaña government, 199; Calvo Sotelo's proposal about, 132; and defascistization, 379, 389–91; and disciplining FET, 379; and elections of 1936, 193; elections to, 449; FET proposal for new, 346–47; Franco's speech about Principles of Movimiento to, 429; and fundamental laws for redefinition of Movimiento, 422; and impeachment of José Antonio, 116–17; José Antonio as member of, 107, 115, 116–17, 123, 127, 154, 159, 168–69, 180–83, 475; José Antonio's views about, 214; and last phase of Movimiento, 435, 446, 447, 454, 458, 461, 467; membership of, 435; and Movimiento in post-fascist era, 409, 418, 422, 429; new, 379, 389–91; and Organic Law (1966), 435; privileges of members of, 113, 117; and prosecution of Dictatorship officials, 75; and recognition of Juan Carlos, 467; reorganization of, 435. *See also specific member*

Cortes de Cádiz (1812), 6–7

Coselschi, Eugenio, 161

Cossío, Bartolomé Manuel de, 75

Costa, Joaquín, 11, 16

Council of Ministers, 297, 349, 365, 438, 441

Council of the Realm, 35, 425, 435, 458–59

Council of Tradition (Carlists), 265

Covadonga: CEDA rallies at, 124

Cruzada Nun' Alvares Pereira, 18, 22, 49

Cuba, 9, 343

Cuéllar, Juan, 111

Cuenca: elections of 1936 in, 183, 193–95

Cueva del Orkompón (Madrid bar), 180

"cultural crisis" (1890), 16

cultural nationalism, 12, 52

culture: and FET, 317–19, 478; Franco's views about, 240; José Antonio's views about, 474–75; and Movimiento in post-fascist era, 412, 413–14; National Dele-

gate of, 451; and weakness of Spanish fascism, 470, 474–75, 479. *See also* neotraditionalism

Dávila, Sancho: arrest of, 268; and elections, 181; and Falange internal politics, 250, 258, 267, 268; and Falange–Carlist fusion, 261–62, 267, 268; and founding of Falange, 81; Franco absolves, 271; and José Antonio, 165, 219; and youth organizations, 303

Day of the Fallen Student, 107, 417, 419

Day of the Mother, 389

Daza, Fermín, 199

defascistization: beginning of, 362; and disciplining FET, 366–87; first phase of (1941–1945), 363–98; and fundamental laws for redefinition of Movimiento, 422, 423; and last phase of Movimiento, 436, 452, 458; and Movimiento in post-fascist era, 422, 423, 425, 428, 429; and political redefinitions, 387–98; and second metamorphosis of Franco regime, 428, 429; and weakness of Spanish fascism, 478

De Gaulle, Charles, 393

Delbos, Yvon, 218, 232

Delegated Council for the Government of the Levant, 212

delegations. *See specific delegation or delegate*

Delgado Barreto, Manuel, 78, 97

democracy: José Antonio's views about, 74, 78, 149; and last phase of Movimiento, 465, 467

Dencàs, Josép, 126–27

DGS. *See* Dirección General de Seguridad

Día de la República, 169

Dictatorship (Primo de Rivera): and authoritarian nationalism, 47; collapse of, 36–37, 72, 290; and constitution of 1929, 34–35, 37; and corporatism, 30–31, 34, 35, 39, 45; crisis of, 35–36; and development of authoritarian nationalism, 38–39; and downfall of monarchy, 41; emergence of, 23–25; and el error de Primo de Rivera, 39, 240, 242, 275, 478; failure of, 38, 47; and fascism of intellectuals, 51, 53; as first step toward

Dictatorship (Primo de Rivera) (*continued*)
Civil War, 38; and Franco, 39, 240, 290,
476; government institutions during,
27–29; Italian Fascism as model for, 22,
23, 27–35, 39–40, 77, 88–89; José Antonio as defender of, 43, 71–77, 88, 116,
117, 236; legacy of, 37–41, 47; legitima-
zation of, 33–34; as political type, 40;
and weakness of Spanish fascism, 470,
476. *See also specific person or topic*
Dirección General de Seguridad (DGS),
187, 188, 192, 376, 387, 390, 391
"disaster literature," 11
*Discurso a las juventudes de España* (*Address to the Youth of Spain*) (Ledesma),
138
DNB (German news agency), 253
Dolz de Espejo, Tomás, 276
Domínguez, Juan, 380
Donoso Cortés, Juan, 18
Doriot, Jacques, 397
d'Ors, Eugenio, 53, 258, 318
"Draft Project of Bases for the Associative
Juridical Regime of the Movement"
(1969), 449–50

Ebro offensive, 294
Eça de Queiroz, Antonio, 177
economic council: FET proposal for new,
346
economy: and authoritarian nationalism,
31–33, 35–36; and authoritarianism,
408; and "definitive program" for Falange, 127–28, 151; and Dictatorship,
31–33, 35–36, 42; and disciplining FET,
371; and early years of World War II,
328–29, 336, 337, 340; and elections of
1936, 179–80; and fascism, 58–59, 426,
472; and F. E. de las JONS, 99–100,
151; and FET between 1939–1941, 328–
29, 336, 337, 340, 354, 355; and FET
during Civil War, 295–301; Franco's
views about, 295; of Italy, 36; José Antonio's views about, 149, 150–52, 196;
and military–FET tensions, 355; and
Movimiento, 405, 408, 409, 412, 425,
430, 431, 432, 433; phases in change in,
408; and Right–FET relations, 254; and
second metamorphosis of Franco regime,
426–30; of Second Republic, 32; and

technocracy, 425, 426–30. *See also* syndicalism; *specific person*
education: and Carlists, 306; and "definitive program" for Falange, 129; and Dictatorship, 45; and fascism, 62, 474–75;
and FET, 278, 304, 320, 369; José Antonio's views about, 159, 474–75; and
Movimiento, 412, 413, 414–16, 435;
and problem of Spanish nationalism, 7,
8; of women, 62. *See also* Popular Education; students; *specific person*
elections: of 1931, 75; of 1933, 93–94,
467; of 1936, 178–84, 193–95, 196,
239, 467, 469, 475; of 1954, 412–13; of
1977, 467; and associations, 449; of
family representatives to Cortes, 449; in
Germany, 195; and students, 415–16,
419–20; and syndicalism, 416, 427, 428;
and violence, 194
Eliseda, marqués de la (Francisco Moreno
Herrera), 82, 87–88, 94, 97, 113, 115,
130, 131, 169
elites, 6, 7, 8, 20, 34, 146–47, 222, 475
Elizabeth II (queen of Great Britain),
415–16
Elola, José Antonio, 323, 389, 419, 428
employers, 122, 300, 351, 352, 406
Enjuto Ferrán, Federico, 227
Enlightenment, 6
*La Epoca* (Right newspaper), 200
*Es así* (*The Right Way*) (publication),
443
Escamots, 126
Escario, José Luis, 276
Escobar, José Ignacio. *See* Marismas,
marqués de las
El Escorial: CEDA rallies at, 124; José An-
tonio's burial at, 233, 308, 418–19,
429–30; SEU congress at, 320
El Escorial agreement, 87
*Escorial* (journal), 318–19
Escrivá de Balaguer, Monsignor, 442
"España: Germanos contra Bereberes"
(José Antonio), 221–22
españolidad: José Antonio's views about,
223–24
Esparza, Eladio, 280
Espinosa de los Monteros, General, 376
Estado Novo (Salazar regime), 45, 175,
176, 178

*El Estado nuevo (The New State)* (Pradera), 48, 133–34

*El Estado totalitario en el pensamiento de José Antonio (The Totalitarian State in the Thought of José Antonio)* (Arrese), 395

Estella, marqués de. *See* Primo de Rivera, José Antonio; Primo de Rivera, Miguel (father)

Estelrich, Joan, 43

*Estilo* (SEU journal), 414

Estraperlo scandal, 179, 371

Ethiopia, 154, 168–69, 177, 211

European Writers' Federation, 389

Extremadura: Falange in, 256, 258

Ezquer Cabaldón, Eduardo, 347, 387

FA (Falange Auténtica), 347, 373–74, 387

FAI (Iberian Anarchist Federation), 104, 166, 218, 221, 226, 231, 260–61

Fal Conde, Manuel, 48, 133, 203, 244, 260, 262, 264–65, 287, 324–25

Falange Autónoma, 347

Falange de la Sangre (Phalanx of Blood), 109, 111, 113, 114, 118

Falange Española (Spanish Phalanx): anniversary of founding of, 456; decline in influence of, 308; dependency of, 476; early leadership of, 88–89; expansion of, 95; and fascism, 93; founding of, 88–114; funding for, 94, 98, 476; German reaction to, 96–97; Italian Fascism as model for, 88–89, 96, 234; Italian reaction to, 96–97; JONS compared with, 93; JONS competition with, 98; JONS fusion with, 98–100; leadership of, 475–76; program of, 92–93; as referring to dissidents, 451; slogans of, 296. *See also* camisas viejas; F. E. de las JONS; FET; Movimiento; *specific person, auxiliary organization, or topic*

Falange Española Auténtica. *See* FEA

Falange Española de las JONS (association), 464, 465

Falange Española de las Juntas de Ofensiva Nacional-Sindicalista. *See* F. E. de las JONS

Falange Española Tradicionalista y de las J.O.N.S. *See* FET; *specific person, auxiliary organization, or topic*

Falange Exterior, 342–44, 376

Falanges Juveniles de Franco, 323, 417, 418

Faraudo, Carlos, 189–90

Farinacci, Roberto, 262, 263, 289

*El Fascio: Haz Hispano* (newspaper), 78, 81, 83

fascism: climax of European, 310–62, 478; and conspiracies against Franco, 347; contradictory aspects of, 157–58, 235, 478; death cults of, 308; Franco's views about, 263, 269, 277, 283, 294, 326, 384, 388, 401, 431, 476–78; of intellectuals, 51–65; José Antonio's views about, 94, 129, 130, 142, 143, 144–58, 162, 224–25, 234–35, 388, 412, 473–75, 478; longevity of Spanish, 469; redefinition of, 392–98; and repression during Civil War, 248; "retrodictive theory" about, 470–79; as revolution of modernity, 319; revolutionary, 473, 475; and second metamorphosis of Franco regime, 426; and Second Republic, 104; as spiritual, 224–25; weakness of Spanish, 469–79. *See also* defascistization; Italian Fascism; *specific person, organization, or topic*

*el fascismo frailuno* (friar fascism), 317–18, 369, 471, 473, 478

Fascist International, 137

Faupel, Wilhelm, 250, 260, 265, 288–89

*F. E.* (Falange newspaper), 95–96, 98, 103, 105, 106–7, 109, 110, 130–31, 167, 253, 321, 395

F. E. de las JONS (Falange Española de las Juntas de Ofensiva Nacional-Sindicalista): Ansaldo's plan for, 118; anthem of, 180; armed revolt of, 170–75, 196–97; arrests and detentions of members of, 188, 191, 203, 204, 255–56, 275; Carlists' fusion with, 259–72; and CEDA, 100; characteristics of, 178; and death of José Antonio, 264; decline of, 134; doctrine and program of, 99–100, 123, 127–29, 134, 141, 151, 159, 165, 167–68, 179–80, 182, 252–56, 259; executions of members of, 246, 249, 256; expansion of, 134, 249–59; and fascism, 129, 154–55, 161, 162–63, 178, 199–200, 253–54, 261–62; as "fashionable,"

F. E. de las JONS (*continued*)
194; first major meeting of, 100–101; formation of, 99–100; funding for, 109, 118, 135, 159, 161, 167, 168, 169–70, 181–82, 190, 191, 219–20; funding of, 161–62, 173, 191; German relations with, 207, 216, 259; goals of, 196–97, 207, 253; Goicoechea agreement with, 118–19; government closure of offices of, 106, 113, 123, 167, 169, 186–87; image of, 178; internal politics in, 134, 249, 256, 258, 264, 266–67; Italian relations with, 160, 161–62, 173, 191, 259, 262–63; José Antonio named Jefe Nacional of, 125; and José Antonio's death, 257; and José Antonio's ideology, 144–58; José Antonio's status in, 122–23, 136, 140, 179, 208; José Antonio's views about, 100, 134–35; leadership of, 125–26, 165–66, 179, 208, 257–58, 264, 267–68; martyrs of, 108; membership of, 141, 160, 164, 165, 189, 199, 207, 256; in 1935, 163–70; organization and structure of, 99, 163, 164–65, 259; outlawing of, 188–89, 192; and re-creation of JONS, 135; reorganization and reconstruction of, 191, 208; repression of, 211, 245–49, 471; slogans and symbols of, 100, 125–26, 166, 186; statutes of, 125, 192; and tentative government list of José Antonio, 172; and violence, 102–14, 189–90. *See also* FET; National Council (F. E. de las JONS); *specific, auxiliary organization, or topic*

FEA (Falange Española Auténtica), 279–80, 306, 347

Federación Cívico-Somatenista, 23

Federación Nacional Aeronáutica, 83

Federación Universitaria Española. *See* FUE

federal republicanism, 8

Feijóo, Padre, 5

Fernández Cuesta, Raimundo: as agriculture minister, 291, 301, 304; ambassadorial appointments of, 345; and Ansaldo's plan, 118; Arrese replaces, 420; and associations, 449; and camisas viejas, 306; and capitalism, 281; and Carlists, 287; and collapse of Italian Fascism, 391; de-

cline in influence of, 308; as exchange prisoner, 236, 264, 281; as executor for José Antonio's estate, 230; and Falange plans for armed revolt, 174; as F. E. de las JONS secretary, 99; and FET, 281–82, 283, 312, 361; Franco's relations with, 281–82; and JAP–Falange collaboration, 191; José Antonio's relationship with, 82, 118, 165; as justice minister, 402, 409–10; and last phase of Movimiento, 447, 448, 449, 464; and law for redefinition of Movimiento, 422; and monarchism, 281; and Movimiento in post-fascist era, 409–10, 411, 413, 418, 420, 422; as Movimiento secretary general, 409–10, 411; and National Council, 283; and outlawing of Falange, 191; and reorganization of Franco's cabinet, 312; as secretary general, 165; and social policy, 297, 299–300; and syndicalism, 281; and youth, 418, 419, 420

Fernández Flórez, Wenceslao, 94, 107

Fernández Miranda, Torcuato, 451–56, 458, 459, 461, 462, 463

Fernando (king of Spain), 4, 46, 80

FET (Falange Española Tradicionalista y de las J.O.N.S.): abolition of, 451; activities of, 273; apogee of, 362; and camisas viejas, 275–77, 279, 281, 282, 283, 284, 309; ceremonies and rituals of, 281, 308, 316, 319; during Civil War (1937–1939), 273–309; and collapse of Italian Fascism, 393; conflict within, 258, 310, 330, 344–62, 376, 380; conspiracies against, 356; criticisms of, 279, 353–58, 365–66; de-emphasis of, 401; and defascistization, 363, 365–98; disciplining of, 366–87; and Falange–Carlist fusion, 240–72; and fascism, 269–70, 272, 276–77, 285, 289, 298, 309, 325–26, 331, 477, 478; foreign image and influence of, 309; formation of, 269; Franco's role in, 277, 284, 361–62, 367, 390; Franco's views about, 272, 304–5, 311, 359–60, 378, 388, 391, 392, 394; functions and goals of, 272, 273, 277, 283–84, 292, 307, 393; German views about, 353; growth of, 284; image of, 377; Italian views about, 280, 289, 304; in last year of Civil War, 304–9; leadership of, 357; membership of, 269, 273, 278, 284–85, 315–16, 345, 365, 370, 376; as "National Movement," 393, 401; under new government of 1938, 290–95; between 1939–1941, 308–9, 310–62; organization and structure of, 269, 277–79, 314, 370–71; and political redefinitions, 387–98; political secretariat of, 276; program and propaganda of, 253, 269; proposals for dissolution of, 401; purge in, 370; reorganization of, 304–5; secretary general of, 281–82, 312, 352, 357, 359, 366–67; statutes of, 277–79, 283, 290–91, 310, 314, 315; symbols and slogans of, 269, 276, 286, 287, 316; and totalitarianism, 285–86, 298, 304–5; ultrabaroque language as characteristic of, 280; unification of, 366–87; and World War II, 326–42, 390–91. *See also* Movimiento; National Council (FET); *specific person, auxiliary organization, or topic*

Fiesta Nacional del Caudillo (1937), 281

Finat, José. *See* Mayalde, conde de

"Flechas" (Arrows) (children's organization), 257, 259

Foix, J. V., 21, 43

foreign relations: and defascistization, 394; Falange influence in, 309; and FET, 278, 329–42; Franco's views about, 332–33, 334, 356; and isolation of Spain, 398, 404; and Italian invasion of Ethiopia, 168–69; José Antonio's views about, 153, 158–63, 168–69; and Movimiento, 423, 465; of Second Republic, 168–69; Spanish rehabilitation in, 405; and weakness of Spanish fascism, 472–73; and World War II, 329–42, 398. *See also specific minister or nation*

Fórmica, Mercedes, 207

Forner, Juan Pablo, 5

*Fotos* (Falange magazine), 253, 391

Foxá, Agustín de, 141, 180, 258, 280, 284, 318, 339

Fraga Iribarne, Manuel, 420, 432, 434–35, 451, 453, 464

France: and execution of José Antonio, 232; fascism in, 397; Franco's views about, 342; and José Antonio in prison, 218; and Spanish archetypes, 10; Spanish imitation of, 6; Spanish relations with, 27, 30; and World War II, 339, 342, 397

Francistes of Marcel Bucard, 161

Franco, Francisco: achievements of, 273; adulation of, 233; anniversary of ascension to power of, 281, 431; basic political attitudes and values of, 240, 242, 268–69, 388, 431, 476–77; as chief of state of Nationalist Spain, 239; conspiracies against, 342, 347–49, 356, 371, 374–75, 382; death of, 457, 465–66, 479; and Dictatorship (Primo de Rivera), 39, 240, 290, 476; and elections of 1936, 193–94; and Falange plans for armed revolt, 170, 172, 173, 174–75; and Falange–Carlist fusion, 259–72; family of, 80; goals of, 273, 307, 330–31; as Jefe Nacional, 269; José Antonio compared to, 239–40, 478; and José Antonio as hero, 232–33; and José Antonio in prison, 216, 218, 219–20, 221, 225, 226; José Antonio as rival to, 307–8; José Antonio's influence on, 144, 263; José Antonio's letters to, 124–25, 170; José Antonio's meetings with, 174–75; José Antonio's views about, 201; Juan Carlos as heir to, 451; and military revolt of 1936, 193, 197, 201, 204–5, 206; Muñoz Grandes as lieutenant to, 431–32; Muñoz Grandes as successor to, 433; on national suffering, 329; plans for death of, 422–25; political base of, 259–72; power and authority of, 242, 290–91, 310, 326, 345, 354, 359, 363, 478; professional background of, 206, 239; as reactionary, 225, 265; reputation of, 124; resumes powers of Chief of State, 460; and Socialist insurrection, 124–25; style of, 345, 356; Suárez's last interview with, 465. *See also* Franco regime; *specific person or topic*

Franco, João, 17

Franco, Nicolás (brother), 216, 259–60, 263, 264, 266, 274, 292

Franco, Ramón (brother), 83

Franco regime: basic values of, 401, 402, 430, 431; Falange dependency on, 476;

Franco regime (*continued*)
and Franco as regent, 404; Franco's design for, 401; influence of José Antonio's ideology on, 144; legitimization of, 404; second metamorphosis of, 426–30; slogan of, 260; and succession, 404, 413; symbols of, 402; third metamorphosis of, 430. *See also* Franco, Francisco; *specific person or topic*
freedom: José Antonio's views about, 147–48
French Revolution, 6, 7, 159–60
Frente de Estudiantes Sindicalistas (FES), 443, 457
Frente de Juventudes (Youth Front), 321, 323, 357, 389, 412, 415, 417, 418, 425, 428, 452
Frente de Trabajo (Labor Front), 305
Frente Español (Spanish Front), 85
Frente Nacional de Alianza Libre (FNAL), 444
Frente Nacional de Trabajadores (FNT— National Workers Front), 443
Frente Sindicalista Revolucionario (FSR), 443–44
Friends of the USSR, 86, 95, 161
FUE (Federación Universitaria Española), 36, 101–2, 106, 107, 109, 114, 415
Fuente, Licinio de la, 462–63
Fuentes de Oñoro (Salamanca province): and Falange plans for armed revolt, 171–75
Fuero de los Españoles, 401–2, 420, 435
Fuero del Trabajo (1938), 297–99, 304, 435
*Fuerza Nueva* (journal), 452, 457
Fueyo, Jesús, 461
Fundamental Laws, 420–25, 435, 436, 448, 454

*La Gaceta Literaria* (journal), 52, 53, 54, 56
Galarza, Valentín, 87, 346, 358, 359, 363, 379, 380, 381
Galicia, 52, 53, 86, 164, 176
Galindo Herrero, Santiago, 440
Galo Ponte prosecution, 76–77
Gamero del Castillo, Pedro: and Carrero Blanco, 364; and conspiracies against

Franco, 349; dismissal of, 359, 368, 390; and Falange–Carlist fusion, 261–62; and FET, 313, 314, 345, 353–54, 356, 359, 362, 367; in Franco's cabinet, 313, 314; and José Antonio in prison, 219; and Junta Política, 345; and National Council (FET), 364; and Serrano, 345; and syndicalism, 352; threatened resignation of, 356
Garcerán, Rafael, 172, 198, 216, 250, 259, 267, 268, 271
García Aldave, José, 210
García Hernández, José, 452
García López, Ignacio, 466–67
García Lorca, Federico, 248
García, Mariano, 190
García Oliver, Juan, 227, 231
García Rebull, General, 444
García Valdecasas, Alfonso, 83, 85, 86, 88, 90, 93, 297, 388–89, 390
García Venero, Maximiano, 220
Gardemann, Erich, 375, 382, 384, 397
Garriga, Ramón, 344
Garrigues, Joaquín, 297, 304, 306, 318
Gaziel (conservative editor), 196
General Military Academy (Zaragoza), 39, 174, 239, 274
Generation of 1870 (Portugal), 17
Generation of 1914 (Spain), 12
Generation of 1927 (Spain), 52
Generation of Ninety-Eight (noventayochistas), 11–12, 14, 17, 47, 101, 413
German Labor Front (DAF), 352, 353
Germany: and Allen's interview of José Antonio, 226; attitudes about Franco in, 337; and Catholicism, 327; collapse of, 398; and conspiracies against Franco, 348; and defascistization, 381–82, 384; and disciplining FET, 381–82, 384, 390–91; and early years of World War II, 329–30, 332–34, 336, 337, 340–41, 342, 352–53; elections in, 195; and Falange–Carlist fusion, 265, 266; and F. E., 96–97; and F. E. de las JONS, 207, 216, 219–20, 259; and FET between 1939–1941, 326, 327, 330, 331, 332–34, 336, 337, 340–41, 342, 352–53; and FET during Civil War, 280, 288–90; and Franco, 240, 260, 266, 284, 288–90, 330, 333,

342, 385; and Great Britain, 327; influence on Spain of, 158, 221–22; and intelligence networks in Spain, 352–53, 354–55; and José Antonio in prison, 216, 218–20; José Antonio's views about, 159–60, 224; José Antonio's visits to, 155, 158–59, 226, 227–28; and military revolt of 1936, 206; Pilar Primo de Rivera visit to, 392; possibility of defeat of, 390, 397; Serrano's visits to, 333; and Soviet Union, 371, 396; Spain withdraws all forces from, 394; Spanish agreements with, 326, 334, 336, 337–38, 342; and Spanish monarchism, 355–56, 372, 373, 381, 382; Spanish workers for, 353; and syndicalism, 352–53. *See also* Nazism; *specific person*

Gibraltar, 339, 415–16

Gil Pecharromán, Julio, 160, 211

Gil Robles, José María: and Allen's interview of José Antonio, 226; and authoritarian nationalism, 44, 45–46; and Catholicism, 178; and elections of 1936, 180, 181, 194; on Falange and Catholicism, 130, 168; and Falange–Carlist fusion, 270; on fascism, 45–46, 470; and F. E. de las JONS, 168, 254; Franco in administration of, 239; German and Italian reactions to, 97; German visit of, 45; and Germany as prototype for Spain, 158; and José Antonio, 71, 89, 115, 168; as monarchist, 44; and National Front proposal, 180; and republicanism, 132; Rome visit of, 45; satire about, 95; slogans about, 124; and violence, 168

Gil Tirado, Vidal, 227

Giménez Arnau, José Antonio, 259, 292, 293

Giménez Caballero, Ernesto: arrest of, 51; and Carlists, 306; and CAUR, 160–61; censorship of, 142; and defascistization, 389; and Dictatorship, 51, 53; early career of, 51–52; and fascism, 51–54, 56, 59, 96, 473, 474; and F. E., 92; and F. E. de las JONS, 125, 254; and FEA, 306; and FET, 276, 277, 319; ideology of, 159; impact of, 54; isolation of, 470; Italian influences on, 51, 52–53, 54, 82, 96; José Antonio's views about, 474; and

Junta de Mando, 277; and military revolt of 1936, 205; and political redefinitions, 389; reputation of, 51, 52; Ruiz de Alda interview of, 83; and theater, 319; writings of, 51, 52, 53, 54, 78, 92, 94–95

Girón, José Antonio: achievements of, 406, 407; and Arias government, 459, 460; and Arrese, 420, 425; arrest and detention of, 256; and associations, 449; and cabinet reorganization, 381; and conspiracy against Franco, 347–48; criticisms of, 377, 380, 427; and defascistization, 380; and Falange internal politics, 258; and Falange–Carlist fusion, 266; farewell speech of, 427; and FET, 273, 279, 313, 359, 361, 374, 377, 380; Franco's relationship with, 359, 368–69, 406, 407, 427; and José Antonio's death, 211, 212; as labor minister, 359, 361, 368–69, 402, 406–7, 409, 427; and monarchism, 374; and Movimiento, 402, 406–7, 409, 420, 427, 449, 456, 459, 463, 464; on National Congress, 412; and press, 441; as proposed successor to Cerrero Blanco, 458; as Right leader, 441, 442; as scapegoat, 427; and second metamorphosis of Franco regime, 427; and social policy, 406–7; and Solís, 428, 441; and syndicalism, 406–7; as Vice Secretariat of Social Works, 420; and World War II, 384

Goded, Manuel, 171–72

Goebbels, Joseph, 336, 353, 385

Goering, Hermann, 327

Goicoechea, Antonio, 47, 87, 118–19, 130, 158, 160, 188, 193, 197, 259

Gomá, Cardinal, 326

Gómez Carbajo, Ursicino, 188

Gómez Jordana, Francisco: and Arrese's trip to Germany, 386–87; and collapse of Italian Fascism, 392, 393; death of, 397; and defascistization, 386–87, 390, 392, 393, 395; and Falange Exterior, 343; and FET, 291, 292, 293, 311, 386–87; as foreign minister, 381, 386–87, 390, 395

González Bueno, Pedro, 291, 297, 299, 300, 350

González de Canales, Patricio, 347, 404
González Vélez, Fernando, 267, 273, 276, 305–6
González Vicén, Luis, 258, 403, 419, 422, 443, 445
Gorría, Romeo, 432
government: Carrero Blanco's views about principles and structure of, 365–66; goals of, 457–58; José Antonio's list for cabinet members for, 214; and Movimiento in post-fascist era, 422–25; municipal, 401; president of the, 457, 458–59, 463; and proposed laws for redefinition of Movimiento, 422–25; vice president of, 431–32, 458
Goya, José María Alonso, 268
Granada: elections in, 183, 193–94; JONS in, 86; and military revolt of 1936, 206; repression during Civil War in, 248
Great Britain: and Carlists, 325; and FET, 325, 332, 333, 340, 355, 395; Franco's views about, 342; and Italian invasion of Ethiopia, 168–69; and José Antonio in prison, 220–21; José Antonio's views about, 157, 168–69; and monarchism, 371; payment of Spanish generals by, 346; Portugese relations with, 327, 339; and Spanish military, 355; Spanish relations with, 397; and World War II, 327, 332, 333, 334, 336, 339, 340, 342, 344, 346, 397
Gredos plan, 171–73, 178
Groizard, Manuel, 112–13
Group of Thirty-Nine, 456
"Gu" (avant-garde painters), 141–42
Guadalajara: battle at, 245
Guadalhorce, conde de, 42
Guardias de Franco, 403, 412, 419, 437, 441, 459
Guariglia, Raffaele, 126
Guerrillas de España, 130
Guipuzcoa: as "enemy" of Franco regime, 404; Falange in, 258
Guitarte, José Miguel, 320, 321

Haartman, Carl von, 243, 267–68
Habsburgs, 4–5, 14
*Haz* (SEU journal), 141, 320, 321, 396
Hedilla Larrey, Manuel: arrest and trial of,

270, 271; and auxiliary organizations, 256; on Canary Islands, 271; and censorship of press, 256; death of, 444; death sentence for, 271; and elections of 1936, 181; and exchange of prisoners, 264; and expansion of Falange, 249–59; and Falange Exterior, 342; and Falange internal politics, 258, 267, 268; and Falange program, 253; and Falange–Carlist fusion, 260, 261–62, 263–64, 265, 266, 267, 268, 269, 270; Franco's relations with, 218, 252, 259, 265, 266, 267, 268, 269, 270; German relations with, 250, 259, 265, 270; on Italian Fascism, 253–54; Italian relations with, 259, 262–63, 264, 265, 270; as Jefe Nacional, 268; and José Antonio in prison, 216, 218; as Junta de Mando jefe, 208, 249–59; and Junta Política, 269, 270, 276; and military, 250, 252; and military revolt of 1936, 205; and Movimiento, 443, 444, 448; on Nazism, 253–54; personal and professional background of, 249; release of, 275; on religion, 253; and repression during Civil War, 248; style and personality of, 249, 250, 264; supporters of, 280; and syndicalism/workers, 255, 443, 444; on totalitarianism, 264
Hendaye, France: Hitler–Franco meeting at, 334–35
Hermandades, 433–34
Hernández, Jesús, 109
Herraiz, Ismael, 395, 420
Herranz, Francisco, 450–51
Herrera, Angel, 28, 29
Herrero Tejedor, Fernando, 439, 440, 446–47, 454, 463–64, 465
Hillers de Luque, Sigfrido, 443, 457
Himmler, Heinrich, 397
history: Carrero Blanco's views about, 365; José Antonio's views about, 144, 222–24
Hitler, Adolf: accession to power of, 77; and Arrese's visit to Berlin, 382, 385; as CEDA model, 46; and conspiracy against Franco, 374–75; defeat of, 397; and F. E. de las JONS, 170; FET praise for, 280; final days of, 394; on Franco, 342, 373, 374; Franco as Spanish, 288;

Franco's correspondence with, 331, 337; Franco's meetings with, 334–35; Franco's views about, 337; and German troops in Spanish territory, 384; Goicoechea's interview with, 87; and Great Britian, 157; influence on José Antonio of, 80, 179; José Antonio compared with, 116, 234–35; and José Antonio's visit to Germany, 158–59; as model for Spanish leadership, 81; and Muñoz Grandes, 372, 374–75, 381, 382, 384, 385, 410; political alliances of, 129; power and authority of, 242, 310; on religion, 373; and Second Republic, 77–78; Serrano's meetings with, 333, 336; style of, 140; and totalitarianism, 474

"Homenaje y reproche a D. José Ortega y Gasset" (José Antonio essay), 141

*La Hora* (SEU journal), 414

humanism, 235, 474

Ibáñez Martín, José, 402

Iberian Anarchist Federation. *See* FAI

*Ideario del Generalísimo* (Franco), 271

imperialist nationalism, 9

individual: and Carlists, 287–88; and "definitive program" for Falange, 127–28; freedom of, 147–48; José Antonio's views about, 74, 147–48, 150, 224, 235; and Movimiento in post-fascist era, 429; and second metamorphosis of Franco regime, 429. *See also* civil guarantees and rights

instauración doctrine, 132, 355, 404, 409, 462

Instituto de Estudios Políticos, 316, 388, 402, 420, 433, 461

Instituto Nacional de Industria (INI), 328

Integralismo Lusitano, 18

Integralists (Portugal), 18, 47, 49, 176

intellectuals: and authoritarian nationalism, 16, 21, 36; and Falange members, 258; fascism of, 51–65, 473; and FET, 317–19; French, 10; José Antonio's views about, 73, 222; and Movimiento, 402, 413, 414, 443; and problem of Spanish nationalism, 6, 13. *See also specific person*

International Anti-Fascist League, 116

Isabel (queen of Spain), 4, 8, 46

Istituto per la Ricostruzione Industriale, 328

Italian Fascism: and authoritarian nationalism, 22, 23, 27–35, 39–40, 42, 43, 45–46, 47; collapse of, 391–92, 394–95; criticisms of, 339, 395–96; and Dictatorship, 22, 23, 27–35, 39–40, 77, 88–89; and early years of World War II, 331; Falange press about, 253; and Falange–Carlist fusion, 261–62; and fascism of intellectuals, 52–53, 54, 58, 59, 60, 61; Franco's views about, 325–26, 476; growth of, 471, 472; and Italian elections of 1921, 180; and José Antonio, 79, 88–89, 142, 148, 151, 154–56, 158, 159, 162, 163, 234, 274, 473; longevity of, 469; and modernization, 53; and Nationalist Association, 264; and party membership, 284; and Portugal, 18, 175; and Socialists, 104; Spanish imitations of, 77–102. *See also* fascism; *specific person*

Italian Social Republic (RSI), 393, 394

Italy: and authoritarian nationalism, 16–17; authoritarianism of, 286; avantgarde culture in, 470; breakdown of liberal system in, 40; Catholicism in, 54, 89, 327; collapse of fascism in, 391–93, 394–95; and early years of World War II, 331–32, 340; economy of, 36; Ethiopia invaded by, 154, 168–69, 177; and Falange armed revolt, 196–97; and Falange–Carlist fusion, 265, 266; and Fascist March on Rome, 22, 27, 77, 172; and F. E., 96–97; and F. E. de las JONS, 160, 161–62, 173, 191, 196–97, 259, 262–63; and FET, 280, 289, 304, 326, 327, 331–32, 340, 376; and Franco, 240, 260, 262–63, 264, 265, 266, 289, 304, 311, 331; Hedilla's relations with, 264, 265, 270; and José Antonio in prison, 219; José Antonio's visits and reports to, 88–89, 161, 173–74, 227–28; and military revolt of 1936, 206; as model for Spanish institutions, 158, 161, 389; and monarchism, 355; Primo de Rivera (Miguel) visits, 27–28; Serrano's visit to, 311, 327, 373, 378; and Spanish

Italy (*continued*)
  monarchism, 160, 161–62, 373, 376;
  Spanish relations with, 30. *See also* Italian Fascism; Mussolini, Benito
Iturmendi, Antonio, 359, 420, 422, 423, 433

JAP (Juventudes de Acción Popular), 46, 48, 134, 168, 189, 191, 267, 274
Jato, David, 104
Javier (Carlist heir), 262, 264–65, 270, 287, 325
Javier Conde, Francisco, 297, 304, 318, 422
Jefe Nacional (National Chief): and F. E. de las JONS, 257–58, 259, 264, 267; and FET, 278, 283, 290–91, 345–46; Franco as, 269, 290–91, 367; Galarza as, 345–46; Hedilla as, 268; and Movimiento, 418, 465; Primo de Rivera (Miguel) as, 29, 39
*Jerarquía* (Falange journal), 258, 318
Jeunesses Patriotes, 92
Jews, 96, 281, 390, 469. *See also* anti-Semitism
Jiménez Millas, Alfredo, 438–39
JONS (Juntas de Ofensiva Nacional-Sindicalista): and anarchists, 86; and birth of syndicalism, 63, 65; and CEDA, 98; commemoration of fusion of Falange and, 453; and conspiracy against Second Republic, 65; decline of, 65, 98; detention of members of, 86; expansion of, 77, 78, 85–86; Falange compared with, 93; Falange competition with, 98; Falange fusion with, 98–100; and fascism of intellectuals, 63; and founding of Falange, 90; and Friends of the USSR attack, 86, 95; funding for, 86–88; leadership of, 63; and monarchists, 86, 87–88; National Council of, 98–99; and Nazism, 96; re-creation of, 135; satire about, 95; slogan of, 86; slogan and symbols of, 63; students in, 85; at Valladolid, 136; and violence, 86. *See also* F. E. de las JONS
"Jons" (local units), 99, 104, 105, 135
*JONS* (publication), 86, 103–4, 152–53
Jordana, Jorge, 418
Jóvenes Mauristas, 19

Joventut d'Esquerra Republicana–Estat Català (JEREC), 126
Juan (monarchy heir), 355, 371, 372, 373, 376, 381, 382, 404, 409, 413, 436–37
Juan Carlos (prince), 28, 404, 417, 418, 436, 451–52, 455, 457, 458, 463, 465, 466, 467
Junta de Defensa Nacional, 207, 216, 240–42, 247, 252
Junta de Mando (F. E. de las JONS): and auxiliary organizations, 256–57; and censorship of press, 255–56; and expansion of Falange, 249–59; expulsion of Alvarez Sotomayor and Ledesma by, 135; and Falange internal politics, 267; and Falange-Carlist fusion, 266, 267, 268, 271; Franco's relations with, 266; and Franco's unification of all militia, 244; functions of, 249; Hedilla as Jefe of, 208, 249–59; leadership of, 258–59; meetings of, 258–59; membership of, 99; and militia training schools, 243; reorganization of, 216; Salamanca as base of, 252–53; suspension of, 123
Junta de Mando Provisional, 259
Junta Directiva Provisional de Fuerzas Económicas, 296
Junta Nacional Carlista, 244, 265
Junta Política (F. E. de las JONS): arrest and trial of members of, 190, 192; and "definitive program" for Falange, 127–29; and elections of 1936, 180; and José Antonio as Jefe Nacional, 125; Ledesma as president of, 125; membership of, 125; and military revolt of 1936, 203; Parador de Gredos meeting of, 171; and plans for armed revolt, 174; police raid on, 186–87; and structure of Falange, 164
Junta Política (FET): and Begoña crisis, 380; and Carlists, 286; Carrero's views about, 365; conflict within, 277; and conspiracies against Franco, 371; criticisms of, 357; and defascistization, 377–78, 379, 380, 390; and disciplining FET, 366–67, 377–78; and early years of World War II, 334; and FET between 1939–1941, 314, 316, 334, 343, 357; and FET reorganization, 304–5; and foreign relations, 334; formation of, 269;

Franco's views about, 304; functions of, 314; functions and powers of, 277, 283; and Hedilla, 269, 270; and introduction of Cortes, 379; membership of, 276, 277, 278, 283, 304, 314, 390; and proposed FET constitution for government, 346–47; role and functions of, 347

Junta Política (Movimiento), 401, 413, 421–22

Junta Suprema del Requeté (Carlists), 325

Junta Técnica del Estado, 281, 291

Juntas Castellanas de Actuación Hispánica (Castilian Committees of Hispanic Action), 62–63

Juntas de Ofensiva Nacional-Sindicalista. *See* JONS

Juntas militares, 23

jurados de empresa, 407, 445

Juridical Statute of the Right to Political Association, 461

justice and law: Cerrero's views about, 366; as FET national service, 279

*Juventud* (SEU journal), 395–96, 414

Juventud Nacionalista, 78

Juventud Socialista Unificada (United Communist–Socialist Youth), 204

Juventud Universitaria (University Youth), 415

Juventudes de Acción Popular (Youth of Popular Action). *See* JAP

Juventudes Mauristas, 47

Karim, Abdul, 24, 25, 27

Keitel, Field Marshal, 374

Keyserling, Count, 71

Kindelán, Alfredo, 330, 355, 358

Kipling, Rudyard, 157

Knobloch, Joachim von, 218, 219, 220

La Jarilla (Seville): Falange training of militia at, 243

labor: and authoritarian nationalism, 33; and FET, 297–99; and Movimiento in post-fascist era, 405, 409. *See also* Ministry of Labor; syndicalism; workers; *specific organization*

Labor Service, 351

Lafuente, Modesto, 7, 8

Laín Entralgo, Pedro, 258, 304, 317–18, 320, 391, 413, 414, 419

Largo Caballero, Francisco: attempted assassination of, 142, 188, 191; and exchange of son for José Antonio, 216; and execution of José Antonio, 231–32; and fascism of intellectuals, 54; and formation of first Popular Front government, 215; imprisonment of, 190; José Antonio's views about, 171; as prime minister, 216; and violence, 114

Larios, Margarita. *See* Primo de Rivera, Margarita Larios

Larra, Mariano José de, 222

Larraz, José, 359

Lateran Pacts (1929), 89

Latin America: Falange Exterior in, 342–44; German–Spanish agreement about, 337–38

Law of the Bases of National Syndicalist Organization (1939), 349–50

Law for the Constitution of Syndicates (1940), 351–52

Law of the Cortes, 435

Law for the Defense of the Republic, 78, 189

Law of the Leadership of the State (1939), 310

Law for the Organization and Defense of National Industry (1937), 328

Law of the Organization of the State, 346

Law for Political Reform (1976), 467

Law for the Protection and Development of National Industry (1939), 328

Law of Public Order, 213

Law of the Referendum, 435

Law for the Structure of Government, 422–25

Law of Succession (1947), 404, 405, 433, 435

Law of Syndical Unity (1940), 350, 352, 357

Law of University Organization (LOU) (1943), 321

Lazar, Hans, 354

leadership: and weakness of Spanish fascism, 475. *See also specific person or organization*

League of Nations, 153, 168–69, 177, 326

Ledesma Ramos, Ramiro: abandons scholarship for politics, 58; achievements of, 69; and Ansaldo's plan, 118; arrests and

Ledesma Ramos, Ramiro (*continued*)
  detentions of, 60, 65, 85, 86, 139; Barcelona as base of, 136; and birth of syndicalism, 54–61, 62, 63, 65; and Calvo Sotelo, 117; and Catholicism, 138; and
  colonialism, 152–53; on communists,
  138; and conflicts within Falange, 134;
  and conspiracy against Second Republic,
  65; death of, 139; declaration at Giménez Caballero's banquet of, 56, 58;
  and "definitive program" for Falange,
  127–29; expulsion of, 135, 136, 140;
  and Falange plans for armed revolt, 170;
  and Falange–JONS fusion, 98, 99, 100;
  and fascism, 82, 136–39, 140, 142, 143,
  155, 195, 269–70, 471, 473, 474; and
  fascism of intellectuals, 53, 54–61, 62,
  63, 65; and founding of F. E., 90; and
  Franco regime, 140; funding for, 58, 60,
  65, 139; ideology of, 136–39; impact of,
  139–40; and José Antonio, 75, 86–87,
  120, 125, 135, 139, 143, 144, 150, 171,
  222; as Junta Política president, 125;
  and leadership of Falange, 125; loyalty
  to ideals of, 441; on Marxism, 137; on
  nationalism, 138; on Nazism, 138; as
  paradigm of radical intellectual, 473; personal and professional background of,
  55–56; and Portugese syndicalism, 175;
  as radical intellectual, 139–40; and re-
  creation of JONS, 135; Redondo compared with, 62; and revolution, 134,
  150; and Right, 200; on Sánchez Mazas,
  314; and Socialist insurrection, 126; and
  students, 135, 136; style and personality
  of, 59, 60–61, 71, 87, 122–23, 136; and
  violence, 103, 105, 107, 109, 114, 122,
  154–55; on working class, 136, 137–38;
  writings of, 53, 55, 56, 58, 78, 136–37,
  139, 140, 152–53. *See also* JONS
Left: and Allen's interview of José Antonio,
  225; and authoritarian nationalism, 16,
  23, 45; defeat of, 310; and elections of
  1936, 179, 183; as enemies of Falange,
  115, 165; executions of, 256; Falangists
  as, 442; and FET, 256, 280; José Antonio's views about, 222, 474; Ledesma's
  views about, 137; and military revolt of
  1936, 206; and Movimiento, 404, 442,
  453–54; and outlawing of Falange, 189;

repression of, 256; and violence, 104–5,
  106, 124, 169, 187, 189–90, 204; and
  weakness of Spanish fascism, 470–71,
  472, 473, 474. *See also specific person
  or organization*
Legion of the Archangel Michael, 175,
  176, 249, 475–76, 477
Legión Española, 163
Legionarios de España (militia), 42, 106
Lenin, V. I., 71, 80, 147
León, 3, 28, 62, 208
Lequerica, José Félix de, 60, 397–98
Lerroux, Alejandro, 95
"Letter to the Military of Spain" (José Antonio), 134, 170, 197
liberalism: and authoritarian nationalism,
  20, 24, 25, 40, 42–44, 48, 49, 50; and
  Carlists, 48; defeat of, 310; and elections
  of 1936, 184; elitist, 6, 7, 8, 20; and failure of Dictatorship, 38; in Falange, 256;
  and FET, 280, 358; Franco's views
  about, 403; in Italy, 40; José Antonio's
  views about, 146, 149, 205, 225, 474;
  Ledesma's views about, 138; and military revolt of 1936, 205; and Movimiento, 403, 413, 414, 424; in Portugal,
  40, 48, 49, 50; and problem of Spanish
  nationalism, 6–7, 8, 14; and weakness of
  Spanish fascism, 471, 472, 474. *See also
  specific person or party*
*Libertad* (Redondo weekly), 62, 96, 166
Libya, 160
Liga de Acción Monárquica, 21
Liga de Actuación Política, 12
Liga Nacional 28 de Maio, 49, 175
Liga Patriótica Española, 20
literature: and FET between 1939–1941,
  317–19
Lliga Regionalista, 15, 21, 22, 43, 52
Llorente, José, 5
Logroño: Falange in, 256
Lope de Vega, Felix de, 319
López Bassa, Ladislao, 265, 266, 269, 276,
  277
López Bravo, Gregorio, 432
López Puertas, Daniel, 271
López Rodó, Laureano, 423, 426, 434,
  438, 440, 446, 447, 455
López-Cancio Fernández, Jesús, 428
Lorente, José, 358–59, 364

Luca de Tena, Juan Ignacio, 78–79
Luna, duquesa de. *See* Azlor de Aragón,
Pilar
Luna Menéndez, José, 258, 368, 380, 381

MacDonald, Ramsay, 116
Macià, Francesc, 22
Macías Picavea, Ricardo, 16
Madariaga, Salvador de, 464
Madrid: Civil War battle for, 227, 240,
241; elections in, 412–13; elections of
1936 in, 183; Falange organization in,
163, 164, 166; and fascism of intellectu-
als, 58; general strike in, 124; JONS in,
85–86; Movimiento membership in,
450; police raid on F. E. de las JONS in,
106, 113; violence in, 109, 110, 111–12,
187, 189–90, 204, 378
Maestú, Cerefino, 444
Maeztu, Ramiro de, 42, 47, 59, 116
Mainer, José-Carlos, 52
Málaga: Falange organization in, 166; and
Falange–Carlist fusion, 270
Malaparte, Curzio, 53, 58, 60, 103–4
Mallol, José Alonso, 188, 192
Mallorca: Hedilla on, 271
Mancisidor, José María, 231
Marañón, Gregorio, 190, 214, 318, 401
Maravall, José Antonio, 318, 358
Marchiandi (Italian labor attaché), 297–98
Mariana, Juan de, 4
Marina, Luys Santa, 166
Marismas, marqués de las (José Ignacio Es-
cobar), 200
Marpicati, Arturo, 89
Márquez Horrillo, Diego, 443
Martín Artajo, Alberto, 402, 403
Martín Echevarría, Leandro, 212, 215,
228
Martín Villa, Rodolfo, 440–41, 456
Martínez Anido, Severiano, 293–95, 297
Martínez Barrio, Diego, 212, 214, 215, 228
Martínez Berasain, José, 265
Martínez de Bedoya, Javier, 136, 256
Marx, Karl, 71, 189, 223, 316
Marxism: and authoritarian nationalism,
46; and defascistization, 391; and "de-
finitive program" for Falange, 127–28;
and Falange plans for armed revolt, 170;
and Falange–Carlist fusion, 261; and fas-
cism of intellectuals, 59, 60, 65; and
FET, 298, 316; Franco's views about,
405; and fusion of Falange and JONS,
100; and Goicoechea–F. E. de las JONS
agreement, 119; José Antonio's views
about, 149, 170; Ledesma's views about,
137; Luca de Tena's views about, 79;
and Movimiento, 405, 453; and weak-
ness of Spanish fascism, 470
Masons, 348, 365, 367, 370, 390, 421
Mateo, Manuel, 135, 172, 444
MATESA Affair (asunto MATESA), 451
Matteotti Affair (Italy), 204
Matthews, Herbert L., 417
Maura, Antonio, 19, 20, 46, 95
Maura, Miguel, 202, 205, 211–12, 214,
215–16
Maurín, Joaquín, 137–38, 469, 470
Maurism, 19–20, 30, 42, 46, 47
Maurras, Charles, 21
Mayalde, conde de (José Finat), 199, 205,
209, 211, 220, 314
Mazón, José Ma., 276, 277
Melquiades Alvarez, D., 193, 214
Menéndez Pelayo, Marcelino, 9, 413
Menéndez Pidal, Ramón, 318
Menéndez Rubio, Tito, 259, 264, 347
Mérimée, Prosper, 10
Merino, Ignacio, 330
MES (Movimiento Sindicalista Español),
85–88
Mexico: Falange in, 343
Miaja, José, 220
Middle Ages, 3, 4, 12, 124, 223
middle class, 38, 470, 471, 472
La Milicia Nacional, 276
militarism, 127–28, 129, 133, 154
military: and authoritarian nationalism,
22–24; and Bilbao incident, 379–80; British relations with, 355; Cerrero's views
about, 365–66; in Civil War, 39; conspiracy against Second Republic by, 65; and
defascistization, 375, 376–77, 378, 379–
80, 381, 393–94; and Dictatorship, 39,
134; and disciplining FET, 365–66, 371,
375, 376–77, 378, 379–80, 381; and
early years of World War II, 327, 331,
336, 338–39, 345–46; and elections of
1936, 183; and Falange plans for armed
revolt, 170, 171–72, 173–75; and fas-

military (*continued*)
  cism of intellectuals, 54; F. E. influence
  in, 97; and FET between 1939–1941,
  311, 312, 314, 327, 328, 330, 331, 336,
  338–39, 345–46, 354–56, 358, 359,
  361; and FET during Civil War, 278,
  280, 283, 307; and FET militia, 345–46;
  and foreign relations, 336; Franco's appointments to, 358; in Franco's cabinet,
  312; Franco's relationship with, 376–77,
  378, 379–80, 393–94; and fundamental
  laws, 423; and Hedilla, 250, 252; José
  Antonio's views about, 149, 170, 197;
  loyalty to Franco of, 478; and monarchism, 311, 355, 358, 371, 393–94; and
  Movimiento, 404, 409, 423; and National Council (FET), 283; and Nazism,
  345–46; in Portugal, 17–18, 49, 178;
  power and influence of, 291, 308, 312,
  328, 361; and syndicalism, 351, 352; titles of nobility for, 407; and weakness of
  Spanish fascism, 471, 472, 473, 475,
  478. *See also* army officers; Dictatorship
  (Primo de Rivera); *specific person*
military rebellion: as charge against José
  Antonio, 227–30
military revolt (1936), 39, 197–208, 239,
  240
militia: arrests of officers of, 244; Carrero's
  views about, 365; command of, 346; criticisms of, 278, 357; and defascistization,
  396; dissolution of, 396; and early years
  of World War II, 345–46; and Falange
  Exterior, 343; and Falange–Carlist fusion, 269, 276; of F. E. de las JONS,
  242–45, 247, 269, 305, 346; of FET,
  276, 304, 305, 343, 345–46, 357, 396;
  and first phase of Civil War, 242–45;
  and Franco, 242–45; Franco's unification
  of all, 244; importance to Nationalists
  of, 245; José Antonio's order to, 242;
  and military, 345–46; organization and
  leadership of, 243, 244; as part of regular army, 269; proposed revival of, 305;
  and repression during Civil War, 247; Ridruejo's proposals for, 304; training of,
  243, 244; university, 346; workers, 351,
  352. *See also* Blue Division; Primera
  Línea; veterans; *specific organization*
Ministry of Agriculture, 312, 349, 350,
  354, 359, 360, 402, 410

Ministry of the Air Force, 312
Ministry of the Army, 342, 355, 410
Ministry of Commerce and Industry, 402,
  426, 451
Ministry of Economics, 354
Ministry of Education, 402, 414, 420,
  427, 451
Ministry of Finance, 359, 426, 451
Ministry of Foreign Affairs, 343–44
Ministry of Housing, 427, 429
Ministry of Industry and Commerce, 349,
  354, 359
Ministry of Information and Tourism, 427,
  432, 459
Ministry of the Interior, 126, 292, 350,
  354, 358–59, 360–61, 364, 369, 440,
  460, 462
Ministry of Justice, 291, 402, 463
Ministry of Labor, 312, 350, 359, 406–7,
  427, 451
Ministry of National Education, 354
Ministry of Public Health, 294
Ministry of Public Order, 293–95
Ministry of Syndical Action and Organiza-
  tion, 299, 349
Ministry of War, 125
Miranda, Joaquín, 208, 250, 276
Modelo prison (Cárcel Modelo): José Antonio in, 190–93, 198
modernization, 9, 40–41, 53, 132, 240,
  319, 426–27
Mola, Emilio: and armed revolt plans of Falange, 171–72, 173; as coordinator of
  military revolt, 197–98; and Falange–
  Carlist fusion, 266; and Franco, 240,
  241–42; Italian views about, 262, 263;
  José Antonio contacts, 198; and José Antonio in prison, 216; and military revolt
  of 1936, 202, 203, 205, 206, 207; and
  militia and paramilitary units, 242; and
  social policy, 295; title of nobility for,
  405
monarchism/monarchists: and authoritarian nationalism, 44, 46–48; and Carlists,
  46, 47–48, 160; and Catholicism, 42,
  43, 46–47; and conspiracy against Second Republic, 65, 77; and corporatism,
  132; and defascistization, 375, 376, 381,
  382, 390, 393–94; and "definitive program" for Falange, 130; and disciplining
  FET, 371–72, 374, 375, 376, 381, 382;

and elections, 94, 412–13; expulsion of, 140; Falange views about, 254; and Falange–Carlist fusion, 262, 270; and Falange–JONS fusion, 100; and FET between 1939–1941, 311, 312, 314, 325, 355, 356, 358; and FET during Civil War, 279, 282, 287, 306–7; and Franco as acting head of insurgent government, 241–42; and Franco as regent, 404; Franco's views about, 240, 269, 270, 325, 371, 372, 390, 393–94, 417; and fundamental laws for redefinition of Movimiento, 423; and funding for Falange, 94, 118; funding sources for, 47, 160, 161–62; and Germany, 355–56, 372, 381, 382; and Goicoechea–Falange agreement, 118–19; and Great Britain, 371; and Italian Fascism, 47; and Italy, 160, 161–62, 355, 373, 376; and JONS, 86, 87–88; and José Antonio, 87–88, 117, 118, 131–32; in Junta Política, 304; and last phase of Movimiento, 432, 436–37, 452, 458, 462, 464; leadership of, 197; and military, 311, 355, 358, 371, 393–94; and Movimiento in post-fascist era, 404, 409, 412–13, 417, 418, 421, 423, 429, 430; and National Council, 283, 314, 390; "neotraditionalist" school of, 42; and Portugese syndicalism, 176, 177; proposed revolution by, 160; realignment among, 46–48; and repression during Civil War, 248; and rivalries within cabinet, 432; and second metamorphosis of Franco regime, 429, 430; and Second Republic, 41–42; and students, 417, 418; and succession, 404, 405, 413; and violence, 378; and working class, 132. *See also specific person or party*

monarchy: downfall of, 41; Franco's views about, 409; future of, 413; and Law of Succession, 404, 405

Monasterio, José, 244

Montero Díaz, Santiago, 86, 100

Montero Rodríguez, Matías, 102, 107–8, 110, 417

Montes, Eugenio, 141, 158, 161, 215–16, 218, 232, 412

Mora Figueroa, Manuel, 396, 404

"Moral Cowardice" (Anson article), 464–65

Moreno, José, 172, 208, 249, 258, 264, 267

Moreno Herrera, Francisco. *See* Eliseda, marqués de la

Morocco: during Dictatorship, 24, 27, 30, 31; and early years of World War II, 329, 332, 339; establishment of protectorate in, 24; Falange in, 220, 250, 253, 279, 342; and fascism of intellectuals, 51, 52; and FET between 1939–1941, 329, 332; and foreign policy, 329; Franco in, 239, 240; high commissioner of, 358; loss of, 426; military in, 23, 24, 39, 109, 329; and military revolt of 1936, 197, 205, 206; Nazis in, 240; Riffi insurrection in, 24, 25, 27, 30

Moscardó, José, 174

Mosley, Oswald, 85, 226

La Motorizada (Socialist militia group), 194, 195

Mourlane Michelena, Pedro, 141, 180

Movimiento: and abolition of FET, 451; activities of, 411–12; anniversary of, 332, 351, 448, 456; anti-Franco sentiment within, 420; Arrese's proposals for advance of, 421–25; and collapse of Germany, 398; as "communion," 446, 448; defascistization of, 478; dissension within, 411–12, 418, 420, 425, 430, 442–44, 452, 456–57; dissolution of, 409, 467; downgrading of, 402–3, 426, 427; and failed revival of Falangism, 408–26; and Falange–Carlist fusion, 260–72; and fascism, 401, 426, 445, 478–79; final years of, 457–68; Franco as essential to, 465, 466; Franco's views about, 403, 410, 411, 412, 413, 421, 427, 436, 448, 461, 465; functions of, 403, 409, 422, 446; funding for, 410–11, 449, 460; goals of, 295; last phase of (1959–1977), 431–68; loyalty to Franco of, 409; membership of, 410, 423, 437, 446, 459–60; National Congress of, 412; between 1945–1977, 399–430; between 1948–1957, 408–26; Principles of, 422–25, 429, 435, 436, 437, 454, 461; and restructuring of FET, 370; role in Franco regime of, 409, 430; and second metamorphosis of Franco regime, 426–30; secretary general of, 402–3, 404, 409–10, 420, 422–25, 427, 437,

Movimiento (*continued*)
440, 446, 447, 451–56, 459, 460, 463, 465; statutes of, 346–47; succession of, 413; symbols and slogans of, 402, 412, 452, 467; uniform of, 411, 412. *See also* National Council (Movimiento); *specific person, organization, or topics*
Movimiento Nacional. *See* Movimiento
Movimiento Sindicalista Español. *See* MES
Mun, Albert de, 30
*Mundo Obrero* (Communist publication), 190
municipal government, 401
Muñoz Grandes, Agustín: as army minister, 410; arrest of, 312; and Cabinet rivalries, 431–33; and camisas viejas, 313; and conspiracies against Franco, 375, 382; and early years of World War II, 336, 340, 342; as Falange military commander, 329; and FET between 1939–1941, 312–13, 327, 336, 340, 342, 345, 357; FET resignation of, 345; as FET secretary general, 345, 361–62; and foreign policy, 394; Franco's relationship with, 313, 345, 385, 394, 433; and Hitler, 372, 374–75, 381, 382, 384, 385, 410; honors for, 385; and last phase of Movimiento, 431–33; and monarchists, 372; and Nazism, 327; personal and professional background of, 312–13; returns to Spain, 384–85; and Spain's entry into World War II, 386; support for Franco regime by, 403; as vice president of government and lieutenant to Franco, 431–32
Muñoz Mates, Juan, 374, 387
Muro, Jesús, 208, 249, 264
Mussolini, Benito: authority of, 242; and Azaña, 54; as CEDA model, 46; and Dictatorship, 22, 25, 27–28, 30, 32–37, 39–40; downfall of, 391–92, 394–95; and early years of World War II, 331, 337; Eliseda's meeting with, 94; and Falange armed revolt, 196–97; and FET between 1939–1941, 337; Foxá's views about, 339; Franco's meetings with, 28, 337; Franco's relations with, 337; Hedilla letter to, 264; and José Antonio, 88–89, 90, 116, 144, 156, 158, 161, 234; Martinez Anido's petition to, 294; as

model for Falange, 96, 101, 170; as model for Spanish leadership, 81; political alliances of, 129; Serrano's meetings with, 373; and Spanish monarchism, 373; style of, 140; and syndicalism, 368; writings of, 90

*La Nación* (UP newspaper), 29, 78, 82, 89, 97
Nacionalismo Lusitano, 18
Napoleonic wars, 14
nation-state: definition of, 149; José Antonio's views about, 145, 149
National Agrarian Council, 352
National Assembly (Dictatorship), 34, 35, 37
National Confederation of Labor. *See* CNT
National Congress of National Movement (October, 1953), 412
National Congress of Press and Propaganda, 253, 263–64
National Congress of Students (Madrid, April 1953), 415
National Congress of Workers, 405, 427
National Council (F. E. de las JONS): and "definitive program" of Falange, 127; and elections of 1936, 179–80; and Falange internal politics, 267, 268, 269; and Falange–Carlist fusion, 268, 269; and José Antonio's death, 257; leadership of, 125–26, 258–59; and membership of Falange, 165; Second, 179; and structure of Falange, 164; suspension of, 123; Third plenary meeting of, 257
National Council (FET): and camisas viejas, 283, 314; and Carlists, 283; and Cortes, 379; criticisms of, 357; and defascistization, 379, 390; and disciplining FET, 371, 379; and early years of World War II, 340; Fernández Cuesta as secretary of, 283; and FET between 1939–1941, 314, 336–37, 340, 357; and FET restructuring, 371; and foreign relations, 329; formation of, 269; Franco's annual messages to, 342, 391; Franco's endorsement of FET before, 391; Franco's speech about fascism to, 384; Franco's views about, 304, 350; functions and powers of, 278, 283, 357; membership of, 283,

364, 390; and military, 283; and monarchism, 283, 307, 390; and social policy, 296–98; statutes of/about, 278, 390; and syndicalism, 349–50
National Council (Movimiento): Arrese's report about Falangist influence given to, 424; and fundamental laws for redefinition of Movimiento, 422–25; goals of, 448; and last phase of Movimiento, 431, 434–35, 446, 448, 449, 453, 454, 456, 458, 460, 461, 463; membership of, 418, 435; and Movimiento in postfascist era, 218, 422–25; power and authority of, 454; Tenth (1964), 446
National Delegation, 315, 357; of Associations, 428, 433–34, 453; of Culture, 451; of Ex-combatants and Ex-prisoners, 405; of the Family, 453; of Health, 438; of Information and Investigation, 409; of Justice and Law, 438; of Political Action and Participation, 453; of Press and Propaganda, 255, 280, 292, 293, 358, 393, 420; of the Provinces, 404, 437; of Social Welfare, 365, 405; of Syndicates, 365, 367–68, 407, 427. *See also specific person*
National Economics Council (Dictatorship), 32
National Front: and elections of 1936, 179–80
National Movement. *See* Movimiento
national referendums, 404, 435, 448
National Socialism. *See* Nazism
National Union (Portugal), 49–50, 175, 176
"National Wheat Syndicate," 136
nationalism: and elections of 1936, 184; factors discouraging modern, 13–14; imperialist, 9; in Italy, 470; and José Antonio, 73–74, 78, 81–82, 145–46, 150, 152, 223–24, 236; Ledesma's views about, 138; peripheral/centripetal, 3, 14, 15, 20, 21; problem of Spanish, 3–15; and weakness of Spanish fascism, 471, 472–73. *See also* authoritarian nationalism
Nationalist Army, 245
Nationalist Association (Italy), 264
nationalization: José Antonio's views about, 179–80

Navarre: Carlists in, 133, 260, 265, 288, 325, 378, 379; Falange in, 256, 258; and FET between 1939–1941, 325; Franco honors Carlists in speech in, 287; historical development of, 3; and problem of Spanish nationalism, 3, 4, 5, 6
Navarro Rubio, Mariano, 426, 433
navy, Spanish, 206, 328, 364
Nazi–Soviet Pact (1939), 329–30
Nazism: and camisas nuevas, 310; and Catholicism, 326, 327; and CEDA, 45; and conspiracies against Franco, 348; and de-fascistization, 397–98; Falange press about, 253; and Falange–Carlist fusion, 261–62; and fascism, 54, 60, 62, 478; and FET between 1939–1941, 325–26; Franco's views about, 325–26, 431; growth of, 471, 472; and JONS, 96; and José Antonio in prison, 218–20; José Antonio's views about, 148, 155–56, 159–60, 225; and José Antonio's visit to Germany, 158–59; and last phase of Movimiento, 453; longevity of, 469; and military, 345–46; and military revolt of 1936, 206; and party membership, 284; and political redefinitions, 397–98; and Portugese syndicalists, 175; racism of, 89, 96; and Radicals, 309, 331; and Socialists, 104; and spirituality, 225; and syndicalism, 317–18, 352; and violence, 106; Winterhilfe of, 257; and Women's Section, 392. *See also* Germany; *specific person*
Negrín, Juan, 186
neo-Nazism, 457, 467
neo-Thomism, 9, 474
neofascism, 457, 467–68
neotraditionalism, 158, 178, 222, 223, 280, 325, 355, 470–71, 474, 478
neutrality, Spanish: in World War I, 472; in World War II, 330, 331, 346, 355, 381, 386, 390, 394
New Order, 331, 332, 333, 387, 391
*New York Times*: Franco interview in, 271–72
Nieto Antúnez, Pedro, 432, 433, 458
*¡No Importa!* (José Antonio paper), 191, 198, 200
nobility: titles for, 405
Nombela-Tayà affair, 179

"Notebook of a European Student" (José Antonio essay), 222–24
noventayochistas. *See* Generation of Ninety-Eight
NSDAP. *See* Nazism

Obra Nacional Corporativa, 261, 300
OJ. *See* Organización Juvenil
Olazábal, José María de, 403
Old Guard. *See* Vieja Guardia del Movimiento
Operación Príncipe (Operation Prince), 451
Opus Dei, 413, 426, 432, 439, 440, 441–42, 451, 459, 463
Orbaneja, Vicente Sergio, 265, 266
*Orden Nuevo* (journal), 444
Organic Law of the Movimiento and Its National Council (Rodríguez Valcárcel proposal), 447–49
Organic Law of the National Movement, 422–25
Organic Law of the National Movement (Solís proposal), 438
Organic Law of the State (1966), 435–36, 446, 447, 448, 449
Organic Statute of the Movimiento (1968), 448, 453
Organización Juvenil (OJ), 303–4, 321, 323, 459
Organización Juvenil Española, 428
Organización Nacional de Excombatientes, 313, 394
Orgaz, Luis, 358, 384
Ortega Díaz-Ambrona, Juan, 461
Ortega y Gasset, José: and authoritarian nationalism, 25, 31; and elites, 146; and fascism of intellectuals, 56; and "Generation of 1914," 12; image of, 142; and José Antonio, 12, 71, 80, 141, 145, 148, 214, 218, 221; "national republicanism" of, 83, 85; and nationalism, 145; and Primo de Rivera dictatorship, 25, 31; and problem of Spanish nationalism, 12–13, 14, 15; satire about, 95; writings of, 141
Ortí Bordás, José Miguel, 441, 455, 456
Ossorio y Gallardo, Angel, 88
Oviedo: Falange in, 131

Oyarzun, Román, 260–61

Pacto de Tortosa (1869), 8
Pais, Sidonio, 18, 40
Pamplona: Carlists in, 288; Falange in, 131, 258; violence in, 378
Panama, 398
papacy. *See* Vatican
Paracuellos del Jarama, 227, 249
Parador de Gredos: Junta Política meeting at, 171
paramilitary and parapolice forces, 19, 202, 320, 396. *See also* militia; *specific organization*
Pardo, Lorenzo, 172
Pardo Sanz, Rosa, 343
Parliament (Dictatorship), 35, 38. *See also* Cortes; *specific person or party*
Parti Populaire Français (PPF), 397
Partido Nacionalista Español (PNE), 42–43, 77–78, 96, 130, 261, 262
Partido Obrero de Unificación Marxista (POUM), 137–38
Partido Revolucionario Institucional (Mexico), 445
Partido Sindicalista Autogestionario (Self-Managing Syndicalist Party), 166, 444
Partido Social Popular, 19–20
Partito Fascista Italiano, 309
*La Patria Libre* (Ledesma publication), 136
Pearl Harbor, 344, 384
Pedregal, Manuel, 189
Pedro Llen (outside Salamanca): Falange training school at, 243, 244, 267–68
Pemán, José María, 34, 42, 283, 318
Pemartín, José, 29–30
Pemartín, Julián, 81, 82
Peña Boeuf, Alfonso, 311
Perales, Narciso, 347, 404, 443–44
Perales Rodríguez, Jorge, 443
Pereira, Pedro Theotonio, 326
Pérez de Cabo, José, 168, 371
Pérez González, Blas, 314, 381, 384
Pérez Pujol, Eduardo, 30
peripheral nationalism, 3, 14, 15, 20, 21
Peronism, 444, 445
Pestaña, Angel, 134, 166–67
Pi y Margall, Francisco, 8
Piasecki, Boleslaw, 309

Picasso, Pablo, 142
Pildain, Bishop, 416
Pimenta de Castro, General, 18
Piñar, Blas, 452, 457
Pinto, General, 226
PNE. *See* Partido Nacionalista Español
political alliances: and "definitive program" for Falange, 129
political Catholicism, 311, 312
political prisoners, 186, 285. *See also specific person*
political redefinitions: and defascistization, 387–98
politics: and weakness of Spanish fascism, 470–71. *See also* associations; *specific person, party, or topic*
Polo, Carmen, 274–75
Polo, Zita, 80, 274–75
Popular Culture: Vice Secretariat of, 378
Popular Education, 369, 370, 402, 404, 410
Popular Front: amnesties granted by, 108; and "belligerance against fascism," 191; and civil rights, 195; and elections of 1936, 185, 194–95; and fascism, 195, 196; formation of first government of, 215; harbingers of, 122; José Antonio's views about, 186; justice system of, 226–30; slogans of, 280; and trial and execution of José Antonio, 227–32. *See also specific person*
Popular Tribunal, 226–27
Portugal: agriculture in, 178; and authoritarian nationalism, 16, 17–18, 21, 30, 45, 48–50; British relations with, 327, 339; Catholicism in, 18, 50, 175, 176, 178; consideration for annexation of, 331; constitution in, 49; corporatism in, 45, 49, 50; coup in, 49; and Falange plans for armed revolt, 171; and fascism, 52, 53, 176, 177, 178; and FET between 1939–1941, 327, 331, 339; First Republic in, 17–18; historical development of, 3; liberalism in, 40, 48, 49, 50; military in, 17–18, 49, 472; and problem of Spanish nationalism, 3, 4, 5, 8, 9; Redondo flees to, 65; Republican movement in, 17–19, 49; Salazar government in, 49–50, 175–78; Sanjurjo exile in, 171; secret plans for invasion of, 339; Spanish friendship treaty with, 327; syndicalism in, 175–78, 469; working class in, 178; after World War I, 18; and World War I, 178; and World War II, 339
Potsdam Conference, 398
POUM. *See* Partido Obrero de Unificación Marxista
Pradera, Victor, 42, 48, 133–34, 263, 405
Prat de la Riba, Enric, 15, 21
president of the government, 457, 458–59, 463
Press Law (1938), 292
Press Law (1966), 434
Press of the Movement, 318, 441–42, 456, 460–61
press and propaganda: and defascistization, 378–79, 387, 393, 396–97; and disciplining FET, 369, 378–79, 387; during Civil War, 278, 280–81, 292–93; and FET between 1939–1941, 317–19, 350, 360–61; and FET during Civil War, 278, 280–81, 292–93; and FET restructuring, 370; and foreign relations, 378–79, 387; Franco's views about, 442; and Movimiento, 402, 409, 420, 434, 441, 447, 448–49; National Delegation of, 280, 292, 293, 358, 393, 420; and political redefinitions, 393, 396–97; Undersecretariat of, 369. *See also* censorship; Press of the Movement
Preston, Paul, 218, 301, 476
Pretender. *See* Juan
Preto, Rolão, 175, 177
Prieto, Indalecio: attempted assassinations of, 112, 142; on Dictatorship, 38; and elections of 1936, 194, 195; and FEA, 280; and Fernández Cuesta exchange, 281; and founding of Falange, 81–82; and José Antonio in prison, 211, 215–16, 218; and José Antonio's defense of his father, 116; and José Antonio's impeachment from Cortes, 117; and José Antonio's outline for government, 214; and José Antonio's proposal for Falange–Socialist fusion, 186; José Antonio's views about, 195–96, 215; and Portugese syndicalism, 177
Prim, Juan, 27

Primera Línea, 111, 163, 164, 174, 191, 198, 210, 243, 247, 415, 417
Primo de Rivera, Carmen, 209–10
Primo de Rivera, Fernando (son of Dictator), 69, 77, 190–91, 201, 205, 209
Primo de Rivera, José Antonio: anniversaries of death of, 418–19, 424, 442–43, 456, 466; arrests and detentions of, 75, 111, 113, 188–208; assassination attempts on, 93–94, 110, 112, 118, 192, 218; bodyguards of, 116–17; cancellation of charges pending against, 186; childhood and youth of, 70–71; contradictory orientations of, 157–58, 235, 478; contribution of, 236; cult of, 284, 307–8; death of, 228–36, 257, 263, 264, 284; early political activities of, 70–77; family and personal life of, 69–70, 71, 80–81, 110, 111, 171; ideology of, 144–58, 212–14; indictments and prosecutions against, 188–89, 191–93, 197, 198; influences on, 71, 80, 88–89, 150, 234; as intellectual, 140; as Jefe único, 140–43; as lawyer, 71, 75–77, 88, 118; leadership abilities of, 234–36, 475; legacy of, 236, 284; loyalty to ideals of, 273, 282, 357, 424, 429, 441; military service of, 71, 73; as national hero, 232–36; official biography of, 159; program of, 73, 79, 90–92; reburials of, 233, 308, 429–30; reprinting of speech of, 255–56; reputation of, 110; self-image of, 116; style of, 71, 73, 77, 83, 95, 115–16, 119–20, 122–23, 136, 140, 142, 157; title of nobility for, 405; trial of, 140–41, 215, 225, 226–30; as university student, 70–71; writings of, 78, 94, 140, 141, 185, 191, 195–96, 197, 198, 200, 212–14, 221–24, 228. *See also specific person or topic*
Primo de Rivera, Lolita, 216
Primo de Rivera, Margarita Larios, 209, 210, 212, 215, 227–30
Primo de Rivera, Miguel (father): death of, 43, 72, 78; failures of, 49; as father, 70; influence on José Antonio of, 97, 150, 234; Italian visit of, 27–28; as "Jefe Nacional," 39; as liberal, 38; Mussolini as model for, 27–28; opposition to, 80; picture of, 26; reputation of, 38; style of,

27. *See also* Dictatorship (Primo de Rivera); *specific person*
Primo de Rivera, Miguel (nephew of José Antonio), 417
Primo de Rivera, Miguel (son of Dictator): as agriculture minister, 360; and armed revolt plans of Falange, 196–97; arrest of, 77; criticism of Franco regime by, 356–58; and FET, 314, 359, 360, 374; and monarchism, 374; and plans for José Antonio's prison escape, 209; in prison, 198–99, 210–11, 212, 215; replacement as agriculture minister of, 402; resignation from Junta Política of, 359; threatened resignation of, 356–58; trial and sentence for, 227–30; and World War II, 384
Primo de Rivera, Pilar: criticism of Franco regime by, 356–57, 358; and defascistization, 389, 392; and dissolution of Movimiento, 467; escape of, 216; and FET, 273; and foreign policy, 392; German visit of, 392; and National Council, 283; and political redefinitions, 389; and SEU, 163; threatened resignation of, 356–57, 358; and Women's Section, 264, 276, 301, 303, 324, 467
Primo de Rivera y Orbaneja, María Jesús "Tía 'Ma,'" 70, 209, 210, 212, 215
Principles of the Movimiento, 422–25, 429, 435, 436, 437, 454, 461
private property: and "definitive program" for Falange, 127–28; and FET, 299
provinces: arrest of Falange leaders in, 203; CONS in, 121–22; and Falange in 1935, 167; Falange in, 201–2, 208, 247, 256, 268; and fascism of intellectuals, 58; redemption of, 14; and restructuring of FET, 370–71. *See also specific province*
*Pueblo* (newspaper), 441, 448, 459
"Puntos Iniciales" (F. E.), 92–93, 102–3, 148, 149
purge: of FET, 370


Quadricentennary: celebration of, 11
Quadrilateral (military group), 24, 25
Queipo de Llano, Gonzalo, 73, 216, 283, 295, 304, 307

racism, 54, 89, 254. *See also* anti-Semitism
Rada, Ricardo, 170, 172
Radicals: criticisms of Franco by, 353–54; and defascistization, 376; and elections of 1936, 178–79; and F. E. de las JONS, 115, 167, 256; and FET, 309, 332, 343, 370, 376; Franco's views about, 477; immorality of, 179; and José Antonio, 117, 179, 186; and military revolt of 1936, 207; and Movimiento, 412, 417, 418, 430, 443, 456; and Nazism, 309, 331; and second metamorphosis of Franco regime, 430; and Socialist insurrection, 124; and violence, 113; and weakness of Spanish fascism, 470–71, 473; and World War II, 332, 343. *See also specific person*
Radio Nacional, 307
Radio Norte, 122
Ravelló, Gabriel, 219
*Razón y Fe* (Jesuit journal), 285
Reacción Ciudadana, 42
Reconquest. *See* Middle Ages
Redondo, Andrés, 208, 250, 258, 259
Redondo Ortega, Onésimo: and birth of syndicalism, 61–63, 65; and colonialism, 153; and conspiracy against Second Republic, 65; and copying of foreign ideologies, 101; death of, 207; distrust of, 166; and elections of 1936, 181; and Falange–JONS fusion, 99, 100; and fascism, 61–63, 65, 163, 474, 478; and JONS, 63, 65; *Libertad* of, 96; loyalty to ideals of, 441; personal and professional background of, 61–62; and re-creation of JONS, 135; reaffirmation of loyalty of, 135, 136; title of nobility for, 405; and violence, 104, 105, 114; widow of, 257; and working class, 254–55
Reforma Social Española, 452
reformists: basic beliefs of, 433; Franco's views about, 442; and last phase of Movimiento, 432–35, 442, 445–46, 452, 454, 455, 456, 460–61; and Organic Law of the State, 435–36; proposals of, 433–35; and rivalries within cabinet, 432–33. *See also specific person*
Regalado, Daniel, 441
Regenerationist movement, 11–12, 14, 16, 24, 71, 240

regentialists, 432. *See also specific person*
Regional Labor Delegations, 407
Rein Segura, Carlos, 402, 410
*Reivindicaciones de España* (Areilza and Castiella), 339, 402
religion: and Carlists, 306; and "definitive program" for Falange, 129, 130; and early years of World War II, 327; and Falange in 1936, 178; and Falange–Carlist fusion, 261–62; and FET, 280, 285–86, 327; Franco's views about, 294, 373; Hedilla's views about, 253; historical role of, 471; Hitler's views about, 373; José Antonio's views about, 148–49, 156, 157–58, 223–24, 474; and Nazism, 327; as part of Falange propaganda, 253; and weakness of Spanish fascism, 471, 473, 474. *See also* Catholicism
Renovación Española: and authoritarian nationalism, 18, 47; in Canaries, 261; and Carlists, 261; dissolution of, 265; Falange competition with, 130; and fascism, 132; founding of, 47; Italian funding of, 160; and JONS and MES, 87–88; José Antonio's agreement with, 118–19; leadership of, 47; and outlawing of Falange, 189; and repression during Civil War, 248; subsidy for F. E. de las JONS from, 135
repression: during Civil War, 245–49; of F. E. de las JONS, 106, 113, 123, 167, 169, 186–87; and Movimiento in postfascist era, 402, 404–5, 419; and weakness of Spanish fascism, 471. *See also* Assault Guards
Republic. *See* Second Republic
República Nova: in Portugal, 40
republicanism, 17–18, 38, 41, 45, 49, 83, 85, 130. *See also* Second Republic; *specific person*
Requetés (Carlists), 160, 202, 203, 232, 242, 244, 245, 269, 325, 379
Restoration era, 8, 10–11, 69
*Revista* (journal), 414
*Revista de Occidente* (Ortega y Gasset journal), 56, 58
revolution: and "definitive program" for Falange, 129; and internal conflict in Falange, 134–35; José Antonio's views about, 127, 150, 151; and Ledesma, 150

revolutionary fascism, 473, 475

Reyes Católicos, 63, 254, 268, 271, 378

Ribbentrop, Joachim von, 333, 334, 340, 373, 382, 385

Rico, Juanita, 111–12

Ridruejo, Dionisio: arrest and detention of, 256; and criticisms of FET, 354; and defascistization, 378; and disciplining FET, 378; dismissal of, 359; and early years of World War II, 340; and Falange anthem, 180; and Falange–Carlist fusion, 266; on Fernández Cuesta, 282; and FET between 1939–1941, 314, 318–19, 340, 354, 359; and FET during Civil War, 273, 304–5; Franco's relationship with, 304–5; German visit of, 290; as intellectual, 141; and José Antonio, 141, 233–34; and Junta Política, 314; and Movimiento, 404, 413, 414, 419; and propaganda, 280, 293; Redondo replaced by, 258; renounces all positions, 378; and Serrano Súñer, 275, 293; and syndicalism, 404; and university reform, 419; as Valladolid chief, 258; writings of, 258, 318; and youth, 303

Riffi insurrection, 24, 25, 27, 30

Right: and alfonsino monarchism, 132–33; arrest of members of, 194, 204; and authoritarian nationalism (1930–1933), 41–46; Calvo Sotelo as spokesman for, 200; and Carlism, 133; and conspiracies against Franco, 348; and elections, 178, 179, 180, 181, 182, 193, 467; Falange as, 442; and Falange–JONS fusion, 100; and F. E. de las JONS, 115, 167, 254; and FET, 297, 311, 320; Franco's views about, 240; influence in Franco's government of, 291; and José Antonio, 101, 117–18, 186, 193–95, 200; and last phase of Movimiento, 441, 442, 444, 449, 452, 467; Ledesma's views about, 137; and militarism, 133; and military revolt of 1936, 198–208; and Movimiento in post-fascist era, 414, 415, 419, 420; and outlawing of Falange, 190; repression by, 419; and repression during Civil War, 247, 248; and social policy, 297–98; and syndicalism, 351, 352; and violence, 204; and weakness of Spanish fascism, 470, 471, 473. *See also* conser-vatism; monarchism/monarchists; *specific person or party*

Rodezno, conde de: and Carlist internal divisions, 264–65; as Carlist leader, 202; and CEDA, 260; and Falange–Carlist fusion, 261–62, 264–65, 270; and FET, 276, 277; and Franco, 265, 288; Italian views about, 262–63; and Junta Política, 277; as justice minister, 291, 306; and military revolt of 1936, 202; and monarchism, 261–62; and National Council, 283; visits José Antonio in prison, 202

Rodríguez de Valcárcel, Carlos María, 403, 415

Rodríguez Tarduchy, Emilio, 82, 170, 347

Rodríguez Valcárcel, Alejandro, 447–49, 455, 458

Romania, 354, 469, 471, 475–76, 477

Romanones, conde de, 232

romanticism, 9–11, 14, 155, 159

Romero, Emilio, 438, 441

Romero, Luis, 195

Roosevelt, Franklin Delano, 384

Ros, Samuel, 141

Rosales, Luis, 318

Rossoni, Edmondo, 350, 368

Royo, Rodrigo, 441

Royo Villanova, Antonio, 45

Rubio, Jesús, 420

Ruggiero, Guido de, 43–44

Ruiz Arenado, Martín, 276

Ruiz de Alda, Julio: and Ansaldo, 109, 118, 122; attacks on, 105; and aviation, 83; and Calvo Sotelo, 117; and elections of 1936, 181; and Falange plans for armed revolt, 170, 171, 172; and Falange–JONS fusion, 98, 99; and founding of Falange, 88, 98; and funding for Falange, 135; and internal conflict in Falange, 134; and José Antonio, 83, 85, 86, 87, 122; and MES, 85, 86, 87; and military revolt of 1936, 207; outlawing of, 123; professional and political background of, 83; reaffirmation of loyalty of, 136; and SEU, 102; and shirt color for Falange, 126; and Socialist insurrection, 126; style of, 122; and Treintistas, 166; and violence, 102, 105, 106, 114, 122, 191; writings of, 191

Ruiz Giménez, Joaquín, 414, 420

Ruiz Jarabo, Francisco, 463
Ruiz Vilaplana, Antonio, 248
"Russia Is Guilty" speech (Serrano), 340
Russian Revolution, 144

Sainz, José, 208, 249, 259
Sainz Rodríguez, Pedro, 87, 118, 119–20,
    304, 306
Sala Argemí, Alfonso, 23
Salamanca: and elections of 1936, 181; Fa-
    lange in, 256, 267–68; and Falange–
    Carlist fusion, 270; José Antonio's
    speech at, 141, 151; Junta de Mando
    base in, 252–53. *See also* Pedro Llen
    (outside Salamanca)
Salas Larrazábal, Ramón, 246
Salas Pombo, Diego, 323, 425
Salazar, Alejandro, 165, 171, 185–86, 191
Salazar, Antonio de Oliveira, 28, 49–50,
    123, 175–78, 265
Salgado Araujo, Francisco Franco, 369,
    408, 416–17, 419
Saliquet, Andrés, 367
Salvador Merino, Gerardo, 305, 315, 350–
    53, 367–68, 376, 405, 445, 451
San Sebastián: artistic elite in, 141; Ger-
    mans invited to, 348; JONS in, 86; José
    Antonio in, 86, 123; violence in, 122
Saña, Heleno, 113–14
Sánchez Mazas, Rafael: and Ansaldo's
    plan, 118; and early years of World War
    II, 332; and elections of 1936, 181; and
    Falange–JONS fusion, 99, 100; and FET
    between 1939–1941, 313, 332, 345;
    José Antonio's relationship with, 118,
    140–41, 314; and José Antonio's Rome
    trip, 161; and Junta Política, 345; Ledes-
    ma's views about, 140, 314; as mentor
    on Italian Fascism, 82; and Movimiento,
    422; and Serrano, 332; writings of, 78
Sánchez Román, Felipe, 205, 214, 215–16
"sanjurjada" (1932), 65
Sanjurjo, José, 65, 95, 134, 171, 226
Santander: elections of 1936 in, 181, 183;
    Falange in, 164, 166; José Antonio
    speech at, 155
Santiago de Compostela: JONS in, 86; vio-
    lence in, 378
Sanz Bachiller, Mercedes, 257, 303
Sanz Orrio, Fermín, 368, 405–6, 407, 427

Saz, Ismael, 37
Schwendemann, Karl, 219
SEAT automobile factory, 405
Sección Femenina. *See* Women's Section
Second Republic: aftermath of, 40; and au-
    thoritarian nationalism, 41–46; and Carl-
    ism, 133; conspiracies against, 65, 77;
    constitution of, 45; Falange revolt
    against, 196–97; and fascism, 61, 104,
    471, 472, 476; foreign relations of,
    168–69; and Goicoechea–F. E. de las
    JONS agreement, 119; inauguration of,
    41–42; José Antonio's views about, 74,
    75–77, 155, 214–15; mass rallies in, 29;
    military revolt against, 197–208; monar-
    chists' revolution against, 160; shutting
    down of Falange during, 188–89; and So-
    cialist insurrection, 113–14, 124–25,
    126, 134; violence during, 102–14,
    187–88
Secretariat of the Movimiento, 427
Segunda Línea (Second Line), 163, 164,
    247
Senate (Dictatorship), 35
Serna, Victor de la, 264
Serrallach, José Antonio, 264
Serrano Súñer, Ramón: and armed revolt
    against Azaña government, 199; Arrese
    compared with, 373; arrest and deten-
    tion of, 274; and Aznar, 305, 306; and
    Begoña crisis, 380; and camisas viejas,
    275–76, 281, 306; and Carlists, 276,
    288, 326; and Carrero Blanco, 364; and
    Catholicism, 275; and CEDA, 100, 274;
    and Cortes (Franco regime), 379, 389;
    criticisms of and conspiracies against,
    282–83, 288, 294, 348, 356, 371, 375,
    376, 377, 380; and defascistization, 363,
    364–65, 378, 380; and disciplining FET,
    366–67, 369, 371, 372, 373, 374, 378,
    380; and dissolution of Falange, 401,
    448; and early years of World War II,
    332–34, 336, 337–38, 339, 340; and
    elections of 1936, 193, 194, 195; and ex-
    change of prisoners, 264; and Falange
    Exterior, 343–44; and Falange goals,
    275; and Falange–Carlist fusion, 266,
    271; and fascism, 274, 275, 325–26;
    and FET between 1939–1941, 311, 314,
    316, 326, 327, 329, 332–34, 336–40,

Serrano Súñer, Ramón (*continued*)
345, 353–54, 356, 358–61, 362; and
FET constitution for government, 346;
and FET during Civil War, 274, 275–76,
281, 282, 285, 306; FET "ultimatum"
to, 354; as foreign minister, 334, 343–
44, 356, 373; and foreign relations, 329,
331, 332–33, 334, 336, 337–38, 339,
340, 372, 374, 378–79; as Franco's adviser, 263; and Franco's cabinet, 311,
313–14; and Franco's death sentences
for Falange members, 271; and Franco's
power and authority, 291; Franco's relationship with, 274–75, 277, 281, 292,
311, 334, 359, 364–65, 380, 478; as
Franco's scapegoat, 356; functions of,
282; and Gamero del Castillo, 333, 345;
and Hitler's Germany, 333, 336, 382;
goals of, 314; as interior minister, 274,
292, 313–14; Italy visits of, 311, 327,
373, 378; and José Antonio, 70, 80,
116, 125, 135, 230, 263, 274, 282; and
Junta Política, 314, 316, 334, 345, 346,
366–67, 380; and military, 356, 378–79;
and monarchism, 282, 307, 355, 356,
372; and Movimiento, 401, 448; and National Council, 283, 364; personal and
professional background of, 70, 274;
power and influence of, 274, 282, 288,
292, 294–95, 304, 343, 354, 360, 361,
363, 364–65, 366–67, 369, 378; as public order minister, 295; radicalization of,
274; resignations of, 359, 371, 372; Ridruejo's relationship with, 293; "Russia
Is Guilty" speech of, 340; and Sánchez
Mazas, 332; and social policy, 297; style
of, 71, 275, 292, 356; and syndicalism,
352
Serrano Súñer family: execution of members of, 263, 274; Franco's relationship
with, 275
service: José Antonio's views about, 148
Service of Fronts and Hospitals, 301
services system, 278–79, 299, 315, 370.
  *See also specific service*
"Servicio EE" (Army Service), 197
Servicio Español de Magisterio (teachers),
437, 438
Servicio Español de Profesorado (profes-
sors), 437
Servicio Exterior, 260, 342–44, 352

Servicio Nacional de Información e Investigación, 285
SEU (Sindicato Español Universitario): and
armed revolt plan of F. E. de las JONS,
171, 186; arrest of leadership of, 188;
and Catholicism, 102; depoliticalization
and defascistization of, 395–96, 428; dissolution of, 441; elections for, 415–16,
419–20; and Falange as clandestine organization, 191; and Falange plans for
armed revolt, 173; and fascism, 395–96;
and F. E. de las JONS, 163, 173; and
FET, 279, 287, 320–23; formation and
functions of, 95, 102, 415; and Franco,
321; FUE as rival of, 102; José Antonio's
relationship with, 165, 171, 186; leadership of, 188, 321, 440–41; and Ledesma, 136; martyrs of, 108; membership
of, 164, 320–21, 415; and Movimiento,
414–19, 428, 440–41, 446; organization
of, 95; and "Plan of Action and Polital
Formation of the SEU," 415; and re-
creation of JONS, 135; reconstruction
and expansion of, 256, 428–29; represented on José Antonio's tentative government list, 172; riots and disorders of,
417–18; and violence, 106, 107, 108,
110, 187; women in, 321; Women's Section of, 163, 164. *See also Haz* (SEU
journal)
Seville: Carlists in, 133; elections in, 185;
Falange in, 109, 164, 208, 218–19, 250,
390; and Falange–Carlist fusion, 270;
Franco's speech about redefinition of
Movimiento at, 421; and military revolt
of 1936, 206; provincial governor in,
440; Sanjurjo revolt in, 65, 95; violence
in, 106, 169, 187
shock troops, 176, 245, 394
*Sí* (journal), 412
Sicherheitsdienst (SD), 353, 354
Silió y Cortés, César, 16
Silvela, Francisco, 13
Sindicato Español Universitario. *See SEU*
Sindicatos Agrícolas Montañeses, 249
Sindicatos Libres (Carlists), 19, 20, 61,
106, 114, 120
social factors: and weakness of Spanish fascism, 471–72
social policy, 283, 295–301, 409. *See also*
social welfare and work

social welfare and work, 257, 279, 343, 365, 370, 405, 406, 409, 435

Socialist General Union of Labor. *See* UGT

Socialists: and authoritarian nationalism, 31, 33, 44; and elections of 1936, 183, 194; and fascism, 78, 104, 123–24, 138, 470; and F. E. de las JONS, 105, 117, 207; financing for, 81; insurrection by, 113–14, 124–25, 126, 134, 170, 173; and José Antonio, 150, 151–52, 158, 186, 199, 218; and Movimiento, 464; and nationalism, 81–82; and Nazism, 104; and Portuguese syndicalism, 177; and repression during Civil War, 248; and students, 419; and violence, 81, 104–5, 111–12, 114, 169, 187, 189–90, 204; young, 111–12, 187

Sociedad Económica de los Amigos del País, 30

*El Sol* (newspaper), 25, 56, 92, 124, 142, 202

Solís Ruiz, José: and cabinet rivalries, 432; criticisms of, 439, 442, 443, 448; dismissal of, 451; and Franco's death, 465–66; Franco's relationship with, 427; and Girón, 428, 441; as leader, 464; and monarchism, 452; and Movimiento, 44, 432, 433–34, 438–39, 441–48, 452; and Opus Dei campaign, 442; and press, 441; professional background of, 427, 437–38; recall of, 465; as reformer, 433–34, 438, 445–46, 447–48; secretary general appointment of Movimiento, 427, 465; and students and youth, 428–29; style of, 427–28, 437, 439; and syndicalism, 427, 428, 438, 444, 445

Somatén de Cataluña, 19, 20, 25, 27, 28

Sorel, Georges, 60

Sotomayor, Enrique, 321–23, 340

Souchère, Elena de la, 246

Southworth, H. R., 139

Soviet Union: authoritarianism of, 286; and fascism of intellectuals, 59, 60; German invasion of, 332, 340–41, 371; German negotiations with, 396; José Antonio's views about, 155; and military revolt of 1936, 206; and Spanish Civil War, 206; in World War II, 371, 372, 375, 381, 390, 396, 478

Spain: German influence on history of, 221–22; José Antonio's views about history and future of, 157, 215, 221–22, 223–24; racial concept in history of, 221–22; role in world of, 127–28, 144–45, 153–54, 182, 330–31

Spaniards: archetype of, 10

Spanish royal family, 218, 355

Spanish-American War (1898), 11

Spengler, Oswald, 71, 144, 197, 223

Stalin, Josef, 242, 310

Statute of Associations, 452

Stohrer, Eberhard von, 290, 293–94, 304

students: and authoritarian nationalism, 36–37; and communism, 419; and fascism, 321; and F. E. de las JONS, 101–2, 141, 164; and FET, 287; in JONS, 85; and JONS re-creation, 135; José Antonio's relationship with, 118, 141; Laín Entralgo's report about, 419; and Ledesma, 135, 136; and Movimiento, 414–16, 419, 437, 443; in Portugal, 175, 176; and rebellion against Redondo, 166; and Socialists, 419; and violence, 102, 104, 105, 106, 107–8, 187, 419–20. *See also* youth; *specific organization*

Suanzes, Juan Antonio, 349–50, 402

Suárez, Adolfo, 440, 463–64, 465, 466, 467

Suevos, Jesús, 125, 397

Superior Council, 330

Superior War College, 339, 346, 385

Supreme General Staff, 332, 346, 432

Swiss Bank Corporation, 346

Syndical Congresses, 351, 367, 445

syndicalism: and agriculture, 301; and authoritarian nationalism, 17, 32; birth of, 63, 65; Bishop Pildain's criticism of, 416; cabinet appointments concerning, 291; and camisas viejas, 275, 305, 350; and Carlists, 288; and Catholicism, 120, 318, 405; and corporatism, 405; and defascistization, 367–68, 387; definition of, 317–18; and Dictatorship, 32; and disciplining FET, 367–68, 387; and early years of World War II, 329; and elections, 416, 427, 428; expansion of, 256; and failed revival of Falangism, 408–9; and Falange Exterior, 343; and fascism, 53, 54–65, 317–18, 368, 473; and FET between 1939–1941, 315, 317, 329, 349–53; Franco regime's adoption of Calvo Sotelo's views about, 132; Fran-

syndicalism (*continued*)
co's views about, 445; and fundamental laws for redefinition of Movimiento, 422; José Antonio's views about, 150–51, 234, 318, 329; and last phase of Movimiento, 435, 438, 443–45, 449, 459; leadership of, 278; and military, 351, 352; and Ministry of Labor, 406–7; and monarchism, 47; and Movimiento in post-fascist era, 403–9, 415, 418, 422, 428, 429; national delegate of, 365, 367–68, 407, 427; as national service, 279; and Nazism, 317–18, 352; in Portugal, 175–78, 469; reform of, 435; and Right, 351, 352; and second metamorphosis of Franco regime, 428, 429; and social policy, 296, 299–301; structure and organization of, 278, 351. *See also* Syndicalist Organization; *specific organization*
Syndicalist Organization: and associations, 449; bureaucratization of, 368; Communist infiltration of, 421; and FET between 1939–1941, 349–52, 353, 368, 370; function and activities of, 405; Girón's views about, 427; lack of worker support for, 408; and last phase of Movimiento, 433, 435, 438, 444, 445, 449, 451, 462; and Movimiento in post-fascist era, 405, 406, 408, 421, 427; Nazi agreement with, 353; reform and restructure of, 349–52, 370; and second metamorphosis of Franco regime, 427
Syndicate of Sugar-Beet Growers of Old Castile, 62
Syndicate of the Cinematographic Industry and Public Spectacles, 319

Tangier, 332
taxi drivers: JONS syndicate of, 120
Teatro Calderón (Valladolid), 100–101
Teatro de la Comedia, 90–92, 95, 102, 141, 412, 448
Technical Services, 259, 315, 343. *See also* auxiliary services
technocracy, 425, 426–30, 432, 434, 442
Tellaeche, Julián, 141
Tellería, Juan, 180
Tenerife: provincial governor in, 440
theater, Spanish, 319

Thomsen, Hans, 336, 348, 352, 353, 355–56, 375
Tierno Galván, Enrique, 464
Toledo: and Falange plans for armed revolt, 174; FET in, 306
Torcuato Fernández, Miranda, 420
Torrente Ballester, Gonzalo, 318, 319, 389
Torreperogil (Jaén province), 111
totalitarianism: ambiguity of meaning of, 286; Arrese's views about, 395; Carrero's views about, 366; components of, 366; and defascistization, 378, 384, 388–89, 393, 395; and "definitive program" for Falange, 127–28; and FET, 285–86, 298, 304–5, 316–17, 346, 393; Franco's views about, 271–72, 294, 378, 384, 477; García Valdecasas's views about, 388–89; Hedilla's views about, 264; Hitler's views about, 474; José Antonio's views about, 149–50, 156, 234, 235, 474; redefinition of, 388–89, 395
Tovar, Antonio, 256, 318, 320, 358, 359, 414, 415
La Traza (The Project), 23, 28
Treaty of Friendship and Conciliation (1926), 30
Treintistas, 166–67
Tribunal de Responsabilidades Políticas de la Dictadura, 76–77
Tribunal de Urgencia, 192
Tribunal Supremo, 192, 193, 198, 213, 227, 390, 447, 463
Tripartite Pact, 336, 340, 375
Triumvirate (Falange), 99, 118, 123, 267, 268
Trotsky, Leon, 80
Tusell, Javier, 35, 37, 277, 298, 355, 478
Twelfth Army Corps, 384
"Twelve Points of the Flecha" (OJ code of conduct), 303
Twenty-Seven Points, 127–29, 130, 152, 153, 188, 192, 235, 269
Twenty-Six Points, 282, 285, 286, 353, 422, 429, 477

Ucelay da Cal, Enric, 7
UDPE (Unión del Pueblo Español), 464, 465, 467
UGT (Socialist General Union of Labor), 33, 61, 104, 121

Ullastres, Alberto, 426
UME (Unión Militar Española), 170, 172, 197, 210, 347
UMN (Unión Monárquica Nacional), 21, 42–44, 73
Unamuno, Miguel de, 11–12, 13, 141, 142, 165
unemployment: and CONS, 120–22
*Unidad* (Falangist daily), 253
Unió Socialista de Catalunya (USC), 22
Unión Ciudadana, 19
Unión de Centro Democrático (UCD), 467
Unión del Pueblo Español. *See* UDPE
Union of Fascists (British), 85
Unión Ibero-Americana, 11
Unión Militar Española. *See* UME
*Unión Monárquica* (journal), 74
Unión Monárquica Nacional. *See* UMN
Unión Patriótica (UP), 28–30, 31, 34, 37, 49, 78, 175, 347
United Nations, 398
United Party. *See* FET
United States, 11, 128, 225, 342, 344, 372, 397
unity: and "definitive program" for Falange, 127–28, 129; José Antonio's views about, 13, 130, 145–46, 147, 152, 196, 215, 223; and Movimiento in post-fascist era, 429; and second metamorphosis of Franco regime, 429; and Socialist insurrection, 126
universities: Cortes representation of, 390; and fascism of intellectuals, 58; and FET between 1939–1941, 320; militia in, 346; and Movimiento in post-fascist era, 414–16, 420; political divisions in, 102; reform of, 320, 414–16, 419; and violence, 107; women in, 41. *See also specific university*
University of Heidelberg, 159
University of Madrid, 85–86, 102, 107, 109, 164, 414, 419–20, 441, 457
University of Salamanca, 414, 415
University of Santiago de Compostela, 100
University of Seville, 102, 106
University of Valencia, 30, 418
University of Valladolid: SEU at, 102
University of Zaragoza: violence at, 106, 107
UP. *See* Unión Patriótica

Uría, Rodrigo de, 297, 304, 318
Urraca Pastor, María Rosa, 301
Uruguay: Falange in, 343
Utrera Molina, José, 459–60, 461, 463
Uzcudun, Paulino, 219

Valdés, Darío, 276
Valdés Larrañaga, Manuel: and defascistization, 392, 397; and Falange plans for armed revolt, 172; and FET, 314–15, 367, 374; and foreign policy, 397; and Germany, 382, 385; José Antonio's relationship with, 165, 368; as labor undersecretary, 368; and monarchism, 374; and Movimiento, 455, 456; as national delegate of syndicates, 368; and SEU, 102
Valencia: as base for Republican government, 227; Falange in, 210; JONS in, 86; and problem of Spanish nationalism, 4; repression in, 346
Valladolid: CONS in, 120; and elections of 1936, 183; Falange in, 163, 164, 166, 207–8, 256, 257, 258, 266; and fascism of intellectuals, 62, 63, 65; and F. E.–JONS fusion, 158; first major meeting of F. E. de las JONS at, 100–101; JONS in, 86; "Jons" in, 135; Movimiento in, 437, 453–54; nationalism in, 61; rallies at, 158; and re-creation of JONS, 135, 136; violence in, 111
Valldecabres, Emilio, 231
Valle de los Caídos (Valley of the Fallen), 429, 436, 439–40, 442–43
Valle-Inclan, Ramón María de, 12
Vallellano, conde de, 423
Valverde, José María, 318
Varela, José Enrique, 172, 348, 355, 374, 375, 376–77, 378, 379–80, 381
Vatican, 218, 327–28, 401, 447, 478
Vázquez de Mella y Fanjul, Juan, 30, 133, 172
Vega, Alonso, 433
Vegas Latapié, Eugenio, 110, 307
Ventosa, Juan (Catalinist financier), 214
*Vértice* (journal), 318
*Vértice, Flechas (Arrows)* (Falange children's journal), 253
veterans, 245, 313, 348, 370, 374, 394, 405, 435, 439–40

vice president of government, 431–32, 458
Vice Secretariat of Popular Education, 369,
378, 402, 404, 410
Vice Secretariat of Press and Propaganda,
361
Vice Secretariat of Social Works of the
Movimiento, 420
Victor Emanuele (king of Italy), 28, 262
Vieja Guardia del Movimiento (Old Guard
of the Movement), 413, 437, 438, 449,
455, 456, 459, 463, 465
Vigón, Jorge, 200, 433
Vigón, Juan, 332, 346, 372–73
Villanueva de la Reina: violence in, 105
violence: and authoritarian nationalism,
20; and elections, 194; expansion of,
122, 187–88, 189–90; and Falange–
Carlist fusion, 271; and fascism, 54, 60,
61, 62, 63, 65, 79, 105, 106, 474; and
F. E. de las JONS, 101, 169; and FET,
317, 359; and Goicoechea–Falange
agreement, 119; and JONS, 86; José Antonio's views about, 79, 90, 103, 105–7,
108–9, 110, 113–14, 118, 142–43, 150,
154, 187, 191, 198, 205, 215, 234–35,
474; justification of, 191; Luca de Tena's
rejection of, 79; and Movimiento, 419–
20, 457; and Nazism, 106; in 1970s,
457; and radicals, 113; during Second
Republic, 102–14, 187–88, 189–90; Socialists' views about, 79, 81; and students, 102, 104, 105, 106, 107–8. *See
also specific person, organization, or
incident*
Vivar Téllez, Rodrigo, 396, 403, 404, 407
Vizcaya: and authoritarian nationalism, 21;
as "enemy" of Franco regime, 404; Falange in, 376; and fascism of intellectuals, 60; and problem of Spanish nationalism, 15; as source of Socialist financing,
81; syndicalism in, 407; workers in, 33
Völckers, Hans Hermann, 96–97, 216,
219, 220

war: definition of, 396; Franco's views
about, 339; José Antonio's views about,
154. *See also specific war*
War of Independence, 6
War of the Spanish Succession, 5
Warlimont, Walter, 219, 220

Wehrmacht, 342, 394
Weizsäcker, Ernst von, 220, 290
women: and authoritarian nationalism, 31,
33, 34, 44; and Catholicism, 44; education of, 62; and Falange as "fashionable," 194; and fascism of intellectuals,
62; and modernization in 1920s, 41; in
SEU, 321; as university students, 41; voting rights of, 34, 154; wages of, 33. *See
also* Women's Section
Women's Section (Sección Femenina): activities of, 257, 301; and Catholicism, 309,
477; conservatism of, 323–24; and defascistization, 390; Delegada Nacional of
the, 324; and dissolution of Movimiento, 467; early leaders and founders
of, 207, 216, 264; expansion of, 257;
and FET, 276, 279, 301, 303, 323–24;
Franco's speech before, 378; functions
of, 323; Italian and German counterparts to, 477; leadership of, 276, 301,
303, 467; loss of support for, 390; membership of, 301, 437, 459; and Movimiento, 437, 443, 445; and Nazism,
392; Pilar Primo de Rivera's threatened
resignation from, 358; political divergence within, 301; Salamanca as base
for, 264; of SEU, 163, 164; seventh congress of, 390; success of, 477
Worker Alliance, 124
workers: and authoritarian nationalism,
22, 45; and Falange propaganda,
254–55; and fascism, 60, 61, 470, 471,
472; Franco's speech to, 405; Hedilla's
views about, 255; José Antonio's views
about, 120; and Ledesma, 136; and monarchism, 132; in Portugal, 176, 178. *See
also* labor; Ministry of Labor; syndicalism; *specific organization*
Workers' Party of Marxist Unification. *See*
Partido Obrero de Unificación Marxista
World War I, 14, 40, 51, 144, 178, 184,
472
World War II: ceremonies and rituals during, 319; and collapse of Germany, 398;
early years of, 326–42; end of, 397, 398;
and Falange dependency, 476; and FET
between 1939–1941, 326–42; Franco's
powers during, 291; possibility of German defeat in, 390; Spain's entry into,

330, 332–33, 334, 336–37, 340, 356, 373, 374, 381, 382, 384, 386, 387; Spain's neutrality in, 330, 331, 346, 355, 381, 386, 390, 394; Spain's nonbelligerence in, 331–32, 394; U.S. entry into, 344, 372; and weakness of Spanish fascism, 478

Ximénez de Sandoval, Felipé, 159, 260, 342, 344, 376, 378

Yagüe, Juan: as air force minister, 312, 328, 348; and armed revolt plans of Falange, 197; and camisas viejas' pardons, 293–94; on Civil War, 293–94; and conspiracies against Franco, 305, 347–48, 375, 382; dismissal of, 348; exile of, 382; and Falange internal conflict, 264; as Falange military commander, 329; and Falange–Carlist fusion, 266; and FET between 1939–1941, 312, 328, 336, 347–48; and foreign policy, 394; Franco's relationship with, 293, 394; and monarchism, 372, 382; in Morocco, 197; and World War II, 382, 384
Yalta Conference, 397

Yanguas Messía, José, 298
Ybarra steamship line, 219
youth: and cult of José Antonio, 307; and Falange–Carlist fusion, 267; and fascism, 321–22; and FET, 279, 286, 303–4, 319–23; José Antonio's views about, 142; Laín Entralgo's report about, 419; and last phase of Movimiento, 435, 443, 457, 460, 461; Ledesma's views about, 138; and Movimiento in postfascist era, 409, 417–18, 419, 421, 430; and second metamorphosis of Franco regime, 430; as Socialists, 111–12, 187. *See also* students; *specific organization*
Yugo y flechas (yoke and arrows), 467
Yzurdiaga, Fermín, 253, 254, 258, 280, 289

Zalamea de la Serena: violence in, 105
Zaldívar, José Ma., 287
Zaragoza: CONS in, 120; Falange in, 207; and Falange–Carlist fusion, 270; Franco's speech in, 293; José Antonio's speech at, 155–56; and military revolt of 1936, 207; repression during Civil War in, 247; violence in, 106
Zugazagoitia, Julián, 226